lonely planet

Walking in Scotland

Sandra Bardwell

Destination Scotland

Walking in Scotland is all about variety and choice, from easy-going coastal strolls to rugged and remote treks in the mountains.

The rolling Southern Uplands are startlingly different from the knife-edged ridges of Skye's Black Cuillin. The voluptuously contoured Cairngorms contrast with the Highlands' steep cliff-lined ridges, and the crumpled and rocky Northern Isles' coasts are utterly different from the Western Isles' long sandy beaches. Heather-carpeted moorlands are worlds away from the surreal rockscapes and waterscapes in the northwest. You'll find tall Scots pine and graceful birch woodlands, broad rivers and tumbling mountain streams, vast lochs and intimate lochans.

Top of the list of walking destinations are Scotland's two national parks, Loch Lomond & the Trossachs and Cairngorm. To find a walkers' paradise on earth head for the wilder, more remote Beinn Eighe and Glen Affric National Nature Reserves.

For long-distance walking fans, the four official waymarked routes include Britain's most popular, the marvellous West Highland Way. If mountains are your thing, there are the 278 Munros (mountains over 3000ft); above all, don't miss Ben Nevis, Britain's highest peak.

For wildlife enthusiasts the great attraction is the teeming birdlife, from the magnificent golden eagle to the mountain-dwelling ptarmigan and the Northern Isles' endearing puffin.

Scotland's reputation for bad weather is largely mythical; across the country, more days are fine than foul, and a Highland suntan is a popular souvenir. From peaks and passes to beaches and glens, Scotland has plenty to keep even the most active walker busy for half a lifetime.

GARETH McCORMACK

The South

NICHOLAS REUSS

Borderline perfect – Coldingham Bay and the village of St Abbs (p83) grace the Borders' rocky and rolling coast

MARTIN MOOS

Track and ruin – Melrose Abbey (p80) is a superlative starting point for a stroll in the Eildon Hills

WAYNE WALTON

An unmissable, craggy lump of volcanic rock, Arthur's Seat (p50) offers remarkable views of Edinburgh

Central, Cairngorms, Lochaber & The Isle of Skye

The Isle of Arran's beautiful Glen Rosa (p99) offers walks on the wild side with its ridges and rapids

PHOTOLIBRARY

CHRIS MELLOR

You can take the high road *and* the low road around Loch Lomond (p93) on the West Highland Way

Introduced reindeer (p143) – Santa's little helpers roam the Cairngorms

DAVID TIPLING

EOIN CLARKE

Skye high – the Black Cuillin mountains dominate the horizon from Glenbrittle (p194)

GRANT DIXON

The Black Cuillin peaks dramatically drop into the waiting waters of Loch Coruisk (p201)

CHERYL FORBES

The Old Man of Storr looks sagely out over the Trotternish escarpment (p208)

Big Ben – Scotland's top destination, Ben Nevis, from An Garbhanach (p129)

GRAEME CORNWALLIS

Western Isles, Wester Ross & Northwest/Sutherland

GRANT DIXON

Hilly Harris boasts the Western Isles' most elevated viewing point, Clisham (p245)

Stone poses – ancient megaliths can be found throughout Scotland and its isles, in the form of prehistoric standing stones

GRANT DIXON

GREG GAWLOWSKI

The coast of Lewis (p237) is exceptionally scenic, with cliffs punctuated by beautiful bays and beaches

GARETH McCORMACK

Rambling soon turns to scrambling along Liathach's exposed edges (p229)

Sublime Sandwood Bay (p258) is combed constantly by Atlantic rollers

PHOTOLIBRARY

Beinn Alligin (p227) ponders its reflection in the waters of Loch Torridon

GARETH McCORMACK

Northern Isles

DAVID TIPLING

Parrots of the high seas – the Shetland isles (p282) have more puffins than people

GRANT DIXON

In contrast to the jagged scenery, the walking is surprisingly smooth on Eshaness (p289), North Mainland

The Old Man of Hoy (p275) stands guard over his rugged Orkney isle

GARETH McCORMACK

Contents

Regional Map Contents

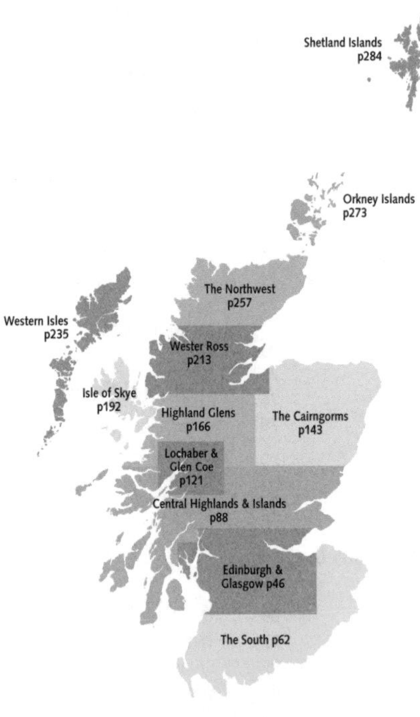

The Author

SANDRA BARDWELL

When I discovered a Scottish great-grandmother, I knew it must be in the genes. The first time I set eyes on the Highlands' hills I felt that I'd come home. When we settled beside Loch Ness I flung myself into the hills and climbed them, walking the glens, loch shores and coast with huge enthusiasm. This happened well into a lifetime of walking in wild, remote and not-so-remote places, mainly in Australia, and writing the odd article and book about bushwalking in that country.

With Lonely Planet I've explored some other wonderful European countries, but Scotland and especially the Highlands, in their infinite variety and ever-changing beauty, are still close to my heart.

My Favourite Walks

Faced with an embarrassment of riches, it's hard to choose, but here goes.

Almost overlooking home, **Meall Fuar-mhonaidh** (p188) is a year-round, old favourite. The path has become a highway, but the extraordinary views up and down Loch Ness are unfailingly rewarding.

You'll either love, as I do, or shun the rock-encrusted, primeval Northwest. Rugged **Quinag** (p267) is an amazingly easy climb, despite its formidable profile, and the sea and mountain vistas are sublime.

Although mountains are my near-obsession, the coast always exerts an irresistible fascination – the sea's untamed power, the birds, the endlessly varied scenery. **Shetland's** (p282) wonderful coastline is without peer, from the black Eshaness crags, to Muckle Roe's red stacks, to Hermaness' green hillsides above the teeming cliffs and the endearing puffins.

LONELY PLANET AUTHORS

Why is our travel information the best in the world? It's simple: our authors are independent, dedicated travellers. They don't research using just the internet or phone, and they don't take freebies in exchange for positive coverage. They travel widely, to all the popular spots and off the beaten track. They personally visit thousands of hotels, restaurants, cafés, bars, galleries, palaces, museums and more – and they take pride in getting all the details right, and telling it how it is. For more, see the authors section on www.lonelyplanet.com.

The Walks	Duration	Difficulty	Best Time	Transport
Edinburgh & Glasgow				
Lothian Coast Links & Bents	2¾-3 hours	easy	year-round	bus
The Pentlands' Scald Law	3¾-4 hours	moderate	Mar-Oct	bus
Along the Greenock Cut	3-3¼ hours	easy	year-round	private
A Campsie Caper	4-4½ hours	moderate	Mar-Oct	bus
Falls of Clyde	4-4¼ hours	easy	year-round	bus
The South				
Southern Upland Way	9 days	moderate-demanding	Apr-Oct	bus, train
The Merrick	4-4½ hours	moderate-demanding	Apr-Oct	private
Grey Mare's Tail & White Coomb	5 hours	moderate-demanding	Apr-Oct	bus
John Buchan Way	5¾-6 hours	moderate	Apr-Oct	bus
Eildon Hills	4 hours	easy-moderate	Feb-Nov	bus
Burnmouth to St Abb's Head	6 hours	easy	year-round	bus
Central Highlands & Islands				
West Highland Way	7 days	moderate	Apr-Oct	train, bus
A Tour Around Goatfell	6-7 hours	moderate-demanding	Apr-Oct	bus, ferry
Cock of Arran	3½-4 hours	easy-moderate	Mar-Oct	bus, ferry
The Cobbler	5 hours	moderate-demanding	Apr-Oct	bus, train
Ben Lomond	4½-5 hours	moderate	Apr-Oct	ferry
Ben Ledi	4 hours	moderate-demanding	Apr-Oct	bus
Ben Lawers	5 hours	moderate-demanding	May-Oct	private
Schiehallion	4 hours	moderate	Apr-Oct	private
Ben Cleuch	5¼-5½ hours	moderate	Apr-Oct	bus
Lochaber & Glen Coe				
Ben Nevis via the Mountain Track	6-8 hours	moderate-demanding	May-Sep	bus
Ring of Steall	7-8 hours	moderate-demanding	Apr-Oct	private
The Road to the Isles	6-8 hours	moderate	Apr-Oct	train, bus
Buachaille Etive Mór	5-6 hours	moderate-demanding	Apr-Oct	bus
Glen Coe & Glen Etive Circuit	5 hours	moderate	Apr-Oct	private
Bidean nam Bian	6-7 hours	moderate-demanding	Apr-Oct	bus
Cairngorms				
Cairn Gorm High Circuit	4½-5 hours	moderate-demanding	May-Sep	bus
Chalamain Gap & the Lairig Ghru	6-6½ hours	moderate-demanding	Apr-Oct	bus
Linn of Dee Circuit	6½-7 hours	moderate	Apr-Oct	private
Blair Atholl to Glenmore	2 days	moderate-demanding	Apr-Oct	train, bus
Lochnagar	6-6½ hours	moderate	May-Sep	private
Highland Glens				
Great Glen Way	4 days	moderate	Mar-Nov	bus, train
Glen Affric	2 days	moderate	Apr-Oct	bus

The Walks	Duration	Difficulty	Best Time	Transport
Five Sisters of Kintail	7-7½ hours	demanding	Apr-Oct	private
Gleouraich	5-5½ hours	moderate-demanding	Apr-Oct	private
Creag Meagaidh	6¾-7½ hours	demanding	May-Sep	private
Isle of Skye				
Bruach na Frithe	6-8 hours	moderate-demanding	May-Oct	bus
Red Cuillin Horseshoe	6-7 hours	moderate-demanding	Apr-Oct	bus
Coast & Cuillin	2 days	moderate	Apr-Oct	bus
Bla Bheinn	5½-5¾ hours	moderate-demanding	May-Oct	bus
The Trotternish Traverse	7-8 hours	demanding	Apr-Oct	bus
The Quiraing	2½-2¾ hours	moderate	Mar-Nov	private
Wester Ross				
An Teallach	7½-8½ hours	demanding	May-Oct	bus
Beinn Dearg Mhór	2 days	moderate-demanding	May-Oct	bus
The Great Wilderness Traverse	2 days	moderate	Apr-Oct	bus
Slioch	7½-8 hours	moderate-demanding	May-Oct	bus
Beinn Eighe Mountain Trail	2½-3½ hours	easy-moderate	Apr-Oct	private
Beinn Alligin	6½-7 hours	moderate-demanding	May-Oct	private
Liathach	7-8 hours	demanding	May-Oct	private
Coire Mhic Fhearchair	4½-4¾ hours	moderate	Apr-Oct	private
Western Isles				
Tolsta to Ness	4-4½ hours	moderate	Apr-Oct	private
Rhenigidale Path	4-4¼ hours	moderate	Apr-Oct	bus
Clisham	3½-4 hours	moderate	Apr-Oct	bus
Eaval	3½-4 hours	moderate	Apr-Oct	private
Hecla	7-7½ hours	demanding	Apr-Oct	private
Heaval	3½-4 hours	moderate	Apr-Oct	bus
Northwest				
Sandwood Bay & Cape Wrath	6½-7 hours	moderate	Apr-Oct	bus
Ben Loyal	6-6 ½ hours	moderate	Apr-Oct	private
Eas a' Chùal Aluinn	5¾-6¼ hours	moderate	Apr-Oct	bus
Quinag	4¼-4½ hours	moderate-demanding	Apr-Oct	private
Northern Isles				
Old Man of Hoy	5½-6 hours	moderate	year-round	ferry
The Yesnaby Coast	5-5½ hours	moderate	year-round	bus
West Westray Coast	3-3½ hours	moderate	year-round	private
Hermaness & Muckle Flugga	3-3¼ hours	easy	year-round	private
Muckle Roe	3¼-3½ hours	moderate	year-round	private
Eshaness	2¼-2½ hours	easy	year-round	private

Summary	Page
A classic, immensely scenic ridge walk including three Munros, far above long, deep glens	180
An exhilarating traverse of a narrow mountain ridge with awesome, mountain-filled views	182
An immensely rewarding and scenic circuit of a magnificent mountain massif	184
A superb outing with spectacular views of the Cuillin peaks, and some exciting scrambling potential	195
Explore these distinctive pink conical peaks, crossing rocky summits and steep, scree-strewn slopes	197
A spectacular coast and glen walk to Loch Coruisk, deep in the rugged Black Cuillin mountains	199
Exceptional views reward a steep climb past a hidden chasm and secluded lochans	203
Lots of ups and downs on the long Trotternish ridge, with plenty of first-class views	207
Explore weird and wonderful pinnacles, crags and bluffs near the northern tip of Skye	209
Classic, airy ridge walk with plenty of exposure and fantastic views	214
A challenging circuit of a spectacular, remote peak, deep in the wilderness	216
A low-level walk through a magnificent, unspoiled fastness of rugged peaks, lonely glens and tranquil lochs	218
From the shores of beautiful Loch Maree to a commanding summit with excellent views	222
Explore the beautiful woodland and wild mountain terrain of a fine nature reserve	225
An exciting mountain circuit, over two distinctive peaks, which could challenge your head for heights	227
A sensational walk with some airy scrambling and unforgettable views	229
Through impressive glens and wild moorland to one of Scotland's finest corries	231
Spectacular coastal scenery, shieling villages and abundant sea birds on Lewis' east coast	237
Historic path through magnificent mountain, glen and coastal scenery to an isolated hamlet	241
Steep, rocky ascent to the Western Isles' commanding highest peak	245
North Uist's highest peak, with superb views of myriad lochans, inlets and tiny islands	246
Challenging but rewarding ascent of South Uist's second-highest peak	249
Very varied climb, over steeply undulating hills, to Barra's highest summit and unsurpassed views	251
From a pristine beach with superb white sand to the dramatic northwestern tip of Scotland	258
One of the north's most attractive and intriguing peaks, topped by weird and wonderful granite tors	262
Scenic walk through wild, remote moorland to the awesome top of Scotland's highest waterfall	265
A surprisingly straightforward walk across a formidably rugged peak with magnificent sea and mountain vistas	267
Through moorland to Orkney's famous landmark and stunning sea cliffs	275
Spectacular cliffs, magnificent sea stacks and long coastal views on Orkney Mainland	278
Tens of thousands of sea birds, easy walking and wonderfully wide vistas	280
Countless sea birds crowding cliffs and crags, and Britain's magnificently wild northernmost outpost	286
An exceptionally scenic, rugged and intricately indented coast on Shetland's Mainland	288
Some of Shetland's finest coastal cliffs, a geologist's paradise, a historic lighthouse and fantastic sea vistas	289

Walk Descriptions

This book contains 66 walk descriptions, ranging from day trips through to multiday megawalks, as well as suggestions for other walks, side trips and alternative routes. Each walk description has a brief introduction outlining the natural and cultural features you may encounter, plus extra information to help you plan your walk, such as transport options, the level of difficulty and time-frame involved, and any permits that are required.

Day walks are often circular and are located in areas of uncommon beauty. Multiday walk descriptions include information on camp sites, mountain huts, hostels and other accommodation, and point out places where you can obtain water and supplies.

TIMES & DISTANCES

These are provided only as a guide. Times are based on actual walking time and do not include stops for snacks, taking photographs, rests or side trips. Be sure to factor these in when planning your walk.

Distances are provided but should be read in conjunction with the altitudes you expect to reach, as significant elevation changes can make a greater difference to your walking time than lateral distance. In this book we have reflected the rather wacky British system of mixing imperial and metric measurements. In route descriptions, daily distances along footpaths are given in miles, with some kilometre equivalents, while shorter distances are given in metres and heights of mountains are given in metres with some feet equivalents.

In most cases, the daily stages are flexible and can be varied. It is important to recognise that short stages are sometimes recommended because of difficult terrain in mountain areas, or perhaps because there are interesting features to explore en route.

LEVEL OF DIFFICULTY

Grading systems are always arbitrary. However, having an indication of the grade may help you choose between walks. Our authors use the following grading guidelines:

Easy A walk on flat terrain or with minor elevation changes, usually over short distances on well-travelled routes with no navigational difficulties.

Moderate A walk with challenging terrain, often involving longer distances and steep climbs.

Demanding A walk with long daily distances and difficult terrain with significant elevation changes; may involve challenging route-finding and periods of scrambling.

TRUE LEFT & TRUE RIGHT

The terms 'true left' and 'true right', used to describe the bank of a stream or river, sometimes throw readers. The 'true left bank' simply means the left bank as you look downstream.

Planning

If Scotland is unknown territory, the question you must ask sooner or later is, 'What kind of walks can I do in Scotland?'. The best answer is, 'Whatever you wish'. You can walk independently, handling all the planning and arranging accommodation and transport yourself, or you can join a guided walk, sitting back while all the arranging is done for you. A good compromise is to have the best of both worlds – enjoy having the accommodation and maps provided, then do the walks by yourself or with friends.

Day walks are the most popular style of walking in Scotland, from a base at a camping ground, hostel or B&B. They can range from easy strolls along clear paths (some feature in this book in the Short Walks boxes) to challenging circuits of several mountain peaks. Some walks are waymarked, though many aren't – these are easy enough to follow with the help of this guide and the recommended maps. If you're looking for walking trips of a few days or more, whether following the official long-distance routes, rights of way or a route of your own, then you're spoilt for choice throughout the country. Accommodation can be in a tent, bothies, hostels, B&Bs or a combination of these. The range of places waiting to welcome you is vast, from rustic hostels in remote locations to B&Bs in grand mansions.

See Climate (p295) for more information

Munro bagging (p108) is a uniquely Scottish pastime and one that's open to anyone keen and fit (some would say crazy) enough to take on climbing 3000ft-plus mountains. Most of these, and the many and varied other mountain walks, are hands-in-pockets outings not requiring rock-climbing skills. Some do call for confidence in exposed places and experience in scrambling (see p216), and if this is exactly your kind of walking then Scotland is for you: there are scores of scrambling routes throughout the Highlands and many of the islands.

WHEN TO WALK

Scotland's peak walking season starts in late April and runs through until the end of September, even sneaking into October for lower-level walks on the mainland. By late April (spring) hours of daylight are generous and snow should have receded from the glens and lower mountains. Wildflowers are at their best during May (late spring) and June (early summer); these are also generally the driest, sunniest months, and the

DON'T LEAVE HOME WITHOUT...

- Industrial strength 24/7 midge repellent (p313)
- Motion-sickness pills for crossing the Minch/Pentland Firth/North Sea (p306)
- Windproof jacket and headgear (p316)
- Tough, easy-to-put-on gaiters (p316)
- Binoculars for bird-watching in the Northern Isles (p272)
- Checking for black holes in your mobile phone's reception (p301)
- Your ID card or passport and driving licence (p307)
- Lonely Planet's *Scotland* guide
- Tartan-coloured haggis net

A carefully planned assault on Carn Mór Dearg Arête (p127)
EOIN CLARKE

massed onslaught of midges (p313) has yet to arrive. Cruelly, the busiest time of the year, the summer high season during July and August, coincides with peak midge activity and unsettled, humid weather. It's not all bad news though; the soft purple heather usually starts to transform the moors from late July.

Autumn (September and October) often brings spells of calm, mellow weather and glorious displays of rich colour in the woodlands and forests. What's more, the midges start to dwindle and have gone by October.

Perhaps surprisingly, there are parts of Scotland where walking is possible year-round. Even in midwinter, plenty of lowland and coastal walks are accessible and safe. Frequent spells of fine weather bring incredibly clear skies, exhilarating low temperatures and light winds, especially in the north and west. Occasional bursts of bitterly cold weather, with snow down to sea level and paths turning to skating rinks, make walking problematic. The best seasons for each walk in this book are given in the walks table (p12–15).

HOW MUCH

Camping ground (tent & person): £8

Night at SYHA hostel: £15

Modest B&B (per person sharing): £28

Bar meal (main course & one drink): £12

1L of unleaded petrol: £1

Ordnance Survey map: £8

COSTS & MONEY

Next to many other European countries, public transport, accommodation and eating and drinking out are quite expensive in Scotland. Petrol in larger towns and cities is on a par with Continental Europe but more expensive in remote areas and the islands, and vastly more costly than in Australia or the USA. While it can be an expensive country to visit, you can save money by self-catering when possible, hiring a small car, staying in hostels and travelling with a partner or friend. Generally, accommodation prices are higher during June, July and August (the so-called high season), but May and September also enjoy good weather.

If you spend most nights in a tent and do your own cooking, expect to spend around £18 per day; upgrade to hostels and you'll be up for around £25. Go for cheaper B&Bs and an evening meal at a pub and you're looking at a minimum of £35.

BACKGROUND READING

Walking Through Scotland's History by Ian R Mitchell reminds us that the gentle pastime of walking is the culmination of a long history in which the Scottish had no choice but to leg it. His light-hearted but erudite survey of the exploits of an extraordinary cavalcade, from Roman legions to fishwives and travelling people, is brought up to date with suggestions about walks you can do today.

By the same very readable and companionable author, *Scotland's Mountains Before the Mountaineers* shifts from the doers to the arena, to look at ideas about Scotland's high places before they became a popular playground. Ever in quest of a new take on the familiar, Mitchell answers such questions as 'How many Munros did Bonnie Prince Charlie bag?' Abundant references open up months and years of further reading.

Dave Hewitt is a zany iconoclast who once set out to walk the full length of Scotland's watershed. Not for him the list-ticking odysseys of Munro and Corbett baggers, but a far more challenging expedition following the watershed's wriggly line from the border several miles south of Jedburgh to Cape Wrath. His very entertaining account, *Walking the Watershed*, is factually a bit out of date, but timeless for its huge enjoyment of life.

Colin Prior is one of two truly outstanding landscape photographers working in Scotland. His *Scotland: The Wild Places* is a magnificent evocation of mountains, lochs, glens, rocks and trees, with his own sensitive, inspirational text. The only disappointment is the exclusion of any of the islands; hopefully they will be the subject of a future volume.

Many walks in this book have a distinctly historical flavour or particular associations, so it's worth having a feel for Scotland's long and

GUIDED WALKS

Many reputable, experienced companies run guided walks throughout Scotland, including on long-distance paths. The many countryside ranger services run guided day-walk programs in their areas, many of which are mentioned in the walk chapters. Including a guided walk or two in your visit gives you a break from doing all the organising, and offers the chance to learn more about the countryside from experienced guides and to meet like-minded people. **Walk Scotland** (http//walking.visitscotland.com) has links to many local companies.

Scotland

- **Transcotland** (☎ 01887 820848; www.transcotland.com) Specialises in long-distance walks, both on official routes and others of the company's own devising.
- **Wilderness Scotland** (☎ 0131 625 6635; www.wildernessscotland.com) Concentrates on wild and remote areas, including the Isle of Rum, Knoydart and the Western and Northern Isles, and is committed to responsible travel.

France

- **Terres d'Aventure** (☎ 01 43 25 69 37; www.terdav.com) Trips to the Orkney Isles and North West Highlands.

USA

- **Backroads** (☎ 800 462 2848; www.backroads.com) Runs a trip to the Western Highlands and Isle of Skye with easy-moderate walks and staying in the best hotels.

To find local operators on specific walks, see the relevant regional chapter. For information on walking clubs around Scotland, see p293.

fascinating history. Fiona Watson's *Scotland from Prehistory to the Present* is very readable, taking an analytical approach to events rather than a mere narrative recitation. She's very positive and forward looking about even the darkest times, though rather brief about the later 20th century.

INTERNET RESOURCES

Best Walks (www.bestwalks.com) A direct route to books and maps for walkers, plus accommodation, guided walks and magazines.

Internet Guide to Scotland (www.scotland-info.co.uk) An excellent travel guide to Scotland.

LonelyPlanet.com (www.lonelyplanet.com) Go to the Thorn Tree link and its walking, trekking and mountaineering branch for discussion about anything and everything.

Ordnance Survey (www.ordnancesurvey.co.uk) Buy your OS maps online – click on the Leisure link.

Traveline (www.travelinescotland.com) Public transport timetables and journey planner for the entire country.

Undiscovered Scotland (www.undiscoveredscotland.co.uk) Another first-rate travel guide with loads of information arranged by area and links to long-distance paths.

Visit Scotland (www.visitscotland.com) Scotland's national tourist board, with an online accommodation service.

Walk Scotland (http//walking.visitscotland.com) About 860 helpful walk descriptions on its database, plus an accommodation guide and mountain weather forecast.

Walking World (www.walkingworld.com) Britain's largest online walking guide, with descriptions of 3200 walks, ranging from rather vague to very useful, and much else. To get the best out of this site you need to become a subscriber.

Environment

SCOTTISH OUTDOOR ACCESS CODE

Scotland has enjoyed a long tradition of mutual tolerance between landowners and walkers about access to the hills and moors, provided walkers observed what was known as the Country Code and respected local restrictions during lambing, deer-stalking and grouse-shooting seasons. During the 1990s the number of people going out into the mountains soared and demand for access to lowland walking areas grew. In 1996 the Access Forum brought together representatives from among land managers, recreation groups and public agencies. They came up with a Concordat on Access, which, essentially, endorsed responsible freedom of access, subject to reasonable constraints for management and conservation. However, it was felt that the agreement merited legal status, and the issue was high on the agenda of the new Scottish Parliament after 1999.

After several years of wide-ranging consultation and, at times, acrimonious debate, the Scottish Parliament passed the pioneering *Land Reform (Scotland) Act* in 2003 and the following year approved the Scottish Outdoor Access Code. This conferred statutory access rights on many outdoor activities, including walking and wild camping, and on farmers and landowners. These rights don't apply to any kind of motorised activity or to hunting, shooting or fishing.

The website www.outdooraccess-scotland.com goes into the Scottish Outdoor Access Code in detail; click on the 'Scottish Outdoor Access Code' link. Leaflets outlining the code are also widely available.

Access rights can be exercised along paths and tracks and across open ground over most of Scotland, from urban parks and paths to hills and forests, from farmland and field margins to beaches, lochs and rivers. The rights don't apply to buildings or their immediate surroundings, houses or their gardens, or most land in which crops are growing. The key points are summarised in the boxed text on p22. The following offers detailed guidance for walkers.

Bothies

- Don't depend on bothies – always carry a tent.
- Space is available on a first-come, first-served basis and for short stays only. Some are private and not open to the public.
- Some are used by shepherds and stalkers during the lambing and stalking seasons when you may be asked not to stay overnight.
- Keep fires small and within the existing fireplaces.
- If there's a toilet, please use it.
- If there's a logbook, enter details of your trip and group; this may help if you require rescue.
- Before you leave, tidy up, ensure the fire is out, replace kindling if possible and close windows and door(s) properly. Take all your rubbish with you and don't leave any food behind – it only encourages rats and mice.
- Check the **Mountain Bothies Association** (www.mountainbothies.org.uk) website for more advice.

Camping

- Seek permission before camping near a farm or house.
- Use a recognised site rather than create a new one, and always camp at least 30m from lochs, watercourses or paths. Move on after a night or two.

- Pitch your tent on well-drained ground so it won't be necessary to dig damaging trenches if it rains heavily.
- Leave minimal or no trace of your stay.

Dogs

- Do not take your dog into fields where there are young animals.
- If you enter a field of farm animals, keep your dog on a short lead or under close control and keep as far as possible from the animals.
- During the bird breeding season (April to July) keep your dog under close control or on a short lead in moorland, forests, grassland, loch shores and the coast.

Fires

- Don't depend on open fires for cooking; any wood may be too wet and it is a precious natural habitat.
- Use a lightweight liquid-fuel stove rather than one powered by disposable gas canisters.
- If you do light a fire, keep it small and use the bare minimum of fallen timber. Extinguish it thoroughly, scatter the charcoal and cover the fire site with soil and leaves.

Human Waste Disposal

- Bury your waste. Use a lightweight trowel or large tent peg to dig a small hole 15cm deep and at least 50m from any path or stream and 200m from a bothy or camp site. Cover it with soil and leaf mould. Use biodegradable toilet paper; it should ideally be burnt, but not if you're in woodland or on dry grassland. Otherwise, carry it out – burying is a last resort.
- Contamination of water sources by human faeces can lead to the transmission of Giardia, a human bacterial parasite; gastroenteritis is probably caused by exposed human faeces. Always check the surrounding area for contamination before collecting water; do so upstream of your camp site.
- Get hold of a copy of *How to Shit in the Woods* by Kathleen Meyer for a good laugh and plenty of useful advice.

Rubbish

- If you've carried something in, you can – and must – carry it back out again. And that means every single thing. Therefore you will need to keep a dedicated rubbish bag to hand and you might want to designate a sealable pocket or compartment of your bag for storing it in.
- Remember, sanitary napkins, tampons and condoms neither burn nor decompose readily, so carry them out.

KNOW THE CODE BEFORE YOU GO

When you're in the outdoors:

- Take personal responsibility for your own actions and act safely.
- Respect people's privacy and peace of mind.
- Help land managers and others to work safely and effectively.
- Care for your environment and take litter home.
- Keep your dog under proper control.

DEER STALKING

Managing Scotland's wild deer population is an organised and ecologically and economically important business. The 750,000-strong population comprises four species – red, roe, sika and fallow. Red deer are the biggest, most numerous and have the greatest impact. A balance must be maintained between deer numbers and their habitat, so they have enough to eat without wrecking the vegetation.

The **Deer Commission for Scotland** (☎ 01463 725000; www.dcs.gov.uk) has fostered the establishment of deer management groups – voluntary groups of landowners covering areas with distinct herds – in most parts of the country. Regular censuses govern the annual cull when older and unhealthy animals are shot by experienced professional stalkers using high-velocity rifles. The sport of deer stalking, a good income-earner for estates and local communities, is integrated into the cull.

During the stalking season, mostly between mid-August and mid-October, you can help to minimise disturbance by doing your best to find out where the activity is taking place and by heeding advice on alternative routes. Avoid crossing land where stalking is taking place. Management groups provide detailed on-site information, usually specifying preferred walking routes. This may also be available through the **Hillphones** (www.hillphones.info) service, or perhaps from local tourist information centres. The National Trust for Scotland, John Muir Trust, Royal Society for the Protection of Birds, Forestry Commission and Scottish Natural Heritage may conduct stalking on their lands but generally maintain access for walkers throughout the year.

Some estates don't belong to deer management groups and some aren't cooperative. It's worth remembering that access along rights of way is always open, and that shooting doesn't happen on Sunday.

Washing

- Don't use detergents or toothpaste, even if they're biodegradable, in or near streams or lochs.
- To wash yourself, use biodegradable soap and a water container, at least 50m from any watercourse. Disperse the waste water widely.
- Wash cooking utensils and dishes 50m from watercourses using a scourer instead of detergent. Strain food scraps and carry them out in your rubbish bag.

THE LAND

Accounting for about one-third of the area of Britain, Scotland's 30,414 sq miles are spread over four geographical areas. The Southern Uplands lie south of Edinburgh and Glasgow, and extend right to the English border. The central Lowlands are a triangular block, from Edinburgh to Stonehaven in the east and across to Glasgow in the west. North of the Highland Boundary Fault (which runs northeast from Helensburgh to Stonehaven) are the Highlands, covering about two-thirds of the country and boasting the major mountain ranges, crowned by Ben Nevis, Britain's highest mountain at 1343m (4406ft). The Highlands is almost split by the largest of several long, deep glens – the Great Glen – which lies on a fault line between Fort William and Inverness and cradles a chain of freshwater lochs, including Loch Ness. To the north are the Orkney and Shetland island groups; the Western Isles (or Outer Hebrides) parallel the northwest coast. The Inner Hebrides are a scattering of mainly small islands further south, including Jura and Islay; the larger islands, Skye and Arran, closer to the mainland aren't usually regarded as part of this group. The western coastline, north of the central Lowlands, is deeply indented with sea lochs, separated by rugged peninsulas. The east coast's profile is smoother, apart from four elongated sea lochs (firths) – Dornoch, Moray, Tay and Forth.

More than 70% of Scotland's population lives within an hour's travel of Loch Lomond & the Trossachs National Park.

It's not difficult to grasp the essentials of Scotland's extremely ancient and diverse geology if you imagine the country being divided into the Highlands and Lowlands regions. Each in turn comprises two districts, defined along geological fault lines, all running northeast and southwest.

Scotland occupies only one-third of Britain's mainland surface area, but has 80% of the coastline and just 10% of the people.

The Highland Boundary Fault separates the two regions, and is a particularly striking feature of the landscape. Within the Highlands, the Moine Thrust (where one layer of rock was shoved over another) is the subdivider, stretching from Skye's Sleat peninsula to Loch Eriboll on the north coast. To its west, the main rock type is Lewisian gneiss, the most ancient rock in Scotland. Here also is reddish, pebbly Torridonian sandstone, eroded to create characteristic isolated, tiered peaks. The Isle of Skye is a world apart, with the Black Cuillins composed of volcanic black gabbro, and the peaks, plateaus and coastal cliffs in the north formed by great lava flows. East of the Moine Thrust, the northern and central Highlands are mainly schist and quartzite. The great granite massifs of the Cairngorms pushed up beneath these rocks and were gradually exposed by erosion.

The central Lowlands lie between the Highland Boundary and Southern Upland Faults. The rocks here, such as coal and limestone, are much younger; remnants of volcanic activity include North Berwick Law and Arthur's Seat. Between the Southern Upland Fault and the border with England, the characteristic rounded mountains consist of sedimentary rocks, interspersed with volcanic remnants, notably the Eildon Hills.

Two land-transforming events wrought great changes in the rocks. About 500 million years ago, over a long period, they were shoved, squashed and folded, creating ridges and mountains, which were then worn down into clusters of mountains and hills. Scotland has been buried under glaciers and ice sheets at least five times, most recently about 10,000 years ago. As these ice masses melted, the courses of rivers were altered, deep lochs created, corries formed and valleys widened and deepened.

WILDLIFE

Billing Scotland as 'Europe's No 1 Wildlife Destination', www.wild-scotland.co.uk promotes an enthusiastic band of wildlife tourism operators. It's a great source of ideas about where to watch an amazing variety of wildlife, with or without a guide.

Although Scotland is home to hundreds of species of mammals, birds and plants, found in a wide range of habitats, the animals don't exactly leap out at you and announce their presence. Most mammals are on the small side and rather secretive; many woodland and moorland birds are small, brown and twittery. Nevertheless, it would be a rare walking day when you didn't see a few birds, and wildflowers and trees are always present. In many parks and reserves there are informative nature trails, which are a great way to broaden your knowledge. The species you're most likely to see on the walks in this book are described in the following sections.

Animals

MAMMALS

The red deer is Scotland's largest land mammal; the stag stands to 1.3m tall and can weigh a hefty 125kg. For most of the year stags and hinds live in separate herds, usually in high, sheltered glens. During the mating season (known as the rut), the stags rope in their harems, accompanying this highly charged period with unearthly, primeval roaring – perhaps the most stirring sound you'll hear in the Scottish wilds.

Much smaller and lighter than the red, the roe deer spends its time grazing in woodlands. In summer its coat is reddish-brown. The roe is most likely to be seen in the Highlands.

During summer the mountain hare has a deep-brown coat with elegant black ear tips. Around October it begins to moult and by December it's completely white; it's back to summer attire between March and May. It's quite common on the mainland, between 300m and 750m, and on Hoy in Orkney, and in Shetland.

Just small enough to put in your pack, *Complete British Animals* by Paul Sterry has excellent photos and a dense page of text for each species and any relatives; sea mammals are in there too.

The hedgehog prefers open areas, rough pastures and the edges of tall forest. It's found in most mainland areas, on the Isle of Skye and in the Northern Isles. It's most active at night, hunting for the mice, lizards, frogs and earthworms that make up its varied diet. When enemies – dogs and foxes – threaten, it curls into a tight ball to maximise its main defence, the coat of sharp quills. Sadly, these are of no use against speeding vehicles and flat hedgehogs are all too numerous on rural roads.

Once common in most parts of Scotland, the red squirrel is now rarely found outside the Highlands. It's at home in coniferous forests, the source of its favourite food, pine-cone seeds, although it will also grab the eggs and chicks of small birds. Reddish-brown almost all over, it has a darker, bushy tail.

The elusive, captivating otter is equally at home in freshwater and the sea. Although it spends most of its time in the water and feeds on fish, it does hunt on land, seeking rabbits and small rodents. The male (or dog) is about 1.3m long, more than half of that being tail. With a superbly streamlined, dark-brown body, it's beautifully agile in the water. The otter's strongholds are the rocky west coast and the Western Isles.

Belying its name, the common seal is much less prevalent than its relative, the grey seal. Adults have dark-grey backs and light-grey undersides, with trademark all-over black spots, blunt noses and slanting eyes. Found all round the coast, they congregate in waters off Shetland and the Western Isles during summer.

The grey seal is Scotland's largest wild animal. The bull is three times heavier than a decent-sized red deer stag and can reach a length of 2.3m. It lives in eastern and western coastal waters and during the summer breeding season gathers on remote islands. The male's pointed noses and the absence of spots marks it out from common seals.

BIRDS

A rather shrill, plaintive mewing high above fields and moors signals the presence of the buzzard. Its broad wings spread in a shallow V-shape and the tail is spread. It often perches on fence posts, where its sandy-coloured chest, light-brown head, darker back and distinctive yellow feet are obvious. It's fairly common throughout mainland Scotland.

In coastal waters anywhere, and around estuaries, there's no mistaking the cormorant, sitting on a rock or buoy, wings bent and hung out to dry. Dark-brown to black in colour, its white lower face and larger size marks it out from the smaller shag. It's a streamlined swimmer, diving frequently to satisfy its huge appetite for fish.

The curlew ranges widely between farmland, low hills, moors and mud flats throughout Scotland. Its long, curved bill and distinctive 'cur-lee' call make identification easy. It congregates in flocks on the coast and in smaller groups inland. The brownish plumage is streaked with darker markings.

The lapwing, a wader, is easily identified, especially in the breeding season when it becomes an aerial acrobat, dipping, diving and rolling. Its black-and-white wings appear rounded in flight and it has a trademark crest. You'll hear its 'pee-wit' or 'peerst' calls throughout the country, most likely on rough grassland.

High in the Cairngorms, the brown back and tawny chest of the small dotterel provide good camouflage on rocky ground; a broad white strip above each eye and on the upper chest are distinctive. It runs along in short bursts, stopping for a feed in between.

The largest resident of Scotland's skies, the golden eagle stands nearly 1m tall. In flight its huge wings, splayed at the edges with white, tapering bands, and the wedge-shaped tail are distinctive. Its plumage is uniformly chocolate-brown. Once hunted to the brink of extinction, the golden eagle is now protected and has made a strong comeback in the Highlands and islands.

Stiff-winged in flight, the fulmar is common around coastal cliffs. It has distinctive tube-like nostrils, a black eye patch, grey wings and white head and chest. Resting on the cliffs where it nests, it cackles noisily to other fulmars.

Diving gannets are one of the most spectacular sights from coastal cliff tops. The bird folds its wings and plunges torpedo-like into the sea when it spots some fish. Its pure white plumage, yellow head and nape and black wing tips are sure identifiers. It nests in large numbers on western and northern islands, especially Unst in Shetland.

Among the crowds of birds on sea cliffs, the kittiwake is the smallest. It has short black legs and a yellow-green bill; the mostly grey wings are long, straight and narrow. Like the gannet, it often dives for fish from a considerable height. The largest colonies are in the Northern Isles.

Still much prized by hunters, the red grouse spends its time in heather moorland, where its rufous, rather mottled plumage provides good camouflage. It can give you quite a fright as it takes off with a clatter of wings, squawking loudly 'go-bak, go-bak'.

The grey heron is often seen standing silently on one leg near river banks and loch shores. Its elongated neck is usually retracted in flight, while its long legs trail behind. Predominantly grey in colour, its neck and chest are white.

The male's black-capped head, white back and part-black, part-white wings distinguish the eider. A large sea duck, it spends all its time cruising and feeding in the shallows around the mainland and on nearby islands. The female is a fairly ordinary mottled brown.

Possibly the most eye-catching of the waders, the oystercatcher has coal-black upper parts, is white underneath and has a trademark red eye and a pointed red bill. It spends the majority of its time on the coast, usually near rivers and on loch shores, though it ventures into fields and moorland fringes throughout Scotland. Its loud 'kleep' is often heard well into the night.

Pocket-sized *Scottish Birds* by Valerie Thom devotes a page to almost all the commonly observed species. Colour illustrations are clear and good enough for identification; the book is handily divided by habitats.

A memorable sound on walks across heather moorland is the rippling 'tlooee' call of the golden plover. This bird is well camouflaged, with golden-brown spangled upper parts and black chest. Its flight is fast and direct and it glides into a landing; it's likely to be seen in the uplands almost anywhere.

Uniquely, the ptarmigan changes plumage three times each year, from mottled brown in midsummer, through autumn greys to winter white. It lives in the mountains year-round, perhaps retreating slightly in severe weather. The harsh rattling croak as its takes off is unforgettable.

Probably Scotland's most unusual-looking bird, and its most endearing, the puffin has a vividly coloured parrot-like beak and white cheeks. It stands erect and waddles, rather than walking about, but flies strongly. It's most numerous in the Northern Isles, where it congregates between April and July.

Notorious for dive-bombing intruders during the breeding season, the great skua (or bonxie in Shetland) spends most of the summer in the Northern Isles, moving south late in the season. It's mainly dark brown in colour with white wing patches.

REPTILES

The adder is coppery brown with a dark zigzag pattern along its back. The adder's bite is poisonous but it's unlikely to be fatal. It's very excitable and more likely to flee than to attack. Adders are found only in mainland Scotland.

Plants

SHRUBS & FLOWERS

Boggy moorlands are enlivened in summer by clumps of flowering bog asphodel. In spring the underground stems sprout narrow, stiff leaves, from which a stem grows to bear the yellow flower spike.

Before the woodland trees are fully in leaf in spring, the ground will be carpeted with wildflowers, including the wood anemone. Its frail stem rises from a cluster of three dark-green, deeply notched leaves, topped by a single white or pinkish flower.

Scottish Wild Flowers by Michael Scott is an ideal walking companion, with a finely detailed illustration for each of 350 species. It also has a good rundown on habitats and the best viewing sites.

On high ground, where heather can't survive in moorlands, blaeberry is the most common plant. It grows to about 60cm, with twisted stems that carry small, bright-green leaves. Its bluish-purple berries are edible and quite tasty, though it would take ages to gather even a cupful.

A member of the pea family, broom grows in dense bushes to 2m high, usually on sandy soils. It has small leaves on its profuse twigs and from early summer is covered with masses of golden-yellow flowers. These then develop into black pods that burst open with a loud 'snap' when they become ripe.

During summer many small moorland ponds will seem to be hanging onto scraps of snow. These are actually balls of white hair on the fruit of cotton grass. Its brownish-green flowers appear at the end of long stems, developing into the cotton balls.

Better known as whin in Scotland, prickly gorse grows widely on rough ground. Its golden-yellow flowers appear among the long, sharp spines, mainly from early spring, and exude an intense, almost intoxicating, perfume.

Cross-leaved heath is the heather most likely to be seen in boggy ground. It has greyish, hairy, needle-like leaves arranged in cross-shaped groups on the stems. Its slightly bell-shaped, pale-pink flowers are larger than those of the other two heathers.

The archetypal symbol of Scotland, heather grows in pine woods and on moorland. The bushy shrub can grow to 1m high without periodic burning to promote new growth for grouse food. Its stems have rows of tiny, needle-like leaves and the spikes of flowers turn the moors a glorious deep-pinkish-mauve during August and September.

The larger, dark-reddish flowers of the bell heather distinguish it from its relations, though the leaf-covered stems are similar in appearance. Bell heather is usually the first to bloom, during July.

Commonly called bluebell, the wild hyacinth carpets woodlands in most areas during early spring. Its stalks rise from a cluster of long, glossy leaves and bear several small, violet-blue, bell-shaped flowers.

A member of the cypress family, common juniper forms dense thickets in pine woodlands and on rocky ground. The needle-like leaves are usually light-grey-green and, when crushed, exude an apple-like perfume.

Bog myrtle is common throughout boglands and heaths. This low-growing plant, its stems bear small green leaves, which, when crushed, have a distinctly resinous aroma.

A colourful sight in woodlands everywhere, the yellow-flowering primrose is also found in grassy areas and on sea cliffs. The flowers form on long furry stems, emerging from a bunch of elongated crinkly leaves.

In early summer the heath spotted orchid is commonly seen, singly or in clumps, on the moors and marshy ground. The white to pale-lilac flowers, with darker pink spots, cluster in a pyramid-shaped head above the darkish-green leaves marked with purple blotches.

Sundews devour insects that land on their leaves, attracted by sweet juice. The insects are trapped by tiny, flexible hairs and then quickly swallowed. The most common species in bogs and on soggy peat is round-leaved sundew. The hairy leaves fan out from the base of a tall stalk on which tiny white flowers may appear.

A remarkably hardy plant, thrift is common on rocky coasts (hence its other name, 'sea pink') and is also found on high inland plateaus. The narrow greyish-green leaves form a thick pad from which the stalk grows, topped with a cluster of small whitish, pink or mauve flowers.

TREES

The widespread silver birch often grows with oak and rowan. A particularly beautiful tree, its branchlets bear shiny green, triangular leaves with notched edges. The bark is white with splotches. This hardy tree can survive extremes of cold and is drought-resistant.

The alder is one of the most common trees along the banks of burns and rivers. Reaching a height of about 20m, it has grey-brown bark arranged in square section, and egg-shaped leaves that are flattened across the top, slightly shiny and very dark green. It sprouts distinctive male catkins up to 5cm long.

The common hazel produces small, tasty nuts, a handy source of wild food in the woodlands, if you have time to collect a handful in autumn. A comparatively small tree, it's quite widespread. The dark-green, hairy leaves are roughly oval-shaped with a sharp point.

Its scarlet fruit, adorning the tree during winter and spring, makes identification of the holly easy. The leaves are also distinctive – glossy, dark-green and edged with sharp spines. It's usually found in oak and beech woods throughout the country, except in the far north.

Both sessile oak and English oak are found in Scotland. The two species are similar in appearance, with the characteristic lobed leaves and grey, cracked bark. The main distinguishing feature is the acorn (fruit); it grows directly on the shoot on the sessile oak but on a stem of the English oak. The sessile has a more open appearance, while the English oak's foliage is more bunched. Oaks can live for up to 800 years.

Rowans are embedded in Gaelic folklore as charms against witchcraft; it's believed that to fell a rowan brings bad luck to the axe wielder. They're traditionally grown by the front doors of houses to ward off evil spirits.

Once widespread throughout Scotland, the Scots pine is a superb-looking tree. Now confined largely to the Highlands, it reaches a height of 35m. The dark-coloured bark is deeply cracked and, on the branches, is a distinctive orange-brown or pink. The dull, grey-brown cone is roughly oval with a marked point, and the leaves are a dark, glossy green (see the boxed text on p175 for details about a Scots pine reserve in Glen Affric).

The red-berried rowan is very hardy – no other tree grows at a higher altitude than its upper limit of 1000m. Masses of white flowers appear in May or June and the fruit starts to colour in September, when it is raided by birds.

WORLD HERITAGE SITES

Four Unesco World Heritage sites have been declared in Scotland.

St Kilda (www.kilda.org.uk) became a natural site in 1986; its designation as a cultural site in 2005 conferred membership of an exclusive group of only two dozen sites around the world enjoying dual status. Owned by the **National Trust for Scotland** (www.nts.org.uk), the archipelago is the remotest part of the British Isles, 41 miles (66km) west of Benbecula in the Western Isles. St Kilda is the most important sea-bird breeding ground in northwestern Europe and has Britain's highest sea cliffs. The native population was evacuated in 1930, ending a unique way of life evolved over hundreds of years.

Edinburgh Old and New Towns (www.ewht.org.uk) was declared in 1996, recognising the superbly preserved medieval old town and the fine Georgian new town. The towns are especially notable for their contrasting architecture, parks, gardens, graveyards, statues and monuments.

The **Heart of Neolithic Orkney** (www.orkneyjar.com), designated a cultural site in 1999, comprises four prehistoric sites: Skara Brae (p278); Maeshowe chambered tomb; the Stones of Stenness, a ceremonial enclosure; and the Ring of Brodgar, a ceremonial enclosure and stone circle. All are in remarkably fine condition for their age (2500 to 5000 years) and have yielded a rich hoard of evidence of life long ago.

New Lanark (www.newlanark.org) is on the route of the Falls of Clyde walk (p56). The most recent addition to Scotland's World Heritage portfolio (declared in 2001), New Lanark is a beautifully restored 19th-century mill village, and the scene of a ground-breaking experiment in social welfare.

NATIONAL PARKS & NATURE RESERVES

In 2002 Scotland caught up with the rest of the world by opening its first national park, Loch Lomond & the Trossachs, more than 50 years after the idea of national parks was first seriously entertained in this country. The more controversial declaration of Cairngorms National Park followed in 2003.

Despite having the finest mountain and coast landscapes in Britain, relatively large areas of undeveloped lands and many sites of national and international ecological importance, Scotland was focussed on other issues until the late 1980s; nevertheless, by the end of the 20th century, protective designations galore had been heaped upon the Scottish countryside. The election of a Scottish Parliament and Executive in 1999 provided the inspiration and opportunity to set up the country's own national parks. After much public debate and consultation, the *National Parks (Scotland) Act* was passed in August 2000, giving the government power to declare parks.

Within Loch Lomond & the Trossachs' (p103) 186,500 hectares are several fine ranges of mountains, including the Arrochar Alps, the Trossachs and the Breadalbane 'hills' with 21 Munros and 20 Corbetts (p108), a score of large and small lochs, woodlands, historic sites, many small towns and villages, major roads and railways, and a fair share of the West Highland Way (p89). Some of these areas were already protected for their natural values, notably Argyll and Queen Elizabeth Forest Parks, designations that are now part of the national park. What benefits can such a large (by local standards) and diverse park bring to residents, the country at large and visitors? Many people's awareness of the park's superb natural heritage has undoubtedly been strengthened by the exhibitions at the visitor centres, publications and the activities programs. Perhaps, too, the problems facing park managers in maintaining – let alone improving – access to lochs, glens and mountains have become more obvious. It's probably too soon to pass judgment; maybe it needs

The well-organised www.lochlomond-trossachs.org offers an excellent introduction to the park, contact details, a load of links to partner organisations, and the lowdown on the Byzantine park-planning process.

a major threat to an outstanding feature (such as power lines across Ben Lomond) to put it to the test!

No-one has ever doubted that the Cairngorms is one of Scotland's finest natural assets (which is saying a lot!) but it seemed that this compelling fact was pushed aside in the wrangling over the boundaries of the national park. When it was finally opened in late 2003 (bizarrely in a restaurant at the top of a much-opposed funicular), many felt that bureaucrats had won and the Cairngorms themselves had lost, or at least been handed second prize. A sizeable swathe of what is generally regarded as Cairngorms country, in the East Perthshire Highlands, had been left out, with the southern boundary generally following that of Highland Council. Nevertheless, the 380,000-hectare park is twice the size of Loch Lomond & the Trossachs; has four of Scotland's five highest peaks; protects 25% of Britain's threatened birds, animals and plants; and is home to more than 17,000 people in seven sizeable towns.

The Cairngorms National Park Authority (www.cairngorms.co.uk) website is easy to navigate and offers a mountain of information about the park's natural and cultural features, organised Countryside Events, public transport services and publications.

The Park does not and will not have a 'Gateway Centre' in the style of Loch Lomond & the Trossachs, nor any dedicated visitor centres. Instead, its many, very attractive leaflets and brochures are, or should be, available from the several tourist information centres (TICs) within its boundaries, notably Aviemore (p145), Ballater (p161) and Braemar (p154).

Also unlike Loch Lomond & the Trossachs, the Cairngorms National Park Authority does not have the last say in development issues within the park, so it remains to be seen how two of the park's four key aims are juggled: 'To conserve and enhance the natural and cultural heritage of the area' and 'To promote sustainable economic and social development of the area's communities'. It's to be hoped that a coalition of Perthshire movers and shakers, led by a local MP, can win its case when the boundaries are reviewed in 2008. Meantime, the park is still incontestably the finest in Britain, judged by natural values alone.

National Nature Reserves

To visitors from North America and the antipodes, Scotland's National Nature Reserves (NNRs) should seem more like the national parks they know and love. Almost invariably they're sizeable areas, more or less wild (or at least uninhabited) and have outstanding natural values. They are established under mid-20th-century legislation that makes Scottish Natural Heritage (SNH) the responsible authority. SNH itself owns or leases about half the 50-plus reserves. The rest are owned and managed by conservation organisations such as the Royal Society for the Protection of Birds or the National Trust for Scotland.

The dedicated website for National Nature Reserves, www.nnr-scotland.org.uk, provides a good lead-in to these 'world-class sites for nature', with a thumbnail sketch of each reserve and details of access, facilities and on-the-ground contacts.

Among SNH's own portfolio, the jewels are Beinn Eighe (p225) – Britain's first NNR – and Creag Meagaidh (p184). Other gems include Hermaness (p286), Ben Lawers (p111) and St Abb's Head (p81). Among the rest, variety is of the essence, from the remote archipelago of St Kilda (p29) and the SNH-owned island of Rum to beautiful Glen Affric (p174), Loch Druidibeg (p254) and Loch Lomond. There's also a vast NNR within Cairngorms National Park. Most are readily accessible, and the majority of popular reserves have a ranger service that can organise guided walks.

ENVIRONMENTAL ISSUES

During the early years of the 21st century, the single issue that has galvanised walkers (and kindred folk) has been proposals for renewable-energy projects. While there is general agreement that, as a nation and as individuals, Scotland needs to act promptly to reduce the use of fossil fuels, the means by which this aim can be tackled, let alone achieved, remain the subject of impassioned debate. Scotland is inevitably swept up in the UK government's commitments and broad policies. Its seemingly empty open spaces, and abundance of places where winds blow frequently and fiercely, make it a prime potential location for wind farms. Proposals to plant large numbers of huge turbines in prominent, hilltop locations, and to build long transmission lines with massive pylons through the countryside, have generally been opposed, especially in areas of outstanding scenery, which are, after all, fairly plentiful in Scotland! Meantime, it has been pointed out that walkers still blithely jump into their cars and drive considerable distances at weekends in pursuit of their hobby. Since public transport services have improved in very recent times, perhaps we should slow down, aim to take longer to do the Munros or whatever, and think about the future.

The Scottish Mountaineering Council (www.smc.org.uk) tirelessly and vigorously represents walkers' interests; its website is a useful source of news and suggestions for individual action. The Ramblers Association (Scotland) is also a dedicated campaigner (check out www.ramblers.org.uk).

With the passage of access legislation (see p21), one consuming issue was more or less laid to rest. While others cause people to jump up and down from time to time (notably payment for parking in popular walking areas), the guarantees provided by the legislation have been underpinned by a quiet revolution in land ownership in rural Scotland. The National Trust has long been a major owner and the John Muir Trust has substantially increased its holdings. At the same time, community-led buyouts of large estates have significantly increased the area of land owned and managed by local people. Starting with the renowned acquisition of the North Assynt Estate by the **Assynt Crofters' Trust** (www.assyntcrofters.co.uk), purchases have included the **North Harris Estate** (www.north-harris.org) on the Isle of Harris in the Western Isles and many others, such as the Isles of Eigg and Gigha, while Barra (p251) was gifted to the nation by its owner. All this is certainly not to imply that individual ownership of estates is undesirable, merely to recognise what is for many Scots the justified return of the land to the people after the brutal Highland Clearances of the late 18th and early to mid-19th centuries.

The major players in the nature conservation arena:

John Muir Trust (☎ 0131 554 0114; www.jmt.org; 41 Commercial St, Edinburgh EH6 6JD) Established in 1983 and commemorating the work of Scots-born US-national-parks-pioneer John Muir, the trust acquires and sensitively and sustainably manages wild areas, and repairs damage, especially to paths. The trust owns eight estates, from Sandwood in northwest Sutherland to the summit of Ben Nevis. Members can get involved by planting trees, repairing paths, collecting acorns and building dry-stone dykes.

National Trust for Scotland (☎ 0131 243 9300; www.nts.org.uk; 28 Charlotte Sq, Edinburgh EH2 4ET) Since 1931 the trust has acted as a guardian of the nation's architectural, scenic and historic treasures. Scotland's largest conservation charity, with more than 270,000 members, it cares for more than 77,000 hectares of land and more than 100 buildings. Its major land-holdings are the Brodick, Glencoe, Kintail & West Affric, Mar Lodge and Torridon Estates, which include some of the finest mountain areas in Scotland.

Royal Society for the Protection of Birds (☎ 0131 311 6500; www.rspb.org.uk; 25 Ravelston Tce, Edinburgh EH4 3TP) The society campaigns for 'wild birds and the environment'. It is Britain's largest conservation charity and owns and/or manages more than 40 reserves in Scotland, including Hoy (Orkney), Balranald (North Uist), Abernethy (Cairngorms), Inversnaid (Loch Lomond) and Loch Gruinart (Islay). Its magazine *Birds* keeps members updated on conservation issues.

Scottish Natural Heritage (SNH; ☎ 01463 725000; www.snh.org.uk; Great Glen House, Leachkin Rd, Inverness IV3 8NW) The government body responsible for caring for the country's natural heritage; its 11 area offices are the best local points of contact. It advises the government on natural heritage matters, owns and manages numerous reserves (notably National Nature Reserves), runs grant schemes to promote nature conservation, supports the countryside rangers services and produces a wide range of publications.

Scottish Rights of Way and Access Society (☎ 0131 558 1222; www.scotways.com; 24 Annandale St, Edinburgh EH7 4AN) The Society has been safeguarding public access since 1845. It works through negotiation and mediation to ensure that access legislation is successful. It publishes the excellent *Scottish Hill Tracks,* a guide to major hill paths and rights of way.

Scottish Wildlife Trust (☎ 0131 312 7765; www.swt.org.uk; Cramond Glebe Rd, Edinburgh EH4 6NS) The trust's mission is to protect Scotland's wildlife. It owns or manages around 110 wildlife reserves, from the Borders to Orkney, and places special emphasis on protecting endangered species. Members are involved in the trust's work and its trainees gain practical experience on the job.

Trees for Life (TFL; ☎ 01309 691292; www.treesforlife.org.uk; The Park, Findhorn Bay, Forres IV36 3TZ) Scarcely a household name but TFL's achievements are outstanding. Its main aim is to restore the Highlands' Caledonian forest, covering an area of 155,000 hectares. Since 1989, staff and volunteers have planted more than 500,000 native trees, grown from seed they collected. The major project is centred on Glen Affric.

Woodland Trust Scotland (☎ 01764 662554; www.woodland-trust.org.uk; Glenruthven Mill, Abbey Rd, Auchterarder PH3 1DP) Originally established in England, the trust's aims are to keep natural woodlands safe from development, and to enhance their diversity with new plantings and removal of exotic species. It cares for more than 50 woods, including Abriachan and two near Drumnadrochit by Loch Ness.

Coasts, Climbs & Canals

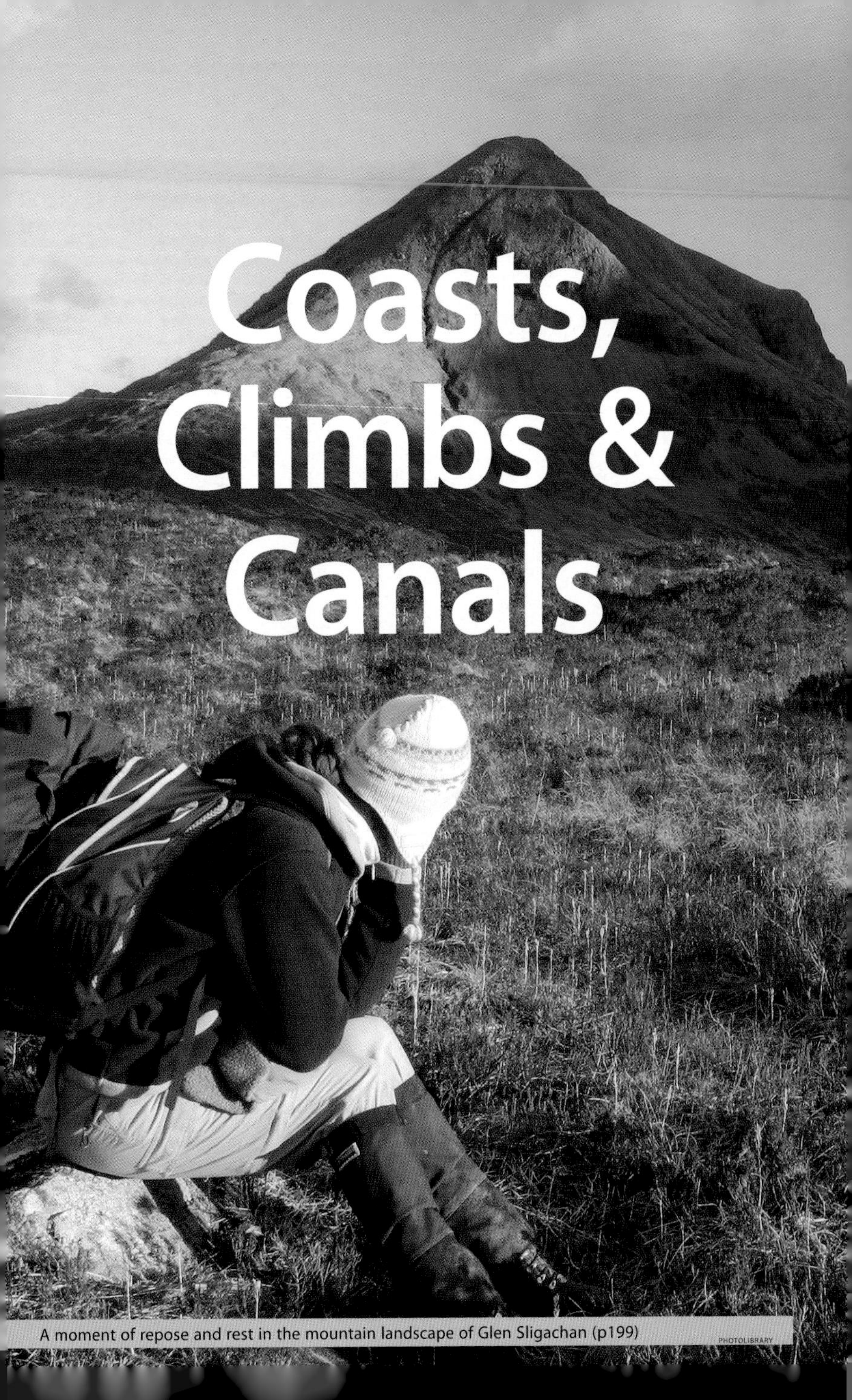

A moment of repose and rest in the mountain landscape of Glen Sligachan (p199) PHOTOLIBRARY

Glencoe's Aonach Eagach ridge (p139) serves up a spectrum of experiences for hikers

GARETH McCORMACK

Walking in Scotland is all about variety, contrast and choice, but if you're new to the country, such diversity could be more bewildering than beneficial.

There are various solutions to this dilemma – such as sticking a pin in a map, drawing names from a hat, picking the oddest names – but, more rationally, we've picked out three themes among the walks: history; coasts and beaches; and the classically Scottish endeavour of Munro bagging. Woven into almost all the walks is another theme: wildlife watching. Sighting sea life is a bonus on coastal walks, and animal encounters are a pleasant surprise everywhere, whether they feature otters, ospreys, golden eagles or red deer.

HISTORY & HERITAGE

There is ample visible evidence of Scotland's long history, right from the border with England to the country's northernmost extremity, and many fascinating examples are to be found on walks in this book – in buildings or other objects that you see, in roads or tracks along which you walk, or simply through association with someone famous.

Dating from prehistoric times, you'll find Iron Age brochs (tower houses) along the **Yesnaby coast** (p278) on Orkney Mainland – a walk that starts close to the best-preserved Neolithic village in northern Europe – and on a small island on the **Eshaness coast walk** (p289) in Shetland. Forts from the same era are dotted along the Great Glen, one of them overlooking the **Great Glen Way** (p168) near Fort Augustus. The Romans occupied the countryside surrounding the **Eildon Hills** (p79), where they too built forts, and from where they

Autumnal evening light lingers on Slioch (p222) in Wester Ross GARETH McCORMACK

counted the miles along their roads. Still with conflict in mind, a particularly bloody period in Scotland's history, the Wars of Independence, is recalled in Bruce's Stone at the start of the **Merrick walk** (p72). The treachery and tragedy of the Massacre of Glen Coe pervades the Lost Valley, through which you pass on the way to **Bidean nam Bian** (p136) in Glen Coe. The 18th-century military roads now make for easy walking along the **West Highland Way** (p89) and **Great Glen Way** (p168), but it's sobering to recall that this extraordinary 1100-mile network of early highways was built mainly to keep rebellious Highlanders under control.

'The treachery and tragedy of the Massacre of Glen Coe pervades the Lost Valley.'

On a much more peaceable note, there is also an abundance of evidence revealing details of old lifestyles long gone, in the silent remains of stone cottages in many now-remote places. Shielings were simple stone-built cottages, which were usually occupied only during the summer, for fishing or tending sheep and cattle. Little clusters of them can be found all along the northeast coast of **Lewis** (p237), beside the historic **Rhenigidale path** (p241) on Harris, and in **Glen Affric** (p174), to name but a few locations.

PUTTING SCOTLAND ON THE MAP

Timothy Pont was possibly the earliest Scottish map maker. Among the many places he visited in the late 16th century were Ben Nevis, Kintail, An Teallach and Torridon. His maps were published in Amsterdam in 1634.

THE TRADITIONAL HIGHLAND CAIRN *Fraser Mackenzie*

Throughout the Highlands, walkers will come across traditional Highland cairns. The best constructed are beehive or conical in shape, and can vary in height from less than 1m to about 2m. Most are built after the fashion of a dry-stone dyke (or wall), but others appear to be no more than a heap of stones. More modern examples, with cemented stones, often bear an inscribed plaque.

Cairns, traditionally built to mark spots of local significance, have long been a feature of Highland culture. Mostly they mark the site of a sudden death, perhaps as the result of an accident or, in more remote times, an inter-clan skirmish. A sudden death was a *bas gun sagart* (death without a priest) and it was believed that the soul of the departed would be consigned to the hottest part of purgatory. As a result, each passer-by was expected to put a stone on the cairn and to pray for the repose of the deceased's soul.

Some cairns mark places where, in the days when coffins were carried from one district to another, mourners stopped for refreshments, placing the remains reverently by the roadside. Again, passers-by were expected to add a stone to the cairn and pray for the departed. Sadly, many old coffin cairns that used to adorn Highland roads have disappeared as roads have been widened.

Tradition also has it that in the ancient days of clan battles, the fighting men would each bring a rock to the place of muster and, after the conflict was over, survivors would each take away a stone. The remainder would be heaped together to form a cairn. Yet again passers-by were expected to add to the cairn.

'Cuiridh mi clach 'nad charn,' a well-known Gaelic saying, literally means 'I will put a stone on your cairn' (and thereby keep your memory fresh). Though the meaning of the expression is now more metaphysical, indicating that the speaker will undertake some action to honour his companion, its continued existence does indicate the importance of the cairn in Highland culture.

Long may the tradition continue.

Two Scottish mountains were the scene of early scientific inquiries: measurements of gravitational pull on **Schiehallion** (p112) inspired the development of those all-important wiggly lines on contour maps, while for many years meteorological data was collected daily at the observatory on the summit of **Ben Nevis** (p123).

Navigation around Scotland's often-treacherous coast was made much safer by the building of lighthouses during the 19th century, many of them in incredibly rugged, seemingly inaccessible locations. Some of the most impressive feature in this book, starting in the southeast with **St Abb's Head** (p81) and finishing with the northernmost of all, **Muckle Flugga** (p286). In between, and way up in the north, are **Stoerhead** (p271), **Eilean Glas** (p254), **Cape Wrath** (p258) at the northwestern tip of mainland Scotland, **Noup Head** (p282) on the Orkney isle of Westray, and **Eshaness** (p289) on Shetland Mainland.

Buachaille Etive Mór (p134), gateway to Glen Coe, where the MacDonalds were betrayed and massacred

MARK DAFFE

The Great Glen Way (p168) follows much of the mighty Caledonian Canal

EOIN CLARKE

One precursor of the long phase of industrial development, which culminated in the so-called industrial revolution of the 19th century, was the short-lived ironworks that plundered the oakwoods on the shores of Loch Maree, at the foot of that fine peak **Slioch** (p222). The Caledonian Canal, which features prominently along the **Great Glen Way** (p168), was an outstanding engineering achievement, especially the flights of locks in Neptune's Staircase at Banavie, and at Fort Augustus. World Heritage–listed **New Lanark** (p58), on the upper reaches of the River Clyde, was not only the site of a large cotton mill but also of Robert Owen's pioneering social-welfare reforms. As the industrial revolution cranked up, fresh water supplies for the rapidly expanding population of Glasgow became a pressing necessity. The **Greenock Cut** (p53), a long canal in the Inverclyde hills, was part of one scheme to resolve the problem; another much larger one brought water from Loch Katrine along a pipeline at the foot of the **Campsie Fells** (p55). Large-scale industry, prompted by the abundant supplies of fresh water, came comparatively late to the Highlands. Aluminium smelters were built, one in the improbable location of **Kinlochleven** (p96) – now on the West Highland Way – where, after the smelter was shut down, one of the buildings was converted to a climbing centre. The other smelter, near Fort William, was supplied by a large hydroelectric scheme. The **Road to the Isles walk** (p129), following a historic cattle-droving route, passes right past one of the dams, Loch Treig, created for the project.

HISTORICALLY TANGLED WEB

A privately maintained website, www.scotshistoryonline.co.uk, emanating from the Scottish History Club, covers several thousand years of Scottish history and scores of topics.

Westray's Noup Head (p282)
GARETH McCORMACK

A BUNCH OF FIVES

Another way to avoid bewilderment is to follow our selection of the best thematic walks. Rather than trawl the Munros on a near-impossible quest for the cream of them, we've shifted down a gear to the Corbetts (mountains between 2500ft and 3000ft), several of which feature in these pages. In fact, many walkers consider the Corbetts to be as challenging as the Munros, lacking only their height. The best coast walks is another obvious thematic choice, and we've distilled a favourite selection from the many short walks outlined in the book.

CORBETTS

- Goatfell (p99)
- Ben Loyal (p262)
- Quinag (p267)
- Beinn Dearg Mhór (p216)
- The Cobbler (p103)

COAST WALKS

- Muckle Roe (p288)
- West Westray Coast (p280)
- Sandwood Bay & Cape Wrath (p258)
- Vatersay (p252)
- Cock of Arran (p101)

SHORT WALKS

- Falls of Kirkaig (p269)
- Lorgill & the Hoe (p210)
- Meall Fuar-mhonaidh (p188)
- The Whangie (p59)
- Arthur's Seat (p50)

COASTS & BEACHES

With 6158 miles (9911km) of coast you'd expect Scotland to do a good line in sea-oriented walks, and it certainly does.

Along the southeast shores there are spectacular cliffs and outstanding outdoor geology case studies separating fishing villages along the **Burnmouth to St Abb's Head walk** (p81). Virtually perched on Edinburgh's doorstep, the shores of **Aberlady** and **Gullane Bays** (p48) offer easy and scenic walking, often in what feels surprisingly like a remote setting. On the Isle of Arran, the north coast is an outstandingly attractive blend of rocky shores, small beaches, impressive cliffs and fine hill and glen panoramas – all seen on the **Cock of Arran walk** (p101). You then have to go a long way north, right up to the Isle of Skye, to find more coastal experiences. The **Coast and Cuillin walk** (p199) offers the best of both worlds, from rugged cliffs and the famous Bad Step, to Loch Coruisk, overlooked by rocky mountains on three sides and separated from the sea by low rocky knolls.

Although the coast of Lewis has few of the beaches that are the glory of the rest of the Western Isles, there is some highly scenic walking along the far northeast coast between **Tolsta** and **Ness** (p237), and over on the **west side** (p239) a fine cliff-top walk finishes at the thatched cottages of a superbly restored crofting village. Some of the best of the famed Outer Hebridean beaches, pristine and gleaming white, are on the small island of **Vatersay** (p252), where on a good day all you need are palms and umbrellas and you could be in the Caribbean.

SEE BIRDS

More than 100,000 sea birds live at Hermaness, including some 50,000 puffins, 32,000 gannets, 28,000 fulmars and 7000 kittiwakes.

A nesting fulmar is unimpressed with all the puffin and blowin' DAVID TIPLING

Sandwood Bay (p258), in the far northwestern corner of the country, lays claim to being the finest beach on the mainland. It's remote and totally unspoiled, a creamy-white insert in a long, cliff-lined coast that ends abruptly at spectacular Cape Wrath.

The coastline of Muckle Roe (p288) is resplendent with red granite GARETH McCORMACK

The Northern Isles offer coast-walking aficionados a magnificent feast. Hoy, the largest of the Orkney Isles, is famous for its **Old Man** (p275), an extraordinary 137m-high sea stack and the highlight of a varied day out on the island. Mile after scenic mile of **Westray's west coast** (p280) are easily accessible, and here, on the **Castle O'Burrian walk** (p282), puffin sightings are almost guaranteed in season. Some of the most stunning cliffs, geos and stacks anywhere line Orkney Mainland's west coast, including **Yesnaby Castle** (p280), a serious sea-stack rival to the Old Man of Hoy.

SIR HUGH'S HUMUNGOUS HILLS

Sir Hugh Munro, whose original list of Munros was published in 1891, didn't climb them all. He was repelled from Skye's Inaccessible Pinnacle by atrocious weather and died before doing the last on his list, in Deeside.

> 'With 6158 miles of coast you'd expect Scotland to do a good line in sea-oriented walks, and it does.'

Almost all the walking in the Shetland Isles is along the coast. Not to be missed is the colourful, indented coast around **Muckle Roe** (p288), the gloriously easy walking across cropped grass above the rugged black cliffs of **Eshaness** (p289) and, furthest north of all, **Hermaness** (p286) – not only for the view of Muckle Flugga lighthouse and Out Stack, the most northerly outpost of the British Isles, but also for teeming colonies of sea birds.

Peering into the jaws of Glen Sligachan from the flanks of Bla Bheinn (p203)

GARETH McCORMACK

Goats go wild on An Teallach (p214) MARK DAFFEY

Peregrine falcons haunt the Highlands DAVID TIPLING

MUNRO BAGGING

The pastime of Munro bagging (done casually or fast-and-furiously, depending on the bagger), is often derided as mere list ticking – more for the sake of the ticks than the mountains themselves – but working through the list of 284 peaks over 3000ft (914m) would mean that you'd travel widely across Scotland; though you'd visit only two of the islands (Skye and Mull) and never go south of the Glasgow–Edinburgh central belt. We've described in detail the ascent of 33 Munros, from Ben Nevis to some only just scraping into the list. There are also pointers to many others in the More Walks sections at the end of several chapters.

The most southerly of the Munros, Ben Lomond, is an early temptation along the West Highland Way; you can escape the crowds on the main route here by following the less-frequented **Ptarmigan route** (p105). Further north, **Ben Lawers** (p111) is the highest peak in the central highlands, a sprawling massif high enough to support unusual alpine flora. Right in the reputed geographical centre of Scotland, the elegant cone of **Schiehallion** (p112) is a comparatively easy climb along an excellent path.

Standing guard at the eastern entrance to spectacular Glen Coe, **Buachaille Etive Mór** (p134) looks to be beyond the reach of mere walkers, but appearances are deceptive and it's really quite straightforward. Nearby to the west, **Bidean nam Bian** (p136), the highest peak in the glen and a mountain of great character, is best explored along a classic circuit route. But the most eye-catching, heart-stopping peak (or rather ridge) in Glen Coe is

...AND I WOULD WALK 500 MILES

If you have the time (and the legs) for it, the ultimate Scottish walking odyssey would be to link the Southern Upland Way, the John Muir Way, the Forth and Clyde Canal from Edinburgh to Glasgow, the West Highland Way and the Great Glen Way – a total stroll of around 490 miles (784km).

LONG DISTANCE WALKS

Scotland has four official waymarked long-distance paths – the Southern Upland, West Highland, Speyside, and Great Glen Ways – and several more recognised long walks. They traverse much of the finest scenery in the country, though the idea has yet to really take hold in the islands. None are particularly difficult walks, though a good measure of stamina is called for at times, making the satisfaction at the end even greater. Three of the four official routes are described in detail in this book; the other long walks are outlined, with details about where you can go for more information. Below are 12 long haul options (at the time of research, the John Muir Way wasn't quite complete).

Walk	Distance	Duration	Page
Borders Abbeys Way	65 miles (105km)	5 days	86
Cateran Trail	64 miles (103km)	5 days	118
Great Glen Way	73 miles (117km)	4 days	168
Fife Coastal Path	81 miles (135km)	5-6 days	118
John Muir Way	50 miles (80km)	4-5 days	85
Kintyre Way	88 miles (143km)	5-7 days	118
Rob Roy Way	79 miles (126km)	5-8 days	118
St Cuthbert's Way	62.5 miles (100.5km)	5 days	85
Southern Upland Way	209.5 miles (338km)	9 days	63
Speyside Way	65 miles (104.5km)	5-7 days	163
West Highland Way	95 miles (153km)	7 days	89
West Island Way	30 miles (49km)	2 days	118

Reaching the summit of Liathach (p229) requires some serious scree scrambling

GARETH McCORMAC

undoubtedly **Aonach Eagach** (p139): feared, admired and aspired to, with few equals among the Munros for challenging scrambling in high, airy places. Near neighbours to the north, dominating the southern side of Glen Nevis, the gracefully contoured **Mamores group** (p128) has four Munros, potentially there for the bagging on a long and rewarding day. No surprises in the next Munro on the list, on the opposite side of Glen Nevis, the mighty Ben Nevis – the only peak among Scotland's many Bens to be known simply as 'the Ben'. The ever-popular **Mountain Track** (p123) is really just a long uphill walk to one of the finest panoramic views in the country. If you're looking for a little excitement en route to the roof of Scotland, the **Carn Mór Dearg Arête** (p127) offers a breezy frisson or two along its knife edge.

Breaking away from the western side of the country to the realms of Cairngorms National Park, **Cairn Gorm** (p147) itself is a bump on the vast and gently undulating plateau; it's well worth the effort to experience the Cairngorms' unique, wide-open spaces. Nearby is **Ben Macdui** (p150), the second-highest summit in Scotland and virtually a must. Moving north, **Sgurr nan Ceathreamhnan** (p177), deep in Glen Affric, commits you to a much longer approach than do the nearby **Five Sisters of Kintail** (p180), which rise directly from the road. Accessible though the sorority may be, a traverse of the quintet, which includes three Munros and a greater total ascent than for Ben Nevis, is no mere doddle. As the raven flies, **Gleouraich** (p182) is only a matter of minutes south of Kintail, and is another Munro that can be tackled directly from the road. It's a fine peak with a much greater feeling of remoteness. **Creag Meagaidh** (p184), beyond the southeastern side of the Great Glen, is more a massif than a peak and provides a classic horseshoe route above a rugged corrie.

'En route to the roof of Scotland, the Carn Mór Dearg Arête offers a breezy frisson or two along its knife edge.'

Airy Corrag Bhuidhe (p216) GARETH McCORMACK

Thrilling Carn Mór Dearg Arête (p127) EOIN CLARKE

Seeing the light at Stoerhead (p271) MARK DAFFEY

Munros on the Isle of Skye don't come easily, though the two in this book (plus a third peak) offer a graduated approach to the really serious stuff. **Bruach na Frithe** (p195) is 'only' an energetic – if rocky – walk, while **Bla Bheinn** (p202), standing slightly apart from the central Black Cuillin mountains, does involve a little modest scrambling. **Sgurr Dearg** (p204), in the heart of the Black Cuillin, is not on the Munro list, but it does offer a good introduction to the scrambling style of ascent and the unavoidable exposure involved in climbing them.

Wester Ross is richly endowed with the big 'hills', most of them leaning towards the challenging end of the spectrum. **Slioch** (p222), which dominates Loch Maree, involves a relatively long approach, and is a good walk in its own right. In the heart of Torridon, **Beinn Alligin** (p227) provides an exhilarating introduction to the skills you will need on **Liathach** (p229) with its pinnacles and knife-edges. Then, if you've enjoyed Liathach, you should be ready for the equally adrenaline-based fun on **An Teallach** (p214), which, like almost all of its fellow Munros, offers a feast of fantastic wide views.

MAKING TRACKS

A good place to start chasing up information about long-distance walks is the VisitScotland website, http://walking.visitscotland.com, where you'll find walk outlines and contact details.

Edinburgh & Glasgow

Scotland's capital, Edinburgh, and its largest city, Glasgow, enjoy contrasting settings, with their own distinctive variations on the themes of hills, waterways and the sea. Within easy reach of both is a wealth of walking opportunities, allowing you to explore these themes. Excellent public transport brings the hills and glens within easy reach of the cities. Even so, there's much to be said for prising yourself away from the cities' rich array of charms and lingering in the small towns near the walks, with their particular claims for your attention. Be prepared for some surprises, and many reasons to return with your walking boots to this often-overlooked part of the country.

Beyond the capital, this chapter picks up two of the pervasive landscape themes. The Pentland Hills are Edinburgh's oasis and its wilderness, especially when the weather is wild and windy. To the east, the delightful Lothian coast is a haven for wildlife, with secluded beaches that tempt you to linger. Short walks take you to two of the emblematic basalt hills rising sharply from the surrounding lowlands.

A short ride or drive from central Glasgow there are some fine walks along routes intimately linked to the industrial past. Not only are they rich in historical interest, they are also strong on attractive scenery and enlivened with occasional wildlife sightings. From the pioneering mill village of New Lanark on the River Clyde to engineering feats that brought water to Glaswegians' homes, both south of the Firth of Clyde, and below the Campsie Fells in the north, these walks can spirit you away from the city's chaos to the stress-free open spaces of the countryside.

HIGHLIGHTS

- Waves, rocks, birds and the surprising remoteness of the **Lothian coast** (p48)
- Scaling **Scald Law** (p49), the highest summit in Edinburgh's Pentland Hills
- Exploring the remarkable **Greenock Cut** (p53) along an easy path with great views near and far
- Wandering across the wild and lonely **Campsie Fells** (p55), high above the crowded Clyde valley
- Sharing the awesome spectacle of the **Falls of Clyde** (p56) with poets and artists

- www.edinburgh.org
- www.seeglasgow.com

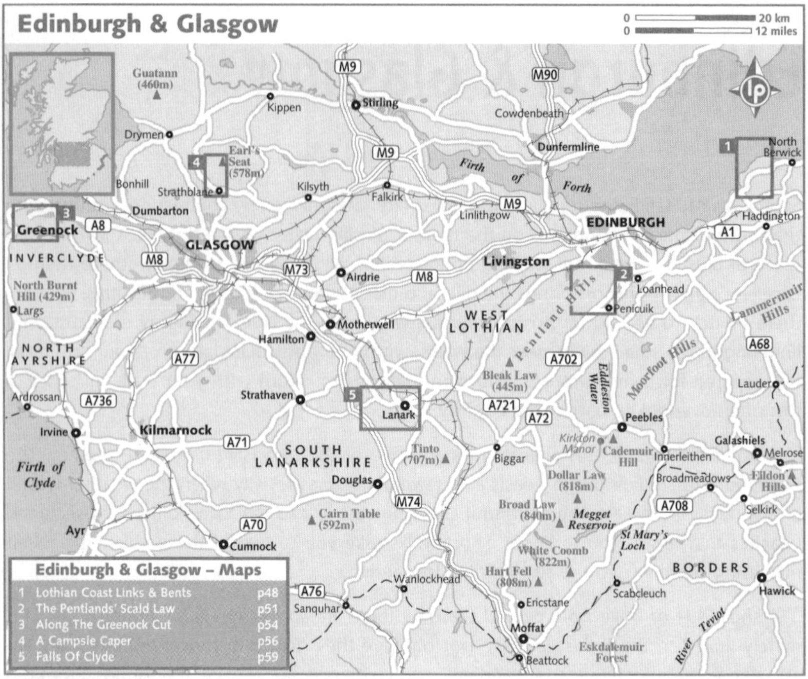

INFORMATION
Maps & Books

For general orientation, the OS Travel – Road 1:250,000 map No 4 *Southern Scotland* is fine.

The Scottish Mountaineering Club's *Southern Uplands* by KM Andrew provides good background for a variety of walks.

EDINBURGH

☎ 0131 / pop 430,000

The thin winding streets of the Old Town and the wide roads of the Georgian New Town, a World Heritage site (see p29) in Scotland's capital, are best explored on foot; reason enough for spending time here. The walks described in this section are all within easy reach by bus or your own wheels.

INFORMATION
Maps & Books

The AA *Edinburgh* street guide, with good clear maps at 1:10,000 and 1:15,000, should avoid the embarrassment of getting lost.

Edinburgh and Lothians by Roger Smith describes 25 walks in the city and further afield. *Edinburgh and Lothians* by Brian Conduit and John Brooks has a slightly wider scope with 28 walks in the city, coast and hills. There's little to choose between the maps in these two books.

Lonely Planet's *Edinburgh* guide is your essential companion and is packed with information on accommodation, restaurants, pubs, bars, transport – it even describes five varied walks around the city.

Waterstone's (☎ 226 2666; 128 Princes St; daily) has a good selection of Scottish titles and a reasonable range of walking guides and maps. There's a coffee shop on the 2nd floor.

Information Sources

The **tourist information centre** (☎ 0845 225 5121; www.edinburgh.org; Waverley Market, 3 Princes St;) is virtually always busy. It stocks a good range of maps, but unfortunately walking-related literature is scarce, as are any similarly themed handouts from the otherwise helpful staff.

EDINBURGH'S SEVEN HILLS

What do Edinburgh and Rome have in common? Nothing to do with grandiose buildings, chaotic traffic or the cat population. It's the more important fact that each is graced by seven hills adorning its horizons. Apart from the well-known Edinburgh Castle, Calton Hill and Arthur's Seat in and close to the city, they are Corstorphine (150m) to the west, Craiglockhart (175m), Blackford (164m) and Braid (208m). The last three are between Edinburgh and the Pentland Hills to the south.

Each June since 1980 runners and walkers have taken part in the 14-mile (22.5km) **Seven Hills Race** (www.seven-hills.org.uk). The route can be of your own choosing and will inevitably involve 2200ft of ascent, which is not even as high as a single Corbett (p108), so not particularly arduous for fit walkers. Full details of the route are on the website, so you can test yourself against the competitors without the stress of a race.

Supplies & Equipment

Both **Nevisport** (☎ 225 9498; edinburgh@nevisport.com; 19 Rose St; ⏰ daily), at one end of the outdoor shopping precinct, and **Tiso's** (☎ 225 9486; edinburgh@tiso.co.uk; 123 Rose St; ⏰ daily), at the other, stock the full range of equipment, books and maps.

The most convenient supermarket is downstairs in **Marks & Spencer** (54 Princes St; ⏰ daily).

SLEEPING & EATING

Consult Lonely Planet's *Edinburgh* or *Scotland* guides or the free *Edinburgh & Lothians Accommodation Guide*, available at the TIC. Alternatively, try **VisitScotland** (☎ 0845 225 5121; www.visitscotland.com), though phone bookings through TICs add £3 to the tariff.

Edinburgh Mortonhall Caravan & Camping Park (☎ 664 1533; mortonhall@meadowhead.co.uk; 38 Mortonhall Gate, Frogston Rd East; unpowered/powered sites for 2 £18/20) is over on the southern city fringe, not far away from the Pentland Hills.

Edinburgh Central SYHA Hostel (☎ 0870 1155 3255; www.syha.org.uk; 9 Haddington Pl; dm £19) opened in 2006 and is SYHA's Edinburgh flagship, complete with bistro and bar. All the rooms, from singles through to the eight-bed dorms, are en suite. It's only around 10 minutes at a walking pace from Princes St.

Acorn Lodge Guest House (☎ 555 1557; www.acornlodge.co.uk; 26 Pilrig St; s/d £50/100), off Leith Walk, is only around 15 minutes' walk from both the train and the bus station. A business-like place, it is tastefully decorated, and is neither bare nor fussy. The street it stands on is nice and quiet, at least by Edinburgh's standards, and the breakfast is better than you will find in a lot of places.

Valvona & Crolla Caffé Bar (☎ 556 6066; www.valvonacrolla.co.uk; 19 Elm Row; mains £9-15; ⏰ lunch) is an Italian oasis, ideal for perfecting the art of the long lunch, but only once you've cruised past its deli (Scotland's oldest), the alluring walls of wines and the baskets of the bar's own bread, baked on site. The menu changes daily and features genuine Italian family recipes and fresh Scottish produce.

Bar Italia (☎ 0131 228 6379; 100 Lothian Rd; mains £7-10; ⏰ lunch Mon-Sat, dinner daily) A classic Italian restaurant, complete with checked tablecloths, candles in Chianti bottles and ebullient waiters. If you love Italian food, this is the place, and it's good value too.

GETTING THERE & AROUND

National Express (☎ 0870 580 8080; www.nationalexpress.co.uk) runs coaches from London Victoria to/from Edinburgh (£32, nine hours, three daily).

GNER (☎ 08457 225225; www.gner.co.uk) operates train services from London Kings Cross (4¾ hours, at least 20 daily); fares vary widely.

Scottish Citylink (☎ 0870 550 5050; www.citylink.co.uk) bus service 900 goes between Edinburgh and Glasgow (£5, 1¼ hours, every 15 minutes).

First ScotRail (☎ 0845 755 0033; www.firstscotrail.com) provides a shuttle-train service between Edinburgh and Glasgow Queen St (£10, 50 minutes, every 30 minutes).

For more information on international flight connections, see p304.

First Edinburgh (☎ 663 9233; www.firstedinburgh.co.uk) operates local buses in and around Edinburgh.

LOTHIAN COAST LINKS & BENTS

Duration	2¾–3 hours
Distance	6.7 miles (10.8km)
Difficulty	easy
Start	Aberlady Bay
Finish	Yellowcraig
Nearest Town	Gullane (below)
Transport	bus

Summary A finely crinkled coastline, a sprinkling of islets, and beaches of sand and shingle, all on Edinburgh's doorstep.

Aberlady Bay (pronounced as if there's a 'y' between the 'a' and 'd') is little more than 10 miles northeast of Edinburgh but is wonderfully wild and natural, a real haven for wildlife. In fact Aberlady Bay Local Nature Reserve was the first such reserve to be established anywhere in Britain, way back in 1952. It protects a remarkable variety of habitats – mudflats, salt and freshwater marshlands, grassland, sand dunes, sand and shingle beaches and the sea – and is a bird-watcher's paradise. There are intrusions, but the relics of WWII defences are partly overgrown, and the golf course blends with the surrounding landscape. On the OS map you'll see the terms 'bent' and 'links'; the former means rough grass, the latter – if you like – 'unrough' grass. This walk takes you through the reserve, along beaches and through low dunes, with views all the way to Yellowcraig and its popular beach, not far from North Berwick.

PLANNING

Maps

Either the OS Explorer 1:25,000 map No 351 *Dunbar & North Berwick*, or the OS Landranger 1:50,000 map No 66 *Edinburgh* cover the walk.

NEAREST TOWN

The closest settlements to the walk are Aberlady and Dirleton, though the former has just a single shop and the Old Aberlady Inn, while the latter has a two hotels and a shop.

Gullane

☎ 01620 / pop 2171

This is definitely the place to aim for if you're inclined to linger in the area.

Kilmory B&B (☎ 842332; margaret@kilmore.fsbusiness.co.uk; Marine Tce; s/d £36/32) has superb views of the beach in a lovely garden setting.

The **Village Coffee Shop** (☎ 842509; 10 Rosebery Pl; light meals £4-9; 10am-5pm) is the best reason for stopping here. Everything is genuinely homemade and fresh, especially the sumptuous afternoon tea, and you can even have a Scottish beer with your scones.

Bangkok Thai (☎ 842233; Rosebery Pl; mains £7-12; dinner Tue-Sun), near the coffee shop, offers an alternative to the handful of pubs.

There's a Co-op supermarket and a bakery in the main street.

First Edinburgh (☎ 0131 663 9233; www.firstedinburgh.co.uk) bus services X5 and 124 to/from Edinburgh stop here (£5, 50 minutes, 12 services Monday to Saturday, 10 Sunday).

GETTING TO/FROM THE WALK

The car park at the nature reserve is beside the A198 Aberlady–North Berwick road, 0.7 miles from Aberlady. **First Edinburgh** (☎ 0131 663 9233; www.firstedinburgh.co.uk) bus services X5 and 124 to/from Edinburgh stop in Aberlady (£4, 45 minutes, 12 services

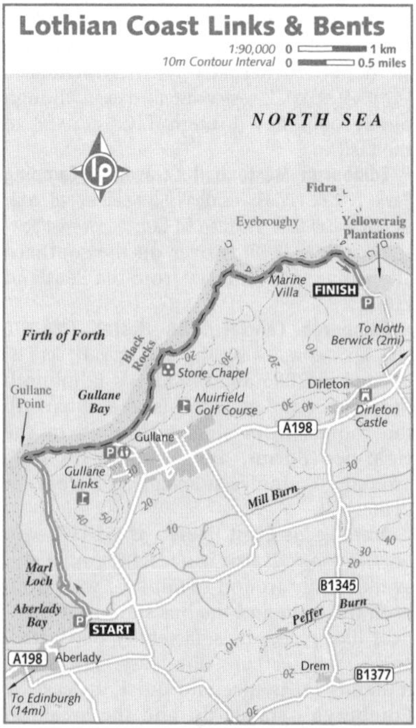

Monday to Saturday, 10 Sunday), from where a roadside footpath provides safe walking to the car park.

From Yellowcraig, simply follow the minor road from the car park south for one mile to the eastern end of Dirleton. The bus stop is 50m to your left. The same First Edinburgh services stop here.

THE WALK

From the car park, cross a long footbridge and set out along the wide path. Within five minutes it bends sharply right through a thicket and passes secluded Marl Loch. Beyond, the varied view takes in the Pentland Hills, the Forth road bridge and the Fife coast to the north. About 10 minutes further on, the path widens to a track. Continue straight ahead at an intersection to a warning sign: 'Beware golf may be in progress'. Cross the fairway speedily, aiming to the right of the concrete block on the far side. The track continues across wavy sand dunes and gains a little height, giving fine views of Gullane Sands to the west. The chunky concrete blocks beside the track, among the thorn bushes, are relics of coastal fortifications thrown up during WWII. Cross a crest, following a sign pointing to Gullane Point, and descend, passing a path on the right, to open ground overlooking the coast. Bear right downhill near **Gullane Point** to a narrow path parallel to the shore. If, however, the tide's in your favour, take to the beach. Continue round a point to a wider, longer beach where a sign marks the eastern boundary of the nature reserve. Wander along the beach, past a large black basalt bluff; alternatively, climb a clear path through the marram grass to a crest. Follow a track, cross a golf course then bear left at the green marker along a cliff-top path, which bears inland to skirt the thorn-bush entanglements. Bear left at an intersection and go down to Gullane Bents car park (about 50 minutes from the golf-course warning). There are toilets here and information about the coast.

Walk down a path to the beach and along the sand. At the far end, a path leads on through the dunes to a small shingle beach. Continue along the edge of the marram grass, past **Black Rocks** to a sandy beach. The path through the dunes passes a ruined ancient stone chapel, to a sandy beach (25 minutes from the car park). From the far end you then cruise along past a couple more beaches separated by shallow points. Low, rocky Eyebroughy Island is just offshore, and all of Fidra and its lighthouse comes into view. Cross flattish rocks at the base of a line of cliffs; about 75m short of a prominent beacon above the shore, climb a sandy path burrowing through the scrub (35 minutes from the beach beyond the chapel). Pass the beacon and a concrete lookout station (another WWII leftover), and emerge into the open beside a fence enclosing the substantial house **Marine Villa**. A path then keeps you off the shingle. From the eastern end of the next beach follow a path across the point to a beach, with a good view of conical North Berwick Law (p50). The direct route to the car park at the end of the walk is via scrub, open ground and scrub to a wide track in the open. **Yellowcraig** is nearby to the right (30 minutes from the beacon).

THE PENTLANDS' SCALD LAW

Duration	3¾–4 hours
Distance	8.2 miles (13.2km)
Difficulty	moderate
Start/Finish	Flotterstone
Nearest Town	Edinburgh (p46)
Transport	bus

Summary A classic, roller-coasting walk over the highest of the Pentland Hills in Edinburgh's backyard with fantastic vistas far and wide.

Only 7.6 miles (12.5km) south of Edinburgh, the Pentland Hills is a fine, compact range, extending from Bleak Law (445m) in the southwest to Allermuir Hill (493m) in the northeast. Its long and bumpy eastern flank borders the A702, which largely coincides with a Roman road, creating a natural barrier to the long, deep Logan Glen running through the centre of the hills' northern section. Here Loganlea and Glencorse Reservoirs feed Edinburgh's water supply, the former dating back to 1851.

Nearly 16 miles long and 6 miles wide, the Pentland Hills are blessed with more than 60 miles of paths. The greater part of the range is within the Pentland Hills Regional Park, established in 1986, a precious area that attracts crowds of city dwellers on weekends, intent on enjoying the many walking, cycling and bridle paths. The walk described here, involving 605m of ascent, takes you over Scald Law (579m), the highest summit in the Pentlands, and back past the reservoirs.

PLANNING

Maps

The OS Explorer 1:25,000 map No 344 *Pentland Hills* or the Harvey Superwalker 1:25,000 *Pentland Hills* map are ideal.

Information Sources

Pentland Hills ranger service (☎ 0131 445 3383; www.pentlandhills.org; Boghall Farm, Biggar Rd) maintains the **Flotterstone Ranger & Visitor Centre** (☎ 01968 677879; Flotterstone). Staff are on hand to answer questions and provide information about the regional park; pick up the *Discover the Pentland Hills Regional Park* brochure, which includes a good map, and check the weather forecast. The centre also has toilets. For details of ranger-led walks, ask for the annual **Outdoor Diary** (www.outdoor-diary.info).

GETTING TO/FROM THE WALK

MacEwan's (☎ 01387 256533) bus service 101 from Edinburgh (Waterloo Place) stops at Flotterstone (30 minutes, three a day Monday to Friday).

By car, take the A702 from Edinburgh to Flotterstone. Turn right for the signposted Flotterstone Inn and drive on to the ranger centre and car park, which is usually full on weekends.

THE WALK

From the ranger centre head west on a path through the woods, past a reconstructed

SHORT EDINBURGH WALKS

You can't possibly visit Edinburgh without climbing **Arthur's Seat** (251m), the unmissable, craggy lump of volcanic rock to the east of the city. It's easy enough to dash up and down, but this longer walk of 3 miles (4.9km) reveals some of its hidden corners and gives plenty of time to absorb the remarkable view. Allow about 1¾ hours; consult OS Explorer 1:25,000 map No 350. The start, a large car park on Queens Drive just south of Holyrood and the controversial parliament building, is on the route of Lothian Buses service 36, which runs along Princes St.

A flight of wooden steps leads to a rough path on your right (southwest). It climbs very steeply for a few hundred metres then levels out beside Salisbury Craigs. Follow the path down to a junction at the southeastern end of the Craigs. Turn left (north), heading uphill briefly; keep to the left and go down the wide valley of Hunter's Bog. At the northern end, descend to a path below a prominent crag. At the base of some crags on your left, bear right up a stepped path then up the side of a grassy glen. Go right up to a saddle and turn right. Follow steps or hard rocks as far as possible (to minimise erosion) to reach the summit. A direction plate helps with identification of the many features, near and far. Return to the saddle and descend to Dunsapie Loch below. Turn left and follow the path beside Queen's Drive back to the start.

Conical **North Berwick Law** (187m) in East Lothian is a prominent landmark for miles around so it's not surprising that the summit yields an amazingly wide view. An easy 1.3-mile (2km) walk of around 50 minutes up to the summit starts and finishes at a car park at the end of an access track 0.9 miles (1.4km) southeast of North Berwick town centre. Follow the A198 to Law Rd, from where signs show the way to North Berwick Law. **First Edinburgh** (☎ 0131 663 9233; www.firstedinburgh.co.uk) bus services X5 and 124 link Edinburgh and North Berwick (£5, one hour, 12 services Monday to Saturday, 10 Sunday). OS Landranger 1:50,000 map No 66 helps with finding your way to the start of the walk.

From the car park go through a gap in the stone wall and turn right along the signposted 'Public Footpath'. An information board here outlines the Law's long history, dating back to the Iron Age. After about 200m, bear left up a narrower path. Where it levels out, follow a wider grassy track bending left, uphill. Follow it around the southern flank to a small waymarker. Turn left; take your pick from multiple paths as you near the summit (187m). This small space is crowded with a trig pillar, a WWII defence lookout, an iron-fenced enclosure, ruins of a small building and a detailed direction plate for the features in the panoramic view. Retrace your steps to the car park.

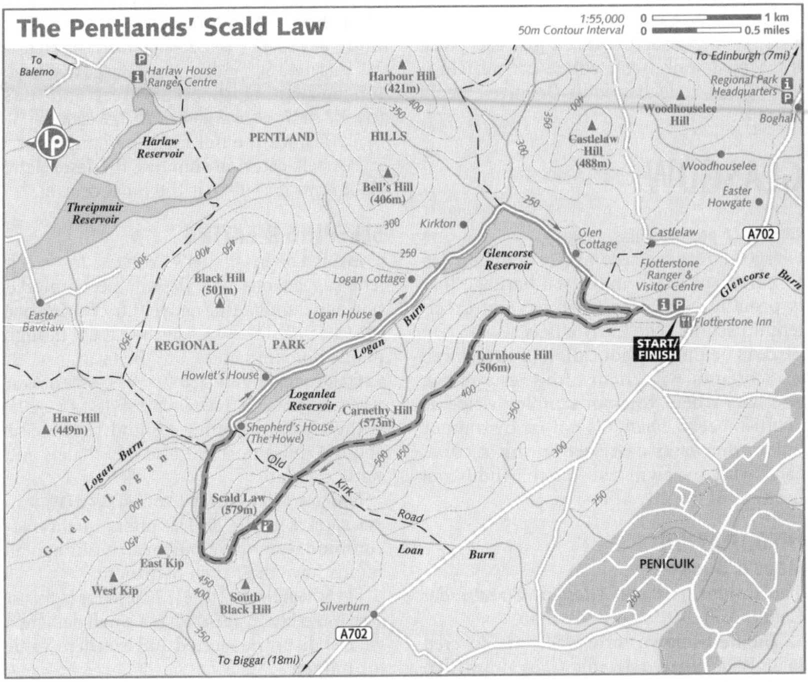

sheep stell (pen), to a road. Follow it for 30m then turn left along a track signposted to Scald Law. About 100m along bear left with another sign for the Law. Go through a gate, across a bridge and up a muddy path to start the climb. The clear path rises along a broad, grassed spur; cross a couple of stiles, pass through a copse of wind-whipped trees then continue steeply up to the main ridge and on to the summit of **Turnhouse Hill** (506m) reached in about 50 minutes.

Charge down, over a minor bump, to a saddle then tackle the steep slope up to the sprawling cairn on **Carnethy Hill** (573m), 30 minutes from Turnhouse Hill. The next descent starts steeply and soon eases but becomes boggy, down to the saddle. Crossing the pass is the once-busy Old Kirk Rd, formerly providing Bavelaw and Loganlea churchgoers with a convenient passage to Penicuik. The main objective is now directly above you, with another steepish pull to the bare summit of **Scald Law**, marked by a trig pillar (40 minutes from Carnethy Hill). The vista embraces a huge armful of hills to the south and the Firths of Clyde and Forth to the north.

Keeping on the northern side of the slope, descend southwest to the col at the foot of East Kip. Turn northeast and follow a rather faint track down, across a minor burn, and soon through a gateway. Steer away from the small plantation ahead and descend to a cluster of sheep pens. Go through a gateway and turn right. Follow the track through another gateway, near which is the tall Shepherd's House (The Howe) and a junction with Old Kirk Rd, which you crossed up in the hills (30 minutes from Scald Law). Cross the burn and bear right along a vehicle track that shortly becomes a road. Follow this for the length of **Loganlea Reservoir** and right around boomerang-shaped **Glencorse Reservoir**. Leave the road to follow a signposted path to Flotterstone via the filter beds; it leads down through woodland to a path parallel to a small stream, and on to rejoin the outward route at a Scald Law sign. It's not far back to the ranger centre (1¼ hours from the Shepherd's House).

The nearby **Flotterstone Inn** (☎ 01968 673717; mains £9-15; ⌚ lunch & dinner) is just the place for a post-walk beer, coffee or meal in a traditional-style bar with Belhaven beers on tap.

GLASGOW

☎ 0141 / pop 629,600

Glasgow, once the second city of the British Empire, has a rich industrial heritage that is proudly celebrated in its several excellent museums. The lively city is also a great place to begin your education in eating well in Scotland, with many fine restaurants, and bars where you can sample delectable Scottish beers. Then, it's not far by train or bus to the walks described in this section, each with its own take on the industrial heritage of the city and area.

INFORMATION

Maps & Books

The Collins 1:10,000 *Glasgow Streetfinder Colour Map* is the best city map.

The best-known local walks are covered in *25 Walks In and Around Glasgow* by Alan Forbes. The Pathfinder series guide *Glasgow, Ayrshire, Arran and the Clyde Valley* is also good. **Waterstone's** (153-157 Sauchiehall St) is well stocked with local and Scottish titles.

Information Sources

Glasgow TIC (☎ 204 4400; www.seeglasgow.com; 11 George Sq) is very helpful but, apart from stocking maps and books, has very little of specific interest for walkers.

Supplies & Equipment

Both **Nevisport** (☎ 332 4814; www.nevisport.com; 261 Sauchiehall St; ⌚ daily), in Glasgow's best, tongue-twisting, shopping street, and **Tiso's** (☎ 248 4877; glasgow@tiso.co.uk; 129 Buchanan St; ⌚ daily) stock the full range of equipment.

For self-catering supplies, the **Tesco Metro** (36-38 Argyle St; ⌚ daily) is the most central.

SLEEPING & EATING

Consult Lonely Planet's *Scotland* for excellent suggestions on Glasgow accommodation and dining. Alternatively, try **VisitScotland** (☎ 0845 225 5121; www.visitscotland.com), though phone bookings add £3 to the tariff.

Craigendmuir Park (☎ 779 4159; www.craigendmuir.co.uk; Stepps; unpowered/powered sites for 2 £12/15) is the closest camping ground to the city, about 4 miles north; it also has chalets and static caravans.

Glasgow SYHA Hostel (☎ 0870 004 1119; www.syha.org.uk; 8 Park Tce; dm £16) offers quality accommodation in a historic building; all rooms have their own bathroom.

Old School House (☎ 332 7600; oschoolh@hotmail.com; 194 Renfrew St; s/d £40/60) is a small detached villa, stylishly decorated and excellent value for money.

Bothy (☎ 334 4040; 11 Ruthven Lane; lunch/dinner mains £8/12; ⌚ lunch & dinner) is light years removed from any bothy you've visited out in the hills. The menu features traditional fare, including pot roast and steak pies, with a uniquely Scottish flavour.

GETTING THERE & AWAY

National Express (☎ 0870 580 8080; www.nationalexpress.com) runs coaches to/from London Victoria

THE RIVER CLYDE

A popular local saying claims that Glasgow made the Clyde, and the Clyde made Glasgow. This city would have remained a rural backwater had it not been for the cathedral, which during medieval times attracted pilgrims, prestige and power. Much later, during the Industrial Revolution, the river was at the heart of Glasgow's growth into a major port and the greatest industrial city in the British Empire.

Scotland's third-longest river, the Clyde flows for 105 miles from its source in the Lowther Hills, tumbling down about 2000ft as it wends through the Clyde valley and Lanarkshire to the centre of Glasgow. It enters the sea in the broad, 28-mile-long Firth of Clyde.

Looking at the Clyde from Glasgow's docks and knowing that 35,000 ships were launched from its once-productive shipyards, it's hard to believe that in the 1700s it was too shallow for the passage of even a rowing boat in places. In the 1690s the city's harbour was 20 miles downstream at Port Glasgow. During the late 18th century the river was dredged and its banks strengthened and development of the port took off.

to Glasgow's Buchanan St bus station (£32, 8¾ hours, three daily).

Virgin Trains (☎ 08457 222333; www.virgintrains.co.uk) link London Euston and Glasgow Central (5¾ hours, at least 15 daily); fares vary widely.

Scottish Citylink (☎ 0870 550 5050; www.citylink.co.uk) bus service 900 links Edinburgh and Glasgow (£5, one hour 20 minutes, every 15 minutes).

First ScotRail (☎ 0845 755 0033; www.firstscotrail.com) shuttles between Glasgow Queen St and Edinburgh Waverley (£10, 50 minutes, every 30 minutes).

For international flight and ferry connections, see p304.

ALONG THE GREENOCK CUT

Duration	3–3¼ hours
Distance	6.5 miles (10.5km)
Difficulty	easy
Start/Finish	Cornalees Bridge
Nearest Town	Inverkip (right)
Transport	private

Summary Explore an early-19th-century engineering marvel in the Inverclyde hills, with magnificent sea and mountain views across the Firth of Clyde.

Serving as the western gateway to Glasgow, the district of Inverclyde includes the major port and industrial towns of Port Glasgow, Greenock and Gourock, as well as the coastal villages of Inverkip and Wemyss Bay, further south and west. Inland, two large reservoirs, Loch Thom and the Gryfe, and an extensive area of rolling moorland are highlights of the 30,000-acre Clyde Muirshiel Regional Park, a popular park in the Renfrewshire hills.

The Greenock Cut walk snakes across north- and west-facing hillsides above the maritime centres, affording superb views of the Firth of Clyde and beyond. Five miles of the walk follow the now-disused aqueduct know as the Greenock Cut, built between 1825 and 1827 to carry water from the Great Reservoir (later renamed Loch Thom) to a booming Greenock. Robert Thom headed this engineering feat, subcontracting the work to teams that excavated countless tons of earth and rock and built 23 bridges. A great deal of work has been done in recent years to clear the aqueduct of masses of vegetation, to improve the path and to repair bridges and the stone bothies where the workmen who de-iced the aqueduct were housed.

PLANNING

Maps

The OS Explorer 1:25,000 map No 341 *Greenock, Largs & Millport* covers the route.

Information Sources

Cornalees visitor centre (☎ 521458; www.clydemuirshiel.co.uk), at the start of the walk, houses a small display about the surrounding area and sells drinks and snacks. Pick up a leaflet about the Greenock Cut.

NEAREST TOWN

Inverkip

☎ 01475 / pop 1598

Once a whisky smugglers' stopover on runs from Argyll and the islands, the conservation village of Inverkip, 2.8 miles from the Cornalees visitor centre, is a quiet haven from the city.

SLEEPING & EATING

Foresters House B&B (☎ 521433; www.forestershouse.com; Station Rd; s/d £35/24, cottage s/d £26/40) extends a very friendly welcome to its superbly appointed rooms, or the Forester's Cottage with bunkhouse-style accommodation.

Inverkip Hotel (☎ 521478; www.inverkip.co.uk; Main St; s/d £45/68, mains £8-17; lunch & dinner), in an old coaching inn, has comfortable rooms. In the dining room (popular with the locals), the extensive menu includes traditionals and an unusually imaginative vegetarian selection.

Kip General Store (Main St) does sandwiches as well as the usual groceries. There's a **Londis** (A78) supermarket at the northern end of the village.

GETTING THERE & AWAY

Strathclyde Passenger Transport (SPT; ☎ 0141 332 6811; www.spt.co.uk) has a suburban train service from Glasgow Central to Wemyss Bay that stops at Inverkip (£7 cheap day return, 50 minutes, at least 12 daily).

It's a 40-minute trip by car from Glasgow, via the M8 (A8) west to Greenock then the A78 to Inverkip.

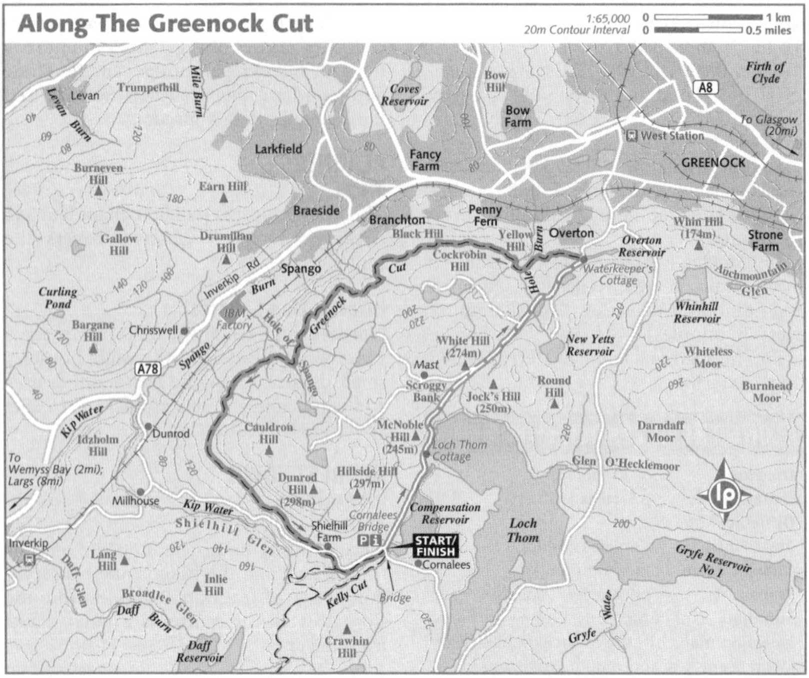

Along The Greenock Cut

GETTING TO/FROM THE WALK

There are no bus services to the start of the walk. From Inverkip train station it's a 3.5-mile walk along rural roads. Walk down Station Rd to the main street, turning right and right again after 200m up Langhouse Rd. Veer left along Millhouse Rd, past a cemetery, to a junction. Continue in the same direction along Millhouse Rd. Turn right at a T-junction and continue to Cornalees visitor centre.

By car, turn left from the A78 into Clyde-Muirshiel Park, 4.2 miles from Greenock (north of Inverkip). Drive 2.5 miles further to the Cornalees Bridge Visitor Centre.

THE WALK

From the Cornalees visitor centre set out northeast through a kissing gate beside a cattle grid and along the road. It follows the shore of Compensation Reservoir (linked to the much larger Loch Thom) to an iron gate, then winds uphill to Loch Thom Cottage. Go through a kissing gate and continue on a gravel road, soon passing a small fountain (drinkable), built by the WWI Gallipoli-bound 5th Battalion Argyll and Southern Highlanders who trained here. Pass a road to the left, though it's worth the 20 minutes or so needed to reach the top of **Scroggy Bank** (topped by a communications mast) for wide views.

Spectacular views open up as the track descends northeast past two small reservoirs. You can see Greenock's busy port with its towering cranes, the Firth of Clyde, Helensburgh and the southern Highlands beyond, including the flattish top of Ben Lomond. Continue to **Overton** and the former waterkeeper's cottage, at the walk's lowest point (50 minutes from the start). Turn left (west) onto Greenock's famous **aqueduct**; just keep to the serpentine footpath for the next 5 miles. The first major feature (10 minutes from Overton) is **Hole Burn** with a sluice gate. About 200m further on, pass the first of Greenock Cut's bridges, which gave access to the now-fallow pastures.

As Greenock recedes from view the sprawling IBM factory begins to dominate the panorama below (30 minutes from Hole Burn). After a while the path crosses the stream hiding in the **Hole of Spango**, a deep and lush valley incised into the hillside. A bit further along, the large tower of a power station near Inverkip appears. The oil-powered station, a 30-year-old eyesore has, disgracefully, only worked once, when a four-day coal-miner's strike coincided with a cargo of oil sitting in the harbour. Beyond the tower the hills on the Isle of Arran (p97) provide a pleasing contrast.

Go on to the road at **Shielhill Farm**, cross and continue along the aqueduct, soon heading through some fine old oaks. A short flight of steps leads to the road, only 50m from the Cornalees visitor centre (two hours from Hole Burn).

A CAMPSIE CAPER

Duration	4–4½ hours
Distance	8.9 miles (14.4km)
Difficulty	moderate
Start/Finish	Blanefield
Nearest Towns	Glasgow (p52),)
Transport	bus

Summary A glorious half-day excursion over the grassy Campsie Fells on Glasgow's gentle northern doorstep, with superb panoramic views.

There are undoubtedly plenty of advantages to living in Glasgow, and one must surely be the proximity of the Campsie Fells. This broad, undulating spread of grassy hills, intersected by deep, peaty glens, sprawls east–west above the city's northwestern suburbs and separates the Clyde valley from that of the River Endrick, which flows into Loch Lomond. Popular on weekends, during the week it feels remote and breezy, and you'll probably have the hills to yourself. Knobbly Dumgoyne stands at the western end of the range, while the highest point, Earl's Seat (578m), the objective of this walk, sits in the western reaches. In the east the hills are broad, with some forested and others bare and grassy. The views north to the edge of the Highlands are inspirational, and there's a keen sense of being on the threshold of real hills. The first part of the walk follows a track that harks right back to Glasgow's boom era in the 19th century (see the boxed text, p57).

PLANNING

Maps

The OS Explorer 1:25,000 map No 348 *Campsie Fells* and OS Landranger 1:50,000 map No 64 *Glasgow* cover this walk.

GETTING TO/FROM THE WALK

The walk starts at the corner of the A81 and Campsie Dene Rd, beside a war memorial. About 150m east of here, on the A81, you'll find the **Pestle & Mortar** (daily), a popular deli-coffee shop, a small Spar supermarket and the **Blane Valley Inn** (☎ 01360 770303).

First Edinburgh (☎ 0131 663 9233; www.firstedinburgh.co.uk) operates bus service 10 from Glasgow Buchanan St bus station to Balfron via Blanefield (£5, 40 minutes, 14 services Monday to Saturday, eight Sunday).

By car, Blanefield is on the A81 Glasgow–Aberfoyle road, 0.5 miles west of the A891 junction in Strathblane. There is very limited roadside parking right at the start of the walk; alternatively, turn right in front of the 'No Entry' sign along a narrow lane that leads to a large car park behind a church.

THE WALK

Set out along Campsie Dene Rd (a private road, closed to vehicles); beyond the large houses and extensive gardens, the road becomes a vehicle track through farmland. It passes a few stone-walled enclosures surrounding exposed sections of the trunk pipeline (see the boxed text, p57). Beyond the third gate across the track, as you start to gain some height, glance down to the left to catch sight of an aqueduct carrying the canal across a burn. Around 200m further on you pass **Cantywheery** farmhouse, cross a stream and turn right through a kissing gate (about 30 minutes from the start). The grassed track gains height straightaway. With a burn nearby to the west, cross a channel and continue on a grassy path, parallel to the burn and still climbing. About 30m above the top of a small wooded gorge sheltering a slender waterfall, ford the burn and cross a stile on the far side of the stone wall ahead. Continue on a lesser path, steeply uphill, more or less northwards, through bracken for a while. Use the fence between you and the burn in Cauldhame Glen as a guide to the line of the path across the steep slopes of Dumfoyn and up to a wide shallow valley. Here the

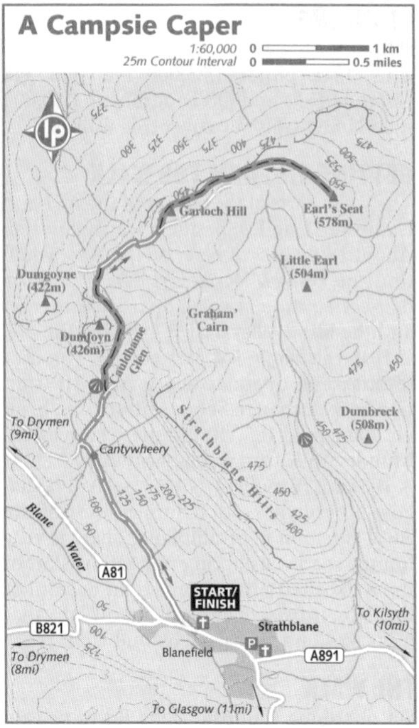

fence turns east; desert it and strike out independently, northwest across the hillside, up to the amorphous ridge on the skyline. Here, close to the escarpment, you'll find a path leading northeast. A vehicle track comes up to the ridge at a saddle and leads northeast between two prominent knolls. This is your route for the next couple of miles (one hour from Cantywheery).

Soon you pass the scant remains of some stone cottages and climb steeply, past a cluster of broken basalt columns. About 10 minutes further on, the track forks; continue along the path northeast up to a small cairn on **Garloch Hill**. The way ahead reveals itself and you can see Earls Seat to the east, distinguished by a fence and pillar. The path drops down, past a tiny lochan among the peat hags nearby. Ignore a track to the right at the start of the next rise, unless you feel like saving some energy and skirting the hillock ahead. On the far side, cross a comparatively wide saddle, keeping to the northern edge of the peaty ground and turn southeast to gain the top of **Earl's Seat** (45 minutes from the two knolls). The panoramic view takes in all of Glasgow and the Clyde valley, Loch Lomond and its surrounding hills to the west, and the Trossachs and many other hills to the north.

The return is simply a matter of retracing your steps, but with a completely different outlook, dominated by Loch Lomond and, from varying angles, the hills to the north and west. Where the track turns north at a saddle, head south to cross the eastern side of the grassy hill east of prominent Dumgoyne; descend to the stile crossed on the way out, continue down to the vehicle track at Cantywheery and back to Blanefield.

FALLS OF CLYDE

Duration	4–4¼ hours
Distance	8.5 miles (13.7km)
Difficulty	easy
Start	Crossford
Finish	New Lanark
Nearest Town	Lanark (opposite)
Transport	bus

Summary Follow the surging River Clyde upstream to the pioneering village of New Lanark and the stunning Falls of Clyde.

The Clyde Walkway, a 40-mile-long (65km) footpath stretching from Glasgow's centre to the Falls of Clyde above New Lanark, has transformed and made accessible the banks of this beloved river (see the boxed text, p52). The most spectacular section links the villages of Crossford and New Lanark through heavily wooded gorges. The clearly waymarked route winds upstream past the once-great Stonebyres Linn (21m high), now harnessed for its power, to New Lanark, a cotton mill village founded in 1785. Hugely successful, it became Scotland's largest mill village in 1799. Visionary Robert Owen introduced revolutionary labour management practices and workers' conditions in what he called his Millennium Experiment. Now a World Heritage site, New Lanark has excellent visitor facilities and a history museum.

The walkway culminates along an 18th-century trail that ascends past Dundaff Linn (3m high), Corra Linn (28m) and, finally, three-stage Bonnington Linn (11m). Ice melt created the gorges and falls 10,000 years ago, carving up the 400-million-year-

KEEPING GLASGOW HEALTHY *Peter Wilkes*

Glasgow's population grew rapidly during the first half of the 19th century, putting an unbearable strain on its water supply. Polluted water caused outbreaks of cholera that killed thousands. Glasgow's city fathers called on John Frederick Bateman, one of the foremost civil engineers of the day, to come up with a plan to provide clean water for Glaswegians. His solution was a large dam that raised the level of Loch Katrine in the Trossachs, 26 miles of trunk pipeline to carry the water to a storage reservoir and a network of pipes to distribute the water around the city. The scheme was officially opened in 1859 by Queen Victoria and is still in use. The Earl's Seat walk follows part of the trunk line, along the road built for its construction. On the road you can see several examples of the various structures of the main aqueduct.

old red-sandstone base. Romantic painters, including JM Turner and Andrew Nasmyth, and the famous writer Sir Walter Scott were enthralled by the falls, especially Corra Linn. According to legend, Corra was a princess who catapulted over the falls on horseback; she became the subject of numerous works. Since the 1920s the Bonnington Power Station has captured the falls' collective force.

The importance of conserving the area surrounding the falls has been recognised in the creation of the Falls of Clyde Wildlife Reserve, cared for by the Scottish Wildlife Trust (SWT).

PLANNING

Maps

The OS Landranger 1:50,000 map No 72 *Upper Clyde Valley* covers the area.

NEAREST TOWN

Lanark

☎ 01555 / pop 8253

Lanark wouldn't score highly for charm or beauty, being cruelly compromised by busy roads. Nevertheless, it can serve as a convenient base for exploring its utterly different neighbour, the World Heritage village of New Lanark. The original cotton mill buildings have been superbly restored and the village is a comparatively quiet haven, despite its well-deserved popularity. **Lanark TIC** (☎ 661661; lanark@visitscotland.com; Horsemarket, Ladyacre Rd) is close to the train and bus stations.

The Scottish Wildlife Trust's **Falls of Clyde Visitor Centre** (☎ 665262; New Lanark; admission £3) has a display about the Wildlife Reserve and sells books about Scottish wildlife. **New Lanark Visitor Centre** (☎ 661345; www.newlanark.org; admission £6) commemorates Owen's work; pick up a village heritage trail leaflet to guide your exploration of the superbly restored village.

SLEEPING & EATING

Summerlea B&B (☎ 664889; 32 Hyndford Rd; s/d £30/50) offers superbly appointed rooms in a central location.

St Catherine's B&B (☎ 662295; 1 Kenilworth Rd; s/d £30/54) is in an impressive building not far from the town centre.

In New Lanark you can stay at **New Lanark SYHA Hostel** (☎ 0870 004 1143; www.syha.org.uk; Wee Row; dm £14), which occupies a former mill building overlooking the river, or in distinctly upmarket **New Lanark Mill Hotel** (☎ 667200; www.newlanark.org; New Lanark Mills; s/d £70/110), in a superbly restored cotton mill.

Prego (☎ 666300; 3 High St; mains £13-16; lunch & dinner Tue-Sun), specialising in Italian cuisine, is definitely the place to eat in Lanark.

Mr A's Cafe (☎ 663797; 90 High St; mains £5-8; lunch & dinner) is a very friendly place, popular with the locals. It's not exactly stylish but servings are generous and it's licensed.

The **Mill Pantry** (New Lanark; snacks & light meals to £5; 10am-5pm) is a cafeteria-style place in former Mill No 3; choose between Broughton ales and Fairtrade coffee.

For self-catering supplies, there's a Somerfield supermarket near the TIC.

GETTING THERE & AWAY

Strathclyde Passenger Transport (SPT; ☎ 0141 332 6811; www.spt.co.uk) trains connect Glasgow Central and Lanark (£5, 55 minutes, half-hourly Monday to Saturday, hourly Sunday).

GETTING TO/FROM THE WALK

McKindless (☎ 01698 386990; www.mckindlessgroup.co.uk) bus service 31 links Lanark and

NEW LANARK – BIRTHPLACE OF SOCIAL WELFARE

New Lanark is incontestably one of the must-see places when you come to Scotland. It's a piece of good fortune that the village is right on the Clyde Walkway. A superb example of an 18th-century planned industrial village, New Lanark became a Unesco World Heritage site in 2001.

The village was founded by David Dale and Robert Arkwright in 1785 to harness the River Clyde's abundant water to power cotton mill machinery. In its heyday the mill was one of the largest in Scotland, employing 2500 people. In 1800 Dale's son-in-law Robert Owen and some business partners purchased the mill and Owen moved into the manager's office, a post he held for 24 years. In 1813 he formed a new company to give him freer rein to put more of his ideas into practice.

Dale had hired hundreds of children, mostly orphans, to help run the mills; Owen abolished child labour and opened a village school (around 50 years before education became compulsory in Scotland) where corporal punishment was forbidden. He introduced free health care, a crèche for working mothers, a cooperative shop and evening classes for adults. As an astute businessman, he also introduced working methods that improved the quality of the cotton produced. Happily, most of Owen's reforms were maintained by his successors.

Towards the end of the 19th century the mill diversified, mainly into rope production. However, it was imprisoned by its site in the narrow, rugged valley, which made expansion or redevelopment prohibitively expensive. The mill closed in 1968. Salvation came with the establishment of the New Lanark Trust in 1974. Restoration of the austerely handsome terrace houses and the mill buildings began and the village has never looked back. New Lanark now welcomes thousands of visitors annually. For more information go to www.newlanark.org and www.robert-owen.com.

Crossford (£1.50, 15 minutes, hourly Monday to Saturday) at the start of the walk. Here, from the intersection of the B7056 (Braidwood Rd) and the A72, walk southeast along the latter for 650m to a riverbank car park.

By car from Glasgow, take the M74 then the A72 south to the B7056 (Braidwood Rd) intersection. Turn right towards Crossford. At a T-junction in the village, turn left along the A72 and continue for 650m to the car park on the left.

Stuart's Coaches (☎ 01555 773533) operates a service between Lanark and New Lanark (£1, 10 minutes, hourly Monday to Saturday, half-hourly Sunday). A well-signposted minor road branches from the A73 just west of the Lanark TIC.

THE WALK

Cross the footbridge over the River Clyde to join the Clyde Walkway; the path parallels a miniature railway for a few hundred metres, then leads on through quiet countryside. After about 35 minutes you close in on the **Stonebyres power station**, and the path skirts steep cliffs. Pass a large water tank and descend to cross the river on the sluice gates. Continue along a path beside a minor road to a junction with the A72.

A road-side path leads into the village of **Kirkfieldbank** (10 minutes from the sluice gates). There are toilets beside the village hall on the right; the Tavern serves snacks and meals and there's a small shop.

Go through the village and, at the threshold of the bridge over the Clyde, continue down Riverside Rd for 30m to a right bend. Turn left across the old bridge above an island in the river. Walk up past some houses and back to the road-side path, uphill. Take the first turn right (not waymarked at the time of research) and walk down the road towards the water treatment works, then left up a Walkway signposted path. This leads to a minor road, which takes you to the edge of **Castlebank Park**. Turn right along a minor road for about 75m, then right again along a path about 60m short of **Castlebank House**. The path winds down almost to river level; further on, climb steps with New Lanark in view, soon coming to a viewing platform (45 minutes from Kirkfieldbank). More steps lead to a road-side path, whereupon you reverse the trend and go downhill into another world at **New Lanark** (15 minutes from the viewing platform).

Go down steps beside the visitor centre to Mill No 3, housing the Mill Pantry. Turn left towards the Falls of Clyde

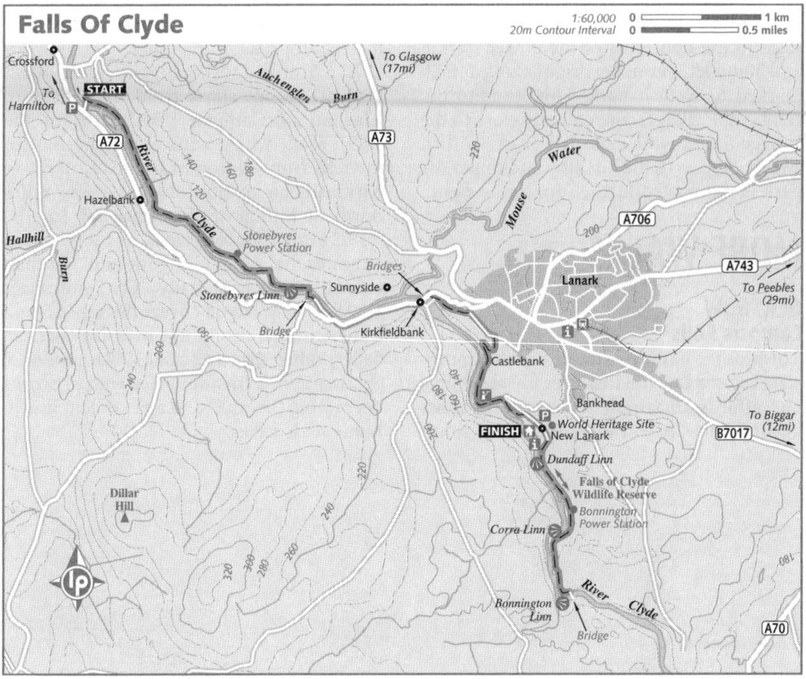

visitor centre, soon passing Robert Owen's school. Bear right to the visitor centre. To continue on the Walkway, go through an archway ahead, up steps, with small **Dundaff Linn** nearby, and follow first a path then a boardwalk through trees, close to the river. Continue past a house then go right at a junction past Bonnington power station and up to the lookout for **Corra Linn**, which, at 28m, is the highest of the three falls. Further on, you may find the SWT's 'peregrine watch' outpost: special fences made of small branches are erected to provide a screen between peregrine falcons nesting on the cliffs opposite and interested passers-by. Then you come to **Bonnington Linn**, perhaps the most impressive of the falls, with at least five separate cascades surging into a large pool (40 minutes from New Lanark).

SHORT GLASGOW WALK

Legend has it that the unusual geological formation known as the **Whangie** was created by the devil flicking his tail as he fluttered past. The long east–west cliff encrusts the northern slope of Auchineden Hill (357m), a few miles south of Drymen. The views of Loch and Ben Lomond and a host of other hills are absolutely superb, even stopping Queen Victoria in her tracks many moons ago. The walk starts and finishes at Queens View lookout, signposted on the A809 Glasgow–Drymen road; you'll need a car for this one. Allow 1¼ hours for the easy 3.2-mile (5.2km) walk. Consult OS Landranger 1:50,000 map No 64. The nearest town is Drymen (p92).

From the car park, cross a stile over a stone wall, follow a boardwalk to a broad, well-trodden path angling up the hillside and on to the base of the cliffs. Here the going becomes rougher, but the path is clear, right along the length of the cliffs. After about 30 minutes, go up through a gap to the moorland plateau and continue west to a trig pillar on the hill's summit for more view feasting. Retrace your steps to the start.

To return to New Lanark, retrace your steps to the house below the power station and 50m further on, bear right along a track marked to New Lanark. This leads to the road in the village, conveniently close to the Village Store, which specialises in Scottish sweets. Access to the bus stop and upper car park is signposted further on, to the right.

MORE WALKS

GLASGOW

Campsie Fells

Towards the eastern extremity of the Campsies, **Cort-ma Law** (531m) is easily accessible and affords amazingly wide-ranging views beyond the Clyde valley, including Edinburgh's Pentland Hills in one direction and the Arran peaks in the other.

A 6.6-mile (10.4km) walk with 400m (1312ft) ascent starts from the village of Clachan of Campsie, just north of the A891 road, which runs along the foot of the fells from Milton of Campsie, north of Kirkintilloch to Strathblane, a few miles north of Milngavie. **First Edinburgh** (☎ 0131 663 9233; www.firstedinburgh.co.uk) bus service 175 operates between Glasgow and Clachan (£3, 50 minutes, 20 daily). OS Landranger 1:50,000 map No 64 covers the walk. Don't leave without dropping in to the **Aldessan Gallery coffee shop** (☎ 01360 313049; mains to £5; 🕑 11am-5pm), a friendly place with artworks decorating the walls and an excellent line in homemade cakes.

The South

Southern Scotland is dominated by an almost continuous range of rolling hills between the west and east coasts and to the border with England. Here, instead of Munros, you can tick off seven Corbetts (2500ft to 2999ft) and no fewer than 82 Donalds (2000ft to 2499ft), which yield nothing in challenge and beauty to the more lofty and better-known peaks further north. These 'hills' may lack the rugged grandeur of Glen Coe or the Wester Ross mountains, but their undemonstrative profiles have a quiet charm that quickly grows on you. By way of contrast, along the crinkled coasts, beautiful beaches hide below rugged, colourful cliffs.

This chapter is divided into three sections. The Southern Upland Way (SUW), Scotland's longest waymarked walk, links the east and west coasts in a demanding and infinitely varied epic. In the Dumfries & Galloway and Borders sections, reminders of the area's long and sometimes bloody history are brought home around the Merrick and in the Eildon Hills, overlooking Melrose, once home to Roman soldiers,. The Borders' John Buchan Way has a more peaceful association, linked to a well-known, early-20th-century writer who loved the area. Among the sites of great value for nature conservation, the walk past the beautiful Grey Mare's Tail waterfall to White Coomb is largely within a nature reserve. St Abb's Head National Nature Reserve is the highlight of the Burnmouth to St Abb's Head walk, in the Borders' easternmost corner. Most of the described walks are conveniently located near the SUW, so you can plan a feast of walking in the south – enough for a month – or more!

HIGHLIGHTS

- Trekking the **Southern Upland Way** (p63) right across the country and sighting the east coast for the first time
- Savouring the panoramic views from the summit of the **Merrick** (p72), the South's highest peak
- Climbing from the cascading torrents of the Grey Mare's Tail waterfall to the lonely summit of **White Coomb** (p75)
- Imagining yourself following Richard Hannay in The 39 Steps along the **John Buchan Way** (p76)
- Tramping along the coast above the wonderfully contorted and colourful cliffs of the Berwickshire coast on the **Burnmouth to St Abb's Head** (p81) walk

- www.visitdumfriesandgalloway.co.uk
- www.visitscottishborders.com

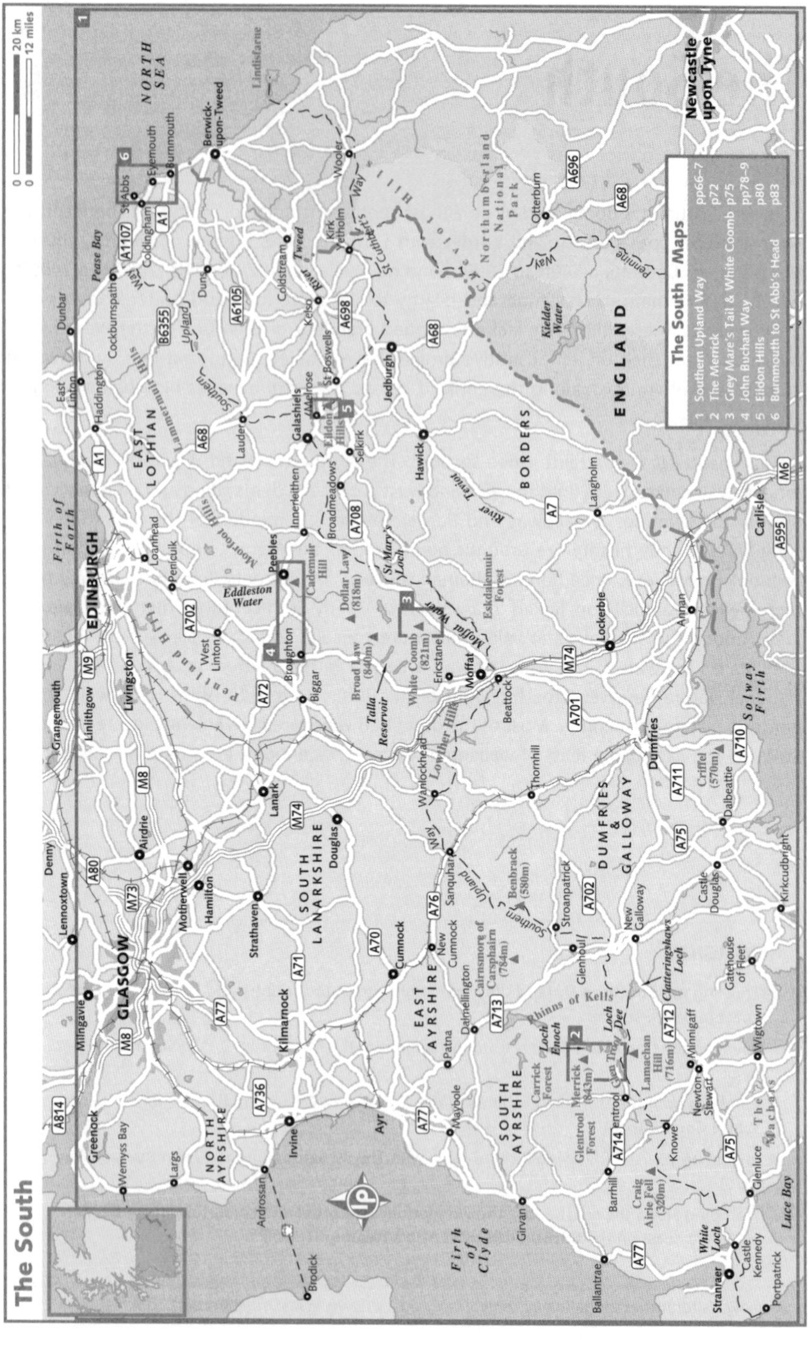
The South
0 20 km
0 12 miles
The South – Maps
1 Southern Upland Way pp66–7
2 The Merrick p72
3 Grey Mare's Tail & White Coomb p75
4 John Buchan Way pp78–9
5 Eildon Hills p80
6 Burnmouth to St Abb's Head p83
NORTH SEA
Firth of Forth
Firth of Clyde
Solway Firth
Luce Bay
Pease Bay
EDINBURGH
GLASGOW
Newcastle upon Tyne
ENGLAND
EAST LOTHIAN
BORDERS
SOUTH LANARKSHIRE
NORTH AYRSHIRE
EAST AYRSHIRE
SOUTH AYRSHIRE
DUMFRIES & GALLOWAY
Northumberland National Park
Lindisfarne
Berwick-upon-Tweed
Burnmouth
Eyemouth
St Abbs
Coldingham
Cockburnspath
Dunbar
East Linton
Haddington
Duns
Coldstream
Kelso
Kirk Yetholm
Wooler
Lauder
Galashiels
Melrose
St Boswells
Eildon Hills
Selkirk
Jedburgh
Hawick
Otterburn
Kielder Water
Langholm
Carlisle
Innerleithen
Broadmeadows
Peebles
Cademuir Hill
Dollar Law (818m)
St Mary's Loch
Eskdalemuir Forest
Moffat Water
Loanhead
Penicuik
West Linton
Eddleston Water
Moorfoot Hills
Lammermuir Hills
Pentland Hills
Broughton
Biggar
Broad Law (840m)
Talla Reservoir
White Coomb (821m)
Ericstane
Moffat
Beattock
Lockerbie
Annan
Lowther Hills
Wanlockhead
Thornhill
Dumfries
Criffel (570m)
Dalbeattie
Kirkcudbright
Castle Douglas
Gatehouse of Fleet
Grangemouth
Linlithgow
Livingston
Airdrie
Lanark
Douglas
Denny
Lennoxtown
Motherwell
Hamilton
Strathaven
Milngavie
Kilmarnock
Cumnock
New Cumnock
Sanquhar
Benbrack (580m)
Stroanpatrick
Glenhoul
New Galloway
Clatteringshaws Loch
Cairnsmore of Carsphairn (784m)
Dalmellington
Rhinns of Kells
Loch Enoch
Loch Dee
Merrick (843m)
Glen Trool
Lamachan Hill (716m)
Minnigaff
Newton Stewart
Wigtown
The Machars
Carrick Forest
Glentrool Forest
Patna
Maybole
Ayr
Irvine
Ardrossan
Brodick
Largs
Wemyss Bay
Greenock
Girvan
Barrhill
Knowe
Craig Airie Fell (320m)
Glenluce
Ballantrae
White Loch
Castle Kennedy
Stranraer
Portpatrick
River Tweed
River Teviot
Cheviot Hills
Southern Upland Way
St Cuthbert's Way
Pennine Way
A1
A1107
B6355
A6105
A698
A68
A696
A7
A708
A702
A72
M9
M8
M74
A701
A80
M73
A71
A77
A70
A76
A713
A702
A711
A75
A710
A712
A714
A736
A814
A77
A75
A595
M6

INFORMATION

Maps

The OS Travel – Road 1:250,000 map No 3 *Southern Scotland* is the one you'll need for general orientation.

Information Sources

The main tourist information centre (TIC) in Dumfries & Galloway is the **Dumfries TIC** (☎ 01387 253862; www.visitdumfriesandgalloway.co.uk; 64 Whitesands, Dumfries). In the Borders contact the **Peebles TIC** (☎ 0870 608 0404; High St) or **Melrose TIC** (☎ 0870 608 0404; Abbey House, Abbey St) or see www.visitscottishborders.com. All three are open year-round.

SOUTHERN UPLANDS

Taking in virtually all the hill country across southernmost Scotland, through Dumfries & Galloway and the Borders, the Southern Uplands is an area of great diversity and interest for walkers. Although none of the mountains reach the much-sought-after Munro height of 3000ft (914m), they offer fine, often challenging, walking.

SOUTHERN UPLAND WAY

Duration	9 days
Distance	209.5 miles (338km)
Difficulty	moderate–demanding
Start	Portpatrick (p64)
Finish	Cockburnspath (p65)
Transport	bus, train

Summary An exceptionally challenging walk from one side of the country to the other, through remote areas in the west and more settled lands in the east, passing fascinating historical sites and with plenty of wildlife-watching opportunities.

The Southern Upland Way (SUW), Britain's first official coast-to-coast, long-distance path, traverses one of the broadest parts of the country. It cuts across the grain of the countryside, roller-coasting over hills and moorland and through conifer plantations, descending to cross rivers and streams, then climbing out the other side. It also passes through deciduous woods and agricultural land, mainly in the eastern half of the walk.

The going underfoot ranges from sealed roads to forest paths. Unfortunately, there are some long (over 2 miles) stretches of bitumen (although not on busy roads), which some walkers feel have no place on official routes. There's much comfort in the fact that they do link some very fine paths across the hills and through woodlands.

Accommodation is sparse in a few areas, so you have to anticipate some long days to get from one night's shelter to the next. Camping or staying in bothies gives more flexibility, but all the necessary gear can weigh heavily after several hours. These factors, combined with the route's length and remoteness, make it a far more serious proposition than the West Highland Way. Nevertheless, the rewards are considerable: you get a real sense of moving across the country, become attuned to the gradual changes in the landscape, meet fellow walkers and have the satisfaction of sighting the North Sea on the last day. It's essential to be fit before you start and preferably to have some experience of long-distance walking. Fortunately, there are many places where you can easily join the Way for shorter, less arduous walks.

Alternatives If you like the sound of the SUW but don't have time to go the whole way, shorter versions are possible. In particular we recommend taking two days to walk the section from St Mary's Loch to Melrose (p70), which has plenty of variety and minimal drawbacks.

PLANNING

The majority of people do the SUW from southwest to northeast. Usually this means the prevailing wind is behind you, but when the Way was originally walked in this direction for this book, the persistent north wind was coming either from the side or head-on. There is much to be said for finishing in the east, which has more open and settled countryside where shorter days are possible, than in the west, which has some unavoidably long daily distances.

The full walk may take as few as nine days or as many as 14 (although some spread the journey over a number of years, doing a bit at a time), depending on your walking speed and number of rest days. We have described the route in nine daily stages;

these are within the reach of fit walkers but should be used mainly as a guide to what's involved. It's worth having some flexibility in your plans as bad weather, likely at any time, may slow you down.

Daily stages between accommodation options can be as short as 8 miles (13km) or as long as 30 miles (50km); the amount of ascent is a significant factor when you're planning an itinerary, especially in the central section between Sanquhar and Beattock. You'll also often have to carry all the food and drink you need for the day – there are precious few watering places en route.

Another factor to reckon with is transport. Many hosts along the Way will pick you up from an agreed spot and return you there the next day. Some people may do this gratis, others may charge, so check first. The Way crosses several main roads with bus services and one railway line with a convenient station, enabling you to reach the SUW from many major centres and to walk parts of it.

The route is well waymarked with a thistle-hexagon logo and signposts, but you should still carry maps and a compass in case visibility deteriorates on the exposed stretches. Distances between markers vary widely, from line of sight across moorland to miles apart along minor roads. Sections of the route are changed (often for the better) from time to time, so waymarkers should always be more trusted over the mapped route.

When to Walk

You can expect a wide range of weather conditions during a complete crossing; thick mist and strong winds, as well as warm sunshine, are likely at any time between April and September – the best, if not the only, time to walk the SUW. Snowfalls over the higher ground are not unknown during winter, when the short hours of daylight make it almost impossible to complete the necessarily long days before dark.

Maps & Books

The Southern Upland Way Official Guide by Roger Smith is invaluable, with loads of background information and pointers to the many short walks near the Way. It comes packaged with separate maps, extracted from the seven OS Landranger 1:50,000 sheets covering the entire Way. The pack's price is less than half the cost of buying the maps individually.

Guided Walks

Make Tracks (☎ 0131 229 6844; www.maketracks.net; 26 Forbes Rd, Edinburgh) can save you a great deal of hassle by organising accommodation, luggage transfer, a pick-up and drop-off service, maps and printed notes.

Information Sources

Start planning your trip with the free brochure *Southern Upland Way* (with an annually updated accommodation list). It's available from the **Dumfries & Galloway ranger service** (☎ 01387 260184; Dumfries) and the **Scottish Borders ranger service** (☎ 01835 830281; Jedburgh), which can also provide leaflets on the wildlife, trees and shrubs, geology, history, archaeology and place names of the area, plus booklets describing short circular walks based on the Way. When you've completed the Way, send your details to one of the ranger services to obtain a free completion certificate.

Accommodation bookings are most conveniently made through **VisitScotland** (☎ 0845 225 5121; www.visitscotland.com).

Make sure you check the invaluable **Southern Upland Way** (www.dumgal.gov.uk/southernuplandway) official website. The commercial site at www.southernuplandway.com is helpful for accommodation and other services.

NEAREST TOWNS

Portpatrick

☎ 01776 / pop 585

The peaceful harbour in the village of Portpatrick was once the port for ferries from Ireland. These days it quietly looks after anglers, sailors and walkers.

SLEEPING & EATING

Galloway Point Holiday Park (☎ 810561; www.gallowaypointholidaypark.co.uk; unpowered sites for 2 £10) is less than 1 mile from town.

Carlton Guest House (☎ 810253; 21 South Cres; s/d £30/52), on the seafront, is recommended among the several B&Bs in the village.

Harbour House Hotel (☎ 810456; mains to £18; 🕑 lunch & dinner) offers the opportunity, with luck, to sit outside and enjoy a dinner of suitably generous proportions for the miles ahead, washed down with real ale.

LAWS & CLEUCHS

As you pore over the maps at home, the names of the hills, rivers and other natural features can help give a clearer picture of the appearance of the landscape, and can also reveal something of the local history.

While Gaelic place names are commonplace in the Highlands and islands to the north, in the Southern Uplands they're largely confined to the southwest, even though Gaelic is now little spoken in these parts. In the Borders, however, the names are mainly from Lowland Scots (Lallans), a distinct language (still in use) with origins in the languages of settlers from the east, rather than the Celtic-Gaelic influences from the west.

Starting at the beginning of the Southern Upland Way, Portpatrick's origin is obvious, given the Irish connection, although it was originally called Portree, from the Gaelic *port righ*, meaning 'harbour of the king'. Killantringan, the location of the fine lighthouse, includes the anglicised version of the common Gaelic prefix *cill*, meaning 'church', in this case of St Ringan or Ninian. Balmurrie, the farm near New Luce, has another widespread Gaelic element, *bal*, meaning 'farm' or 'small township', in this case of the Murray family.

Laggangairn, the site of the two prehistoric cairns beyond Balmurrie, means 'hollow of the cairns' (*lag* meaning 'hollow'). A bit further on you climb over Craig Airie Fell – a hybrid of Gaelic and Norse. Craig is derived from *creag*, Gaelic for 'cliff' or 'crag'; *áiridh* is Gaelic for 'shieling' (a temporary dwelling); and fell, once a Norse term, is commonly used in the English Lake District to mean 'mountain'. Dalry is from the Gaelic *dail righ* or 'meadow of the king'. Benbrack, the hill between Dalry and Sanquhar, is the speckled *breac* or 'hill', while Fingland comes from the Gaelic *fionn gleann*, meaning 'white glen'.

In the east, the Lammermuir Hills feature prominently in the latter stages of the Way; the name comes from Old English for lamb – still appropriate today.

Among the most common names for geographic features is cleuch, which comes directly from the Lowland Scots for ravine; the similar-sounding *heugh* is a cliff. The name law pops up all over the Borders and is the equivalent of the Gaelic *beinn*, meaning 'mountain' or 'hill', often isolated and conical in shape. A *knowe* is also a high sort of place (a small hillock), while a *dod* is a bare round hill.

Scottish Hill and Mountain Names by Peter Drummond, the Scottish place-names guru, should answer almost any query you come up with.

THE SOUTH

There's a small shop, which has a good range of the sorts of things you will need during the first day on the track.

Stranraer, 8 miles northeast of Portpatrick, is a large town with plenty more accommodation. Contact **Stranraer TIC** (☎ 702595; Harbour St) for more information.

GETTING THERE & AWAY

Stagecoach Western (☎ 01292 613500) operates bus service X77 from Glasgow to Ayr (£5, 1¼ hours, every 30 minutes) connecting with route 358 to Stranraer (£6, two hours, six services Monday to Saturday). **First ScotRail** (☎ 0845 755 0033; www.firstscotrail.com) runs trains from Glasgow Central to Stranraer (£17, two hours, five services Monday to Saturday, two Sunday).

Stagecoach Western's route 358 links Stranraer to Portpatrick (£2, 20 minutes, six services Monday to Saturday).

For details of ferries between Northern Ireland and Stranraer and Cairnryan, see p306.

If you're travelling by car from Glasgow, follow the M77 and the A77 to Stranraer and on to Portpatrick.

Cockburnspath

☎ 01368

Cockburnspath is a tiny village just inland from the coast, unfortunately with minimal facilities for walkers – you have been warned.

SLEEPING & EATING

Chesterfield Caravan Park (☎ 830459; www.chesterfieldcaravanpark.co.uk; The Neuk; unpowered/powered sites for 2 £8/10), a very well appointed site, is a couple of miles from town.

There are a couple of B&Bs on nearby farms: **Mrs Hood** (☎ 830620; The Cornbarn, Cove

Farm; d £40), who opens her B&B on weekends only, and **Mrs Russell** (☎ 830465; townhead@ecosse.net; Townhead Farm; d £40).

Unfortunately the nearest pub is at Grantshouse, a few miles south along the A1, but the small shop in Cockburnspath is licensed.

GETTING THERE & AWAY

Perryman's Buses (☎ 01289 380719) service 253 between Edinburgh and Berwick-upon-Tweed (on the main east-coast railway line) stops here (£6, one hour, at least three daily). The village, just off the A1 between Edinburgh and Berwick-upon-Tweed, is 35 miles from Edinburgh and 20 miles from Berwick.

THE WALK

Day 1: Portpatrick to New Luce

8½–9 hours, 22.5 miles (36.5km), 370m ascent

In Portpatrick the Way starts at the foot of a flight of stairs at the northwestern end of the small harbour. From here it heads northwest above impressive cliffs (take care, especially in poor visibility) and around scenic coves. The route ahead isn't always obvious but trust the thistle waymarkers to show the way from the shore back up to the cliff top. Killantringan lighthouse comes dramatically into view and the SUW joins the minor road leading inland.

Minor roads and farm tracks lead to a high point with fine views on a clear day. From here, more minor roads, farm tracks

Southern Upland Way

and short, sometimes muddy, paths take you down past the outskirts of Stranraer to **Castle Kennedy**. This village has a small shop (at the garage) and the **Plantings Inn** (☎ 01581 400633; unpowered sites for 2 £5, s/d £35/60, mains to £17), where you can choose a comfortable room or camp in the grounds and eat at the hotel.

From Castle Kennedy a bitumen drive takes you through the pleasant, wooded grounds of the ruined castle to a minor road. You soon leave this to follow farm tracks to another minor road, then right round the edge of a cleared conifer plantation. The route descends to a footbridge over a railway line, then goes down to a suspension bridge over the Water of Luce. New Luce is off the Way, 1 mile north along a nearby road. If you feel like covering a few more miles before stopping at New Luce, continue across open moorland, past deserted Kilhern and down to a minor road about 1 mile east of New Luce.

NEW LUCE

☎ 01581

Here you'll find the fine old **Kenmuir Arms Hotel** (☎ 600218; 31 Main St; s/d £35/56) and its adjacent **camping ground** (unpowered sites for 2 £5; breakfast £5). There's a small shop in the village.

A limited bus service (No 410) operated by **Irvine's Coaches** (☎ 300345) links New Luce with Stranraer (£1, 27 minutes, one service Tuesday, Wednesday, Friday).

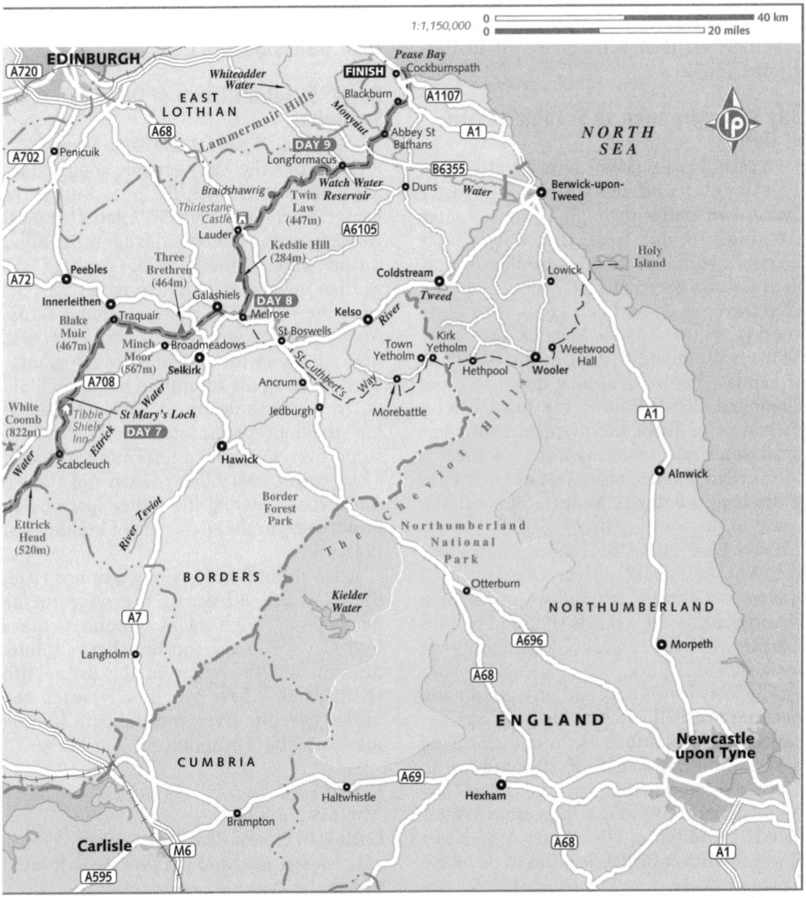

Day 2: New Luce to Bargrennan

6¾–7¼ hours, 17.5 miles (28km), 340m ascent

Follow very quiet roads to Balmurrie farm, from where the route rises across moorland and then follows a wide, heathery firebreak through a plantation. Artfield Fell has been taken over by a wind farm with around 15 large swirling turbines. A short stretch of forest road leads to an open area with a timber, beehive-shaped bothy, which only has sleeping platforms; there is a fresh water supply nearby. Also nearby are the 4000-year-old **Laggangairn** standing stones, complete with information about their history. Beyond a large cairn the Way climbs over **Craig Airie Fell** (320m) providing an excellent view all round. It then descends past Derry Farm and follows minor roads past Knowe and Glenruther Lodge, over Glenvernoch Fell and down to Bargrennan (p72).

Day 3: Bargrennan to St John's Town of Dalry

9–9½ hours, 22 miles (34km), 500m ascent

This day starts off along mossy and partly overgrown paths through conifers. After crossing a minor road, the route passes through some pleasant woodlands and then follows the Water of Trool. The Way then traverses above Loch Trool, with some good views towards the Merrick – which at 843m is the highest point in the Southern Uplands – before dropping down to cross Glenhead Burn. Follow the burn briefly then diverge from the mapped route and head southeast across country to meet a forest road about 1 mile west of Loch Dee. **White Laggan Bothy** is about 350m off the route to the south.

Once past Loch Dee Angling Club's hut, the Way crosses the River Dee and then traverses a conifer plantation, much of it clear-felled. It then meets the road to Mid Garrary, which you proceed to follow west for a short distance.

The Way leaves the road on a good path, heading north through wide clearings between more plantations, and then rising across moorland before descending to Clenrie Farm. Further on, well down Garroch Glen, the Way cuts east across Waterside Hill and follows the Water of Ken to a fine suspension bridge leading to St John's Town of Dalry.

ST JOHN'S TOWN OF DALRY

☎ 01644

Often shortened to Dalry, this large village has two hotels and a small shop.

Clachan Inn (☎ 430241; www.theclachaninn.com; Main St; s/d £30/60, mains to £18) is the place to go for a comfortable night.

Mrs Findlay's B&B (☎ 430420; fjames441@aol.com; Main St; s/d £25/50) is a good alternative.

MacEwan's (☎ 01387 256533) operates bus route 520 to Castle Douglas (£2, 43 minutes, three services Monday to Saturday), where route 502 connects to Dumfries (£3, 35 minutes, six services Monday to Saturday). Route 520 also continues from Castle Douglas to Dalmellington (£2, 1½ hour, two services Monday to Saturday), where **Stagecoach Western** (☎ 01292 613500) runs route 52 to Ayr (£3, 50 minutes, at least 12 daily) on the coast with good onward connections.

Day 4: St John's Town of Dalry to Sanquhar

10–10¾ hours, 25 miles (40km), 900m ascent

From Dalry the Way crosses rough grazing land, past Ardoch Farm, to Butterhole Bridge. Friendly **Kendoon SYHA Hostel** (☎ 01644 460680; www.syha.org.uk; dm £12) is about 1.5 miles further west, off the SUW, at Glenhoul (the warden may be able to help with transport from the Way). The route continues across rough grazing ground to Stroanpatrick, then climbs a wide clearing through plantations, skirting the summit of Manquhill Hill (421m). Continue up to **Benbrack** (580m) for excellent panoramic views. You descend over a couple of lesser tops, through a plantation, past Allan's Cairn and along a forest road, passing the rather spartan **Polskeoch Bothy** to the scattering of buildings at Polskeoch.

After about 2 miles along a minor road, the Way sets off across the ridge to the north along rough tracks. Sanquhar comes into view from the top but there's a long descent into the valley of the River Nith (Nithsdale), where you finally reach the bridge over the river and the path leading into Sanquhar (pronounced 'san-ker').

SANQUHAR

☎ 01659 / pop 2028

Castle View Caravan Park (☎ 50291; ireneriddall@aol.com; Townfoot; unpowered sites for 2 £5) is located beside the Way.

Mrs McDowall (☎ 50751; marymcdowell@aol.com; Town Head; s/d £25/44) offers weary walkers a warm welcome.

Blackaddie House Hotel (☎ 50270; www.blackaddiehotel.co.uk; Blackaddie Rd; s/d £40/70, mains to £20) could tempt you for a bit of well-earned pampering.

First ScotRail (☎ 0845 755 0033; www.firstscotrail.com) operates trains to Glasgow (£10, 1¼ hours, six services Monday to Saturday, two Sunday), and **Stagecoach Western** (☎ 01292 613500) runs bus service 246 to Dumfries (£3, 50 minutes, at least five daily).

Day 5: Sanquhar to Beattock

10½ –11½ hours, 28 miles (45km), 1550m ascent

Leaving Sanquhar there's a short climb straightaway, then two more bumps to cross, with Cogshead, a ruined farmhouse, set between them in a steep-sided valley. A steep descent on a good track leads into **Wanlockhead**, the highest inhabited village in Scotland (467m). It is an old lead-mining village with plenty of industrial archaeology, and a striking contrast to the bare, lonely moorland. Here you'll find a couple of B&Bs and **Wanlockhead Inn** (☎ 01659 74535; 🕑 lunch Sat & Sun, dinner Wed-Sun). The **Museum of Lead Mining** (☎ 01659 74387; www.leadminingmuseum.co.uk; £6; 🕑 Apr-Oct) and its tearoom are worth a visit.

From here the Way climbs to **Lowther Hill**, crossing and recrossing the sealed road to the surreal golf-ball-like domes (containing radar equipment) in a fenced enclosure on the summit (725m). Here, on a good day atop the highest point on the Southern Upland Way, it's possible to see the Pentland Hills (near Edinburgh) to the north. The Way continues over high ground, steeply up to Cold Moss (628m). It then drops down to the A702 at Over Fingland.

Just beyond the A702, in **Watermeetings Forest**, you reach the halfway point of the SUW. Cross the wall holding back Daer Reservoir (drinking water for Glasgow's southern suburbs) then tackle the long climb over Sweetshaw Brae, Hods Hill and Beld Knowe (507m), overlooking the reservoir. This is inevitably followed by an equally long descent through the plantation to Cloffin Burn. **Brattleburn Bothy** is out of sight, about 400m west of the Way. The SUW continues generally downhill, still among dense conifers, across a large clearing and Garpol Water, eventually reaching a minor road at Easter Earshaig. Follow this down to Beattock.

EATTOCK

☎ 01683

Craigielands Country Park (☎ 300591; www.craigielandsleisure.co.uk; unpowered sites for 2 £12), about 1 mile south of the Way, has its own restaurant; there's a shop nearby.

Barnhill Springs Country Guest House (☎ 220580; s/d £35/60), in a historic building, is beside the Way.

Moffat (p74), just over 1 mile north of Beattock, has more accommodation, restaurants and shops, but the A701 is very busy, so try for a place that provides vehicle transfers. Buses link Moffat with Edinburgh and Glasgow.

Day 6: Beattock to St Mary's Loch

9–9½ hours, 21 miles (33.5km), 1200m ascent

From Beattock the Way goes under the A74(M), across the River Annan, over a small hill, then beside Moffat Water. It then winds through a plantation on a forest road to a path up a deep valley. This leads to the **gorge** carved by Selcloth Burn; the path traverses this dramatic cleft then climbs to **Ettrick Head** (520m), the boundary between Dumfries & Galloway and the Borders. Beyond here you soon meet a forest road, which leads down to **Over Phawhope Bothy** and a minor road beside Ettrick Water. Follow this valley – whose natural beauty is slightly compromised by a blanket of conifers – for six miles.

Turn off at **Scabcleuch** along a signposted public path, which climbs up a narrow glen then over Pikestone Rig to **Riskinhope Hope**, a once-solid stone house now a bramble-covered ruin. The route then turns around Earl's Hill and picks up a forest track for the descent to St Mary's Loch.

By the loch is historic **Tibbie Shiels Inn** (☎ 01750 42231; www.tibbieshielsinn.com; s/d £35/60, mains to £10), scene of the Way's opening in 1984, offering relatively luxurious accommodation and excellent bar meals. There's also a **camping ground** (unpowered sites for 2 £6) nearby, run by Tibbie.

Nearby **Glen Cafe** (☎ 01750 42241; mains to £15; 🕑 breakfast & lunch daily, dinner Sat) is also a great place to relax and unwind over a drink.

A summer-only Saturday bus service to Moffat (p74), operated by **Houston's Minibuses** (☎ 01576 203874), stops at the café.

Day 7: St Mary's Loch to Melrose

12–13 hours, 30 miles (50km), 1120m ascent

This ultra-long day could be split into two, with an overnight stop at Traquair, 12 miles (20km) from St Mary's Loch. Of the total climb, 800m comes between Traquair and Melrose.

From the inn, pass in front of the St Mary's Loch Sailing Club building and follow a path, then a vehicle track, beside the loch. Further on cross Yarrow Water to the A708. The Way crosses the road and returns to open country. Good paths and tracks climb over a spur to Douglas Burn then it's up again, across heathery Blake Muir and down to the hamlet of **Traquair**, near Innerleithen, in the Tweed valley. **First Edinburgh** (☎ 0131 663 9233; www.firstedinburgh.co.uk) bus service 62 links Innerleithen with Peebles (p76) and Edinburgh (£5, 15 minutes, every 30 minutes Monday to Saturday, 12 services Sunday).

There are a couple of B&Bs in the village, including the **School House** (☎ 01896 830506; http://old-schoolhouse.ndo.co.uk; s/d £30/56); alternatively, try **Traquair Mill Bunkhouse** (☎ 01896 830515; dm £13). There's more accommodation and several shops in Innerleithen, about 1 mile north along the B709.

Turning your back on Traquair, follow a lane climbing steadily into a plantation. Just inside its boundary is a log cabin, which can be a welcome haven in bad weather. **Minch Moor** (567m) rises on the right and the short detour is well worth the effort for the panoramic view, which includes the Eildon Hills near Melrose to the east. The SUW continues through a plantation and rises to **Brown Knowe** (523m), which also provides good views. The tops ahead are skirted on the right and left. The turn-off to **Broadmeadows SYHA Hostel** (☎ 01750 725506; www.syha.org.uk; dm £13), Scotland's first youth hostel, is signposted; the hostel is 1 mile to the south, though the nearest shops are in Selkirk, 5 miles away. The route continues up to the three massive cairns known as the **Three Brethren**. Then it's down to Yair and a bridge over the River Tweed.

You then climb over a fairly broad ridge and go down across fields, crossing numerous stiles, to woodland on the outskirts of **Galashiels**. The Way follows a rather circuitous route through parklands and along suburban streets, skirting Gala Hill. Cross the busy A7 and follow river-side paths and the hard-surfaced bed of the old Waverley railway to Melrose (p80).

Day 8: Melrose to Longformacus

9½–10 hours, 25 miles (40km), 900m ascent

From Melrose cross the River Tweed, this time on a 19th-century chain suspension bridge for pedestrians and 'light carriages' only. The Way goes back up beside the river then heads north, steadily gaining height. There are fine views on a good day from the highest point around flat-topped **Kedslie Hill**. The route passes through several fields occupied by grazing cows – very inquisitive but not aggressive. The descent into **Lauder** skirts the local golf course.

Lauder has three hotels and a couple of nearby B&Bs, of which **Thirlestane Farm** (☎ 01578 722216; s/d £40/60), about 1.5 miles east of the Way beside the A697, is particularly recommended. **Thirlestane Castle Caravan & Camp Site** (☎ 01578 718884; thirlestanepark@btconnect.com; unpowered sites for 2 £6) is superbly sited near splendid Thirlestane Castle. In the main street you'll find an excellent baker, a small supermarket and the Flat Cat Coffee Shop, which is just as well since Lauder is the last place where you can stock up on chocolate and other walking staples before Cockburnspath at the end of the Way. **Munro's of Jedburgh** (☎ 01835 862253) buses can take you to Earlston on route 51 (£2, 45 minutes, five services Monday to Saturday) and on to Galashiels on route 66 (£2, 25 minutes, one a day Monday to Saturday).

From Lauder the Way weaves through the grounds of **Thirlestane Castle** (open to visitors). Cross the A697 and follow a lane up through the curiously named Wanton Walls Farm and steeply up to a small plantation. The Way then wanders up and down across open grassland before crossing Blythe Water on a substantial bridge. Continue on to Braidshawrig, part of the Burncastle Estate grouse moor. It's essential to keep to the track, especially during the grouse shooting season, which always starts on 12 August. The track climbs across the vast empty moors, dotted with shooting butts and old tin sheds providing shelter for stock, to the ridge crest. It then turns right to the high point of **Twin Law** (447m), topped with two giant cylindrical cairns, each with a sheltered seat facing southeast.

From there the Tweed valley is spread out before you and the sea is in sight at last. The descent towards Watch Water Reservoir is easy – a good track leads to Scarlaw and onto a sealed road. If the weather is fine you should find a small **tearoom** (Easter-Sep) at the reservoir. Continue down to the tiny village of **Longformacus** (pronounced 'long-for-may-cus').

Whinmore B&B (01361 890669; junren26@tiscali.co.uk; s/d £35/60, dinner £15) also offers three-course evening meals.

Day 9: Longformacus to Cockburnspath

7–8 hours, 18.5 miles (30km), 450m ascent

About one mile along a minor road east of Longformacus, the Way branches off to climb over moorland, going past some small plantations and down to the B6355. From here the route follows steep-sided Whiteadder valley through mixed woodland to the hamlet of **Abbey St Bathan**. Cross Whiteadder Water, just below where it joins Monynut Water. The Way follows the Whiteadder for a while then turns north; the **Riverside Restaurant** (01361 840312; Tue-Sun) is just across the river. The route here follows paths and lanes, crossing some fields in the process. From a minor road at Blackburn you can catch a last glimpse back to the hills. Then it's down to the busy A1 (cross with care) to follow an old road between the A1 and the railway to a pleasant green track into Penmanshiel Wood. It seems cruel at this stage but the route climbs through the wood – fortunately it leads to a very rewarding **view** of the North Sea and the Firth of Forth. A flight of steps takes you down to the A1107, beyond which is Pease Dean Wildlife Reserve, the site of a native woodland regeneration project.

Skirt the serried ranks of vans in Pease Bay Holiday Home Park and walk up the road above the bay. The final cliff-top walk, mirroring the start, is blessed with impressive coastal scenery, along to colourful Cove Harbour tucked below. Turn inland, under the A1 and the railway line, to the mercat (market) cross at **Cockburnspath** (pronounced 'co-burns-path' or just 'co-path'), the official end of the Way. It takes a while for the realisation to sink in that you really have walked almost 210 miles from Portpatrick – congratulations!

DUMFRIES & GALLOWAY

Often described as Scotland's hidden gem, this sparsely populated area's rugged hills, extensive forests and varied wildlife make for a fascinating backdrop while walking on its often-remote paths. Within one of Scotland's most densely forested regions, the 290-sq-mile Galloway Forest Park, are the highest and most challenging mountains in the south, notably the Merrick (843m). The Southern Upland Way, Scotland's first coast-to-coast long-distance path, marches across the region from Portpatrick through the hills, glens and forests. The walks we've selected are but a tiny taster of the wealth of potential Dumfries & Galloway has to offer.

PLANNING

Books

Walking in the Galloway Hills, by Paddy Dillon, describes 33 circular walks. Also look out for *Southern Upland Way Western Section Short Walks* published by Dumfries & Galloway Council and describing 30 walks close to the Way. It's available from TICs.

Information Sources

Dumfries & Galloway Tourist Board (01387 253862; www.visitdumfriesandgalloway.co.uk) is the first point of call for information and accommodation bookings.

Dumfries & Galloway Council (01387 260184; www.dumgal.gov.uk) countryside ranger service produces a free comprehensive guide, *Countryside Events*, available from TICs.

GETTING THERE & AWAY

Virgin Trains (0845 722 2333; www.virgintrains.co.uk) operate services between Glasgow Central and Dumfries (£12, 1¾ hours, at least eight daily). **First ScotRail** (0845 755 0033; www.firstscotrail.com) runs the same route (£12, one hour 50 minutes, at least five daily).

Stagecoach Western (01292 613500) runs bus service X77 from Glasgow to Ayr (£5, 1¼ hours, every 30 minutes), from where service 246 departs for Dumfries (£5, two hours 20 minutes, five services Monday to Saturday).

Dumfries & Galloway is a two-hour drive from Glasgow and Edinburgh.

THE MERRICK

Duration	4–4½ hours
Distance	8 miles (12.9km)
Difficulty	moderate–demanding
Start/Finish	Bruce's Stone car park
Nearest Towns	Bargrennan (right) and Glentrool (right)
Transport	private

Summary Classic walk to the Southern Uplands' highest peak along a stunningly scenic ridge above dark forests, tumbling burns and myriad lochs.

Standing at 843m (2766ft) the Merrick is the highest peak in the entire Southern Uplands – there's nothing to top it heading north until you come across Goatfell (on the Isle of Arran) and Ben Lomond. It's a big, bulky hill with a classic, highly scenic ridge route to the west and a string of wild lochs to the east. Part of the Range of the Awful Hand, its southwestern satellite Benyellary (Hill of Eagles) represents the Hand's thumb, while Merrick itself (from the Gaelic for 'branched finger') and the smaller hills to the north form the Hand's other fingers.

The surrounding area has its fair share of gory history. In Caldons Wood, at the southern end of Loch Trool, a memorial stone commemorates three Covenanters murdered for their religious beliefs. Bruce's Stone, at the start of the walk, perpetuates the victory of Robert the Bruce, King of Scotland, over the English army in 1307 during the Scottish Wars of Independence.

The good-quality path to the Merrick, which is quite steep at times, is easy to follow during the 750m ascent from Loch Trool. Rather than retracing your steps, you can return along the well-made path from Loch Enoch to Loch Neldricken (see the Alternative Route, opposite).

PLANNING

Maps

The best maps for this walk are either the OS Explorer 1:25,000 No 318 *Galloway Forest Park North* or the Harvey Superwalker 1:25,000 *Galloway Hills*. Alternatively, use the OS Landranger 1:50,000 map No 77 *Dalmellington & New Galloway*.

Information Sources

The Forestry Commission's **Glentrool visitor centre** (☎ 01671 840302; Easter-Oct), in a Swedish-style log cabin 1.8 miles from the A714 and Glentrool village (where the bus stops), has maps and books for sale, and can provide information about surrounding Galloway Forest Park. There's also a small café where you can stoke up with light meals and hot drinks.

NEAREST TOWNS

Bargrennan & Glentrool

☎ 01671

Bargrennan and the nearby small village of Glentrool, just west of Loch Trool, offer limited facilities but no shortage of warm hospitality.

Glentrool Holiday Park (☎ 840280; www.glentroolholidaypark.co.uk; Bargrennan; unpowered sites for 2 £11, holiday homes per night £47, minimum 2 nights) is a small, peaceful park with quality facilities, including a small on-site shop. Holiday homes are not available July and August.

Lorien B&B (☎ 840315; morag.lorien61@btinternet.com; 61 Glentrool; s/d £22/44) is second-to-none

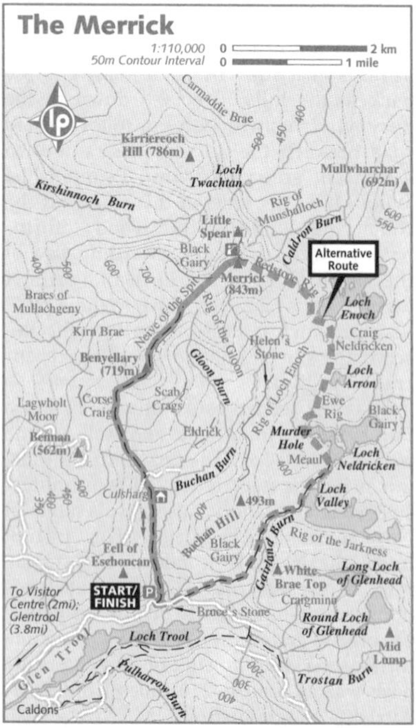

for hospitality; Morag will set you up for the day with the heartiest of breakfasts.

House O'Hill Hotel (☎ 840243; www.houseohill.co.uk; Bargrennan; s/d £35/60; mains to £9; lunch & dinner) may have featured in John Buchan's thriller *The Thirty-Nine Steps* (see the boxed text, p77). In the informal bar, tuck into plenty of good, solid pub fare.

The nearest shops are in Newton Stewart, 8.7 miles southeast.

GETTING THERE & AWAY

King's Coaches (☎ 01671 830284) operates bus service 359 (four services Monday to Saturday) between Bargrennan and Newton Stewart (£2, 23 minutes) and Girvan on the east coast (£2, 50 minutes). From Bargrennan it's 1.4 miles to Glentrool village.

By car from Newton Stewart, take the A714 Girvan road for 8.7 miles to Bargrennan; turn right to Glentrool Village. From here it's 1.8 miles to the Glentrool visitor centre.

GETTING TO/FROM THE WALK

Bruce's Stone car park is 3 miles east from the Glentrool visitor centre.

THE WALK

At the eastern end of the Bruce's Stone car park look left for a sign to Merrick and follow the path ascending northeast. After 500m of moorland, birch and hawthorn trees, pass through a kissing gate. The trail borders Buchan Burn's western side. A bit further, take the recommended high path, which heads left, slightly above the burn. Another kissing gate and a 'forest trail' sign mark the entrance to the woods.

After just over 0.5 miles of easy going, the path emerges from the forest and passes an abandoned bothy at Culsharg, good for emergency shelter only. The path becomes rocky and the ascent more difficult. Reaching a forestry road, turn right, cross a bridge over a Buchan Burn tributary, and then bear left onto an ascending path through trees, marked 'Merrick Climb'. After 800m of very steep going, the trail leaves the forest and continues northwest along Benyellary's open slopes. Continue through a kissing gate to a dry-stone dyke and follow it northeast up to **Benyellary** (719m). Follow the wall for just under 1 mile towards Merrick's summit, along the scenic **Neive of the Spit** ridge crest.

Where the wall separates from the trail, head northeast to the summit of the **Merrick** (843m), marked with a view indicator. Northern Ireland's Mountains of Mourne, Ben Lomond and the Lake District fells are visible in the distance; nearby are Mullwharchar (northeast), Craignaw (southeast) and Muldonoch and Lamachan Hills (south). Retrace your steps to Bruce's Stone.

Alternative Route: via Loch Enoch

3 hours, 5 miles (8km)

From the Merrick summit, descend steeply along Redstone Rig to Loch Enoch's southwest shore. Go southeast along a col above Loch Arron, then descend to the lake. Follow the western slopes of Ewe Rig along a wall heading south to Murder Hole. Cross a wall then follow the outflow of Loch Neldricken to the Loch Valley outflow. Descend Gairland Burn glen from a gate in the wall. Buchan Hill is to the right. Cross a field southwest and follow the path to a stile on the right; once over, cross a bridge and go west along the road to the Bruce's Stone car park.

GREY MARE'S TAIL & WHITE COOMB

Duration	5 hours
Distance	8.3 miles (13.4km)
Difficulty	moderate–demanding
Start/Finish	Grey Mare's Tail car park
Nearest Town	Moffat (p74)
Transport	bus

Summary From the supremely beautiful Grey Mare's Tail waterfall to a classic horseshoe ridge walk high above spectacular Loch Skeen.

Celebrated by two of Scotland's best-known writers, Sir Walter Scott and Robert Burns, Grey Mare's Tail waterfall plunges 61m over rugged cliffs in a steep-sided glen on the northwestern side of Moffat Dale. Its tributaries, including Tail Burn, flow from the precipitous flanks of a horseshoe of broad-backed hills, of which White Coomb (821m) is the highest, impressively embracing brooding Loch Skeen.

Moffat Water's classic U-shaped valley reveals its glacial origins. At the end of the last Ice Age, glacial debris dammed Loch Skeen. Tail Burn was stranded in a glen hanging above the main valley, so forced its way down by becoming a waterfall.

Almost the whole walk is within the National Trust for Scotland's (NTS) Grey Mare's Tail Nature Reserve, dedicated to the protection of many rare plants and animals, and to enabling visitors to explore this magnificent corner of the Southern Uplands.

The total ascent on this walk is 750m.

PLANNING

When to Walk

This is a walk for all seasons, unless there's more than a few inches of snow on the ground, which would make the steep path across the precipitous slopes above Tail Burn potentially treacherous. Crossing the burn above the falls could be difficult after heavy rain.

Maps & Books

The OS Explorer 1:25,000 map No 330 *Moffat & St Mary's Loch* is ideal. *Dumfries & Galloway Walks* by Brian Conduit includes many other fine walks in the area.

Information Sources

At the small **NTS visitor centre** (☎ 01683 222714; Apr-Oct), you'll find countryside rangers, who are on hand to answer any questions and to take bookings for their program of guided walks.

NEAREST TOWN

Moffat

☎ 01683 / pop 2135

Famous as a Victorian spa town and for its woollen products, Moffat is also close to the Southern Upland Way. The **TIC** (☎ 220620; www.visitmoffat.co.uk; Churchgate; Mon-Sat Apr-Oct) is near the town entrance from the A74(M) and stocks OS maps and several local history books; ask for the brochure *Walking in and around Moffat*, a handy guide to several short walks.

SLEEPING & EATING

The **Moffat Camping and Caravanning Club site** (☎ 220436; www.campingandcaravanningclub.co.uk; Hammerland's Farm; unpowered/powered sites for 2 £12/13) has flat, grassy sites close to the town centre.

Berriedale House B&B (☎ 220427; Beechgrove; s/d £25/44), in a large 19th-century villa, has huge, comfortable bedrooms in a quiet location.

Dell-Mar B&B (☎ 220260; dell-mar@tiscali.co.uk; 6 Beechgrove; s/d £35/54) offers a friendly welcome to weary walkers.

Bombay Cuisine (☎ 220900; Main St; mains to £11; lunch & dinner) specialises in unique Laziz Khama cuisine from Samarkand (Uzbekistan), in which each dish has its own sauce; the helpful waiter will explain these absolutely delicious dishes.

Claudio's Italian Restaurant (☎ 220958; Old Police Station; mains to £20; dinner daily Jun-Aug, Tue-Sun Sep-May), on the Selkirk road, has a lovely conservatory dining room where you can try a haggis-adorned Robbie Burns pizza.

For delicious cakes and filled rolls or sandwiches don't miss **Little's Bakery** (Main St). The Co-op supermarket is next to the well-signposted Moffat woollen mill, off the A701 near the TIC.

GETTING THERE & AWAY

Located just north of the M74 on the A701, Moffat is 30 miles southeast of Glasgow via the M74, and 50 miles southwest of Edinburgh via the A701.

MacEwan's (☎ 01387 256533) bus service 100 travels regularly between Edinburgh and Moffat (£5, two hours, three services Monday to Saturday, one Sunday). From Glasgow, **Stagecoach Western** (☎ 01292 613500) runs service 974 to Moffat (£6, 1½ hours, three services Monday to Saturday, two on Sunday).

GETTING TO/FROM THE WALK

Houston's Minibuses (☎ 01576 203874) operates a summer-only Saturday service between Lockerbie and Selkirk via Moffat and the Grey Mare's Tail car park (£4 return from Moffat, 30 minutes); the timetable allows plenty of time to do the walk using this service.

By car follow the A708 from Moffat towards Selkirk for 9 miles to the signposted Grey Mare's Tail Nature Reserve. There's a pay-and-display (£2) car park on the northwest side of the road.

THE WALK

From the car park follow a well-made path with steps rising steeply above Tail Burn; soon you're high above **Grey Mare's Tail** – an awesome experience. Follow the path past the upper cascades as it levels out beside the burn. Cross it to follow a prominent stone

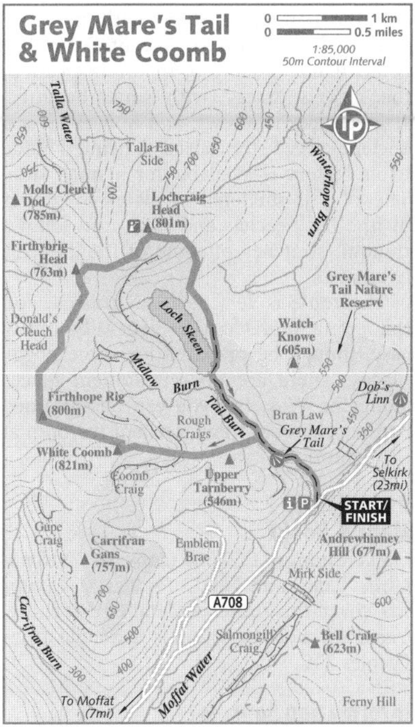

wall generally westwards, with the wall on your left. The wall arrows up a broad spur to a saddle. Now the going gets tougher as you ascend steeply past Rough Craigs where the wall vanishes briefly. Continue gaining height until you see the rounded summit of **White Coomb** about 150m to the south – a short stroll to bag another Corbett (2¾ hours from the car park).

Return to the wall and then follow a fence west across superb grasslands for just over half a mile to **Firthhope Rig** (800m). Make a 90-degree turn (north) and traverse the pleasantly undulating Donald's Cleuch Head ridge, following a fence and a wall for about one mile. At **Firthybrig Head** (763m) turn east at a T-junction in the wall and plunge down to a soggy saddle before rising steeply to **Lochcraig Head** (801m), one hour from White Coomb. The views continue to be impressive: White Coomb lies to the south, the three Eildon Hills are clearly visible over to the east and Loch Skeen shimmers below. Descend beside the wall towards the loch for just over one mile. The wall ends in a morass and a fence continues across the peat hags. After about 10 minutes the fence turns southeast; turn south and make your way down to meet the path just below Tail Burn's outflow from Loch Skeen (45 minutes from Lochcraig Head). Follow the path back down to the car park.

THE BORDERS

The Borders is a hill-walkers' delight, a seemingly vast area of southeast Scotland laid out in rolls between the Moorfoot and Lammermuir Hills in the north and the Cheviot Hills on the English border in the south. In this sparsely populated area (compared with central Scotland), it's easy to feel that you're a long way from anywhere as you traverse the broad ridges and cross deep, lonely glens. The western fringe reaches 840m at Broad Law, the highest of the multitude of Borders' hills. Eastwards, the rugged cliffs and sheltered coves of the Berwickshire coast face the North Sea. Through the centre runs the River Tweed, a silver thread travelling 96 miles steadily eastward through several towns to the sea at Berwick-upon-Tweed in England.

The day walks described here explore the lush Tweed valley and nearby hills, and a magnificent stretch of coast. There's also the eastern section of the Southern Upland Way (p63) across the full breadth of the area to Cockburnspath, and Melrose is also the starting point for St Cuthbert's Way (p85).

PLANNING

Books

The Scottish Borders: 25 Walks by Peter Jackson concentrates on circular walks in the Tweedsmuir, Moorfoot and Lammermuir Hills. *Short Walks on the Eastern Section of the Southern Upland Way*, describing more than 35 walks, and the excellent Borders Council *Walks Around* series of booklets cover Peebles and Melrose (among others), and are available from TICs. The Borders Council also publishes a Heritage series of four titles, including *Christian Heritage in the Borders*, all by John Dent and Rory McDonald; also available at TICs, they represent great value and background reading.

Information Sources

The Borders' **TICs** (☎ 0870 608 0404; www.visitscottishborders.com) are very helpful and stock a veritable mountain of information for walkers, including the useful booklet *Walking Guide to the Scottish Borders*. They can also book accommodation for you.

The **Scottish Borders Council ranger service** (☎ 01835 830281; rangers@scotborders.gov.uk; Harestanes by Ancrum), in conjunction with several other agencies, issues the **Outdoor Diary** (www.outdoor-diary.info) describing loads of ranger-led walks and activities.

GETTING THERE & AROUND

Amazingly, the Borders is bereft of train stations; bus services link the train stations at Berwick-upon-Tweed and Edinburgh to the main towns. By road the western Borders is most easily accessed from the A74(M). The A708 (Moffat–Selkirk) takes you to the heart of the region; the A7 and the A68 bisect the region as they beeline north to Edinburgh. The A1 traverses the eastern part of the region. Most of the Borders' major towns are within a one-hour drive of Edinburgh and 1½ hours from Glasgow.

JOHN BUCHAN WAY

Duration	5¾–6 hours
Distance	13.5 miles (22km)
Difficulty	moderate
Start	Peebles (right)
Finish	Broughton (opposite)
Transport	bus

Summary A vigorous and varied walk through the opulently rolling hills and eerily quiet, remote glens that inspired a noted Scottish writer.

Proving that size doesn't matter when it comes to hill walking, the John Buchan Way eschews climbing to any tick-me-off summit, taking you instead through irresistibly alluring hills and glens on either side of the Tweed valley west of the attractive town of Peebles. If ever a walk served to entice people back to the area, this is it.

Commemorating author John Buchan (see the boxed text, opposite) the route links Peebles to the village of Broughton, passing through farmland, both past and present, and the hamlet of Stobo with its 12th-century kirk (church), one of the oldest in Scotland. Usually open for inspection, the kirk is graced with some beautiful stained-glass windows, and houses several ancient carved stone slabs. A printed guide to its history is available for a small sum. The Way is sheltered in places by groves of fine old beeches and oaks, and follows tranquil stretches of some of the Tweed's tributaries.

The route is very well waymarked, and the going underfoot is generally pretty easy, though be prepared for some boggy places. There are no refreshment places along the Way, but you can be sustained by the prospect of the excellent tearoom at Broughton.

PLANNING

Maps & Books

OS Landranger 1:50,000 maps No 72 *Upper Clyde Valley* and No 73 *Peebles & Galashiels* cover the route. A detailed brochure, *The John Buchan Way*, is available from Peebles TIC.

Information Sources

The **Scottish Borders Council ranger service** (☎ 01835 830281; rangers@scotborders.gov.uk; Harestanes by Ancrum) looks after the Way.

NEAREST TOWNS

Peebles

☎ 01721 / pop 8065

Peebles TIC (☎ 0870 608 0404; www.visitscottishborder.com; High St; daily Apr-Dec, Mon-Sat Jan-Mar) stocks a wide range of publications. The **Great Outdoors** (☎ 724263; High St) sells outdoor clothing and basic equipment.

SLEEPING & EATING

Crossburn Caravan Park (☎ 720501; www.crossburncaravans.co.uk; Edinburgh Rd; unpowered/powered sites for 2 £7/12) is a short walk or drive from the centre of town with plenty of space for tents.

Whitestone House (☎ 720337; www.aboutscotland.com/peebles/whitestone.html; Innerleithen Rd; s/d £28/50) in a beautifully kept 19th-century manse offers large, well-appointed rooms and a comfortable guest lounge.

Rowanbrae (☎ 721630; www.aboutscotland.com/peebles/rowanbrae.html; Northgate; s/d £30/50) sits surrounded by a luxuriant garden, producing fresh flowers to bedeck the beautifully

THE THIRTY-NINE STEPS & OTHER TALES

John Buchan would be pleased to know that a walking route in the Borders is named in his honour. Buchan (1875–1940), a prolific writer of fiction, historical works and biographies, and a man of many other parts, spent youthful summer holidays in the Borders. Exploring the hills and glens on foot, he nurtured a lifelong passion for their wild, wide spaces.

His prodigious output of more than 100 books, plus short stories and articles, is all the more surprising considering that writing was not always his full-time calling. A varied career in government, parliament and newspapers culminated in his appointment as governor general of Canada in 1935 with the title of Lord Tweedsmuir (after the Borders' river). However, he is best remembered for *The Four Adventures of Richard Hannay*, which were pioneers in the realm of thriller-cum-detective stories.

Set in the years before, during and after WWI, the stories evoke a bygone era, imbued with ideas about duty, loyalty, race and class relations that are way out of step with the 21st century. That matters little, for his clear, uncluttered, engaging style, and his ability to paint landscapes, delineate all kinds of characters and to pile up the tension and excitement, make for compulsive reading. Scenes in *The Thirty-Nine Steps* (famously and incomparably filmed by Hitchcock in 1935) are set in the Borders, probably near Dollar Law, not far south of the John Buchan Way. In those days people lived in the sad, ruined cottages you'll pass today. A gripping interlude in the much longer *Mr Standfast* is set in the Cuillin hills on the Isle of Skye and on the nearby mainland, and is vividly and convincingly evoked.

The **John Buchan Society** (www.johnbuchansociety.co.uk) website is a rich source of 'Buchanalia' and well worth browsing if you're hooked. And don't forget the John Buchan Centre in Broughton (see below).

furnished rooms of this traditional Victorian home.

Prince of India (☎ 724455; 86 High St; mains to £10; lunch & dinner) features tasteful Indian décor and a wide selection of vegetarian dishes.

The award-winning **Sunflower Restaurant** (☎ 722420; www.thesunflower.net; 4 Bridgegate; mains £12-16; lunch & dinner) uses top-quality local ingredients in delectable combinations of Scottish, Mediterranean and Far Eastern cuisine.

For groceries head to **Somerfield** (38 Northgate) supermarket; there's a second Somerfield on Dovecote Rd, off the Edinburgh road. People come from Edinburgh to buy bread at **Forsyth's Bakers** (21 Eastgate).

GETTING THERE & AWAY

First Edinburgh (☎ 08708 727271) bus service 62 links Peebles and Edinburgh (£4, 1¼ hours, every 30 minutes Monday to Saturday, hourly Sunday).

Broughton

☎ 01899

There's no accommodation in Broughton, but there is an excellent tearoom and a brewery – who needs anything else!

The **John Buchan Centre** (☎ 880258; Moffat Rd, Broughton; £2; 2-5pm May-Oct) houses photographs and other memorabilia relating to John Buchan.

Laurel Bank Tea Room (☎ 830462; light meals to £5; lunch & afternoon tea) offers a good range of snacks and superb homemade cakes; cold drinks include Australia's incomparable Bundaberg ginger beer.

Broughton Brewery (☎ 830345; www.broughtonales.co.uk; Mon-Fri) sells gift packs and ales by the dozen.

Broughton Stores in the main street stocks Broughton ales (and much else).

MacEwan's (☎ 01387 256533) operates bus route 91 between Peebles and Broughton (30 minutes, six services weekdays, five Saturday). Cars can be parked next to the village hall at the northern end of Broughton, or outside the primary school at the southern end.

THE WALK

From the car park below the southeastern corner of the Tweed Bridge, cross Caledonian Rd and follow waymarked lanes and minor roads through the southern fringes of Peebles to a minor road leading south, up past Tantah House, hiding behind a stone

John Buchan Way

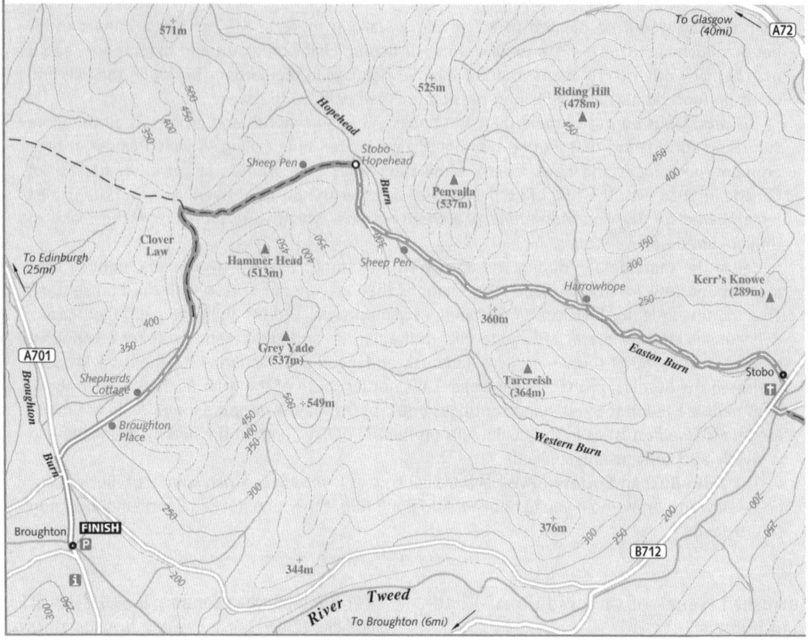

wall. Go through a gate in a wall on your right (west) and start ascending, soon following a path southwest across the open slope of a wide valley with Peebles in view. Veer west up to a minor saddle and continue on a grassy path steering southwest. Maintain that direction up to the ridge extending northeast from prominent **Cademuir Hill**. Though the official route bypasses the summit, it's worth taking an extra 25 minutes or so to climb it, if only for the fantastic views of huge rounded hills and deep, deep valleys.

The path pursues a generally southward route as it meanders downhill, with a dyke on the left. It then swings west and descends past a Scots pine plantation almost to the road (1¼ hours from Peebles). Follow the path until you're just past the more westerly of two entrances to Cademuir farm, then take to the grassy verge leading to the levee bank beside Manor Water, where there are a couple of very enticing picnic tables. Cross over a bridge, turn right then left and continue west, past Croftlea cottage to a T-junction at the **Glack**.

Go through a gate between a stone cottage and barn and keep walking west, aiming for the forest corner on the skyline. From there, go on to a stile then descend to a point just short of a gate in a dyke. Turn left, and continue up past the corner of the dyke and a small plantation to a fence corner; change direction to west and descend to cross a footbridge over a burn. Follow a short path then a farm track; turn right and follow the waymarked route across a field, over stiles and through gates to a vehicle track; turn left to reach the B712 (1¾ hours from the Glack).

Walk northeast along the road, diverging to **Stobo Kirk** if you wish. To continue along the Way, take the second turn left (west). Shortly, at a fork, bear left over a stile and follow a delightful track beside **Easton Burn** for 1 mile or so to a ruined cottage at **Harrowhope** (30 minutes from the B712). Cross a footbridge to a very pleasant spot for a decent break before tackling the next stage.

Continue west up the slope, through a belt of trees, over a giant stile and then

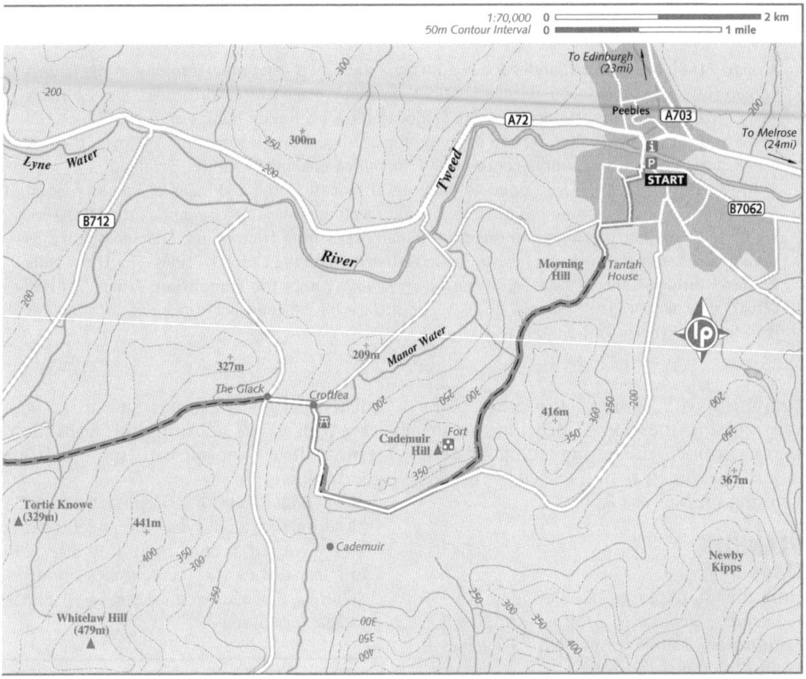

along a track leading northwest towards the massive bulk of Penvalla. Walking up the wide valley it's easy to imagine you are Richard Hannay (see the boxed text on p77). From a small saddle, bear northwest into the valley of Hopehead Burn along a track across the hillside. Descend steadily, past a curious circular stell (stone-built sheep pen). Cross the burn on a footbridge then follow the farm access track past lonely **Stobo Hopehead** cottage. Bear left along a path, soon ascending west to the head of the valley, past an unusual hexagonal stell. At the saddle (around 1¼ hours from Harrowhope), continue west briefly then turn south and descend steeply. Cross a burn for one last ascent on a wide track. Go down to Shepherds Cottage on the right, through a gate then along a track and road, past the imposing mansion **Broughton Place**, which was built in 1937. Continue down past Broughton Place Farm, where there's an old water mill beside the road on your left, to the A701. Turning left, it's only 800m into Broughton (about one hour from the saddle).

EILDON HILLS

Duration	4 hours
Distance	7.9 miles (12.7km)
Difficulty	easy–moderate
Start/Finish	Melrose Abbey
Nearest Town	Melrose (p80)
Transport	bus

Summary Check out local history by scaling the Eildon Hills (once occupied by Romans), exploring the Roman fort Trimontium, and following an ancient path back to Melrose.

The charming town of Melrose sits at the northern foot of the Eildon Hills, a trio of distinctively shaped hills that seem to say, from near and far, 'Come and climb me'. Visible from miles around, and rising steeply from the broad Tweed valley, their volcanic rock cores are blanketed in sandstone with a coverlet of heather and grass.

Centuries ago, the pushy Romans commandeered the strategic summits and the saintly Cuthbert (see p85) moved through these parts. Today, the Eildon Hills Walk,

ALL ROADS LED FROM TRIMONTIUM

Around AD 80 the Romans, under Julius Agricola, established what grew into one of the largest Roman forts in Scotland: 370-acre Trimontium, meaning 'place of the three hills', just 1.5 miles east of Melrose. He ousted the locals, the Selgovae tribe, from their homes on top of Eildon Hill North and set up a signalling station or shrine there. Named on Ptolemy's AD 145 map, the fort was a strategic base and supply centre in the Roman campaigns to subdue Scotland.

It was also used as the zero point to measure distances. Of the 500 miles of Roman road in Scotland, only one milestone has been found. Engraved upon it is '*MP Trimontio*', the MP standing for *milia passum*, meaning 'thousands of Roman paces' from Trimontium. Archaeological digs have unearthed metalwork, ditches and more settlements on the Eildon hillsides. The **Three Hills Roman Heritage Centre** (Market Sq, Melrose; £2; ⌚ Apr-Oct), run by the **Trimontium Trust** (☎ 01896 822651; www.trimontium.net), houses displays about daily life on the Roman frontier; local guides lead the free weekly Trimontium Walk.

combined with some of the other paths crisscrossing the slopes, provides an extremely scenic, exhilarating outing. The last stretch is along Priorswalk, used by masons working on Melrose Abbey.

PLANNING
Maps

Both the OS Explorer 1:25,000 map No 338 *Galashiels, Selkirk & Melrose* and the OS Landranger 1:50,000 map No 73 *Peebles & Galashiels* cover the walk.

NEAREST TOWN
Melrose

☎ **01896 / pop 1656**

Dominated by the beautiful 12th-century Cistercian abbey, Melrose makes a particularly attractive base for this walk. **Melrose TIC** (☎ 0870 608 0404; www.visitscottishborders.com; Abbey House, Abbey St; ⌚ Apr-Oct), opposite the abbey and next to a car park, stocks the useful *Walks Around Melrose* booklet, OS maps and local history references.

SLEEPING & EATING

Gibson Park Caravan Club Site (☎ 822969; High St; sites for 2 £18), close to the town centre, has a few tent sites and excellent facilities.

Melrose SYHA Hostel (☎ 0870 004 1141; www.syha.org.uk; Priorwood; dm £14) occupies a fine Georgian mansion, overlooking Melrose Abbey.

Braidwood B&B (☎ 822488; www.braidwoodmelrose.co.uk; Buccleuch St; s/d £35/56) offers high-standard facilities and a friendly welcome to this 19th-century townhouse.

Marmion's Restaurant (☎ 822245; Buccleuch St; mains to £17; ⌚ lunch & dinner Mon-Sat) is both a quietly elegant restaurant and an art gallery, with works adorning the walls. Substantial dishes cooked with some flair are good value.

King's Arms Hotel (☎ 822143; High St; mains to £10; ⌚ lunch & dinner), a 300-year-old coaching inn, offers a varied menu, including Mexican and curry dishes and has real ales on tap.

There are two supermarkets: **Co-op** (High St) and **Spar** (High Street).

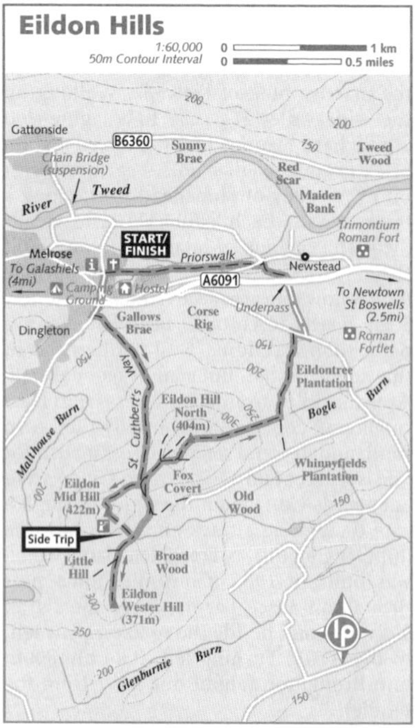

GETTING THERE & AWAY

First Edinburgh (☎ 08708 727271) bus route 62 links Edinburgh and Melrose (£5.50, 2¼ hours, eight services Monday to Saturday, six Sunday).

By car from Edinburgh, take the A7 south to Galashiels and then head east on the A72 to Melrose.

THE WALK

From the car park opposite Melrose Abbey walk south up Abbey St. Cross Market Sq, then head up Dingleton Rd, following the St Cuthbert's Way markers (Celtic cross). Pass under the A6091 and in 150m turn left between houses, following an 'Eildon Walk' sign. Cross a stream and climb steps to a grassy path. Follow it up, passing through two gates on either side of a track, and up with a hedge on your left. A kissing gate leads to open ground; shortly turn south to reach a saddle between Eildon Hill North and Eildon Mid Hill (40 minutes from the start). Even though the Eildon Way sign directs left, turn west and soon bear right at a fork for a gentler ascent. Continue up to the summit of **Eildon Mid Hill** (422m), where you can identify the many features in the view on a direction plate.

To reach Eildon Wester Hill descend southeast on a narrow path to a wider path; turn right. Reach the **summit** (371m) via the second path on your left. Return downhill, past the path from Mid Hill and follow a track into woodland to a T-junction; turn north. At a fork, St Cuthbert's Way continues north; instead go straight on to the saddle you crossed earlier. Continue northeast along a grassed track and fork right (east) at the start of the main ascent; then a few minutes further on bear left (north) and follow the broad path up to the summit of **Eildon Hill North** (404m), one hour from the saddle, for an equally good view.

Head east, very steeply downhill, through gorse; a few Eildon Hills Walk waymarker posts indicate the route. Go through a kissing gate to a woodland path beside a burn and continue to a road (25 minutes from Eildon Hill North); turn right. A short distance beyond an information board about the 13th-century poet Thomas the Rhymer, turn left through a gate. Follow the track to an underpass beneath the A6091, then a disused railway. Turn left and follow a path down to the western fringes of **Newstead**. You could break off here to explore Trimontium, the Roman encampment.

Follow a minor road to the left then go right onto a path between a house and stables. Beyond fields on the right, you reach a bitumen path leading to a road; bear right downhill and continue along beside a quiet road. Where it bends left, continue along **Priorswalk**, soon through a park and to the road opposite the car park (35 minutes from Newstead).

BURNMOUTH TO ST ABB'S HEAD

Duration	6 hours
Distance	11.9 miles (19.2km)
Difficulty	easy
Start	Burnmouth (p82)
Finish	St Abb's Head Nature Centre
Nearest Town	Eyemouth (p82), Burnmouth (p82), Coldingham (p83), St Abbs (p83)
Transport	bus

Summary Riveting cliff and beach walk, passing through fishing villages, a wealth of extraordinary geological formations, flocks of seabirds and abundant wildflowers.

Some of the finest coastal scenery in Scotland awaits you along this walk, part of a cross-border waymarked route linking Berwick-upon-Tweed and St Abb's Head. Small villages, tiny beaches, secluded harbours and the towering cliffs make for an exceptionally varied day out.

St Abb's Head National Nature Reserve, owned and managed by the NTS, protects a coastline of exceptional geological significance. In Burnmouth, sedimentary Silurian mudstone (greywacke) and siltstone, laid down on the sea bed 440 million years ago, appear in dramatic, swirling layers along the cliffs of Fancove. Around Burnmouth's harbour the same rock has been transformed by wave action into neatly packed layers rising vertically from the sea floor, and is bent and twisted at Linkim Kip and Coldingham Bay. Rusty-red sandstone sedimentary rocks, laid down in river beds 380 million years ago, form the cliffs north of Eyemouth. Between these two periods, harder igneous rocks, produced from lava flows, created the steep, erosion-resistant St Abb's Head.

THE SAINTLY EBBE

If you're wondering how St Abb's Head acquired its name, the answer is an amazing woman who lived 1300 years ago.

Born into a ruling pagan family in Northumbria (England) around AD 615, Ebbe arrived in Scotland as a young girl with her widowed mother and family. Following her conversion to Christianity she was hotly pursued by a persistent suitor but was saved by divine intervention. Later, the same force helped her to escape would-be captors, then sailed her boat to an isolated promontory on the Berwickshire coast, perhaps St Abb's Head. Monks in a nearby church witnessed her landing and promptly renamed their church in her honour. They then joined the unisex monastery she founded.

A pious woman, she drew kindred folk to the monastery, including the reputed misogynist St Cuthbert (see p85). Soon after her death in AD 683, the monastery was destroyed by fire.

Sea birds are the reserve's pride and joy. Puffins nest in the cliffs from May to July, and it's easy to spot shags, fulmars, guillemots and herring gulls. Grey seals, porpoises and even dolphins make an appearance from time to time.

PLANNING

The walk is described from south to north, so that you reach the main highlight, St Abb's Head, in the closing stages. Excellent public transport connections make it easy to pick and choose starting and finishing places.

When to Walk

May and June are best for wildflowers, and July and August for butterflies. For nesting sea birds plan a visit between May and July, while migratory sea birds pass through in May and from September to mid-October.

Maps & Books

The OS Explorer 1:25,000 map No 346 *Berwick-upon-Tweed* covers the walk. The free pamphlet *The Berwickshire Coastal Path* is a mini-guide to the complete 15-mile (24km) route, starting in Berwick-upon-Tweed.

Information Sources

St Abb's Head Nature Centre (🕒 Apr-Oct) is at the end of the walk. Contact the **NTS head ranger** (☎ 01890 771443) for more information and to arrange a guided walk. The NTS booklet *St Abb's Head National Nature Reserve* is available at the nature centre.

NEAREST TOWNS

There are plenty of options near this walk, the largest of them being Eyemouth, though you can also choose to base yourself in tiny Burnmouth, Coldingham or St Abbs.

Burnmouth

☎ 01890

Burnmouth is a tiny village divided into Upper Burnmouth, Partanhall (a string of cottages at the foot of the cliff), Cowdrait and Ross (just south, nearer the harbour).

White Craggs B&B (☎ 781397; www.whitecraggs.co.uk; d £70) is an attractively furnished bungalow above the tiny harbour.

The **Flemington Inn** (☎ 781277; mains to £15; 🕒 lunch & dinner) prominently stakes its claim to be Scotland's last inn before the English border.

GETTING THERE & AWAY

GNER (☎ 0845 722 5225) trains from Edinburgh to London stop in Berwick-upon-Tweed (£17, 45 minutes, at least 10 daily), the closest train station to Burnmouth.

Perryman's Buses (☎ 01289 308719) operates two convenient services: route 253 Edinburgh to Berwick-upon-Tweed stops in Coldingham, St Abbs, Eyemouth and Burnmouth (£8, two hours, at least three daily); and route 235 Berwick-upon-Tweed to St Abbs, stops in Burnmouth (£1.50, 10 minutes, six services Monday to Saturday, three Sunday).

By car take the A1 either north from Berwick-upon-Tweed or east from Edinburgh to the A1107, which links (from south to north) Burnmouth, Eyemouth and Coldingham.

Eyemouth

☎ 01890 / pop 3383

Eyemouth, the only town along the way, is an active fishing port with an attractive town centre where you'll find the **TIC** (☎ 0870 608404; Auld Kirk, Manse Rd; ⏲ Apr-Oct).

Hillcrest B&B (☎ 750463; Coldingham Rd; d £46) is conveniently located and offers comfortable rooms with shared bathrooms.

The **Ship Hotel** (☎ 750224; Harbour Rd; s/d £25/56; mains to £12; ⏲ lunch & dinner) is a homely place; there's a good choice of real ales in the bar.

Giacopazzi's (☎ 750317; 20 Harbour Rd; mains to £14) is famous throughout the land for its fish and chips, oven-fired pizzas and home-made ice cream.

There's a **Co-op** (High St) supermarket.

See Getting There & Away for Burnmouth (opposite) for transport details.

Coldingham

☎ 01890 / pop 600

This delightful large village sits between lush undulating farmland and a beautiful crescent-shaped sandy beach.

Coldingham Sands Youth Hostel (☎ 0870 004111; www.syha.org.uk; dm £14) overlooks the ocean.

Priory View B&B (☎ 771525; prioryview@btinternet.com; Eyemouth Rd; d £60) has a lovely sea view from one of its rooms.

For a meal, try the New Inn on the main road in the centre of the village. There's a Spar supermarket in the village.

See Getting There & Away for Burnmouth (opposite) for transport options.

St Abbs

☎ 01890

St Abbs was named after the 7th-century monastery founded here by Ebbe or Abb (see the boxed text, opposite).

Murrayfield B&B (☎ 771468; 7 Murrayfield St; d £36) is a former fisherman's cottage.

Castle Rock B&B (☎ 771715; www.castlerockbandb.co.uk; d £58), on the route at Murrayfield, must enjoy the most spectacular B&B location on the coast. Evening meals are available by prior arrangement.

At the western entrance to the nature reserve at Northfield Farm is **Old Smiddy** (☎ 771707; lunch £6; ⏲ lunch daily, dinner Fri & Sat), ideally located for a post-walk refresher.

See Getting There & Away for Burnmouth (opposite) for transport options.

GETTING TO/FROM THE WALK

There are car parks at Burnmouth harbour (space is limited) and in the village, in the centre of Eyemouth and at the walk's end near the visitor centre (£2.50 for a car with two passengers). Once in Burnmouth, walk to the northwest edge of the village where the main and harbour roads meet. On the ocean side of the main road you will see the primary school and, to the right, a sealed road descending steeply to the harbour. Locate the 'Coastal Footpath' waymarker.

The walk ends at the St Abb's Head Nature Centre. To reach the bus stop in St Abbs, walk down the B6438 Coldingham–St Abbs road or take the clear path into the centre of St Abbs village.

THE WALK

Set out eastwards along the signed coastal path and reach the cliffs in five minutes. To the south you can see Burnmouth's harbour and its curious combed rock. Once on the cliffs the way ambles north for 1.4 miles, past cultivated fields to the cliffs' highest point, Fancove Head. In 10 minutes the path reaches the golf course. Ignore a trail that heads off left and continue just over 0.5 miles along the cliffs, to a sign offering

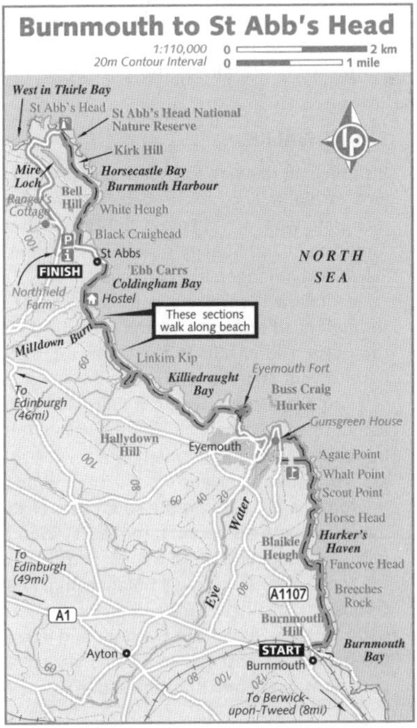

THE SOUTH

a choice: either turn left towards the clubhouse and then right onto the sealed road to Eyemouth, or continue along the cliffs. Along the latter, beware of wayward golf balls at the seventh tee sign. Cross the course and exit through an opening in the wall. Turn right onto the sealed road to Eyemouth, joining the alternative route.

After a hairpin turn you reach Eyemouth's fish market. Keep the lifeboat station and **Gunsgreen House** – a renowned 18th-century smuggler's house – off to the left, cross a footbridge and continue along the quayside. At a road junction turn right towards **Eyemouth** and in 200m you reach Manse Rd and the TIC a few steps away. Continue along the harbour road and turn left onto the maritime walkway bordering the half-moon beach. Turn right at the swimming pool and go down to the beach. Leave it after 100m by a flight of steps up to the caravan park. About 50m further on, leave the coast path by turning right to inspect two rusting cannons at **Eyemouth Fort**, reminders of Eyemouth's past importance as a military centre in Borders' conflicts.

Follow the contour of the red sandstone cliffs west. The trail rejoins the path bordering the caravan park. Cross a grassy clearing and continue along the cliff edge for 500m; the path swings round to the right, passing above Killiedraught Bay and cultivated fields to the left. Continue straight across the field on the path to a gate and a red sandstone wall between the trail and the cliff edge. Follow the field edge path for 600m to a stile. Cross it then descend steps through a gully to Linkim Shore. Walk along the beach and at the far end go back up to the cliffs. In 15 minutes descend more steps to a pebble beach; cross it then climb out at the other end. Descend again and cross the sandy beach at **Coldingham Bay**, exiting at its northern end to rejoin the obvious trail, which is paved to St Abbs.

Entering St Abbs, a sign directs you left, but continue straight on the road fronting the cliff-side homes. Once you reach a phone box, turn right and then left past the Heritage Museum and church (both left), walking parallel to a high stone wall. At the wall's corner turn right and continue towards the sea and a kissing gate at the entrance to **St Abb's Head National Nature Reserve**. The cliffs soon begin to rise gently, offering splendid views of St Abbs village and Mire Loch from the crest. For the next 20 minutes the path undulates along the cliffs, passing the pebbly beaches of Burnmouth Harbour and Horsecastle Bay, before reach-

THE SOUTH

SHORT WALKS

It's uphill all the way to **Broad Law** (840m), the highest summit in the Borders, in a wonderful area of big, rolling, steep-sided hills and deep glens. Allow 2¼ hours for this 4.7-mile (7.6km) moderate walk. It starts and finishes at the Megget Stone on the narrow minor road linking Tweedsmuir and St Mary's Loch (p69). The nearest towns are Moffat (p74) and Broughton (p77). Take OS Landranger 1:50,000 map No 72.

Just follow the walkers' path paralleling a fence line, generally northwards from the road, up through heather moorland and grass to the flattish summit. The view includes the lowlands to the north, Eildon Hills to the southeast, St Mary's Loch, White Coomb and much, much more. Retrace your steps to return.

From near Peebles you can follow the delightful riverbank **Tweed Walk** and take in an easy ascent to a fine viewpoint over the valley. This easy–moderate walk of 4.5 miles (7.1km) takes 2½ hours and starts and finished from the river-side car park in Peebles (p76). You'll need the *Walks Around Peebles* booklet from the TIC and/or OS Landranger 1:50,000 map No 73.

From the car park on the south side of the river, cross the river and follow the Tweed Walk river-bank path upstream, through Hay Wood Park, past imposing Neidpath Castle, under an old railway viaduct and on to a road. Turn left (southeast), cross Manor Bridge then, in 100m, turn left (northeast) to cross Old Manor Brig. Follow the quiet road up to Manor Sware viewpoint. Opposite a small car park and picnic area, turn left (west) into the forest and bear left down a path. Ignore two paths to the right and descend steeply to meet a wider path. Turn right, follow the path down past the end of the viaduct then along the river bank. Continue along a paved path from near Fotheringham Bridge to the road bridge near the car park.

ing a summit and, finally, the lighthouse on St Abb's Head appears. Skirt left round the houses near the lighthouse to a sealed road. Turn left and in about 2 miles the road reaches the reserve car park and the nature centre.

MORE WALKS

DUMFRIES & GALLOWAY

Arthur's Seat & Hart Fell

A classic Moffat Hills walk is the double ascent of Arthur's Seat (731m) and Hart Fell (808m), returning above the Devil's Beef Tub, a steep-walled, enclosed valley. Taking the A701 (north) from Moffat turn right after the Moffat Academy and continue 3 miles to a 'Hart Fell Spa' sign before Ericstane. The moderate–demanding 7.2-mile circular route ascends steeply along Auchencat Burn, past the purportedly medicinal waters of Hart Fell Spa and up to the ridge crest. Continue northeast, reaching first Hart Fell then Arthur's Seat. The trail then uses the regional border fence to continue west to Whitehope Knowe (614m), Chalk Rig Edge (499m) and Great Hill (466m). Overlooking Devil's Beef Tub, look for the southbound trail to reach Corehead and Ericstane. OS Landranger 1:50,000 map No 78 covers this walk.

THE BORDERS

John Muir Way

Dunbar, a small coastal town in East Lothian, has been at the centre of the awakening of interest in one of Scotland's least-recognised famous sons, John Muir. Acknowledged in the USA, his adopted home, as the 'Father of National Parks', his name is perpetuated by the John Muir Trust (p31). Muir was born in Dunbar in April 1838; his birthplace houses an excellent **visitor centre** (☎ 01368 865899; www.jmbt.org.uk) featuring his passionate evocation of the importance of preserving wilderness areas. The John Muir Country Park, on the western side of the town, is a small, more-or-less-natural oasis along the coast with a scenic 2-mile cliff-top path.

The John Muir Way, a coastal path of approximately 50 miles, will eventually link Cockburnspath (at the end of the Southern Upland Way, p65) and Edinburgh. By mid-2006 two sections were open: Musselburgh to Aberlady (18.6 miles/25.2km) and Dunbar to Dunglass (10 miles/16km). While you can't help but wonder what Muir would think of a path that passes through or very close to two power stations (one of them nuclear) and an unsightly quarry, the route does offer plenty of varied, often scenic, coastal walking. Long-distance enthusiasts will probably be lured by the prospect of walking from Portpatrick on the southwest coast to Edinburgh, combining the Southern Upland and John Muir Ways, a distance of around 260 miles. The best parts of the Dunbar-to-Dunglass section are between Dunbar and Barns Ness, and between Thorntonloch and Dunglass. For copies of the superbly illustrated leaflets (with maps), contact **East Lothian Council** (☎ 01620 827199; www.eastlothian.gov.uk) or drop into the **Dunbar TIC** (☎ 01368 863353; www.dunbar.org.uk; 143 High St) or John Muir's birthplace.

St Cuthbert's Way

St Cuthbert was a 7th-century Celtic saint whose vocation with the church began at Melrose in AD 650. He was eventually appointed Bishop of Lindisfarne (Holy Island), just off the Northumberland coast in England. For Cuthbert, walking was a time for peaceful contemplation.

St Cuthbert's Way links Melrose (p80) and Lindisfarne in a route of great variety and interest, passing through places associated with Cuthbert's life and ministry. It crosses the Eildon Hills and the Cheviot Hills in Northumberland National Park, follows sections of the beautiful Tweed and Teviot Rivers and part of the ancient Roman road, Dere Street, and traverses fertile farmland. At low tide you can cross to Lindisfarne by the causeway or by the Pilgrims' Route across the sands. The route is waymarked with the Way's Celtic cross logo. There's a reasonable supply of accommodation along the way.

The distance of 62.5 miles (100.5km) includes 1200m of ascent. It could be walked in four days but you'll probably need to allow five or six to fit in with safe crossing times to Lindisfarne. The Way links with the Pennine Way at Kirk Yetholm and the Southern Upland Way at Melrose, thus making possible a grand long-distance walk.

The official trail guide, *St Cuthbert's Way* by Roger Smith and Ron Shaw, comprises a detailed guidebook and a 1:40,000 Harvey map. The OS Landranger 1:50,000 maps are Nos 73, 74 and 75.

Information about accommodation is available from **VisitScotland Borders** (☎ 0870 608 0404; www.visitscottishborders.com) and the **Berwick-upon-Tweed TIC** (☎ 01289 330733; www.berwick-upon-tweed.gov.uk). For public transport details go to **Traveline** (☎ 0870 608 2608; www.travelinescotland.com). Vital information about safe crossing times to Lindisfarne is available from **Wooler TIC** (☎ 01668 282123) and is displayed there out of hours – tide times are given for the coming fortnight.

Borders Abbeys Way

This 65-mile (105km) circular route connects the towns of Kelso, Jedburgh, Melrose and Dryburgh, each with a superbly preserved 12th-century abbey. The route, which divides easily into five sections, follows paths, tracks and quiet roads and is clearly waymarked with a distinctive AW logo. There are many other interesting historical features along the way, which also passes through the town of Hawick. A set of five information-rich leaflets, each with a detailed map covering the Way, is available from local TICs; alternatively, contact **VisitScotland Borders** (☎ 0870 608 0404; www.visitscottishborders.com).

Central Highlands & Islands

Scotland's central Highlands and islands form an area of exceptional beauty, brimful of contrasts and rich in alluring challenges. In the far west, the rugged Isle of Arran has something for everyone, from spectacular ridges and peaks (notably Goatfell, the island's highest) to a peaceful, scenic and very accessible northern coastline. Scotland's first national park, Loch Lomond & the Trossachs, embraces a wonderful array of glens, lochs and mountains, including Ben Lomond, the southernmost Munro, and the Cobbler, which offers a test of nerves and skill almost second to none. Around Loch Tay, mighty Ben Lawers, one of Scotland's 10 highest summits, is a naturalist's delight and a superb mountain in its own right, while nearby Schiehallion, reputedly right in the centre of Scotland and a distinctive landmark peak, has interesting and varied historical associations. To press the contrasts even further, the rolling grassy uplands of the Ochil hills in the east afford magnificent views in all directions, from Edinburgh in the east to the Isle of Arran in the west. The southern section of the West Highland Way, the most famous and most popular of Scotland's long-distance paths, quickly escapes from suburban Glasgow to thread its way through gently undulating countryside, then beside Loch Lomond and towards the wilds of Rannoch Moor in Lochaber.

This superb slice of Scotland is compact and easy to reach from Glasgow or Edinburgh. We have divided it into five manageable sections: the West Highland Way, Isle of Arran, Loch Lomond & the Trossachs National Park, Around Loch Tay and the Ochil hills.

HIGHLIGHTS

- Sharing the day's experiences over a beer with fellow **West Highland Way** (p89) walkers
- Weaving through jumbled boulders on the ascent of Arran's **Goatfell** (p100)
- Scrambling to the top of the fearsome boulders on the summit of the **Cobbler** (p103)
- Summiting **Ben Lomond** (p105) for an eagle's-eye view of the divide between the Highlands and lowlands
- Finding that Ben Ledi's lush **Stank Glen** (p110) does not live up to its name
- Exercising your photographic skills with **Schiehallion's** (p112) summit mantle of rose quartz
- Striding along the broad, grassy ridges of the Ochil hills towards **Ben Cleuch** (p115)

- www.visitscottishheartlands.com
- www.perthshire.co.uk

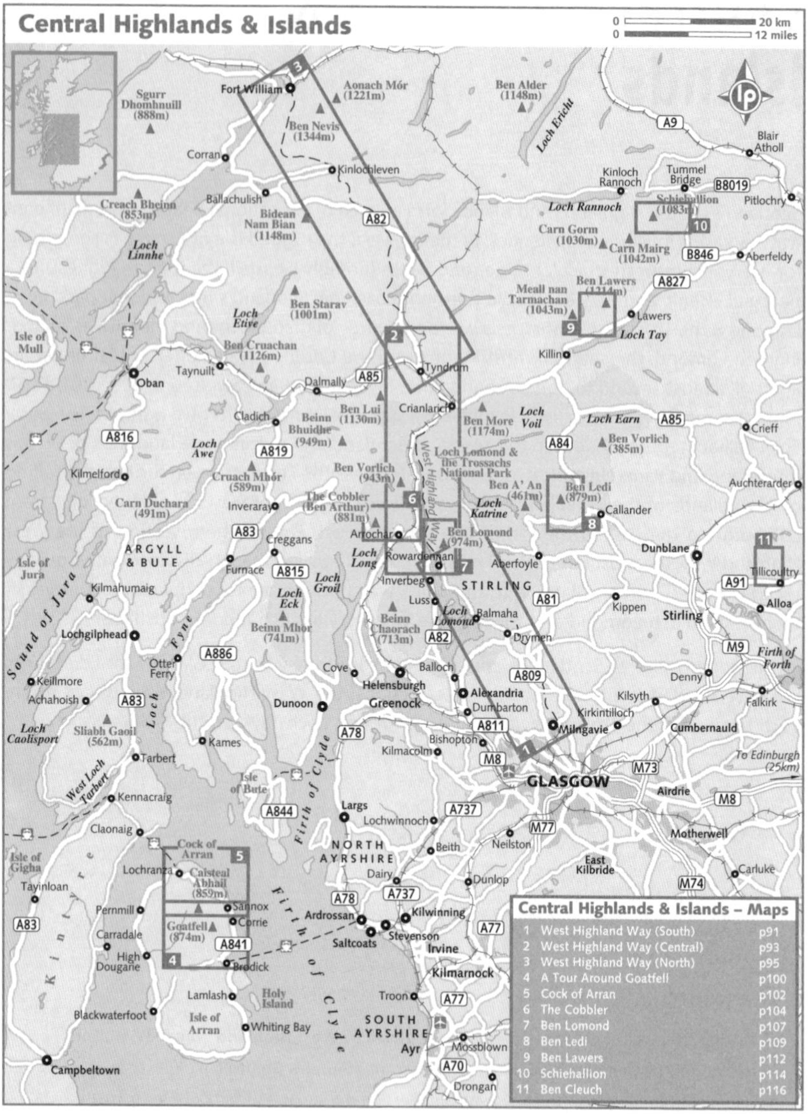

ENVIRONMENT

Convulsions of the earth's crust shaped Scotland's topography eons ago, and nowhere more impressively than along the Highland Boundary Fault. It arcs across central Scotland in an unwavering line southwest, from Stonehaven, on the east coast to Helensburgh on the shore of Gare Loch. Geologists call it a fault line, a weakness in the earth's crust. About 600 million years ago the tough ancient schists of the Highlands collided with the younger, softer sandstones of the lowlands; the fault is the collision zone. From Conic Hill (p92) on the West Highland Way there's a clear view of this line arrowing across the landscape.

INFORMATION

Maps & Books

The OS Travel – Road 1:250,000 map No 3 *Southern Scotland* covers the area neatly.

The Southern Highlands by KM Andrew is a rich source of information about geology, geography and routes long and short.

WEST HIGHLAND WAY

Duration	7 days
Distance	95 miles (153km)
Difficulty	moderate
Start	Milngavie (p90)
Finish	Fort William (p121)
Transport	train, bus

Summary Scotland's most popular long-distance path, passing through some of the country's finest landscapes, from suburban Glasgow to the foot of the highest mountain in Britain.

From the outskirts of Glasgow, Scotland's biggest city, the West Highland Way leads through fertile, populous lowland countryside to the shores of Loch Lomond, on the threshold of the Highlands. From there it carries you north through glens, beside fast-flowing streams and past wild moorland where magnificent mountains are never out of sight. The very names have an alluring ring: Rannoch Moor, Glen Coe, Devil's Staircase. Not only is the Way a rich sensory experience, it's also steeped in history. The route follows long stretches of drove roads, along which cattle were once taken to market, the flat beds of old railway lines, roads along which horse-drawn coaches once jolted, and the 18th-century military road built to subdue rebellious Highlanders. This is the most popular long-distance path in Scotland (and Britain for that matter); something like 15,000 walkers go the full distance each year, so you'll rarely be short of like-minded company from around the world.

The walk begins in the south, at Milngavie, easing you into it with the two least strenuous days, before you hit the harder going north of Rowardennan. Spreading it over seven days means only one long day (between Tyndrum and King's House) and a majority of comfortable days; don't overlook the fact that it's not only horizontal distance that matters – the Way involves a total of 3543m (11,624ft) of ascent.

Of course, you can take much longer, by doing shorter days or by taking time out to knock off some of the nearby Munros – Ben Lomond and Ben Nevis being the obvious candidates.

If your time is limited and you just want to walk a day or two of the West Highland Way, we recommend a couple of day walks in the box on p90.

The Way is clearly waymarked with the official thistle-and-hexagon logo, and there is a shelf-full of guidebooks and maps to enlighten and entertain you along the way.

By the time you reach Fort William you might even be supremely fit and ready to continue along the Great Glen Way to Inverness (see the boxed text on p96).

PLANNING

Maps & Books

Four OS Landranger 1:50,000 maps – No 64 *Glasgow*, No 56 *Loch Lomond & Inveraray*, No 50 Glen *Orchy & Loch Etive* and No 41 *Ben Nevis* – cover the Way, although it's much easier to use a purpose-designed, all-in-one route map. The excellent Harvey 1:40,000 Route map *West Highland Way* and the superbly designed Rucksack Readers guide *The West Highland Way* are more than adequate, and include lots of practical information for walkers.

The official guide, *West Highland Way* by Bob Aitken and Roger Smith, comes with a Harvey Route map in a plastic wallet.

Information Sources

The Official West Highland Way Pocket Companion, a free booklet listing accommodation and facilities on the West Highland Way, is available from the **West Highland Way office** (☎ 0845 345 4978; www.west-highland-way.co.uk; Balloch) at the national park headquarters. The *Pocket Companion* should be available as a download on the website.

Accommodation

Along the northern part of the walk, accommodation is widely spaced so your days may be longer or shorter than you'd prefer. Happily, there are numerous B&Bs and hotels along the rest of the route; some B&B hosts, particularly those not right on the route, will meet you and drive you back to the trail next morning for a small charge. If you're on a tight budget, there are also SYHA hostels, bunkhouses and formal and informal camp sites. If you do use the 'wild camping' sites (listed on the website but not in the *Pocket Companion*), it's absolutely essential that you follow the guidelines set out on p21. During the peak period, from May to August, you must book all accommodation in advance. The accommodation places listed in our route description represent a selection from a fairly crowded field.

Guided Walks & Baggage Services

Rather than doing all the organising, you can take advantage of the services offered by a few small companies that will organise all your accommodation and carry your luggage between overnight stops. Some outfits go a step further and will provide you with sheafs of information about the Way and the places through which you pass.

Easyways (☎ 01324 714132; www.easyways.com) has years of experience in organising accommodation and baggage transfer. **Transcotland** (☎ 01887 820848; www.transcotland.com) also has a good track record and will provide reams of directions and background information for the traveller.

NEAREST TOWNS

See Fort William (p121).

Milngavie

☎ 0141 / pop 14,000

Milngavie (pronounced 'mullguy') is a bustling outer suburb of Glasgow so there's no shortage of shops, restaurants and accommodation. The nearest information centre is the **Glasgow TIC** (☎ 204 4400; www.seeglasgow.com; 11 George Sq).

The **Iron Chief** (☎ 956 4597; 5 Mugdock Rd), 100m from the start of the walk, stocks much of the stuff you're likely to have forgotten.

SLEEPING & EATING

Bankell Farm Camping & Caravan Site (☎ 956 1733; www.bankellfarm.co.uk; Strathblane Rd; unpowered sites for 2 £8) is a small, sheltered site 1 mile or so northeast of town, off the A81; you can leave your car here while you're doing the walk (£2 per day).

Best Foot Forward (☎ 956 3046; BFFMorag@aol.com; 1 Dougalston Gardens South; s/d £35/56) is only a few minutes from the start of the Way; all rooms are en suite.

Laurel Bank B&B (☎ 584 9400; adam.96@ntlworld.com; 96 Strathblane Rd; s/d £35/25), in a large Edwardian home, is only five minutes' walk from the train station.

Toscana Bistro (☎ 956 4020; 44 Station Rd; mains £10-13; dinner Thu-Sat), a cosy establishment in the heart of things, offers a good-value, extensive, Italian-themed menu.

Primo Restaurant (☎ 955 1200; 14 Stewart St; lunch mains £4-7, dinner mains £8-15; lunch & dinner;) is all contemporary style and genuine Italian cuisine; start the day with an espresso fix and one of its energy-giving cakes.

For last-minute supplies, there's a Tesco supermarket next to the train station.

GETTING THERE & AWAY

Milngavie is 7 miles north of Glasgow. At exit 17 from the M8, follow the A82 then the A81. A **Strathclyde Passenger Transport**

ROUTE HIGHLIGHTS

If you'd like to sample the West Highland Way without attempting the whole thing, the best section (in our opinion) is between Kings House Hotel and Glen Nevis. It is possible to go the full distance, a hefty 19 miles (30.5km), in a single day, though you'll need to allow about nine hours. Paths are good all the way.

Start at the Altnafeadh car park on the A82, 3 miles west of Kings House Hotel. **Scottish Citylink** (☎ 0870 550 5050; www.citylink.co.uk) buses from Glasgow and Fort William pass the car park, and the driver will stop if you ask when you board the bus. At the end of the day you can either stay at Glen Nevis (p124) or catch a bus to Fort William (p121).

Another highlight of the route is the walk along the wooded shores of Loch Lomond, past several spectacular waterfalls; the 7-mile (11km) section from Inversnaid to Inverarnan makes an easy day walk. A **passenger ferry** (☎ 01877 386223) from Inveruglas on the western side of the loch will take you across the water to the start of the section. Both Inveruglas and Inverarnan are request stops on the Scottish Citylink Glasgow–Fort William bus service.

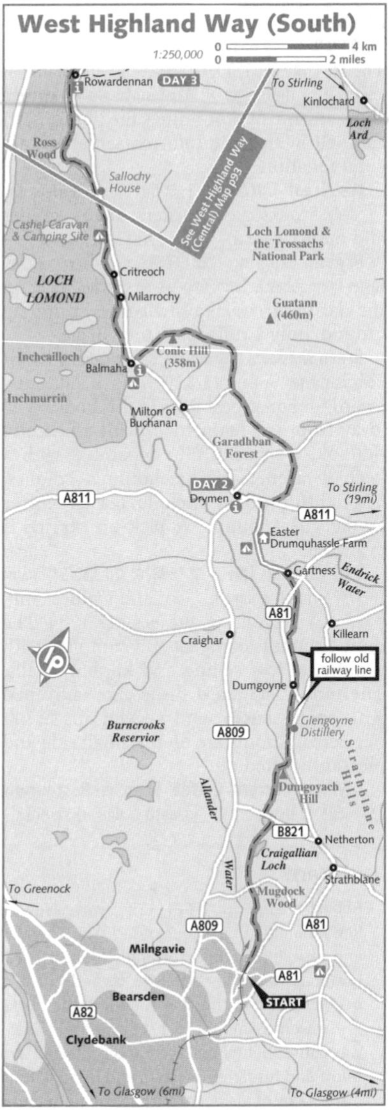

(SPT; ☎ 0845 601 5929; www.spt.co.uk) suburban train service from Glasgow Central terminates at Milngavie (£3, 25 minutes, every 30 minutes).

GETTING TO/FROM THE WALK

The official start of the West Highland Way is a granite obelisk (unveiled in 1992) beside the bridge over the Allander Water on Douglas St, Milngavie, but for most people the journey begins at Milngavie train station. Buses stop here and there's a car park near the station, just off Station Rd. To reach the obelisk from the station, go through the underpass and up a flight of steps to the pedestrianised centre of Milngavie. Bear left at the underpass exit to join Douglas St, passing through a shopping precinct before reaching the Allander Water and the official start point.

If you plan to walk just a section of the Way, Crianlarich, Tyndrum and Bridge of Orchy are well served by trains; contact **First ScotRail** (☎ 0845 755 0033; www.firstscotrail.com) for details. **Scottish Citylink** (☎ 0870 550 5050; www.citylink.co.uk) buses on the Glasgow–Fort William route stop at Crianlarich, Tyndrum and Bridge of Orchy.

THE WALK

Day 1: Milngavie to Drymen

4½–5½ hours, 12 miles (19km)

From the obelisk on Douglas St, a small sign on a nearby building indicates a turn upstream. Cross the river and continue beside Allander Water, to **Mugdock Wood**. At the end of the wood, paths and a track take you past some holiday homes to the B821. Turn left and follow the road for about 300m to a stile giving onto a path to the right. As you skirt Dumgoyach Hill watch out for Bronze Age standing stones to your right just before the hill. Well past Dumgoyach Bridge you pass **Glengoyne Distillery** (🕑 Apr-Oct); 800m further on you reach the Beech Tree Inn at Dumgoyne, a pub that serves food all day. In the village of Killearn, 1.5 miles to the right, there's accommodation, shops, pubs and a post office.

Follow the old railway track to Gartness, from where you're on a road most of the way to the edge of Drymen. A mile beyond Gartness is **Easter Drumquhassle Farm** (☎ 01360 660893; juliamacx@aol.com; unpowered site for 2 £10, wigwam for 2 £14, B&B s/d £33/50, dinner £16), from where Loch Lomond makes its first appearance.

Pass a quarry and continue along the road; just past a sharp left bend, the Way leaves the road and follows a path to the right. If you're going to Drymen, continue along the road and cross the A811 to enter the village.

DRYMEN

☎ 01360 / pop 681

The **TIC** (☎ 0870 720 0611; www.visitscottishheartlands.com; Library, The Green; May-Sep) has a relatively short season; at other times the library staff can help with basic information about accommodation.

It's Great Outdoors (☎ 661148; 1 Stirling Rd; daily) stocks gas canisters, maps, guides and outdoor gear.

Drymen Camping (☎ 660893; juliamacx@aol.com; Easter Drumquhassie Farm; unpowered sites for 2 £20), on the Gartness road, is a small grassy camping ground, only 1 mile from the village.

Green Shadows (☎ 660289; greenshadows@hotmail.com; Buchanan Castle; s/d £28/50) wins the author's award for equal-best B&B in this book. Well away from the main road, with a peaceful outlook, it's beautifully decorated with a keen awareness of harmonious colours. Thoughtful extras include tea or coffee in the guest lounge. A pick-up service is available.

The **Clachan Inn** (☎ 660824; s/d £30/54, mains £8-17; lunch & dinner), Scotland's oldest inn, has been welcoming guests since 1734. The dining room is compact and complete with traditional low ceiling and knobbly walls. The mostly standard dishes are enlivened with spicy sauces, and vegetarians aren't neglected. Rooms are on the small side and pleasantly fitted out.

Drymen Pottery Coffee Shop & Restaurant (☎ 660458; mains £5-9; lunch & dinner) specialises in lunches in the conservatory or outdoors; evening meals are available in the adjacent bar upstairs.

For self-catering supplies, there's a Spar supermarket and the smaller Village Shop.

Day 2: Drymen to Rowardennan

5–6½ hours, 14 miles (22.5km)

From near the A811 just outside Drymen, a forest track gradually climbs to Garadhban Forest (there is wild camping here with no facilities). Just over an hour from Drymen, a side path runs left to the village of Milton of Buchanan; it's also the alternative route when Conic Hill is closed during the lambing season (late April to early May). There are a couple of B&Bs in the village but no pubs or shops.

The Way climbs then contours north of the summit of **Conic Hill** (358m), but it's worth the short detour for the wonderful panorama over Loch Lomond. This viewpoint also has a special, even unique, significance. From the summit you can make out the unmistakeable line of the Highland Boundary Fault, separating the lowlands from the Highlands, so from here on you really are in the Highlands.

Descend to Balmaha, a small village usually thronged with people messing about in boats. As well as the **National Park Centre** (☎ 01389 722100; Easter-Oct) there's also a small shop and the **Oak Tree Inn** (☎ 870357; www.oak-tree-inn.co.uk; dm/s/d £25/50/70, mains £7-14), which

ROB ROY

Robert MacGregor (1671–1734) was given the nickname Roy from the Gaelic *ruadh*, meaning 'red', thanks to his shock of red hair. The MacGregor clan was notorious for violent lawlessness and rebellion so, unsurprisingly, Robert became a cattle trader, making occasional raids to the lowlands to rustle cattle. He owned much of the land around Inversnaid and had effectively become head of the clan soon after he turned 30.

He went bankrupt in 1711 when his head drover absconded with his annual profits, and he was subsequently betrayed and outlawed by the Duke of Montrose, a former ally. His home was burnt and his family evicted, and he took to the hills to begin a campaign of revenge against the duke. Tales of his generosity to the poor and daring escapes from the clutches of the law earned him a reputation as a Scottish Robin Hood; legends and romantic stories have since ensured him a place among the characters of popular Scottish history. The Hollywood film *Rob Roy* (largely shot in Glen Nevis) added a contemporary layer to the legend.

A natural rock cell in a crag about 1.5 miles north of Ptarmigan Lodge is given the distinction of being Rob Roy's prison, where he is said to have kept kidnap victims. The cave where he is supposed to have hidden from the duke's men is north of Inversnaid. Both sites can be visited from the West Highland Way, but there is little of real interest to see, and tales of his use of them can be attributed more to mythology than hard fact.

has comfortable rooms and a four-bed, en suite bunkroom. You can dine in style in the restaurant, or informally in the bar.

Continue along the shore of **Loch Lomond**, passing a marker commemorating the Way's 1980 opening, to Milarrochy (one hour from Balmaha). From Critreoch, about 800m further on, the path dives into a dark forest and emerges to follow the road for about 1 mile. Just after you join the road is the popular **Cashel Caravan and Camping Site** (☎ 870234; www.forestholidays.co.uk; sites for 2 £14). A mile beyond Sallochy House, the Way climbs through **Ross Wood**, its magnificent oaks making it one of Scotland's finest natural woodlands, to Rowardennan (p106).

Day 3: Rowardennan to Inverarnan

6–7½ hours, 14 miles (22.5km)

From Rowardennan follow the unsealed road that parallels the loch shore. Just past private Ptarmigan Lodge an alternative path branches left and follows the shoreline, but it's rough and not recommended. Stick to the much easier official route along a track higher up the hillside. From both routes you can reach **Rowchoish Bothy**, a simple stone shelter; it's free and always open.

Not far beyond the bothy the forestry track gives way to a path, which dives down to the loch for a stretch of difficult walking to Cailness. From here the going improves to Inversnaid, shortly before which the path crosses Snaid Burn just above the impressive Inversnaid Falls. The huge **Inversnaid Hotel** (☎ 01877 386223) could be a good place to stop for refreshments before you tackle the next and toughest section of all.

For a couple of miles north from Inversnaid, the path twists and turns around large boulders and tree roots, a good test of balance and agility. A mile or so into this, the Way passes close to **Rob Roy's cave** (see the boxed text, opposite), although there's little to see. Further on, **Doune Bothy** provides basic accommodation. Almost 1 mile beyond the bothy, at Ardleish, there's a landing stage used by the ferry across to **Ardlui Hotel** (☎ 01301 704243; www.ardlui.co.uk; unpowered sites for 2 £10, s/d £45/60).

From Ardleish, you leave the loch and climb to a col below Cnap Mór, where there are good views on a clear day, north towards the Highlands and south over Loch Lomond. The path descends into Glen

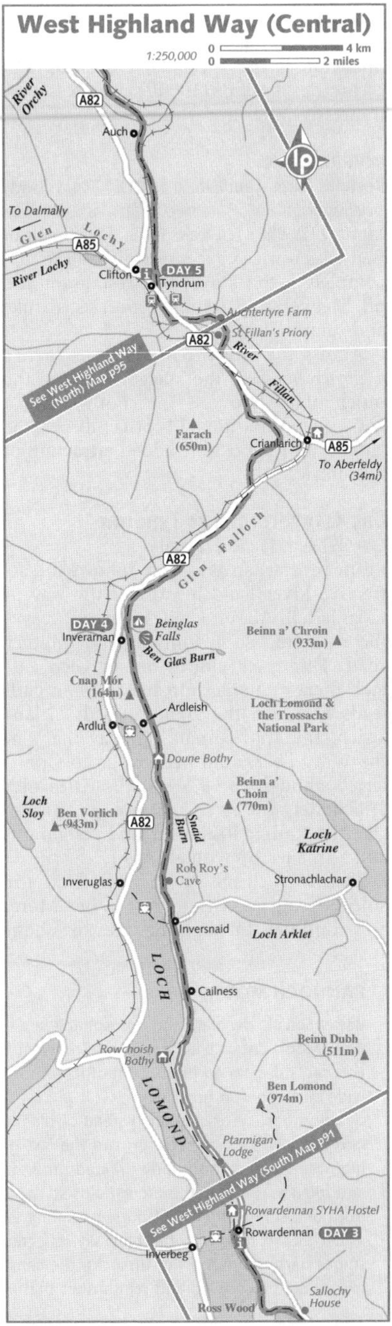

Falloch; a footbridge over Ben Glas Burn heralds your arrival at Inverarnan. Just upstream is the spectacular **Beinglas Falls**, a cascade of 300m (1000ft), which is very impressive after heavy rain.

INVERARNAN

Beinglas Farm Campsite (☎ 01301 704281; www.beinglascampsite.co.uk; unpowered sites for 2 £10, wigwam for 2 £25, B&B d £60, mains £6-10), just north of Ben Glas Burn, is exceptionally well set up, complete with its own bar, restaurant and off-licence shop selling groceries, drinks and camping supplies.

Across the river, in the village, there's a choice between the Stagger Inn and the much older Drover's Inn, both doing a good line in traditional Scottish dishes, the latter with the possible added attraction of live music.

Day 4: Inverarnan to Tyndrum

4½–5½ hours, 13 miles (21km)

From Inverarnan the route follows the attractive River Falloch most of the way to Crianlarich. About 4 miles along, it leaves the river and soon joins an old military road. This track climbs out of Glen Falloch then, at a stile into the forest, a path leads down to the right towards Crianlarich, the approximate halfway mark of the Way. There's no need to go to Crianlarich, though there are B&Bs, **Crianlarich SYHA Hostel** (☎ 0870 155 3255; www.syha.org.uk; dm £16), the Rod & Reel's bar and restaurant, and a small shop with an ATM.

The Way climbs to the left from the stile, offering good views east to Ben More, and continues through the trees for about 2 miles. Next, it crosses under the railway line, goes over the road and crosses a wooden bridge over the River Fillan, where there is a wild camp site (no facilities) on the west bank. Pass the remains of **St Fillan's Priory**, turn left and go on to **Strathfillan Wigwams** (☎ 01838 400251; www.sac.ac.uk/wigwams; wigwam for 2 £25) at Auchtertyre Farm. The route crosses the A82 once more and, in less than an hour, you make it to Tyndrum.

TYNDRUM

☎ 01838

This village, originally a lead-mining settlement and now a popular staging point between Glasgow and Fort William, is strung out along the A82.

The **TIC** (☎ 08707 200626; www.visitscottishheartlands.com; Easter-Oct) is opposite the Invervey Hotel. The **Green Welly Stop** (☎ 400271; www.thegreenwellystop.co.uk; daily) includes an outdoor gear store (that sells maps), an off-licence and a cafeteria-style **restaurant** (mains to £8), which is liable to be flooded by bus parties, and offering generous servings of standard dishes. The weather forecast is prominently displayed at the store.

By the way (☎ 400333; www.tyndrumbytheway.com; sites for 2 £5, cabin beds £8-10, dm £15) provides excellent facilities, including a campers' kitchen.

Strathfillan House B&B (☎ 400228; www.tyndrum.com; s/d £24/48) does a special deal for walkers, including pick-up and drop-off.

Inverey Hotel (☎ 400219; www.inverveyhotel.co.uk; s/d £28/48, bar meals £6-8) has comfortable rooms and a large bar.

Brodie's (daily) mini-market is an off-licence sell hot takeaway snacks and camping gas.

RANNOCH MOOR

Barren, bleak, desolate and inhospitable are epithets often flung at the 50 sq miles of wild Rannoch Moor, Britain's largest moor. The West Highland Way merely skirts its western fringes but you can still gain an impression of its atmosphere – unwelcoming in bad weather, wonderfully wide and open on good days.

The moor is a triangular plateau of blanket bog framed by mountains. It sits on an ancient bed and owes its present form to the last glacial period, when ice gathered here. Since then, high rainfall and the poorly drained ground have combined to create a dense mosaic of bog and lochans. Indeed, the moor holds so much water that it has been said it's possible to swim from one side to the other during summer and to skate across it in winter!

On a calm day, with the blue sky reflected in the lochans, and curlews, golden plovers and snipes darting among the tussocks, the sense of open space is inspiring. In poor weather, the low cloud, fierce wind and rain ensure that it lives up to its reputation.

Day 5: Tyndrum to Kings House Hotel

6½–8 hours, 19 miles (30.5km)

From Tyndrum the route soon rejoins the old military road and crosses the railway line, affording easy walking with lovely views. Three miles from Tyndrum, you cross a burn at the foot of Beinn Dòrain (1074m), the 'hill' that dominates this section of the path.

The path climbs gradually to pass the entrance to Glen Orchy, crossing the railway again, heralding the beginning of the really mountainous scenery. The Bridge of Orchy settlement is dominated by the **Bridge of Orchy Hotel** (☎ 01838 400208; www.scottish-selection.co.uk; dm £15, s/d £55/90), where you can live it up in the hotel or stay in the bunkhouse. The latter doesn't have a kitchen but the bar serves good food. The **West Highland Way Sleeper** (☎ 01838 400548; www.westhighlandwaysleeper.co.uk; dm £15), in the old station building, does have a kitchen, and en suite dorms. There is a free camp site (no facilities) just over the bridge on the right.

Cross the old bridge (built in 1750) and climb through the trees onto moorland, from where there are superb views across to Rannoch Moor. The path here has been upgraded and is now very good. It winds down to the secluded **Inveroran Hotel** (☎ 01838 400220; www.inveroran.com; s/d £38/70). There's another free camp site (no facilities) beside a stone bridge 400m west of the hotel.

The Way follows the road, which soon becomes a track, climbing gently past some plantations and out onto **Rannoch Moor** (see the boxed text, opposite). There's no shelter for about 7 miles, and Bà Bridge, about 3 miles beyond the plantations, is the only real marker point. It can be very wild and windy up here, and there's a real sense of isolation. A cairn marks the summit at 445m and from here there's a wonderful view down into Glen Coe.

As the path descends from the moor to join the road again, you can see the chairlift of the Glen Coe Ski Centre to the left. There's a café and skiing museum at the base station, about 500m off the West Highland Way. **Kings House Hotel** (☎ 01855 851259; www.kingy.com; s/d £35/60, bar meals £8-12) is just over 1 mile ahead across the A82. Dating from the 17th century, the building was used as barracks for George III's troops, hence the name. If you can't get a bed here

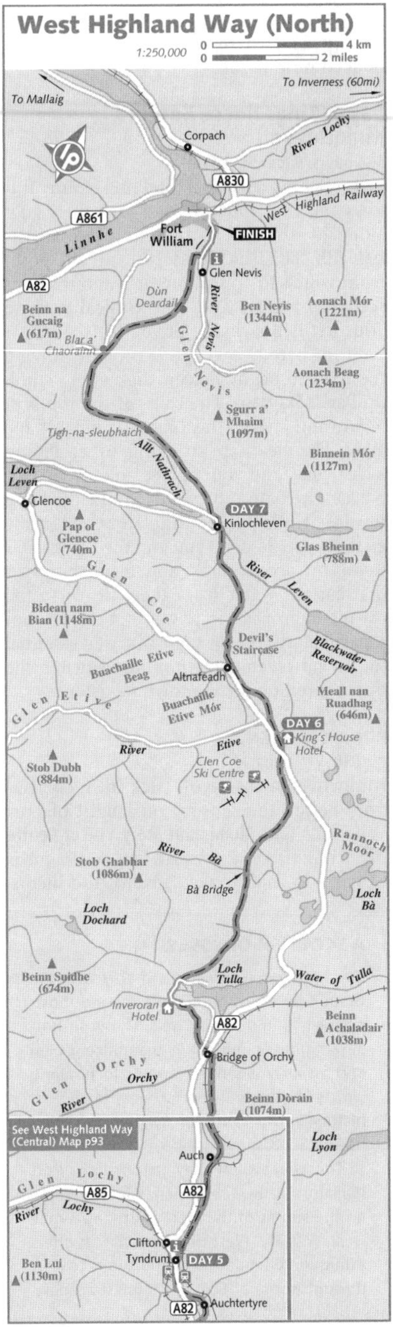

you could catch a bus to Glencoe, 11 miles west (p133), where there's a wider selection of accommodation.

Day 6: Kings House Hotel to Kinlochleven

3–4 hours, 9 miles (14.5km)

From Kings House Hotel the route follows the old military road and then goes alongside the A82 to a parking area at Altnafeadh. This is a wonderful vantage point from which to appreciate the mountainous scenery of Glen Coe. The conical peak to your left is Buachaille Etive Mór (p134).

From here the Way turns right, leaving the road to begin a steep, zigzagging climb up **Devil's Staircase**. The cairn at the top is at 548m and marks the highest point of the Way. The views are stunning, especially on a clear day, and you may be able to see Ben Nevis. The path now winds gradually down towards Kinlochleven, hidden below in the glen. As you descend you join the Blackwater Reservoir access track, and meet the pipes that carried water from there down to the town's hydroelectric power station. It's not a particularly pretty sight but was essential for the now-defunct aluminium smelter, the original reason for the town's existence.

KINLOCHLEVEN

☎ 01855 / pop 897

Kinlochleven eases you back into 'civilisation' before the sensory onslaught of Fort William. The **Aluminium Story Visitor Centre** (☎ 831663; Linnhe Rd; admission free; Mon-Fri) is worth a look to make sense of the incongruously massive buildings dominating the village.

Blackwater Hostel & Campsite (☎ 831253; www.blackwaterhostel.co.uk; Lab Rd; unpowered sites for 2 $10, dm £12) has well-maintained, pine-panelled dorms with en suite, and grassy tent pitches.

Tailrace Inn (☎ 831777; www.tailraceinn.co.uk; Riverside Rd; s/d £40/70, bar meals £8-14) has tastefully furnished rooms and features live music some evenings.

Macdonald Hotel and Lochside Campsite (☎ 831539; www.macdonaldhotel.co.uk; Fort William Rd; unpowered sites for 2 £10, cabin s/d £20/24, B&B s/d £55/80) is at the northern end of the village. The camping ground is small and well grassed; the cabins have four bunk beds. Campers' breakfast (£4 to £7) is served in the bar.

Ice Factor (☎ 831100; www.ice-factor.co.uk; Leven Rd; mains to £8; to 6pm, later Tue, Wed & Thu), in part of the former smelter, houses the world's largest indoor ice-climbing wall plus a 'normal' climbing wall so you can watch people performing amazing vertical feats while you hoe into a large pizza.

Both the Co-op supermarket and the village store are open daily.

> **A SCOTTISH ODYSSEY**
>
> Combine the West Highland Way with the Great Glen Way, Scotland's second-most-popular long-distance walk, throw in Britain's highest mountain, a magnificent glen and an internationally famous loch, along with some magnificent scenery, a slice of history and a touch of mystery, and you have a Scottish odyssey.
>
> The Great Glen Way (p168) links Fort William, via the Great Glen, with Inverness on the shores of the Moray Firth, a 73-mile walk. With the West Highland Way, it offers a unique, 168-mile-long opportunity to walk through some of Scotland's finest scenery.

Day 7: Kinlochleven to Fort William

5½–7 hours, 14 miles (22.5km)

From Kinlochleven follow the road north out of town and turn off opposite the school. The path climbs through woodland to the old military road out in the open, from where you can see the way ahead for the next couple of miles. Climb gradually to the crest, just beyond which are the ruins of several old farm buildings at **Tigh-na-sleubhaich**. From here the Way continues gently downhill and into conifer plantations 2 miles further on. You emerge at Blar a' Chaorainn, which is nothing more than a bench and an information board.

The Way leads on and up, through more plantations; occasional breaks in the trees provide fine views of Ben Nevis. After a few miles, a sign points to nearby **Dùn Deardail**, an Iron Age fort with walls that have been partly vitrified (turned to glass) by fire.

A little further on, cross another stile and follow the forest track down towards Glen Nevis. Across the valley the huge bulk of Ben Nevis fills the view. A side track leads down to the village of Glen Nevis (p124), which can make a good base for an ascent of 'the Ben' (p123).

Continue along the path if you're heading for Fort William, passing a small graveyard just before you meet the road running through Glen Nevis. Turn left here and, soon after, there's a large visitor centre on the right. Continue along the roadside down into Fort William. The end of the West Highland Way, like many other long-distance paths, is a bit of an anticlimax: just a sign by the busy, rather anonymous road junction on the edge of town, but you can look forward to an end-of-walk celebration in one of the town's several restaurants and bars (p122).

ISLE OF ARRAN

Arran's popular alternative name, 'Scotland in miniature', isn't just a slick advertising gimmick. The steeply angled hills, the long, deep glens and the wild, remote feel of the northern half of the island certainly bring to mind many parts of the Highlands. The southern half's rolling moorlands and scattered farms resemble parts of the Borders or Dumfries & Galloway in microcosm. To emphasise the likeness, Arran has its own Great Glen in the long, straight valley separating the two halves of the island. Goatfell (874m), the highest peak, lords it over Brodick, the island's capital on the mid-east coast.

All this is packed into a chunk of land little more than 20 miles (32km) from north to south. Arran is only an hour-long ferry ride across the Firth of Clyde from Ardrossan, itself a stone's throw from Glasgow. Unsurprisingly therefore, the island swarms with visitors from Easter to October, including many walkers, for whom Goatfell tops their must-do list. For something completely different, the north coast offers just as much wildness, plus scenery equally as fine, but a little less up and down. A short walk (p103) offers a taster of the wealth of walks Arran has to offer.

ENVIRONMENT

Arran's geology is amazingly varied – you will find all kinds of rock types and evidence of different geological processes, which have taken place over countless millennia. In fact, a trip to Arran is virtually compulsory for geology students from all over the world; one of the most famous features is Hutton's Unconformity, named after its discoverer Dr James Hutton. An unconformity is the occurrence, side by side, of rocks from different geological eras at a discordant or unexpected angle. On the north coast, about 1 mile northeast of Newton Point, Hutton identified such an area, where ancient metamorphic rock (schist, altered from its original form) was overlain by less ancient sandstone.

The granitic northern peaks and ridges and the deep glens were sculpted by glaciers during the last Ice Age. This granite mass is almost surrounded by much older schist, slate and some river sediment. Sedimentary rock, limestone and sandstone monopolise the north coast. The southern half of the island has a more mixed array: granite (most prominently on Holy Island in Lamlash Bay), extensive outcrops of ancient lava and shale, and widespread sedimentary rocks.

A small brochure, *Isle of Arran Trails: Geology*, available from the TIC, should demystify the complexities of Arran's geology.

PLANNING

Wild camping is not permitted anywhere on Arran without the landowner's permission.

When to Walk/Stalking

Generally walkers are free to roam throughout Arran. However, deer control measures (stalking) are carried out from mid-August to mid-October in the north of the island. Call the **Hillphones** (☎ 01770 302363) service for daily updates on where stalking is to take place and which paths should be used or avoided. Access to National Trust for Scotland properties (Glen Rosa, Goatfell and Brodick Country Park) is unrestricted at all times.

Maps

Arran is covered by OS Landranger 1:50,000 map No 69 *Isle of Arran* and OS Explorer 1:25,000 map No 361 *Isle of Arran*. Harvey's *Arran* map shows the whole island at 1:40,000 and the northern half at 1:25,000.

Books

25 Walks Ayrshire & Arran by Alan Forbes includes 10 varied walks on the island; the maps are superior to those in Paddy Dillon's *Walking in the Isle of Arran*, which

THE CROOKED STRAIGHT AND THE ROUGH PLACES PLAIN

This title, borrowed from Handel's *Messiah*, neatly sums up the work of the National Trust for Scotland and the Arran Access Trust on the island. It's all too easy to take for granted the well-built paths and various bits of outdoor furniture that make walking on Arran easier than many other places (though they haven't yet worked out how to make all walks downhill).

Seriously though, the Trust, a major landowner on the island, has done a huge amount of work to repair worn paths on its Brodick Castle estate, and to build bridges and install signs. The Access Trust's remit covers the whole island and it has completed major projects near Lochranza and Brodick in particular. Contact the **National Trust Ranger Centre** (☎ 01770 302462; Brodick Castle) for more information.

describes 41 day walks. *The Islands* by Nick Williams describes five adventurous Arran outings. *Arran Behind the Scenes* by Gillean Bussell delves into the island's colourful history.

GETTING THERE & AWAY

For all public transport timetables contact **Traveline** (☎ 0870 608 2608; www.travelinescotland.com).

Stagecoach Western (☎ 01292 613500) bus service X15 links Glasgow to Ardrossan (£3, 1¼ hours, twice daily), the ferry terminal on the Ayrshire coast.

First ScotRail (☎ 0845 755 0033; www.firstscotrail.com) operates trains from Glasgow to Ardrossan Harbour (£6, 55 minutes, four services Monday to Saturday, three Sunday).

Caledonian MacBrayne (☎ 0870 565 0000; www.calmac.co.uk) runs the car ferry between Ardrossan and Brodick (passenger/car £5/37, 55 minutes, four services Monday to Saturday, three Sunday). It also does a seasonal service between Claonaig (on the Mull of Kintyre, between Lochgilphead and Campbeltown) and Lochranza (passenger/car £5/21, 30 minutes, at least seven daily March to October).

Ardrossan is about 40 miles southwest of Glasgow via the M8, and A78 roads.

ACCESS TOWN

Brodick

☎ 01770 / pop 621

This surprisingly large town is the best base for island walking, being the ferry port and the hub of the island's bus services.

The well-organised **TIC** (☎ 303774; www.ayrshire-arran.com; The Pier; daily Easter-Oct, Mon-Sat Oct-Easter) offers an array of leaflets, accommodation lists, maps and guidebooks. All bus timetables are detailed in the free *Area Transport Guide*. The local weather forecast is displayed daily.

Arran Active (☎ 302416; www.arranactive.co.uk; Cladach Visitor Centre; daily), next to Arran Brewery and opposite the walkers' entrance to Brodick Castle, is the one place where you can purchase the full range of fuel for camping stoves, and much else besides.

SLEEPING & EATING

For accommodation bookings, go to www.ayrshire-arran.com.

Glen Rosa Farm Campsite (☎ 302380; unpowered sites for 2 £4), on the Glen Rosa road about 2.5 miles northwest of Brodick Pier, is just a grassy field on the banks of Glen Rosa Burn with a basic toilet block and running water. Check in at the first cottage on the western side of the Glen Rosa road.

Lochranza SYHA Hostel (☎ 0870 004 1140; www.syha.org.uk; Lochranza; dm £14) is the nearest hostel, in a small peaceful village. It's not ideal for Goatfell but the island's bus service enables you to get around fairly easily. The nearest shops of any size are in Brodick.

Orwin B&B (☎ 302307; Shore Rd; s/d £25/50) has four comfortable rooms, including a single with lovely views across the golf course; your hostess is very helpful and obliging.

Hotel Ormidale (☎ 302100; Knowe Rd; mains £8-12; lunch Sat & Sun, dinner daily) hosts the local Mountain Rescue Team so the atmosphere is entirely compatible for sampling its varied dishes featuring local produce, washed down by draught Arran ales.

Oscars of Arran (☎ 302427; breakfast £5, mains £6-10, breakfast, lunch & dinner) sits beside Glen Cloy Burn just off the main road, scarcely a mile northwest of Brodick. It's a small but well-lit place, with nice outside tables, where you can sink your teeth into a whole range of snacks, or order more substantial, hunger-satisfying dishes. It also stocks a fair selection of health foods.

Fill your trolley at one of the two Co-op supermarkets along Shore Rd but save bread purchases for **Wooleys Bakery** (Shore Rd). **Arran Brewery** (☎ 302061; www.arranbrewery.com; Cladach; daily) is very conveniently located beside the end of the Goatfell walk; tours and tastings tempt you to linger.

GETTING THERE & AWAY

For Brodick transport details, see opposite.

A TOUR AROUND GOATFELL

Duration	6–7 hours
Distance	11 miles (18km)
Difficulty	moderate–demanding
Start & Finish	Brodick (opposite)
Transport	bus, ferry

Summary Take the connoisseur's route to Arran's highest peak, through superbly scenic Glen Rosa and along steep, rock-encrusted ridges to spectacular wrap-around views from the summit.

You can't really visit Arran and not climb Goatfell; it beckons from Ardross and it's ever-present once you reach Brodick. Most walkers tramp up the eastern routes, from Cladach or from Brodick Castle. However, there's a less crowded and more satisfying approach from the west, via beautiful Glen Rosa, North Goatfell and along Stacach Ridge. The descent is through the steep, rocky eastern face to moorland and forest paths.

The National Trust for Scotland (NTS) has done a superb job of repairing and building paths; the descent is completely mud-free. The cliffs on both sides of the west ridge and Stacach Ridge are precipitous so extra care is needed.

This route can be done in either direction but we recommend clockwise. The overall ascent is more gentle, with some steep bits, and the summit comes in the latter part of the route. There are signposts where paths leave the road but not on Goatfell itself. The route includes at least 800m of ascent and some minor scrambling.

It can turn very cold, wet and windy on Goatfell very quickly, at any time of the year, and the mountain creates its own weather – Brodick can be basking in hot sunshine while Goatfell is mist-bound.

PLANNING

Guided Walks

The **NTS countryside rangers** (☎ 01770-302462; Brodick Country Park), located about 2 miles (3km) north of Brodick, organise a program of walks from May to October, ranging from afternoon wildlife strolls through low-level forests to days out on Goatfell.

GETTING TO/FROM THE WALK

Stagecoach Western (☎ 302000) bus 324 stops at Cladach, near the end of the walk (£1.50, 10 minutes, three daily). There is a car park nearby.

THE WALK

From Brodick TIC, walk mainly north beside the main road (A841) for about 1.5 miles (along a path for all but the last 200m) to a major junction. Turn left along the B880 towards Blackwaterfoot. After about 100m, turn right down the narrow 'Glen Rosa Cart Track' to the Glen Rosa Farm Campsite (opposite) – above which there's a small car park and the bitumen ends. Continue along a clear vehicle track into **Glen Rosa**. There are superb views of the precipitous peaks on the western side of the glen, culminating in Cir Mhòr (799m) at its head.

The track becomes a path at the crossing of Garbh Allt, the boundary of the NTS property. Aiming unerringly for the Saddle, the low point between Cir Mhòr and the massive, rock-encrusted bulk of Goatfell, the path climbs gently then quite steeply. From the **Saddle** (2½ to three hours from the start) there's a fine view among the granite boulders down Glen Sannox to the sea. Cir Mhòr's alarmingly steep crags rise immediately to the left. To the north are the castellated ridge of Caisteal Abhail (859m), Arran's second-highest peak, and the notorious cleft, Ceum na Caillich (Witch's Step). To the right the features of the next section of the walk are clearly visible: the bouldery west ridge, leading steeply up to North Goatfell; and Stacach Ridge, which is crowned by four small, rocky peaks.

From the Saddle, the path leads up the ridge towards North Goatfell. There are some narrow, exposed sections and a few near-vertical 'steps' where you'll need to

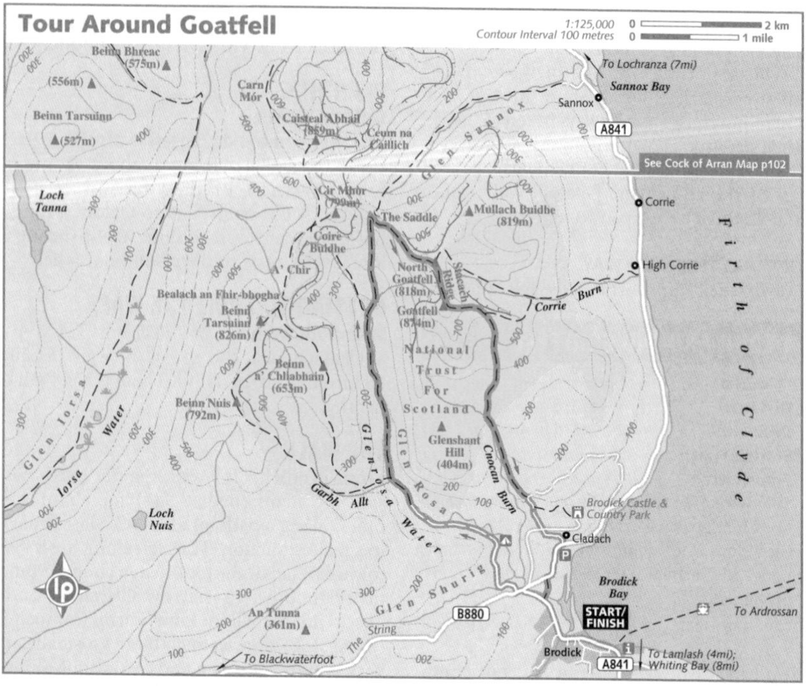

use your hands. More tricky, though, are the patches of loose granite gravel. About an hour from the Saddle the route nears the summit of **North Goatfell** (818m). The final section is a scramble but if this is too intimidating, pass below the top, keeping it on your left, then return to the ridge. Turn back to gain the summit from the east, over large slabs and boulders.

From North Goatfell you can keep to the crest of the ridge, scrambling over the rocky knobs. Alternatively, drop down to the less exposed eastern side of the ridge and follow paths below the knobs. The final section involves hopping giant boulders to the summit of **Goatfell** (874m), 45 minutes from North Goatfell. Here there's a trig point and direction plate, from which you can identify features in the panoramic view – sometimes including Ben Lomond and the coast of Northern Ireland. All Arran is spread out below, with the conical Holy Island rearing up from the sea in Lamlash Bay.

From the summit a path winds down the steep eastern face, then straightens out as the ridge takes shape. At a shallow saddle the path changes direction and leads southeast then south across moorland, down Cnocan Burn glen and into scattered woodland. At a junction in a conifer plantation, continue straight ahead then turn right at a T-junction. Descend through conifers, cross a road and go on to Cladach and Arran Brewery; the main road is a little further on.

The last leg starts along a footpath on the western side of the main road. Where the path ends, cross the road to a signposted path beside, and then briefly across Brodick golf course, leading back to the main road beside Arran Heritage Museum. Follow the roadside path into town (2½ hours from Goatfell summit).

If you'd like to have a look around **Brodick Castle and Country Park**, turn left 30m after the T-junction in the conifer plantation mentioned above. Follow Cemetery Trail past the eponymous site (the resting place of the 11th and 12th Dukes of Hamilton and a wife), over bridges and into the castle grounds. The ranger service office is in the first building on the right; continue straight on to the NTS shop and tearoom.

COCK OF ARRAN

Duration	3½–4 hours
Distance	8 miles (13km)
Difficulty	easy–moderate
Start	North Sannox
Finish	Lochranza (right)
Nearest Town	Sannox (right)
Transport	bus, ferry

Summary Easy walking spiced with rock-hopping interludes along Arran's wild and beautiful north coast, with superb horizon-wide views across the Firth of Clyde.

If there's cloud on the hills, don't despair, head for the north coast and a wonderfully scenic walk between North Sannox and Lochranza. Steep hillsides sweep down to the rocky shore, and there are some impressive cliffs, shingle beaches and scattered pockets of birch woodland, as well as plenty of geological interest and the ever-restless sea. The Cock of Arran, a prominent block of sandstone, isn't named after a rooster but probably comes from the Lowland Scots word meaning 'cap' or 'headwear'. Views across the Sound of Bute to the mainland, the Isle of Bute and part of the Kintyre peninsula can be excellent. There's also a good chance of seeing common seals.

Ideally, set out soon after high tide (a tide-times booklet is available from the Brodick TIC), for though the rise and fall isn't unusually great, there's one section best done near low tide.

Alternatives If time is short, you can do an out-and-back walk from North Sannox to Millstone Point; allow 2½ to three hours for the 5-mile (8km) outing.

Alternatively, add 1 mile or so by starting at Sannox. Alight from the bus opposite the start of the Glen Sannox path. Follow a path nearby, indicated by an Arran Coastal Way waymarker, to large stepping stones across Sannox Burn. Continue along the path parallel to the coast, past a beacon and through woodland to a small burn. It may be possible to ford it to reach the start of the main walk at North Sannox; otherwise, follow a path upstream to the road bridge, then the minor road down to North Sannox.

You can also leave the main walk at Laggan cottage and follow a path west and uphill from the north side of a small wind pump; there's neither a signpost nor a waymarker. The path, which could be partly hidden under bracken in summer, climbs over the ridge rising from the coast and up the hillside, to a high point (261m) on the moorland ridge, then descends across to a minor road at Narachan. Follow this to a junction and turn left to reach the main road through Lochranza and the bus stop. The distance is 9 miles (12.9km); allow about four hours.

NEAREST TOWNS

Sannox

☎ 01770

Sannox, 7 miles from Brodick and Lochranza, is just a handful of homes beside the main road, and is a peaceful alternative to the comparative bustle of Brodick. It's way too small to have a shop so come with all the snacks you'll need.

Gowanlea Guest House (☎ 810253; www.arran.net/sannox/gowanlea; s/d £28/50, dinner £10-12), a traditional-style large home in a scenic setting, offers plenty of home comforts and represents excellent value.

Sannox Bay Hotel (☎ 810225; www.sannoxbayhotel.com; s/d £35/60, mains £8-12; lunch & dinner) looks straight across the bay. The restaurant menu extends only to standard mains, though more traditional Scottish fare, using local produce, is offered in the bar.

Corrie Golf Club Tearoom (☎ 810223; mains to £5; lunch & dinner), on the north side of the bridge over Sannox Burn, is a real find. Snacks and lights meals use local and Fairtrade produce whenever possible and you're welcome to bring your own wine or beer.

Sannox is on the **Stagecoach Western** (☎ 302000) route 324 from Brodick (£2, 25 minutes, at least three daily). Alight at the stop opposite the signposted start of the Glen Sannox path or ask the driver to drop you further on at the turn-off to Sannox.

Lochranza

☎ 01770

This scattered village on the shores of Loch Ranza, sheltered by hills to the west, looks out towards the low-lying Mull of Kintyre. Bring all your supplies – sadly, there aren't any shops in the village.

Lochranza SYHA Hostel (☎ 0870 004 1140; www.syha.org.uk; Lochranza; dm £14) occupies an impressive mansion overlooking Loch Ranza.

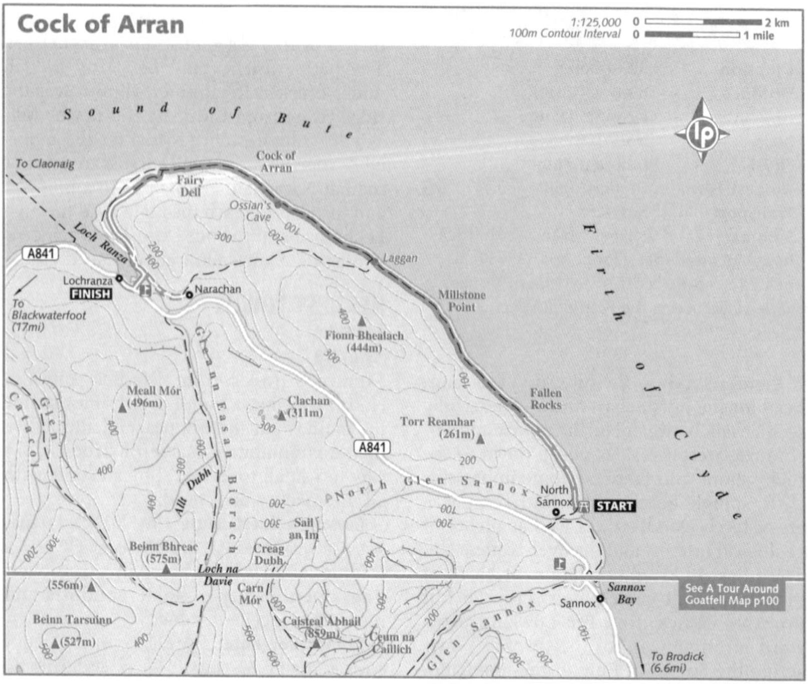

Castlekirk B&B (☎ 830202; www.castlekirkarran.co.uk; s/d £25/50) is worth the journey to stay in a century-old former Free Church; the bedrooms occupy the space under the soaring pitched roof.

Lochranza Hotel (☎ 830223; www.lochranza.co.uk; s/d £50/84, mains £9-12) is a dignified two-storey place overlooking the loch, with comfortable, spacious rooms. The restaurant offers standard dishes and daily specials.

See p98 for details of the ferry service from Claonaig. The **Stagecoach Western** (☎ 302000) service 324 passes through Lochranza from Brodick (£2.50, 40 minutes) and Sannox (£2, 20 minutes) at least three times daily.

GETTING TO/FROM THE WALK

The walk starts at a picnic area (with toilets) at the end of a minor road, which branches from the A841 about 800m northwest of Sannox.

The walk ends in Lochranza village. There's a car park by the shore at the southeastern corner of Loch Ranza; the turn-off from the main road is signposted 'Public Footpath'.

THE WALK

The forest track leading north from the picnic area gives fine views across the Firth of Clyde to the multitude of hills draped right across the horizon, a theme sustained for the whole walk. After nearly 2 miles the track gives way to a footpath along the shore. At the far end of a shingle beach thread your way through Fallen Rocks, a jumble of massive conglomerate boulders (studded with pebbles and resembling Christmas pudding) reclining at the foot of a steep, bracken-covered hillside. The path, mainly grassy and occasionally boggy, keeps close to the high-tide mark to **Millstone Point** (1½ hours from North Sannox), where white-painted Laggan cottage comes into view,.

Less than 1 mile beyond the cottage, the local scene changes, with birch-oak woodland on the lower slopes. In summer, tall bracken hides the remains of stone cottages and the coal pits and salt pans that were excavated here to support local fishing in the 18th century. Ignore paths climbing into the trees and stick to the rocky shore, where you might find scraps of blackish coal. Further

SHORT WALK

Heights of North Sannox

Forest and moorland paths lead from North Sannox to fantastic views of Arran's rugged peaks. Colour-coded, waymarked routes from the North Sannox car park (shown on the information board there) provide walks with scenic and archaeological highlights. To reach the high point (224m), follow the yellow route and return down the blue route. The red and green markers lead to a shieling (rough cottage) and a prehistoric burial cairn. Allow about 1½ hours for the 2.8-mile (4.5km) walk.

on, Ossian's Cave, although marked on the map, is invisible from the shore. The pinkish-red sandstone cliffs then start to close in. Around the **Cock of Arran** flat, red slabs of sandstone line the shore. Change down into rock-hopping gear to get through a confusion of conglomerate boulders; soon you're back on grass. Then, between the two cottages at **Fairy Dell**, follow a path from the corner of a dyke, up through trees and bracken to moorland. The path drops down to a gravel road between two cottages; there's a signpost here back to Fairy Dell. Continue down to the minor road along Loch Ranza's northeast shore. A short distance along, turn right to reach the main road in Lochranza village, opposite a church and near the bus stop (two hours from Laggan).

LOCH LOMOND & THE TROSSACHS NATIONAL PARK

Established in 2002, 720-sq-mile (1865-sq-km) Loch Lomond & the Trossachs was Scotland's first national park, gathering together the northern section of the Argyll Forest Park (the first forest park to be declared in Britain, in 1935), including the Arrochar Alps and its *pièce de résistance*, the Cobbler. To this, add the 'hills' south of Crianlarich, notably Ben More and Stob Binnein; the ranges east of Strathyre, including Ben Vorlich and Stuc a' Chroin; the Trossachs; Queen Elizabeth Forest Park; and almost all of Loch Lomond. The park is more than mountains – it's rich in glens and lochs, there are numerous villages and a few small towns, and Scotland's most popular and best-known long-distance path, the West Highland Way, strides across a long strip of the park.

PLANNING

Maps

Harvey's spiral-bound *Loch Lomond & the Trossachs National Park* atlas has waterproof map pages (at 1:40,000) and lots of background information and contacts.

Information Sources

The Loch Lomond & the Trossachs National Park's **Gateway Centre** (☎ 0845 345 4978; www.lochlomond-trossachs.org; Loch Lomond Shores, Balloch) is an excellent first port of call for information about the park, including accommodation. There's also the **Balmaha National Park Centre** (☎ 01389 722100; Easter-Oct), more in the heart of things.

THE COBBLER

Duration	5 hours
Distance	8 miles (13km)
Difficulty	moderate–demanding
Start/Finish	Forestry Commission car park on the A83, 0.5 miles west of Arrochar
Nearest Town	Arrochar (p104)
Transport	bus, train

Summary Climb one of Scotland's most famous and unforgettable peaks; don't forget to pack your head for heights for the final scramble.

Ben Arthur (881m), is more commonly and fondly referred to as the Cobbler. With its distinctive three-pronged rooster crown, it stands majestically apart from its rounded neighbours. While not the highest of the six Arrochar peaks (which include four Munros), the Cobbler is without a doubt the favourite among both hillwalkers and climbers. It dominates the southernmost section of the Arrochar Alps, bounded by Glen Loin, the head of Loch Long and Glen

WARNING

The final ascent of the central peak is potentially dangerous, especially when the rock is damp. Take the greatest care if you decide to squeeze through to the narrow ledge and scramble to the top – it's a long way down from the edge of the ledge.

Croe (along the A83) in the south, Loch Lomond in the east and Glen Kinglas in the west. The popular story of the mountain's name tells of how a cobbler was hunched over (forming the north and centre peaks) listening to his wife, Jean (the south peak). Very much part of the development of Scottish rock climbing, especially among young, working-class Glaswegians, the Cobbler Club (1866) was Scotland's first climbing group. The last Ice Age littered the mountain with moraine, leaving behind the prominent Narnain Boulders below the Cobbler's peaks.

The well-used path gains 850m and ends with a steep and rocky section from the corrie at the peaks' base and then what is – for some – a short and exhilarating scramble. The south peak's steep sides, seen from the corrie, are a popular haunt for climbers. The north peak is easily reached along its northern face. The centre peak's final ascent is dramatic and, depending on your experience and the conditions on the day, potentially dangerous. You must squeeze through a body-sized hole (known as the 'needle') in a huge, box-shaped rock to reach the top via a narrow shelf (potentially lethal if it is damp) above a steep drop. People hang out around the centre peak gathering their nerve or watching the brave and nerveless (or foolhardy) few 'threading the needle'.

PLANNING

Maps

The OS Landranger 1:50,000 map No 56 *Loch Lomond & Inveraray* covers the area; a better bet is the Harvey Superwalker 1:25,000 map *Arrochar Alps*.

Information Sources

The **Ardgartan visitor centre** (☎ 01301 702432; www.visitscottishheartlands.com; Ardgartan; Easter-Oct), 2 miles west of Arrochar, is a good source of maps and information about local walks; staff can also help with accommodation bookings.

NEAREST TOWN

Arrochar

☎ 01301 / pop 650

A rather scattered village along the shores of Loch Long, Arrochar suffers somewhat from the passing of heavy vehicles, but has an unbeatable view across Loch Long to the Cobbler.

There's at ATM in the service station, otherwise the nearest is in Inveraray, 22 miles to the west.

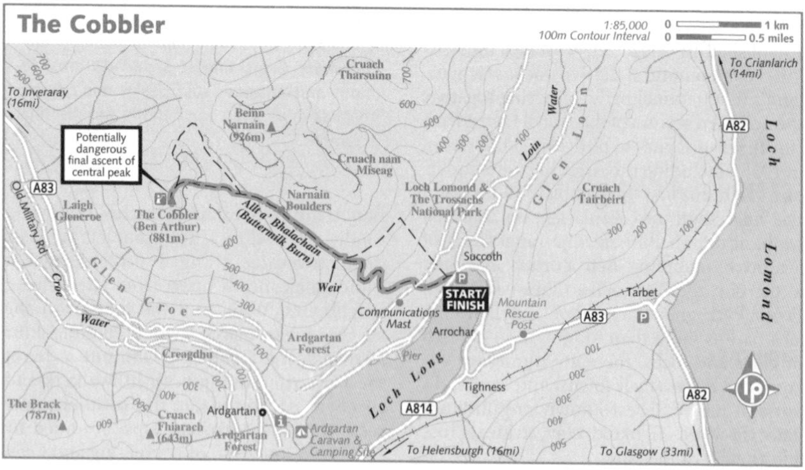

SLEEPING & EATING

Ardgartan Caravan & Camping Site (☎ 702293; www.forestholidays.co.uk; A83; sites for 2 £15), run by the Forestry Commission, is 2 miles west of Arrochar, right beside Loch Long.

Inveraray SYHA Hostel (☎ 0870 004 1125; www.syha.org.uk; Dalmally Rd, Inveraray; dm/d £14/28), 22 miles west of Arrochar in a historic town, is the nearest hostel. It has doubles and small dorms.

Ferry Cottage (☎ 702428; www.ferrycottage.com; Ardmay; s/d £35/56, dinner £12), a superbly restored old ferryman's cottage, is 1 mile south of the village. Expect a warm welcome and good home cooking; all rooms have views of Loch Long.

Greenbank Licensed Restaurant (☎ 702305; Main St; mains £7-14; lunch & dinner) is a small, friendly place, offering standard fare, including vegetarian dishes, and a special Taste of Scotland menu; you certainly won't leave here feeling underfed. It's wise to book a table during the busy season.

The **village shop** (Main St) stocks a reasonable range of supplies; if you've forgotten your map, try the post-office shop.

GETTING THERE & AWAY

Scottish Citylink (☎ 0870 550 5050; www.citylink.co.uk) Glasgow–Campbeltown buses stop at Arrochar (£7, 1¼ hours, three daily).

First ScotRail (☎ 0845 755 0033; www.firstscotrail.com) trains on the West Highland line from Glasgow to Fort William stop at Arrochar & Tarbet station (£11, 1½ hours, three daily), 20 minutes' walk from Arrochar. Overnight sleeper trains between London Euston and Fort William also call here.

By car from Glasgow, take the M8 (Greenock) towards Loch Lomond and then the highly scenic A82; continue on the A83 to Arrochar.

GETTING TO/FROM THE WALK

The walk starts from a pay-and-display (£1) car park on the A83 west of Arrochar. It's a good five-minute walk from the village to the car park, around the head of Loch Long.

THE WALK

From the car park, cross the A83 and pass through the timber vehicle barrier signed 'Access to Ben Narnain and Cobbler'. Follow the well-made path as it zigzags its way uphill to a forestry road; first turn left towards a communications mast then right in front of it. The zigzags continue up through the conifer plantation to a forest track and Allt a' Bhalachain (Buttermilk Burn). A fine vista of the Cobbler's famous three peaks welcomes you to the halfway mark. Follow the clear path upstream, crossing numerous tributaries, to the distinctive **Narnain Boulders**. Over the next half-mile or so the well-made path steers clear of a morass and climbs to the rocky corrie below the three peaks. Scramble up to the saddle between the central and north peaks, marked with a cairn. For a less arduous, though slightly longer route, follow the path up the valley for another 1 mile to the watershed, where it divides. Take the southern branch, climbing steeply up the north ridge on well-built zigzags, to reach the saddle between the central and north peaks.

The central and highest peak lies to the left, while the more easily accessed **north peak** is to the right. The superlative view takes in Loch Long, Gareloch, the Firth of Clyde, the Isles of Bute and Arran, Ben Lomond and dozens of other peaks to the east. Return the same way to the car park.

BEN LOMOND

Duration	4½–5 hours
Distance	7 miles (11km)
Difficulty	moderate
Start/Finish	Rowardennan (p106)
Transport	ferry

Summary A circuit over one of the most popular 'hills' in central Scotland, via the quiet Ptarmigan Route; the views of 'the bonnie, bonnie banks of Loch Lomond' are magnificent.

There's no freshwater loch in Scotland larger than Loch Lomond, which is 22 miles long and up to 4.5 miles wide. Standing guard over the loch is Ben Lomond (974m), the most southerly Munro. It's thought that the name Lomond comes from an old Lowland Scots word *llumon*, or the Gaelic *laom*, meaning a 'beacon' or 'light'. Loch Lomond is a very popular venue for water sports and on fine weekends the droning of powerboats and jet skis is all too audible, even on the summit.

Ben Lomond is the most popular of all Scotland's mountains – more than 30,000 people climb it each year. Most follow the 'tourist route' up and down, which starts at Rowardennan car park. It's a straightforward climb on a well-used and maintained path; allow about five hours for the 7-mile (11km) walk. The scenic Ptarmigan Route, described here, is less crowded and follows a narrower, clearly defined path up the western flank of Ben Lomond, directly overlooking the loch, to a curving ridge leading to the summit. You can then descend via the popular main-ridge route, making a satisfying circuit.

There are no easy alternative routes. Ben Lomond slopes very steeply down to the loch and tracks through the forest on the eastern side aren't particularly attractive. The West Highland Way (p89) passes between the loch and the Ben, and many Way walkers take a day off to do the climb.

PLANNING

Maps & Books

Harvey's 1:25,000 map *Glasgow Popular Hills* includes Ben Lomond but isn't much help for identifying surrounding features. For this purpose, use either the OS Landranger 1:50,000 map No 56 *Loch Lomond & Inveraray* or the OS Explorer 1:25,000 map No 364 *Loch Lomond North*.

Loch Lomond, Trossachs, Stirling & Clackmannan by John Brooks covers a wide variety of walks and is recommended.

Guided Walks

Ben Lomond National Trust for Scotland rangers (☎ 870224) lead guided walks on Ben Lomond during summer.

NEAREST TOWN

Rowardennan offers a smattering of accommodation and dining, though Drymen (p92), about 10 miles southeast, has the nearest shops of any size and a good selection of pubs and places to stay.

Rowardennan

☎ 01360

At the end of the sealed road in Rowardennan is a large white building housing toilets and an unstaffed display about the park.

SLEEPING & EATING

Cashel Caravan and Camping Site (☎ 870234; www.forestholidays.co.uk; sites for 2 £14), right on the loch shore about midway between Balmaha and Rowardennan, has a small café and a shop, and is usually busy. A special backpacker rate (£5 for two) is available if you arrive on foot.

Rowardennan SYHA Hostel (☎ 0870 004 1148; www.syha.org.uk; dm £14), in a former lodge, has a superb outlook. Being very convenient, it's also very popular, so it pays to book ahead.

Rowardennan Hotel (☎ 870273; www.rowardennanhotel.co.uk; s/d £60/110; lunch & dinner) does reasonably priced bar meals in the lively Rob Roy Bar.

LOCH LOMOND

Loch Lomond is the largest body of fresh water in Britain, covering 27 sq miles. It is also an area of great beauty, and is besieged by visitors during summer.

The loch is believed to have been gouged by a glacier flowing from the ice sheet that covered Rannoch Moor during the last Ice Age. At its deepest, just south of Inversnaid, the water depth is 190m. The loch straddles the boundary between the lowlands and the Highlands, and two distinct environments can be seen along its shores. Botanical studies have found that 25% of all known British flowering plants and ferns can be found along the eastern shore.

The southern part of the loch is bordered by relatively flat, arable land, and is wide, shallow and dotted with 38 islands, some of which contain early Christian sites. This part of the loch freezes over during severe winters, and islanders have managed to access the mainland by foot on several occasions over the last 50 years.

The northern end of the loch is deeper, generally less than 1 mile wide, and is enclosed by steep hillsides. It is unknown for this part of the loch to freeze. The slopes at the loch shore are covered by Scotland's largest remnant of oak forest, mixed with newer conifer plantations. These are being felled, to be replaced by native broad-leaved species to help regenerate the native forest.

GETTING THERE & AWAY

The only public transport to Rowardennan is the small summer-only ferry (operated by the Rowardennan Hotel) that plies the loch to and from Inverbeg, on the western shore. Use the regular **Scottish Citylink** (☎ 0870 550 5050; www.citylink.co.uk) bus service to Inverbeg from Glasgow (£6, one hour, five daily) or Fort William (£12, 2¼ hours, five daily), then catch the passenger ferry (£5) to Rowardennan. The ferry departs at 10.30am, 2.30pm and 6pm, and returns at 10am, 2pm and 5.30pm.

THE WALK

With your back to the toilet block, walk towards Loch Lomond, where there's a view of the distinctive rounded knob of Ptarmigan, a couple of miles due north. Turn right (north) along the loch-side path, soon passing a granite war-memorial sculpture. The path becomes a gravel road; in a few minutes swing right through a gate in front of the youth hostel, then turn left, following the West Highland Way with its thistle-and-hexagon waymarker.

Pass Ardess Lodge National Trust for Scotland Ranger Centre and Ben Lomond Cottage on the right, cross a burn and immediately turn right along an unmarked path up through the trees. It climbs beside the burn for a short distance to a small cascade, then veers left up the bracken-covered hillside. As you climb steadily across the slope, you're treated to views of the loch and the hills on its western side and, further on, Ptarmigan summit comes into view. Higher up, above some rock outcrops, go through a kissing gate. The path gains more height on an open spur then zigzags steeply up a grassy bluff to the ridge and on to the summit of **Ptarmigan** (731m), near a small lochan (1½ to two hours from Rowardennan). The fine views include virtually the full length of the loch and its cluster of islands, and the Arrochar hills to the west.

The path continues on, along the bumpy ridge and through a chain of grassy rocky knobs, to a narrow gap where stepping stones keep you out of the mud. The final steep climb starts through formidable crags, but natural rock steps and the well-maintained path make it comparatively easy. From a grassy shelf there's one

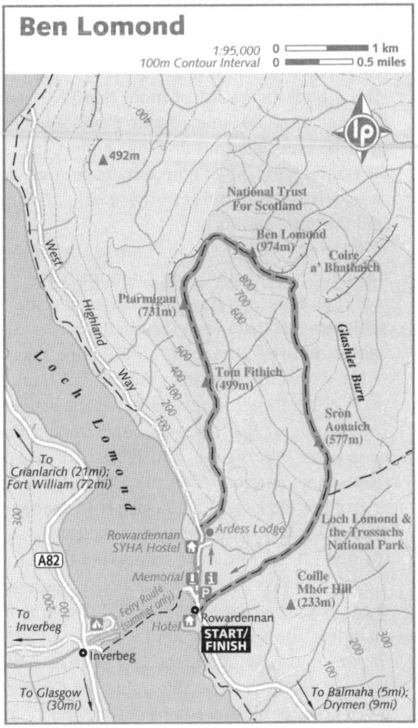

more straightforward rocky climb to the trig point on the summit of **Ben Lomond** (974m), less than one hour from Ptarmigan summit. The all-round view includes Ben Nevis on the northern horizon, the Isles of Arran and Jura in the southwest, the Firth of Clyde, the Arrochar hills immediately across the loch (notably the awl-like profile of the Cobbler) and the Campsie Fells and Glasgow to the south.

The wide, well-trodden path starts to descend immediately, going past the spectacular, north-facing cliffs on the left. Soon it swings round to the right and makes a series of wide zigzags down the steep slope to the long ridge stretching ahead, which it follows south. Eventually the grade steepens over Sròn Aonaich (577m) and the path resumes zigzagging through open moorland. Cross a footbridge and continue into the pine forest, along an open clearing. The path steepens, becoming rockier and more eroded as you go down through mixed woodland. Eventually it emerges at the toilet block at Rowardennan, two hours from the top.

MUNROS & MUNRO BAGGING

It all began in 1891 when Sir Hugh Munro, a member of the Scottish Mountaineering Club (SMC), published a list of more than 500 Scottish summits over 3000ft, the height at which he believed they became proper mountains. Never mind modern metrication, this figure is still quoted, especially because the equivalent, 914m, lacks the imperial measurement's neatness. Sir Hugh identified 283 'mountains in their own right' (those with a significant drop on all sides or widely separated from other peaks), though his original list has been revised over the years and the total stands at 284.

Reverend AE Robertson climbed the lot in 1901, initiating the sport of Munro bagging, which has become something of a national pastime. More than 3550 people have completed the full round and are therefore entitled to join the Munro Society. Records have been set and unique achievements have been recorded, such as continuous rounds (no breaks at all) in summer and in winter, and self-propelled rounds using bikes between climbs and canoes to reach the islands.

List or no list, the great majority of Munros are outstanding walks with superb views; 33 of them are featured in this book. Of the several guides on the subject, two stand out. The SMC's *The Munros* by Rab Anderson and Donald Bennet is a weighty tome of absolutely reliable and exhaustive information, and is best for whiling away winter evenings planning next summer's campaign. Cameron McNeish's *The Munro Almanac* slips into your map pocket easily, is written by one of the most respected walkers in Scotland and has all the basic information you'll need. The **Munro Society** (www.themunrosociety.com), founded in 2002, is another useful source of information. It's open to all who have completed the full 'round' of 284 summits.

Once you've bagged the Munros, there are other collections of summits to tackle, such as the 219 Corbetts – Scottish 'hills' over 2500ft (700m) with a drop of at least 500ft (150m) on all sides. The guide for these is *The Corbetts & Other Scottish Hills* by Rob Milne and Hamish Brown. And how about the 224 Grahams, hills between 2000ft and 2499ft? Andrew Dempster has compiled the inevitable guide *The Grahams: A Guide to Scotland's 2,000ft Peaks*. With even just a selection of all these behind you, you'll have a fair idea of why Scotland is such a wonderful walking destination.

BEN LEDI

Duration	4 hours
Distance	7.4 miles (12km)
Difficulty	moderate–demanding
Start/Finish	Ben Ledi car park
Nearest Town	Callander (opposite)
Transport	bus

Summary A circular walk through lush woodland, along enchanting Stank Glen, past rushing cascades and across a spectacular ridge to sweeping summit views.

The Trossachs is a wild region ringed by several lochs: Loch Ard and Lake of Menteith in the south, the north end of Loch Katrine to the west, Loch Doine and Loch Voil hem in the north and Loch Lubnaig rounds out the east. To the west of Loch Lubnaig, the Trossachs' highest mountain, Ben Ledi (879m), makes a formidable backdrop to Callander and Loch Venachar, and is deserving of its name 'God's Hill'; an account from 1791 links it to an annual summer-solstice celebration. A less dramatic definition, 'hill of the gentle slope', perhaps refers to the broad grassy ridge running north from the summit down to Lochan nan Corp – the wee loch of the dead bodies! Local legend suggests that the lochan is named for an ill-fated funeral party, which fell through the ice as it crossed the apparently frozen surface.

While fairly straightforward in good conditions, Ben Ledi should be taken very seriously if the weather turns nasty. This circular walk includes around 740m of ascent and a steep descent. Only initially waymarked, the path is generally easy to follow.

PLANNING

Maps & Books

Use OS Landranger 1:50,000 map No 57 *Stirling & the Trossachs*. The pocket-sized Hallewell guide *Walks in the Trossachs* by Mike Williams describes 40 walks in the area from mountain climbs to riverside rambles.

Information Sources

Much of the Trossachs is within Queen Elizabeth Forest Park; the **David Marshall Lodge Visitor Centre** (☎ 01877 382258; car park £1; 🕑 Mar-Dec), 800m north of Aberfoyle on the A821, has information about walks in the park. Callander (below) also has a well-stocked TIC.

NEAREST TOWN

Callander

☎ **01877 / pop 3000**

Long popular with day trippers from Stirling and Glasgow, Callander sits on the eastern edge of the Trossachs and serves as an amenable base for walks in the area.

Rob Roy and the Trossachs Visitor Centre (☎ 0870 720 0628; www.robroyvisitorcentre.com; Ancaster Sq) has loads of information; you can listen to the story of the renowned 17th-century outlaw Rob Roy (see p92) and watch a film about the area.

If you've forgotten your walking socks, head for **It's Great Outdoors** (☎ 339743; Main St).

SLEEPING & EATING

Keltie Bridge Caravan Park (☎ 330606; unpowered/powered sites for 2 £11/12) is east of town on the A84 but within walking distance.

Trossachs Backpackers (☎ 331200; www.scottish-hostel.co.uk; Invertrossachs Rd; dm/tw £16/42) is about 1 mile from town. The dorms are spacious and breakfast is included in the tariff.

Linley Guest House (☎ 330087; www.linleyguesthouse.co.uk; 139 Main St; s/d £30/48), in an old, stone-built terrace, has comfortable rooms and serves up a good breakfast.

Jaan Restaurant (☎ 339111; 25 Main St; mains £8-13; 🕑 lunch & dinner) has smart blue-and-white décor and offers a wide range of curry-style dishes, from mild kormas to searing vindaloos.

Callander Meadows (☎ 330181; 24 Main St; dinner mains £13-15; 🕑 lunch & dinner), in a well-preserved Victorian building, has a small dining room. The set two-course dinner (£15) is good value in a superior restaurant.

For supplies, there's a **Tesco supermarket** (Main St).

GETTING THERE & AWAY

First (☎ 08708 727271; www.firstgroup.com) operates a bus service between Stirling and Callander (£4, 45 minutes, at least 10 services Monday to Saturday).

By car from Glasgow (on the M80) or Edinburgh (M9), head to Stirling and then Callander (A84).

GETTING TO/FROM THE WALK

From Callander it is 3 miles to the start of the walk, close to the A84, at the Forestry Commission's Ben Ledi car park, signed to Strathyre Forest Cabins. The car park, along a track immediately to the left across the bridge, is small and often full; if so, there's more parking on the A84, north of the turn-off. You can easily walk this distance (which passes the Falls of Leny) along the cycle route connecting Callander and Killin.

The **First Edinburgh** (☎ 0131 663 9233; www.firstedinburgh.co.uk) Stirling–Killin bus service passes the trailhead; ask to be dropped near the bridge.

THE WALK

From the car park, walk past the bridge and continue straight on (north) along the sealed road, marked with green posts, parallel to the Garbh Uisge river, for just over

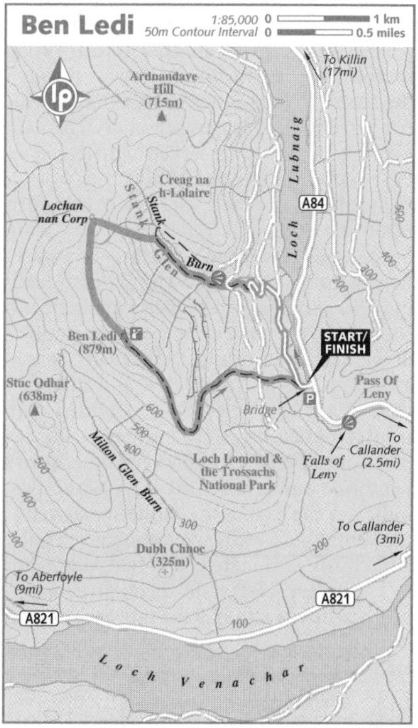

SHORT TROSSACHS WALK

Diminutive **Ben A'an** (461m), in the heart of the Trossachs, epitomises all that's so attractive about the area – woodlands, deep glens and rocky peaks. Originally called Am Binnein (small pointed peak), its name was changed by the 19th-century Romantic poet Sir Walter Scott in his poem *Lady of the Lake*. Though it's really only a prominent knob in the jumble of humps and bumps between Glen Finglas Reservoir, Loch Achray and Loch Katrine, it affords surprisingly good views, including nearby Ben Ledi (east) and Ben Venue (west). The 3.7-mile (6km) walk involves about 360m ascent; allow 1¾ to two hours. Consult either OS Landranger 1:50,000 map No 57 or the Harvey Superwalker 1:25,000 map *Glasgow's Popular Hills*.

To reach the Forestry Commission car park opposite the start of the walk, follow the A84 west from Callander (p109) and turn left along the A821 at Kilmahog; the car park is on the south side of the road, close to the western end of Loch Achray.

The all-too-clear path climbs steeply at first through forest, emerging after a while at a small clearing, where you can glimpse a sliver of Loch Katrine. About 100m further along, the serious climb starts on well-made steps, up a gully, crossing and recrossing a small burn, to a saddle. From here, beaten paths lead to the knobbly summit. Retrace your steps to the start.

800m. Turn left onto a forestry road that makes a curving ascent to a fork. Head left here through a broad-leaved forest. After five minutes, abandon the forestry road at a sharp curve and turn right (west) onto a footpath through a magical birch wood that ascends alongside the rushing **Stank Burn**. About 200m further on, spruce (a conifer species) dominates the forest, and the route reaches and crosses another forestry road to continue its northwest course through the forest. Five minutes later, a natural balcony overlooks a leaping cascade. The path for Ben Ledi is waymarked with green or brown posts with a red band.

Reaching another forestry road, turn right for 30m and then head left again onto a narrow road that ascends west. After a tough, steep stretch, the path leads into breathtaking **Stank Glen**. Stank Burn's source, at the end of the valley, tumbles down in a series of spectacular falls. Ignore a road going up to the left and continue west along the valley floor, studded with stumps. After crossing another road, follow a footpath that approaches the burn's winding course and ford it. A white post indicates the end of the modern waymarking. From here the waymarking is irregular and clearly antiquated. The footpath heads to the valley's left side through a boggy, heather-lined section. Reaching a wire fence, cross it by a stile and continue along its right side to a gate. The real back-breaking work, a 800m-stretch to reach the ridge crest, now begins. Once on the crest, iron fence posts run along the ridge marking old boundary estates. A five-minute detour right (north) leads to Lochan nan Corp.

To reach the **Ben Ledi** summit, follow the posts about 1 mile south. The sweeping views, especially south and east towards Stirling's Castle and Wallace Monument and the upper reaches of the Firth of Forth, are just reward after the long uphill pull.

To descend, follow the posts southeast along a heavily eroded trail for almost 1.5 miles, where the trail swings sharply left (northeast). Descend towards the forest below Ben Ledi's abrupt east face; the steep path can be icy in cold weather. From the foot of this steep section, the path is much better. Use the stile to cross a wire fence, ford a stream and follow the path down its bank through a recently felled area into the forest. Follow this path (marker posts with blue bands) down for 1 mile, crossing a forestry road, to emerge at the bridge near the car park.

AROUND LOCH TAY

A Munro bagger's delight, the area bounded by Loch Tay in the south, Lochs Rannoch and Tummel to the north, the River Tummel to the east and Loch Lyon in the west is packed with incredible scenery and has a fascinating history. Glen Lyon, one of Scotland's best glens, bisects the area east–west and separates the two largest massifs in the southern Highlands: Carn Mairg to the north and the 7.5-mile-long ridge of the Ben Lawers group, with seven summits exceeding 900m, to the south. The Tarmachans range, topped by Meall nan Tarmachan (1043m), lies to the west of the Lawers group, separated by the Lochan na Lairige pass. Just two of the dozens of possible walks in this marvellous area are described in this section – ascents of Ben Lawers (1214m) and Schiehallion (1083m), an outlier of the Carn Mairg range. These two walks should be enough to send you straight back to the map and start planning the next visit.

PLANNING

Maps & Books

The OS Landranger 1:50,000 map No 51 *Loch Tay & Glen Dochart* covers both Ben Lawers and Schiehallion. Harvey's 1:25,000 map *Ben Lawers: From Loch Tay and Loch Rannoch* includes both peaks, the important massifs and a visitor guide. Felicity Martin's useful *Walks: North Perthshire* succinctly covers 26 walks on Loch Tay's eastern end.

Information Sources

For information about other walks, walker-friendly accommodation and events in the area go to the Walking Wild link at the **Perthshire** (www.perthshire.co.uk) website.

GETTING AROUND

Unfortunately this is not an area where you can readily use public transport, with services being limited to inconvenient postbuses and occasional school-day runs.

BEN LAWERS

Duration	5 hours
Distance	8.2 miles (13km)
Difficulty	moderate–demanding
Start/Finish	Ben Lawers Mountain Visitor Centre
Nearest Town	Killin (right)
Transport	private

Summary A direct ascent along well-made paths to one of Scotland's highest 10 mountains, a veritable alpine flower garden.

Reigning mightily over Loch Tay's north shore, handsome Ben Lawers (1214m) is Perthshire's highest Munro and the central feature of a national nature reserve protecting an extraordinary array of Arctic alpine plants that thrive in the high ground's unusually rich soil. The best time to do this walk, especially if you're a keen botanist, is between June and August. The NTS cares for 3374 hectares of its southern slopes, and 1348 hectares of the Tarmachans to the west. Following a well-used path, the walk climbs 940m to reach the rocky summit, a remnant of an attempt by 30 men in 1878 to elevate Ben Lawers height by 5m to reach Scotland's elite 4000ft club.

PLANNING

Information Sources

The NTS maintains the **Ben Lawers Mountain Visitor Centre** (☎ 01567 820397; ⌚ May-Sep), up on the mountainside, with displays on geology and fauna and a shop. The *Ben Lawers Nature Trail* booklet describes the flora and fauna. The ranger service based here runs guided walks during July and August. The car park has a pay-and-display system (£2).

NEAREST TOWN

Killin

☎ 01567 / pop 700

Killin is strung out along the main A827, on either side of the River Dochart.

The **TIC** (☎ 0870 720 0627; www.visitscottishheartlands.com; ⌚ Easter-Oct) is in the Breadalbane Folklore Centre, an old water mill overlooking the Falls of Dochart; it sells maps and books and can help with accommodation arrangements.

Killin Outdoor Centre (☎ 820652; Main St) stocks a reasonable range of gear.

SLEEPING & EATING

Cruachan Farm Caravan & Camping Park (☎ 820302; www.cruachanfarm.co.uk; North Loch Tay Side by Killin; unpowered/powered sites for 2 £10/12) is a spacious, sheltered site, close to the Ben Lawers turn-off. The on-site **licensed coffee shop and restaurant** (☎ 820700; ⌚ lunch & dinner) offers home baking and light meals; the menu features old favourites and more imaginative dishes.

Killin Youth Hostel (☎ 0870 004 1131; www.syha.org.uk; Aberfeldy Rd; dm £13), in a Victorian mansion at the northern end of the village, has up-to-date facilities and can offer advice on local walks.

Drumfinn Guest House (☎ 820900; www.drumfinn.co.uk; Manse Rd; s/d £35/29) is a friendly place with light, airy rooms in an early Victorian building that served as a bank for more

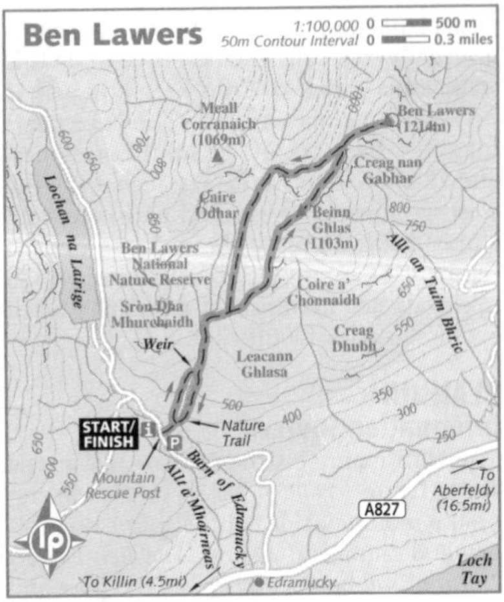

than a century. Look forward to being entertained by the frog musicians.

Falls of Dochart Inn (☎ 820270; Falls of Dochart; mains £10-15; dinner) overlooks the falls and has a small, enticing dining room where you can sample excellent Scottish-inspired dishes.

For supplies, there's a Co-op supermarket, a greengrocer and the Bake Shop for pies and snacks, all along Main St.

GETTING THERE & AWAY

By car from Edinburgh/Glasgow, take the A84 road via Stirling and Callander. If you're coming by car from Arrochar, take the A82 to Crianlarich then the A85.

GETTING TO/FROM THE WALK

Ben Lawers Mountain Visitor Centre is located 6.5 miles east of Killin. At Edramucky on the A827, turn up the road signposted to Ben Lawers Mountain Visitor Centre; it's 1.5 miles to the car park. The NTS operates a pay-and-display system (£2).

THE WALK

From the Ben Lawers Mountain Visitor Centre take the Nature Trail that heads northeast. Clearly visible in the distance is the footpath that ascends the open hillside of Beinn Ghlas. After the boardwalk protecting the bog, cross an elevated, double-staired stile (and fence, which keeps the hungry sheep and deer out of the lush protected area), fork left (northeast) and ascend along a burn. At the next rise fork right and cross the burn.

A few minutes later, ignore the Nature Trail's right turn and ascend parallel to the burn's true left bank for about 800m. Leave the protected zone by another double stile and steeply ascend Beinn Ghlas' shoulder. Reaching a couple of large rocks, ignore a northbound footpath and continue zigzagging uphill. The rest of the 1.5-mile ascent is a straightforward succession of three false summits. The last and steepest section alternates between erosion-sculpted rock and a meticulously crafted cobbled trail. A cairn marks the summit of **Beinn Ghlas** (1103m), with a great view of Ben Lawers ahead.

Descend northeast along the ridge crest for 20 minutes to the base of Ben Lawers. The initial segment of the 800m ascent is made easier by the cobbled sections reminiscent of ancient Roman highways. Beyond a small plateau the ascent continues along an eroded path up to the rocky summit of **Ben Lawers** (1214m).

Return the same way, or take one or both of two decent detours. Instead of continuing along the ridge crest and climbing Beinn Ghlas again, take a track from the base of Ben Lawers that heads southwest, gently descending along the contour of Beinn Ghlas' north face. After about 1 mile, old iron fence posts appear and soon you see Loch Tay and the visitor centre. In just over 1 mile the alternative rejoins the main trail. Another good option is to finish along the eastern segment of the Nature Trail, near the start of the route. At the 'To Car Park' sign, turn left and you will soon reach the double stile.

SCHIEHALLION

Duration	4 hours
Distance	7.6 miles (12km)
Difficulty	moderate
Start/Finish	Braes of Foss car park
Nearest Town	Aberfeldy (opposite)
Transport	private

Summary Ascend the famous landmark in Scotland's centre, the 'hill' that also sired the contour lines on topographical maps.

Famed for its symmetrical conic appearance, especially when viewed from Loch Rannoch's north shore, Schiehallion (1083m), 'the fairy hill of the Caledonians', is an isolated whale of a mountain. Designated a Site

BIRTH OF CONTOUR MAPS

Contour lines, the bread and butter of map-crafting, were indirectly born due to Schiehallion's famous symmetry and a 1774 attempt to calculate the earth's mass. Applying Isaac Newton's theory of the universal gravitational constant, Astronomer Royal Nevil Maskelyne set up observatories on the north and south sides of the mountain 'to measure by how much plumb lines would be pulled out of the vertical and towards the mountain by gravitational force due to its mass'. At the time this was known as the attraction of mountains. (Nowadays the attraction of mountains isn't measured by gravitational pull but by eroded paths!) Apparently the project took a huge effort over two years, moving a 10ft telescope around the mountain in order to take highly accurate sightings of stars. The apparent and true differences in latitude were then compared. While analysing the results, mathematician Charles Hutton began to connect similar heights on the mountain with lines, pioneering the concept of contours.

Maskelyne built several cairns during his experiments; if you continue west from the end of the path at the summit, you'll soon come to a horseshoe-shaped cairn, probably on the site of one of the Astronomer Royal's cairns.

of Special Scientific Interest, it's a distinctive landmark from many viewpoints; even the great chronicler Ptolemy, in the 2nd century AD, listed it in his landmark work *Geography*. Look for the limestone pavements and ptarmigans, and the yellow saxifrage and wild thyme scenting the hillsides.

The John Muir Trust (p31) owns and manages the summit, path and eastern slopes and has re-routed the path to the summit ridge, providing a narrow but firm walking surface. This has allowed vegetation to grow along the former route, which was heavily eroded with deep, wet, peaty troughs. The all-encompassing views are especially fine in summer when the setting sun makes the Highlands glow in the west.

PLANNING

Information Sources

The **John Muir Trust** (www.jmt.org) website has details of the path restoration work. There's also an on-site information board and toilets near the car park.

At the **Queen's View Centre** (☎ 01796 473123; Tay Forest Park; car park £1; ⏰ Mar-Nov), at the east end of Loch Tummel, 7 miles from Pitlochry on the B8019, the eponymous view is of Schiehallion.

NEAREST TOWN

Aberfeldy

☎ 01887 / pop 1897

Quiet, riverside Aberfeldy is immortalised in Robert Burns' 1787 poem *The Birks O' Aberfeldy*, a paean to the nearby Falls of Moness and birch wood (birk).

The **TIC** (☎ 820276; aberfeldytic@visitscotland.com; The Square; ⏰ daily Apr-Oct, Mon-Sat Nov-Mar) sells guidebooks and maps.

Munros (☎ 820008; 1 Bridgend) stocks a fair range of outdoor equipment.

SLEEPING & EATING

The **Bunkhouse** (☎ 820265; www.thebunkhouse.co.uk; Glassie Farm; dm £12) is 1.3 miles off the B846 (towards Schiehallion) and has great views from its hillside site; facilities are excellent.

Balnearn House (☎ 820431; www.balnearnhouse.com; Crieff Rd; s/d £40/64) welcomes walkers to this late-Victorian home in a lovely garden setting.

Kiwis (☎ 829229; The Square; lunch mains £6, dinner mains £11-13; ⏰ lunch daily, dinner Thu-Mon) is a refreshing alternative to pub food; it uses fresh local ingredients wherever possible, with antipodean flair.

Black Watch Inn (☎ 820699; Bank St; mains £6-12; ⏰ lunch & dinner) offers good basic fare enlivened by the occasional gesture towards Thai cuisine.

For supplies, there's a **Co-op** (The Square) supermarket.

GETTING THERE & AWAY

By car, take the A9 out of Stirling and Perth, connecting to the A822 (then A826) or the A827 to Aberfeldy.

GETTING TO/FROM THE WALK

To reach the start of the walk, take the B846 and turn down Braes of Foss Rd between Coshieville and Tummel Bridge. Continue 2 miles on Braes of Foss Rd and turn left

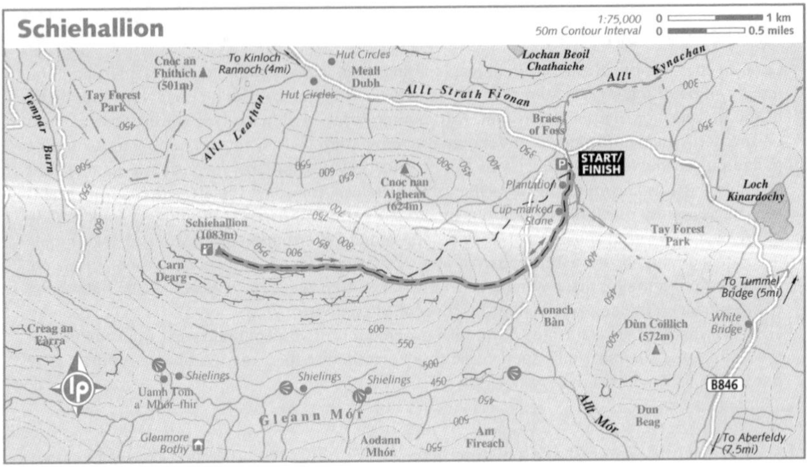

into the well-marked Braes of Foss car park, which has metered parking.

THE WALK

The new path, established in 2003, was not marked on most maps at the time of research, so follow our description rather than the maps.

Leave the car park by the marked gate and follow the path climbing gently south between a small conifer plantation on the right (west) and a much larger expanse of commercial forest on the left (east). The narrow path is perfectly clear ahead, curving right past the wood to climb southwest past a prehistoric, cup-marked rock close to the path on the right (not easy to spot – look for small hollows, the purpose of which is uncertain). Continue towards a rough hill track and cross it near a former sheep pen. From here the path begins to climb more steeply southwest, up onto Schiehallion's east ridge, swinging gradually to the right (west). Once on the crest, it is about 1.5 miles west to the summit. The trail disappears in places on the rocky ridge but cairns guide the way. You'll notice an abundance of rose and white quartz veining the rocks. The upper part of the ridge can be awkward as the rock strata dip away at an angle to the line of ascent. There's no real danger of a dramatic plunge, though it would be all too easy to twist an ankle here. The final rise to the **Schiehallion** summit is on bare, gently sloping rock. On sunny days the top is transformed into a high-level outdoor bistro, and you may have to wait a few minutes for the party ahead of you to finish taking photos at the cairn atop this popular hill.

Enjoy the 360-degree views from the numerous stone-built windbreaks. Return by the same route.

THE OCHIL HILLS

The Ochils are a precious pocket of wilderness immediately north of the Forth Valley, extending northeast for about 12 miles (20km) from the fringes of the historic town of Stirling, itself around 20 miles east of Loch Lomond & the Trossachs National Park. The precipitous southern ramparts of the broad, grassy, undulating massif rise most impressively from the broad valley. The hills are composed mainly of basalt, exposed in deep clefts on its southern slopes, sheltering a rich array of mosses and lichens, trees and shrubs. The unusual name (pronounced 'owe-kills') isn't, for a change, of Gaelic origin, but comes from Brittonic, an older language, and means 'high'.

The string of towns along the southern fringe is collectively known as the Hillfoots. In earlier times it was at the heart of thriving industries based on silver mining and woollen mills, now most evident in the variety of architectural styles among houses large and small.

PLANNING
Maps & Books

The OS Landranger 1:50,000 map No 58 *Perth & Alloa* provides a useful overall impression of the area.

The pocket-sized guide *Stirling & District Walks* by Alistair Lawson describes 24 mostly easy outings. More wide-ranging is Patrick Baker's *Walking in the Ochils, Campsie Fells and Lomond Hills*, covering 33 jaunts.

Information Sources

The **Mill Trail Visitor Centre** (☎ 08707 200605; www.visitscottishheartlands.org; West Stirling St, Alva; 🕑 daily Easter-Oct, Mon-Sat Nov-Easter) sells maps and books, including several on the local architectural heritage of woollen mills, mining and railways. It can also help with accommodation bookings. There's also an exhibition featuring wool, tartan and tweed making and a small café offering standard snacks and drinks.

The **Friends of the Ochils** (www.sites.ecosse.net/ochils/index.html) group works hard to maintain awareness of the great importance of the Ochil hills as a relatively wild area in central Scotland, and strives to protect them from intrusive, inappropriate developments, especially wind farms.

BEN CLEUCH

Duration	5¼–5½ hours
Distance	6.8 miles (11km)
Difficulty	moderate
Start/Finish	Mill Glen car park, Tillicoultry (right)
Transport	bus

Summary A magnificent circuit over the glorious rolling uplands of the Ochil hills, crowned by Ben Cleuch, with amazingly varied views.

Of the several possible walks in the Ochils, one that takes in the highest point, Ben Cleuch (721m), is a pretty obvious choice. It's no mere dash up and back; the comparatively long approach gives you time to become imbued with the spirit of these fine rolling hills, and to savour the superb panoramic views. There's more to the Ochils than uplands, as this walk also reveals. Mill Burn is one of the several streams biting deeply into the southern flanks of the range, tumbling through a secretive, steep-sided glen. Ben Cleuch, by the way, takes its name from the Scots word meaning gully.

Be prepared for steep ups and downs during the walk, involving 680m of ascent. Paths are generally clear enough and fences can be useful navigation handrails, but shouldn't be relied on. In poor visibility you would need finely honed navigation skills to stay on course.

PLANNING
Maps

The best map is the Harvey Superwalker 1:25,000 map *Ochil Hills*. Alternatively, consult OS Explorer 1:25,000 map No 366 *Stirling & Ochil Hills West*.

NEAREST TOWN
Tillicoultry

☎ 01259 / pop 5400

A former mill town at the foot of the hills, Tillicoultry is rather dour and depressing but is saved by the hills themselves and three local bright spots. The nearest TIC is in Alva (see left).

SLEEPING & EATING

Wyvis B&B (☎ 751513; www.wyvisbandbscotland.com; 70 Stirling St; s/d £36/62), in a superbly modernised mill-worker's cottage, has surprisingly large, and beautifully decorated, rooms. Your hostess is charming and very helpful. Breakfast is superb.

Westbourne House B&B (☎ 750314; www.westbournehouse.co.uk; 10 Dollar Rd; s/d £36/56) is a onetime mill-owner's mansion, crammed with the owners' memorabilia from worldwide wanderings. The rooms are on the small side and the breakfast is excellent.

The **Bridge Inn** (☎ 750252; www.maclay.com/bridge-inn-tillicoultry.html; 1 High St; mains £8-15; 🕑 lunch & dinner) passes muster as a traditional-style pub with plenty of framed vintage ads on the walls. It can be busy on Fridays, but the tables aren't too close to each other for comfort.

The **Harviestoun Restaurant** (☎ 752522; Dollar Rd; mains £8-18; 🕑 lunch & dinner) occupies a restored steading (barn). Don't be put off by the fact that it attracts suited types during the week, as the menu ventures away from standard pub fare to some Thai dishes.

For on-the-walk supplies, there's a **Co-op supermarket** (High St).

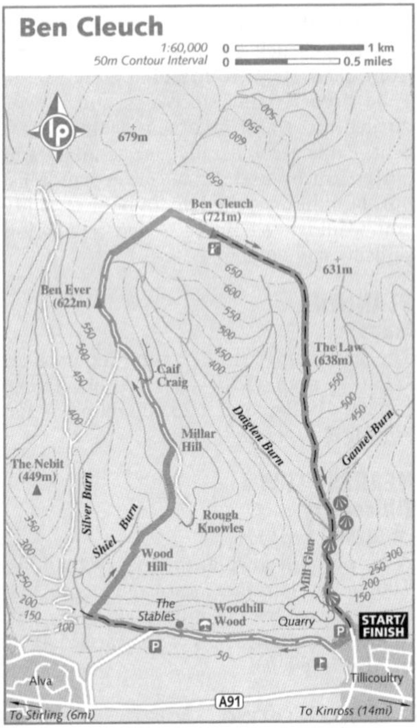

GETTING THERE & AWAY

Tillicoultry is on the routes of the **First** (☎ 08708 727271) 62 and 63 services from Stirling to Alloa (£3, 40 minutes, every 20 minutes Monday to Saturday, hourly on Sunday).

By car, Tillicoultry is on the A91 between Stirling and Kinross, accessible from the M9 near Stirling and the M90 at Kinross.

GETTING TO/FROM THE WALK

From the main road in Tillicoultry, walk or drive up Mill St, at the western edge of town, signposted 'Mill Glen'. There's a small car park at the end of the street; if this is full, you can park near the designated parking area about 150m downhill, still in Mill St.

THE WALK

From the top car park, walk down Mill St for about 150m and turn right along the signposted 'Public Path' to Alva. Cross a stream and continue along Scotland Pl to a T-junction. Turn right and soon left along a vehicle track signed to Alva. The track traverses the steep hillside above Tillicoultry golf course and leads into woodland, soon passing an imposing building known as the Stables (see the boxed text, below). A little further on (30 minutes from the start) you come to an information board featuring the Clackmannanshire Countryside Path Network; it tells you that you're on the red-marked Hillfoots Link. A few metres along, turn right to follow a vehicle track into the Woodland Trust's Woodhill Wood. Pass a track junction on the right and then, just short of a footbridge across Silver Burn, veer right up a steep path through bracken. It swings generally northeast and uphill in open woodland and soon bursts into the open and becomes clearer. The path rises unflinchingly across the flank of a spur, ever higher above Shiel Burn. When you reach a stone wall, follow it up east to a north–south vehicle track about 150m short of Rough Knowles, a line of crags. Follow the track generally north, with occasional minor flirtations northeast, up past a curious hollow on the right and onto the spur at Millar Hill. Continue to a fence line intersection and go through a gate (1½ hours from the information board). Follow the vehicle track (generally paralleled by a fence) past Calf Craig and on to a track intersection. Continue northwest up to the flat summit of **Ben Ever** (622m), 30 minutes from the gate. The wonderful view takes in the serpentine meanderings of the River Forth, as well as Ben Lomond, the Trossachs and Ben Ledi.

Drop down northeast to a saddle, cross a stile and start the stiff ascent northeast, with the fence on your left, up to the survey pillar on the summit of **Ben Cleuch** (721m),

THE STABLES

This handsome building was completed at the beginning of the 19th century for the owners of the surrounding Alva Estate. It housed 17 horses and incorporated coach houses and housing for grooms, a coachman, butler and gamekeeper. Though Alva House was demolished more than 50 years ago, the stables survived and have been beautifully restored. After an interlude as Farriers Hotel, the building is now a private residence.

40 minutes from Ben Ever. An excellent direction plate helps to identify Arran on the southwestern horizon, North Berwick Law far to the east and, on especially clear days, Ben Nevis to the north.

Set out downhill (southeast) with the fence. At a junction turn right (south) and follow it over the Law (638m). Then comes a steep descent on a rough path that becomes – or seems to become – nearly vertical on the nose of the spur, towards the confluence of Gannel Burn to the east and Daiglen Burn to the west. Near the end, scramble down small crags to a footbridge across Gannel Burn. Go up to the right briefly then turn right again and go down to cross the Mill Glen burn on another footbridge. The narrow path sneaks through **Mill Glen** well above the burn. Ignore a junction on the right and continue down; go through gates, past a quarry and on down to the car park from where the walk started (two hours from Ben Cleuch).

MORE WALKS

ISLE OF ARRAN

Glen Rosa to Lochranza

The extremely rugged ridge on the western side of Glen Rosa, and its extension from Cir Mhòr via Caisteal Abhail towards the north coast, offers as fine a ridge walk as you'll find anywhere in Scotland. Although it looks impossible from below, there are miraculous ways around those crags and peaks, which only experienced rock climbers can traverse. The views all along are tremendous, especially to the west. The 11-mile (18km) walk includes 1360m of climbing, much of which is precipitous and rocky; allow at least seven hours. The recommended map is Harvey's 1:40,000 *Arran*, which includes coverage of this walk at 1:25,000. See p102 for transport details from Lochranza.

ISLE OF JURA

Paps of Jura

Jura is a magnificently lonely island, the wildness of its uplands only matched on the Isle of Rum and on Harris in the Western Isles. Fewer than 200 people live here, mostly in the southern corner; the rest of the island is uninhabited and unspoiled.

In Craighouse you'll find the excellent **Jura Hotel** (☎ 01496 820243). To reach Jura catch the **CalMac** (☎ 08705 650000; www.calmac.co.uk) ferry from Kennacraig to Port Askaig on the Isle of Islay then the small **Argyll & Bute Council** (☎ 01631 562125) boat to Feolin. From there a bus goes to Craighouse and north to Inverlussa (twice daily, Monday to Saturday).

The OS Landranger 1:50,000 map No 61 is the one to have. The Scottish Mountaineering Club's *The Islands of Scotland including Skye* by DJ Fabian, GE Little and DN Williams covers the mountains with a short section on path walks. Much of the island is managed for deer stalking, so the best time for a visit is early May to early July. For more information about Jura, visit www.isle-of-islay.com.

The three conical Paps of Jura – Beinn a' Chaolais (734m), Beinn an Oir (784m) and Beinn Shiantaich (755m) – dominate the island. A circuit of their summits provides a fairly energetic and outstandingly scenic day; the distance is 11.6 miles (18.5km), with about 1500m of ascent. Allow eight hours – the going is generally rough. A convenient place to start is by the bridge over the Corran River, about 3 miles (5km) north of Craighouse.

ISLE OF ISLAY

Although separated from Jura by the narrow Sound of Islay, this island is remarkably different. Together, Jura and Islay can provide an extremely varied two-island walking holiday.

Larger and more settled, although much less rugged, Islay (pronounced 'i-lay') has opportunities for plenty of easy and medium walks, plus some more demanding ones. The west coast has fine beaches, especially Machir and Lossit Bays, and there are numerous historic and prehistoric sites to visit, notably Finlaggan, the ancient seat of the Lords of the Isles. The highest peak, Beinn Bheigeir (491m), can be climbed from near the hamlet of Ardtalla. In the far south is the Oa, a bumpy area with some fine sea cliffs; a short walk leads to the American Monument. One longer walk on the east coast follows an old track to the deserted settlement of Proaig, then crosses the mountains above the Sound of Jura to Storakaig and a minor road to Ballygrant.

For further information contact the **Bowmore TIC** (☎ 08707 200617; info@islay.visitscotland.com); the local website www.isle-of-islay.com is another useful resource. A locally produced walks booklet describes a dozen varied walks. OS Landranger 1:50,000 map No 60 is the one to take. For details of ferry services see the Isle of Jura section on p117; the ferry also calls at Port Ellen.

ISLE OF BUTE

West Island Way

This 'long-distance' path – the first on a Scottish island – encompasses some of the best walking the Isle of Bute has to offer. As well as a changing landscape, including coast, moors, farmland and forest, the Way showcases the island's natural attractions, geography, geology and history. It is 30 miles (50km) long, the walking is easy and it can be split into two comfortable days. The Way is signposted and navigation is straightforward, using a brochure with map available locally. For more information contact the **Rothesay TIC** (☎ 08707 200619); check the **Isle of Bute Discovery Centre** (www.visitbute.com) website for more local background.

KINTYRE PENINSULA

Kintyre Way

At the time of research, this was Scotland's newest long-distance path. Opened in 2006, the **Kintyre Way** (www.kintyreway.com) winds its way for 88 miles (143km) through the long, slender Kintyre peninsula, which reaches out to the Atlantic Ocean immediately west of the Isle of Arran. The fully waymarked way follows paths, tracks and various minor roads through low hills and forests and beside beaches, from the large village of Tarbert to Southend on the peninsula's south coast. Accommodation is available throughout the five to seven days of the walk. The website is the only point of contact and includes a good description of the route, with accompanying maps, an accommodation list and up-to-date news about the Way.

AROUND LOCH TAY & BEYOND

Rob Roy Way

This imaginative long-distance route links Drymen and Pitlochry via Aberfoyle, Callander, Lochearnhead, Killin, Loch Tay and Aberfeldy. The 79-mile (126km) Way follows forest and moorland tracks, paths and some minor roads, through some of the finest mountain and glen scenery in central Scotland. It can be crammed into five days or taken at a more leisurely pace across seven or eight. Accommodation is readily available; Drymen and Pitlochry are well served by public transport. The superb guide, *The Rob Roy Way*, by Jacquetta Megarry, who was closely involved in developing the Way, includes a map and detailed description of the route.

Cateran Trail

This is a scenic, circular walk of 64 miles (103km) based around the town of Blairgowrie, at the foot of the southernmost Cairngorms, and reaching into the hills as far north as Spittal of Glenshee. The route commemorates the caterans, the fighting men of Highland clans (who specialised in cattle stealing), and irregular soldiers and marauders who were active during the 15th and 16th centuries generally. The mostly low-level, waymarked route passes through countryside that has been farmed for centuries, woodlands and moorland, along tracks, paths and forest or minor roads. It can easily be completed in five days, making use of accommodation in the villages and small towns along the way. *The Cateran Trail* by Jacquetta Megarry, in handy spiral-bound format, is a beautifully illustrated guide with all the information you'll need for the walk, including a drop-down route map. Contact **Blairgowrie TIC** (☎ 01250 872960; blairgowrietic@visitscotland.com) for more information about the trail.

FIFE

Fife Coastal Path

Although Fife isn't a major walking area, it does have a scenic and varied coastline, much of it accessible along long-established paths. **Fife Coastal Path** (FCP; www.fifecoastalpath.co.uk) incorporates these paths in a fully waymarked route linking North Queensferry on the Firth of Forth (across the water from Edinburgh) in the south with Tay Bridge on the Firth of Tay in the north, a distance of 81 miles (135km).

Fife's coastal landscape bears the imprints of its industrial and maritime heritage, and one or two stretches of the FCP are better seen from the window of a bus. However, the pluses easily outweigh the minuses – the constantly changing vistas across the Firth of Forth and along the subtly indented coast, and the fascinating fishing villages of Elie, Pittenweem and Crail on the east coast. Bird life is plentiful, common seals bask on rocks and the route passes through many fine woodlands.

With the most walker-friendly section in the northeast, North Queensferry is the place to start, saving the best until last; allow at least five days to go the full distance. The FCP website has plenty of useful information, detailed maps and contacts for the five TICs that can help with accommodation bookings. *Along the Fife Coastal Path* by Hamish Brown, both a local and one of Scotland's best-known walkers, will be an excellent companion. OS Landranger 1:50,000 map Nos 59, 65 and 66 cover the walk.

Lochaber & Glen Coe

The name Lochaber may not send out a particularly positive signal but if you link it to Glen Coe, it should soon become obvious that we're looking at some of the most spectacular mountain scenery and many of the finest walks in the country. The heartland of this area lies in Glen Coe and in Glen Nevis just next door, with the less known but little less impressive areas of Ardgour, Morvern and Moidart to the west across Loch Linnhe. As Britain's highest mountain, Ben Nevis is the biggest drawcard in more ways than one, and the curvaceous Mamores range dangles an irresistible temptation in the multiple-Munro Ring of Steall walk. At much lower levels, the historic Road to the Isles walk, following an ancient route used by cattle drovers, crosses some of the remotest country in the region. In Glen Coe the magnificent Bidean nam Bian massif and Buachaille Etive Mór, the spectacular guardian of the glen's eastern entrance, both provide memorable days out on their rugged ridges, though for a truly unforgettable experience, the fearsome Aonach Eagach ridge is without peer. Striking a gentler note, the Glen Coe & Glen Etive Circuit displays impressive evidence of the glen's icy geological history. The northern half of the West Highland Way, Scotland's most popular long-distance walk, finishes in fine style in Lochaber; you'll find a full description on p89. We're sure you'll agree that there are many more reasons than just Ben Nevis for Lochaber to be on your must-visit list.

HIGHLIGHTS

- Summiting **Ben Nevis** (p126), Britain's highest mountain
- Getting the adrenaline pumping on the exposed scramble along the **Aonach Eagach** (p139) ridge
- Exploring the hidden beauty of Nevis gorge and Steall Meadows on the **Ring of Steall** (p128) and **The Road to the Isles** (p129) walks
- Stealing through tragic Lost Valley on the way to the lofty ridge of **Bidean nam Bian** (p136)

- www.visithighlands.co.uk
- www.outdoorcapital.co.uk

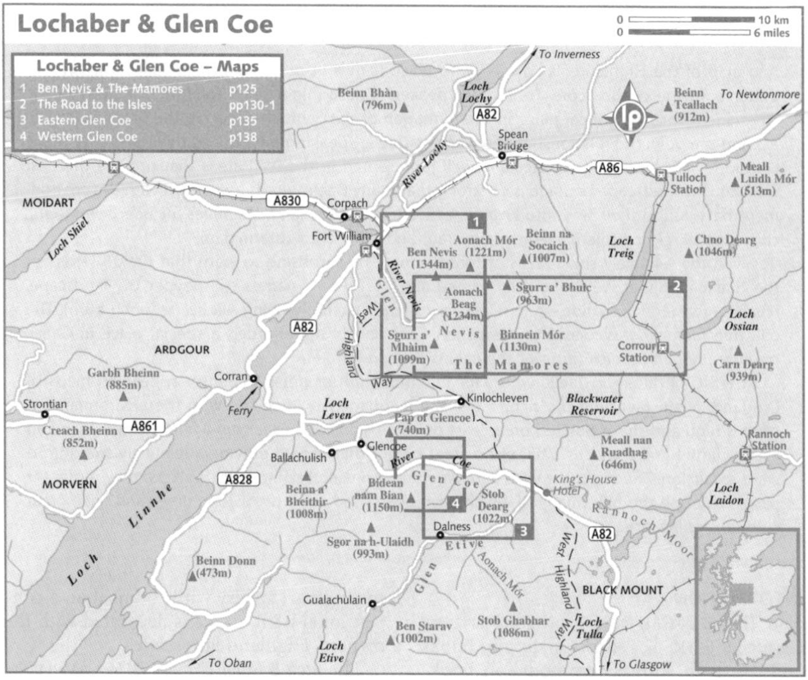

CLIMATE

The Lochaber and Glen Coe region is one of the wettest areas in Scotland, with an average rainfall of 200cm in Fort William, increasing to more than 400cm on the summit of Ben Nevis. Lower, the proximity of the sea makes for a milder climate but conditions become increasingly severe with altitude; high winds and low cloud are common on the summits. Some years, patches of snow survive in sheltered corries on the region's higher peaks until late summer. The steepness of the glens can cause frequent temperature inversions, when the valley floors are bitten by hard frosts or shrouded in fog.

December and January are the wettest months, though rainfall during August (usually the busiest month) can match that in February. May is the driest and July the warmest month, when the low-level daily maximum averages 16°C.

INFORMATION

Maps & Books

OS Travel – Road 1:250,000 map No 3 *Western Scotland* provides an overview of the region. *Walks Fort William* by John and Tricia Wombell, in the excellent Hallewell series, describes 26 walks in the area. Nick Williams' *Central Highlands* Pocket guide covers the Glen Coe area, among others.

Information Sources

Outdoor Capital (www.outdoorcapital.co.uk) is an immensely rich lode of information about a huge range of outdoor activities.

For all public-transport timetable information, consult **Traveline Scotland** (☎ 0870 608 2608; www.travelinescotland.com).

GATEWAY

Fort William

☎ 01397 / 9910

Fort William, near the head of Loch Linnhe and famously in the shadow of Ben Nevis, was established as a garrison for the king's troops during the 17th century. These days it promotes itself, with considerable justification, as Scotland's Outdoor Capital, and is an unrivalled destination for walkers, climbers and all sorts of outdoor-sports enthusiasts.

HILLWALKERS & SCOTLAND'S GAELIC HERITAGE *Roddy Maclean*

Any map of the Highlands is covered with place names in or derived from Gaelic, the original Celtic language of the Scots. To English speakers, Gaelic might seem foreign, but study of the language reveals its critical place in the formation of the Scottish nation in the first millennium AD and the powerful relationship between the Gaelic-speaking people and their land over many centuries. This heritage is particularly well represented in the wild areas that provide the best walking. The landscape heritage is so strong that many Gaelic words associated with the environment have found their way into English, as it's used in Scotland. Examples include *beinn* (ben), *coire* (corrie), *gleann* (glen), *creag* (craig, crag) and *tármachan* (ptarmigan).

Given the relatively small areas of forest, it may be surprising to learn that the 18 letters of the Gaelic alphabet were originally named after trees. Tree names still pepper the landscape, recalling former woodlands – one relatively common example being *Allt Beithe* (birch burn). The oak tree *(darach)* was sacred to the pagan Celts and is still afforded a special place in Gaelic tradition; *Allt an Daraich* (burn of the oak) is in Torridon.

At least 42 different Gaelic words for hill, mountain or upland country appear on maps of Scotland, again revealing the richness of the language's relationship with the environment. A *sgúrr* is high and sharp-pointed on at least one side, a *meall* is usually much less shapely (and an easier climb!) and a *cnoc* is a hill of no great height that should provide a relatively straightforward excursion. The words *bealach* and *láirig* are also useful pointers for walkers; they represent passes through the hills, many of which have been used since prehistoric times and have great cultural significance.

INFORMATION

The **TIC** (☎ 703781; fortwilliam@visithighlands.com; Cameron Sq, High St; 💻) stocks maps and books and can help with accommodation bookings. Pick up a copy of Highland Council's *Public Transport Timetable – Lochaber*.

SUPPLIES & EQUIPMENT

Among the clutch of outdoor gear shops in town, the easiest to find is **Nevisport** (☎ 70493; www.nevisport.co.uk; Airds Crossing; 🕓 daily), a short stroll from the train and bus stations. Its **café-bar** (snacks to £6, mains to £13; 🕓 lunch & dinner) offers standard dishes and makes a feature of big steaks; not surprisingly, the atmosphere is very relaxed and congenial.

Morrisons supermarket is next to the train and bus station.

SLEEPING & EATING

The nearest camping ground is in Glen Nevis (p124).

Calluna (☎ 700451; www.fortwilliamholiday.co.uk; Heathercroft; r per person £15) is run by a highly experienced mountain guide and his wife. They offer comfortable accommodation in modern, semi-detached, self-contained apartments, available for short stays or week-long bookings.

Lime Tree Studio (☎ 701806; www.limetreestudio.co.uk; Achintore Rd; s/d £40/70) is, refreshingly, more an art gallery with rooms than a conventional B&B, its walls decorated with the owners' Highland landscapes.

The **Grog & Gruel** (☎ 705078; 66 High St; mains £10-15; 🕓 lunch Mon-Sat, dinner daily) claims to offer the best range of Scottish real ales anywhere, including the wonderful ales from nearby Atlas Brewery in Kinlochleven. Match this with a pizza in the Alehouse, or steaks and seafood in the traditional pub-style restaurant.

Crannog Seafood Restaurant (☎ 705589; Town Pier; mains £13-19; 🕓 lunch & dinner), with an uninterrupted view over Loch Linnhe, is a great place to go for a celebration seafood feast. The marine menu includes local mussels and langoustines.

GETTING THERE & AWAY

Fort William, on the A82, is 146 miles from Edinburgh, 104 miles from Glasgow and 66 miles from Inverness.

First ScotRail (☎ 0845 755 0033; www.firstscotrail.com) operates the *Caledonian Sleeper* from London to Fort William (seat/sleeper £75/115, 13 hours, daily Sunday to Friday), and the service from Glasgow (£24, 3¾ hours, three service Monday to Saturday, two Sunday). From Edinburgh (£35, five hours, three services Monday to Saturday, two Sunday), change at Glasgow Queen St.

Scottish Citylink (☎ 0870 550 5050; www.citylink.co.uk) provides bus services from Glasgow (£15, three hours, three daily), Edinburgh (£21, four hours, three daily), Inverness (£10, two hours, five services Monday to Saturday, two Sunday) and Portree on the Isle of Skye (£18, three hours, three daily).

BEN NEVIS VIA THE MOUNTAIN TRACK

Duration	6–8 hours
Distance	9 miles (14.5km)
Difficulty	moderate–demanding
Start/Finish	Ionad Nibheis Visitor Centre
Nearest Towns	Fort William (p121), Glen Nevis (p124)
Transport	bus

Summary A great feeling of camaraderie pervades the most famous climb in Britain, which is steep and unrelenting but worth every step for the finest bird's-eye view around.

Ben Nevis (1344m) is the highest mountain in Britain and attracts hordes of walkers and climbers. Like the highest peak in many countries, the Ben tempts visitors with barely any walking experience to have a go, and many discover they have taken on more than they expected. For reasons many and various, there are several mountain rescue call-outs on Ben Nevis each year.

The mountain is a compelling and alluring presence above Fort William, often capped in cloud and presenting a rugged profile from any and every viewpoint. The ascent is bound to be one of the more memorable events in any walker's career, so it's worth allowing a few days in which to stage your climb, to allow for the vagaries of the weather.

The climb starts almost at sea level and continues relentlessly all the way to the summit. The main route follows the Mountain Track, along the old bridle path. It's very well maintained as far as the junction near Halfway Lochan, from where it's rougher, crossing steep, rocky slopes. Conditions on the top can be extreme – mist envelops everything like a thick blanket, and strong winds gust and eddy about, making normal walking difficult. What's more, navigating safely past the deep, sheer-sided gullies that cut into the summit plateau very close to the path is notoriously dangerous in poor visibility.

There are other walking, or at least non-climbing, routes up the Ben, of which the Carn Mór Dearg Arête (see the boxed text on p127), on its northern flanks, offers a certain amount of excitement along its slender spine, without being beyond the reach of anyone with some experience of scrambling and a reliable head for heights.

HISTORY

The Gaelic name Nibheis can be traced back to words meaning 'dread' and 'terrible'. The mountain first appeared on a map in 1654 with the name Bion Novesh, and by the early 1700s ascents were mentioned in literary records.

Much later, scientists in the Scottish Meteorological Society began to take an interest in the mountain. During the summers of 1881 and 1882, a member of the society, Clement Wragge (soon nicknamed 'the inclement rag'), climbed to the summit every day to take weather measurements. In 1883 a summit observatory was built, and was maintained until it closed in 1904. A bridle path, the origins of today's Mountain Track, was forged up the mountainside to supply the observatory, and a small hotel, little more than an annexe, materialised.

BEN NEVIS – AN EXTREME CLIMATE

As you might expect, the weather on Britain's highest mountain can be the most extreme in the country. The temperature on the summit is typically 9°C colder than at the base of the mountain, and this figure does not allow for wind chill. An average of 261 gales per year rip across the summit and wind speeds well in excess of 100mph have often been recorded. Even if skies are clear when you set out, don't be lulled into complacency, as the weather can turn arctic at any time. The mean annual summit temperature is below 0°C and snow often lies on the mountain until early summer – the summit is only a couple of hundred feet below what would be the permanent snow line. If the views are superb, the chances of seeing them are not – the summit, on average, is cloud-covered six days out of seven.

Two local women provided B&B at the hotel for 10 shillings (50p) a head until it closed in 1918.

The idea of a race up the mountain was originally intended as a distraction from the daily routine of life at the observatory. William Swan, a local tobacconist, made the first timed and recorded ascent in October 1895, taking two hours 41 minutes for the return trip from Fort William. The race soon captured public imagination and became an institution, the **Ben Nevis Race** (www.bennevisrace.co.uk). These days, as many as 500 people enter the annual 'Ben Race' on the first Saturday of September. By 2006 the records stood at one hour 25 minutes for men and one hour 43 minutes for women, both set way back in 1984.

The Ben Nevis Estate was put on the market in 1999, and the John Muir Trust (JMT; p31) snapped up the property for approximately £500,000. The estate extends east into the Grey Corries and west past the upper Glen Nevis gorge. The Trust is a member of the **Nevis Partnership** (www.nevispartnership.co.uk), committed to sustainable environmental and visitor management of the Ben Nevis massif and Glen Nevis, in particular footpath repair projects. Aware that, in many people's eyes, the Ben's summit had become the highest rubbish tip in Britain, the JMT has organised several clean-up days; on one, the remains of a grand piano were found beneath a cairn. It turned out that it had once been carried up the mountain to raise funds for charity. The summit also became a popular place for leaving mementos of people who had come to grief on the mountain (and elsewhere), a practice that proved to be highly controversial, with many walkers and climbers believing that the mountain was being desecrated. In response, the JMT opened a Garden of Remembrance near the visitor centre (in August 2006) where the many and various memorials placed on the summit over the years were brought together.

GETTING DOWN SAFELY

The most hazardous part of the Ben walk is the descent from the summit plateau. Particular care is needed if there is snow on the ground or in poor visibility. To reach the top of the Mountain Track safely, use the following bearings:

From the trig point, walk 150m (count your paces – probably about 200 paces) on a grid bearing of 231 degrees. Then follow a grid bearing of 281 degrees. This should take you safely off the plateau and onto the path. Remember to allow for magnetic variation – this is given on the recommended maps and must be *added* to the grid bearing.

Two useful leaflets, *Ben Nevis Safety Information* and *Navigation on Ben Nevis*, are available from the visitor centre at the start of the walk.

PLANNING

When to Walk

The best month for an ascent is August, by which time the summit plateau is normally free of snow, although it should be safe enough from June until late September.

What to Bring

Carry plenty of warm and waterproof clothing – protection for your head and hands is particularly important – and a copy of the bearings needed to descend safely, as given in the boxed text, left.

Maps & Books

The walk is covered by OS Landranger 1:50,000 map No 41 *Ben Nevis*, OS Explorer 1:25,000 map No 392 *Ben Nevis & Fort William* and two Harvey maps: 1:25,000 Superwalker *Ben Nevis* and 1:12,500 Summit *Ben Nevis*. Local leaflets covering this route include *Ben Nevis – walking the path from June to September*, produced by the ranger service, and *Great Walks No 2* by Fort William and Lochaber Tourism.

Guided Walks

The JMT organises walks in the area; contact the **Nevis Conservation Officer** (☎ 705049) or the Ionad Nibheis Visitor Centre (p126) for details.

NEAREST TOWNS

See Fort William (p121).

Glen Nevis

☎ 01397

The village of Glen Nevis is really a collection of amenities, 2 miles from Fort William. It can be extremely busy in summer.

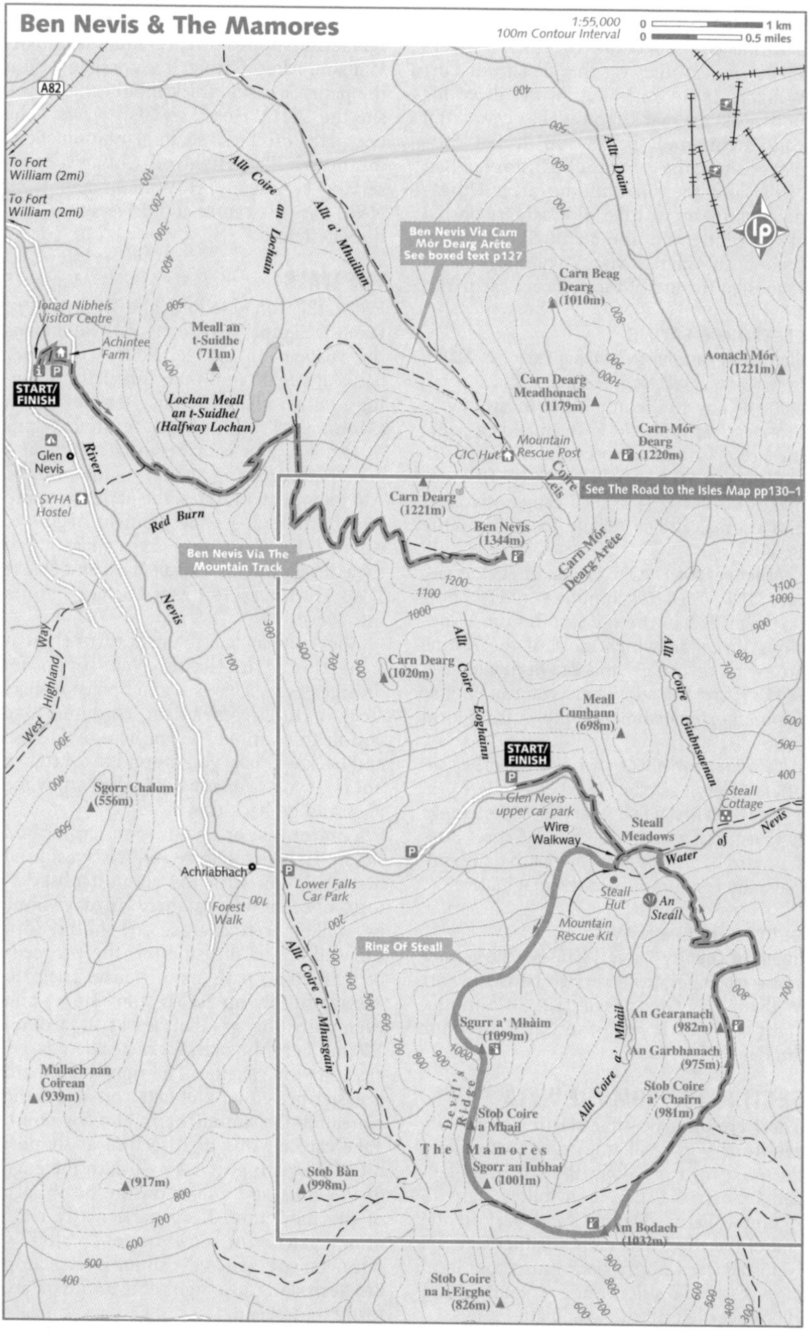
Ben Nevis & The Mamores
1:55,000
100m Contour Interval
0 1 km
0 0.5 miles
A82
To Fort William (2mi)
To Fort William (2mi)
Ionad Nibheis Visitor Centre
Achintee Farm
START/ FINISH
Meall an t-Suidhe (711m)
Lochan Meall an t-Suidhe/ (Halfway Lochan)
Allt Coire an Lochain
Allt a' Mhuilinn
Allt Daim
Ben Nevis Via Carn Mór Dearg Arête See boxed text p127
Carn Beag Dearg (1010m)
Carn Dearg Meadhonach (1179m)
Aonach Mór (1221m)
Carn Mór Dearg (1220m)
Mountain Rescue Post
CIC Hut
Coire Leis
See The Road to the Isles Map pp130–1
Glen Nevis
River
SYHA Hostel
Red Burn
Carn Dearg (1221m)
Ben Nevis (1344m)
Ben Nevis Via The Mountain Track
Carn Mór Dearg Arête
Nevis
West Highland Way
Carn Dearg (1020m)
Allt Coire Eoghainn
Allt Coire Giubhsaenan
Meall Cumhann (698m)
START/ FINISH
Glen Nevis upper car park
Steall Cottage
Wire Walkway
Steall Meadows
Water of Nevis
Sgorr Chalum (556m)
Achriabhach
Lower Falls Car Park
Forest Walk
Steall Hut
An Steall
Mountain Rescue Kit
Ring Of Steall
Allt Coire a' Mhusgain
Sgurr a' Mhàim (1099m)
An Gearanach (982m)
An Garbhanach (975m)
Allt Coire a' Mhàil
Stob Coire a' Chairn (981m)
Devil's Ridge
Stob Coire a Mhail
The Mamores
Sgorr an Iubhai (1001m)
Mullach nan Coirean (939m)
(917m)
Stob Bàn (998m)
Am Bodach (1032m)
Stob Coire na h-Eirghe (826m)

INFORMATION

Ionad Nibheis Visitor Centre (☎ 705922; Easter–mid-Oct) is 1.5 miles up the glen from Fort William. It stocks leaflets with advice for Ben walkers, maps, books, basic walking equipment, trail snacks and drinks. Displays feature the geology and history of Ben Nevis and the surrounding area. Up-to-date mountain weather forecasts are posted at the centre and also at the SYHA hostel (below) in Glen Nevis. A voluntary fee is requested for use of the adjacent car park.

SLEEPING & EATING

Glen Nevis Caravan & Camping Park (☎ 702191; www.glennevis.co.uk; unpowered/powered sites for two £10/12.50) has an incomparable location and top-class facilities, so is swamped in summer; reservations are recommended.

Glen Nevis SYHA Hostel (☎ 0870 004 1120; www.syha.org.uk; dm £14;) has a range of rooms and dorms, and is ideally located for the Ben.

Achintee Farm (☎ 702240; www.achinteefarm.com; dm/d £11/13, B&B d £60) combines a very comfortable B&B in the old farmhouse, a spacious hostel in which most of the rooms are twins or triples, and **Ben Nevis Inn** (mains £8-14; lunch & dinner), where you can choose from an extensive menu emphasising local products.

Cafe Beag (☎ 703601; mains £6; lunch & dinner) offers pretty basic but inexpensive fare.

Glen Nevis Restaurant & Bar (☎ 705459; bar mains £9-15, restaurant mains £10-18; lunch & dinner) does standard bar meals, leavened with daily specials; the restaurant is more imaginative.

GETTING THERE & AWAY

Highland Country Buses (☎ 01463 710555; www.rapsons.com) operates a service between Fort William and Glen Nevis (£2, 20 minutes, eight services Monday to Saturday, four Sunday).

GETTING TO/FROM THE WALK

There are three possible starting points. By car from Fort William, head north along the A82; turn off along the road to Claggan Industrial Estate then follow signs to Achintee Farm. There's a car park at the end of the road. The daily weather forecast is posted on a notice board next to a local map. Climb a stile beside a gate; within 100m bear left up the wide path.

In Glen Nevis, you can park at Ionad Nibheis Visitor Centre, 1.5 miles from Fort William. Alternatively, it is possible to join the path via a side track that begins opposite the SYHA Hostel in Glen Nevis – the two paths meet at a small plantation above the hostel. The Highland Country Buses service between Fort William and Glen Nevis pass the centre and drivers may stop if requested.

THE WALK

Map p125

From the Ionad Nibheis Visitor Centre take the signed 'Ben Nevis Path' and cross the suspension bridge. Follow the river bank upstream and then turn left, following a stone wall to reach the Ben Nevis Path (Mountain Track), where the climb begins in earnest. You gain height steadily on a good path, crossing a couple of footbridges. After about 40 minutes, the path turns into Red Burn glen. As the gradient begins to ease a little, the path zigzags sharply and then levels out as **Lochan Meall an t-Suidhe** (also known as Halfway Lochan) comes into view.

Above the lochan the path turns right at a junction – the Classic Walk (opposite) diverges here. This is a good place to take stock. Is the weather fit to continue? Are you fit to continue? From here to the top and back will take you around three to five hours. If you're in any doubt, just enjoy the view and go back down.

Continuing on, you soon cross Red Burn. Halfway House, which was used in association with the summit observatory, once stood near here. In days gone by, walkers were charged one shilling (5p) for walking to the summit, the proceeds being used for path maintenance. The path zigzags steeply up across stony slopes and eventually the gradient eases at around 1200m; here the path forks beside a large, circular stone shelter. The right-hand path is easier but either will take you across the plateau to the summit cairn and trig point. Take care on this final section as the last bit of the path goes very close to the edge of the cliffs and gullies on the north face of the mountain. Keep particularly clear of any patches of snow. In poor visibility, once you've reached the summit cairn atop **Ben Nevis** don't lose sight of it until you are ready to descend.

CLASSIC WALK – CARN MÓR DEARG ARÊTE

The connoisseur's route up Ben Nevis is via Carn Mór Dearg Arête, a tough walk involving a thrilling rock ridge; the views throughout are superb. Allow eight to nine hours for the very demanding 9.5-mile (15km) walk, involving 1660m ascent. It starts and finishes at the Ionad Nibheis Visitor Centre (opposite) in Glen Nevis and makes a horseshoe circuit of the Ben Nevis massif, approaching from the satellite peak of Carn Mór Dearg to the northeast. The two peaks are linked by a wonderful narrow rock-ridge, Carn Mór Dearg Arête, the traverse of which provides the highlight of the day.

The walk is covered by OS Explorer 1:25,000 map No 392 *Ben Nevis* and Harvey's 1:12,500 Summit map *Ben Nevis* and its Superwalker 1:25,000 *Glen Coe*.

Follow the Ben Nevis via the Mountain Track description (p123) to Lochan Meall an t-Suidhe. From a junction above the lochan, follow a well-made path leading north. Several minutes along, turn right onto a narrower path, which is rougher than the virtual highway you've been following so far and has a few potentially boggy spots. It contours the steep slope below the Ben's western cliffs then swings round into the long, deep glen carved by Allt a' Mhuilinn and leads to the CIC Hut at the head of the glen, marked out by a small wind pump. You could walk right up to the hut but it's quicker to drop down to the stream and climb the slopes of Carn Beag Dearg. A well-marked path traverses below its summit, and leads to the summit of Carn Dearg Meadhonach (1179m). Press on over a slight dip to Carn Mór Dearg. From here the ridge narrows and descends slightly to the beginning of the Carn Mór Dearg Arête. The drop to either side of the fairly easy scramble is steep; an easier path, mostly on the left, avoids some of the exposure. Beyond a subsidiary top, the ridge rises to meet the eastern flanks of Ben Nevis. A worn path then zigzags for 300m up the steep, rocky slope to the rounded summit plateau. Make sure you have a note of the bearings needed to descend safely from Ben Nevis (see the boxed text on p124) then descend along the Mountain Track (p123).

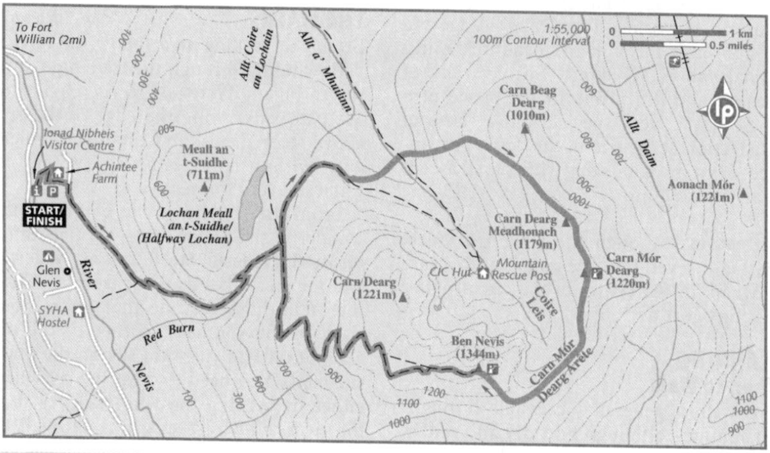

The summit isn't perhaps the most scenic of places, containing the remains of the substantial walls of the observatory, several cairns and the trig point amid the boulder-strewn moonscape. But the views are exceptional, with the islands of Mull, Rum and Skye to the west, and a myriad of mountain peaks as far as the eye can see.

The return is 'simply' a matter of retracing your steps. Remember to watch out for the dangerous summit gullies that cut into the mountain near the path and, in poor visibility, use the bearings listed in the boxed text on p124 to reach the top of the path. Take care once you're on the path – most accidents occur during the descent.

RING OF STEALL

Duration	7–8 hours
Distance	8.5 miles (13.5km)
Difficulty	moderate–demanding
Start/Finish	Glen Nevis upper car park
Nearest Towns	Fort William (p121), Glen Nevis (p124)
Transport	private

Summary A challenging circuit, with a knife-edged ridge, which increases your Munros 'bag' by four and provides views of mountains galore.

The Mamores is a shapely mountain range in an incredible location, though easily overlooked in favour of Ben Nevis and the more famous peaks of Glen Coe, especially if you're not in hot pursuit of all the Munros in the area. The name almost certainly comes directly from the Gaelic *mám mór* meaning big, breast-shaped hills – as always with Gaelic names, a concise and apt description.

The route described is the best circuit the Mamores has to offer, featuring several Munros, a crossing of the Devil's Ridge and an approach through the beautiful, mini-Himalayan Nevis gorge. Such variety of scenery and situations in the space of a single day is very special, and a sense of satisfaction at the end of the day is guaranteed. It's a strenuous day with a total ascent of around 1500m.

Alternatives Although the terrain is steep, there are several escape routes into Coire a' Mhàil, in the centre of the circuit, after passing Sgorr an Iubhai.

PLANNING

When to Walk

This walk is generally accessible throughout summer, although fine, dry and settled weather is pretty well essential. The path through the Water of Nevis gorge crosses rocky ground and can be treacherous when icy, though this is unlikely during summer.

If the Water of Nevis is in spate, which is possible at any time, you'll have no choice but to cross on a wire walkway consisting of two thick strands of wire with small footplates and shoulder-high 'hand rails', for which balance and sure-footedness are more important than a head for heights.

High winds will make the crossing of Devil's Ridge dangerous.

Maps

The walk is covered by OS Explorer 1:25,000 map No 392 *Ben Nevis* and Harvey's Superwalker 1:25,000 map *Glen Coe*.

GETTING TO/FROM THE WALK

A **Highland Country Buses** (☎ 01463 710555; www.rapsons.com) seasonal service from Fort William goes up to the Glen Nevis Lower Falls car park (£2.50, 15 minutes, eight services Monday to Saturday, three Sunday), 1.5 miles (2.5km) downhill from the upper car park at the start and finish of this walk.

If you don't make the last bus, you'll have to walk either 4 miles to Glen Nevis village or 6 miles to Fort William. There's a track through the forest starting at Achriabhach, about 250m west of where the road crosses to the other side of the river. Alternatively, you can leave the road in places to follow the river bank along informal paths.

THE WALK

Map p125

From the parking area follow the obvious path winding through the trees high above the turbulent Water of Nevis. Higher up, the path runs along the edge of the river above steep drops, and the huge boulders and swirling rock features carved by the water are very impressive.

From the far end of the gorge, another wonderful sight opens up – the flat plateau of **Steall Meadows**. Steall means 'waterfall' and the area takes its name from An Steall, the 100m-high cascade that pours down slabs in the southeast corner of the plateau. Steall Hut (private) sits on the opposite bank. You need to cross the river here, either by braving the wire walkway or, if the river is low, by splashing through the shallows slightly upstream. From Steall Hut head west through long grass, soon skirting a thicket of trees. Gain the northeast shoulder of Sgurr a' Mhàim and veer to the south, climbing between craggy outcrops on the ridge. You will soon pick up a path that leads up the shoulder to a scree-filled corrie, where a well-worn path leads onto the northwest ridge and the summit of **Sgurr a' Mhàim** (1099m), 3½ to four hours from the

THE WEST HIGHLAND RAILWAY

The West Highland Railway runs between Glasgow, Fort William and Mallaig, passing through some of Scotland's most wild and spectacular mountain scenery. Stations such as Arrochar & Tarbet, Crianlarich, Bridge of Orchy and Spean Bridge allow you to set off on a seemingly endless range of wonderful mountain walks direct from the platform. There are several opportunities for circular walks, or you can get off at one station, have a good walk, then catch the train from another station up or down the line.

Possibly the most intriguing place to get off is at Corrour, which, at 408m above sea level and 11 miles from the nearest road, is the highest and most remote station in Britain. From Corrour there are plenty of peaks to climb and remote valleys to explore, including the Road to Isles (below) walk described here.

Work on the line began in 1889 and 5000 men were employed to build it, laying foundations of brushwood and earth across miles of bog to support the tracks. It's a tribute to the railway's Victorian engineers that the line is still used.

Beyond Fort William the train runs through the rugged country around Glenfinnan and on to Mallaig, from where it's a short ferry ride to the Isle of Skye.

start. The view across to Ben Nevis is hard to beat and, ahead, the horseshoe of peaks you are about to cross should be visible.

From Sgurr a' Mhàim the path drops down to a saddle, and meets the fearsomely named **Devil's Ridge**. The ridge is very narrow and airy in places, with considerable exposure, but easily negotiable by using your hands here and there. It leads up to Stob Coire a' Mhàil, where the ridge broadens. Drop down to a saddle and then climb once again to reach the flat summit of **Sgorr an Iubhai** (1001m); the Gaelic name means 'peak of the yew tree', which grows wild in the area.

From Sgorr an Iubhai descend to a col, ignoring a path that contours around Am Bodach's northwestern slopes, and climb the rocky slope to the **Am Bodach** (1032m) summit. There are fine views to the south over Loch Leven, and most of the Mamores should be visible. A steep path now heads down the northeast ridge, weaving its way between boulders and stones. The path is well worn for the rest of the route. Cross Stob Coire a' Chairn (where the main spine of the Mamores range heads east), descend slightly then climb steeply, possibly using your hands in places, to **An Garbhanach** (975m). Between here and An Gearanach, the last summit, the ridge narrows briefly to a knife-edge; from **An Gearanach** (982m) follow the path steeply down to Steall Meadows.

At the bottom, swing round to the west, clambering over rocks and tree roots to avoid the many wet, boggy sections of the path. The lower reaches of this path are badly eroded and some parts have been swept away by small landslips. Take great care here, but once past the tumbling cascade of An Steall, any difficulties are behind you. Recross the Water of Nevis and follow the path back to the Glen Nevis upper car park.

THE ROAD TO THE ISLES

Duration	6–8 hours
Distance	14.5 miles (23km)
Difficulty	moderate
Start	Corrour (p130)
Finish	Glen Nevis upper car park
Nearest Towns	Glen Nevis (p124), Fort William (p121)
Transport	train, bus

Summary A long and remote low-level walk following a historic route from the wild expanses of Rannoch Moor to spectacular Nevis gorge.

The Road to the Isles means, to most people, the 46-mile route following roads westward from Fort William to the fishing port of Mallaig on the west coast. For walkers it means something a little more adventurous – the eastern section of this ancient route through the western Highlands, linking central Scotland to the Isle of Skye via Fort William. It was much used by cattle drovers heading for the cattle trysts (fairs) at Crieff and Falkirk. Armies, their quarries and refugees have also marched and fled along the route.

The Road To The Isles

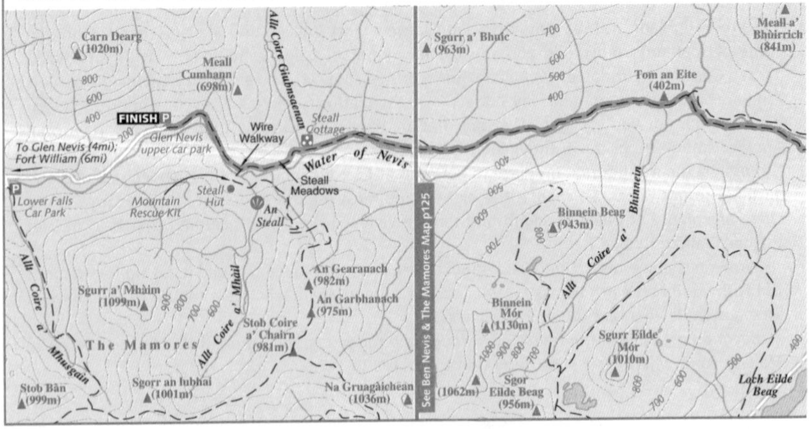

The walk starts at Corrour station, 11 miles from the nearest public road, in the heart of Rannoch Moor. The route then follows a right of way to Glen Nevis, past the southern shores of Loch Treig, across wide, grassy, treeless moorland backed by comparatively low 'hills'. Once you cross the watershed, the scenery becomes much more dramatic, as the lightly wooded glen narrows right down to a small gorge, the spiky Mamores ridge soaring steeply to the south, and mighty Ben Nevis and the rugged Grey Corries towering above to the north. Simple bothies at Staoineag and Meanach can provide shelter, temporarily or overnight, if you bring all the necessary equipment. Both are open and free to walkers year-round.

Although the route can be done in either direction, there's more downhill and the views are better in the direction described.

PLANNING

When to Walk/Stalking

This route passes through Corrour and Grey Corries-Mamore Estates, where stalking usually takes place between mid-August and the end of October. Nevertheless, you're free to follow the right of way at any time.

Maps

The route is covered by OS Explorer 1:25,000 maps No 392 *Ben Nevis & Fort William* and No 385 *Rannoch Moor & Ben Alder*, and OS Landranger 1:50,000 map No 41 *Ben Nevis.*

NEAREST TOWNS

See Glen Nevis (p124) and Fort William (p121).

Corrour

Corrour begins and ends at the train station, a surprisingly busy place when trains arrive and depart, being popular with walkers, hostellers and train spotters keen to watch a steam train that passes through during summer.

SLEEPING & EATING

Corrour Station House B&B & Restaurant (☎ 01397 732236; www.corrour.co.uk; s/d £26/52, breakfast £3, mains £8-15; 🕐 breakfast, lunch & dinner) is a friendly, relaxed place offering pleasantly unfussed accommodation, and satisfying meals in the former station waiting room. It hopes to reopen the refurbished bunkhouse in 2007.

Loch Ossian SYHA Hostel (☎ 0870 004 1139; www.syha.org.uk; dm £13) is 1 mile east of Corrour station. As an eco-hostel, it has many environmentally friendly features. Bring your own sleeping bag and supplies.

GETTING THERE & AWAY

First ScotRail (☎ 0845 755 0033; www.firstscotrail.com) trains from Glasgow (£17, three hours) and Fort William (£6, 50 minutes) stop at Corrour. There are four trains Monday to Saturday, and two Sunday. First ScotRail's *Caledonian Sleeper* service from London stops here on request (seat/sleeper £80/130, 11½ hours, daily service Sunday to Friday).

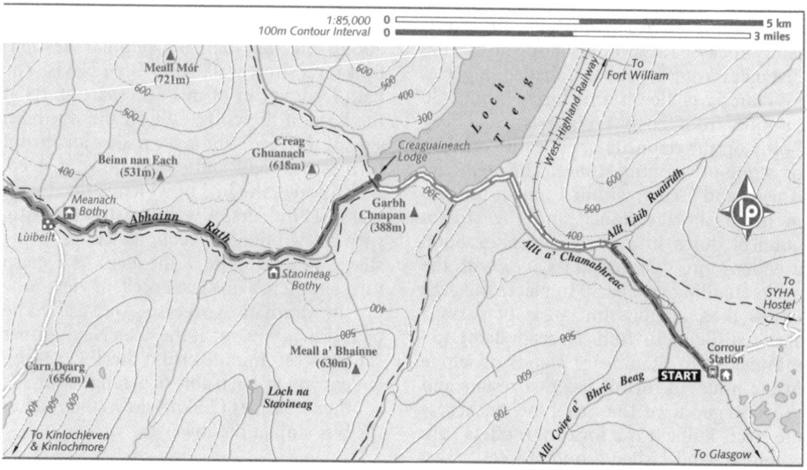

The platform at Corrour is so small that only one door of the train can be opened to let passengers off; the conductor will tell you where best to sit.

GETTING TO/FROM THE WALK

For transport information from the finish, see p128.

THE WALK

From Corrour station on a clear day you can actually see Ben Nevis and its satellites. Cross to the western side of the railway line and follow the track leading northwest, signposted to Fort William (and other destinations). Old railway sleepers help to keep your feet dry across some soft spots and several small burns.

About 20 minutes out, cross a substantial bridge over Allt Lùib Ruairidh and join a wide, firm vehicle track linking Loch Ossian and Loch Treig. Soon the track descends steeply to the shores of **Loch Treig.** This is actually an artificial loch, contained by a dam at its northern end. The level of the original loch was raised as part of the hydroelectric power scheme to supply the aluminium smelter at Fort William. Opened in 1929, the scheme also involved a huge, 15-mile-long tunnel through Ben Nevis to the prominent pipes on its western slope carrying water towards the turbines in the smelter's power station. The last thing you'd expect to see out here is a house, but **Creaguaineach Lodge**, at the loch's southwest corner, just survived Treig's enlargement. Before you reach the lodge, you need to decide whether to continue along the northern side of the stream, following the right of way and the wider path, or to stay on the southern bank, chasing a much narrower and rougher path. The latter route avoids having to ford the stream much further west – only a problem if it's in spate.

Choose the northern route and cross the substantial bridge over the burn (1¼ hours

CATTLE DROVING

The Road to the Isles is a famous route used by drovers on their way from the north to Tyndrum, a key stop for the cattle-droving trade during the 18th and 19th centuries. Herds of small black Highland cattle and their drovers – who had usually trekked hundreds of difficult miles to this point, sometimes swimming across tidal narrows to get to the mainland in the first place (as from the Isle of Skye), and then crossing mountain passes and traversing remote glens – passed through Tyndrum on their way to the 'trysts' (cattle markets) at Crieff or Falkirk, northeast of Glasgow.

Cattle often continued on foot with their new owners to cross the border into England, leaving drovers with the long return journey home. The cattle rustling, thieving and celebrations that accompanied the marches are still celebrated today.

from Allt Lùib Ruairidh). The intermittently rocky path wanders along at varying distances from the stream, shaded in places by clumps of beech and birch. About 30 minutes from Loch Treig, pass Staoineag Bothy on the opposite bank, easily reached by a line of stepping stones. The glen here is wide and grassy; within 1 mile it pinches in for a short distance and the stream bounces down in a run of cascades. Soon it widens into vast, flat grasslands with the peaks standing well back. In places the path is less than obvious but signs of passage aren't difficult to find. **Meanach Bothy** (50 minutes from Staoineag) stands all alone in the midst of this; it has two rooms and provides good, weatherproof shelter. Across the river, Lùibeilt is a forlorn, roofless ruin among a wind-lashed group of trees.

A track leads west from the bothy to a stream, where it's possible to hop across; alternatively, continue upstream on a narrow path until you find a suitable ford. If you do cross here, pick up a rather rough track leading northwest. About 1 mile beyond Lùibeilt the track becomes a path and fades. The easiest going is close to the stream. About 40 minutes from Meanach, cross Allt Coire a' Bhinnein and head north along the western side of Allt Coire Rath for a couple of hundred metres to pick up a path leading generally westwards. It cuts across the slope of **Tom an Eite**, an amorphous lump lying above the narrow watershed between the east-flowing Abhainn Rath and the Water of Nevis. The path is generally easy to follow, and heads downstream in a fairly determined fashion. After 1 mile or so there is, theoretically, a choice between an upper level (and drier) path and a lower, more clearly defined one, but the parting of the ways is very obscure. Unless there's been a lot of rain recently, the lower path isn't too bad, and you can easily keep your feet dry.

As you descend towards Glen Nevis, many more fine peaks of the Mamores come into sight and there's a dramatic view of Ben Nevis' northeast profile. Eventually you reach a substantial footbridge over a burn, beside the ruins of Steall Cottage (1¾ hours from Tom an Eite). You'll soon discover the origin of the cottage's name, on the far side of the Water of Nevis: the beautiful **An Steall** waterfall, a skein of long cascades down more than 100m of rock slabs. There are usually plenty of people about, the falls being a popular destination for a short walk from Glen Nevis. The path leading out of this sanctuary starts at the base of the cliffs, still on the northern side of the glen. The river makes an abrupt turn to the right and surges down a steep, rocky gorge, the bed of which is filled with massive boulders. A well-constructed path, with a few bouldery sections, clings to the steep, wooded slope of the glen. At a sharp turn left there's one last excellent view back up the dramatic gorge to An Steall. The path brings you out at the Glen Nevis upper car park (40 minutes from Steall Cottage). Unless you've been able to arrange a lift, it's another 1.5 miles (2.5km) down the road to the bus stop at the lower car park.

GLEN COE

Glen Coe is among the most popular destinations for walkers and climbers in Scotland. It is one of the most dramatic valleys in the country, and most visitors approach Glen Coe from the east, on the A82. From that direction you descend off Rannoch Moor, pass the pyramidal sentinel of Buachaille Etive Mór, and drop into the narrow Pass of Glencoe, a notch between Am Bodach (at the eastern end of Aonach Eagach) and Beinn Fhada. Ahead, the valley floor is pancake-flat and no more than 500m wide. To the north, sweeping up from sea level to more than 900m, the ramparts of the Aonach Eagach ridge are so steep that you must crane your neck to see the top. To the south, the massive, jutting buttresses known as the Three Sisters throw shadows across the valley. Partially hidden behind them are the tantalising peaks of Bidean nam Bian and Stob Coire nan Lochan. The view is one of the most arresting in Scotland – and that's just from the car!

Glen Coe was among the National Trust for Scotland's (NTS) early land acquisitions. In 1935 Aonach Eagach and Signal Rock were purchased, and two years later the mountains on the south side of the valley were donated to the NTS. The estate now covers approximately 14,000 acres. The Trust's mandate is simple: to protect the natural and cultural heritage of the area and to ensure open access for walkers (and climbers).

ENVIRONMENT

The event that makes Glen Coe geologically significant occurred towards the end of a period of volcanic activity 60 million years ago. A circular piece of the earth's surface, roughly 6 miles in diameter, fractured and sank into the hot magma below, a phenomenon known as cauldron subsidence. The discovery of the cauldron at Glen Coe marked an important development in geological knowledge. A small quarry near Clachaig Inn exposes the fault line of the cauldron, which then follows the prominent gully west of Achnambeithach Cottage.

Around 25,000 years ago, Glen Coe was blanketed by ice. The Lost Valley (see p137) between Gearr Aonach and Beinn Fhada is a good example of a hanging valley, formed when a higher glacier is cut off in its downhill journey by a larger glacier in the valley below. The Lairig Gartain and Lairig Eilde valleys (see p136) are classic U-shaped glacial valleys.

PLANNING

Maps & Books

All the walks in Glen Coe are covered by OS Landranger 1:50,000 map No 41 *Ben Nevis*, OS Explorer 1:25,000 map No 384 *Glen Coe* and Harvey's Superwalker 1:25,000 map *Glen Coe*. Chris Townsend's *Ben Nevis & Glen Coe* is a reliable guide by one of the most experienced walkers in Scotland.

Information Sources

A site sponsored by a local inn, www.glencoe-scotland.co.uk, is particularly useful for background information and links to useful sites, including transport and mountain weather forecasts.

ACCESS TOWN

Glencoe

☎ 01855 / 360

Glencoe is a picturesque village at the western end of the Glen Coe valley. Fortunately, most of it is bypassed by the A82, so it remains fairly quiet, away from the heaviest traffic.

INFORMATION

The National Trust for Scotland Visitor Centre (☎ 811307; www.glencoe-nts.org.uk; Mar-Oct), 1 mile east of the village, is in an award-winning eco-building, and houses displays (£5) about conservation issues and local geology. Videos explore the Glen's natural and cultural history, a shop stocks a good range of walking guides and maps (including the NTS's own guide, *Glencoe*), and a **cafeteria** (mains to £3; 10am-5pm) sells packaged sandwiches and the like. The daily weather forecast is prominently displayed. A richly diverse program of guided walks and many other events is staged from the centre; bookings are advisable.

SUPPLIES & EQUIPMENT

Mountain Sports Equipment (A82) stocks outdoor gear and maps. There is a small Spar supermarket in the village.

SLEEPING & EATING

Red Squirrel Campsite (☎ 811256; www.redsquirrelcampsite.com; Leacantium Farm; unpowered sites for two £7), beside the River Coe, offers the rare

SHORT WALK

Part-hidden by tall forest, just north of Glencoe village, **Glencoe Lochan** sits at the foot of the western end of the ridge bounding the northern side of Glen Coe. On fine days its waters display beautiful reflections of the distinctive profile of Sgorr na Ciche, better know as the Pap of Glencoe. Three colour-coded, waymarked walks around the lochan and through the forest, owned and managed by the Forestry Commission, make for a pleasant, easy-going afternoon. The walks start at a car park at the end of a rough track, branching from the minor road at the Bridge of Coe at the eastern end of the village.

Follow markers for the blue route steeply up to a lookout for views of peaks in western Glen Coe, and in Morvern and Ardgour across Loch Linnhe. Soon descend steeply to a junction and turn right to follow the lochan shore. Cross the outlet and a retaining wall to a junction; turn right and go down to the car park. This 1.8-mile (3km) walk should take about 45 minutes. Although a map's scarcely necessary for this stroll, the OS Landranger 1:50,000 No 41 would be useful for orientation from the lookout.

opportunity to sit around the perfect midge repellent – a campfire.

Glencoe SYHA Hostel (☎ 0870 004 1122; www.syha.org.uk; dm £14; 🖳), about 1.5 miles from the village, has largish dorms.

Glencoe Hostel & Bunkhouse (☎ 811906; www.glencoehostel.co.uk; camp sites for 2 £10, dm £10; 🖳), 1¼ miles from the village, offers a variety of hostel-style accommodation and a small camp site. There's also a small on-site shop.

Clachaig Inn (☎ 811252; www.clachaig.com; s/d £38/42; bar meal mains £9-15) is 2.5 miles west of the village. The inn really comes into its own during the evening, when most outdoor people in the area congregate in the climbers' bar. The selection of real ales, to wash down the very generous meals, is bewilderingly wide and all too temping (including the local Atlas Brewery's ales from Kinlochleven); there's the added attraction of regular live music.

GETTING THERE & AWAY

The A82 linking Glasgow and Fort William slices though Glen Coe, but bypasses the village. **Scottish Citylink** (☎ 0870 550 5050; www.citylink.co.uk) buses between Glasgow (£14, 2½ hours, three daily) and Fort William (£5, 30 minutes, three daily) stop at the Glencoe crossroads. **Highland Country Buses** (☎ 01463 710555; www.rapsons.com) provides a service between Fort William and Kinlochleven via the Glencoe junction (£5, 40 minutes, at least seven services Monday to Saturday, three Sunday).

BUACHAILLE ETIVE MÓR

Duration	5–6 hours
Distance	6.5 miles (10.5km)
Difficulty	moderate–demanding
Start/Finish	Altnafeadh
Nearest Town	Glencoe (p133)
Transport	bus

Summary A classic exploration of the ridges and peaks of the most commanding mountain in Glen Coe.

Standing sentinel at the head of Glen Coe, Buachaille Etive Mór, meaning 'big herdsman of Etive', is one of the most distinctive landmarks in the Scottish landscape. At first sight, from the east on the A82 or from the start of the walk at Altnafeadh, it's a daunting, seemingly impregnable pyramid of buttresses and chasm-like gullies. But looks are often deceiving and Coire na Tulaich provides a steep but reasonably straightforward ascent.

The summit is commonly called Buachaille Etive Mór but, strictly speaking, is Stob Dearg (1022m). From there a high-level ridge extends southwest, linking three more summits; the name Buachaille Etive Mór properly refers to this entire massif. With deep valleys on either side, the views and the feeling of space from the ridge and summits are exceptional. The walk along the ridge above Coire na Tulaich is quite easy with only a few short ascents to reach the summits. The route described here continues along the ridge across Stob na Doire and then descends into Lairig Gartain via Coire Altruim, giving a total ascent of 1080m.

Alternative For a shorter walk, you can simply return down Coire na Tulaich after bagging Stob Dearg; allow three to four hours.

GETTING TO/FROM THE WALK

The walk starts and finishes at the Altnafeadh parking area on the A82. Buses operating along the A82 (see left) should stop here if requested in advance.

THE WALK

From Altnafeadh car park, follow the wide 4WD track to a large footbridge and then set out along a good path past Lagangarbh Cottage. Continue gently upwards into Coire na Tulaich and ignore a path going off to the left – this leads to the many scrambles and rock climbs on the buttresses further east. Follow the path along the right bank of the Allt Coire na Tulaich, which in all likelihood will be dry in summer.

As you get higher up, the ground on both sides steadily becomes steeper and the stream bed is gradually choked with boulders. The path climbs up to the right, on to easier ground heading towards the scree slopes up above. Once you are actually on the scree, stick to the righthand side, where a well-constructed path leads you to the top of some small rocky outcrops below the rim of Coire na Tulaich.

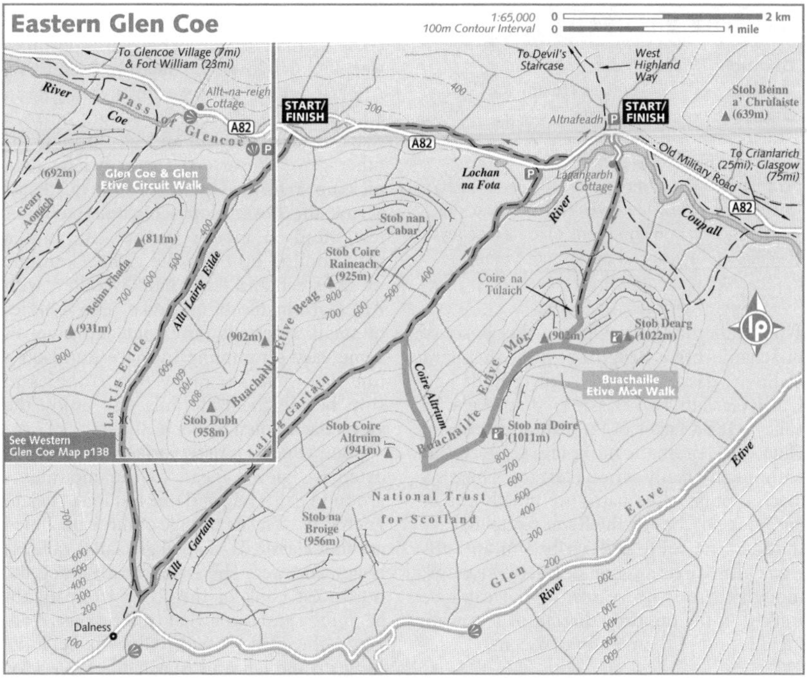

Following that, it is only a short scramble to the top, where you emerge somewhat suddenly on the ridge between Stob Dearg and Stob na Doire (around 1½ hours from the start).

Turn east and climb steadily for about 20 minutes over stony, frost-shattered ground to the summit of **Stob Dearg** (1022m). There are fine views to the east across exposed Rannoch Moor, and to the north and northwest across the shapely summits of the Mamores as far as the unmistakable, whale-backed profile of Ben Nevis. Closer to home, the eye is drawn to the steep, northeast face of Stob na Doire, which is next on the agenda.

Descend back to the top of Coire na Tulaich and head west and then southwest across a lovely, broad ridge with many small lochans filling the depressions between the grassy hummocks. Around 10 or 15 minutes of walking on this ridge should see you reach the base of the short, steep haul to **Stob na Doire** (1011m). A well-defined path clearly shows the way to the small summit cairn. The views over to the west across Bidean nam Bian dominate here, and there is also an excellent vista south into Glen Etive.

The Buachaille Etive Mór ridge continues southwest to Stob na Broige, while immediately below, in a col, you can make out the red erosion scar of a path heading down into Coire Altruim. Descend steeply to the col; from here you can take the option of extending the walk out to Stob na Broige, where there are some great views of Loch Etive.

From the col, the descent into Coire Altruim is steep but straightforward, except for a few wet and rocky steps towards the bottom, where a little extra care should be taken. Allow an hour to reach the River Coupall, which may be difficult to ford if it is in spate. If so, simply follow the river back to Altnafeadh and cross it on the footbridge that you used at the start of the walk. If the river is low, cross and follow the well-defined but boggy path that takes you to the A82 just a few hundred metres west of Altnafeadh (around one hour from the river crossing).

GLEN COE & GLEN ETIVE CIRCUIT

Duration	5 hours
Distance	10 miles (16km)
Difficulty	moderate
Start/Finish	Pass of Glencoe
Nearest Town	Glencoe (p133)
Transport	private

Summary A low-level walk across two dramatic passes in magnificent glaciated valleys overlooked by rugged peaks and ridges.

This walk circumnavigates the base of Buachaille Etive Beag, the 'little shepherd of Etive', passing through Lairig Eilde and Lairig Gartain, two classic U-shaped glacial valleys. It's a taster of the wilder reaches of Glen Coe's dramatic mountain scenery, but without any really serious terrain. There's a catch though – the paths are mostly rough and rocky or, beside the River Coupall, very muddy. The route is described in an anticlockwise direction for aesthetic reasons, though there is no reason why it can't be walked in the opposite direction. The walk includes more than 600m of ascent.

GETTING TO/FROM THE WALK

The walk starts and finishes at a car park beside the A82, immediately east of the Pass of Glencoe.

THE WALK Map p135

At the car park a Scottish Rights of Way & Access Society sign points to Loch Etiveside. With excellent views across Glen Coe to the spiky, precipitous ridge of Aonach Eagach, the path leads southwest up to Allt Lairig Eilde. If the river is in spate it is dangerous to cross, and even in average conditions it can be difficult so, if in doubt, continue along the east bank until you rejoin the path higher up. On the other side of Allt Lairig Eilde, the well-defined path continues for around 1 mile then crosses back to the east bank. The way, marked by a few cairns, now leads up, bending round to the south, with views of increasingly wild country – the jagged ridges of Stob Coire Sgreamhach to the west with rocky gorges below. You might be lucky and see red deer here. When you eventually reach the top of **Lairig Eilde** (489m) the views open up across Glen Etive to the mountains beyond.

Descend from the top of the pass and cross a small stream. The path continues steeply down towards **Dalness** in Glen Etive. After about 0.6 miles go through a gate in a high fence and cross the stream on rock slabs. Bear left, uphill and go through another gate. Traverse the spur briefly then pick up a formed path leading northeast across the lower slopes of Stob Dubh. A few hundred metres further on, join a path coming up from the right. Continue up the steep and fairly narrow valley, with Allt Gartain tumbling down it in a series of small waterfalls. The route up involves some easy scrambling in places, and on a fine day there are many opportunities to stop beside the waterfalls and enjoy the views back down to Loch Etive.

Soon you reach **Lairig Gartain** (489m), with extensive views ahead to the mountains around Loch Treig and one last look back to Loch Etive. The next stage of the walk, down another classic, U-shaped glaciated valley is boggy and wet. The eroded path along the northwest bank of the River Coupall can be muddy and somewhat treacherous. Walk down the glen, between Buachaille Etive Beag on the left and Buachaille Etive Mór on the right, to a car park beside the A82. Cross the road and follow a path that leads to an old road; turn left to follow it west for about 1 mile to where it meets the A82. Then you've little choice but to walk beside the road for several hundred metres, back to the car park at the start of the walk.

BIDEAN NAM BIAN

Duration	6–7 hours
Distance	6 miles (9.5km)
Difficulty	moderate–demanding
Start/Finish	parking area west of Allt-na-reigh Cottage
Nearest Town	Glencoe (p133)
Transport	bus

Summary From the beautiful and atmospheric Lost Valley, tackle a stunning circuit of a rugged mountain massif with wonderful views.

The ascent of Bidean nam Bian, which at 1150m is the highest mountain in Argyll, is one of the Glen Coe classics. The route squeezes up and down the steep-sided valleys that divide the Three Sisters, the

GLEN COE MASSACRE

The history of Glen Coe is stained by a massacre that happened in the valley in 1692. King William III extended an olive branch to rebellious Highland clans by offering pardons for their participation in a recent Jacobite uprising, provided they swore an oath of allegiance in front of a magistrate before 1 January 1692. Eventually, some chiefs did comply, but Alastair Maclain, 12th Chief of Glencoe (and head of a sept of the Clan MacDonald) left it to the very last minute. Fatefully, he was turned away by the governor in Fort William and sent south to Inveraray, with assurances for his safety. Although he was unable to swear until 6 January, both sides were satisfied that he had complied.

However, some people in high places saw an opportunity to get rid of some enemies and hatched a plot in which the king was complicit. Around 120 soldiers, under the command of Captain Robert Campbell, were housed with the MacDonalds in Glen Coe, supposedly on a mission to collect certain new taxes; naturally they enjoyed traditional Highland hospitality. After a couple of weeks Campbell received orders to 'fall upon the Rebels' and to 'put all to the sword under 70'. Accordingly, on 13 February, Maclain and 37 other men were murdered and 40 women and children perished of cold after their homes were torched.

Despite a verdict of murder by an official inquiry into the massacre, and the Scottish parliament's petition to the king, no one was punished – for a crime sanctioned at the highest level.

The event is remembered each year at a memorial in Glencoe; happily the long-held animosity between MacDonalds and Campbells has all but disappeared.

towering buttresses that enclose Glen Coe on its southern side. It then ascends the massif of Bidean nam Bian, which rears up at the head of the valleys. Appropriately enough, the name probably means 'chief of the hills'. The walking conditions on the massif itself are fine – mainly on rocky ridges, which are narrow enough to feel airy without being dangerous or difficult. The route largely follows maintained paths, although foot-worn trails rather than purpose-built paths mark the way along the high, rocky ridges. The total ascent on the route is 1150m.

The approach includes a crossing of the Lost Valley, a bowl-like hanging valley that was created sometime during the last Ice Age. In more recent years this mountain sanctuary was used as a hiding place for cattle stolen by the MacDonald clan from the Campbells (see the boxed text on above). A walk to the Lost Valley is worthwhile in its own right; allow three hours for the return trip.

GETTING TO/FROM THE WALK

The walk begins and ends at the large parking area on the south side of the A82, a short distance west of the cottage at Alltna-reigh. Buses operating along the A82 may stop here if requested in advance – see p134 for details.

THE WALK

From the parking area drop down the grassy slope south of the road and join a track that follows the banks of the River Coe upstream. Cross the river on a wooden footbridge and join a well-maintained path. This path leads up the rocky gorge that cuts between the towering crags of Beinn Fhada and Gearr Aonach, and hands are needed in several places to help mount easy rock steps. The path soon crosses onto the east bank of the Allt Coire Gabhail, and a short climb brings you over a rise and into the **Lost Valley**.

The floor of the valley is a jumble of rocks and boulders – pick your way diagonally across the muddle to join a more distinct path to the right. At the head of the valley a steep rock wall seems to rise almost vertically – the route ascends directly up this wall, although the terrain is not as steep as it first seems. The path continues up the valley, contouring above a gorge that has been chiselled out by the burn. Care is needed here in wet or icy weather.

The terrain steepens as you reach the headwall of the valley, and the ground becomes less stable underfoot. The climb itself is not easy-going, over a mixture of steep earth, scree and boulders rising sharply up to the ridge. Hands may be needed for balance in one or two places, and great care

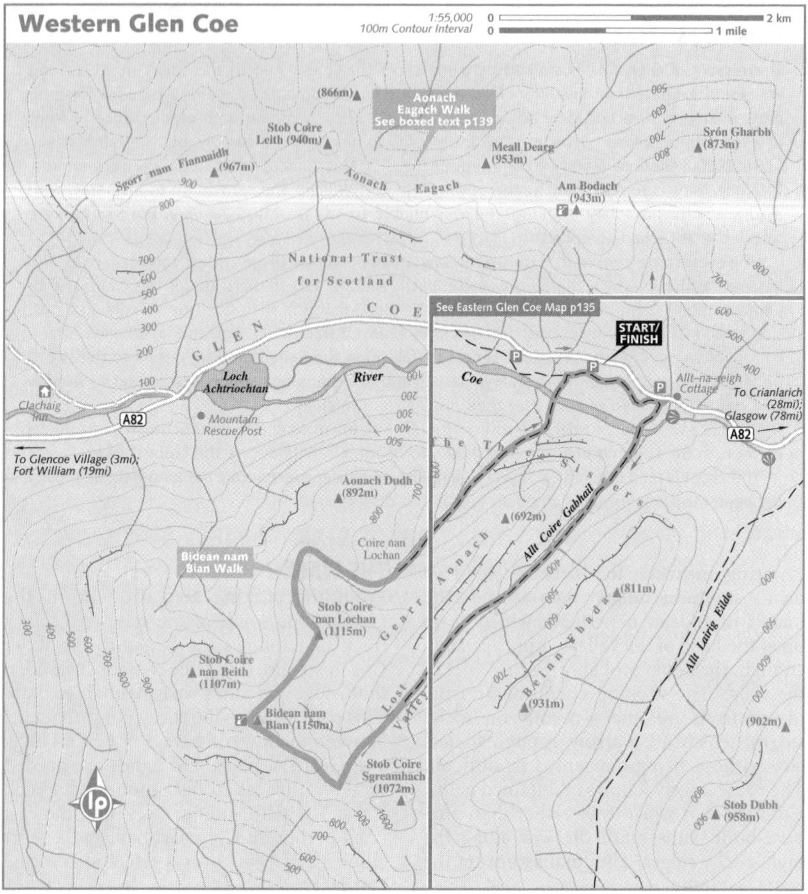

must be taken if you descend this way. Once on top of the ridge, however, the views suddenly open out in all directions.

The summit of Bidean nam Bian is now about 1.2km away, along the ridge to the west. Stick to the crest of the ridge and climb over the boulders of several rises and subsidiary peaks, crossing one narrow section, before making a final ascent to the large cairn on the **Bidean nam Bian** summit (1150m), about four hours from the start. The views are exceptional and, on a clear day, the panorama includes the Western Isles, Ben Nevis and many of the peaks and ranges of the western Highlands.

Descend northeast from Bidean nam Bian, following a narrow, rocky spur down to a col between Bidean nam Bian and Stob Coire nan Lochan; care is needed here in poor visibility. Climb up to the summit of **Stob Coire nan Lochan** (1115m), where the view is dominated by the Aonach Eagach ridge on the other side of Glen Coe.

To descend from Stob Coire nan Lochan it is necessary to walk northwest for a few hundred metres and then north for about the same distance, following the rim of some impressive cliffs. At a col turn east, descending into Coire nan Lochan. Cut across the grassy hollow and pick up paths beside the many small streams flowing towards the River Coe below. The streams soon converge and the path becomes clear, descending steeply on the eastern banks

CLASSIC WALK – AONACH EAGACH

A spectacular ridge-line scramble, Aonach Eagach ('the notched ridge') forms a nearly sheer, 900m-high, 1.5km-long wall on the northern side of Glen Coe. Beyond the knife-edge ridge, the mountain falls away precipitously. You need to be fit, have a head for heights and some serious scrambling experience, as it's either sensational or terrifying, depending on your vertigo tolerance. Though it's only 6 miles (9.5km), allow seven to eight hours for this demanding outing, involving a 1000m ascent. It starts at a parking area just west of Allt-na-reigh cottage, a few miles east of Glencoe (p133). Once on the ridge there is no easy way to bypass difficulties at the crest and no simple escape routes into the valleys on either side. The route is generally completed from east to west because rock steps are less problematic in this direction. Take great care not to dislodge rocks as the route is popular and there's bound to be someone below. It's advisable to carry a decent length of climbing rope.

From the parking area, pick up a good path climbing steeply onto the southeast ridge of Am Bodach. After about 15 minutes the path flattens out beneath some crags and then turns to the east, skirting the base of these cliffs to reach the Allt Ruigh. Follow the stream on either side and continue to gain height, reaching the ridge between Am Bodach and Sròn Gharbh 1½ hours from the start. Turn to the southwest and clamber up a broad, rocky ridge to reach the summit of **Am Bodach** (943m) at the beginning of the ridge (10 minutes further on). Now the fun starts.

Descending the rock step there's one awkward manoeuvre that is exposed on the right. If you find this stressful, don't continue – there are more difficult sections ahead. Once off this rock step the narrow ridge provides superb walking to **Meall Dearg** (953m), 30 minutes from Am Bodach.

Descend from Meall Dearg onto the ridge, which narrows and often calls for the use of hands. Edge across an exposed notch and then tackle the crux of the route – a gendarmed section of the ridge with vertical exposure on both sides. Move to the right (north) side and use a ledge to bypass a block before regaining the crest and easier ground. Descend steeply into a notch, where another difficult section begins; scramble up an exposed ramp on the left (south) side of the ridge. Descend again into another notch and scramble steeply but easily up a prominent gully to escape the final difficulties. You'll need about an hour for this section; longer if you rope-up anywhere.

Climb a rocky ridge to the summit of **Stob Coire Leith** (940m). A broad ridge descends gently then sweeps around for the day's final climb to the highest summit on the ridge, **Sgorr nam Fiannaidh** (967m). Descend steeply to the south from the summit, picking up a faint path in the scree and working around rock outcrops. The descent is steep and unrelenting; if the grass on the lower half is wet, be extra careful. Back at the A82 (one to 1½ hours from Sgorr nam Fiannaidh) turn left and walk east along the road for 1.5 miles to the parking area, avoiding some of the road by following a track below the road to the right.

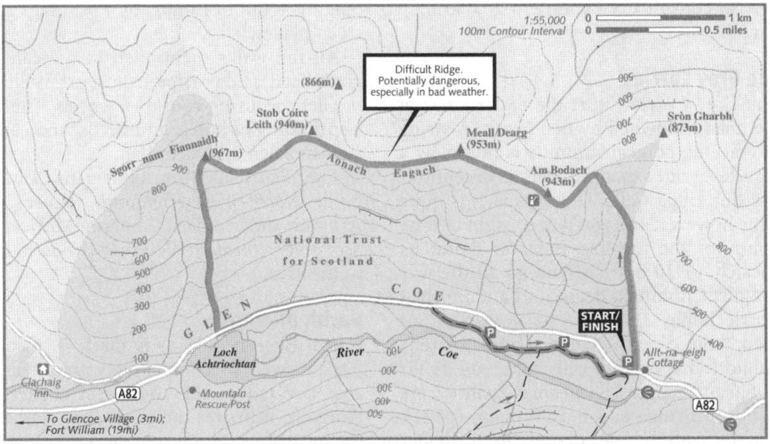

of the burn. At the bottom of the descent, cross a wooden footbridge over the River Coe, from where it's a few hundred metres up the grassy slopes to the parking area.

MORE WALKS

LOCHABER

The Aonachs

The Aonachs dominate the nearer eastwards view from Ben Nevis; Aonach Beag, at 1234m (4048ft), is the sixth-highest mountain in Scotland (despite its name – 'beag' means small). The flatness of the summit plateau contrasts with the exceptionally rugged crags that plummet into the eastern corries. The connoisseur's route begins at the Nevis Range car park, 6.5 miles northeast of Fort William along the A82; **Nevis Range** (☎ 01397 705825; www.nevisrange.com) is a commercial downhill ski centre and is clearly signposted. **Highland Country Buses** (☎ 01463 710555; www.rapsons.co.uk) operates a service from Fort William (£1.50, 15 minutes, six services Monday to Saturday, three Sunday).

The route approaches Aonach Mór along its fine northern spur; continue from there to Aonach Beag then traverse the summit plateau and descend across the ski fields. The distance is 11 miles (18km), for which you should allow around eight hours. You could also take advantage of the cable car (open all year), which will take you about halfway to the top of Aonach Mór.

Also consult OS Explorer 1:25,000 map No 392.

The Grey Corries

The Grey Corries lie at the eastern end of the massif crowned by Ben Nevis. A string of graceful, conical summits is linked by a high-level ridge that provides an exceptionally fine ridge walk. The approach is quite long, however, and you'll need eight or nine hours for the traverse as far as Beinn na Socaich, or 10 hours if you go all the way to Sgurr Chòinnich Beag. Start and finish at Corriechoille, 2.5 miles east along a minor road from Spean Bridge. Unfortunately, public transport will only take you as far as Spean Bridge. The nearest facilities are in Spean Bridge and Fort William (p121). For the truly heroic, there's the Lochaber Traverse, beginning at Corriechoille and traversing the Grey Corries, Aonachs and Carn Mór Dearg, and finishing with an ascent of Ben Nevis. All in one day of course! Consult OS Explorer 1:25,000 map No 392 and either of the recommended Munros guides (p108).

GLEN COE

Beinn a' Bheithir

The Beinn a' Bheithir massif offers a route every bit as good as Bidean nam Bian or Buachaille Etive Mór. Summit views take in Morvern and Ardgour to the west. The walk starts and finishes at the forest car park in Glenachulish, near Ballachulish, 1 mile west of Glencoe village on the A82. The aim is first to reach the saddle between Sgòrr Dearg (1024m) and Sgòrr Dhonuill (1001m) then pick off the two summits. You'll need six or seven hours for the 8-mile (13km) outing, involving more than 1300m of ascent. Consult OS Explorer 1:25,000 map No 384 and Cameron McNeish's *Munro Almanac*.

MORVERN, ARDGOUR & MOIDART

These rugged and less-frequented districts are separated from Lochaber by Loch Linnhe. Morvern and Ardgour can be reached most easily on the Corran ferry southwest of Fort William, while Moidart and the Rois-bheinn Ridge are most easily reached via Fort William. These areas have a quiet, wild charm, and although the peaks are not particularly high, the terrain is challenging – full of lumps, bumps, crags and steep places.

All the walks mentioned below can be completed as day trips from Fort William or Glencoe, using your own wheels. There's a sprinkling of hotels and B&Bs, and camp sites in Salen and Strontian.

The Scottish Mountaineering Club's guide *North-West Highlands* focuses on Ardgour and Moidart; Cameron McNeish's *Scotland's 100 Best Walks* describes routes in the area.

Garbh Bheinn

Garbh Bheinn (885m) is the fine, distant peak viewed so compellingly from Glencoe. Located in the southwest corner of Ardgour, it proves the point that Corbetts (below 914m) can be at least as demanding as any Munro. This is a bonus for those who can ignore such arbitrary judgments of worth, because Garbh Bheinn is a superb peak with some demanding terrain and great views. A good circuit starts on the A861, just west of Inversanda, not far from the Corran ferry. With more than 1000m of ascent, the 9 miles (14.6km) should take seven to eight hours. Consult OS Explorer 1:25,000 map No 391.

Rois-bheinn Ridge

Dominating Moidart, Rois-bheinn (882m) is the highest point on a ridge spiked with several summits over 800m. A long and strenuous circuit (with 1500m of ascent) of the rocky ridge can be made from Inverailort on the A861. The terrain is complex and navigation in poor weather may be difficult. Consult OS Explorer 1:25,000 map No 390.

The Cairngorms

The Cairngorms is the wildest and most extensive area of uplands in Scotland and embraces the largest tracts of land over 600m and up to 1300m high. For this chapter 'Cairngorms' is interpreted very broadly – from Strathspey in the north, to Braemar and central Deeside in the east and south, and around the edge of the uplands to Blair Atholl in Glen Garry, according to the authoritative Scottish Mountaineering Club guide. Originally the Cairngorms was called Am Monadh Ruadh, meaning 'red rounded mountains' (referring to the big outcrops of pinkish-red granite) but the name of the summit most visible from Strathspey was adopted for the entire area in the 19th century. Oddly, the name of this summit – Cairn Gorm – means 'blue rocky mountain'.

With its central plateau generally above 1000m, the Cairngorms is a place to be taken seriously and not where you'd go for a casual stroll. The area offers some of Scotland's finest opportunities for long-distance walks along the network of public paths, and for magnificent treks across rolling mountains and plateaus. In winter it's one of Scotland's two main mountaineering and ice-climbing venues, and very popular with cross-country and downhill skiers. The greater part of the area is within Cairngorms National Park (see the boxed text on p144), the larger of Scotland's two parks, set aside in 2003.

The Cairngorms can seem intimidatingly bleak and featureless. However, once you have spent some time here, you may understand what Henry Alexander, an early Scottish Mountaineering Club guidebook author, meant when he wrote, 'the greatness and dignity and calm of the Cairngorms cast their spell over the spirit'.

HIGHLIGHTS

- Magnificent views to distant horizons from **Cairn Gorm** (p147), a vast alpine plateau seemingly on top of the world
- Following centuries-old pathways through remote glens to **Lairig Ghru** (p152), Scotland's most dramatic mountain pass
- Marvelling at Glen Derry's beautiful Caledonian pine woodlands, with purple carpets of heather in late summer, on the **Blair Atholl to Glenmore** (p156) walk
- Seeing mysterious, darkly beautiful lochans cradled by the towering cliffs of glacier-sculpted corries on **Lochnagar** (p159)

- www.cairngorms.co.uk
- www.visithighlands.com

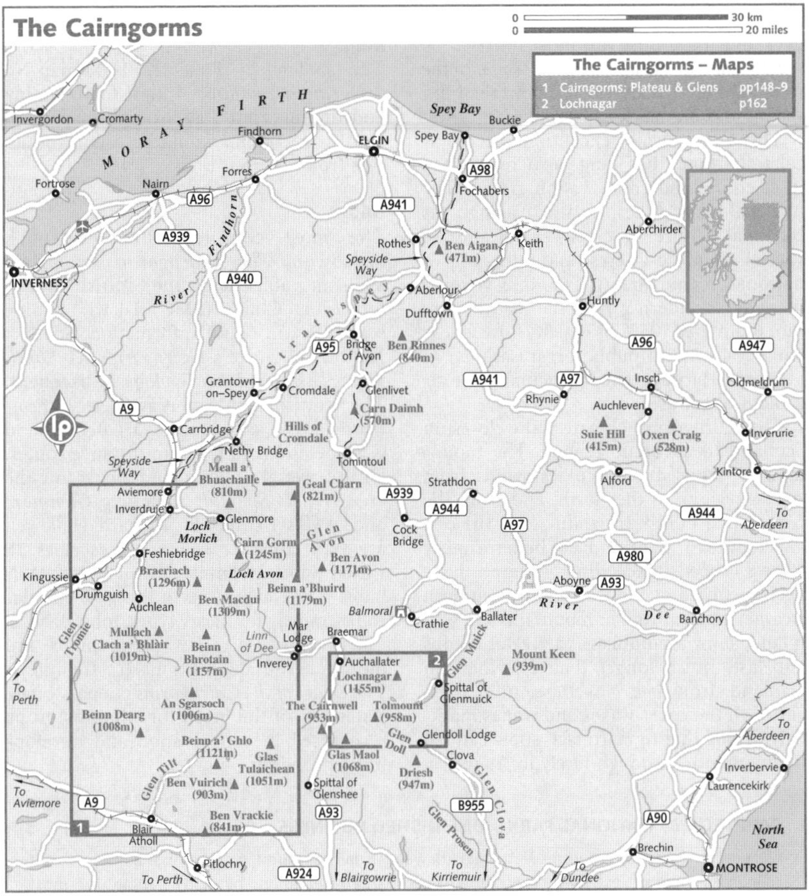

ENVIRONMENT

Granite and schist have created two basic types of Cairngorms' landscapes. The plateau and the big, rounded mountains with smooth, contoured slopes consist principally of granite, which commonly weathers into vast sheets of scree and fine gravel. Crags, bluffs and broken slopes and cliffs indicate the presence of schist (and gneiss and diorite). The landforms have glaciation and the ice age written all over them: long, deep, U-shaped glens, great cliff-lined trenches, scores of stunning corries gouged out of the mountain slopes, and curiously shaped mounds of moraine in the glens.

The Caledonian woodlands, which include birch and juniper, in Rothiemurchus, Glen Derry and Glen Feshie in particular, are but remnants of the once-extensive tree cover. The arctic-alpine vegetation of the Cairngorms is outstanding in its variety and extent. Tiny flowering plants, mosses and liverworts survive in areas where snow lingers into summer and on the crags and the gritty plateaus. Heather moorland is widespread below 750m (higher in some areas, lower elsewhere); the heather species are mixed with grasses and sedges.

Only a few birds and mammals live on the high ground: long-legged mountain hare, introduced reindeer on the Cairngorm plateau, golden plover, dotterel, snow bunting and the remarkable ptarmigan, which changes plumage three times a year and is a permanent resident. Red and roe deer and red grouse are most likely to be seen on the moors and in woodlands. In the trees, bird life is plentiful, notably crossbills, siskins and big black capercaillies.

The Cairngorms' exceptional ecological importance has long been recognised in scientific and conservation circles. The national park takes in the Cairngorms National Nature Reserve, several sites of special scientific interest and parts of two national scenic areas. The UK government is considering nominating the core mountain area (25% of which is owned by conservation and public organisations) as a World Heritage site, principally for its geological features.

The Cairngorms' climate is the closest in Scotland to an arctic regime. The mountains are exposed to the coldest winds, from Arctic regions to the north, and from the continental European landmass to the east and southeast. The wind can be ferociously strong; speeds exceeding 150mph have been recorded at the Cairn Gorm summit weather station. As the mountains are well inland, snow accumulates to greater depths and lasts much longer than elsewhere in Scotland, from late November until May, although the cover waxes and wanes markedly during that time. In fact, snow can fall in any month, although rarely in August.

INFORMATION

Maps

The OS Travel – Road 1:250,000 map No 2 *Northern Scotland* is ideal for planning and finding your way around; map No 4 *Southern Scotland* would be useful for access from the south.

Books

The most comprehensive guidebook around is *The Cairngorms* by Adam Watson, published in the Scottish Mountaineering Club's (SMC) District Guide series. For in-depth information, Scottish Natural Heritage's *Cairngorms: A Landscape Fashioned by Geology* is excellent. The Scottish Rights of Way Society's *Scottish Hill Tracks*, edited by DJ Bennet and C Stone, is useful for long-distance routes. Of the several walking guides covering the area, *Walks Speyside including Glenmore* and *Walks Deeside* by Richard Hallewell are very compact and each describes 25 varied walks. In similar format, Nick Williams' *The Cairngorms* outlines 40 circular walks, mostly for hardy types. John Brooks' *Cairngorms Walks* has better maps and more generous descriptions. Jim Crumley's *The Heart of the Cairngorms* is a passionate statement of the 'need for wildness' to be recognised in conservation and development proposals.

CAIRNGORMS NATIONAL PARK – UNFINISHED BUSINESS

After much debate, Cairngorms National Park was officially declared in September 2003, an event welcomed more or less universally, though with large reservations by many people. The most contentious of these was to do with the park's southern boundary, which follows the watershed between the River Dee and south-flowing steams, but excludes several fine glens and hills, leaving the park without an accessible southern gateway. The only reason the Scottish Executive, which decided to draw this boundary, would give was that it needed to reduce the number of local government authorities involved – never mind anything to do with nature conservation. Widespread dissatisfaction coalesced in the PARC (Perthshire Alliance for the Real Cairngorms) but to no avail (yet), the Executive saying only that the issue will come up for debate again when the park is reviewed in 2008.

Meantime, life goes on. There are plenty of roadside signs welcoming visitors to the park and a shelf-full of attractive and informative brochures about the park, but unlike most (if not all) national parks, it has no dedicated visitor centre (go to the local TICs instead) and no national park rangers. The several existing ranger services, run by local estates and councils, remain in business, continuing to do excellent work.

To end on an upbeat note, in August 2005 the park received the European Charter for Sustainable Tourism in Protected Areas, the first British park to do so. It is only given to areas that match exacting standards for sustainable development and tourism management, based on an action plan drawn up by the park authority.

Information Sources

Cairngorms National Park (www.cairngorms.co.uk) does not have a dedicated visitor centre; instead, local TICs carry a selection of the park's publications.

For accommodation bookings throughout the area, contact **VisitScotland** (☎ 0845 225 5121; www.visitscotland.com). **Traveline Scotland** (☎ 0870 608 2608; www.travelinescotland.com) is the most direct source for detailed public transport timetables.

NORTHERN CAIRNGORMS

The focus of this section is mainly on the vast, central Cairn Gorm-Macdui plateau, crowned by Ben Macdui (1309m, 4294ft), Scotland's second-highest mountain, rising to the south of Cairn Gorm (1245m, 4084ft). The plateau is separated from neighbouring mountain massifs by the deep gash of Lairig Ghru in the west and Lairig an Laoigh in the east, and is pitted with spectacular, cliff-lined corries on its northern and southern faces. The weather on the plateau is notoriously fickle, with low cloud, mist, strong winds and sleet likely at any time. Visibility can quickly deteriorate to zero and, although the paths are well worn, prominent landmarks are scarce so route-finding can be difficult. Navigation skills – using a map and compass – are therefore essential.

Don't be put off if you're not keen on climbing mountains. On the northern slopes of the plateau, in Rothiemurchus Estate (privately owned) and Glenmore Forest Park (managed by Forest Enterprise), there are many low-level walks suitable for all and ideal for days when the mountains are shrouded in cloud.

Extensive snow cover can persist on the high plateau until well into May and start to build up again in November, so the best months for the area are May to September.

Two walks – a high-level circuit over the summit of Cairn Gorm with an optional extension to Ben Macdui, and a medium-level route deep into the range through Lairig Ghru – provide a good introduction to the scale and wildness of the Cairngorms. There's an outline of a beautiful short walk around Loch an Eilein (p151) and the More Walks section (p162) includes outlines of the ascent of nearby Braeriach, third only to Ben Nevis and Ben Macdui and a truly magnificent peak; a much shorter climb over Meall a' Bhuachaille, with fine views of the plateau; a long, low-level walk to beautiful Loch Avon; and an outline of the Speyside Way, a long-distance path linking Aviemore and Buckie on the North Sea coast.

PLANNING

Maps

Harvey's Superwalker 1:25,000 *Cairn Gorm* map covers both walks in this section very well.

Information Sources

At the Cairngorm funicular's base station at Coire Cas – generally known as Cairngorm – the **Cairngorms countryside ranger service** (☎ 01479 861703) can give expert advice about walks on the plateau; the local weather forecast is posted there daily. The service runs a program of guided walks during summer. Whatever your opinion is about the funicular (see the boxed text on p150), the website of its operator, **Cairn-Gorm Mountain Ltd** (www.cairngormmountain.com), is worth a look.

ACCESS TOWNS

Aviemore

☎ 01479 / pop 2397

Aviemore sees itself as the gateway to the Cairngorms, with the full range of facilities, but lacks the atmosphere of a real mountain town.

The **TIC** (☎ 0845 225 5121; www.visithighlands.com; The Mall), in the town centre, has a good range of maps and guides, and can look after accommodation bookings.

The several gear shops in the centre of town, all open daily and with similar ranges of stock, include Cairngorm Mountain Sports, Nevisport and Ellis Brigham.

SLEEPING & EATING

The nearest and most amenable camping ground is at Rothiemurchus (p146).

Aviemore SYHA Hostel (☎ 0870 004 1104; www.syha.org.uk; 25 Grampian Rd; dm £14; 💻) is a superior hostel, five minutes' walk from the town centre.

Old Bridge Inn (☎ 811137; 23 Dalfaber Rd; bar meals £9) is a largely unspoiled, traditional pub specialising in Scottish fare; local ales are on tap.

For supplies, the Tesco supermarket has all you're likely to need.

GETTING THERE & AWAY

First ScotRail (☎ 0845 755 0033; www.firstscotrail.com) services from both Edinburgh and Glasgow to Inverness stop at Aviemore (£36, 2½ hours, nine Monday to Saturday, five Sunday) as does the **GNER** (☎ 0845 722 5225; www.gner.co.uk) midday service from London Kings Cross to Inverness via Edinburgh (7½ hours, daily); fares for these trips are variable. There is also a suburban service from Inverness (£9, 40 minutes, 11 services Monday to Saturday, five Sunday). The First ScotRail *Caledonian Sleeper* from London Euston to Inverness calls at Aviemore.

Scottish Citylink (☎ 0870 550 5050; www.citylink.co.uk) buses from Edinburgh and Glasgow (both £16, 3¼ hours, six services Monday to Saturday, five Sunday) stop at the train station; the TIC handles bookings and inquiries. **Highland Country Buses** (☎ 01463 811211; www.rapsons.co.uk) links Aviemore and Cairngorm Ski Centre (£3, 25 minutes, at least 10 daily).

By car, turn off the A9 between Kingussie and Daviot to reach Aviemore.

Glenmore

☎ 01479

Glenmore (7 miles from Aviemore), beside the Ski Rd up to Coire Cas, is the closest settlement to the start of the walks. Forest Enterprise's **Glenmore Forest Park Visitor Centre** (☎ 861220) concentrates on the surrounding forest park. The *Guide to Forest Walks*, available from the centre, includes maps and notes for waymarked walks in the park. There is also a **café** (breakfast £7, lunch £6, dinner £8; breakfast & lunch daily, dinner Jun-Sep) here.

SLEEPING & EATING

Glenmore Camping & Caravan Site (☎ 861271; unpowered/powered sites for 2 £10/19) is run by Forest Enterprise. Pitches are mostly flat and well grassed; the views are superb.

Cairngorm Lodge SYHA Hostel (☎ 861238; www.syha.org.uk; dm £14;), in a spacious former lodge, has excellent facilities, as well as a great outlook.

Glenmore Lodge (☎ 861256; www.glenmorelodge.org.uk; s/d £20/40, mains £6-10; lunch & dinner), about 1 mile east of Glenmore, houses the National Sports Training Centre. The Lochain Bar has a marvellous view of the Cairngorm plateau and – when you can't see the view – stunning posters of more distant peaks. Accommodation availability (shared bathroom) depends on courses in progress.

Cas Bar (Cairngorm car park), near the funicular station, is primarily a watering hole, although it does also serve snacks and light meals.

Glenmore shop (☎ 861253), next to the camping site, stocks a small range of supplies and liquid fuel and gas; the local forecast is posted outside. It has an adjacent **café** (breakfast £5, lunch mains £5, dinner mains £8; lunch daily, dinner Jun-Sep).

GETTING THERE & AWAY

Highland Country Buses operates services between Aviemore and Glenmore; see opposite for details.

Inverdruie & Coylumbridge

☎ 01479

These two tiny settlements beside the road to Cairngorm can serve as quiet alternative bases to Aviemore.

Rothiemurchus Visitor Centre (☎ 812345; www.rothiemurchus.net; Inverdruie) is run by Rothiemurchus Estate and provides information about the estate, including guided walks led by the estate's own rangers. Under the same roof is the Farm Shop and Larder, stocked with seriously tempting Scottish delicacies.

Rothiemurchus Camp & Caravan Park (☎ 812800; Coylumbridge; unpowered/powered sites for 2 £10/15) is set in pine woodland beside the Lairig Ghru path.

Junipers B&B (☎ 810405; Inverdruie; s/d £28/50) is welcoming and comfortable.

The **Einich** (☎ 812334; mains £7-14; lunch daily, dinner Wed-Sat), in an old stone building next to the visitor centre, is a pleasantly informal restaurant. Local produce is to the fore on the small menu; the soup is second-to-none.

For public transport to Inverdruie and Coylumbridge, see opposite.

CAIRN GORM HIGH CIRCUIT

Duration	4½–5 hours
Distance	7.5 miles (12km)
Difficulty	moderate–demanding
Start/Finish	Cairngorm car park
Nearest Town	Glenmore (opposite)
Transport	bus

Summary An outstanding mountain walk across a sprawling alpine plateau, with magnificent wide-ranging views; take in even higher Ben Macdui for good measure.

This is the most popular high walk in the Cairngorms, the highlights being the summit of Cairn Gorm, the dramatic peaks of Stob Coire an t-Sneachda and Cairn Lochan, and the awesome corries. It can't be stressed too strongly that this walk is not a doddle. The vast plateau drops precipitously in almost all directions and severe weather is possible at any time; conditions may be fine at Glenmore but up on top it can be completely different. If you haven't done much walking, then solicit some experienced company for this great walk. Ben Macdui provides even wider views and a greater sensation of remoteness, out of sight of the developments on the northern slopes; what's more, at 1309m it's Scotland's second-highest peak.

Although this walk can be done in either direction, it's described clockwise, going up to Cairn Gorm from the northeast, around the rim of Coire an t-Sneachda, over Cairn Lochan then down the ridge and back to the start. The ascent to Cairn Gorm's summit is about 645m and there's an additional climb of about 155m over Cairn Lochan; for Ben Macdui add another 200m of climbing. Realistically, the only escape route is down Fiacaill a' Choire Chais, the ridge between Coire Cas and Coire an t-Sneachda. The main Cairn Gorm walk isn't a particularly long day, so you'll have plenty of time to enjoy the views; adding Ben Macdui makes for a full day but if you're fit – no worries!

GETTING TO/FROM THE WALK

Highland Country Buses (☎ 01463 811211; www.rapsons.co.uk) links Aviemore and Cairngorm Ski Centre (£3, 25 minutes, at least 10 daily), via Inverdruie and Coylumbridge.

By road from Aviemore, take the B970 via Inverdruie to Coylumbridge, then continue along the Ski Rd to Glenmore and the Cairngorm car park.

THE WALK

Map p143

Start by walking back (north) down the road, away from the car park, to a road junction; take the road to the right for about 90m to a stonework drain on the right. A small cairn in the heather marks the start of a narrow path on the other side of the ditch, parallel to the road. Follow this entrenched old track for about 200m and you'll find that it becomes wider and clearer, up the heather-clad slope. After a while cairns mark the route, which continues steadily up, with views unfolding of the corries and spurs of the Cairngorm plateau. The path goes beneath a ski lift and past the top of another, weaving in and out of the picket fences lining the routes of the lifts. Having left the heather behind, the path then crosses gravelly ground and skirts the Ptarmigan restaurant. Beyond the restaurant, a stone-paved path leads fairly steeply up to a boulder field where cairns and poles clearly mark the route across this minor obstacle course and up to the large cairn on the summit of **Cairn Gorm** (1245m), with a weather station nearby.

Among the multitude of features in the view are the long, flat plateau of Ben Wyvis (just west of Inverness) to the north; the sprawling bulk of Ben Macdui nearby; beyond it, the sharper profile of Braeriach; and, to the southeast, flat-topped Ben Avon, dotted with granite tors.

Descend sharply west over a jumble of big boulders – initially there's no clear path – towards a wide path on clearer ground below. Then, on a broad saddle, diverge a little to the right to a prominent cairn (1141m) at the head of Fiacaill a' Choire Chais (the escape route mentioned earlier) for a great view of the crags on the eastern side of Cairn Lochan.

To continue, follow the broad path around the rim of Coire an t-Sneachda, which is lined with cliffs. Its flat floor is decorated with swampy lochans. A cairned route, rather than a path, leads up to **Stob Coire an t-Sneachda** (1176m) and more great views. Drop down west to a small gap. The path to Ben Macdui (see the Side Trip on p150) leads south from here. Otherwise, climb steeply to **Cairn Lochan** (1215m) with

Cairngorms: Plateau & Glens

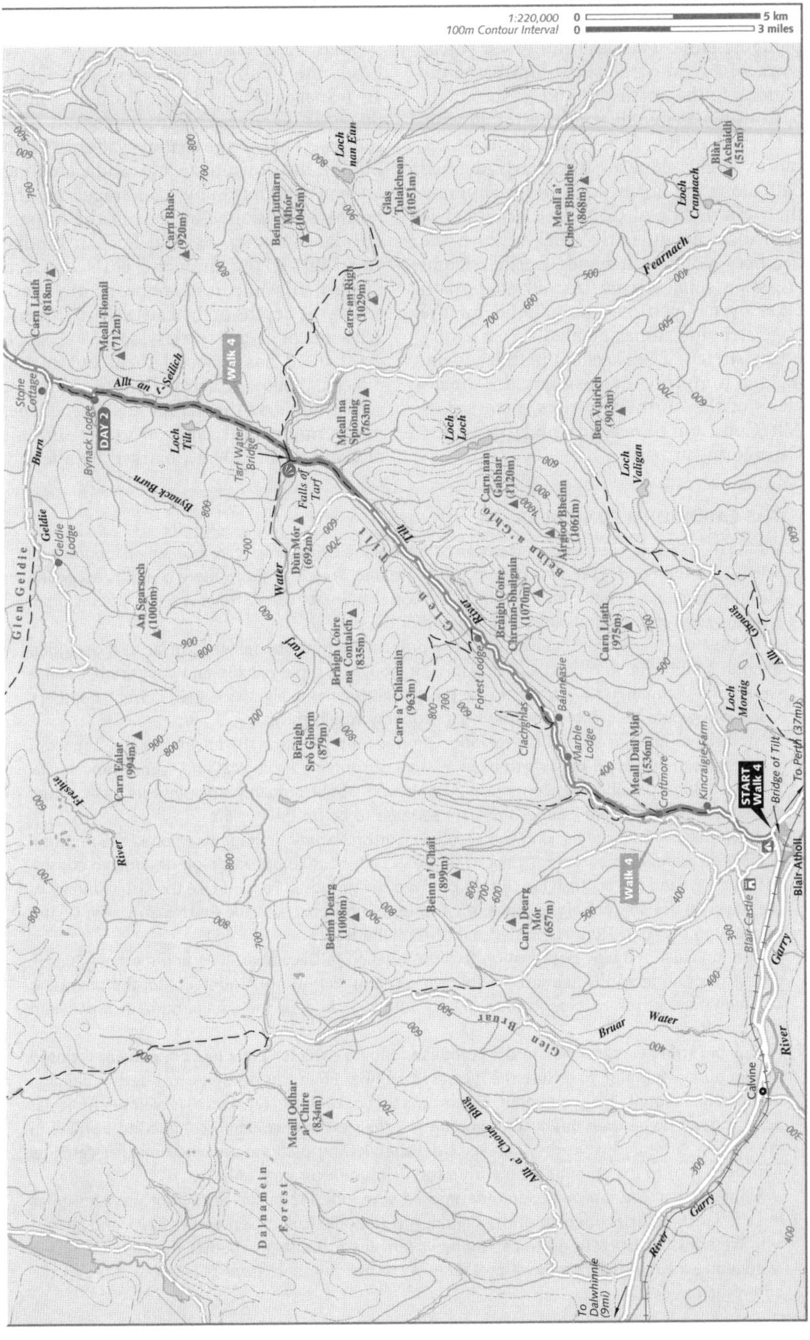
1:220,000
100m Contour Interval
0
5 km
0
3 miles
Stone Cottage
Bynack Lodge
DAY 2
Allt an t-Seilich
Walk 4
Loch Tilt
Tarf Water Bridge
Falls of Tarf
Bynack Burn
Geldie Burn
Geldie Lodge
Glen Geldie
Carn Liath (818m)
Meall Tionail (712m)
Carn Bhac (920m)
Beinn Iutharn Mhór (1045m)
Loch nan Eun
Glas Tulaichean (1051m)
Meall a' Choire Bhuidhe (868m)
Loch Crannach
Blàr Achaidh (515m)
Fearnach
Carn an Righ (1029m)
Meall na Spionaig (763m)
Loch Loch
Ben Vuirich (903m)
Loch Valigan
Carn nan Gabhar (1120m)
Airgiod Bheinn (1061m)
Beinn a' Ghlo
Dùn Mór (692m)
Glen Tilt
River Tilt
An Sgarsoch (1006m)
Tarf Water
Bràigh Coire Chruinn-bhalgain (1070m)
Forest Lodge
Carn Liath (975m)
Bràigh Coire na Conlaich (835m)
Carn a' Chlamain (963m)
Balaneasie
Clachghlas
Marble Lodge
Allt Girnaig
Loch Moraig
Kincraigie Farm
Meall Dail Min (536m)
Croftmore
START Walk 4
Bridge of Tilt
To Perth (37mi)
Bràigh Sròn Ghorm (879m)
Carn Ealar (994m)
Feshie River
Blair Atholl
Blair Castle
Beinn a' Chait (899m)
Beinn Dearg (1008m)
Walk 4
Carn Dearg Mór (657m)
Garry
Bruar Water
Glen Bruar
River Garry
Calvine
Meall Odhar a' Chire (834m)
Allt a' Choire Bhig
Dalnamein Forest
River Garry
To Dalwhinnie (9mi)

its sprawling cairn close to the rim of the plunging cliffs. The beautiful green patchwork of broad Strathspey dominates the outlook to the northwest and west.

Continue generally southwest, following a cairned route, then descend the steep, mostly rocky slope to the clearly defined path along the north–south ridge rimming the western side of Coire an Lochain. The path loses height fairly quickly down the heathery slope as it bends northeast and crosses a small stream. A well-made path takes over – you may be grateful for the huge stepping stones planted across a very boggy stretch. The excellent path leads on, making it much easier to enjoy the superb views of the northern corries, then across Allt Coire an t-Sneachda and on to the Cairngorm car park.

SIDE TRIP: BEN MACDUI

2½ hours, 5 miles (8km), 200m ascent

From the small gap between Stob Coire an t-Sneachda and Cairn Lochan, follow the clear, narrow path leading south then southwest above the shallow valley of Féith Buidhe and down to a wide saddle cradling Lochan Buidhe. Snow can linger on the north-facing slope, just east of the lochan, into late summer. Beyond Lochan Buidhe you can see the dramatic cliffs of Carn Etchachan, while in the opposite direction, across the depths of the Lairig Ghru, Braeriach's magnificent corries look as if some giant hand has scooped them out of the plateau. Follow a cairned route southeast across boulders then climb the steep slope, past a minor peak, and on to the summit of **Ben Macdui** (1309m), marked by a lonely

THE CAIRNGORM FUNICULAR

During the 1960s the northern (and eastern) slopes of the Cairngorms were opened up for downhill skiing with the building of a road from Glenmore into Coire Cas. From there chairlifts ascended via an intermediate station to Ptarmigan, the top station at 1080m. However, the lift was often closed by the strong winds that regularly buffet the plateau.

In 1994 the Cairngorm Chairlift Company proposed a funicular railway similar to those operating in continental European alpine resorts. It would be more reliable and comfortable and it would, the company said, attract up to 100,000 visitors annually, twice then-current numbers. Many jobs would be created and the local economy would thrive.

Walkers, mountaineers and conservation groups protested that the environmental impact of the development would be disastrous in an area of supreme ecological and scenic importance, that it couldn't possibly be economically viable and would probably drive visitors away rather than draw them in. What's more, snowfalls seemed to be on the decline.

Nevertheless, financial backing was secured, Scottish Natural Heritage sanctioned the proposal (subject to mandatory access restrictions to protect adjacent European Union-designated conservation areas) and the Scottish Executive approved the proposal. To minimise the visual impact of the funicular and its support columns, the top 250m of the track to the Ptarmigan Visitor Centre go through a shallow tunnel, blasted out of the hillside.

The funicular and new base-station facilities opened in December 2001 and the new Ptarmigan Visitor Centre and restaurant the following spring. CairnGorm Mountain Ltd, the operating company, undertook to plough money back into the ski area, including footpath repair and construction.

One big string was attached to the European funding – the funicular must operate as a closed system during summer, to ensure the increased number of visitors doesn't cause severe damage to the fragile mountain environment. This means that between 1 May and 30 November funicular riders are not be allowed out onto the mountain, their experience being confined to displays in the visitor centre and what they can see from the viewing platform and the funicular carriage. Access on foot to the summit is now from the Cairngorm car park only.

Opponents of the funicular were not amused when the Ptarmigan restaurant was chosen as the site for the official opening of the Cairngorms National Park in September 2003, and several who were invited boycotted the ceremony. It remains to be seen whether the summer access restriction withstands commercial pressures, as visitor numbers have fallen way short of the optimistic forecasts.

survey pillar, near which is a low stone shelter and a geographic direction plate erected by the Cairngorm Club (Aberdeen) in 1925. It helps identify the features in the extraordinarily wide view – from Ben Nevis and Creag Meagaidh (just south of west) to Lochnagar (slightly south of east) and Ben More Assynt (a bit west of north).

To return to the Cairn Gorm High Circuit route, retrace your steps to the saddle at Lochan Buidhe. From there, keep to the left or westerly path over the broad spur, then it's down – with an awesome view straight into the Lairig Ghru, overlooked by rugged Lurchers Crag. Follow this path back to Cairngorm car park as described in the main route.

CHALAMAIN GAP & THE LAIRIG GHRU

Duration	6–6½ hours
Distance	14 miles (22.5km)
Difficulty	moderate–demanding
Start	Sugar Bowl car park
Finish	Coylumbridge (p146)
Nearest Town	Glenmore (p146)
Transport	bus

Summary An energetic walk over a low pass into one of the wildest and most spectacular glens in Scotland.

Far from any road, the Lairig Ghru is widely regarded as the finest mountain pass in Scotland. Cut by a massive glacier slicing right through the mountain mass, it provides a natural route from Strathspey to upper Deeside. Lairig Ghru means 'pass of Druie' – the stream that drains its northern side. It has been used for centuries as a trade and cattle-droving route, and is a public right of way. Traditionally, people walked the full 28 miles (45km) from Aviemore to Braemar, but these days many start from Coylumbridge or Glenmore. The walk described here is a day's outing from just south of Glenmore, through dramatic Chalamain Gap and up to the top of Lairig Ghru then back to Coylumbridge through Rothiemurchus pine woodlands.

The best way to do the walk is as described, starting at a point higher than the finish. Crossing Chalamain Gap involves a climb of 240m and it's another 225m up to the top of Lairig Ghru.

SHORT WALK

Secluded **Loch an Eilein**, part hidden in tall forest, sits at the foot of a long ridge to the northwest of the main Cairngorms massif, within both the Rothiemurchus Estate and Cairngorms National Park. Well-made paths through birch and pine woodland provide an easy 3-mile (5km) circuit of the beautiful loch, for which you should allow 1½ hours. To reach the start, follow the B970 southwest from Inverdruie (p146) for about 1 mile to the signposted turnoff to Loch an Eilein. The parking area (£2) is 1 mile further on. For more information, call at the main Rothiemurchus Visitor Centre (p146).

From the car park follow a wide path south to the small **visitor centre** (Easter-Oct), where you can learn something of what you'll be seeing during the walk. The large, partly grassed mound nearby is the remains of a lime kiln. Continue south along the track, close to the shore and soon the islet that gave the loch its name comes into view, monopolised by the brooding, grey ruins of a 14th-century castle. Further on, close to the path on the left, is a memorial to Walter Rice, who drowned while skating here in 1882, reputedly because he misjudged the thickness of the ice. From the end of the track, a path leads on to the left. Beyond the bridged crossing of the stream joining Loch Gamhna to Loch an Eilein, the path leads along the eastern shores, and there are more good views of the castle. At the northern end of the loch, bear left along a shoreline path to the visitor centre and turn right to reach the car park.

Alternatives One possible alternative for the return is to walk back to Herons Field car park on the Ski Rd near Glenmore, a distance of 14.8 miles (23.5km); Forest Enterprise charges £1 for the use of this car park. Or, you can reach the Ski Rd near the western end of Loch Morlich via the Rothiemurchus Estate road, although car parking there is less satisfactory. The distance for this version is 12.8 miles (20.5km). There's an outline of these alternatives after the main walk description.

If you have plenty of time, there are several interesting possibilities to consider. You could continue down Lairig Ghru to

BENNACHIE – THE CAIRNGORMS' EASTERN SENTINEL

Bennachie is a range of lowish mountains overlooking the lowlands northwest of Aberdeen. The highest point is Oxen Craig (528m); of its various satellites, Mither Tap (518m) is much loved by the locals and affords an incredibly far-ranging view on a good day, from Morven (a mountain in eastern Sutherland) far to the north, to the Cairngorm plateau and around to Aberdeen's urban sprawl.

Heather moorland carpets the ridge's higher ground, dotted with characteristic granite tors; the lower slopes are given over to conifer plantations and small-scale farms. People have lived on and around Bennachie for thousands of years. There's an Iron Age fort on Mither Tap, and crofters were evicted from the eastern slopes in the 19th century.

Much of the range is owned by the Forestry Commission, which has developed a web of waymarked walks across Bennachie, from short woodland strolls to the scenic, 11.5-mile-long West Gordon Way. Following forest tracks and footpaths, these walks fan out from the **Bennachie Centre** (☎ 01467 681470; bennachie.warden@aberdeenshire.gov.uk; 🕑 10.30am-5pm Tue-Sun) and from car parks on the northern and southern sides of the mountain. The waymarked Way, from the Bennachie Centre to the Suie car park in the west, is shown on OS Landranger 1:50,000 map No 37, and extends onto map No 38.

The Bennachie Centre has displays and a forest shop; rangers lead guided walks from the centre during summer.

The centre is a few miles west of Inverurie; access from there, via Burnhervie, is signposted. For information about accommodation and facilities in Inverurie and nearby Alford, contact the **Inverurie TIC** (☎ 01467 625800; 18 High St).

the Luibeg path, and on to Derry Lodge and Linn of Dee, from where it's possible to reach Braemar, or keep going south, right through Glen Tilt, to Blair Atholl (see the walk on p156).

GETTING TO/FROM THE WALK

The walk starts at Sugar Bowl car park, on the northeastern side of the Ski Rd, 1.75 miles south of Glenmore. You could use the Highland Country Buses service from Aviemore to Cairngorm Ski Centre (see p147), although the driver will probably stop below the car park for safety's sake.

At the end of the walk, there's a small roadside car park nearby. Alternatively, the same bus service to the start of the walk stops in Glenmore and Coylumbridge on the way to Aviemore.

THE WALK

Map p143

From the car park cross the road and follow the path down to a footbridge across Allt Mór. Climb up to the right then, on the rim of the bank, veer left along a stone-paved path and continue past a sign warning that you're entering a wild mountainous area. The views along the moorland here are great, taking in the deep corries and sharp spurs of the northern face of the Cairngorm plateau. The path dips to cross a small stream then climbs steadily to narrow **Chalamain Gap**. Clamber over the boulders filling its narrow cleft, keeping to the lowest level to avoid the peaty, heathery slopes. It's an eerily quiet place, where rock falls seem to occur fairly frequently. On the far side there are magnificent views across Lairig Ghru to mighty Braeriach and the cairn-topped Sgòran Dubh Mór beyond. The wide, rocky and occasionally wet path crosses a shallow valley then descends steeply to the Lairig Ghru path beside Allt Druidh.

The path crosses the stream on big boulders and climbs the heathery slope, before emerging onto more open ground overlooked by steep slopes. Elongated mounds of moraine, left behind by the retreating glaciers, partly block the valley as you climb towards the pass. The path is marked by occasional cairns; follow these carefully, keeping to the left (east) for the final stretch to the **Lairig Ghru** crest. Ahead, the rugged peaks of Cairn Toul and the Devil's Point come into view. Continue for another 650m or so to the **Pools of Dee**, the headwaters of the River Dee, from where you can look far down the southern side of Lairig Ghru.

Retrace your steps to the point where you joined the Lairig Ghru path and continue downstream. The rough path crosses steep, rocky slopes with Allt Druidh far below in a deep trench cut through the moraine. Continue past a path to the right (to Rothiemurchus Lodge), with fine views of the Monadhliath Mountains on the western side of Strathspey and Meall a' Bhuachaille above Loch Morlich. After about 1.25 miles you come to some beautiful Scots pines, the outliers of the Caledonian woodland and a precious remnant of the great forests that once covered much of the Highlands. The path junction, known unofficially as **Piccadilly**, has direction signs to Aviemore (to the left/west) and Loch Morlich (to the right/east).

Follow the Aviemore track, beside Allt Druidh, past a stream junction and down to the footbridge, built in 1912 by the Cairngorm Club, over Allt na Beinne Moire (mapped as Am Beanaidh). A short distance further on, bear right along a path to Coylumbridge. This leads through dense pines then more-open pine woodland (where the displays of purple heather in August are magnificent), across small burns and through gates. Pass a path to the left (to Glen Einich) and continue along the broad track, past Rothiemurchus Camp & Caravan Park, to the road at Coylumbridge. There is a small roadside car park to the left.

ALTERNATIVE FINISH: PICCADILLY TO GLENMORE

1¼ hours, 3 miles (5km)

Turn right at Piccadilly along the wide path towards Loch Morlich. This leads through pine woodland to a high deer fence, just beyond which you meet the wide gravel road to Rothiemurchus Lodge. Bear left and continue along the gravel road for nearly 1 mile to an unsigned junction.

To reach the Ski Rd near the western end of Loch Morlich directly from here, just continue ahead for 300m. There is some roadside car parking here and there's a Forest Enterprise car park (£1), 200m to the right. Glenmore is 1.25 miles along the Ski Rd.

For Herons Field, follow the path from the unsigned junction to a footbridge across a small burn then go through a tall gate and go left along a wide forest track, skirting the shore of Loch Morlich. Near its eastern end turn left along a path marked with a red-banded post. Follow the route, marked with these posts, north and east through cleared land and pines to the car park just west of Glenmore. Sugar Bowl car park is 1.25 miles further south along the Ski Rd.

SOUTHERN CAIRNGORMS

The highlights of this area, south of an east-west line roughly through Ben Macdui, are the lengthy public footpaths through the glens, which serve to unify the entire Cairngorms area. For walkers, these pedestrian 'highways' offer outstanding opportunities for extended walks in remote, uninhabited country, and easy access to scores of mountains. Many of the walks pass through the large Mar Lodge Estate, owned by the National Trust for Scotland (NTS). The estate is rich in archaeological evidence of past

MAR LODGE ESTATE – A WORK IN PROGRESS

The National Trust for Scotland's purchase of the 29,500-hectare Mar Lodge Estate in 1995 was hailed by many conservationists as a victory for the protection and better management of natural areas. All too frequently estates had been acquired by wealthy people with no real understanding of the natural values of the land. In the mid-1990s, the estate's red deer population was too high to allow the precious Caledonian woodlands to regenerate naturally (a problem since the 1830s), magnificently wild and lonely glens were blighted with exotic conifer plantations (although not on a large scale) and bulldozed tracks scarred some hillsides.

The main thrust of the Trust's program to rehabilitate the landscape is reducing the numbers of deer from 3300 in 1995 to around 1650. This will enable the Caledonian pines to regenerate and the heather moorland to recover from the intensive grazing by deer. At the time of research, Trust staff monitoring new tree growth had found fairly restricted, slow progress. To put a positive spin on this, it will probably take more than a decade to make good the neglect of more than 170 years!

settlement and many hundreds of sites have been identified. Examples of these, such as the foundations of stone cottages and stone-walled enclosures, are quite common through Glen Dee.

This section features walks along some of the public footpaths and a mountain walk to beautiful Lochnagar in Deeside, the area centred on the River Dee and its broad strath. Under More Walks (p163) are notes about a walk around Loch Muick (near Lochnagar) and another up Morrone, a fine mountain above Braemar.

LINN OF DEE CIRCUIT

Duration	6½–7 hours
Distance	16 miles (26km)
Difficulty	moderate
Start/Finish	Linn of Dee
Nearest Towns	Braemar (right), Inverey (opposite)
Transport	private

Summary A generally low-level exploration of two beautiful glens and superb Scots pine woodlands, with awesome views of the Braeriach massif above Lairig Ghru.

This is a superbly scenic, comparatively low-level walk, exploring Glen Dee and Glen Lui, west of Braemar. It's a good way to familiarise yourself with the area and its special feeling of remoteness and isolation. With a high point of 610m (only 250m of ascent), it is ideal for a misty day. A clockwise direction is recommended so you walk up the ever-narrowing Glen Dee towards spectacular Lairig Ghru, and the best of the going underfoot is concentrated in the second half of the walk. The walk can be extended further up Lairig Ghru as far as the Pools of Dee; this involves an extra 7 miles (11km) return.

The NTS has a policy of encouraging the long walk-in to the mountains – the reason for the car park being at Linn of Dee rather than Derry Lodge.

This walk is the key to several mountain climbs (or Munro-bagging excursions): massive Beinn Bhrotain (1157m), rising from the western side of Glen Dee; the Devil's Point (1004m), towering over Corrour Bothy; Carn a' Mhaim (1037m), opposite the bothy; Ben Macdui (1309m) via Glen Luibeg and Sròn Riach; and Derry Cairngorm (1156m). All are very fine walks, although adding any to the route described here makes for a long day, best kept for good midsummer weather. Spreading these walks over a couple of days would be better; small Corrour Bothy, renovated by the Mountain Bothies Association (p21), could serve as a base, and there's plenty of tent space nearby. During the renovation, seven large sacks of rubbish were lifted out by helicopter; please help to ensure that this expensive clean-up is never necessary again. Elsewhere, being in NTS territory, there's no problem with wild camping for a night or two, although open fires are strictly prohibited.

During the walk you see plenty of evidence of the NTS's work to restore the magnificent pine woodlands, with fenced areas (exclosures) in Glen Luibeg where the native woodland, safe from hungry deer, is slowly making a comeback. In Glen Dee, conifer plantations and their enclosing fences are being removed, to make way for native species and to give capercaillie and black grouse a better chance of thriving without the hazard of lethal fencing. Less obviously, the number of red deer has been greatly reduced.

PLANNING

When to Walk/Stalking

The walk is entirely within the NTS Mar Lodge Estate, where estate staff do the stalking, but never on weekends. Walkers' access is not affected by stalking activities.

Maps & Books

The OS Landranger 1:50,000 map No 43 *Braemar & Blair Atholl* covers this walk. The Harvey Superwalker 1:25,000 *Cairn Gorm* map excludes the area northwest from Linn of Dee, between Glen Luibeg and the River Dee.

The SMC's guide *The Cairngorms* contains some relevant information. The NTS booklet about Mar Lodge Estate is available from the rangers' office at Mar Lodge or, more conveniently, from the TICs in Braemar and Ballater.

NEAREST TOWNS

Braemar

☎ 01339 / pop 400

Braemar, internationally famous for its annual September Highland Gathering, is a compact village deep in the mountains, just off the A93. The **TIC** (☎ 741600; www.aberdeen-grampian.com; ⌚ daily Jun-Sep, Mon-Sat Oct-May) carries a good range of guidebooks, and the local weather forecast is usually on display. The one bank does not have an ATM – the nearest is in Ballater (p161).

Braemar Mountain Sports (☎ 741242; 5 Invercauld Rd; ⌚ daily) has a comprehensive range of stock, including stove fuels.

SLEEPING & EATING

Invercauld Caravan Club Site (☎ 741373; www.caravanclub.co.uk; Glenshee Rd; unpowered/powered sites for 2£15/24) is open to nonmembers. It's well laid out with plenty of trees and grass; facilities include a drying room.

Braemar SYHA Hostel (☎ 0870 155 3255; www.syha.org.uk; 21 Glenshee Rd; dm/d £13/26; 💻), beside the A93 just south of the village, has smallish dorms and a few doubles, an excellent drying room and a large kitchen. The mountain weather forecast is displayed daily.

Schiehallion House (☎ 741679; www.schiehallionhouse.com; Glenshee Rd; s/d £25/52), run by two keen walkers, provides a touch of luxury without too much fuss; look forward to a warm welcome.

Fife Arms Hotel (☎ 741644; Mar Rd; mains £8-12; ⌚ lunch & dinner) is the walkers' pub, and the lounge bar serves bar meals that are better than average.

For self-caterers there's an Alldays supermarket, Strachan's grocery for Scottish delicacies, and a good butcher where you can also buy delicious fresh bread, a great start to a fortifying picnic lunch.

GETTING THERE & AWAY

Stagecoach (☎ 0870 608 2608; www.stagecoachbus.com) operates service 201 between Aberdeen and Braemar (£8, 2¼ hours, eight services Monday to Saturday, five Sunday) via Ballater.

Braemar is on the A93, 59 miles (96km) from Aberdeen and 17 miles (28km) west of Ballater.

Inverey

Inverey can't even be called a settlement – it consists simply of a couple of buildings, one of which is the small **Inverey SYHA Hostel** (☎ 01339 741969; dm £12), just west of the village on the Linn of Dee road. There's always plenty of hot water on tap to compensate for the lack of a shower.

The postbus service from Braemar (see below) passes Inverey on the way to Linn of Dee; ask the driver to drop you at the hostel.

GETTING TO/FROM THE WALK

The walk starts at the NTS Linn of Dee car park (£2 per day), 6.4 miles (10.5km) west of Braemar, just north of the River Dee bridge. A **Royal Mail postbus** (☎ 01246 546329) service, route 072, links Braemar and Linn of Dee (£2, 20 minutes, Monday to Saturday) via Inverey but doesn't reach Linn of Dee until 1.40pm.

THE WALK Map p143

From the car park head west along the road and continue on past a barrier, along a vehicular track. You soon leave a pine plantation behind, entering wide, steep-sided Glen Dee. Follow the road, past many former settlements and scattered Scots pines, almost to White Bridge (about 1¼ hours from the start). Just before the bridge, leave the track on the well-made path to the right (west). In about 250m you pass close to the picturesque clear pools and cascades of the **Chest of Dee**. The path – generally pretty rough but properly constructed in places and easy to follow – leads northwest up Glen Dee, with the river in view. About 1.2km beyond the Chest of Dee, the path fords a small burn, beside which are the remains of two small dwellings. After a couple of miles the route drops down to the river bank where the glen narrows. From here, splendid views of the mighty cliffs of the Devil's Point, the gateway to Lairig Ghru, and Cairn Toul beyond begin to unfold. As the glen widens again, near the cliff-lined Glen Geusachan to the west, the path rises across the heathery-peaty slope and leads to a junction. This is spectacularly overlooked by the Devil's Point and is just about opposite **Corrour Bothy** (about 2½ hours from White Bridge).

To reach the bothy, go down a narrow path on the left to a bridge across the river. Pick your way through the peat hags up to the bothy, standing more or less high and dry above the peaty morass. The small bothy, which was built in 1877 to house an estate deer watcher on the lookout for poachers, was renovated in 2006 by the

Mountain Bothies Association. The outlook to Ben Macdui is most impressive and the bothy is dwarfed by the surrounding mountains.

From the path junction it takes a good three hours to continue up through the magnificent depths of Lairig Ghru to the Pools of Dee and to return – it's well worth the effort if time is on your side.

The route back to Linn of Dee heads south from the path junction. The path rises steadily up the lower slopes of Carn a' Mhaim to the divide between the Dee and Luibeg Burn. Around here the quality of the path improves dramatically, with sections of stone paving and beautifully built culverts. The path descends into **Glen Luibeg** to an exclosure – go through the gate. There's a choice to be made here; the dry-feet option is to turn left (north), cross 300m of muddy ground to Luibeg Bridge, then go back downstream through an exclosure, past a path junction (to Ben Macdui) on the left (1½ hours from Corrour Bothy). The alternative, when Luibeg Burn is low, is to carry on straight ahead and cross the stream on widely spaced stepping stones, before joining back up with the main path.

From here, the track rapidly becomes wider and seems well made. It winds its way east through Glen Luibeg, where the scattered pine woodlands are a dramatic change from the moors and crags earlier. After about 1.5 miles you reach the edge of a flat stretch of open grassland. Follow a rough path east from here to a bridge over Derry Burn, near boarded-up Derry Lodge (around one hour from Luibeg Bridge). There is a telephone for public and emergency use here, in a red box on the side of a brown timber building near the lodge. It's coin-operated and maintained (at a loss) by the volunteer Braemar Mountain Rescue Team.

The last hour of walking is nice and easy, down Glen Lui on a vehicular track, past exclosures, areas cleared of exotic conifers and the scattered remains of former settlements. Beyond the Black Bridge, the track rises a little then falls, passing a fenced plantation on the left. On the downhill section, look out for the sign indicating the path to the right, heading through a plantation to the car park.

BLAIR ATHOLL TO GLENMORE

Duration	2 days
Distance	44 miles (71km)
Difficulty	moderate–demanding
Start	Blair Atholl (opposite)
Finish	Glenmore (p146)
Transport	train, bus

Summary Two magnificent days through the length of the Cairngorms, skirting the eastern slopes of the plateau through isolated glens and beautiful Caledonian pine woodlands.

Glen Tilt provided a natural, low-level route between Blair Atholl and Braemar for centuries. The Duke of Atholl tried to frustrate this tradition by closing the glen in the 1840s but lost his court case, ensuring the right of way's integrity. Forest Lodge is a long-standing centre for hunting; Queen Victoria was a visitor in 1844, and she and Prince Albert drove through Glen Tilt to Braemar in 1861.

The unswerving southwest to northeast trend of Glen Tilt betrays its location on a major geological fault line. The rocks here, predominantly schist and limestone, have produced relatively fertile ground so the glen looks much greener than others in the Cairngorms. You can never get away from the ice age in the Cairngorms; the unusual evidence in Glen Tilt is the sharp bend in the course of Tarf Water, where a bank of moraine rerouted its original flow into the River Dee.

This walk takes you across three major watersheds: between the River Garry and the River Dee north of Glen Tilt, between the Dee and the River Avon over Lairig an Laoigh, and between the Avon and Strathspey north of the Fords of Avon. Typical of the Cairngorms, there is clear evidence of glaciation in the wide, flat-bottomed glens and in the great mounds of moraine in upper Glen Derry. The amount of ascent involved is about 820m, the greater part of which is in the stretch north from Linn of Dee.

The recommended place to camp, near the ruins of Bynack Lodge, is within the NTS's Mar Lodge Estate.

Glen Derry pine woods are one of the outstanding features of this walk – the NTS's work to restore their vigour is outlined in the boxed text on p153.

Alternatives Some of the finest camp sites in the Cairngorms are in Glen Derry, beneath the Scots pines, not far from deserted Derry Lodge. This is in the heart of the NTS's Mar Lodge Estate, where wild camping is perfectly OK – provided you leave the area as you find it (see p21). However, Derry Lodge is 27 miles (43.5km) from Blair Atholl – on the long side for a day's walk. If you're tempted by the Munros within easy reach of Glen Derry – Derry Cairngorm (1156m), Carn a' Mhaim (1037m) and Ben Macdui (1309m) – then a short day to Glen Derry from Bynack Lodge makes sense. As you walk through Glen Derry and over Lairig an Laoigh, you'll also pass Beinn Mheadhoin (1182m) and Bynack More (1090m) to the west, not to mention the magnificent mountains to the east, foremost among which is Beinn a' Bhuird (1196m). For these it would be worth considering making a base at Hutchison Memorial Hut on upper Derry Burn.

Another possibility is to stay at Inverey SYHA Hostel (p155), just over 1 mile east of Linn of Dee (23 miles/37.3km from Blair Atholl). And lastly, if you have five or six days to spare, there's a grand Cairngorms tour worth contemplating. From Glenmore, it's easy to reach the path through Lairig Ghru (p151), then to follow it all the way down to White Bridge, where you pick up the path followed earlier from Blair Atholl.

Shorter walks include the stroll up Glen Tilt to Forest Lodge, which would make a good 16-mile (26km) day out from Blair Atholl.

PLANNING

When to Walk/Stalking

In **Atholl Estates** (☎ 01796 481646) the most sensitive period for stalking is from mid-August to mid-October. While it's fine to follow the path through Glen Tilt, for walks elsewhere you should check with the estate office about daily activities.

The central part of the walk is in the NTS's Mar Lodge Estate where access is open at all times.

Maps

The OS Landranger 1:50,000 maps to carry are No 43 *Braemar & Blair Atholl* and No 36 *Grantown & Aviemore*. The eastern boundary of Harvey's Superwalker 1:25,000 *Cairn Gorm* map coincides with the path northward from Glen Derry, so it's worth having this map if you are planning to climb any of the Munros west of the route described here.

NEAREST TOWNS

See Glenmore (p146).

Blair Atholl

☎ 01796 / pop 300

Blair Atholl is a large village on the southern fringe of the Cairngorm uplands, close to the A9 and ideally placed for exploring the area.

Atholl Estates countryside ranger service (☎ 481355; www.athollestatesrangerservice.co.uk; Easter-Oct), provided by the major local landowner, is based in a building next to the large car park near the Bridge of Tilt. The rangers can provide details of guided walks and waymarked routes on the estate.

There's an ATM at Atholl Stores, close to the main road and next to the Atholl Arms Hotel.

The website www.blairatholl.org.uk is a good first port of call for information. The nearest information centre is the **Pitlochry TIC** (☎ 01796 472215; pitlochrytic@visitscotland.com; daily Apr-Oct, Mon-Sat Nov-Mar), about 6 miles (10km) south of Blair Atholl along the A9.

SLEEPING & EATING

Blair Castle Caravan Park (☎ 481263; www.blaircastlecaravanpark.co.uk; unpowered/powered sites for 2 £14/16;) is exceptionally well set up and maintained. There's a small shop on site. Pick up a copy of the brochure *Discover Atholl Estates*, outlining local waymarked walks.

The nearest hostel is **Pitlochry SYHA** (☎ 0870 004 1145; www.syha.org.uk; dm £13), about 6 miles (10km) south on the A9.

The **Firs B&B** (☎ 481256; www.firs-blairatholl.co.uk; St Andrew's Cres; s/d £35/50) has beautifully furnished rooms in a fine old house; breakfast is first-rate.

The **Loft Bistro** (☎ 481377; Golf Course Rd; mains £12-15; lunch & dinner Tue-Sun) is an experience in itself. One of the better restaurants around, the house speciality is Aberdeen Angus steak; vegetarian choices are limited.

The **Atholl Arms Hotel** (☎ 481205; www.athollarmshotel.co.uk; r £80, mains £8-14; lunch & dinner) serves superior-quality bar meals in the

New Bothy Bar. Staying here, in understated luxury, would be a rather special treat.

For self-caterers, there are two mid-sized supermarkets, Atholl Stores and a Spar.

GETTING THERE & AWAY

First ScotRail (☎ 0845 755 0033; www.firstscotrail.com) trains stop at Blair Atholl from Edinburgh, Glasgow (both £19, two hours, six services Monday to Saturday, three Sunday) and Inverness (£16, 1½ hours, six services Monday to Saturday, three Sunday).

Blair Atholl is on the B8079, directly accessible from the A9, 32 miles (52km) north of Perth and 33 miles (54km) south of Kingussie.

THE WALK

Map p143

Day 1: Blair Atholl to Bynack Lodge

6½–7 hours, 19 miles (30.5km)

The walk starts at the Bridge of Tilt on the main road (B8079) through Blair Atholl. Cross the bridge to the eastern side of the River Tilt and go left down some steps to a river-side path through mature woodland. The path follows the river for just over 800m then leads up to the road; follow the road for 100m then turn right at the Scottish Rights of Way Society sign towards 'Deeside by Glen Tilt'. There's another of these signs at the next road junction; turn left then, shortly, cross a bridge and go steeply up to the final turn, left towards Kincraigie Farm. From here there's a fine view of white Blair Castle amid trees to the southwest. Follow the gravel road and soon, at a bend, cross a stile and follow a grassy track to a gate. This leads through woodland and across open ground; just past Croftmore (a stone house with well-tended gardens) ignore a track going up to the right and continue gently down to a gravel road (1½ hours from Blair Atholl).

Soon, a grassy track offers a short cut from the road. A few hundred metres further on is the solitary stone cottage Marble Lodge. The steep, scree-strewn slopes of Beinn a' Ghlo are starting to dominate the view ahead. The road crosses the River Tilt and leads along the bank. Almost opposite deserted Balaneasie cottage, bear left along a grassy track to cut off another bend in the road, with Glen Tilt opening up invitingly ahead. The startling sound of roosters crowing leaves you in no doubt that Clachghlas is lived in. A good mile further on you reach the imposing entrance to Forest Lodge (a map shows preferred walking routes during the stalking season). Walk past the lodge, along the edge of a small conifer plantation and into the ever-narrowing glen. The road becomes a vehicular track, which eventually ends about 3 miles from Forest Lodge. The **Falls of Tarf** and Tarf Water Bridge are about 200m further north along a path (2¾ hours since joining the road). The bridge was originally built in 1886 by the Scottish Rights of Way Society to commemorate a drowning there in 1878. Just beyond the bridge, a stone in the ground bears the figure '13' – the miles from Blair Atholl.

A good path continues up the glen, more of a narrow defile, for about 1 mile. It widens suddenly around the source of the River Tilt, where the new outlook is towards big, sprawling mountains. About an hour's walk from Tarf Water you reach the start of a rough vehicular track; it's another 20 minutes to the rather forlorn remains of **Bynack Lodge**, with a few windswept larches.

Day 2: Bynack Lodge to Glenmore

10 hours, 25 miles (40km)

The first stage of this long day is comparatively easy, along the path on the eastern side of Bynack Burn, soon crossing Allt an t-Seilich. A vehicular track continues to the Geldie Burn crossing, which shouldn't present any problems unless the burn is in spate. Continue north along the track, past a conifer plantation, to White Bridge and the River Dee. After crossing the bridge head east down broad Glen Dee to the sealed road near Linn of Dee (1¾ hours from Bynack Lodge).

Continue east along the road to the car park and, from its northern edge, turn onto a signposted path to Glen Lui. This leads through the conifer plantation to a vehicular track in Glen Lui and another straightforward stretch up the broad glen, dominated by the bulk of Derry Cairngorm ahead. After about an hour, you reach **Derry Lodge**, standing silently with boarded-up windows in the open pine woodland. There is a telephone for public and emergency use in a red box on the side of a brown timber building near the lodge. It's coin-operated and maintained (at a loss) by the volunteer Braemar Mountain Rescue Team.

Cross the bridge over Derry Burn and follow a path leading north away from the burn (rather than along the faint and discontinuous path beside the burn). Go through the woodland, past an exclosure, over a low, heathery hillock and then down to a footbridge over Derry Burn. The path meets a vehicular track about 200m further on. The glen soon starts to close in. There are inspirational views ahead to the tors on the broad summit plateau of Beinn Mheadhoin, rising impressively above Stob Coire Etchachan's cliffs.

The vehicular track ends beside an exclosure. A wide track continues through another exclosure, but follow the path leading on and starting to climb. Soon, large stepping stones provide an easy crossing of Glas Allt Mór and a good path leads on to the junction with the path to Hutchison Memorial Hut below Stob Coire Etchachan (1½ hours from Derry Lodge).

From the path junction, continue heading north. A steepening climb on a rougher path, across a few muddy patches, takes you up to **Lairig an Laoigh** (30 minutes from the path junction). A new outlook unfolds down a wide glen, with boulder-strewn slopes cradling Dubh Lochan, and across the Fords of Avon to the great bulk of Bynack More. Follow the path down, past the well-named Dubh Lochan ('small dark lake') to the **Fords of Avon** (45 minutes from the Lairig). Boulders, rather than stepping stones, should enable you to keep your feet dry on the two crossings, separated by a tiny grassed island. The nearby refuge is small, dark and windowless, and could only be inviting in foul weather.

The path leads on up the glen of Allt Dearg, past Lochan a' Bhainne and across the low divide between the allt and a stream called Glasath, which you soon cross on good stepping stones. The path rises rather muddily from the crossing, around the broad shoulder of Bynack More, wanders around a bit and then drops down to cross Uisge Dubh Poll a' Choin on treacherous, mossy stones. Then it's a short, steep pull up to the broad northern spur of Bynack More – a bleak, windswept place in poor weather, but has the classic Cairngorms feel of open space on a good day. To the south-east, Ben Avon's great tor-studded summit plateau, and Beinn a' Bhuird's crag-lined top dominate the view. The path, muddy and badly eroded in places, soon sets out on the long descent to the bridge over the **River Nethy** (about 1½ hours from Fords of Avon).

A stony vehicular track leads on from here and, about 1 mile from the bridge, joins a track from the right at the base of the steep scree- and heather-clad slopes of Meall a' Bhuachaille. The rest is easy, walking south-west down the vehicular track or forest road, past beautiful **An Lochan Uaine**, through pine woodlands and some conifers. Glenmore Lodge (p146), just over 1 mile from the lochan, seems large and incongruous after the emptiness of the moors and glens, but it does have a good bar! Glenmore village is another 1 mile along the sealed road (1½ hours from the River Nethy).

LOCHNAGAR

Duration	6–6½ hours
Distance	14 miles (22.7km)
Difficulty	moderate
Start/Finish	Spittal of Glenmuick
Nearest Town	Ballater (above)
Transport	private

Summary The best-known peak in the Deeside Cairngorms, with spectacular panoramic views and a descent beside a dramatic waterfall to Loch Muick, in the heart of an outstanding nature reserve.

A magnificent mountain, with huge corries scooped out of its northern face, Lochnagar (1155m, 3788ft) is the highest of the peaks to the south of Deeside. It provides a dramatic backdrop to the town of Ballater and is the feature of a huge, roughly horse-shoe-shaped ridge embracing Loch Muick. The name Lochnagar can be confusing – it refers to the twin peaks of Cac Carn Beag and Cac Carn Mòr, as well as a lochan in one of the northern corries.

The walk described here follows a vehicular track, then a well-used and maintained path, with long sections of stone paving and steps, steeply up to the gap between Lochnagar and its outlier, Meikle Pap (980m). Another steep, rocky climb leads to the spectacular rim of the corrie cradling Lochnagar; the summit (Cac Carn Beag) stands on a spur between Lochnagar and Loch nan Eun to the west. To make an excellent circular walk, the return is down a steep, stone-built path beside Glas Allt to the shore of Loch Muick, where a vehicular track leads back to the start. The total ascent for the walk is 800m.

Alternatives If you're fit and experienced, it will be hard to resist the temptation to 'do the round' of Loch Muick – and, perhaps, to bag another four Munros. To do this, continue from Lochnagar's secondary summit (1150m) southwest and west over the Stuic (1093m) above Loch nan Eun (and/or Carn a' Choire Bhaidheach at 1110m, if you're in bagging mode) to Carn an t-Sagairt Mór (1047m), then southeast to Cairn Bannoch (1012m) and on to Broad Cairn (998m).

From there it's a long descent to a boggy saddle; then you can either follow a path down to Loch Muick, or the vehicular track, which keeps to high ground for another 2 miles then drops down across Black Burn to the loch and back to the start. This superb walk of around 16.5 miles (26.5km) involves at least 1130m of ascent and would take around nine hours.

HISTORY

Lochnagar means 'loch of noise' or 'laughter', or perhaps 'noisy' or 'laughing loch' – possibly describing the sound of falling scree on the cliffs.

Glen Muick (pronounced 'mick') once supported many crofting families and the Spittal of Glenmuick ('a resting-place') was used by drovers taking cattle along the Capel Mount route over the mountains to Glen Clova. The famous Romantic poet George Lord Byron, a native of Aberdeenshire, fondly remembered Lochnagar with the lines:

> England! Thy beauties are tame and domestic
> To one who has roved o'er the mountains afar:
> Oh for the crags that are wild and majestic!
> The steep frowning glories of dark Lochnagar!

The nucleus of the Balmoral Estate, which extends from the River Dee southeast to well beyond Loch Muick, was purchased by Queen Victoria in 1878. She added the Ballochbuie Forest to the royal portfolio, so saving it from imminent felling. She was very fond of the estate, and Glen Muick was a particular favourite; she had Glas-allt-Shiel Lodge built beside the loch soon after her beloved husband Prince Albert died. The estate still belongs to the royal family, who are regular summer visitors to nearby Balmoral Castle.

ENVIRONMENT

Lochnagar is essentially a granite mountain, the originally grey-pink rock taking on darker tones as lichen accumulates on exposed surfaces. Evidence of the work of glaciers during the last Ice Age is clearly seen in Loch Muick's U-shaped valley and in the corries where, even now, snow lies well into spring.

Mountain hares are occasionally seen bounding about on the higher ground and you'd be unlucky not to see ptarmigan, which are not at all shy and easily identifiable by their croaking call.

PLANNING

When to Walk/Stalking

Within **Balmoral Estate** (☎ 01339 742534) the stalking season is from mid-August to mid-October. Although access to Lochnagar is maintained throughout the season, stalking takes place around the other mountains in the area. Detailed information is available daily from the estate and at the Spittal of Glenmuick visitor centre (below).

Maps & Books

Harvey's Superwalker 1:25,000 *Lochnagar* map is the one to use for this walk and its possible extensions. The relevant OS Landranger 1:50,000 map is No 44 *Ballater & Glen Clova.*

Naturally, Lochnagar features in all the Munros guides (see the boxed text on p108); the SMC's guide *The Cairngorms* devotes a chapter to 'Dark Lochnagar'.

Information Sources

At Spittal of Glenmuick, the starting point for the walk, Balmoral Estate has a small, information-packed **visitor centre** (☎ 01339 755059; www.balmoralcastle.com; 🕑 daily Easter-Oct), where you'll often find one of the countryside rangers; information about stalking activities is displayed there. The rangers run guided walks in and around the glen from May to September.

NEAREST TOWN

Ballater

☎ 01339 / pop 1450

Very much aware of being in Royal Deeside, Ballater sits on a wide bend in the River Dee. The **TIC** (☎ 755306), in the renovated train station, is very helpful and well organised. **Lochnagar Leisure** (☎ 560008; Station Sq; daily) stocks a good range of outdoor gear, including fuel.

SLEEPING & EATING

Anderson Road Caravan Park (☎ 755727; unpowered/powered sites for 2 £7/18) is well set up and can be very busy.

Netherley Guest House (☎ 755792; www.netherleyguesthouseballater.com; 2 Netherley Pl; s/d £35/50), with its trademark blue shutters, is centrally located; the atmosphere is friendly and relaxed.

Celicall Guest House (☎ 755699; celicall@tiscali.co.uk; 3 Braemar Rd; s/d £33/54) is a friendly B&B centrally located opposite Station Sq.

The nearest hostel is the SYHA at Braemar (p154).

La Mangiatoia (☎ 755999; Bridge Sq; mains £6-13; lunch & dinner), off the A93 on the eastern side of town, offers an Italian-inspired menu that includes some Scottish dishes, and is good value for this part of the world.

Rowan Tree Restaurant (☎ 755509; 43 Bridge St; mains £5-16; lunch & dinner) is quite a stylish place, offering a strongly Scottish-flavoured menu, though with limited temptations for vegetarians.

For self-catering, there are two supermarkets, Strachan's (a superior grocery) and a fruit-and-vegetable shop.

GETTING THERE & AWAY

Stagecoach (☎ 0870 608 2608) operates bus service 21 between Aberdeen and Ballater (£7, 1¾ hours, 11 services Monday to Saturday, seven Sunday).

By road, Ballater is on the A93, 42 miles (68km) west of Aberdeen and 17 miles (27km) east of Braemar.

GETTING TO/FROM THE WALK

The walk starts at the Spittal of Glenmuick, at the end of the public road through the glen. From Ballater, cross the River Dee bridge and turn right. About 1.2km further along, bear left at a junction to Glen Muick (as signposted). The car park is 8 miles (12km) from here. A pay-and-display system (£2 per day) operates here; the proceeds are channelled to mountain path repair work.

THE WALK

From the car park, cross the bridge and walk down the track to the visitor centre, passing toilets in the trees. A short distance further on, turn right along the path signposted to Lochnagar. Ahead, the scree-encrusted Meikle Pap, the cliffs on Lochnagar's northeast face and the broad plateau of Cuidhe Crom are framed in the V formed by nearer, heathery mountains. Follow the track across River Muick in its flat-bottomed glen and, where the track bends right, continue straight ahead across a road and to the left of a stone cottage, along a signposted path. This passes a plantation on the left and goes through pine woodland, merging with a wider track from the left; soon you're out in heather moorland. The wide track rises beside Allt na Giubhsaich, crossing it on stepping stones and continuing to gain height steadily in the rather bleak heather moorland. About an hour from the start you reach a fairly broad col between Conachcraig to the northeast and Lochnagar.

Leave the track and drop down a well-made stone path, which then climbs the slope of Meikle Pap, strewn with granite boulders. Well up, just before the path turns west under the slope of Cuidhe Crom, a short path to the left leads to **Foxes' Well**, the last source of water on the climb. Beside it is a memorial (with a rather intrusive photograph) to a man who died climbing in the corrie in 1953. The steep, stone-built path continues to the col south of Meikle Pap, from where there are spectacular views of the cliff-girt corrie sheltering Lochnagar's loch. The path then bears left and rises south through the boulder field (where it's discreetly waymarked), well back from the corrie rim, and up to the spacious plateau. Skirt the corrie rim and cross a shallow gap; a line of cairns marks the route, which then swings away from the edge to mount the slope leading to Cac Carn Mòr. Despite its name, it's not Lochnagar's highest point –

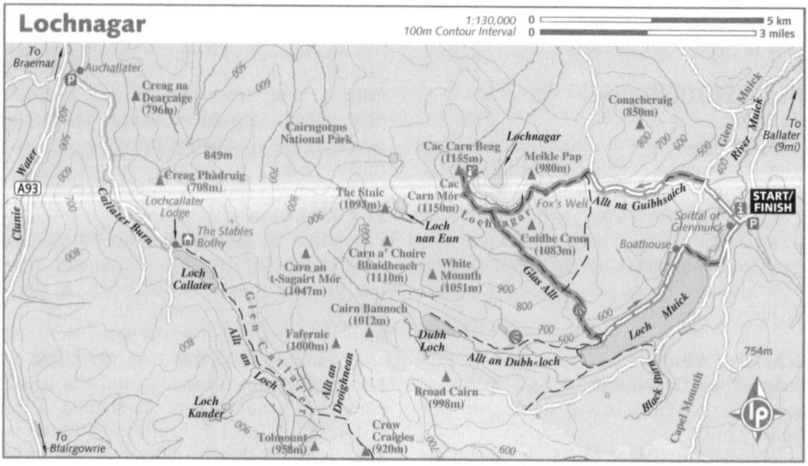

this honour goes to **Cac Carn Beag**, 500m north, topped by a massive cairn (about two hours from the Conachcraig col). A direction finder installed in 1924 and, remarkably, still in fair condition helps identify the features of the amazing panorama of mountains and glens. Among the more distant are the Pentland Hills (near Edinburgh), Ben Lomond, Creag Meagaidh and Ben Nevis.

Retrace your steps over Cac Carn Mòr and, ignoring a path leading right by a small cairn, drop down its southeastern flank to a prominent path junction; descend steeply into the deep glen of Glas Allt. Extensive path repairs have made this descent into a particularly peaty and heathery place relatively easy. The path follows the stream closely, crossing on a good bridge after nearly 1 mile. Here a track leads away northeast across the hillside but continue in a southeasterly direction. Glas Allt plunges into a dramatic gorge and the path clings miraculously to the steep, rocky slope as it descends towards the deep trench of Loch Muick. The **Falls of Glasallt** aren't particularly high but are attractive nonetheless, pouring down grey, blocky cliffs with long cascades below. The path descends to a pine woodland; go past the end of a dyke beside the stream, cross a footbridge and continue down to the loch-side vehicular track (two hours from Cac Carn Beag). Follow this northeast to the end of Loch Muick and turn right beside the boathouse onto the path along its northern shore. Cross River Muick and follow the vehicular track north, which takes you back to the start (1¼ hours from where you met the loch-side vehicular track).

MORE WALKS

NORTHERN CAIRNGORMS

Braeriach

Braeriach (1296m, 4251ft), meaning 'the brindled upland', is the second-highest peak in the Cairngorms and the third-highest in Scotland. It's the culmination of a great, undulating plateau, with Lairig Ghru on its precipitous eastern side and its western flank rising almost as steeply from lonely Gleann Einich. This magnificent massif, with dark, mysterious corries scooped out of its northern and eastern slopes, is unspoiled by any developments. For Munro enthusiasts the extra lures are Sgòr an Lochain Uaine (1258m) and Cairn Toul (1293m), perched on the rim above Lairig Ghru.

The climb to Braeriach starts only after a fairly long walk in, so you'll need a fine midsummer day. The distance is 18.75 miles (30km) and the ascent is 1000m; allow about nine hours. The best map is Harvey's 1:25,000 *Cairn Gorm*. The SMC's guide *The Cairngorms* is an invaluable reference.

The most popular approach is from the Lairig Ghru path by Allt Druidh (see p151) to a minor track junction about 150m south of the Chalamain Gap path junction. Rather than return the same way, a descent west into Glen Einich, returning down that valley, makes a much more interesting walk. Extending the walk to Sgòr an Lochain Uaine and Cairn Toul would add 4 miles (6.5km), 300m ascent and about two hours to the walk. The route described is the one Rothiemurchus Estate prefers walkers to take during stalking season (September and October); for more information contact the estate's **visitor centre** (☎ 01479 812345).

Meall a' Bhuachaille

This shapely mountain (the name means 'shepherd's hill') overlooks Glenmore and Loch Morlich and gives superb views of the Cairngorm plateau and Braeriach from its summit. A waymarked path leads north from behind the Glenmore Forest Park Visitor Centre and climbs steeply through the pines to open moorland. From here a well-made path leads up to a broad saddle between Creagan Gorm (782m) to the west and the Meall (810m) itself, then on to the summit. To make a circuit, continue east down the broad spur to Ryvoan Bothy then follow a vehicular track past beautiful An Lochan Uaine ('green lake'), Glenmore Lodge and back to the village. Allow three hours for this 6-mile (9.5km) walk, which includes 480m of climbing. Use Harvey's 1:25,000 map *Cairn Gorm* or the OS Landranger 1:50,000 map No 36 *Grantown & Aviemore*.

Speyside Way

This long-distance path links Aviemore (p145) in Strathspey and Buckie on the North Sea coast, and generally follows the course of the River Spey, Scotland's second-longest river and one of its most scenic. Overlooked by the Cairngorm mountains at its Strathspey end, the Way passes through Boat of Garten, Nethy Bridge, Grantown-on-Spey, Cromdale, Aberlour (where you'll find the Way's excellent visitor centre), Craigellachie, Fochabers and Spey Bay to reach its end at Buckie. A spur route, from Bridge of Avon to Tomintoul (the highest village in the Highlands) provides an attractive walk in its own right and is definitely worth the extra time. The Way is well signposted and waymarked with the official thistle-hexagon logo.

The Way, which can be followed in either direction, is 65 miles (104.5km) long; the Tomintoul spur is 14.3 miles (23km). It is possible to do the whole lot in five days, but six or seven allows time for visiting whisky distilleries and the famous Strathspey Steam Railway.

The **Speyside Way Ranger Service** (☎ 01340 881266; www.speysideway.org; Aberlour visitor centre) publishes a free annual accommodation brochure and a public transport guide.

The 1:40,000 Harvey map *Speyside Way*, the official map for the route, shows facilities and some features of interest. For coverage of the surrounding area you'll need OS Landranger 1:50,000 map Nos 28 and 36, which show the route of the Way.

The official brochure is invaluable, as it indicates which accommodation hosts offer a pick-up and drop-off service – useful where there are long gaps between shelter of any type (particularly between Cromdale and Aberlour). Camp sites are spaced so you could camp each night.

For transport to Aviemore, see p145. Buses link Buckie, Aberdeen and Keith, which is on the train line connecting Inverness and Aberdeen. Several intermediate towns are served by buses from major centres.

SOUTHERN CAIRNGORMS

Glen Tilt & Glen Feshie

This two-day, 38.7-mile (62km) walk, linking Blair Atholl and Kingussie, follows two of the Cairngorms' marvellous public footpaths through remote glens. Only 500m of ascent is involved, mostly on the first day. The recommended camp site, near the ruins of Bynack Lodge, is within the NTS's Mar Lodge Estate. For a second night out, Ruigh-aiteachain Bothy in Glen Feshie offers simple but comfortable shelter. As the route follows public footpaths, access during the stalking season isn't an issue (the three estates involved are Atholl, Mar Lodge and Glen Feshie).

You'll need OS Landranger 1:50,000 map Nos 43 and 35.

Contact **Aviemore TIC** (☎ 0845 225 5121; www.visithighlands.com) for help with accommodation. Most First ScotRail services from Edinburgh and Glasgow to Inverness stop at Blair Atholl and Kingussie. Scottish Citylink buses on the Edinburgh to Inverness service stop at Kingussie, which is on the A86, close to the A9, 15 miles (24km) southwest of Aviemore and the same distance north of Dalwhinnie.

The first day matches that of the Blair Atholl to Glenmore walk (p156). Day two involves about 7½ hours and 19.7 miles (31.5km) of walking; route finding is straightforward, except perhaps for the last few miles from Stronetoper Cottage. Take the next turn left along a forest road signposted to Kingussie. A few hundred metres along, at a crossroads, go straight ahead and on to a gate into open moorland. Ignore tracks to the left. Cross a small burn then a channel; continue across a bridge, bear left for about 50m and go over another bridge. Turn left along the forest road; at a crossroads continue ahead, soon through Drumguish (1¾ hours from the River Feshie). At a T-junction, turn left. Follow this minor road into Kingussie (1¼ hours from Drumguish).

Morrone

Morrone (859m) dramatically presides over Braemar from the southwest and offers a good introduction to the area, with fine views that include Braeriach and Ben Macdui. Well-made and waymarked paths make the climb relatively easy. The communications tower on the summit isn't overly intrusive and makes possible a good round walk, following the gravel road built to construct and maintain it.

To reach the start of the walk, turn off the Linn of Dee road on the western edge of Braemar, along Chapel Brae, signposted to 'Forest Walk'. There's a large car park at the end of the sealed road, beside a small lochan. The first part of the walk goes through the Morrone Birkwood, a National Nature Reserve protecting an unusual community of birch, juniper and lime-loving herbs. From the summit, go down the road on the eastern flank of the mountain to a minor road. Follow this north for almost 1.2 miles to a narrow gravel road on the left; beyond a large stone house and in open ground, fork right and continue to Chapel Brae and back to the start. Allow about three hours for this 7.5-mile (12km) walk. You'll need OS Landranger 1:50,000 map No 43.

Loch Muick & Dubh Loch

If cloud and strong winds rule out walking to Lochnagar, then a circuit of Loch Muick, with a side trip to mysterious and dramatically beautiful Dubh Loch, is a very worthy substitute. The walk starts and finishes at the Spittal of Glenmuick car park (for access details, see p155) and is best done clockwise, heading out on the vehicular track along the southeastern shore of Loch Muick, then along the path from Black Burn to the head of the loch.

The path to the western end of Dubh Loch takes off from the northwestern corner of Loch Muick – where the main path turns east to follow its northwestern shore. The Dubh Loch path climbs above Allt an Dubh-loch, past a spectacular waterfall on Stulan Burn. The Loch Muick circuit involves very little ascent and is 7 miles (11km) horizontally; the Dubh Loch extension adds about 5 miles (8km). The visitor centre at Spittal of Glenmuick (p160) has plenty of information about the area, including a *Loch Muick Circuit Walk* leaflet; carry OS Landranger 1:50,000 map No 44.

Highland Glens

Highland and glens are two of the most evocative words associated with Scotland – touchstones for images of misty, rugged mountains and long, lonely valleys. These are, in fact, the essential features of the Highland Glens area, extending from Glen Garry and Glen Spean in the south to Strathconon in the north, and west from the Monadhliath Mountains to the east coast. Here you'll find several beautiful and very different glens and straths (broader valleys); scores of mountains of all shapes and sizes; waterfalls, lochs and tumbling rivers; and, of course, dozens of first-class walks at high and low levels. In this chapter we offer a tempting sample of these riches.

The Great Glen Way is a first-class long-distance path through the grandest glen of all, from Fort William to Inverness, following some long stretches of the historic Caledonian Canal, the line of an old railway and traversing high above famous Loch Ness. Glen Affric is generally regarded as the most beautiful of all the glens. Here we describe a two-day walk through this wild, road-free glen to Morvich, very close to the west coast, with suggestions for alternative routes and side trips, including the spectacular Falls of Glomach. A small selection from the wealth of mountain walks on offer takes in the Five Sisters of Kintail, one of the finest ridge walks anywhere in Scotland; Gleouraich, a remote Munro above Loch Quoich in western Glen Garry; and Creag Meagaidh, a magnificent massif cradling an awesome corrie in Glen Spean.

HIGHLIGHTS

- Striding along the Caledonian Canal and wondering about the legend of Loch Ness on the **Great Glen Way** (p168)
- Wandering through Caledonian woodland in beautiful **Glen Affric** (p174) as you follow the footsteps of early travellers over a pass towards the west coast
- Traversing the **Five Sisters'** (p180) slender, scenic ridge above dramatic Glen Shiel
- Mountain-filled views from the summit of ice-sculpted **Creag Meagaidh** (p184)

- www.visithighlands.com
- www.greatglenway.com

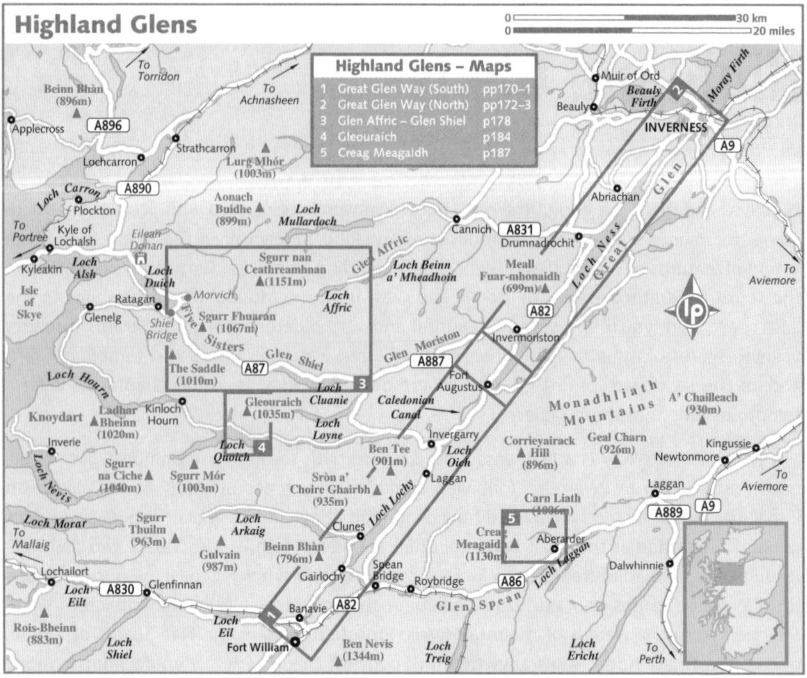

ENVIRONMENT

Putting it simply, these mountains were formed when two enormous plates of the earth's crust rammed together and the plates were bent and folded into peaks and ranges. Much later, ice sheets and glaciers, which accumulated in successive ice ages, enlarged the glens and sculpted the mountains.

The Great Glen – a near-straight-sided trench running from Inverness in the northeast to Fort William in the southwest – almost splits the Highlands asunder. It's the result of massive shifts along a geological fault line eons ago; Loch Ness and Loch Lochy, the largest of the Glen's chain of lochs, were later gouged out by glaciers. To the north and northwest of the Great Glen, the rocks are almost universally metamorphic (altered sediments), of ancient origin and known as schist. This produces poor soil that supports vast tracts of heather and grass moorland. Small remnants of the native Caledonian woodland survive, mainly in Glen Affric (see the boxed text on p175). You're never far from a conifer plantation, although none are of any great size.

INFORMATION

Maps & Books

For overall planning the best bet is the OS Travel – Road 1:250,000 map No 2 *Northern Scotland.*

The most comprehensive guide to the area for walkers is the Scottish Mountaineering Club (SMC) Hillwalkers' Guide *North-west Highlands* by Dave Broadhead, Alec Keith and Ted Maden; it is beautifully illustrated and has colour maps.

For delving into historical background, you can't do much better than James Hunter's books, fired by a passionate commitment to devolution of power to Scotland, and those by John Prebble on the Clearances. To understand something of the traditional Highland ways of life, Calum I Maclean's *The Highlands*, an insider's view of this unique culture, is peerless.

Information Sources

The local branch of **VisitScotland** (www.visithighlands.com) is a fruitful source of information for planning your trip, including accommodation bookings. For public transport information, the most direct source is **Traveline Scotland** (www.travelinescotland.com).

GATEWAY

Inverness

☎ 01463 / pop 41,000

Scenically located on the shores of the inner Moray Firth, Inverness is the bustling, thriving capital of the Highlands, proudly proclaiming its status as a city.

The **TIC** (☎ 234353; www.visithighlands.co.uk; Castle Wynd; daily Easter-Oct, Mon-Sat Nov-Mar;) provides a comprehensive service, including accommodation bookings.

Highland Council's **countryside ranger service** (☎ 724312) runs an extensive program of guided walks in the Inverness area between March and December.

SUPPLIES & EQUIPMENT

Several of the major outdoor gear shops have a branch here, including **Tiso's** (☎ 716617; 41 High St; daily), which is also the best place in town for maps. **Waterstone's** (☎ 717474; 50-52 High St; daily) stocks a wide range of Scottish titles and travel and walking guides.

The most central of Inverness' large collection of supermarkets is **Morrisons** (Millburn Rd), near the train station; there's also a good **health food shop** (Baron Taylor's St).

SLEEPING & EATING

Bught Park Caravan Park & Campsite (☎ 236920; www.invernesscaravanpark.com; Bught Park; unpowered/powered sites for 2 £9/10) is very close to the Great Glen Way, on the southern edge of town. Pitches are flat and grassy, and it's very popular in the high season.

Inverness SYHA Hostel (☎ 0870 004 1127; www.syha.org.uk; Victoria Dr; dm £15;) is in a large, rather soulless modern building in inner-suburban Inverness. The tariff includes a continental breakfast; some rooms have their own bathroom.

Ardconnel House (☎ 240455; www.ardconnel-inverness.co.uk; 21 Ardconnel St; s/d £35/60) is a terraced Victorian house with comfortable en suite rooms in a comparatively quiet street, only a couple of minutes from the city centre.

When it comes to eating out, you're seriously spoilt for choice these days in Inverness. Most of the best places, including the three recommendations, are alongside the River Ness, where there are a few first-rate Italian restaurants.

The **River Cafe & Restaurant** (☎ 714884; 10 Bank St; breakfast £6, lunch mains £5-8, dinner mains £9-15; breakfast, lunch & dinner) enjoys a good location overlooking a quiet stretch of the River Ness. The menu and the daily specials reflect both Mediterranean and Scottish influences; presentation and service are excellent.

Shapla Tandoori (☎ 241919; 2 Castle Rd; mains £7-13; lunch & dinner) offers an extensive menu featuring tandoori and biryani dishes; book early for one of the tables directly overlooking the River Ness.

Mustard Seed (☎ 220220; 16 Fraser St; lunch mains to £8, 2 courses to 7pm £12, dinner mains to £15; lunch & dinner) is a lively, busy place for which booking is almost essential. Fish features prominently on the menu (changed weekly – always a good sign), and vegetarian dishes are imaginative rather than token gestures.

GETTING THERE & AWAY

Air

easyJet (☎ 0870 600 0000; www.easyjet.co.uk) operates daily flights from London Luton and

> **LOW-FLYING JET AIRCRAFT**
>
> It's a perfect sunny day, the breeze is a mere whisper and you're enjoying a peaceful walk. Suddenly, without warning, an ear-splitting roar destroys the tranquillity and one or two sinister-looking military aircraft flash past at an alarmingly low altitude, possibly even below you. This unwelcome intrusion can happen almost anywhere in the Highlands and in many places elsewhere. During walks research for this book, they howled through Glen Sligachan and over Loch Coruisk on Skye, raced down Loch Ness, roared past Quinag in the northwest and screamed through Glen Shiel and above the Road to the Isles.
>
> Fortunately not a daily presence, though seemingly permanent and totally unpredictable, these supersonic jets of the Royal Air Force (RAF) and/or the North Atlantic Treaty Organization (NATO) are practising low flying manoeuvres, mainly from Scottish bases. These skills, we are told, are put to good use overseas in combat zones.
>
> Protests have proved futile, and despite the massive consumption of fuel and consequent pollution, the authorities insist it's vital for national security.

Belfast International (three per week) to Inverness. **British Airways** (☎ 0870 850 9850; www.britishairways.com) flies to Inverness from London Gatwick, Edinburgh and Glasgow. **British Midland** (☎ 0870 607 0555; www.flybmi.com) provides the sole link with London Heathrow. Other airlines fly between Inverness and Dublin (Aer Arann), Liverpool (Ryanair), and Newcastle and Leeds Bradford (Eastern Airways).

Inverness airport is at Dalcross, about 6 miles (10km) northeast, off the A96; **Highland Country Buses** (☎ 01463 710555; www.rapsons.co.uk) connect with many flights (£3, 20 minutes, at least hourly).

Bus

National Express (☎ 0870 580 8080; www.nationalexpress.com) operates a direct overnight service from London (£40, 13 hours).

Scottish Citylink (☎ 0870 550 5050; www.citylink.co.uk) provides direct services from Glasgow (£18, four hours, four daily), Edinburgh (£18, four hours, five daily), Fort William (£11, two hours, five daily), Ullapool (£8, 1½ hours, two services Monday to Saturday) and Portree on the Isle of Skye (£13, 3¼ hours, three daily).

Megabus (☎ 0900 160 0900; www.megabus.com) offers cheap fares from Glasgow, Edinburgh and London.

Car

The main arterial roads to Inverness from Glasgow are the A82 via Fort William, or the M80 then A roads and motorways via Stirling to the A9. From Edinburgh take the M9/A9 via Perth and Pitlochry.

Train

First ScotRail (☎ 0845 755 0033; www.firstscotrail.com) trains arrive in Inverness from Glasgow (£35, 3¼ hours, eight services Monday to Saturday, three Sunday) and Edinburgh (£35, 3¼ hours, nine services Monday to Saturday, three Sunday), as well as the *Caledonian Sleeper* from London Euston (seat/sleeper berth £129/132, 12½ hours, daily except Saturday).

GNER (☎ 0845 748 4950; www.gner.co.uk) operates a daily service from London King's Cross (£115, eight hours); book well ahead and save money. The frequent services linking London with Edinburgh and Glasgow can connect with onward journeys to Inverness.

GREAT GLEN WAY

Duration	4 days
Distance	73 miles (117km)
Difficulty	moderate
Start	Fort William (p121)
Finish	Inverness (p167)
Transport	bus, train

Summary A magnificently scenic walk through the Highlands' most famous glen, above three superb lochs, beside a historic canal and through wildflower-rich woodlands.

The Great Glen is the wide, deep trench that almost severs the Highlands from the rest of Scotland. With Ben Nevis and the Nevis Range at the southwestern end, Loch Ness and the Moray Firth at the northeastern outlet, and the superb Loch Lochy and Loch Oich and several fine 'hills' in between, it's magnificently scenic. The whole glen is rich in historical associations dating from prehistoric times. It's a natural route for a long-distance path, and the Great Glen Way is one of the finest in the country.

It can be walked in either direction and there are good arguments in favour of each. By starting from Inverness you are walking towards the best of the views, to the high peaks around Loch Lochy and beyond to Ben Nevis. On the other hand, Inverness probably has more to offer at the end of a long walk. More importantly, the Way provides the opportunity to undertake a truly world-class long walk, following the West Highland Way (p89) from Glasgow to Fort William, and continuing through to Inverness along the Great Glen Way, a total of 170 miles (274km). Although the prevailing wind is from the southwest, it's as likely to be coming from the north or northeast.

The Way is 73 miles (117km) long, which, spread over four or five days, makes a reasonably comfortable walk. Most of the ascent is at the northeastern end between Invermoriston and Drumnadrochit and between Drumnadrochit and the Abriachan plateau. The Way follows long stretches of the historic Caledonian Canal's towpath, an old railway formation, and quiet roads and tracks. Some sections are, in theory, shared with cyclists and trail bike riders, so you need to be alert on the narrower paths. There's relatively little walking along sealed roads, most of this being around Drumnadrochit and across the Abriachan plateau. The Way is well signposted and waymarked, with the official thistle-hexagon logo, and adorned with numerous stone and timber monoliths. Dozens of interpretation panels focus on history, archaeology, plants and wildlife, forest management and folklore.

Alternatives If you don't have time to do the whole walk, any one of the sections described (or parts of them) could be done as a day walk, making use of the good bus services through the glen.

There are many tempting side trips if you can extend the walk to a week or so. From Fort William, you're spoilt for choice, one option being Ben Nevis (p123). The Munros and Corbetts above Loch Lochy are easily accessed from the Way. Also directly accessible is Meall Fuar-mhonaidh (699m) – 'hill of the cold moor', pronounced 'me-awl foorvonee' – the highest point overlooking Loch Ness, which offers extraordinarily wide views. From Drumnadrochit you can wander through the woodlands overlooking the village, and there's a scenic network of mainly woodland paths at the southern end of the Abriachan plateau, developed and maintained by the community-owned Abriachan Woodland Trust. To complete the Caledonian Canal traverse, the walk from Dochgarroch to the Clachnaharry sea lock (see p188) sustains its scenic diversity and historical interest to the end.

HISTORY

There's plenty of evidence of prehistoric occupation of the Great Glen, most visibly as Iron Age forts (dùns): Torr Dhùin near Fort Augustus (and in view from the Way) is an excellent example. Perhaps the earliest recorded visitor was St Columba, the Irish Christian missionary, who travelled through the Glen in AD 565 (see the boxed text on p173). A few castles gaze down on the lochs, most much reduced from their original dimensions. Invergarry Castle, largely destroyed in the 18th century, can be seen across Loch Oich on Day 2; while Urquhart Castle, dating from about the 13th century and virtually destroyed 400 years later, is a short walk south from Drumnadrochit.

Jacobite disturbances raged up and down the Great Glen and led to the building of military roads along its southeastern side to link forts near Inverness with those at Fort Augustus and Fort William. Even now, 260 years later, the formation is still clear in many places. The Caledonian Canal, planned by Thomas Telford to make the glen navigable from end to end, opened for through traffic in 1822. Until WWII it provided the main means of transport through the glen, when roads made for faster and easier travel. Fishing vessels were a common sight along the canal for many years, as were passenger steamers carrying visitors from Glasgow. A Great Glen railway seemed a logical development but the dream fell to disputes and underfunding; only a line from Spean Bridge to Fort Augustus (part of which the Way follows) carried trains, from 1903 until the 1930s.

Large industries have been few. An aluminium smelter operated at Foyers for more than 60 years until 1967. A hydroelectric power station there is now one of the few sizable buildings, and probably the ugliest, on the shores of the lochs.

PLANNING

This is one walk that can be done at almost any time. It offers the opportunity to see the magnificent spectacle of snow-covered mountains, especially Ben Nevis, during winter. The only serious hazard at that time could be ice on the paths and tracks.

The recommended stages can easily be shortened to make a five- or six-day walk by staying at Gairlochy between Fort William and Laggan, and at Invermoriston between Fort Augustus and Drumnadrochit.

You can make life much easier, and probably even more enjoyable, by signing up with one of the several entrepreneurs who arrange accommodation and baggage transfer along the Way. Among several such businesses, **Transcotland** (☎ 01887 820848; www.transcotland.com; 6/7 nights £340/360) has long experience in the business and also provides maps and background information.

Before you set out each day, make sure you have plenty to eat and drink; there are no shops or cafés along the Way on the first, second and last days.

Maps & Books

OS Landranger 1:50,000 maps No 41 *Ben Nevis*, No 34 *Fort Augustus* and No 26 *Inverness*

& Loch Ness cover the route. However, the Harvey 1:40,000 map *Great Glen Way*, on a single sheet with town/village maps and other information, is more practical.

Rucksack Readers' illustrated guide *The Great Glen Way* has detailed maps and a handy notebook format.

Information Sources

For up-to-date information about the Way, check the information-rich **Great Glen Way** (www.greatglenway.com) website; it includes details of accommodation and services. The Way's **rangers** (☎ 01320 366633; Auchterawe) are based at Fort Augustus.

GETTING TO/FROM THE WALK

Scottish Citylink (☎ 0870 550 5050; www.citylink.co.uk) and **Highland Country Buses** (☎ 01463 710555; www.rapsons.co.uk) operate daily services through the Great Glen, stopping at the villages along the A82.

To start the walk in Fort William, using the train station as a reference point, cross the adjacent supermarket car park, then a road just north of a large roundabout. The start of the Way, on the site of the old fort, is marked with a stone plinth and plaque.

From Inverness Castle, head east to reach Castle St and turn left. About 100m along, turn right along pedestrianised High St. Follow it to similarly car-free Inglis St; this leads to Academy St. Cross at the lights and bear left to reach the train station, or continue for about 150m to Margaret St, a short distance along which is the bus station.

THE WALK

Day 1: Fort William to Laggan

7½–8 hours, 22.5 miles (36.1km)

Take the minor roads and paths as they cross River Nevis, run briefly beside Loch Linnhe, then skirt River Lochy's estuary. Cross a bridge beside the railway then follow roadside paths around the fringes of the suburb of Caol. The route swings away from the loch to the Caledonian Canal but before continuing along the bank you can follow a path to the left to Corpach sea lock, the southwestern extremity of the canal.

Cross a road to the remarkable **Neptune's Staircase**, a flight of eight locks that raises (or lowers) boats by 64ft (21m), about an hour from the start. From here, the next section is easy – simply follow the towpath mostly northeast to Gairlochy. The views of the Ben Nevis massif and the Aonach Mòr ski slopes to the south are excellent. About 4 miles (6.5km) along, you pass the Moy swing bridge, each half of which is opened separately. **Gairlochy** is 1 mile further (two to 2½ hours from Neptune's Staircase).

Although there isn't a shop in Gairlochy, there is **Gairlochy Holiday Park** (☎ 01397 712711; www.theghp.co.uk; unpowered sites £6) and **Dalcomera B&B** (☎ 01397 712778; www.dalcomera.co.uk; s/d £30/50).

Cross the road bridge and walk along the minor road for about 800m; continue along a path beside **Loch Lochy**. This takes you back to the road, which you must follow through the hamlet of Bunarkaig and on to the handful of houses at Clunes. A short distance beyond the village the Way leaves the road to follow a forest track for several miles above Loch Lochy to Kilfinnan. Continue along a minor road for 1 mile or so then follow a path to reach **Laggan Locks** and the next stretch of the Caledonian Canal at South Laggan. The towpath leads on for 1.4 miles to just short of Laggan swing bridge, between the canal and Loch Oich (4½ hours from Gairlochy).

LAGGAN
☎ 01809

Loch Lochy SYHA Hostel (☎ 0870 004 1135; www.syha.org.uk; South Laggan; dm £14; Apr-Oct;) is close

Great Glen Way (South)

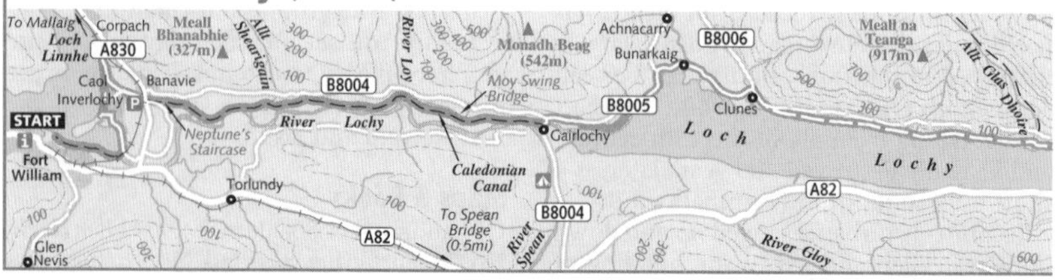

to the Way, between Laggan Locks and the swing bridge.

Forest Lodge Guest House (☎ 501219; www.flgh.co.uk; South Laggan; s/d £30/52, dinner £15) offers compact en suite rooms and a satisfying four-course dinner.

Loch Oich Restaurant (☎ 501383; lunch mains to £8, dinner mains to £15; 🕑 lunch & dinner), in the Great Glen Water Park, close to the Way and a short distance beyond the swing bridge, is a pleasant place to go for a meal; the menu is a cut above the ordinary.

The **Seven Heads store** (🕑 daily) is about 400m along the A82 from the swing bridge.

Day 2: Laggan to Fort Augustus

4–4½ hours, 10.5 miles (16.8km)

From Laggan swing bridge, follow the minor road to the Great Glen Water Park then continue along a track following the line of the short-lived Spean Bridge–Fort Augustus railway, through Leitirfearn Nature Reserve. In spring the woodland is carpeted with primrose and dog violet. After a while you leave the track to follow a stretch of military road, built during the 18th century. From time to time there are fine views across **Loch Oich** – look out for the romantic sight of the ruins of Invergarry Castle. The Way emerges from the forest at Aberchalder; follow the route close to the loch shore to the A82 (two hours from Laggan). Cross and continue along the vehicle track leading to Cullochy Lock, past the impressive **Bridge of Oich**, built in 1850 to a pioneering double-cantilever design.

Follow the towpath beside the canal with the River Oich nearby, past a long slender loch, to secluded **Kytra lock**. Above, to the west, is steep-sided, forested Torr Dhùin, an Iron Age fort. The Way leads on between the canal and the river to the top of the flight of five locks at Fort Augustus (two hours from Aberchalder).

FORT AUGUSTUS

☎ 01320 / pop 510

This large village straddles the Caledonian Canal and has plenty of accommodation. The **TIC** (☎ 366367; fortaugustus@host.co.uk; 🕑 Easter-Oct) is beside the car park on the main road at the northern end of town. The **Caledonian Canal Heritage Centre** (☎ 366493; admission free; 🕑 daily Apr-Oct) is well worth a visit.

Fort Augustus Caravan & Camping Park (☎ 366618; www.campinglochness.co.uk; Market Hill; unpowered/powered sites for 2 £11/14) is a spacious, grassy site. To find it, walk along the A82 to the southern edge of town.

Morag's Lodge (☎ 366289; www.moragslodge.com; Bunoich Brae; dm/d £14/52) is close to the Way on the north side of town with a great outlook. Most rooms have en suite.

The **Lock Inn** (☎ 366302; Canalside; mains to £9; 🕑 lunch & dinner) offers good, traditional dishes such as mince 'n' tatties, and a vegetarian option.

The **Bothy** (☎ 366710; Canalside; mains £9-13; 🕑 lunch & dinner) doesn't take bookings but there's a bar where you can try one or two of its cask ales if you have to wait for a table. The menu makes a feature of fish, though you could try the Isle of Rum venison.

There are two small supermarkets: one beside the canal locks, the other in the petrol station nearby.

Day 3: Fort Augustus to Drumnadrochit

7½–8 hours, 22 miles (35.2km)

Leave Fort Augustus along the minor road signposted to Jenkins Park. It curves around through the outskirts of the village, to just short of the A82. Turn sharply left and climb through mixed forest to a track; turn right. The track undulates through a conifer plantation with occasional views of Loch Ness. About 2½ hours from Fort Augustus, pass a track to the right leading

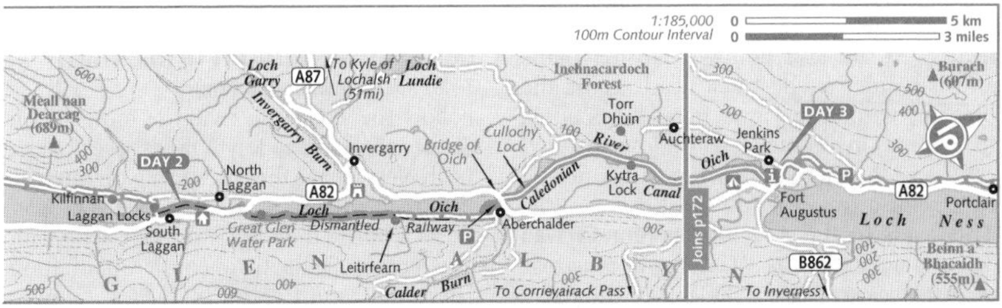

Great Glen Way (North)

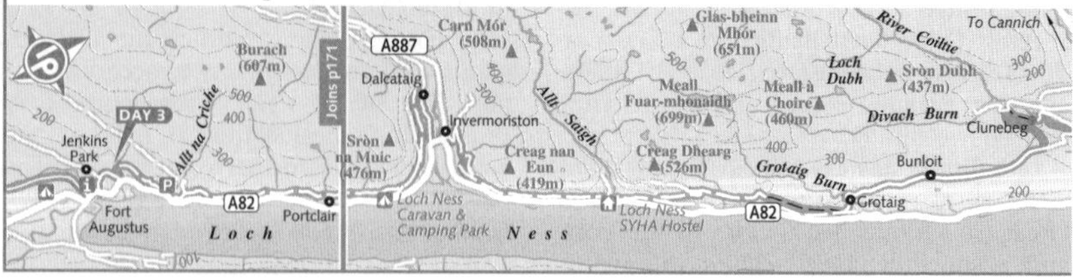

to the well-run **Loch Ness Caravan & Camping Park** (☎ 01320 351207; www.lochnesscaravanandcampingpark.co.uk; unpowered sites for 2 £12, bar meal mains to £7). Soon you glimpse the village of Invermoriston below, but the Way teases you with a westerly diversion up Glen Moriston for a good mile, to a short path leading to a forest track, which becomes a road at Dalcataig and carries you past **Lann Dearg Studios** (☎ 01320 351353; www.lanndearg.co.uk; Dalcataig; s/d £45/60) to the A82 (three hours from Fort Augustus). Turn left and within 200m, at a major junction in Invermoriston, go left again for a short distance.

There's a handful of B&Bs here, including **Bracarina House** (☎ 01320 351258; s/d £35/50). The **Glenmoriston Arms' Tavern** (☎ 01320 351206; lunch & dinner) does excellent homemade pies and Isle of Skye beers, or there's the **Pig's Nose Restaurant** (☎ 01320 351352; lunch & dinner) nearby. Top up your snack supplies at the small **shop** (daily).

Cross the road and climb up to a steep road through forest to a junction. Now you start on another roller-coaster ride, along forest tracks and paths and across a bridge over Allt Saigh. **Loch Ness SYHA Hostel** (☎ 0870 004 1138; ww.syha.or.uk; dm £14; Apr-Oct;) is nearby, right beside Loch Ness (1½ hours from Invermoriston). The Way climbs again, up to a high point with superb views along Loch Ness and the Great Glen, descends then rises again to a minor road at Grotaig (two hours from Allt Saigh). The path to Meall Fuar-mhonaidh (p188) is nearby to the left. Follow roadside paths and the quiet single-track road across the plateau, with fine views in all directions, to a junction on the left. Follow the forest track, then a path down past Clunebeg, to a vehicle track beside the River Coiltie. This leads to the A82; **Borlum Farm Caravan & Camping Park** (☎ 450220; www.borlum.com; unpowered/powered sites for 2 £10/12) is to the right, with grassy pitches in an open field. Drumnadrochit is to the left. Follow the roadside path into the village (1½ hours from Grotaig).

DRUMNADROCHIT

☎ 01456 / pop 820

Famed for its association with the Loch Ness Monster, the village has much more to offer, with plenty of accommodation and a handful of pubs and restaurants. The small, helpful **TIC** (☎ 459086; drumnadrochit@visitscotland.com; The Car Park; daily Apr-Oct, Mon-Sat Nov-Mar) can help with accommodation and local information.

Loch Ness Backpackers (☎ 450807; www.lochness-backpackers.com; East Lewiston; dm £12), about 200m east of the A82, has compact dorms in an 18th-century farmhouse and adjacent bunkhouse.

Glenkirk B&B (☎ 450802; www.lochnessbandb.com/glenkirk; Cannich Rd; s/d £45/55) is a friendly place in a former church, with superbly decorated, spacious rooms.

Benleva Hotel (☎ 450080; Kilmore; mains £8-14; lunch & dinner) is an award-winning pub where you can sample a fine range of Highland cask ales. The food is a cut above the usual bar supper fare and features local ingredients whenever possible.

Fiddlers Highland Market has a tempting range of Highland delicacies and snacks. There's a small supermarket, and the post office shop stocks groceries.

Day 4: Drumnadrochit to Inverness

7–7½ hours, 18 miles (28.9km)

Follow the A82 on a roadside footpath out of the village for nearly 2 miles, overlooking Loch Ness. Leave the road up a path opposite the small marina at Temple Pier. The path skirts a house then leads through woodland and across fields to a conifer plantation. Here, the ascent starts in earnest, along a

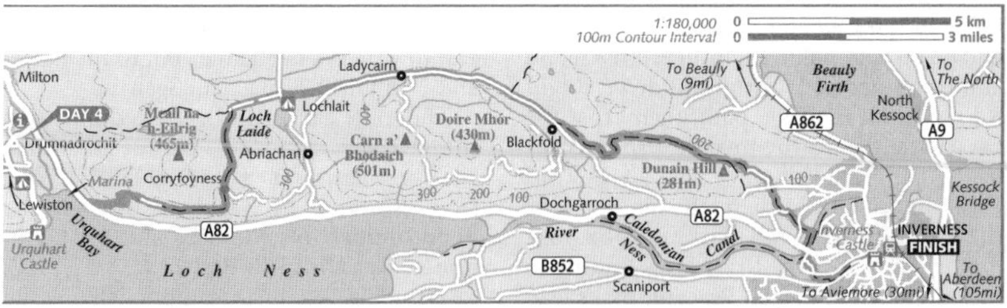

wide, well-graded path. At length it meets a broad forest track, which leads on through cleared areas to an isolated cottage at **Corryfoyness**. Here, the track turns west and continues to gain height, through a gate and on to a junction near Achpopuli. Turn right here along the straight-as-an-arrow track, past the Abriachan Community Woodland car park (where there are toilets) to a road near Loch Laide (two hours from Drumnadrochit).

Cross directly and follow a path that curves gently, past **Wester Laide Agro Forestry Campsite** (☎ 01463 861462; unpowered sites for 2 £10, caravan B&B d £20), to meet a minor road at Ladycairn. Turn left and follow the single-track road across the Abriachan plateau for about 5 miles (8km), with fine views west across mountains and deep glens, to a junction on the left at Blackfold (about two hours from Loch Laide). Follow tracks through conifer and broad-leaved forests and out into the open, with fine views across Inverness (1½ hours from Blackfold). Descend to the grounds of the former Craig Dunain mental hospital, slated for housing redevelopment. Walk past a handful of buildings to a road; turn left then soon right along a minor road, past the headquarters of Scottish Natural Heritage, to a path that takes you down to suburban Inverness. Follow waymarkers across grass and along hard-surfaced paths between houses to an underpass. On the far side continue along a path between a golf course and playing

LOCH NESS – LEGEND & SCIENCE

The Great Glen Way provides an unrivalled opportunity to contemplate the famous and mysterious Loch Ness, from the shore to several hundred metres above, right along its 22.6-mile (36.6km) length.

Although St Columba is said to have repelled a large creature in the River Ness in AD 565, it wasn't until 1932 that claims of sightings of large, plesiosaur-like creatures were publicly made, hoaxes were perpetrated and the name 'monster' was first used in print. The excitement fizzed briefly then died away until the 1960s. A vigil was mounted along the loch in 1962 but only deepened scepticism about the chances of a large creature living in the cold, dark waters, which reach a maximum depth of 754ft (227m). Since the 1970s the legend has been sustained with regular, though declining, sightings of 'Nessie' and popular fascination with the unknown.

Scientific interest in the loch, first formally expressed early in the 20th century with the making of a remarkably accurate underwater map, has intensified. The loch's habitats have been accurately described, down to the icy-cold depths where tiny creatures, relics of the ice age, survive the enormous pressure. Comparatively few aquatic species live in the loch, the largest of which is the wild salmon. It's been shown that the loch simply doesn't contain enough food to support even one sizable reptile, let alone a small family of them. The Rosetta Project during the 1990s extracted cores from the loch bed, which revealed 10,000 years of environmental change – a fascinating chart of the loch's history. The Chernobyl disaster left its mark even here, but in recent years deposits from chemical pollution have diminished.

The **Loch Ness 2000** (☎ 01456 450573; www.loch-ness-scotland.com; admission £6; 🕑 9.30am-5pm Easter-end of May, 9am-6pm Jun & Sep, 9am-8pm Jul & Aug, 9.30am-5.30pm Oct) exhibition in Drumnadrochit delves into this intriguing story and is worth a visit as you pass through. Alternatively, pick up a copy of Adrian Shine's book *Loch Ness*, a serious look at the loch and its long history.

fields to the Caledonian Canal. Turn right and go on Tomnahurich bridge; cross it and almost immediately turn right down Bught Rd. Follow a roadside path, then cross the car park at the nearby Inverness sports centre to the **Floral Hall coffee shop** (daily until 5pm). Continue right then left, soon passing the entrance to Whin Park, and on to a footbridge across the River Ness leading to the wooded **Ness Islands**. Peaceful paths lead across the islands to a riverside path. Turn left for the last stretch, along what is Lady's Walk then Ness Bank. Cross at Ness Bank Church and go up to View Pl. **Inverness Castle** and the official end of the Way is a short distance up to your left, with a highly satisfying view back down the Great Glen (1½ hours from near Craig Dunain).

GLEN AFFRIC

Duration	2 days
Distance	17 miles (27.4km)
Difficulty	moderate
Start	River Affric car park
Finish	Morvich (p176)
Nearest Town	Cannich (p176)
Transport	bus

Summary One of the finest long-distance walks in Scotland, through beautiful, untouched Glen Affric, across a dramatic pass to the shores of Loch Duich and past some tempting Munros.

Glen Affric could be called the brightest and finest star in the Highland Glens constellation. Its claim to first place is strong: no public roads; the superbly beautiful Loch Affric, uncompromised by dam walls; a major Caledonian woodland revival; public right of way; and it has one of the very few youth hostels you can't drive to. With Loch Cluanie and Glen Shiel to the south and remote Loch Mullardoch and Glen Cannich to the north, it's centred in a magnificent, road-free area extending north to Strathcarron in Wester Ross.

This remote and rewarding walk through the glen follows public footpaths virtually all the way, although it isn't waymarked. While it's described from Loch Affric in the east to Loch Duich in the west, from the mountains to the coast, it can just as well be done in the opposite direction, although this would involve more ascent. The height gained going east to west is a negligible 70m to the hostel and 230m over Bealach an Sgàirne.

The route can easily be walked in a long summer day; indeed, it's part of an annual charity marathon, the Highland Cross, from Morvich to Beauly. However, the opportunities for side trips and to stay in remote **Glen Affric SYHA Hostel** (0870 155 3255; dm £13; Apr-Oct), or to camp locally, easily justify lingering for a day or three. If you plan to stay at the hostel it's best to book ahead, if possible at least a week before your arrival. For its isolated location, amenities are luxurious – running water, hot shower, electricity (thanks to a wind turbine) and gas for cooking. You'll need a sleeping bag, all your own food, a bag to carry out your rubbish and indoor footwear.

Alternatives Two alternative Day 2 routes from the hostel are also described. Gleann Lichd, immediately south of the main route, is perhaps a little less dramatic but beautiful nonetheless, flanked by the Five Sisters of Kintail (p180) on one side. It also leads to Morvich and involves only 100m of ascent, although it's slightly longer than the more northerly route. The other route takes you south through a broad pass and down An Caorann Mór to the A87 near Cluanie Inn. It's the shortest route, with 150m of ascent (190m in the opposite direction), but has by far the worst going underfoot – bogs and morasses joined by short dry bits of path.

With time on your side you could do a grand Affric tour. Walk to Morvich from Loch Affric as described. Stay there overnight, then return to the hostel via Gleann Lichd and back to the River Affric car park via the south side of the loch, along the forest road from Athnamulloch. The total distance is 34 miles (55km).

Two of several possible side trips are also described. Sgurr nan Ceathreamhnan (1151m, 3775ft) is the third-highest peak above Glen Affric (and is a Munro). Its tongue-twisting name means 'hill of the quarters' (land divisions) and is pronounced 'kay-ravan', although colloquially it's known as 'Chrysanthemum Hill'. Secondly, the Falls of Glomach is perhaps the most spectacular waterfall in the country, with a total drop of 123m.

It's also possible to experience much of the beauty and remoteness of Loch Affric on a day walk around the loch, starting and finishing at the River Affric car park. Follow the route described below along the northern side of the loch to the junction with a vehicular track. Walk down this to Athnamulloch, and cross a small stream on stepping stones to a path beside the River Affric. This leads to a forestry road along the south side of the loch and back to the car park. The distance is 10.4 miles (16.5km).

HISTORY

There's little, if any, definite evidence of prehistoric settlement in the glen. It's likely that the Irish missionary St Dubhthach (Duthac) crossed Bealach an Sgàirne during the 11th century in the course of travels between his parishes in Kintail and Tain (on the southern shore of Dornoch Firth, north of Inverness). The bealach (pass) appears on a map dated 1725 and was the main route from Kintail east until the military road was built through Glen Shiel after 1746.

As you walk through the glen, you can't miss the many low rectangles of stones – the remains of small cottages, some with adjacent stone-walled enclosures (for sheep and cattle) and probably dating from the early to mid-19th century. These are particularly prominent above Loch Affric and in Gleann Gnìomhaidh, west of the hostel. A substantial survivor is Camban Bothy. It was used by a shepherd as early as 1839 and was later occupied by stalkers; the last residents left in 1920. More recently, the bothy has been restored by the Mountain Bothies Association. People were living at Alltbeithe in 1841, and there has been a hostel there since 1949, although the present premises are much modified from the original.

Glen Affric was cleared of sheep and farmers after the estate was acquired by Lord Tweedmouth in the mid-19th century, after being in the hands of Clan Chisholm for 400 years. He turned it into a deer 'forest' for stalking and built Affric Lodge in 1870. Forest Enterprise purchased a large holding in 1951; the National Trust for Scotland (NTS), with its 3650-hectare West Affric Estate and the adjacent Kintail Estate, is also a major local landowner.

ENVIRONMENT

In marked contrast to Glen Shiel, just over the mountains to the southwest, Glen Affric is relatively broad and flat-bottomed. It is also flanked by towering peaks, which are less jagged but no less beautiful in a grand, majestic style. The main reason for this difference is believed to be that during the last Ice Age, the glen (and others to the north) sheltered beneath an ice cap, safe from gouging glaciers.

Glen Affric National Nature Reserve protects a large remnant of native Caledonian woodland, which is benefiting from a long-term project for its restoration and expansion, led by Forest Enterprise (see below).

PLANNING

When to Walk/Stalking

The greater part of this walk is within the NTS' West Affric Estate; public access is unaffected by stalking activities. The eastern part of the walk, above Loch Affric, passes through North Affric Estate, and provided you keep to the path (a public

A FUTURE FOR CALEDONIAN PINE WOODLAND

When you realise that 'only' 10,000 years ago, thousands of square kilometres of Highlands' land was covered with Caledonian pine woodlands, and that the area has since shrunk to a mere 180 sq km, the vital significance of Caledonian forest reserves hits home.

The 14,150-hectare reserve in Glen Affric, the largest in northern Scotland, protects a richly diverse community of Scots pine, birch, aspen, rowan and willow, many shrubs and wildflowers, mammals (including red and roe deer and red squirrel) and about 100 species of bird, notably crossbill and golden eagle. Many of the Scots pines are far beyond pensionable age; some around the River Affric car park are more than 300 years old.

Even in the relatively short time since the reserve was established, it's easy to see the positive impact of the fencing that keeps grazing animals at bay, in the proliferation of Scots pine and birch across the hillside. Glen Affric will never be the same again!

right of way), you shouldn't encounter any problems during the mid-August to mid-October stalking season.

Maps

The coverage of Harvey's excellent 1:25,000 *Kintail* map extends west from Allt Coulavie, near the western end of Loch Affric, and so misses most of the first day of this walk. It also stops short of the descent to the Falls of Glomach from Bealach na Sròine. For both of these you'll need OS Landranger 1:50,000 map No 25 *Glen Carron & Glen Affric*; map No 33 *Loch Alsh, Glen Shiel & Loch Hourn* covers the western part of the walk.

NEAREST TOWNS

Cannich

☎ 01456

The village of Cannich, at the start of the only road to Loch Affric, was originally established to house forestry workers in the 1950s. The nearest TIC is in Drumnadrochit (p172). In lieu, the locally sponsored website www.glenaffric.info has accommodation pages and plenty of other useful information.

SLEEPING & EATING

Cannich Caravan & Camping Park (☎ 415364; www.highlandcamping.co.uk; unpowered/powered sites for 2 £9/12), near the road to Drumnadrochit, has a sheltered, well-grassed area for tents.

Glen Affric Backpackers Hostel (☎ 415263; rob@cannich.freeserve.co.uk; dm £10), just southeast of the village centre, is well set up with two- or four-bed rooms and a large kitchen.

Westward B&B (☎ 415708; www.westwardbb.co.uk; s/d £30/50) is a traditional Highland home near the junction at the Cannich bridge.

Tomich Hotel (☎ 415399; www.tomichhotel.co.uk; Tomich; s/d £50/90; mains £8-15; 🕑 lunch & dinner) is a former hunting lodge in a small conservation village a couple of miles from Cannich. It's well worth the trip – the bar meals are excellent and Highland ales are on tap. The menu includes curries as good as in any 'Indian' restaurant, and a range of traditional dishes, notably venison casserole.

The small **post office shop** (🕑 daily) is also an off-licence.

GETTING THERE & AWAY

Highland Country Buses (☎ 01463 710555; www.rapsons.co.uk) operates a service to Cannich from Inverness via Drumnadrochit (£4, one hour, at least three services Monday to Friday, three Saturday).

Cannich is on the A831 between Drumnadrochit and Beauly.

Morvich, Ault a' chruinn & Shiel Bridge

☎ 01599

At the end of this walk these three hamlets offer a reasonable choice of accommodation and restaurants. The nearest TICs coming from the east are in Drumnadrochit (p172) or Fort Augustus (p171).

At Morvich the **NTS** (☎ 511231; kintail@nts.org.uk) maintains a small, unstaffed visitor centre featuring the Kintail Estate; the weather forecast is displayed daily. Countryside rangers based here run guided walks during the summer.

SLEEPING & EATING

Morvich Caravan Club Site (☎ 511354; www.caravanclub.co.uk; Inverinate; sites for 2 £19) is closest to the end of the walk. Pitches at this secluded, sheltered site are flat and grassy.

Shielbridge Caravan & Camping Site (☎ 511211; Shiel Bridge; unpowered/powered sites for 2 £5/13) is flat and open, with great views of the Five Sisters. Facilities are clean and well maintained.

Kintail Lodge Hotel (☎ 511275; www.kintaillodgehotel.co.uk; dm/s/d £13/50/58, breakfast £10; lunch & dinner mains to £10) offers superior hotel accommodation and the Trekkers' Lodge, with twins and singles, and the Wee Bunk House, offering dorm-style accommodation. Meals are available in the hotel.

Jac-O-Bite Restaurant (☎ 511347; breakfast £7, lunch £4-7, dinner £9-20) has a superb outlook; the smallish menu features plenty of local produce, and daily specials are available.

Five Sisters Restaurant (☎ 511221; Shiel Bridge; breakfast £4-7, lunch £4-7) offers standard fare in cheerful surroundings. The adjacent **Shielshop** (🕑 daily) stocks a reasonable range of supplies and local maps.

GETTING THERE & AWAY

Scottish Citylink (☎ 0870 550 5050; www.citylink.co.uk) buses stop at Shiel Bridge from Glasgow (£23, 4¾ hours, three daily) and the Isle of Skye via Fort William (£12, 1½ hours, three daily) as do its buses on the Inverness–Portree service (£14, 1½ hours, three daily).

You can reach Shiel Bridge by train and bus, travelling to Kyle of Lochalsh on the scenic line from Inverness (£16, 2½ hours, at least three Monday to Saturday, two Sunday) then catching a Scottish Citylink bus on the route from Skye to Shiel Bridge.

Shiel Bridge is on the A87, which branches from the A82 Inverness–Fort William road at Invergarry. From Inverness, turn off the A82 at Invermoriston along the A887 to join the A87 near Loch Cluanie.

GETTING TO/FROM THE WALK

From Cannich a single-lane road winds its way west for 10 miles (16km) to the River Affric car park at its end, where there are toilets and picnic tables. From July to mid-September **Ross's Mini-Buses** (☎ 01463 761250) operates between Cannich and Glen Affric (£2, 30 minutes, two Monday to Friday, three Saturday and Sunday).

From the end of the walk at Morvich, it's 1.5 miles to the A87 then just over 1 mile south along that road to Shiel Bridge. Buses to/from Shiel Bridge (see opposite) also stop at Cluanie Inn near the end of alternative Day 2B.

THE WALK Map p178

Day 1: River Affric Car Park to Alltbeithe

3½–4 hours, 8.5 miles (13.5km)

Set out along the gravel road leading west and shortly bear right at a fork. The road follows the course of the broad River Affric to the access road to private Affric Lodge and a nearby house. From here a path, signposted to Kintail and the hostel, continues in the same direction. A few hundred metres along, a single, creaky plank crosses a small stream and from here you can see the impressive Affric Lodge, backed by tall Scots pines, gazing down Loch Affric. Further on, you pass through a fenced pine-regeneration area. The path maintains a good height above the loch, revealing wonderful views west to the mountains around the hostel.

Succeeding streams are crossed on stepping stones and footbridges, and the path rises across the steep slope, passing vigorously regenerating clumps of birch and scattered remains of stone buildings. A substantial bridge takes you across Allt Coire Leachavie (a short distance west, a cairned path leads into the corrie – the route to Màm Sodhail and other nearby Munros) then it's generally down towards Loch Coulavie. On the way, the crossing of Allt Coulavie, which tumbles down through the fine waterfall of Sputan Bán, could be difficult after heavy rain. The path, now rather boggy and eroded, curves around **Loch Coulavie** and down to a vehicle track (2½ hours from the start).

The track leads west in undulating fashion, across the broad, flat-based glen of the River Affric, rising steeply on both sides. A substantial bridge over Allt Coire Ghaidheil marks the boundary of the NTS' West Affric Estate. The track continues close to the river and soon the reddish roof of the hostel and the wind turbine come into view. You should reach **Alltbeithe** and the hostel about an hour after meeting the vehicle track.

SIDE TRIP: SGURR NAN CEATHREAMHNAN

4 hours, 7.5 miles (12km), 940m ascent

The path starts at the back of the upper hostel building. Go up beside the burn for about 200m then head east to cross Allt na Faing, which could be difficult if it's in spate. The narrow, mostly clear path climbs beside the burn, passing through two gates in an exclosure, to Coire na Cloiche. Cross two burns flowing down from the left and continue up towards the headwall of the corrie along a series of broad 'steps', skipping past peat hags. The path fades in a morass of peat hags, as the crags close in on the left, but it's easy enough to go up, just above the burn, to the unnamed gap on the main ridge (about 1¼ hours from the hostel).

The crags of Stob Coire na Cloiche seem to bar the way as you climb southwest from the gap. The way over it is straightforward enough, just to the left then right, closer to the northern edge. The fine ridge then opens up ahead, rising to the graceful *sgurr* (pointed hill). Continue along the undulating ridge and up the final, steep pull to the summit of **Sgurr nan Ceathreamhnan** (1151m) with its large cairn (1¼ hours from the gap). The all-round view is quite awesome: the Kintail and Affric hills, and multitudes more as far north as Torridon, and south across Glen Shiel to Knoydart and the 'hills' above Loch Quoich.

If you decide to make this a circuit, rather than retracing your steps to the hostel, head west along the narrow ridge, cross a confined gap then climb up a gully to the right to the broad summit of Ceathreamhnan's satellite, only a few metres lower at 1143m.

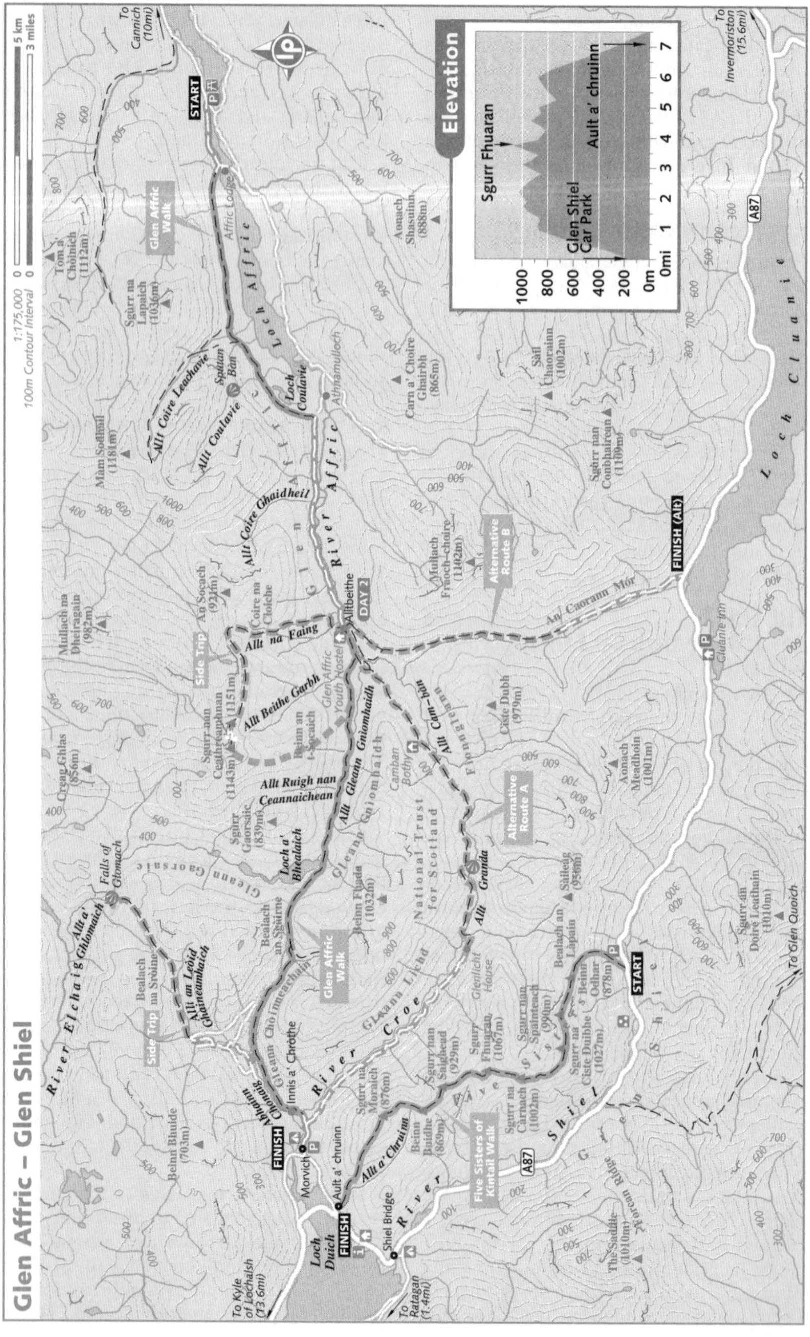

Glen Affric – Glen Shiel

Head down, southwest, generally keeping close to the rim of the spur on your left, and on to Beinn an t-Socaich. From here, plot a route down to the path through Gleann Gnìomhaidh below, avoiding the extensive fencing. Once safely on the path, just follow it back to the hostel (about two hours from the summit).

Day 2: Alltbeithe to Morvich via Bealach an Sgàirne

4 hours, 8.5 miles (13.5km)

Head towards the River Affric and follow a track upstream along the bank. Cross the bridge over Allt Beithe Garbh ('rough stream of the birches') and turn right on a stone-paved path, which follows the stream for a few hundred metres then turns west to head up Gleann Gnìomhaidh. The path is joined by a wide, eroded vehicle track. Although there is also a path of sorts close to the stream below, it's better to stick with the higher track, which is mostly grassed but wet in places and not consistently clear. Aim for a prominent circular stone enclosure (shown on the Harvey map) beside Allt Ruigh nan Ceannaichean (about an hour from the hostel). About 500m further on, the path (as it is now) becomes clear and leads west, across the potentially hazardous stream draining beautiful Loch a' Bhealaich and round its southern shore. It's a steep climb on a good path up to dramatic, narrow **Bealach an Sgàirne** (1½ hours from the stone enclosure).

The descent through spectacularly rugged and steep-sided Gleann Chòinneachain is mostly on a good path. After about 3 miles go through a fenced (and gated) exclosure and continue downstream, above Abhainn Chonaig. The path veers away from the stream to a gate; continue across fields to a stile and junction. Turn left and cross a bridge over the River Croe at Innis a Chrótha. Soon, opposite a junction on the left (to Gleann Lichd), leave the road to follow paths through woodland, close to the river, eventually back to the road about 100m from the NTS visitor centre and car park at Morvich (1½ hours from the top of the bealach).

SIDE TRIP: FALLS OF GLOMACH

4 hours, 7.5 miles (12km), 600m ascent

As you're coming down Gleann Chòinneachain from Bealach an Sgàirne, you pass through a gate in a fenced exclosure (an area planted with trees and fenced to keep out leaf-chomping deer). About 200m beyond the second (lower) gate, bear right at a path junction down the field to a path through trees, which leads to a bridge over Abhainn Chonaig. Go on up, through a gate to a forest track, turn right and follow the track across open ground to a gate.

Turn left at the nearby forest track, up to another junction where you turn right. Follow the track up the glen, keeping right at a fork. The track ends just short of a bridge over Allt an Leòid Ghaineamhaich (35 minutes from Abhainn Chonaig). On the far side a footpath leads up and across the steep slope then up the deep glen. It loses a bit of height then regains it up to the narrow defile that is Bealach na Sròine. Out onto open moorland, you soon start to descend gradually then steeply to Allt a' Ghlomaich (1½ hours from the last bridge). An eroded path descends beside the **Falls of Glomach** to truly breathtaking viewpoints of the thundering water. The falls plunge in two leaps; the uppermost is enclosed between dark crags encrusted with mosses and ferns, and the lower is more open. The water crashes into a churning pool, from where the stream surges through a deep gorge.

Retrace your steps to return.

Day 2A: Alltbeithe to Morvich via Gleann Lichd

4½ hours, 9.5 miles (15.5km)

Head towards the River Affric and follow a track upstream along its bank. Cross the bridge over Allt Beithe Garbh and continue beside the river. A little further on, bear right along a narrow path, just before a ford on the main track, and continue for about 200m to a footbridge. Rejoin the main track about 40m beyond the ford. Nearly an hour's walk from the hostel brings you to a short path leading to **Camban Bothy**.

The main track soon becomes a narrow, well-made footpath for a few hundred metres. Climb to the watershed between Glen Affric and Gleann Lichd, marked by a large cairn. The path loses height gradually, across some boggy bits and some rocky ground, then climbs over a spur and wanders up and down to the top of the real descent into **Gleann Lichd** (an hour from Camban Bothy).

The path, much of it stone-paved, winds down the steep hillside. Pass a narrow gorge with a fine waterfall on Allt Granda, crossing the main stream and a tributary near Glenlicht House, a securely locked stone building. From here a vehicle track makes for easy walking down the scenic glen to the end of the sealed road near Morvich (about 1½ hours from Glenlicht House).

Day 2B: Alltbeithe to Loch Cluanie

2½ hours, 7 miles (11.5km)

Follow a path beside the burn next to the hostel for a short distance south then swing left to the bridge across the River Affric. The path is vague across boggy ground but it becomes clearer as you climb fairly gently up the hillside. Keep to higher paths (not as wet) and press on across the gap and down to the start of the vehicle track through An Caorann Mór. Follow this for about 1.5 miles to the A87; **Cluanie Inn** (☎ 01320 340238; www.cluanieinn.com; dm/s/d £32/45/60; lunch & dinner) is 1 mile west along the road, and offers comfortable rooms in the hotel or the adjacent Club House and good food in the bar and restaurant.

FIVE SISTERS OF KINTAIL

Duration	7–7½ hours
Distance	7.5 miles (12km)
Difficulty	demanding
Start	Glen Shiel car park
Finish	Ault a' chruinn (p176)
Transport	private

Summary One of the finest ridge walks in Scotland – an immensely scenic walk over rough ground, traversing narrow ridges along mostly clear, well-used paths.

Travelling west to the Isle of Skye you pass through what appears to be impenetrable Glen Shiel. The winding road snakes between steep-sided, rock-encrusted mountains, soaring skywards to the north, and rising almost as steeply and ruggedly to the south. The western end of the long, spiky ridge to the north is known as the Five Sisters of Kintail, and is quite different in character from the more rounded, less dramatic chain of summits on the south side of the glen. The name Kintail comes from the Gaelic *cean da shaill*, meaning 'head of the two seas', ie Loch Duich and Loch Long, which in turn are inlets from Loch Alsh.

This chain of elegant, precipitous summits, separated by slits of passes (or bealachs), falls away vertiginously to Glen Shiel on one side and to the more remote and peaceful Gleann Lichd on the other. To the northwest, the ridge drops a little less steeply to the shores of beautiful Loch Duich. Three of the sisters are Munros (peaks over 3000ft/914m): Sgurr Fhuaran (1067m), Sgurr na Càrnach (1002m) and Sgurr na Ciste Duibhe (1027m). The other two, at the northern end of the ridge, are Sgurr nan Saighead (929m) and Sgurr na Moraich (876m). There are two peaks to deal with before you even reach the first, southernmost sister – Beinn Odhar (878m) and Sgurr nan Spainteach (990m).

The ridge commands fine views, with the Torridon 'hills' punctuating the horizon to the northwest, the Isle of Skye spread-eagled across the western skyline and the islands of Canna, Eigg and Rum sailing between the rugged peaks to the southwest – and much, much more. Far and away the better direction to walk is from east to west – walking towards the views, starting at a higher point than where you finish, and with a slightly less steep and knee-jarring descent. The overall distance isn't unusually long but the ascent of 1530m is nearly 100m more than a romp up Ben Nevis. Keep in mind that even when you've reached the highest point on the walk (Sgurr Fhuaran) the climbing isn't over – there are still two peaks to go.

THE SPANISH CONNECTION

In the long struggle between government and Jacobite forces, which ended at the Battle of Culloden in 1745, a lesser-known battle took place in Glen Shiel. In June 1719 Jacobite troops, including a Spanish regiment, landed at Eilean Donan castle beside Loch Duich. Government troops came from Inverness and the two sides met about 1 mile west of the starting point of this walk (there is a National Trust for Scotland interpretive sign at the site). The government side routed the Jacobites, of whom the last to flee were the Spanish who dashed up the hillside to the pass now called Bealach nan Spainteach, and down into Gleann Lichd.

Alternatives Once you're on the ridge, escape routes are few. People do go down to Glen Shiel via the spur from Sgurr Fhuaran but this is seriously steep. Routes to and from Gleann Lichd, on the other side, are feasible and, indeed, have much to recommend them. There is a clear path up to the ridge at Bealach an Làpain from Glenlicht House, and the long ridge thrusting east from Sgurr Fhuaran offers a fairly straightforward climb or descent.

PLANNING

When to Walk

The Five Sisters are very exposed and could be extremely hazardous in poor visibility, strong wind or rain, so it's worth waiting for the right day for this classic ridge walk. This is also important because there's a lot of loose rock along the ridge, especially on the descents into and climbs out of the bealachs, so considerable care is needed for your own and others' safety. The best times are May and June, and September to early October. The whole ridge is within the NTS' Kintail Estate, so access is open at all times.

Maps

Harvey's 1:25,000 map *Kintail: Glen Shiel* covers the Five Sisters and has some background information and local contacts. In the OS Explorer 1:25,000 series, the relevant map is No 414 *Glen Shiel*.

GETTING TO/FROM THE WALK

The walk starts at a car park on the A87 5 miles west of the Cluanie Inn (opposite). This car park (not signposted at the time of research) is about 100m west of the one marked on the OS 1:50,000 map. Scottish Citylink bus services through Shiel Bridge (see p176) stop at Cluanie Inn, about 5 miles (8km) east of the start.

The walk finishes in the hamlet of Ault a' chruinn, on the minor road (which branches off the A87, 1.5 miles from Shiel Bridge) to Morvich. The closest parking area is at the nearby Jac-O-Bite Restaurant.

THE WALK

Map p178

Just uphill of the car park, go through a small gate, immediately right of a burn, and follow a path up to a forest track. Just 12m to your right, immediately before a burn, bear left along a clear path. It follows a generally zigzagging route up beside the burn, through a young conifer plantation, climbing fairly steeply, to a gate in a high fence, giving onto open moorland. Continue on the path, soon bearing left to cross a burn at the foot of a small waterfall. The path leads northwest, up below a crag, zigzags then pursues a rising traverse to the remains of an old stone wall. Climb beside or on it for a few minutes then bear left and cross a small stream. From there, in the absence of a clearly defined path, climb up the steep grassy slope to the main ridge, reaching it west of Bealach an Làpain, in the vicinity of Beinn Odhar. Suddenly you're in a wholly different world – surrounded by mountains and deep glens and, for the moment, out of earshot of the traffic on the road below.

Continue along the ridge crest and follow the well-worn path across a shallow dip to the start of a rocky climb to **Sgurr nan Spainteach**. A scrambly descent down the face of a bluff takes you to the amazingly narrow Bealach nan Spainteach (see the boxed text, opposite).

Make your way up through the boulders to the neat summit cairn on **Sgurr na Ciste Duibhe** ('peak of the black coffin'), the first of the Five Sisters (2½ to three hours from the start). Here you can look east towards Glen Affric across the gap at the top of Gleann Lichd and, in the opposite direction, contemplate the serrated skyline of the Isle of Skye beyond Loch Duich.

The ridge changes direction, leading northwest down to Bealach na Craoibhe. Keep to the highest ground in the absence of a clear path. The line of ascent then turns north, climbing to **Sgurr na Càrnach** ('rocky peak'), the second Sister. From here new features in the panorama include Lochs Affric and Beinn a' Mheadhoin to the east. The first bit of the descent is through a narrow cleft to the left, then bearing right to regain the line of the ridge and going down to Bealach na Càrnach. A steep, rocky and twisting path takes care of the climb to **Sgurr Fhuaran** ('peak of the springs or small stream'), the highest point on the ridge and the third Sister (about 1½ hours from Sgurr na Ciste Duibhe). From here the view is no less absorbing than those from her siblings.

Leaving the summit cairn, take care to head northwest then north on this awesome and spectacular descent to Bealach

Buidhe. The path then traverses above the dramatic sheets of cliffs leading up to **Sgurr nan Saighead** ('arrows peak'), Sister number four. The ridge now changes character with more small, rocky knobs to negotiate on the way down and then up to Beinn Buidhe. A rough path drops down to a narrow gap, with fine views of Gleann Lichd below. Climb straight up and soon the path follows a more even course among rocky outcrops and (for a pleasant change) across grass and finally up to **Sgurr na Moraich** ('mighty peak'), Sister number five (two hours from Sgurr Fhuaran).

Having led northwest from the summit, straight towards Skye Bridge, the path fades. Keep well to the left of the broad spur, generally northwest (or about 300 degrees magnetic) as you descend very steeply over grass and heather, steering away from the small cliffs bristling on the crest of the spur. Keep your eye on the crags on the western side of Allt a' chruinn as a guide to the best route down to a narrow path high above the stream. Follow it down to a stile over a fence and continue to a water-treatment works. Turn right along a vehicle track, which becomes a sealed road, meeting the Morvich road in Ault a' chruinn, about 200m from its junction with the A87 (about an hour from Sgurr na Moraich).

GLEOURAICH

Duration	5–5½ hours
Distance	7.5 miles (12km)
Difficulty	moderate–demanding
Start/Finish	Loch Quoich car park
Nearest Town	Invergarry (opposite)
Transport	private

Summary An exhilarating traverse of a narrow mountain ridge, with awesome views of multitudes of peaks, near and far.

Glen Garry reaches west from the village of Invergarry in the Great Glen. It contains two large lochs, Loch Garry and Loch Quoich, both enlarged for hydroelectric power generation. Between Glen Shiel to the north, and Glen Kingie and Loch Arkaig in the south, it lies in the heart of a large, sparsely populated and mountainous area.

There are plenty of excellent mountains around the head of Glen Garry, mostly above both sides of Loch Quoich. The highest, Gleouraich (1035m, 3395ft), which means 'roaring' or 'bellowing' (a reference, perhaps, to the autumnal roaring of red stags during the rut or mating season), and its neighbour Spidean Mialach (996m, 3269ft), probably meaning 'peak of the deer', are both Munros. Together they make a top-class circuit walk.

Their rugged, linking ridge and the spurs extending generally south towards Loch Quoich enclose three coires (Coire Peitireach, Coire Mhèil and Coire Dubh) and Loch Fearna, perched on the spur below Spidean Mialach. It's a remarkably varied cluster of scenic features in a relatively small area. While Loch Quoich can betray its artificial size during summer, when its level drops, it still provides a fine foreground. So, with little Glen Quoich to the west and the South Kintail mountains to the north, this walk has as scenic a setting as you'll find anywhere.

The best way to do the circuit is clockwise, so you can enjoy climbing the superbly engineered stalkers' path up the western spur, which makes the ascent relatively painless. The path stops short of the final climb to the summit but the way is clear. The narrow ridge linking the two summits drops precipitously to the north, so good weather is a must for this walk. It's not a particularly long day, although it does involve 1180m of ascent.

Alternatives There are two possible routes down from Spidean Mialach: one on the western side of Allt a' Mhèil and the other following the spur on its eastern side. As you will see on an information board at the start of the walk, the Glenquoich Estate asks walkers not to use the western route, particularly during the stalking season (24 August to 10 October).

The walk could be cut short by descending into Coire Dubh, west of Spidean Mialach, or you could simply return to the start from Gleouraich, leaving Spidean for another day.

PLANNING

When to Walk/Stalking

Stalking takes place in Glenquoich Estate between 24 August and 10 October each year. During that time the estate asks walkers not to use the path that crosses Allt a' Mhèil below Coire Mhèil.

ROYAL GLEN QUOICH LODGE

Only the massed thickets of rhododendrons and a few tall pines on the shores of Loch Quoich give any clue of previous habitation. So it needs a considerable leap of the imagination to 'see' a large two-storey building, with others nearby, right on the shore where Allt Coire Peitireach enters the loch.

The lodge was well established by 1872 and it had at least 10 bedrooms, many with a dressing room attached. The walls of the billiard room were decorated with heads of stags shot on the estate (a common practice in those days). Nearby were a large cottage, coach house, carpenter's shop and gardeners' 'bothies'. There was even a school room for a handful of local pupils.

The lodge was clearly fit for a king, as a fragment from the Glen Quoich Stags logbook (itemising the number of stags shot during the stalking season) for the 1904 season reveals. The tally for the North Forest, directly above Loch Quoich, was 77 stags, of which 'The King' (George V) shot three, and Grand Duke Michael of Russia, nine.

However, royal patronage ultimately counted for nought in preserving the lodge – it was eventually demolished and the site drowned by the rising waters of an enlarged Loch Quoich, part of a hydroelectric power scheme in the late 1940s.

Maps

Harvey's 1:25,000 *Kintail* map extends as far south as Loch Quoich, so is ideal. For identifying peaks to the south and west (and for local use), OS Landranger 1:50,000 map No 33 *Loch Alsh, Glen Shiel & Loch Hourn* is the one to have.

NEAREST TOWN

Invergarry

☎ 01809

Invergarry is a dot on the map with limited facilities.

Faichemard Touring Caravan & Camping Site (☎ 501314; www.faichemard-caravancamping.co.uk; unpowered/powered sites for 2 £9/11) is a superbly set-up and long-established site. It has an adults-only policy so peace and quiet is all but assured.

Ardgarry Farm B&B (☎ 501226; www.ardgarryfarm.co.uk; Faichem; unpowered sites for 2 £10, s/d £24/48), in a peaceful location just west of the village, offers excellent value in a small B&B in spacious grounds.

Tomdoun Hotel (☎ 511218; www.tomdoun.com; dm/s/d £10/35/45, 3-course dinner £23; dinner), on the minor road through Glen Garry (en route to the walk), is a traditional, century-old lodge. Accommodation is available in the hotel or in the adjacent bunkhouse. The menu in both the restaurant and bar emphasises local shellfish and other top-quality produce. Bunkhouse guests can get breakfast for £5.

Invergarry Hotel (☎ 501206; mains £7-16; lunch & dinner) serves excellent bar meals (try the Highland game pie) and offers a selection of real ales.

There's a tiny shop at the service station beside the A82, about 220m northeast from the A87 junction.

GETTING THERE & AWAY

Invergarry is on the junction of the A82 and A87, 7 miles (11km) southwest of Fort Augustus and 15 miles (24km) north of Spean Bridge.

GETTING TO/FROM THE WALK

From Invergarry drive west along the A87 for 5.3 miles (8.2km) to a junction signposted to Tomdoun and Kinloch Hourn. Follow this single-lane road (look out for wandering sheep, which don't have much road sense) for about 15.3 miles (24.6km) to an informal car park on the south side of the road, close to the bridge over Allt Coire Peitireach. The walk starts and finishes here.

THE WALK

The path leads away from the road through rhododendrons for about 200m then emerges onto open, grassy moorland, climbing fairly gently. Once on the narrow crest of the spur the view north takes on new and dramatic dimensions as the mountains of the South Kintail ridge take shape. The path skirts the rocky crest of the spur on its western side to reach a shallow saddle, from which the final and steeper climb starts; ignore a large cairn by the path. Here you can look down to lonely Alltbeithe Cottage beside the River Quoich far below. The stalkers' path ends at a stone shooting butt (a low, roofless shelter used by stalkers). Continue straight up the steep slope, mostly over rocky ground but on a clear path, to the neat summit cairn of **Gleouraich** (about 1¾ hours from the start). On a good day you can easily see Ben Nevis to the southeast.

Continue along the rocky crest for about 100m then lose a bit of height before going up and over a secondary summit (Creag Coire na Fiar Bhealaich). Here you join a well-made path to descend to a bealach above rugged Coire Dubh to the south and steep cliffs on the northern side (about 45 minutes from the top). The ensuing climb to the next summit (977m) isn't unduly steep. From here a narrow ridge, with near vertical cliffs below on the left, leads to the final climb to the sprawling cairn on **Spidean Mialach** (40 minutes or so from the bealach above Coire Dubh). The stunning view extends as far as Ben Nevis to the southeast, west to Skye's Cuillin mountains, and to the dramatic corries scooped out of the South Kintail mountains nearby.

The descent starts straight away along a clear path on the south side of the cairn, heading towards Loch Fearna over shattered slabs then grass. Head generally west across the slope, intersected by several boggy burns, to a well-defined spur. Follow the spur on its eastern side over grass and scattered rocks and continue down to the road just east of Allt a' Mhèil. Turn right to return to the start in 1.2km. The descent, from where you joined the spur, takes about an hour.

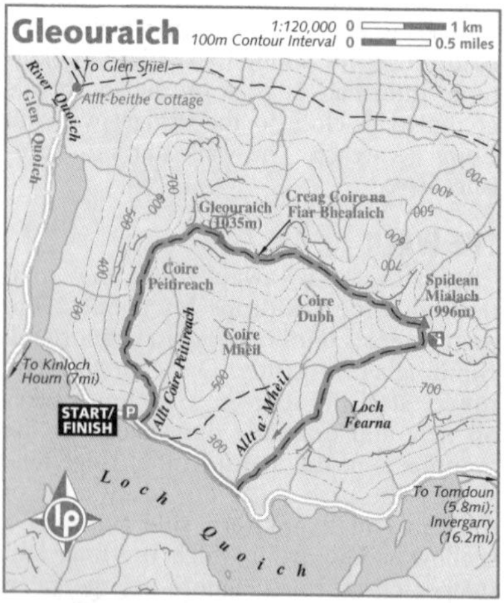

CREAG MEAGAIDH

Duration	6¾–7½ hours
Distance	11.8 miles (19km)
Difficulty	demanding
Start/Finish	Aberarder
Nearest Towns	Roybridge (p186), Laggan (p186)
Transport	private

Summary A strenuous, immensely rewarding and scenic circuit of a magnificent mountain massif in one of Scotland's finest national nature reserves.

Glen Spean extends southwest to northeast for around 25 miles (40km), from Spean Bridge, near the southern end of the Great Glen, along the River Spean and through to the head of Loch Laggan, close to the divide between the glen and Strathspey to the northeast. Along its southern side two groups of sprawling, high mountains are separated by Loch Treig. On the opposite side of the glen, above Loch Laggan, is a smaller cluster of peaks, dominated by Creag Meagaidh. The mountain, in the Creag Meagaidh National Nature Reserve, owned and managed by **Scottish Natural Heritage** (SNH; www.snh.org.uk/nnr-scotland), offers one of Scotland's classic circuit walks.

The walk can be done in either direction, depending on whether you prefer to reach the highest point, Creag Meagaidh (1130m, 3706ft), before or after a longish ridge walk. The more popular direction is probably anticlockwise, climbing generally north from Allt Coire Ardair to Carn Liath (1006m), the easternmost summit on the ridge. Although it's not a particularly long walk, the 1240m of ascent easily puts it in the difficult class, as does the roughness of the ground on the long southern spur over Sròn a' Ghoire (1001m) and down to Allt Coire Ardair. The route gives Munro baggers three summits: Carn Liath, Stob Poite Coire Ardair (1053m) and Creag Meagaidh, which is pronounced 'krayk megee' and means 'crag at the bog'.

Alternatives If Creag Meagaidh alone will satisfy your desires, then the quickest approach is the mostly good path (along which railway sleepers keep you out of most of the bogs) all the way from Aberarder to Lochan a' Choire in Coire Ardair. From there an informal path skirts the northern side of the lochan and wriggles up the steep, scree-filled gully to the gap between Stob Poite Coire Ardair and the Creag Meagaidh. This entails around 900m of ascent and can take up to six hours.

If the weather isn't suitable for a high-level walk (which it often isn't), or if there's too much snow on the ridge for your tastes, you can walk to Lochan a' Choire and back (10 miles/16km, 370m ascent). The view of the corrie's cliffs, likely to be crawling with ice climbers, is well worthwhile – Coire Ardair's cliffs offer some of the best snow and ice climbing in Britain and have attracted climbers since the end of the 19th century.

ENVIRONMENT

Creag Meagaidh is a spectacular example of a landscape moulded by snow and ice, created by two million years of advancing and retreating glaciers and ice sheets. Coire Ardair is a classic glaciated corrie, with its almost sheer headwall cliffs, the lochan below and the wavy mounds of glacial debris or moraine in the glen of Allt Coire Ardair. The stream is almost encircled by the ridge this walk traverses. The massif, crowned by Creag Meagaidh, is more complex, with corries gouged out on all sides and ridges fanning out from the summit, from the west round to the east.

The national nature reserve protects a diverse range of plants and wildlife, from the woodlands to the near-arctic, tundra-like summit plateau. One of SNH's aims is to eventually restore the native birch woodland. The results of reducing the number of grazing animals can be seen in the dense regrowth along the lower reaches of Allt Coire Ardair (see the boxed text, below). There are also plenty of rowan and willow, some alder and hazel, and many smaller flowering plants.

On the high ground, camouflaged ptarmigan are common, but it's more difficult to spot dotterels, a rare species in Scotland. You're more likely to see golden plovers, readily identified by their haunting, lonely call.

PLANNING

When to Walk

Snow can lie on the ridge until well into spring but usually the best times for this walk are from mid-May until mid-June and in September. In poor visibility finding your way across Creag Meagaidh's relatively featureless summit plateau can be difficult, so take particular care to check the forecast when planning this walk.

STALKING

SNH staff carry out an annual deer cull between July and February, but access within the reserve is open at all times. It may happen that you'll be asked to consider an alternative route but not to leave. Contact **SNH** (☎ 01528 544265) at Aberarder for more information.

CARING FOR CREAG MEAGAIDH

The geological significance of Creag Meagaidh's glaciated landscape was officially recognised by the declaration of the area as a Site of Special Scientific Interest in 1975. Nearly a decade later the threat of a conifer plantation on the lower slopes prompted the Nature Conservancy Council (Scottish Natural Heritage's predecessor) to buy the land and the adjacent mountainous ground, covering about 3948 hectares; it became Creag Meagaidh National Nature Reserve in 1986.

Most of the Aberarder farm buildings, at the eastern entrance to the reserve, date from the 19th century when the sheep population was huge. Numbers dwindled after 1918 and never really recovered, apart from a brief revival in the late 1940s. All surviving sheep were taken away after the national nature reserve was created.

In 1986 little native woodland was left. Its restoration has been outstandingly successful and there has been a spectacular improvement in the diversity of animal species. This success is partly due to the substantial reduction of the red deer population, by live catching and traditional culling.

Maps & Books

The OS Explorer 1:25,000 map No 401 *Loch Laggan* and OS Landranger 1:50,000 map No 34 *Fort Augustus* cover the walk.

The Scottish Mountaineering Club's Hillwalkers Guide *The Munros*, edited by Donald Bennet, is useful. The SNH leaflet about the reserve can be downloaded from www.snh.org.uk/nnr-scotland.

NEAREST TOWNS

Laggan

☎ 01528

Laggan is a small village 10 miles (16km) northeast of Aberarder, which emerged from its seclusion during the internationally popular TV series *Monarch of the Glen*. The community-run **Information Office** (☎ 544383; www.laggan.com; May-Sep) serves as a TIC and sells maps and local guidebooks.

SLEEPING & EATING

The **Pottery Bunkhouse** (☎ 544231; www.potterybunkhouse.co.uk; A889, Caoldair; dm £11), just east of the village centre, is a well-designed place with dorms and en suite family rooms. Bedding can be hired (£4). The facilities are excellent and include a hot tub with mountain views. The adjacent coffee shop serves first-class cakes, baked on the premises.

The **Monadhliath Hotel** (☎ 544276; www.lagganbridge.com; s/d £35/60), originally a manse (minister's house) close to the Pottery, has bright, elegantly furnished rooms. For a meal, choose between the bar and small dining room.

The **village shop** (daily) has a good range of supplies.

GETTING THERE & AWAY

Laggan is on the A86 (Spean Bridge–Newtonmore road), 29 miles (47km) from Spean Bridge and 7 miles (11km) from Newtonmore.

Roybridge

☎ 01397

Roybridge is a larger village on the A86, 16 miles (26km) southwest of Aberarder and about 4 miles east of Spean Bridge. There is a bus and train service to the village, but unless you have a vehicle you will still be stranded a long way from the walk.

Bunroy Caravan & Camping Site (☎ 712332; www.bunroycamping.co.uk; sites for 2 £10) is about 300m south of the main road on the banks of the River Spean; the facilities are well maintained.

Station Lodge (☎ 732333; www.stationlodge.co.uk; Tulloch; dm/tw £11/24, breakfast £5, dinner mains £8), on the Fort William–Glasgow train line between Roybridge and Aberarder, is a first-rate bunkhouse. It has thoughtfully appointed dorms and a small shop. The dinner menu always includes a vegetarian option and the lodge is licensed.

The **Stronlossit Inn** (☎ 712253; www.stronlossit.co.uk; s/d £75/90, dinner mains £11; lunch & dinner) is a family-run establishment in the centre of the village. The menu features local produce wherever possible and vegetarians are catered for.

There is also a small **shop** (daily) in the village.

GETTING TO/FROM THE WALK

The walk starts at the car park beside the A86, near SNH's Aberarder office, nearly 20 miles (32km) from Spean Bridge and 10 miles (16km) from Laggan.

THE WALK

From the car park walk northwest along the vehicle track, passing to the right of the white-painted, two-storey house and a small information shelter. A well-made track, with sections of railway sleepers across boggy ground, leads towards Allt Coire Ardair. After about 500m it swings away to the north to climb the partly wooded hillside, soon entering dense birch woodland. Just over 800m miles further on, and a few metres past an old metal fence post on the right, a narrow, informal path, marked by a small cairn, leads uphill and generally follows the intermittent line of posts up to the crest of the spur just northwest of Na Cnapanan (623m). The terrain is rough underfoot and in places the path is overgrown with regenerating birch and rowan crowding in on the steep hillside. From Na Cnapanan the clear path climbs steadily to the main ridge, over mainly rocky ground. Diverge to the east, over shattered rock, for a few hundred metres to the sizable cairn on the summit of **Carn Liath** (1006m), almost two hours from the start. The fine panorama takes in scores of 'hills', notably the Glen Shiel ridge to the northwest and part of Ben Nevis to the southwest; the Cairngorms are draped across the eastern skyline.

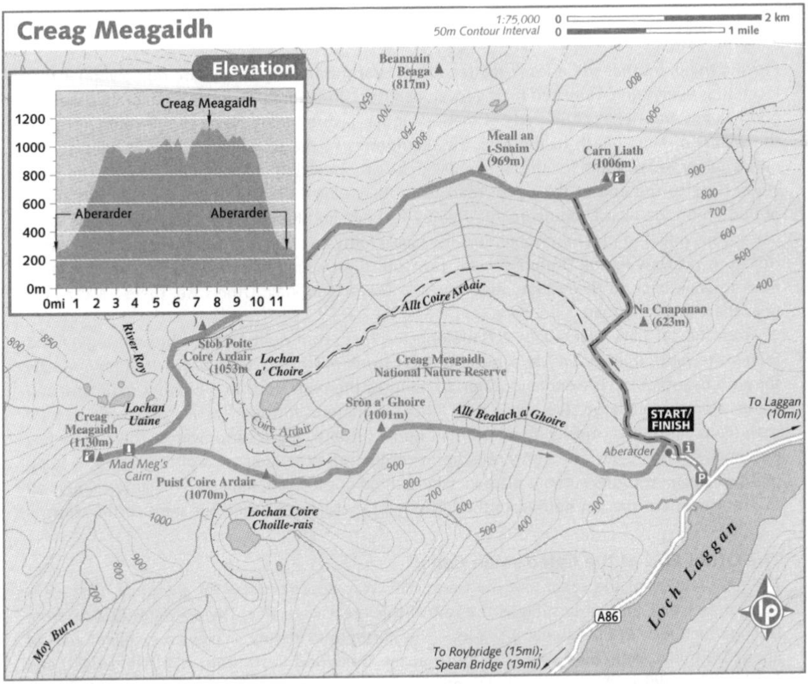

Descend the broad ridge, soon leaving the rocky ground for grass, skirt a narrow gap on the left and then wander over a string of small bumps. The way is still down to a deep, narrow gap, from where there's a good view of Loch Spey, at the head of the River Spey in the glen far below to the north. Inevitably a climb follows, leading to a fine, narrow ridge and on to **Stob Poite Coire Ardair** (1½ hours from Carn Liath).

Then it's steeply down into the divide between the ridge and the main mountain massif, hitting the lowest point on the north side of the twin gaps here. A not-too-steep pull takes you up to the sprawling summit ridge. Here the path keeps to the northern edge, past the huge Mad Meg's Cairn, to the summit of **Creag Meagaidh** (about 45 minutes from the Stob). The extraordinary view includes Loch Ericht and the Glen Coe and Nevis Range 'hills' to the south.

Return to Mad Meg's Cairn then descend east and across a shallow, dry valley. Go over Puist Coire Ardair, crowned with a small cairn, and on to the cliff-edge path, which yields excellent views of Loch Laggan and upper Strathspey. Then comes a steep descent to skirt a corrie cradling a tiny lochan; a discontinuous path leads on and up to Sròn a Ghoire. Then it's down with a vengeance – keep well to the right (south) for the best way around the small streams and marshy ground on the hillside. Aim to reach a pair of old fence posts, from where a fairly clear path leads generally east, across Allt Bealach a' Ghoire and marshy ground. At a distinct path intersection turn left (northeast) and continue to a bridge across Allt Coire Ardair. A bit further on, ignore a track leading to the Aberarder buildings and head towards the stone wall ahead to join the main path, about 100m west of the information shelter. You should reach the car park about 2½ hours from the summit.

MORE WALKS

There are scores of other first-rate high- and low-level walks in the Highland Glens. As well as the following suggestions, browse the SMC Hillwalkers' Guide *North-west*

SHORT WALKS

Proving the point that size doesn't matter, **Meall Fuar-mhonaidh** (699m) also demonstrates that location is everything. Hunched high above Loch Ness, its summit provides a panoramic view as good as any from peaks hundreds of metres higher, taking in Ben Nevis to the southwest and the waters of Moray Firth to the east, the Cairngorms to the south and a host of 'hills' to the north. Allow 3–3¼ hours for the 6-mile (9.6km) walk, involving around 500m ascent. The walk starts close to the end of the minor road to Grotaig, which branches from the A82 just south of Borlum Bridge near Drumnadrochit. Nearby is the delightful Loch Ness Clay Works, the ideal place from which to purchase some genuine local craft work. Carry OS Landranger 1:50,000 map No 26. A postbus leaves Drumnadrochit post office at 8.30am, but returns directly, so you'd have to walk back to the village, following the Great Glen Way. Otherwise, there's a car park near the end of the road.

From the car park walk about 200m along the road; turn right and go through a gate and follow the path, initially beside a burn. It soon turns northwest to follow a tributary, mostly through beautiful birch woodland. After 20 minutes the path leads into heather moorland and climbs steadily to a large stile over a deer fence (15 minutes further). The all-too-clearly-defined path leads southwest, mostly along a broad ridge, onwards and ever upwards. There are a few potentially boggy places, and only one dip to compromise the directness of the ascent. A steep pull takes you up to the summit plateau, where the highest point, marked by a large cairn, is on the southwestern rim (an hour from the big stile). Eventually, retrace your steps to the start.

The Other End of the Caledonian Canal

The only section of the canal that the Great Glen Way doesn't follow for any great distance is at least as scenic and interesting as the rest of this great waterway. The 5.7 miles (9.2km) from Dochgarroch lock to Clachnaharry sea lock, the northern extremity, makes an excellent walk of about 2½ hours. You could start with lunch at the **Oakwood Restaurant** (☎ 01463 861481) and finish with a pint or two at the traditional **Clachnaharry Inn** (☎ 01463 239806). The **Highland Country Buses** (☎ 01463 710555; www.rapsons.co.uk) service to Drumnadrochit stops at Dochgarroch (four services Monday to Saturday); from Clachnarry, it's about 40 minutes on foot into the centre of Inverness, or you can pick up a bus on the A862 (Stagecoach Inverness–Dingwall service, hourly Monday to Saturday). There's a car park beside Dochgarroch lock but nowhere convenient to park at the end of the walk.

Set out along the track on the northern side of the canal, but not without saying hello to the very old Mediterranean spur-thighed tortoises in the garden of a nearby house. Beyond the diverse collection of moored boats, the vehicle track ends; continue along an informal path beside fields and dense masses of gorse and other bushes. Along here there are good views west of the Craig Dunain hillside and the prominent buildings, formerly a mental hospital. About 55 minutes out, just past houses at Hythe Quay, are some fine Scots pines beside the path. Soon you can see the broad River Ness below to the east. About 25 minutes from Hythe Quay you reach a jetty and Tomnahurich swing bridge. Cross the bridge to the opposite bank and continue past a large cemetery. Soon you'll see the reason for crossing the bridge – the large marina and ship repair yards opposite. Then comes the flight of five locks at Muirtown; cross the top lock gate and walk down to a gap in a white-painted wall on the left. Cross the busy road and go through a kissing gate to follow the broad tow path, past another marina on the far side. From here you can see graceful Kessock Bridge (across Beauly Firth) silhouetted against timbered Ord Hill ahead. The wider section of the canal a little further on was originally a swing basin, used to manoeuvre vessels in the days of commercial shipping along the canal. Just past Clachnaharry works lock, Beauly Firth comes into view. Negotiate the pedestrian crossing on the Inverness–Kyle of Lochalsh train line and continue to the meeting of the canal and the firth at Clachnaharry sea lock (25 minutes from Muirtown). To reach the bus route and/or inn, retrace your steps almost to the train line. Turn right along a street to a foot bridge over the railway. Cross it to reach the main road; the inn is nearby.

Highlands to find out more about the South Kintail ridge, a fiercely undulating string of mountains opposite the Five Sisters; Glen Dessary, west of Loch Arkaig, leading to the remote and beautiful shores of Loch Nevis and overlooked by several great mountains (notably Sgurr na Ciche); and Strathfarrar, north of Glen Affric, with plenty of 'hill' and glen walks. Another that can't be overlooked is Ben Wyvis, the big, sprawling mountain dominating the view west from Inverness. It is similar to the Cairngorms with its spacious, undulating summit plateau and affords magnificent views.

STRATHCONON

This long, broad valley reaches west along the River Conon from near Dinwall on the Cromarty Firth. A public road through the strath passes two artificial lochs, scattered farms and woodland, and follows the River Meig to Scardroy, a lone, large house. The 'hills' on either side are relatively unassuming until you reach Scardroy and the start of a right of way into the mountains.

Scardroy to Glen Carron

This path follows the River Meig generally west through Gleann Fhiodaig to its head, deep in the mountains near Glenuaig Lodge. It then descends through a spectacular gorge beside Allt a' Chonais and a plantation to a bridge over the River Carron, near the hamlet of Craig on the A890 (Achnasheen–Lochcarron road). The distance is about 13 miles (21km) one way, best done as a two-day walk, perhaps camping in the vicinity of Glenuaig Lodge. Gleann Fhiodaig is overlooked by towering peaks on both sides, including several fine crag-girt hills, notably the formidable Maoile Lunndaidh (1007m) and Sgurr a' Chaorachain (1053m) to the south – good reasons for taking more than a day. Use OS Landranger 1:50,000 map No 25. The most useful reference is the SMC's guide *The Munros*.

There's a **bunkhouse** (☎ 01520 766232; www.gerryshostel-achnashellach.co.uk; dm £21) at Craig, otherwise the nearest accommodation is at least 10 miles (16km) further west at Lochcarron. Unfortunately there isn't a postbus service through Strathconon. At the other end, trains on the Inverness–Kyle of Lochalsh line stop at Achnashellach (£12, 1½ hours from Inverness, three services Monday to Saturday, one Sunday), about 2.5 miles west of Craig.

KNOYDART

Knoydart is a wild, rugged, virtually road-free area on the west coast, between Loch Nevis to the south and Loch Hourn, at the head of Glen Garry. It's defined as much by these lochs and its remoteness as it is by the marvellous glens leading into and within its confines, notably Glen Dessary and Glen Barrisdale. After long years of mismanagement and conflict, Knoydart is now cared for sympathetically by a group of landowners comprising the **Knoydart Foundation** (www.knoydart-foundation.com), on behalf of the local community, the John Muir Trust and private individuals. There's a **ferry** (www.knoydart-ferry.co.uk) from Mallaig to Inverie, Knoydart's port; Mallaig, in turn, is served by First ScotRail trains and Scottish Citylink buses from Fort William.

Kinloch Hourn to Inverie

This route follows a public right of way, generally along the southern shore of Loch Hourn to Barrisdale Bay, then across the pass of Mam Barrisdale and down to the village of Inverie, overlooking Loch Nevis. From the pass it's possible to climb the magnificent peak of Ladhar Bheinn (1020m, 3346ft), pronounced 'larven', and its southern neighbour Luinne Bheinn (939m). The distance for the through walk, without side trips, is 15 miles (24km). OS Landranger 1:50,000 map No 33 covers the area and the SMC's *The Munros* book is your guide. There's a bothy at Barrisdale Bay and a choice of accommodation at Inverie.

GLEN URQUHART

Drumnadrochit, roughly midway along the northwestern side of Loch Ness, is famously associated with the legendary Loch Ness Monster and is a staging point on the Great Glen Way. It's much less known as the 'capital' of Glen Urquhart, and is the crucial link to a string of forest paths and tracks leading to Loch Affric and through to Loch Duich (see the walk on p174).

From the western edge of the village, paths lead through Craig Mony woodland to forest tracks, which go west along the south side of beautiful Glen Urquhart to Corrimony. Then, forest and farm tracks lead up the River Enrick's glen, and generally west to the village of Tomich (about 16 miles/26km from Drumnadrochit). The route continues generally southwest along forest roads past Plodda Falls and Cougie to a forest road on the south side of Loch Affric, from where the car park is about 1.5 miles to the northeast (about 11 miles/18km from Tomich). Alternatively, sections of this route can be done as day walks from local bases.

Accommodation is available around Balnain and Shenval in Glen Urquhart, and at Tomich; otherwise it's OK to camp in Forestry Commission areas, for one night in each place. The walk is covered by OS Landranger 1:50,000 map Nos 25, 26 and 33. The Highland Country Buses service from Drumnadrochit to Cannich/Tomich goes through Glen Urquhart (four services Monday to Saturday). Contact **Forest Enterprise** (☎ 01320 366322) for more information.

Isle of Skye

The Isle of Skye is blessed with incontestably the finest scenic splendour and variety in Scotland, assets that have drawn writers, artists and travellers to the island for centuries. Since the early 20th century walkers and climbers have also flocked to Skye to revel in the glorious array of hill and coast walking. All manner of visitors also come in search of the island's mystical atmosphere, little diminished in many quiet corners, at a safe distance from the seemingly unstoppable growth of tourism and construction of new houses.

The Black and Red Cuillins, Skye's trademark among hill folk, are all about adrenalin-drenched challenge and sublime hill and sea vistas, and immensely rewarding for that. They're the subject of the first part of this chapter with two walks, both involving a modest amount of rock scrambling, in the angular Black Cuillin and one in the rounded Red Cuillin. A third Black Cuillin outing, to Sgurr Dearg, and involving a hefty swag of scrambling, is outlined in the boxed text on p204. Proving that height isn't everything, the Coast & Cuillin walk, into the heart of the Black Cuillin, combines superb coast and hill scenery.

North of the Cuillin, beyond the island's capital of Portree, lies the Trotternish peninsula, the centrepiece of which is an undulating, mostly grassy ridge, encrusted with crumbling cliffs and fantastic pinnacles. The walking here is over gentler gradients and on grass. The Quiraing, close to the northern tip of the island, is an extraordinary assemblage of pinnacles, bluffs and secret places.

HIGHLIGHTS

- Venturing into the remote sanctuary of **Loch Coruisk** (p201)
- Finding the way along on the airy ridge of **Bla Bheinn** (p203) in the Black Cuillin
- Savouring the magnificent views far and wide from the **Storr** (p208)
- Romping along the roller-coaster Trotternish ridge on the **Trotternish Traverse** (p207)
- Not getting lost among the weird pinnacles of the **Quiraing** (p209)

- www.visithighlands.com
- www.isleofskye.net

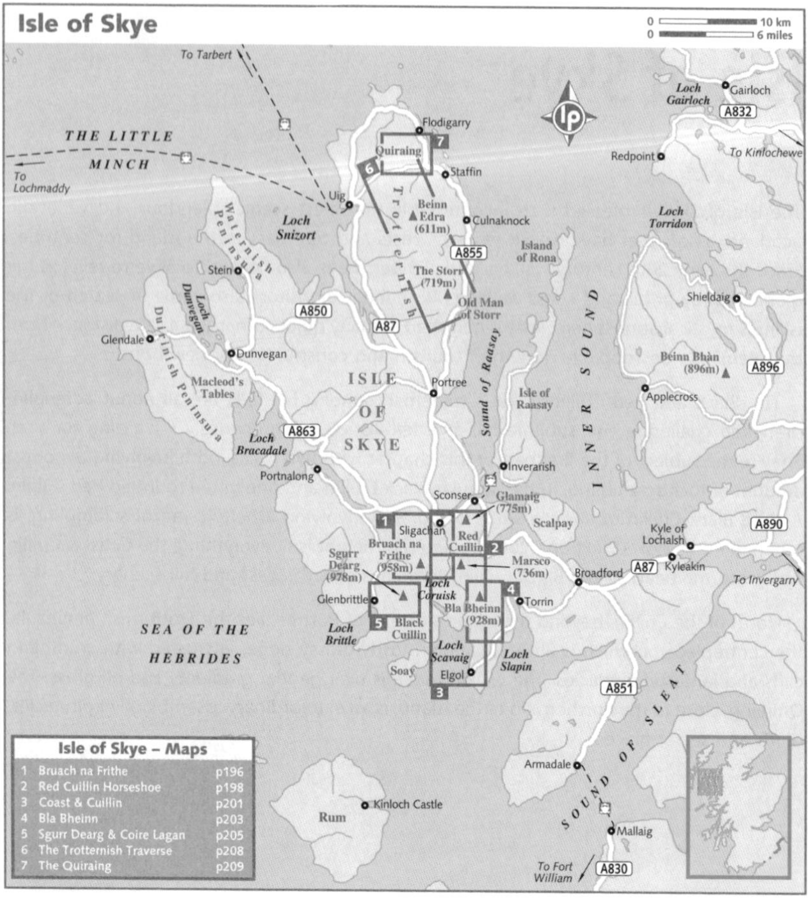

INFORMATION

Maps & Books

For a topographic overview of the island the OS Travel – Road 1:250,000 map No 2 *Western Scotland* is ideal.

Skye & the North West Highlands by John Brooks and Neil Wilson covers 15 varied walks on Skye. The Ramblers' Association's *Guide to the Isle of Skye* by Chris Townsend describes 30 walks, ranging from easy strolls to challenging Cuillin scrambles. *Isle of Skye including Raasay* by Paul Williams concentrates on walks at the easier end of the spectrum. *Skye 360, Walking the Coastline of Skye* by Andrew Dempster is a personalised account of a month-long journey with just enough details to follow in his footsteps. *A Long Walk on the Isle of Skye* by David Paterson, in coffee-table format, offers a description of his walk, inspired by his superb photos.

Guided Walks

Highland Council's countryside rangers (☎ 01471 822905; Old Corry Industrial Estate, Broadford) run varied programs of guided walks, with particular emphasis on Skye's natural heritage, from around March until October. Pick up a printed program from local tourist information centres (TICs).

Cuillin Guides (☎ 01478 640289; www.cuillin-guides.co.uk; Glenbrittle) has years of solid experience behind it, and an unrivalled knowledge of the hills. Its program includes five days of ridge walking and scrambling with a guide-to-client ratio of 1:5); the staff are qualified mountain leaders.

Hebridean Pathways (☎ 07092840603; www.hebrideanpathways.co.uk; PO Box 6340, Broadford IV49 9AE) offers a varied program, including six energetic days doing the Cuillin Munros. With a guide-to-client ratio of 1:4 the cost is £350. The principal guide is a member of the Association of Mountaineering Instructors.

Information Sources

VisitScotland's (www.visithighlands.com) comprehensive website is a good place to start, especially for accommodation bookings. For a local take on the island, go to www.isleofskye.net.

For all public transport information contact **Traveline** (☎ 0870 608 2608; www.travelinescotland.com).

GATEWAY
Portree

☎ 01478 / pop 1920

Portree, the largest town on the island and the recognised capital, sprawls along the western shore of a deep inlet on the east coast. It's important to remember that most businesses are closed on Sundays; exceptions are noted.

The **TIC** (☎ 612137; www.visithighlands.com; Bayfield House, Bayfield Rd; daily Jun-Sep, Mon-Sat Oct-May;) sells maps and books and can answer all your questions about staying on Skye.

SUPPLIES & EQUIPMENT

Island Outdoors (☎ 611073; The Green; daily) stocks gear, maps and books.

MacIntyre's (☎ 612918; 14 Wentworth St; daily) has the best range of books about Skye and Scotland generally.

For self-catering supplies, there's a large **Co-op supermarket** (Dunvegan Rd; daily) and a small **Somerfield supermarket** (Bank St; daily). There is also **Granary Bakery** (Somerled Sq; Mon-Sat), which is recommended.

SLEEPING & EATING

Although there's a wide and plentiful range of accommodation in and near the town, it's wise to book ahead during summer.

Torvaig Camping & Caravan Site (☎ 611169; Staffin Rd; unpowered/powered sites for 2 £6/8), about 1 mile north of town on the A855, has few level pitches but is grassed and sheltered.

Bayfield Backpackers (☎ 612231; www.skyehostel.co.uk; Bayfield; dm £13) enjoys a scenic location; some of the dorms have their own bathroom.

The **Pink Guest House** (☎ 612263; www.pinkguesthouse.co.uk; 1 Quay St; s/d £35/60) is a tour de force of interior decoration in almost every imaginable shade of pink, stopping short of the electric variety. It's quiet and particularly comfortable.

Apart from the several hotels in town, all serving their own variations on the bar-meal theme, there are two tempting alternatives.

Prince of India (☎ 612681; Bayfield Rd; mains £9-12; lunch & dinner Mon-Sat), in a large white traditional cottage close to the bay shore, offers a large and varied menu, specialising in Balti dishes.

Café Arriba (☎ 611830; Quay Brae; breakfast £4, mains £7-10; lunch & dinner) is a cheerful place with chefs who inhabit a different planet from the creators of pub fare, offering a constantly changing menu especially strong on vegetarian dishes.

GETTING THERE & AWAY

Scottish Citylink (☎ 08705 505050; www.citylink.co.uk) operates bus route 916 from Glasgow via Fort William to Portree (£26, 6¼ hours, three daily), and route 917 from Inverness to Portree (£16, 3½ hours, three daily).

A highly recommended variation from Inverness is to take the outstandingly scenic **First ScotRail** (☎ 0845 755 0033; www.firstscotrail.com) train trip to Kyle of Lochalsh (£17, 2½ hours, four services Monday to Saturday, two Sunday) and connect with the local **Highland Country Buses** (☎ 01463 710555; www.rapsons.co.uk) service to Portree (£5, one hour, at least four services Monday to Saturday, two Sunday).

By car, follow the A82 from Inverness to Invermoriston then the A887 and A87, across the once-controversial bridge. From the south, the A82 from Glasgow via Fort William lands you at Invergarry, from where you continue on the A87.

THE CUILLIN

The Black and Red Cuillin mountains are rarely out of sight all over southern Skye. Their name Cuillin (pronounced 'coolin') most likely derives from the Norse *kjolen*, meaning 'high rocks'.

The Black Cuillin is the most visually awe-inspiring mountain range in Scotland and, indeed, Britain. The main ridge is 7.5 miles (12.2km) in length and averages about 700m in height, the highest peak being Sgurr Alasdair (993m/3257ft). It's typically spiky, with knife-edged ridges, and is exceptionally challenging – the ultimate test for many walkers. Fortunately there are a couple of routes to seemingly impossible summits that aren't the exclusive domain of rock climbers. All the while, it's salutary to recall that there was a time, not so very long ago as far as the rock itself is concerned, when the Cuillin were considered unassailable (see the boxed text on p197).

The nearby Red Cuillin mountains are completely different, being lower, more rounded and tending to conical profiles. Their red granite, from which they take their name, seems less intimidating and alien than the rough black gabbro of their neighbours. Glamaig (775m/2542ft) reigns supreme.

Basing yourself at Sligachan puts you within striking distance of the summit of Bruach na Frithe, a comparatively easy Black Cuillin peak. Another path from Sligachan leads to the Red Cuillin horseshoe; if the cloud is down or you fancy a low-level walk, you can walk through to Loch Coruisk and back, as fine a low-level walk as you'd want.

From the shores of Loch Slapin, west of the hamlet of Torrin, you can climb the great gabbro massif of Bla Bheinn (Blaven), a Black Cuillin outlier and a superlative viewpoint from which to view all the Cuillin mountains. Further down the road from Torrin is the hamlet of Elgol, from where you can follow a coastal path to the magnificent Loch Coruisk and on through Glen Sligachan to the main island road at Sligachan itself.

Head down to remote Glenbrittle to take up the challenge of the scramble to the summit of Sgurr Dearg, some of the most airy and exhilarating walking around.

ENVIRONMENT

Millions of years after violent volcanic activity created the Cuillin, Skye was in the grip of a great ice age. Glaciers formed on the highest parts of the island and sculpted the landscape, carving deep basins, now the characteristic corries, in the gabbro rock. The basalt has eroded more readily than the hard gabbro, creating gullies and chimneys, and a finely sculpted, jagged ridge line.

MOUNTAINS FOR SALE?

During the early part of 2000, John MacLeod (chief of the Clan MacLeod) put the Black Cuillin mountains on sale for an asking price of £10 million. Typical of the local reactions reported in the press was the comment of a young lass: 'You cannae sell a mountain'. Environmental and outdoor-interest groups had only just defeated plans for scenic flights to be operated over the same mountains from Sligachan, and were horrified by rumours that wealthy foreigners had expressed interest in purchasing the range. Some feared the Black Cuillin would be turned into a mass-tourism theme park, or that the long history of public access to the mountains would be threatened. The move prompted an even stronger reaction from islanders, who were angered by MacLeod's assumption of title, and a suggestion at a public meeting that the government would buy the estate for the people was booed. Their view was that MacLeod should not profit from the sale and it was unclear whether he actually owned the mountains. MacLeod, on the other hand, stated that he simply needed the money for repairs to the roof of Dunvegan Castle, one of the island's leading tourist attractions.

Later in the year the property was withdrawn from the market pending an investigation by the Crown Estate Commission, which looks after state-owned land, into legal title to the mountains. If the commission found that MacLeod did not own the estate then title would fall to the Crown and, hence, become public property. However, the commission decided not to contest MacLeod's claim to the title and, despite the strength of feeling, MacLeod put the estate back on the market. In July 2001 MacLeod offered to give the Cuillin to the nation in exchange for acceptable arrangements to restore his castle. At the time of research, eight government and private organisations were immersed in an assessment of what needed to be done to the castle. The community at large was to be consulted about how best to handle guardianship of the mountains. As the John Muir Trust says: 'It is likely to be some time' before the whole thing is sorted out.

The most common rock type in the Black Cuillin rock is gabbro, with surface outcrops of smooth basalt. This dark gabbro is a coarse crystalline rock, once described as similar to a nutmeg grater in texture. Being rich in iron, it does strange things to magnetic compasses – you have been warned (see the boxed text, right). The Red Cuillin mountains comprise granite and quartz, with flakes of pink feldspar providing the characteristic red colour.

WATCH YOUR COMPASS

The magnetic properties of the Black Cuillin gabbro rock distort compass readings, so this small piece of equipment is virtually useless. Thus you are thrown back on your map-reading skills, or GPS bearings and/or route-notes interpretation on cloudy days. If you're a bit uncertain about these skills, then ensure that the weather is fine and settled for your summit attempts. Even then, extreme caution is necessary as the mountain climate is notoriously changeable.

PLANNING

Maps

OS Explorer 1:25,000 map No 411 *Cuillin Hills* and Harvey's Superwalker 1:25,000 map *Skye: The Cuillin* cover the hill walks. The latter includes a 1:12,500 enlargement of the Cuillin ridge, offering probably the clearest picture of the complex terrain.

BRUACH NA FRITHE

Duration	6–8 hours
Distance	8.5 miles (13.5km)
Difficulty	moderate–demanding
Start/Finish	Sligachan (below)
Transport	bus

Summary A superb, energetic outing, with spectacular views of the Black and Red Cuillin and the chance of some exciting scrambling for the cool-headed.

Standing on an apex of the main Black Cuillin ridge, Bruach na Frithe (958m/3142ft) is a superlative viewpoint from which to appreciate the outstanding rock architecture of this amazing range, without getting involved in the serious scrambling most Black Cuillin routes demand. From Sligachan good paths lead right into Fionn Choire, from where a short and steep, but very straightforward, ascent takes you up to the summit. This may be the easiest peak in the Black Cuillin to climb but it still requires considerable effort, involving a total ascent of more than 900m.

NEAREST TOWN

Sligachan

☎ 01478

Historic Sligachan is just a large hotel, a bunkhouse, camping ground and a bus stop. It has been the gateway to the Cuillin for more than a century and seethes with activity during summer; in fact it's rarely quiet here. You'll search in vain for a shop, so bring all you need from Portree (p193) or Broadford, also the locations of the nearest TICs.

SLEEPING & EATING

Sligachan Campsite (☎ 650204; unpowered/powered sites for 2 £8/11), opposite the hotel at the head of Loch Sligachan, enjoys an outstandingly scenic setting.

Sligachan Bunkhouse (☎ 650204; www.sligachan.co.uk; dm £10), on the eastern side of the main road, has that all-important Skye facility – a drying room.

Sligachan Hotel (☎ 650204; www.sligachan.co.uk; s/d £48/96) is a must, if only for a look at the walls of historic photos of early climbers. The comfortable rooms have either mountain or lake views and you can eat in lively **Seamus Bar** (mains £6-12; breakfast, lunch & dinner) or go upmarket at **Cairidh Seafood Restaurant** (mains £12-18; lunch & dinner).

GETTING THERE & AWAY

Scottish Citylink (☎ 08705 505050; www.citylink.co.uk) bus route 916 from Glasgow, via Fort William, to Portree stops at Sligachan (£26, six hours, three daily), as does route 917 from Inverness (£13, three hours, three daily) to Portree.

A **Highland Country Buses** (☎ 01463 710555; www.rapsons.co.uk) service from Portree (£2, 20 minutes, at least three Monday to Saturday, one Sunday) stops at Sligachan.

By car, Sligachan is 9 miles from Portree and 23 miles from the Skye Bridge. There is a small car park on the south side of the A863 Dunvegan road about 500m west of the hotel, beside a footpath sign pointing to Glenbrittle.

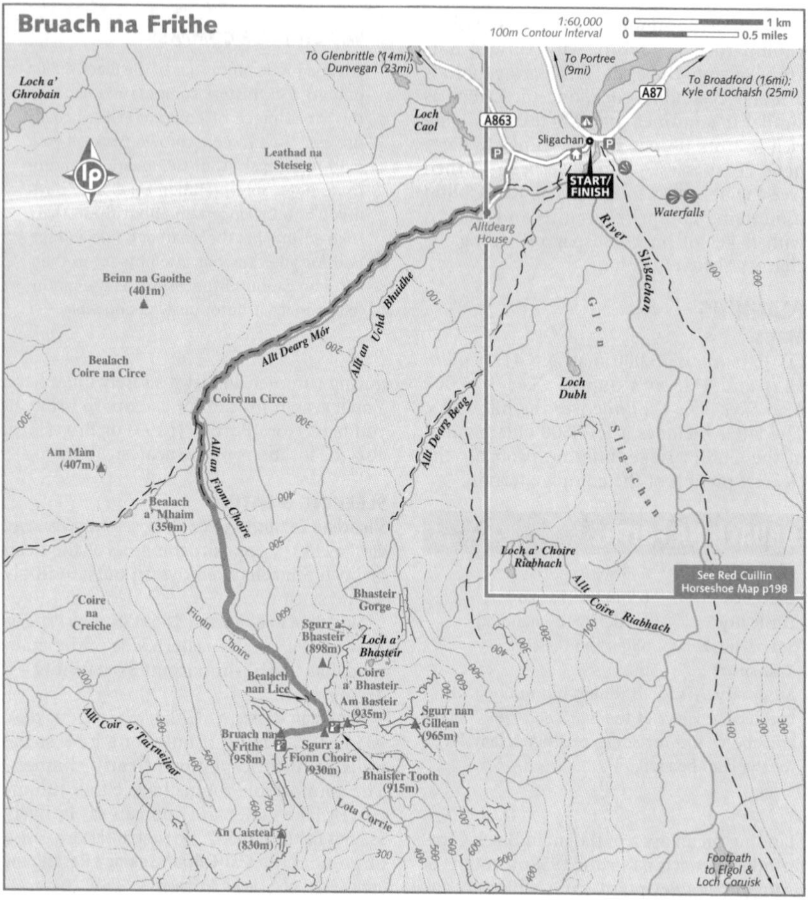

THE WALK

From the roadside car park on the A863, follow the track signed 'Footpath to Glenbrittle', heading towards Alltdearg House. A signed path diverts you around the grounds north of the house, crossing boggy ground. The firmest route keeps close to the fence on the left.

You soon pick up a stony path that runs alongside Allt Dearg Mór, a burn that tumbles down a series of rock ledges, forming some beautiful pools and small waterfalls that invite a swim on a hot day. After 2 miles the path begins to level out in Coire na Circe. Continue on, fording a sizable tributary to reach a large cairn. Here the path for Bruach na Frithe, fainter than the one you've been on, forks left across boggy ground and crosses another burn, 200m after the cairn. If the weather is clear you will be able to see the summit of Bruach na Frithe and grassy, boulder-strewn slopes running up into Fionn Choire. Follow the ascending path for about 30 minutes, keeping Allt an Fionn Choire (a burn with small waterfalls pouring from the corrie above) on your left, until you reach a substantial cairn on top of a rock slab. This is a good place for a rest while you decide which route to take to the summit.

Fionn Choire has not been gouged out as deeply as most Scottish corries and does not hold a lochan. Nonetheless, it is a beautiful and impressive place. You should be able to make out a path climbing the steep scree

IT'S ATTITUDE THAT MATTERS

Standing on the summit of Bruach na Frithe or Sgurr Dearg on a good summer's day, it is difficult to imagine that the Black Cuillin were considered to be unattainable as recently as the early 19th century. Between then and now, when people regularly traverse the entire Cuillin ridge, some even making nonstop traverses of the Greater Cuillin (including Bla Bheinn), lies a fundamental shift in attitude. It wasn't modern climbing gear, boots or clothing that made the difference but the development of a different approach to the mountains.

Most of the summits were considered unclimbable until 1835 when Reverend Lesingham Smith and local forester Duncan MacIntyre visited Loch Coruisk and returned to Sligachan by scrambling across the ramparts of the Druim nam Ramh ridge into Harta Corrie. The following year Professor James Forbes hired MacIntyre as a guide and together they made the first recorded ascent of Sgurr nan Gillean by the now popular (but still tricky) southeast ridge.

With the psychological barrier broken, local men quickly knocked off the other peaks in the Cuillin, with Sheriff Alexander Nicolson claiming the first ascent of Sgurr Alasdair, the highest summit on Skye. Many of these local men became guides to members of the Alpine Club, and John Mackenzie became the first local professional guide on the island. In 1859 an Admiralty surveyor, Captain Wood, mapped the south Cuillin and identified a pinnacle at 986m as being unclimbable, but it only needed that tag to ensure that the first ascent of what is now known as the Inaccessible Pinnacle soon followed. Today it's one of the most popular climbing challenges in the Black Cuillin, involving one pitch of easy rock climbing and a short abseil. Another popular climbing challenge is the Cioch, on the face of Sron na Ciche above Glen Brittle, which was first climbed by Norman Collie (a scientist credited with the first X-ray photograph) and John Mackenzie. The first traverse of the Black Cuillin ridge fell to Shadbolt and Maclaren in 1911, taking nearly 17 hours. It has since been completed in a less than 25% of that time.

on the corrie headwall to reach Bealach nan Lice, just east of the summit. This is the normal route. To your right a grassy shoulder leads up onto the jagged and impressive northwest ridge.

Continuing on the normal route, the path to the base of the headwall is not very distinct but there are a couple of small cairns to look out for as you tend southeast, gently climbing over easy terrain. Cross a small gully and pick up an intermittent path that leads towards the steeper ground, where the path again becomes quite distinct. From here a short, steep climb brings you to the dramatic **Bealach nan Lice**, in the shadow of Am Basteir and Bhasteir Tooth. Turn right and follow a distinct trail around the base of a pinnacle and onto the final, rocky ridge leading to the summit of **Bruach na Frithe**. The peak is marked by a trig point and the view on a clear day is one of the best on Skye. To the west the main section of the Black Cuillin ridge cuts back on itself in a spectacular Z shape, ending in the prominent, thumb-like summit of Gars-bheinn. To the east the fang of rock rising above Am Basteir is Sgurr nan Gillean, and beyond it are the bright scree slopes of the Red Cuillin.

The easiest way back to Sligachan is to reverse the route of ascent. Alternatively you can continue past Am Basteir and drop into Coire a' Bhasteir for a more direct but more difficult descent back to Sligachan.

RED CUILLIN HORSESHOE

Duration	6–7 hours
Distance	7.5 miles (12km)
Difficulty	moderate–demanding
Start/Finish	Sligachan (p195)
Transport	bus

Summary A tour over the distinctive pink conical peaks, crossing rocky summits and steep, scree-strewn slopes, and giving expansive views of the entire island.

This circuit takes in the main Red Cuillin peaks, including the highest, Sgurr Mhairi (775m), part of the Glamaig massif. Although access is easy, the distance covered is not great and the summits themselves are quite modest in height, the gaps between the hills are far below the summits so, not surprisingly, the walk involves a total ascent of 1207m. The final climb is particularly demanding, and if you don't fancy climbing 300m of steep, loose scree then maybe this isn't the walk for you: perhaps consider an alternative return from Bealach na Sgairde. However, if you do make it to the top you will be rewarded (or confronted) with a 500m-long scree run on the descent, a quick and exhilarating way to end the day.

This route has become the scene of a race, in which the competitors finish the circuit in around 1½ hours. Mere mortals can count on taking a little longer. The meanings of the Gaelic names of the summits are typically descriptive and colourful. Beinn Dearg Mheadhonach and Beinn Dearg Mhór can be translated as 'middle red mountain' and 'big red mountain' respectively. Glamaig itself is of Norse origin and generally regarded as meaning 'gorge mountain', which is less evocative than another interpretation, 'greedy woman', on account of her voluptuous shape perhaps?

THE WALK

Cross the old stone bridge east of Sligachan Hotel and follow the path signed to Loch Coruisk. After approximately 200m, the gorge of the Allt Daraich comes up on the left. Leave the main path here, go through a gate and follow a path along the fenced southern rim of the ravine. The gorge soon dwindles in height and the path strikes out across open moor towards the shoulder of Sròn a' Bhealain. This section can be boggy but the path can be seen zigzagging encouragingly up drier slopes ahead beyond the fence.

The ascent of the shoulder is initially steep and passing feet have cut high steps into the muddy ground. The gradient eases as you climb higher, until you join the grassy, undulating terrain of the Druim na Ruaige ridge. Several cairns mark the crest of the ridge and there is an excellent perspective over the circuit of peaks ahead. The peak of Sgurr Mhairi, on the Glamaig massif to the north, looks ominously steep.

Leaving the ridge the path enters the stone and scree-covered terrain that dominates the high ground of the circuit. Zigzag up the loose rock to a cairn at the top. The official summit of **Beinn Dearg Mheadhonach**

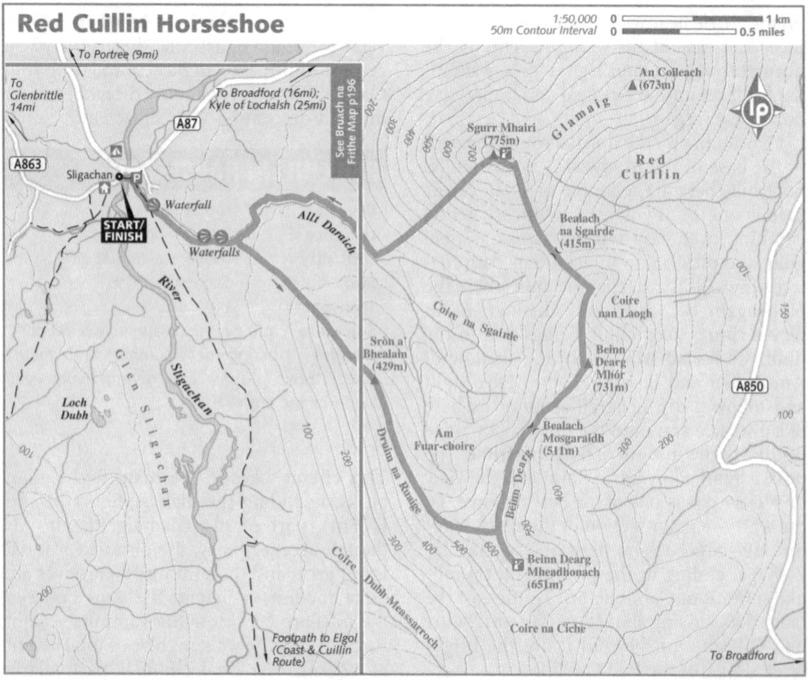

(651m) is actually a short detour to the southeast, but the views from both cairns are impressive. Flat-topped MacLeod's Tables and the broad Trotternish peninsula lie to the northwest and north, while the peaks of Glen Shiel and Torridon are clearly visible to the east and northeast on the mainland. The dark, barren peaks of the Black Cuillin dominate the scene to the southwest.

Return to the cairn that marked your arrival on the summit ridge and continue north, following a faint path over easy ground to the Bealach Mosgaraidh between Beinn Dearg Mheadhonach and Beinn Dearg Mhór. The path becomes more obvious as it climbs up the other side, over steeper, rocky ground, to reach the summit cairn on **Beinn Dearg Mhór** (731m). Finding the descent from here can be tricky and care is required in poor visibility. Follow the northern spur of the mountain for around 500m to a subsidiary rise marked by a cairn. From this cairn take a few steps backwards (south) and drop steeply down to the northwest. A rough path descends over several worn scree chutes at first, before joining a jumble of larger rocks and boulders towards the bottom of the slope.

The grassy saddle of **Bealach na Sgairde** offers a short break from the rock. The route then goes directly up the steep and crag-studded scree slope of Sgurr Mhairi, roughly following the line of a dry burn. The climb is sustained and the rock is often unstable, and it is a relief to reach the grassy summit plateau of **Sgurr Mhairi** (775m). Another excellent panorama presents itself from the large summit cairn, including a bird's-eye view of the Isle of Raasay.

Descend from Sgurr Mhairi in a southwesterly direction, sliding down long scree slopes to the grass below. The best way to descend scree chutes is to dig in your heels to maintain balance over the sliding rocks. Continue until you meet Allt Daraich then turn right to follow a faint path along its northern bank. The burn soon becomes a series of picturesque falls and pools. Cross the stream at one of many fords before you reach the ravine and continue down the opposite bank. You will rejoin the path that you started the day on, and from here it doesn't take long to retrace your steps back to Sligachan Hotel.

COAST & CUILLIN

Duration	2 days
Distance	14 miles (22.5km)
Difficulty	moderate
Start	Elgol (p200)
Finish	Sligachan (p195)
Transport	bus

Summary A spectacular coast and glen walk that takes you deep into the heart of the Black Cuillin to Loch Coruisk, via the notorious 'Bad Step'. There's also a superb alternative, out and back from Sligachan.

The combination of magnificent coast walking, from Elgol to the supremely beautiful Loch Coruisk, and dramatic Glen Sligachan make this one of the finest walks on Skye. Loch Coruisk is the jewel in the crown of the Black Cuillin. The jagged arc of peaks rising precipitously from the shore suggests a formidable fortress guarding its beauty. There are only two feasible routes into the loch that don't demand rock-climbing skills; this walk links the two. It can be completed in a single long day (allow seven to nine hours) but by taking two you can immerse yourself in the incomparable scenery. Camping in the wild at Loch Coruisk is an unforgettable experience; don't forget the guidelines for wild camping (p21). There is a bothy at Camasunary, but in a tent at Loch Coruisk you're much closer to the essential spirit of the place.

There's only one problem: about 500m short of Loch Coruisk there's one section of scrambling, along the Bad Step. This is a 6m-long, 60-degree slab with a narrow ledge for the feet and small handholds for support. It is exposed but lurks about 8m above deep water, so is not necessarily dangerous if you can swim well! A cool head is required, especially if you're carrying a bulky, heavy pack.

If prospect of the Bad Step is too daunting, there are two possible alternative ways of reaching Loch Coruisk.

The easier of the two is to go by boat to Loch Coruisk and then walk out. **Bella Jane Boat Trips** (☎ 0800 731 3089; www.bellajane.co.uk; £14) sail from Elgol across Loch Scavaig to the landing steps near Loch Coruisk, a trip of about 45 minutes. Here you can join the path and walk the 8 miles out to

Sligachan, following the Day 2 route. This option would fit easily into a single day and make for a very memorable trip.

Alternatively, walk in and out from Sligachan (see the Alternative Route on p202), but instead of descending to the loch shores, climb the modest hill of Sgurr na Stri (497m), overlooking Loch Coruisk to the southeast for a magnificent view of the Black Cuillin, the loch and various offshore islands.

NEAREST TOWNS

See Sligachan, p195.

Elgol

☎ 01471

This tiny village, dependant on fishing and visitors, sits close to the end of the Strathaird peninsula with an incredible view of the Cuillin across Loch Scavaig.

SLEEPING & EATING

Accommodation is in short supply here, but it's not far from Torrin (p203), where there are a couple more possibilities.

Rose Croft (☎ 866377; www.isleofskye.net/rosecroft; s/d £30/44) is a long-established and friendly B&B with a beautiful garden and lovely views. A light evening meal (£6) is available by arrangement.

Rowan Cottage (☎ 866287; www.rowancottage-skye.co.uk; 9 Glasnakille by Elgol; s/d £30/60, dinner £20-23) is a traditional cottage with pleasingly furnished rooms a couple of miles along a narrow, winding road east of Elgol.

Coruisk House (☎ 866330; www.seafood-skye.co.uk; s/d £38/76, mains £10-25; lunch & dinner;) is a restaurant northeast of Elgol village with rooms in what was originally a small thatched cottage to which travellers were first welcomed a century ago. These days, historic photos adorn the walls, the bedrooms are superbly decorated and the restaurant specialises in locally caught fish and seafood, though without neglecting vegetarians.

Cuillin View Gallery & Coffee Shop (snacks to £3; lunch), above the harbour, is licensed and offers sandwiches and home baking, and the chance to contemplate the work of local artists, as well as the eponymous view.

The **Post Office Shop** (9am-5pm Mon-Sat) has basic supplies and serves home baking and hot and cold drinks.

GETTING THERE & AWAY

Highland Country Buses (☎ 01463 710555; www.rapsons.co.uk) operates a bus service from the Broadford post office to the Elgol post office (£3, 40 minutes, two services Tuesday and Thursday). This is supplemented by the **Royal Mail postbus** (☎ 08457 740740; www.postbus.royalmail.com) service (one hour, two services Monday to Friday, one Saturday). Good connections are available at Broadford to Sligachan (p195) and Portree (p193).

The A881 to Elgol branches from the A850 Kyleakin–Portree road in the small town of Broadford. There's a car park at the bottom of the first steep descent to the harbour and more parking space opposite the nearby village hall.

THE WALK

Day 1: Elgol to Loch Coruisk

4–5 hours, 6 miles (9.5km)

The walk begins about 300m northeast of the Elgol post office along a lane leading north from the A881, and clearly signposted as a footpath to Camasunary and Sligachan. The road soon disappears, leaving a dirt track that ends at two houses. A footpath, signed to Loch Coruisk, continues directly ahead between the fences of the houses. It crosses through a gate and leads out onto open hillside. The views are immediately impressive: the small isles of Soay, Eigg, Rum and Canna lie to the south, while the Black Cuillin dominate the skyline to the northwest.

The well-trodden path basically contours across grass and heather slopes all the way to the beach at Camasunary, with ever-improving views. The drop-off to the west is steep in places as the lower slopes of Ben Cleat and Beinn Leacach are passed, and care is required over these sections. At Glen Scaladal a stile is crossed before descending to a pebbly cove. A steep climb from the back of the beach leads to the broken cliff top. Duck under the branches of a grove of stunted trees, and soon follow a track that skirts a drop by climbing slightly higher up the cliff. Easier ground then leads down to the bridge over the Abhainn nan Leac and a substantial junction of paths, about 3 miles from Elgol.

Of the two buildings at Camasunary, the larger house by the bridge is private. The smaller building, 500m west, is a bothy which is maintained by the **Mountain Bothies**

Association (www.mountainbothies.org.uk), providing free accommodation for hillwalkers. At the junction of paths, the 4WD track descending from the shoulder to the east leads to Kirkibost, 1.5 miles away. The path that forks right, between the bridge and house, leads directly up the glen to Sligachan, avoiding Loch Coruisk.

To continue to Loch Coruisk take the path leading west along the top of the beach, passing in front of the bothy. Ford the Abhainn Camas Fhionnairigh by following its banks upstream for 100m or so and then cross on stepping stones. The path on the other side soon climbs slightly to contour around the craggy lower slopes of Sgurr na Stri. The terrain is rougher than previously, and you cross several rock steps and angled slabs. As you round the headland another wonderful vista opens up – rocky islands nestle in the azure water at the mouth of the Scavaig River, backed by the looming Cuillin.

The slabs become more frequent as the path veers north and care must be taken not to lose the main trail as it splits in various places. Continue towards the white sand and turquoise water of Loch nan Leachd cove. The notorious Bad Step is the very last slab that needs to be negotiated before the beach. A cairn marks the stony path that descends to the difficulties. It could be a good idea to undo pack straps if you are worried, just in case of a slip into the water below. Duck under an overhang and scramble out onto the seaward rock face. Pull yourself up to balance on a ledge that skirts around the slab, using handholds for support. Shuffle along, taking care to drop diagonally down to the boulders at the beach rather than continuing up the slab at a convergence of fault lines.

Cross the boulders to the sand of Loch nan Leachd beach, and follow the path inland across the low saddle at the back of the cove. **Loch Coruisk** is suddenly revealed in all its glory and its banks make a fine rest spot. If you are spending the night here, flat ground for camping can be found just over the stepping stones that cross the Scavaig River.

Day 2: Loch Coruisk to Sligachan

3–4 hours, 8 miles (13km)

The path from Loch Coruisk to Sligachan leads around the southeastern shore of the

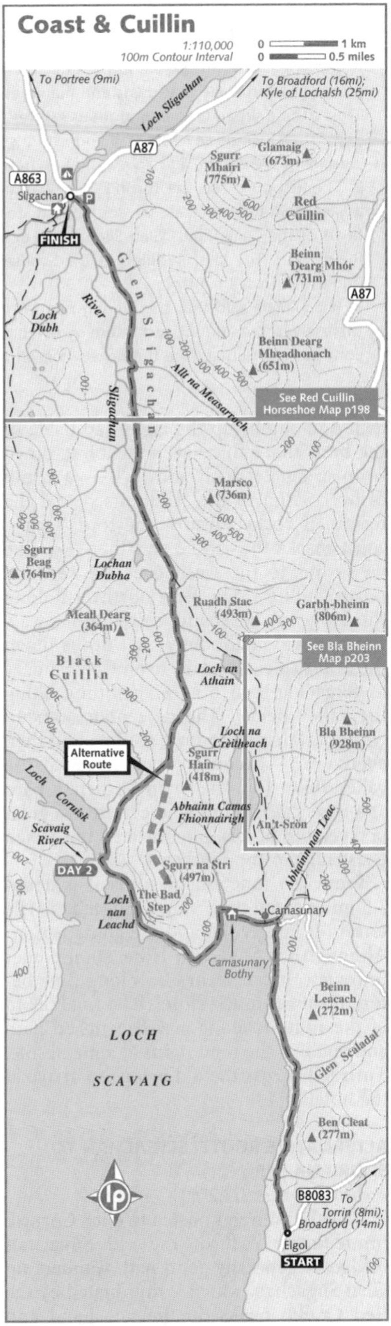

SKYE IN TRUST

A good deal of south Skye and the Cuillin is owned and managed by the John Muir Trust (p31), a conservation body that owns and manages several other areas on the Scottish mainland. The Trust's three separate but contiguous estates total around 30,000 acres of mountainous and rural Skye. They include several small and active crofting communities, which are directly involved in managing the estate, and a wealth of archaeological sites and plant and animal species.

The first purchase, the Torrin Estate, was made in 1991. Three years later, the much larger and adjacent Strathaird Estate was purchased, ensuring the preservation of land extending into the heart of the Cuillin, plus Glen Sligachan, Loch Coruisk and the peaks of Bla Bheinn, Marsco and Ruadh Stac. The later addition of the Sconser Estate brought more summits in the Red Cuillin under the Trust's control.

It could be said that the glaring gap in the Trust's Isle of Skye portfolio is the Black Cuillin themselves, the current and future ownership of which is the subject of a drawn-out and highly controversial debate (see the boxed text on p194).

loch and climbs up the right-hand side of the burn that can be seen tumbling down from a smaller loch above. It is a climb of over 300m to the saddle itself and the terrain is rocky towards the top. A large cairn marks the saddle and there are fine views out to the west, over the serrated north Cuillin ridge. Veer northwest along the ridge to a second cairn 20m away, where a wide and stony trail drops down the other side. The path from Camasunary to Sligachan can be seen winding along the valley below. The descent to join up with it is fairly steep for a section, and then evens out – becoming rather wet at the valley floor. Join the main Sligachan path at a large cairn, from where there is a great perspective of Bla Bheinn and the Clach Glas ridge to the southeast.

From the junction of paths it is about 3.5 miles along the valley to Sligachan. The terrain is largely flat and the going is easy. Although the Sligachan Hotel soon comes into view, it can seem like a long time before it moves much closer. The final 500m of the route is along a well-benched path and you exit the mountains at a metal stile. Turn left across the old bridge to arrive at the hotel.

ALTERNATIVE ROUTE: SLIGACHAN TO SGURR NA STRI

7½ hours, 15 miles (24.2km)

Follow the path signposted to Loch Coruisk immediately east of the old Sligachan bridge. A generally good path wanders up Glen Sligachan, which is dominated by the Red Cuillin peaks on the one hand and Sgurr nan Gillean and its Black Cuillin satellites on the other. The path becomes rockier and wetter as it gradually rises towards the watershed, past the imposing crags on Marsco's precipitous flanks. Bla Bheinn comes into view and soon you cross the watershed (1¾ hours from the start) and start to descend. Shortly, at a fork marked by a large, sprawling cairn, bear right and go down to cross Allt nam Fraoch on stepping stones. The rough path climbs steadily, through a steep, eroded stretch, to easier going, then on to the ridge crest, from where a sliver of Loch Coruisk can be seen (one hour from the watershed).

Swing left (south); a line of cairns marks the steep descent to the loch's shores. However, continue generally south across the steep, grassy slope, which is strewn with boulders, across three gullies, trending generally downhill. At the top of a short ascent from the third gully (about 30 minutes from the ridge crest), with more of Loch Coruisk visible, leave the path. Head south then southeast, along intermittent paths, up shallow, damp gullies and across huge, rough, dark slabs. Edge west towards the precipitous drop to the loch's outlet and continue up to a large cairn on the summit of **Sgurr na Stri** (1¼ hours from the ridge crest). The superb view here takes in Elgol, Camasunary, three of the four Small Isles, the Old Man of Storr and the Trotternish ridge, and the incomparable Loch Coruisk.

Retrace your steps to Sligachan (3½ hours from the summit).

BLA BHEINN

Duration	5½–5¾ hours
Distance	5.2 miles (8.4km)
Difficulty	moderate–demanding
Start/Finish	Allt na Dunaiche car park
Nearest Towns	Torrin (right), Elgol (p200)
Transport	bus

Summary Plenty of steep uphill work past a hidden chasm and two secluded lochans to exceptional views from the summit of a Black Cuillin outlier.

Standing slightly aloof from the central Black Cuillin ridge, and rising impressively from the northwestern shores of Loch Slapin, Bla Bheinn (928m/3045ft), or Blaven as it is often Anglicised, looks pretty daunting. With sheets of steep scree, two massive buttresses of black, fissured gabbro split by a deep gully, and looking precipitous from every angle, it seems to be strictly for rock climbers. However, a well-made path leading generally west from the Elgol road, and built by the John Muir Trust – the peak stands on the Trust's Strathaird Estate (see the boxed text, opposite) – takes you up into hidden Coire Uaigneich. From here, if you don't mind skittering about on steep scree slopes, the ascent is fairly straightforward, at least to the southern summit (924m). The main top, 4m higher, is only a short distance away, but reached on an exposed scramble.

This is definitely not a place to be in poor weather, and a compass is virtually useless (see the boxed text on p195). The only reliable method of route-finding is your own observation, so make sure to check the weather forecast before setting out.

NEAREST TOWNS

See Elgol, p200.

Torrin

☎ 01471

This small settlement at the head of Loch Slapin has retreated from the edge of extinction since the John Muir Trust purchased the land it occupies. It has only a couple of B&Bs, with the nearest hostel being in Broadford, 7 miles to the east, where you'll also find shops, restaurants and an ATM.

Fearnoch (☎ 822717; www.fearnoch-skye.com; ½ of 16 Torrin; s/d £40/70) is a modern cottage with superb views. Evening meals are available by arrangement.

Slapin View (☎ 822672; d £19) is a renovated croft (farm) house. The owner will cook an evening meal if requested when booking.

Blue Shed Coffee Shop (☎ 822000; snacks £3; 🕑 10am-5pm) is a well-dressed shed beside the main road at the western end of the village. Art prints adorn the walls and it's a popular drop-in place with the locals.

Torrin is on the A881, 7 miles west of Broadford; the Broadford–Elgol bus stops here (£2, 10 minutes, two services Tuesday and Thursday).

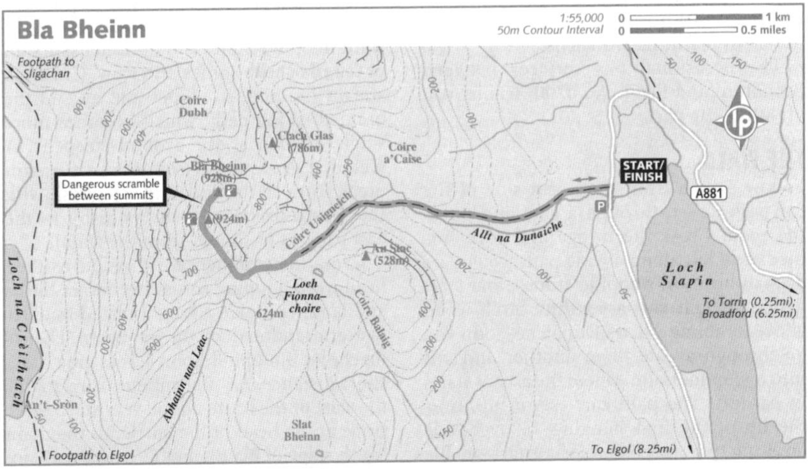

CLASSIC WALK – SGURR DEARG & COIRE LAGAN

This challenging, exhilarating ascent of Sgurr Dearg (978m/3208ft) on the main Black Cuillin ridge involves some scrambling and a descent to one of the most impressive corries in Scotland. It provides a taster of Cuillin 'walking' and is less technical than other routes on the main ridge. It takes in the summit of Sgurr Dearg, scuttles around the base of the Inaccessible Pinnacle then descends an exhilarating scree chute into Coire Lagan. Allow 5½ to 6½ hours for the 5-mile (8km) demanding walk, which has 990m of ascent.

The walk begins in Glenbrittle, where accommodation is available at either **Glenbrittle SYHA Hostel** (☎ 01478 640278; www.syha.org.uk; dm £13) or **Glenbrittle Campsite** (☎ 01478 521206; unpowered sites for 2 £9); the small shop stocks basic supplies, stove fuel, maps and books.

Highland Country Buses (☎ 01463 710555; www.rapsons.co.uk) and M Macdonald operate a bus service from Portree to Glenbrittle via Sligachan (55 minutes, two return services daily) between 15 May and 30 September. By car, turn off the A863 5 miles west of Sligachan along B8009; 2 miles along, turn off for Glenbrittle, which is 7 miles ahead.

Begin the walk across the road from Glen Brittle Hut (private), just north of the village. Follow a signposted path and then cross a footbridge over Allt Coire na Banachdich. A clear path climbs gently over the bog to a lookout above Eas Mor waterfall. Continue heading southeast up the main path, passing under the western spur of Sgurr Dearg. At any stage here you need to leave the path and strike out towards the spur, across rough and sometimes wet ground. The gradient soon steepens and the terrain becomes rockier as you gain the spur. Paths zigzag around outcrops as far as a short and steep section. Either bypass this on the left (north) or complete the easy scramble up a prominent gully to emerge on a flat and partially grassy shoulder (around one hour from the start).

The ascent continues steadily along a broad ridge to another short, steep section. A little easy scrambling puts you on top and within sight of the summit of Sgurr Dearg. Between you and the summit, however, is a knife-edge ridge, the crux of this route. The scrambling across it is straightforward but the exposure is considerable. There's an easier alternative just to the right (south) side of the ridge crest. Once past this, a short climb leads to the sharp summit of **Sgurr Dearg** (two hours from the partially grassy shoulder).

Even sharper than the summit of Sgurr Dearg is the adjacent Inaccessible Pinnacle (986m), a great fin of rock usually called the 'In Pin', which can only be reached by a rock climb. Further

GETTING TO/FROM THE WALK

The car park is on the western side of the A881, 2 miles from Torrin, just past the bridge over Allt na Dunaiche.

The occasional bus services between Broadford and Elgol (see p200) will let you off at the car park.

THE WALK

Follow a path from the north side of the car park down, through a gate and on to the road. Cross the bridge and turn immediately left along a wide path. Negotiate a small burn on stepping stones, and start gaining height past a youthful birch wood above tumbling Allt na Dunaiche. Soon you go through a gate, then another and out into open moorland, where the ascent starts in earnest. The path carries you up, over the lip of the first hanging valley beside an attractive waterfall, closing fast on Bla Bheinn's huge black bluffs, leaning woozily to the north. The path leads on, up beside the burn, which you cross on slightly awkward stepping stones and the inner sanctum of **Coire Uaigneich** comes into view. Cross the stream draining its slopes and ascend the braided, stony path, which becomes more single-minded as the ground steepens. A secluded grassy bowl comes as a pleasant break from all the rock and steepness, with **Loch Fionna-choire** on a shelf nearby to the east (one to 1¼ hours from the start).

Cross the confluence of two burns then head west, hopping across two larger burns and landing beside a huge isolated boulder (a useful landmark on the way back). There's no choice but uphill, soon across grass for a short distance. An amorphous cairn marks the start of the route up the very steep scree slope at the head of the corrie, to the main south ridge of Bla Bheinn (30 minutes from afield the stunning view takes in the northern Cuillin ridge, and Sgurr Alasdair and Sgurr Mhic Choinnich across Coire Lagan to the south.

Take great care to find the correct route down into Coire Lagan. Descend a prominent ramp running down to the right (south) of the In Pin, dropping down from the main ridge beneath the cliffs of An Stac. Be careful on the slabs, where loose gravel and stone act like ball bearings underfoot. Go round a corner to the left, pass beneath the cliffs, and contour for a short distance to the top of An Stac Scree plunging down from Bealach Coire Lagan. You should be able to see a clean run down to Loch Coire Lagan, but if the cloud is down and you can't see the bottom, go cautiously. **Coire Lagan** is very impressive, its cliffs falling more than 300m directly from the summit of Sgurr Alasdair. A well-defined path descends steeply from the rim of Coire Lagan. After a few hundred metres turn right at a fork marked by a small cairn and follow the smaller path (rough and boggy in places) back to the start (one to 1½ hours from Coire Lagan).

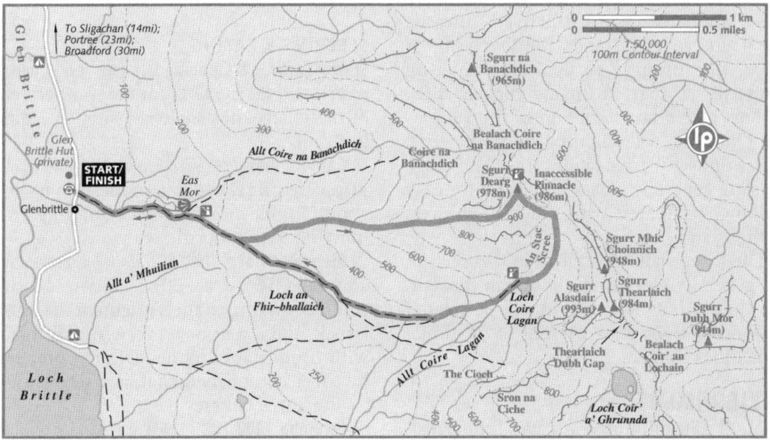

near Loch Fionna-choire), where there's a small pond and even some grass.

The path onwards is faint at first, following the crest briefly then swinging to the western flank and becoming clearer, snaking through lines of small cliffs, mostly on scree. Pause to contemplate the fine view straight down to the beach and lonely white cottage at Camasunary. It's a surprisingly straightforward, though steep, route on scree and broken rock but take care to keep to the main, fairly well-worn line to avoid any chance of finding yourself in an awkward situation. After a while the ridge broadens and the route angles up across the slope to a cairn on the edge of a small plateau, from where it's a short distance to another cairn on the south summit (one hour after reaching the south ridge). The views from here extend to Knoydart and even as far as Ben Nevis on a good day.

Not far to the northeast, a cairn and trig point mark the slightly higher main summit of Bla Bheinn, but reaching it is not straightforward. Continue along the spine of the ridge, descend steeply into a notch, then go up to the right across exposed, sloping ledges and on to the main summit of **Bla Bheinn** (928m), 15 minutes from the south summit. The views north across Garbh-bheinn and the Red Cuillin are stunning.

Retrace your steps, over the south summit then down, aiming for the prominent lochan on the bealach. Take great care to steer well clear of a deep, precipitous gully on your left, down to the pond. Once you've crossed the burn, the Torridon and Knoydart peaks come into view, and much further down a small, narrow canyon on Allt na Dunaiche is right beside the path, much more obviously than on the way up. Continue down to the car park.

ISLE OF SKYE

TROTTERNISH

The Trotternish – a 25km-long sinuous, precipitous escarpment snaking across the middle of the peninsula – dominates the northern end of Skye beyond Portree. It rises abruptly from the narrow coastal fringe in the east while in the west the indented slopes are longer and less steep. The peaks are not as high or dramatic as the Cuillin, but an unusual sequence of geological happenings has created the escarpments, pinnacles and landslides that make the Trotternish so distinctive. Towards the southern end stands the Old Man of Storr, the instantly recognisable tapering pinnacle set apart from the rugged cliffs. Almost at the northern end of the ridge is the Quiraing, a fascinating maze of weird and wonderful rock sculptures. The ridge tops are generally grassy and make for easy walking, compared with much of the rest of the island.

The three walks described in this section are generally less demanding than those in the Cuillin but they should still be treated with respect and may present navigational difficulties in mist.

ENVIRONMENT

Around 150 million years ago Trotternish was a coastal lagoon colonised by sea reptiles and dinosaurs – footprints have been found on the east of the peninsula and fossils can be seen in abundance along the shore. Then the whole peninsula was covered with lava, up to 1300m deep, from huge volcanic eruptions further south on the island. The massive weight of basalt convulsed the softer, more pliable sedimentary rocks, causing them to crack and slip. The Trotternish ridge and its chaotic crags are the result of this huge landslide, and the geological upheaval continues to this day. It is under such conditions that pinnacles of rock have sheered off from the main cliff face and been squeezed and eroded into positions that seem to defy natural laws. The 2300m-long landslide that runs from the scarp on Meall na Suiramach, the peak above the Quiraing, down to Staffin Bay is the largest single slip in the British Isles. It is generally stable, though the road at Flodigarry still shifts occasionally.

PLANNING

Maps

The OS Explorer 1:25,000 map No 408 *Trotternish & The Storr* covers all walks on the Trotternish peninsula.

ACCESS TOWNS

Staffin

☎ 01470

The white-painted houses of the several hamlets that belong to Staffin are spread out on either side of the main road just inland from Staffin Bay. The nearest bank or ATM is in Portree.

SLEEPING & EATING

Staffin Caravan & Camping Site (☎ 562213; unpowered/powered sites for 2 £7/13), at the southern end of the village, has sheltered sites in a quiet location.

Gairloch View (☎ 562718; www.gairlochview.co.uk; 3 Digg, Staffin; s/d £24/48) is a modern bungalow about 1 mile north of the Quiraing road junction with fantastic sea views.

Glenview Hotel (☎ 562248; www.glenviewskye.co.uk; s/d £45/90, dinner £25) is about 4 miles south of Staffin, in the settlement of Culnaknock, and is a homely, very friendly place, with comfortable rooms. Dinner, prepared by the accomplished chef, is a set menu of two or three courses.

Columba 1400 (☎ 611400; mains to £5; lunch & dinner Mon-Sat;) is a large, comparatively new but sympathetically designed community centre in which you'll find an excellent café with superb views, serving great-value snacks and light meals.

Staffin Bay Stores (Mon-Sat) and the smaller **Village Shop** (Stenscholl; Mon-Sat), about 1.5 miles further north, stock basic supplies.

Hidden Treasures and the adjacent **Pieces of Ate** (☎ 562787; lunch mains £4, dinner £8; lunch Easter-Sep, dinner Mon-Sat Jul-Aug, Fri & Sat Sep-Jun), at the junction of the A855 and the Quiraing road, are definitely worth a stop. The former is a licensed deli, while the latter is a takeaway sandwich bar that also does takeaway evening meals.

GETTING THERE & AWAY

Highland Country Buses (☎ 01463 710555; www.rapsons.co.uk) operates service 57 between Portree and Uig (on the west coast) via Staffin (£3, 33 minutes) and Flodigarry (£4, 45 minutes). There are eight services Monday to Saturday. The Flodigarry Taxi Bus, operated by **Uig Taxis** (☎ 01470 542342), connects with Scottish Citylink's evening arrivals from Inverness and Glasgow – see p193 for details.

Flodigarry

☎ 01470

A tranquil hamlet strung along the coast in the far northeastern corner of the peninsula, Flodigarry's claim to fame is as the birthplace of Flora MacDonald, who lived here between 1751 and 1759. She helped Bonnie Prince Charlie (the Young Pretender) to escape from the mainland to Skye after his defeat at the Battle of Culloden in 1746. Her cottage is now part of the hotel. The nearest bank and ATM is in Portree. For transport details see opposite.

SLEEPING & EATING

Dun Flodigarry Hostel (☎ 552212; hostel.flodigarry@btopenworld.com; unpowered sites for 2 £5, dm/tw £11/26; 💻) is a large building in a beautiful position overlooking Staffin Bay. The friendly staff can help with advice about walking in the Quiraing and around the coast.

Flodigarry Country House Hotel (☎ 552203; www.flodigarry.co.uk; s/d £55/80, with dinner £85/106), an award-winning small hotel with large, view-oriented rooms and superb Scottish-style cuisine, is a great place for a special celebration.

THE TROTTERNISH TRAVERSE

Duration	7–8 hours
Distance	14 miles (22.5km)
Difficulty	demanding
Start	Storr Woodlands car park
Finish	Quiraing road car park
Nearest Towns	Staffin (opposite), Flodigarry (above)
Transport	bus

Summary A superb crossing of the long, undulating central ridge of the Trotternish, with lots of ups and downs, rewarded by plenty of first-class views.

The crumbling black cliffs and the extraordinary pinnacles and bluffs of the Storr (from the Norse *staur*, meaning 'stake') are one of the most popular places on the island. The tapering, nearly pointed Old Man of Storr, all 50m of him, is a landmark for miles around. Unnervingly, he seems to be leaning rather drunkenly seawards and will probably topple completely one day as the friable rock at his base gradually erodes away. The Storr (719m/2358ft) is the highest point on the Trotternish peninsula, and from here this classic ridge walk crosses the greater, and best, part of the peninsula. From the Storr you gradually lose height as you progress north, crossing several summits. At the end, you'll have polished off about 1450m of ascent. Paths, such as there are, have been made by the ubiquitous sheep, and walkers.

WARNING

Massive rock falls, once a rarity, have become more frequent in the area around the Old Man of Storr. Warnings signs have been posted advising visitors not to go beyond the edge of the forest. The route described here does not seem to go perilously close to the danger zone. Nevertheless, take the greatest care in the area, especially after heavy rain.

Alternatives If time is short, or the transport arrangements for the full walk are too complicated, there's no shame in just walking up to the Storr and back. Allow 4½ to five hours for the 5.5-mile (9km) walk.

Two paths leading generally west from the ridge provide alternative routes off the ridge to the village of Uig on the west coast. You can descend from Bealach a' Mhòramhain via Glen Uig or from Bealach Uige via Glen Conon. Either gives a similar distance to the main walk but less ascent, and the advantage of finishing on a bus route (see opposite).

GETTING TO/FROM THE WALK

The walk starts from the signposted Storr Woodlands car park, beside the A855, 6.5 miles north of Portree. Highland Country Buses service 57 (see opposite) will stop here on request; the car park is about 15 minutes from Portree.

The route ends at a parking area on the crest of the steep, narrow Quiraing road, 1.1 miles west of its junction with the A855 at Brogaig, which is about 1 mile northwest of Staffin. Highland Country Buses service 57 also passes through Brogaig.

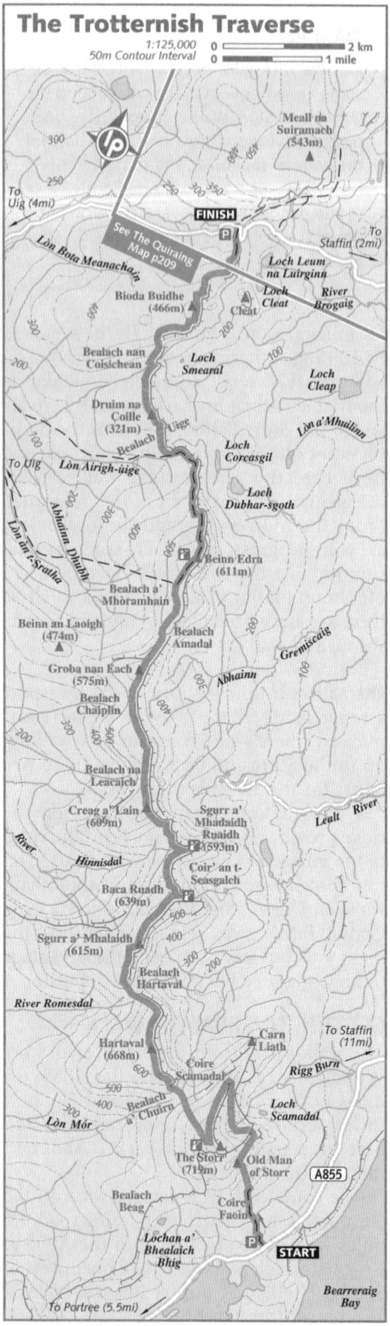

THE WALK

From the car park follow the wide, well-constructed path up through the conifer plantation, steadily gaining height. At the forest edge the Old Man comes into view, standing aloof from the main ramparts beyond. Go through a gate (15 minutes from the start) and continue up across open grassland to a path junction. Turn right (north) here (the clearer path to the left goes up almost to the foot of the Old Man). Continue up the grassy slopes to the right of the Old Man, gradually gaining the classic perspective of the pinnacle from a position slightly above and to the north of him. Follow the path, crossing a fence on a rocky spur, and continue around to the west where a short, steep climb leads to the grassy bowl beneath the northern cliffs of the Storr. The path becomes fainter as it skirts the bowl and climbs onto the broad skyline ridge, where the views of Trotternish really begin to open out. From here a 20-minute climb south should see you on the summit of the **Storr** (719m).

The panoramic views embrace most of Skye. The long line of cliffs of the Trotternish ridge stretches north to the Quiraing, and the jagged profile of the Cuillin is unmistakeable to the south. To the east, across the waters of the Minch, the mainland mountain ranges of Torridon, Applecross, Glen Shiel and Knoydart are spread out across the horizon. More immediately, there is a dizzying view across the cliff edge to the Old Man of Storr and the pinnacles of Coire Faoin 300m below.

From the cairn, descend northwest down the steep slope to Bealach a' Chuirn. Then it's up the broad grassy back of **Hartaval** (668m), with rather craggy ground higher up on the rock-strewn summit.

Descend close to the cliff edge to Bealach Hartaval. A short, steep climb leads back up onto the ridge. Go up the right side of a sheep pen and scramble up a short gully to the top. The terrain is less bumpy now, even though you cross Sgurr a' Mhalaidh and Baca Ruadh. **Sgurr a' Mhadaidh Ruaidh**, an impressive tongue of cliff, juts out from the ridge to the east; it is possible to walk to its very end for views back along the main cliffs.

The ridge now veers to the west and a descent, a climb and then another descent lands you in Bealach na Leacaich, where there's an old stone wall and a wire fence. Cross the fence by a stile about 100m to the west and continue over three more tops and down to **Bealach a' Mhòramhain** (the start of one of the two alternative routes to Uig) at the foot of the ascent to **Beinn Edra** (611m).

The next 2.5 miles or so, north from Beinn Edra, are tougher going, over heathery, boggy ground. Keep close to the cliff edge for the easiest passage. It's a long descent from Beinn Edra to **Bealach Uige** (and the second possible route west down to Uig). Less than 1 mile further on, you have to find a way through thick tussock grass on the seriously steep pull up to the summit plateau of **Bioda Buidhe** (466m), but console yourself with the thought that this is the last climb of the day. The Quiraing road soon comes into view over the other side, beyond which the pinnacles of the Quiraing can be clearly seen. Veer away from the cliff edge to avoid a crag on the descent then return to the ridge to join a clear path that will guide you down to the car park beside the road.

THE QUIRAING

Duration	2½–2¾ hours
Distance	3.5 miles (5.6km)
Difficulty	moderate
Start/Finish	Quiraing road car park
Nearest Towns	Staffin (p206), Flodigarry (p207)
Transport	private

Summary Explore the weird and wonderful pinnacles, crags and bluffs at the northern end of the Trotternish ridge.

The pinnacles, cliffs and landslides of the Quiraing (pronounced 'kweer-yng' and meaning 'pillared enclosure') are a compact and easily explored example of the features that make the Trotternish peninsula unique. Generally easy paths give access to the summit of Meall na Suiramach (543m/1781ft) with fine views of islands, the mainland and to the base of the towering escarpment.

GETTING TO/FROM THE WALK

The walk starts at a car park on the Quiraing road, 1.8 miles west of its junction with the A855 at Brogaig, which is about 1 mile northwest of Staffin.

THE WALK

Set out along the well-worn path, signposted to Flodigarry. Follow it for a few hundred metres to the first burn crossing then strike up north and northeast across country to a grassed stone wall. Follow this northeast for a few hundred metres until it disappears then zigzag up the steep slope to find a clear path leading northeast across the hillside. Wet in places, it leads into a wide, shallow and grassy glen; go through a gate in the fence there (35 minutes from the start). Continue northeast up the slope. About 10 minutes further on, the path swings north to parallel the cliff edge. From the nearby rim there's a fantastic view down into the heart of the Quiraing and a row of flat-topped rock outcrops between the cliff and a row of massive bluffs. Continue past a cairn (the summit of Meall na Suiramach is further west) with fine views of the many offshore islets and the Western Isles. Keeping close to the edge, start to descend (15 minutes from the gate) and you'll soon reach a large cairn. A clear path descends north near the

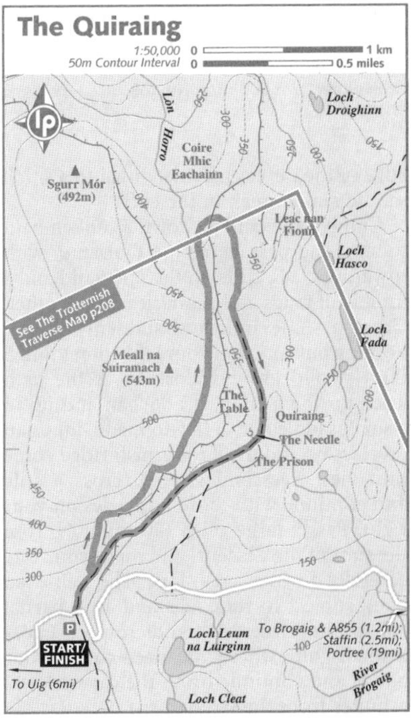

SHORT WALKS

Waternish peninsula

Follow a clear track across the northern end of the remote Waternish peninsula, past two Iron Age brochs to Unish house, the oldest residential building still standing on Skye. Allow 2¾ hours for this 5.6-mile (9km) easy walk. It starts and finishes at Trumpan church car park; turn off the A850 Portree–Dunvegan road 19 miles from Portree along the B886. Turn right at a T-junction and continue along a minor road to the car park. Take OS Explorer 1:25,000 map No 408.

From the car park, follow the road northeast for 600m to a right-angle bend. Turn left (northwest) along the vehicle track, going through a gate. The track can be muddy in places after wet weather. About 1.2 miles along, a commemorative cairn on the left is a good vantage point for a view of Dun Borrafiach on the hillside to the northeast. It looks like an untidy heap of stones but is worth the diversion; it's an Iron Age broch, built about 1500 years ago. Approximately 800m further on you'll find another broch, perched on a small hilltop. An hour from the start, Unish house comes into view. Go through two gateways and down to the building. Built during the 17th century, it was occupied for around 200 years. The long crack in the eastern wall is locally reputed to have been caused by a lightning strike. The remains of several smaller stone buildings nearby suggest that a substantial community once lived here. Retrace your steps to the start.

Stein is the only settlement that really resembles a village found on the Waternish peninsula. At the T-junction (mentioned in the first paragraph) turn left – about 400m on is the **Stein Inn** (☎ 01470 592362; www.steininn.co.uk; s/d £35/54, mains £9-14; lunch & dinner), the oldest inn on Skye and highly recommended. It has real ales on tap and does hearty bar meals, specialising in locally caught fish.

Coral Beaches

Explore one of Skye's gems – beaches of white, crunchy, crushed-shell sand with beautiful coastal views. Allow two hours for this 5-mile (8km) easy walk. It starts and finishes at the Coral Beaches car park – from Portree follow the A850 to Dunvegan on the west coast. Continue on to Dunvegan Castle then continue on a single-track road to the hamlet of Claigan and the car park. Take OS Explorer 1:25,000 map No 408.

edge of the outer cliff line, down to a small saddle and a break in the cliffs.

Climb a stile and go down a sunken path to start the passage of the Quiraing, with towering black cliffs on the one hand and a jumble of crags and pinnacles on the other. Cross a stone wall and suddenly there's nothing but space on your left! Soon though there's solid ground close by as the path leads up the glen, past a lochan and up to a small saddle. Here, flat-topped Dun Caan on Raasay, and the Trotternish ridge come into view. Descend steeply; cross a stile and continue with more pinnacles on your right. Pass a large cairn (30 minutes from the start of the descent) and make your way carefully down a scree slope. The well-used path, subject to rock falls and even partial collapse in places, demands respect. Cross a small gully where you need to use your hands and continue on to the car park (40 minutes from the large cairn).

MORE WALKS

MACLEOD'S TABLES

On the Duirinish peninsula in westernmost Skye is a large and rugged expanse of wild and windswept moorland dominated by the unusual, flat-topped summits of Healabhal Mhor (MacLeod's Table North) and Healabhal Bheag (MacLeod's Table South). These twin tops are commonly referred to as MacLeod's Tables. Legend has it that the chief of the MacLeod clan once hosted a banquet on the summit of Healabhal Bheag in order to prove the superiority of his dining hall. Both tops can be visited on a 7-mile (11km) circuit starting and finishing from a small stream about 1.2km north of the hamlet of Orbost, on a minor road branching from the B884 Glendale road, which in turn branches from the A863 Dunvegan–Sligachan road, 1.3 miles southeast

Follow a vehicle track down to the shore and the first beach, with its scraps of coral among the black shingle. Here the track turns inland; continue on grass beside the shore. Soon cross a low cliff, descend to the shore and the second beach, with a grassy foreshore. Soon you reach the third and finest of the beaches, a gentle white crescent overlooked by a low rocky mesa, characteristic of this area. The Western Isles fill the horizon, while Dunvegan Head rises sharply to the northwest. To explore further, walk across grass from the end of the beach to the point (Groban na Sgeir), from where the Waternish peninsula comes into view. Go round a stone wall at the seaward end, step over a fence and follow paths across the steepish slope and down to tranquil Lovaig Bay. Retrace your steps to the start.

Lorgill & the Hoe

This walk affords magnificent views of the highest sea cliffs on Skye, and passes the remains of a village deserted in the 1830s. Allow two hours for the moderate 4-mile (6.4km) walk. It starts and finishes at Ramasaig farm; turn off the A863 Dunvegan–Sligachan road 1.3 miles southeast of Dunvegan along single-track B884. Eight miles along (and beyond Glendale village), turn left along a road signposted to Ramasaig. There's limited parking at the end of the road near the farmhouse. Glendale has two shops and the An Strupag licensed café. Use OS Explorer 1:25,000 map No 408.

Walk down the farm track (muddy for about 250m), past farm buildings and an old stone byre on the left, and through a gate. The track climbs to the divide; descend to a gate with new views of the wide Lorgill River glen. You can spot the remains of at least 20 stone buildings and enclosures below. Leave the track and head south on intermittent sheep paths. Gain height south and southwest to overlook a green shelf below. An hour out, an isolated rocky knoll is a useful landmark and lookout. The wide views include the Cuillin, Western Isles, Macleod's Tables and Macleod's Maidens – delicate rock pinnacles offshore from Idrigill Point to the southeast. Keep as close as safely possible to the cliff edge on cropped grass. From the crest the dramatic vista of Waterstein Head (296m) and Neist Point is revealed. Descend into a wide glen, crossing a burn about 50m above the shore. Go through a gate then aim just right (east) of the farmhouse, up across the field on a track of sorts. Cross another burn near a cluster of ruined stone buildings, skirt a sheep pen and go through a small gate to the farm track and back to the start.

of Dunvegan. Parking here is very limited. The walk should take around 5½ hours to complete and involves 800m of ascent over some steep, rough ground. Use OS Explorer 1:25,000 map No 407.

ISLE OF RAASAY

Raasay is the quiet island sandwiched between Skye and the mainland. The bulk of the island is undulating upland and forest, and a circuit taking in the best features can be made in around seven hours from the pier where the ferry docks near Inverarish. The circuit is 11 miles (18km) and involves 570m of ascent to the top of Dún Caan (443m), from where there are excellent views of the Cuillin, Trotternish and the mainland ranges. There are also several options for shorter walks. There is a hostel, a camp site, a hotel and a small shop on the island. The **Caledonian MacBrayne** (www.calmac.co.uk) car ferry (passenger/car £3/11, 15 minutes, at least nine services Monday to Saturday, two Sunday) sails from Sconser, a few miles northeast of Sligachan. Consult OS Landranger 1:50,000 map No 24.

Wester Ross

Wester Ross is heaven for hillwalkers: a remote and starkly beautiful part of the Highlands with lonely glens and lochs, an intricate coastline of rocky headlands and white-sand beaches, and some of the finest mountains in Scotland. If you are lucky with the weather, the clear air will provide rich colours and great views from the ridges and summits. In poor conditions the remoteness of the area makes walking a much more serious proposition. Whatever the weather, the walking can be difficult, so this is no place to begin learning mountain techniques. But if you are fit and well equipped, Wester Ross will be immensely rewarding – and addictive.

The walks described here offer a tantalising taste of the area's delights and challenges. An Teallach's pinnacle-encrusted ridge is one of Scotland's finest ridge walks, spiced with some scrambling. Proving that there's much more to walking in Scotland than merely jumping out of the car (or bus) and charging up the nearest mountain, Beinn Dearg Mhór, in the heart of the Great Wilderness, makes an ideal weekend outing. This Great Wilderness – great by Scottish standards at least – is big enough to guarantee peace, even solitude, during a superb two-day traverse through glens cradling beautiful lochs. Slioch, a magnificent peak overlooking Loch Maree, offers a comparatively straightforward, immensely scenic ascent. In the renowned Torridon area, Beinn Alligin provides an exciting introduction to its considerable challenges, epitomised in the awesome traverse of Liathach, a match for An Teallach in every way. And to recover from this expenditure of adrenaline, we recommend the gentle walk to one of Scotland's finest corries, Coire Mhic Fhearchair.

HIGHLIGHTS

- Revelling in the scrambling along the lofty ridges of **An Teallach** (p214) and **Liathach (p229)**
- Losing track of time in the remote and spectacular **Great Wilderness** (p218)
- Looking for hobbits in the Caledonian woodland of the **Beinn Eighe National Nature Reserve** (p225)
- Being knocked sideways by the views of Scotland's west coast from atop the **Horns of Alligin** (p228)

- www.visithighlands.com

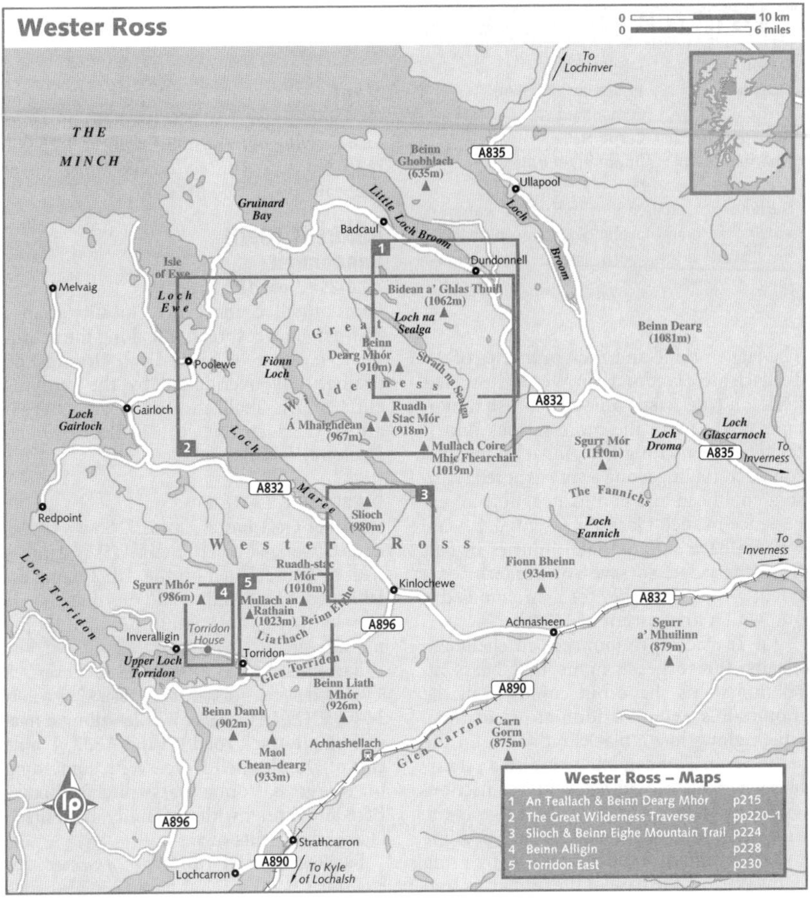

INFORMATION

Maps & Books

OS Travel – Road 1:250,000 map No 3 *Western Scotland* provides an excellent topographic overview of the region.

The Scottish Mountaineering Club's Hillwalkers' Guide *North-West Highlands* by Dave Broadhead, Alec Keith and Ted Maden is exhaustive (but not exhausting!) and the best source of comprehensive background information. For more specialised enlightenment about the landscape you can't do better than *Northwest Highlands, A Landscape Fashioned by Geology*, published by Scottish Natural Heritage (SNH) and the British Geological Survey. It's well illustrated and anything but dry and academic. Straightforward walking guides include *Skye & the North West Highlands* by John Brooks and Neil Wilson, which describes a range of low-level and easy routes in the area.

Information Sources

VisitScotland (☎ 0845 225 5121; www.visithighlands.com) is the main resource for accommodation information and reservations in the area.

Traveline Scotland (☎ 0870 608 2608; www.travelinescotland.com) provides full timetable details. Alternatively, the **Highland Council** (☎ 01463 702660; public.transport@highland.gov.uk) *Wester Ross & Lochalsh* public transport timetable is a handy reference.

AN TEALLACH

Duration	7½–8½ hours
Distance	11.5 miles (18.5km)
Difficulty	demanding
Start/Finish	Corrie Hallie
Nearest Town	Dundonnell (right)
Transport	bus

Summary A challenging mountain walk involving a scramble along an airy, pinnacle-encrusted ridge, with spectacular, wide-ranging views.

The jagged ridge and rock pinnacles of An Teallach are a landmark in Wester Ross. The peak is a true classic among Scottish mountains, and one of the more serious undertakings. Negotiating the pinnacles involves some scrambling along a very exposed ridge, so a cool head and confidence, born of experience in such places, is essential. Several walkers have suffered fatal injuries in falls from the ridge, so save An Teallach for a fine, dry day. It makes for a strenuous day out, with a total ascent of 1370m.

An Teallach (pronounced 'an chelluck') means 'the forge', a name that bears no relation to its shape but comes from the mountain's red Torridonian sandstone, which glows like a blacksmith's fire in the setting sun. This sandstone is also a scrambler's delight, providing plenty of friction. The most difficult part of the ridge is the notorious 10m-high 'bad step'. It's possible to avoid almost all the scrambling by using paths skirting the base of the pinnacles, and you can choose if and when to venture onto the rocky ridge. Even by taking the most cautious paths, it's still impossible to complete the walk without crossing some steep and exposed ground.

The traverse is described in a clockwise direction, which means scrambling up, rather than down, the most difficult parts of the ridge. Paths on the high ground are well worn, making navigation in mist relatively straightforward. A short rope may be handy if you're familiar with the techniques required to use it safely.

PLANNING
When to Walk/Stalking

An Teallach is within **Eilean Darach Estate** (☎ 01854 633203), where stalking traditionally takes place between mid-August and mid-October.

Maps

Os Landranger 1:50,000 map No 19 *Gairloch & Ullapool* and OS Explorer 1:25,000 map No 435 *An Teallach & Slioch* cover the walk.

NEAREST TOWN
Dundonnell

☎ 01854 / pop 170

Dundonnell is more of a locality than a distinct village, spread out along the southwestern shore of Little Loch Broom and dramatically overlooked by the outlying cliffs of An Teallach. The nearest ATMs are in Gairloch (between Kinlochewe and Poolewe) or Ullapool.

SLEEPING & EATING

Sàil Mhór Croft Hostel (☎ 633224; www.sailmhor.co.uk; Camusnagaul; dm £11, breakfast £5) is 2 miles west of Dundonnell on the A832. Long established and family-run, the owners are very knowledgeable about the surrounding mountains.

Badrallach (☎ 633281; www.badrallach.com; Croft 9, Badrallach; unpowered sites for 2 £7, bothy £6, caravan for 2 £40, B&B £25, dinner £25) is 7 miles along a narrow single-track road off the A832, 1 mile east of Dundonnell Hotel. With something for everyone, from a grassy pitch to luxury B&B and dinner with the family, Badrallach is in a class of its own.

Dundonnell Hotel (☎ 633204; www.dundonnellhotel.com; s £35-45, d £70-90, mains £7-10; lunch & dinner) is superbly furnished and most rooms have glen or loch views. You'll eat well in the Broombeg bar, where the menu reflects an imaginative approach to standard dishes.

Dundonnell Stores (Mon-Sat), the only shop, is actually 5.5 miles west at Durnamuck, half a mile along the Badcaul road from the A832.

GETTING THERE & AWAY

Westerbus (☎ 01445 712255) operates a bus service between Inverness and Gairloch via Dundonnell (£7, one hour 40 minutes, one service Monday, Wednesday and Saturday), stopping outside the hotel. The driver will also stop elsewhere if you ask nicely.

WESTER ROSS

GETTING TO/FROM THE WALK

Corrie Hallie parking area is 2 miles south of Dundonnell on the eastern side of the A832. The Westerbus driver may drop you here with sufficient notice.

THE WALK

Map below

From Corrie Hallie cross the road and follow the track signposted to Kinlochewe. Go through a gate and follow the track up through a grove of silver birch. About 1.2 miles out, cross a footbridge. Soon the track zigzags up the hill beside the burn to a cairn, about 100m beyond which, two smaller cairns mark a path to the right. After 800m it crosses a hollow, and the most direct route up An Teallach leaves the established path (which leads on to the bothy at Shenavall) and heads west across open ground. Pass **Lochan na Bradhan** then head straight up the shoulder of Sàil Liath, or you can avoid the scree by following a grassy slope towards the north of the shoulder. This steep route is slippery when wet; there's a slightly more gradual line further to the south.

Join the ridge and turn northwest up the rocky slope to the summit cairn on **Sàil Liath** (954m). The wonderful panorama extends southwest to Beinn Dearg Mhór, and nearby Loch Toll an Lochain far below is framed dramatically by an impressive amphitheatre of buttresses. A worn path leads along the ridge from here; descend to the west to the steep, exposed ridge – a taste of things to

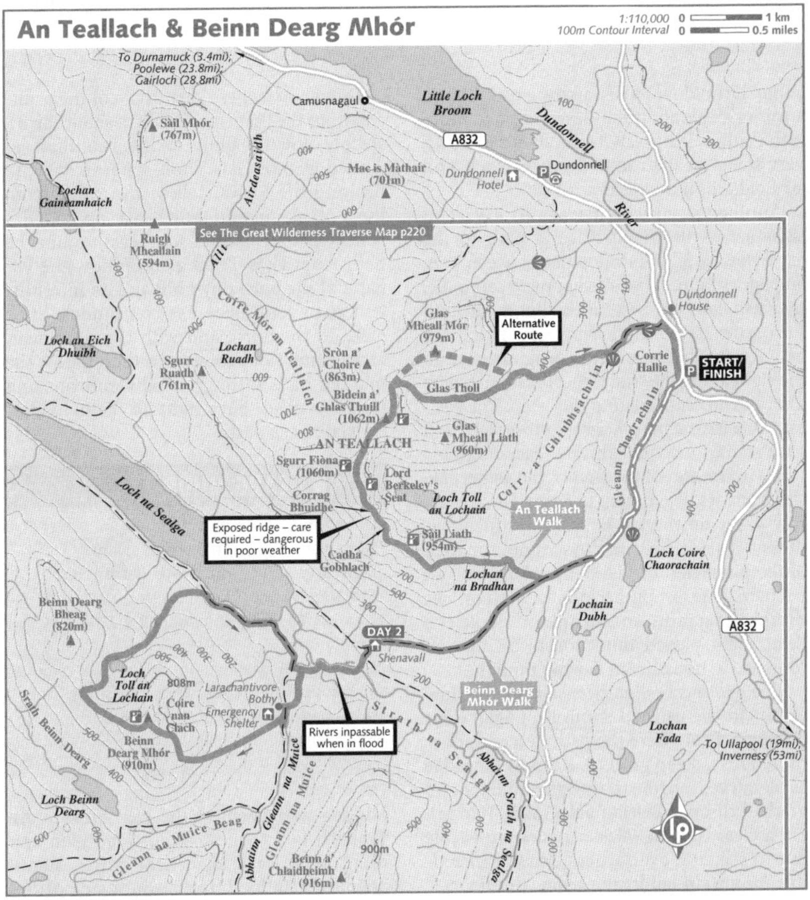

SCRAMBLING

Between the world of walking and the world of rock climbing there is a region of increasing exposure, increasing verticality and increasing adrenaline. Scrambling is the term used for sections of a route that require the significant use of hands for balance and to move upwards. It may be a small rock-step on an otherwise easy ridge, it might be a knife-edge narrowing on a ridge or, at the extreme end, it could be several hundred feet of quite steep rock. Essentially, scrambling ends where technical rock climbing begins. Mostly scrambling depends on your head for heights, and previous climbing experience helps a great deal. Most scramblers go without ropes but they do offer reassurance on harder moves, provided they're used correctly.

The Aonach Eagach (p139), Ben Nevis via Carn Mór Dearg Arête (p127) and An Teallach (p214) walks are classic scrambling routes, while the Ring of Steall (p128) walk and the Beinn Alligin (p227) horseshoe provide less-challenging introductions to the art. Any route will be that much harder if the rock is wet or the wind is strong. Pick dry, calm days for scrambles and enjoy the friction. Hiring a guide would be a good way to get going. Alternatively, take one of the courses run at the National Outdoor Training Centre at **Glenmore Lodge** (☎ 01479 861256; www.glenmorelodge.org.uk) near Aviemore. For guidance, chase up *The Hillwalkers Guide to Mountaineering* by Stuart Johnston, and for a fund of ideas *Classic Mountain Scrambles in Scotland* by Andrew Dempster is your guide.

come. Drop down to a narrow gap, climb to a minor peak and then descend once more into Cadha Gobhlach, from where there's a very steep escape route, down to Loch Toll an Lochain, if necessary.

Another steep ascent leads to a wall of slabs across the main ridge; a path to the left bypasses all the difficulties between here and Sgurr Fiòna. If you're happy to scramble, the first slabs are best taken slightly around the corner to the left, leaving you on a ledge beneath the 'bad step'. Any progress back to the right along the true ridge line is barred by a very steep, intimidating rock step. The easiest route is straight up, across more slabs and rock steps. Once past this, an easy scramble puts you on top of the first of the **Corrag Bhuidhe pinnacles**. From here to Sgurr Fiòna, narrow paths on the left bypass all difficulties, though it's relatively easy to scramble up each of the pinnacles for views into Coire Toll an Lochain. The last pinnacle is the vertiginous, overhanging prow known as Lord Berkeley's Seat, again passed innocuously on the left (one to 1¼ hours from Corrag Bhuidhe).

The ground is slightly easier for the final ascent to the cairned summit of **Sgurr Fiòna** (1060m). From here the path descends over more loose, steep ground. Keep to the ridge as it curves northeast for the final, more gradual climb to **Bidein a' Ghlas Thuill** (1062m). On a clear day the Western Isles are visible out to sea, and everywhere else the incredible mountain landscape seems limitless.

Descend steeply north to a col then take a path to the east (marked by a small cairn), steeply down a gully to the beautiful secluded glen of Glas Tholl. Alternatively, to prolong the views, follow the ridge from the col north and northeast up to Glas Mheall Mór. Descend southeast to join the path from Glas Tholl glen. Follow the left bank of the burn downhill and an intermittent path soon becomes continuous. Stick close to the burn, and with the road near, cross some sandstone slabs then follow the marked path through rhododendrons and on to the road. Turn right for 650m to Corrie Hallie car park.

BEINN DEARG MHÓR

Duration	2 days
Distance	16 miles (25.5km)
Difficulty	moderate–demanding
Start/Finish	Corrie Hallie
Nearest Town	Dundonnell (p214)
Transport	bus

Summary A challenging circuit of a remote and spectacular peak. River crossings, steep slopes and a night at Shenavall Bothy make this a trip to remember.

Hidden away behind the vast bulk of An Teallach is a rugged, steep-sided glen cradling Loch na Sealga, near which stands Shenavall Bothy. On the south side of this wild glen, the steep crown of Beinn Dearg Mhór (910m/2985ft) rises resplendent. A finely chiselled massif standing above the head of the loch, the mountain rises like a beacon to walkers.

Its challenging ascent involves steep slopes, several river crossings and tricky navigation if the weather is poor, so you need to be right up to the mark with these techniques and skills. The complete circuit from Corrie Hallie takes 10 to 11 hours, which could feasibly be fitted into a summer's day. However, this strenuous route really should be spread over two days with a night at or near Shenavall Bothy. The rivers are impassable even in minor flood so postpone your trip if possible during or just after heavy rain.

PLANNING

When to Walk/Stalking

The route passes through the **Eilean Darach Estate** (☎ 01854 633203), where the traditional stalking season is from mid-August to mid-October.

Maps

Use OS Explorer 1:25,000 map No 435 *An Teallach & Slioch* or OS Landranger 1:50,000 map No 19 *Gairloch & Ullapool*.

GETTING TO/FROM THE WALK

To get to Corrie Hallie see p215.

THE WALK Map p215

Day 1: Corrie Hallie to Shenavall

2 hours, 4 miles (6.5km)

From Corrie Hallie cross the road and take the vehicle track signposted to Kinlochewe. Pass through a gate and follow the track up through a grove of silver birch trees. The track fords a stream, and there is a wooden footbridge if water levels are high. The ground becomes steeper, the stream forms into a series of picturesque waterfalls, and the track zigzags up the hill beside it. The top of the climb is marked by a cairn and inspirational views of a wilderness of peaks and glens.

About 100m after the cairn, two smaller cairns mark a path to the right. This path is well worn, although after about 1.2km miles it passes the shoulder of Sàil Liath and the ground becomes wetter and rougher. Pick your way alongside a stream as the path descends through a narrow valley to reach Shenavall and the bothy.

Shenavall Bothy is maintained by the Mountain Bothies Association and is open and free for all mountain users. It is simply a shell of an old stone house and has no facilities except a fireplace. It can serve as an alternative to camping, although you'll still need camping gear (sleeping mats and stove etc). If you do stay in the bothy (or camp near it), be sure to walk well upstream before collecting water – the bothy is very popular and there isn't a toilet, so the water nearby is definitely *not* drinkable.

Day 2: Shenavall to Corrie Hallie via Beinn Dearg Mhór

8 hours, 12 miles (19km)

The first challenge is to cross the two rivers that snake towards Loch na Sealga. If they're in spate, crossing will be impossible, but generally the water is calf- to knee-deep in the shallows and wading is cold but not difficult.

Leave Shenavall and cross Abhainn Srath na Sealga just southwest of the bothy. Stick to the river bank on the other side to avoid the worst of some very wet ground between the two rivers, then cross the bog to Abhainn Gleann na Muice. Follow its bank south and cross in front of the private Larachantivore Bothy, a place with a sad history (see the boxed text on p218). Close by is a small building, as the sign on the door says, for walkers' use in an emergency; this would be most welcome if you were coming from the west and the river was impassable. Once on the western bank of the Abhainn Gleann na Muice, start straightaway to traverse southwest up and across the steep eastern flanks of Beinn Dearg Mhór to reach a prominent gully and stone chute. Follow the chute to where it is bounded on the left by some small crags. Cross the chute and traverse left (south) above the crags, ascending gradually across boulder fields and heather to reach easier ground at the lip of a corrie (1½ to two hours from Larachantivore cottage). Immediately in front of you is an impressive cleft, where a few hardy ash trees grow from ledges in the rock walls. The route to the summit is now quite apparent and straightforward, but a promontory on the summit ridge hides the top.

TRAGEDY AT LARACHANTIVORE BOTHY *Fraser Mackenzie*

Near the present Larachantivore Bothy, the death of two Highland ghillies (employees of the estate who guide hunters and anglers) in a fatal fire is commemorated by a modest plaque. Set firmly into a large rock, the plaque is inscribed with the names of Finlay Maclennan and Tony Roberts. Also recorded is Smudge, Roberts' golden retriever.

The tragedy occurred on the evening of Friday 11 October 1985 when Roberts and Maclennan had completed a day's deer stalking with two Dutch guests of Letterewe Estate owner Paul Van Vlissingen.

Finding the dinghy that had brought them up Loch na Sealga capsized and the outboard motor submerged, the party transported the flooded engine up into the bothy, where Roberts and Maclennan attempted to dry it out. While they were doing this, it appears that the heat from a paraffin lamp caused petrol vapour to ignite. In the resulting fire the bothy, lined with pitch pine, was burned to the ground and the ghillies, who were trapped in the storeroom, perished in the flames. The Dutch guests, who had retired to the nearby lodge, where unable to rescue them. With the permission of the victims' families, Van Vlissingen erected the plaque in May 1986.

Climb steadily northwest to reach the summit ridge in 20 to 30 minutes. The ground falls away abruptly here, with buttresses, gullies and overhanging prows of rock dropping away for 300m into the corrie below. The pinnacled ridge of An Teallach stands framed beyond Loch na Sealga. You can turn right (east) here and follow the ridge out to the east summit (15 minutes return). From where you reach the ridge, a short, steep climb brings you to the summit of **Beinn Dearg Mhór** (910m). An Teallach dominates the view to the north; to the south are the spellbinding ridges, valleys and summits of the Great Wilderness.

Walk south from the summit for a couple of hundred metres and pick up an eroded path that zigzags northwest down the steep, stony slope towards the bealach (pass) between Beinn Dearg Mhór and Beinn Dearg Bheag. Below and to the right (north) the waters of Loch Toll an Lochain are your next goal, but don't be tempted to descend directly. It is easier to continue along the bealach almost to the beginning of the ascent to Beinn Dearg Beag and then follow grassy slopes northeast down to the lake shore.

Skirt the western shores of the loch and descend gently at first, and then more steeply, along the west bank of the burn that drains it. Cross over the burn where the descent begins to ease, and then cut across rough ground to pick up a good path on the shores of Loch na Sealga. Follow this path southeast until it reaches Gleann na Muice, where you should be able to ford the waters without walking too far upstream. Cross the Srath na Sealga in front of Shenavall Bothy and then follow the path back out to Corrie Hallie.

THE GREAT WILDERNESS TRAVERSE

Duration	2 days
Distance	23 miles (37km)
Difficulty	moderate
Start	Corrie Hallie
Finish	Poolewe (opposite)
Nearest Town	Dundonnell (p214)
Transport	bus

Summary A scenic low-level route crossing the beautiful and isolated heart of a magnificently unspoiled fastness of rugged peaks, lonely glens and tranquil lochs.

The Great Wilderness is a particularly remote area of the western Highlands, stretching from Little Loch Broom in the north to Loch Maree in the south, and from the Fannichs in the east to the west-coast village of Poolewe. With an area of about 180 sq miles, it's rather small by many standards, but in Scotland (and Britain for that matter) this is wilderness indeed.

The landscape is mountainous, with some fine, austere peaks. Between the mountains there are lochs of all shapes and sizes, rivers, waterfalls, peat bogs and grassy valleys. The one thing that the landscape lacks is trees, so it may seem a bit strange when you see Fisherfield Forest, Letterewe Forest and

Dundonnell Forest on the map. Forest, as used here, means hunting ground, and the names indicate different estates.

The route itself follows well-trodden, though unmarked, paths for its entirety. It involves one ascent of 500m to a mountain plateau that is roughly half the height of the major peaks surrounding it. It is a long route but, for the second half, the terrain is largely flat and the going is quick. While it could conceivably fit into one long summer's day, it is well worth taking your time and spreading the route over two days, both for the sake of your legs and to fully appreciate the beauty and atmosphere of your surroundings. There are two shelters for walkers' use along the route: the bothy at Shenavall and a barn at Carnmore. Alternatively, you can camp anywhere along the route. The walk involves the crossing of two rivers that are impassable in spate, so avoid walking during or after heavy rain.

PLANNING

When to Walk/Stalking

The route passes through the **Letterewe Estate** (☎ 01445 760311). Contact the estate for advice during its main stalking season, which is between mid-September and mid-November. The route also passes through the **Eilean Darach Estate** (☎ 01854 633203), where the traditional stalking season is mid-August to mid-October.

Maps

Use OS Explorer 1:25,000 map No 435 *An Teallach & Slioch* or OS Landranger 1:50,000 map No 19 *Gairloch & Ullapool.*

NEAREST TOWNS

See Dundonnell, (p214).

Poolewe

☎ 01445

A compact, picturesque village at the head of Loch Ewe, Poolewe has a modest array of facilities. **Slioch Outdoor Equipment** (☎ 781412; www.slioch.co.uk; Clifton; ⏲ Mon-Fri), one of the quiet success stories on the Scottish outdoor scene, makes high-quality outdoor clothing; its shop stocks camping and walking equipment, maps and books.

The nearest ATM and TIC are in Gairloch, about 5 miles southwest along the A832.

SLEEPING & EATING

Poolewe Camping & Caravanning Club Site (☎ 781249; www.campingandcaravanningclub.co.uk; Inverewe Garden; unpowered/powered sites for 2 £14/18) welcomes nonmembers and is close to the end of the walk.

Craigdhu B&B (☎ 781311; s/d £15/30) is a good old-fashioned B&B where you're welcome in the family home. Rooms are neatly furnished with a minimum of fuss. It's a short step along a lane in the centre of the village.

Poolewe Hotel (☎ 781241; www.poolewehotel.co.uk; s/d £42/80, bar meals £8-12; ⏲ lunch & dinner), once a coaching inn, enjoys a great location, so most of the comfortable rooms have loch and sea views. Locally caught seafood is a speciality.

The **Bridge Cottage Cafe & Gallery** (breakfast £5, light meals £4-5; ⏲ 10.30am-5pm) is licensed and does particularly good cakes and coffee.

There's just one **shop** (⏲ Mon-Sat) with a fair range of supplies.

GETTING THERE & AWAY

Westerbus (☎ 01445 712255) operates a service between Inverness and Gairloch via Poolewe (£8, 2½ hours, Monday, Wednesday and Saturday). **Scotbus** (☎ 01463 224410; www.scotbus.co.uk) runs the same route (£8, 2¼ hours, daily).

GETTING TO/FROM THE WALK

For transport details to Corrie Hallie see p215.

THE WALK

Day 1: Corrie Hallie to Shenavall

2 hours, 4 miles (6.5km)

Follow the Day 1 description of the Beinn Dearg Mhór walk (above).

Day 2: Shenavall to Poolewe

8–9 hours, 19 miles (30.5km)

The first challenge is to cross the two rivers that snake towards Loch na Sealga. If they're in spate crossing will be impossible, but generally the water is calf- to knee-deep in the shallows and wading is cold but not difficult.

Leave Shenavall and cross Abhainn Srath na Sealga just southwest of the bothy. Stick to the river bank on the other side to avoid the worst of some very wet ground between the two rivers, then cross the bog to Abhainn Gleann na Muice. Follow this river's bank

The Great Wilderness Traverse

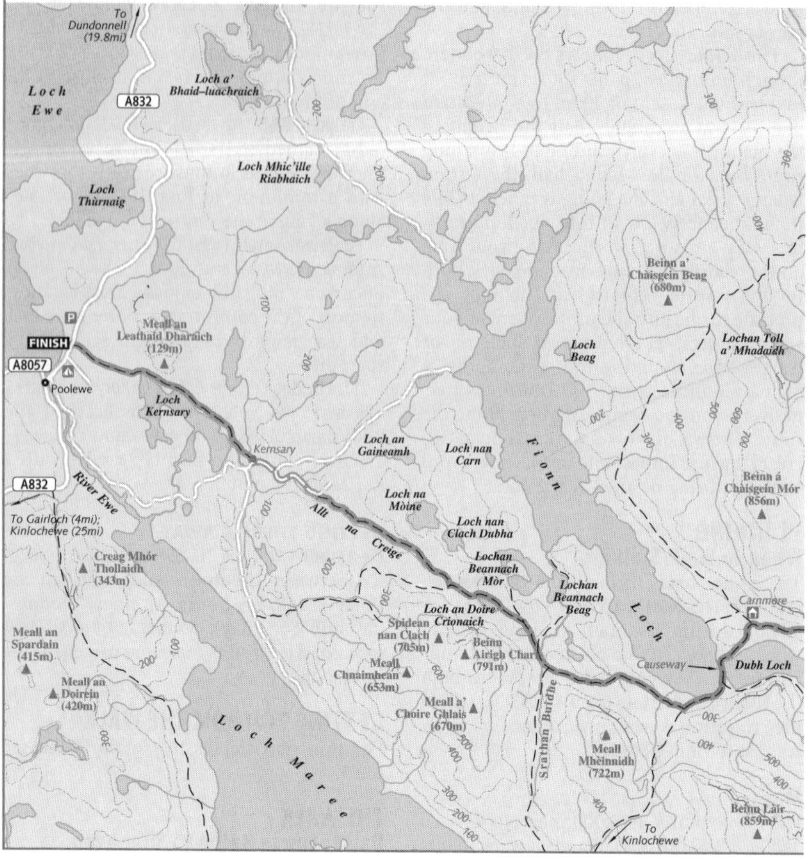

south and cross in front of the private Larachantivore Bothy. Close by is a small building, as the sign on the door says, for use by walkers in an emergency, particularly if nearby streams are impassable. About 50m west of the cottage you may notice a memorial plaque on a rock – see the boxed text on p218. Once on the western bank of the Abhainn Gleann na Muice, join a path that passes in front of the cottage and follows the river upstream. Pass the slopes of Beinn Dearg Mhór and the valley of Gleann na Muice Beag opens up to the west. A burn runs down the centre of the steep-sided valley; take the path that leads off to the right (west) about 50m before the confluence of this burn with the main river.

This path is narrower and drier than the previous one. Follow it up the northern bank of the burn, which cascades down steep rock walls at the head of the valley. The path zigzags its way up the side, passing the beautiful Loch Beinn Dearg halfway up. Gain the plateau and the path is fairly flat for the next 1.5 miles, past numerous lochans. On the western side of the plateau the path forks; keep right (west) and begin the descent, on an excellent path, towards Carnmore. Just as you leave the plateau the most stunning **view** of the route opens up ahead: Allt Bruthach an Easain is framed in the perfect bowl of a glacial valley, then drops suddenly away to reveal the steep walls of the massif opposite. As you descend slightly further and

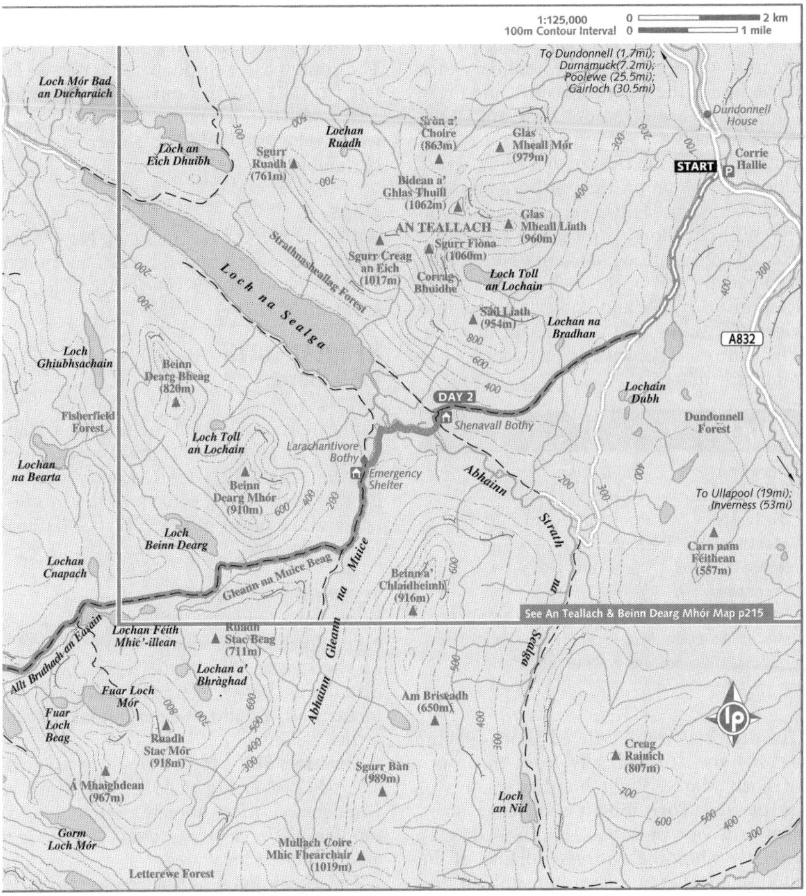

round a corner towards the west, another vista is spread before you, with Dubh Loch and Fionn Loch stretched out below.

The descent is fairly gentle as the path contours down the steep slope towards the buildings at Carnmore (about 8 miles from Shenavall). These buildings are part of the Letterewe Estate and are not maintained by the Mountain Bothies Association. A sign invites climbers and walkers to use the barn (always open and without charge) situated 50m northwest of the main house. The shelter is pretty basic, with just four iron bedsteads, but could be very welcome in bad weather.

The trail veers to the southwest at Carnmore and leads down to a rock and concrete causeway crossing the lochs. Follow round the top of a series of pebble beaches on the opposite (southern) shore of Fionn Loch. The path forks about 1.2km beyond the causeway. The path to the south leads to Kinlochewe over the Bealach Mheinnidh. Take the path to the right (west) along the shore of the loch. Bear away from the loch slightly and pass several small lochans. At a cairned fork, 1.5 miles beyond the Kinlochewe junction, keep right (northwest) and cross directly over the Srathan Buidhe burn (a path amendment not marked on the OS map). The trail from here is well benched and level.

Continue to a conifer plantation; go through a turnstile and join a vehicle track at a cairn. Turn left (west) along the track;

where it leaves the plantation, take the west fork at a junction. This will bring you to the farm at Kernsary. At the boundary turn north beside the farm enclosures and make for a metal bridge across a stream. Walk north for about 150m, almost to a ruined cottage, to join the clear path leading across a heathery slope on the northern shore of Loch Kernsary. Halfway along the loch, on the southern shore, you can see a splendid example of a crannog (ancient island dwelling). At the end of the loch a short climb leads to a turnstile and Poolewe comes into view. Continue to the A832, turning left. The centre of Poolewe is just a couple of minutes' walk away.

SLIOCH

Duration	7½–8 hours
Distance	12 miles (19km)
Difficulty	moderate–demanding
Start/Finish	Incheril car park
Nearest Town	Kinlochewe (right)
Transport	bus

Summary A beautiful approach along the shores of Loch Maree leads to a compact mountain horseshoe with excellent views.

The dramatic, double-tiered Slioch (980m/3214ft) rises majestically from the shore of Loch Maree. Eight hundred metres of purple-red Torridonian sandstone soars skywards out of a bed of rounded, grey gneiss – when the buttressed flanks of the mountain reflect the evening sunlight, the effect is dramatic. It is well named, the most likely meaning being 'spear'.

Unusually among mountain walks in most parts of the country, this one starts with a comparatively long walk to the start of the ascent, providing plenty of time to become imbued with the spirit of the place. This is, surely, far preferable to the usual routine of piling out of the car and heading straight up the path to the top. The route to Slioch follows the picturesque Kinlochewe River to Loch Maree, then climbs through wild moorland to the cluster of peaks that make up the Slioch massif. From the summit ridge, views range from the remote heart of the Great Wilderness to the Western Isles. The walk involves a total ascent of 1160m and crosses some rough ground.

PLANNING

When to Walk/Stalking

The route passes through the **Letterewe Estate** (☎ 01445 760311). Contact the estate for advice during its main stalking season, which is between mid-September and mid-November.

Maps

Both OS Explorer 1:25,000 map No 435 *An Teallach & Slioch* and the OS Landranger 1:50,000 map No 19 *Gairloch & Ullapool* cover this route.

NEAREST TOWN

Kinlochewe

☎ 01445

Kinlochewe is a dot on the map in a magnificent location. It sits right at the foot of steep, dramatic Glen Docherty and the head of Loch Maree, with views towards Slioch and the peaks of Beinn Eighe National Nature Reserve.

SLEEPING & EATING

Beinn Eighe Campsite (☎ 760254; free) is 1.5 miles north of the village along the A832, on the eastern side of the road; check the distance as there's no sign indicating where to turn off. Facilities are minimal but the setting is fantastic.

Cromasaig B&B (☎ 760234; www.cromasaig.com; A896; s/d £24/48, evening meal £16), just south of Kinlochewe, offers homely, simple accommodation. The owners are very knowledgeable about the local area.

Kinlochewe Hotel & Bunkhouse (☎ 760253; www.kinlochewehotel.co.uk; dm £10, s £33-35, d £66-70, mains £9-11; 🕑 lunch & dinner) offers a warm welcome. The bunkhouse has a kitchen, or all meals are available in the hotel. In the bar, Isle of Skye beers are on tap, or you can try one of Harviestoun's or Heatherale's brews. The menu changes daily so everything is freshly prepared; hope that the popular steak and real ale pie, and bean stew are on.

The **village shop** (🕑 Mon-Sat, 10am-1pm Sun) sells maps, among other things. You can obtain cash from the post office.

There's a tiny shop and the **Tipsy Laird coffee shop** (☎ 760227; mains £3-5; 🕑 10am-4pm Wed-Sun), good for a quick snack, next to the petrol station a little way north along the main road.

HEAVY INDUSTRY BESIDE LOCH MAREE

Anything remotely resembling industrial development around Loch Maree would be most unwelcome, of course, but rest assured, it all happened during a brief interlude at least 400 years ago.

On the way to Slioch you cross Abhainn an Fhasaigh; here, between the path and the shore of Loch Maree, largely hidden by thick heather, are the remains of a fairly primitive ironworks (buildings, hearths and furnaces). Using local bog iron ore, the works probably operated around the end of the 16th century. It is likely that the works helped to encourage entrepreneur George Hay to develop what was probably the first charcoal-fired blast furnace in Scotland, near Letterewe, about 3 miles west of Slioch. Hay shipped iron ore from Fife and felled most of the oak woodlands on the loch shore to produce charcoal. It's not clear just what he did with the iron produced but there were ready markets at home and abroad. All activity had ceased by about 1670, leaving the works to crumble almost to nothing, as well as a decimated oak wood and the seemingly incongruous place name 'Furnace' near Letterewe.

GETTING THERE & AWAY

Westerbus (☎ 01445 712255) operates a service Inverness and Gairloch via Kinlochewe (£7, 1½ hours, Tuesday, Thursday and Friday). **Scotbus** (☎ 01463 224410; www.scotbus.co.uk) runs the same route (£6, 1½ hours, daily).

GETTING TO/FROM THE WALK

Follow the A832 east from Kinlochewe for about 800m, then turn left along the signposted road to Incheril. Continue for 800m to the large car park at the end of the road.

THE WALK

Map p224

From the cairn and plaque (about the Letterewe Estate) on the northern side of the car park, go up steps and through a gate. Turn left with the sign to 'Poolewe by Letterewe'. After a few minutes the track ends; continue along a path and soon go through a gate. The path leads on past fields and through bracken to another gate, below which is a wide wooden bridge over Allt Chnàimhean. The well-worn path now climbs slightly and in less than 10 minutes leads into the first of several lovely mixed woodlands along the way. Soon you're down beside the river, where you catch sight of the mighty ramparts of Slioch for the first time. Just past the end of this first woodland is a faint path junction. Bear right and cross grassland, soft in places, or continue straight on, through bracken, for a slightly longer, though generally better, path. The two unite a short distance beyond a stony burn. Further on, about 50 minutes from the start and a short distance beyond another wooded area, you come to another fork. Bear left along a grassy path, generally close to the shore. Cross a pebble beach, pass through a silver birch grove and soon you come to the footbridge across thundering **Abhainn an Fhasaigh** (about an hour from the start).

Go through a gap in the wire fence on the far side of the bridge and immediately turn right along a path that follows the river upstream. After 150m the path turns sharp right; this is in fact a fork, which may be marked by a low cairn. Bear left, up across rock slabs and follow the clear path northeast, soon across generally flat ground. About 1.2km further on, bear left at a prominent junction, marked by a large cairn. The path leads more or less north, soon near a burn in the shallow depression between Meall Each and Sgurr Dubh.

At the col between these two hills, the main path veers west around the bottom of Sgurr Dubh directly towards Slioch. Leave the path at the col and strike out over open ground across Coire na Sleaghaich towards the grassy eastern slopes of Sgurr an Tuill Bhàin. Cross the stream that runs down the centre of the corrie and climb the heathery lower slopes of the mountain. Veer west to gain easier ground on a rocky shoulder and then climb to **Sgurr an Tuill Bhàin** (934m), where there is a wonderful view north over Lochan Fada to the remote heart of the Great Wilderness.

Pick up a path from the summit and follow it west, dropping down onto a narrow ridge. The ridge widens as it climbs towards the northern summit of **Slioch**. In poor visibility stick to the northern edge of the ridge and you will be guided to the top. The northern and southern summits are actually the same height (980m), although the south summit enjoys official status as the higher one. Views from both points are stunning, with a panorama of Loch Maree stretching out to the Atlantic below you and the Western Isles visible on the horizon beyond. From the northern summit make a major change in direction turning south then swinging slightly east around the top of a steep drop to reach the trig point on Slioch's southern summit.

From the summit descend southeast on a grassy slope. The path becomes slightly confused through rocky ground; cross a rise and then veer further east to drop down the left side of a steep rock spur and reach the col below, just east of two lochans. The main path heads east into Coire na Sleaghaich. If you want to complete the entire horseshoe, climb the rise to the south of the lochans, veering west slightly to locate the path that descends to the broad col below Sgurr Dubh. A straightforward climb up the shoulder ahead brings you to the summit of **Sgurr Dubh** (738m). To descend, cross to the northeast of the summit plateau and go down steeply towards Meall Each. Join back up with the main path at the bottom, turning south and retracing your route back to Loch Maree and the Incheril car park.

Slioch & Beinn Eighe Mountain Trail

1:80,000 · 50m Contour Interval · 0–1 km · 0–0.5 miles

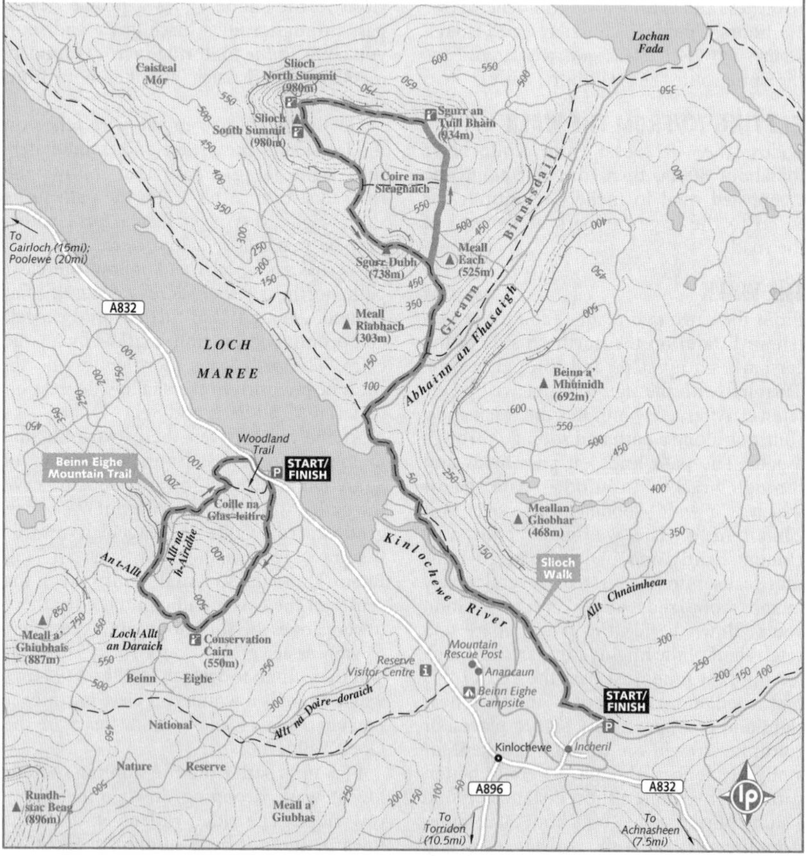

WESTER ROSS ROCKS

Many of the peaks of Wester Ross have exposed, rocky flanks and summits, and the geological processes that created the region can be clearly seen. Ancient Lewisian gneiss, up to 2500 million years old, is the bedrock. It was subsequently eroded and then, when the area was situated south of the equator around 800 million years ago, was smothered by desert sands up to 4 miles thick. This sedimentary material hardened to form a rock so specific to the area that it has been named red Torridonian sandstone, although in real life it looks more purple than red. Slioch, with its distinctive double-tiered silhouette, displays these rocks particularly well, with a broad, grey base topped by an 800m-high mound of red sandstone.

Much of this relatively soft sandstone has been eroded, mainly by successive ice ages, wind and rain, sculpting wonderful pinnacle formations on high ridges. The pinnacles of An Teallach and the Horns of Beinn Alligin are superb examples of this process, and today the glue-like friction of the fine-grained sandstone provides a perfect rock playground for scramblers.

The third main geological component of the area, Cambrian quartzite, was formed by sediments laid down by tropical seas that flooded the sandstone around 600 million years ago. At the end of the last Ice Age, this rock was the first to emerge from beneath the ice. It was riven into pinnacles and the scree on Beinn Eighe, which makes it appear snow-covered, even in mid-summer.

BEINN EIGHE MOUNTAIN TRAIL

Duration	2½–3½ hours
Distance	2.5 miles (4km)
Difficulty	easy–moderate
Start/Finish	Glas Leitir car park
Nearest Town	Kinlochewe (p222)
Transport	private

Summary A short, steep walk that explores the beautiful woodland and wild mountain terrain of the Beinn Eighe National Nature Reserve.

Beinn Eighe (pronounced 'ben ay') National Nature Reserve was established in 1951, the first such reserve in Britain. It was created to help safeguard the largest remnant of ancient Caledonian pine woodland in the western Highlands, and covers 4750 hectares between the shore of Loch Maree and the mountain massif of Beinn Eighe (probably meaning 'file mountain', for its long, slender ridge). The whole reserve is managed by SNH. Two walking trails explore the best of the area's habitats. The Mountain Trail is longer and ventures higher up the slopes of Beinn Eighe for some great views; the Woodland Trail is only 1 mile long and explores the Caledonian woodland bordering Loch Maree. Both trails are well marked by stone cairns with 'indicator points', showing features of interest that are fully explained in the trail guidebooks, available from the visitor centre (see right). The trails are open during the short stalking season, when signs will request walkers to keep strictly to the defined path.

The Mountain Trail leads up from the shores of Loch Maree, through Scots pine, to the bare and rocky mountain slopes above. It might be relatively short, and it might be waymarked, but don't underestimate the walk; the terrain is steep (one section gains 320m in height over a horizontal distance of 500m) and you need to use your hands to haul yourself up high rock steps in several places. The trail offers an ideal introduction to mountain walking, and is an informative and exciting place to bring older children. It's also a worthwhile alternative to the high peaks if they're cloud-covered.

PLANNING

Maps

The walk is covered by the OS Landranger 1:50,000 map No 19 *Gairloch & Ullapool*. For more detail use the OS Explorer 1:25,000 map No 433 *Torridon*.

Information Sources

Beinn Eighe National Nature Reserve Visitor Centre (☎ 01445 760254; www.nnr-scotland.org.uk; A832; 🕓 10am-5pm Easter-Oct) is 1.2km north of Kinlochewe, housing displays about the reserves habitats and selling maps and natural-history guides. These include two of SNH's own publications. One is *Beinn Eighe: Britain's First National Nature Reserve*, a beautiful coffee-table volume with photos by Scotland's best-known outdoor photographer, Colin Baxter, and others; the other, *Beinn Eighe: First Among Equals,* is more down-to-earth and provides a comprehensive introduction to the area.

The *Beinn Eighe National Nature Reserve: Mountain Trail* guide is available from a vending machine at the Glas Leitir car park.

GETTING TO/FROM THE WALK

The walk starts and finishes at the Glas Leitir car park, about 2.5 miles north of Kinlochewe along the A832.

THE WALK

Map p224

From the information board at the Glas Leitir parking area, cross under the road on a walkway beside the river. Keep left at the trail junction just after the tunnel, following the direction of the mountain symbol on a marker post. The stony path follows along the banks of Allt na h-Airidhe for a short time then veers away to cross through a silver birch grove densely carpeted with bracken. The trail begins its ascent almost immediately, although the gradient is easy at first. As you climb, the bracken is interspersed by heather and the silver birch gives way to Scots pine.

The path joins up with a tumbling burn and climbs more steeply up its banks on stone steps, then crosses it on a wooden footbridge. The steps become more continuous as the trees dwindle in size and the path emerges onto open slopes. Views of Loch Maree and Slioch open up to the north. The rock steps gradually give way to natural slab and loose stone and the terrain becomes wilder. Just beyond the 305m marker cairn you'll need to use your hands to haul yourself up a couple of rock ledges as you climb a very steep section of the trail.

As you climb, views of the Beinn Eighe massif open up ahead and the steepest section of ascent is now over. The path weaves its way uphill between craggy outcrops of rock and finally reaches the **Conservation Cairn**. At 550m this is the high point of the trail and there is a real feeling of being in the heart of the mountains. The 360-degree panorama embraces the precipitous Torridon peaks, in a cluster to the southwest, and the lofty landscape of the Great Wilderness spread out to the north. In good visibility a total of 31 Munros (mountains over 914m/3000ft) can be seen from this excellent vantage point.

The trail drops down to the west and weaves its way past several beautiful lochans. An t-Allt is crossed on stepping stones and the path turns north to follow the burn and begin the descent. The terrain is more gently graded than it was on the climb up. The burn soon disappears into a gorge to your right and, as you descend further, there are impressive views into the deep, sheer-sided chasm.

After a right bend and small rise the path leads to the rim of the gorge; take care here because the drop to the burn below is sheer. Continue on, back into the forest below. The path joins the Woodland Trail and turns left, soon reaching a wooden conservation cabin and a trig point. It leads on through silver birch woodland, across a boardwalk over marshy ground and back to the road. Cross the road and pass through trees to a beautiful pebble beach on the shore of Loch Maree. Turn right and walk along the top of the beach, crossing a wooden bridge, and back to the car park.

TORRIDON

The National Trust for Scotland's (NTS) 6450-hectare Torridon Estate embraces some of the most impressive peaks of Wester Ross: the massifs of Beinn Alligin and Liathach and parts of Beinn Dearg and Beinn Eighe, renowned for their deep corries, imposing buttresses, airy pinnacles and magnificent views. Parts of the eastern boundary of the NTS' estate, purchased in 1967, adjoin SNH's Beinn Eighe National Nature Reserve.

Walks over Torridon's high ground are no mere strolls, and call for considerable fitness and mountain skills. Happily, there are also several low-level routes that explore the deep valleys between the mountain massifs. Whatever the route, given a little luck with the weather, Torridon is a magnificent area that will surely draw you back many a time.

PLANNING

Maps

The OS Explorer 1:25,000 map No 433 *Torridon* neatly covers all of the walks in this section, as does Harvey's 1:25,000 Superwalker map *Torridon*. Most of the walks are covered by OS Landranger 1:50,000 map No 24 *Raasay & Applecross*, although this map overlaps with OS Landranger 1:50,000 map No 19 *Gairloch & Ullapool* on Beinn Alligin.

Books

Torridon, the Nature of the Place by Chris Lowe provides all you need to know about the area's flora, fauna and geology.

ACCESS TOWN

Torridon

☎ 01445

The village of Torridon, along Loch Torridon's northern shore, is the main settlement in the area. The nearest TIC and bank are 31 miles away in Gairloch, though the shop may be able to provide a cash-back service for small amounts from UK bank cards.

INFORMATION

The NTS Countryside Centre (☎ 791221; exhibition £3; 🕑 10am-5pm Easter-end Sep) is at the entrance of the village, just off the A896. It stocks maps and a very good range of walking and environment books relating to the local area. Displays feature the scenery and wildlife of Torridon and Loch Torridon. Mountain weather forecasts are posted beside the entrance. Countryside rangers lead short walks between June and August aimed at introducing the natural and cultural landscape of Torridon, and high-level guided mountain walks are available by appointment; contact the centre for details.

SLEEPING & EATING

Torridon Campsite (free) is opposite the Countryside Centre. It's basic; use the nearby public toilets.

Torridon SYHA Hostel (☎ 0870 004 1154; www.syha.org.uk; dm $13) has mainly smaller-than-average rooms, two lounges with panoramic views and a first-rate drying room.

Ben Damph Inn (☎ 791242; www.bendamph.lochtorridonhotel.com; s/d £50/74, mains £7-12; 🕑 lunch & dinner) occupies a former stable that has been converted to motel-style accommodation but without the sterile atmosphere such places can have. The bar, where you can sample some of the 60 malt whiskies on offer, is the centre of evening activity in the area.

Torridon Stores (🕑 Mon-Sat), despite being small, is well stocked and carries camping gas, books, maps and a great array of Scottish beers. It's 800m northwest along the Inveralligin–Diabaig road.

GETTING THERE & AWAY

Torridon village is at the eastern end of Loch Torridon, on the A896 between Kyle of Lochalsh and Kinlochewe. It is possible to arrive by public transport, if you're prepared to fit in with limited connecting services. The nearest train station is Strathcarron, reached with **First ScotRail** (☎ 08457 484950; www.firstscotrail.co.uk) from Inverness (£12, 1¾ hours, four services Monday to Saturday, two Sunday) and Kyle of Lochalsh (£5, 45 minutes, four services Monday to Saturday, two Sunday).

Donnie Maclennan (☎ 01520 755239) runs a bus service from Strathcarron station to Torridon via Lochcarron and Shieldaig. He waits for the trains from both Kyle and Inverness that arrive around 12.40pm Monday to Saturday. For the return journey the bus leaves Torridon about 10.30am, arriving at Strathcarron in time for the 12.35pm trains to Kyle and Inverness. The times and services can change, so contact Donnie beforehand.

BEINN ALLIGIN

Duration	6½–7 hours
Distance	6 miles (9.5km)
Difficulty	moderate–demanding
Start/Finish	Torridon House Bridge
Nearest Town	Torridon (left)
Transport	private

Summary An exciting circuit of a horseshoe ridge with two major summits that could challenge your head for heights and your scrambling techniques.

The circuit of ridges and peaks of Beinn Alligin is one of the most popular mountain walks in Wester Ross. A steep ascent allows access to excellent, airy walking, and the traverse of the Horns of Alligin offers a little slightly exposed scrambling. This route is a good warm-up for the difficulties encountered on An Teallach (p214) and Liathach (p229). If you find Beinn Alligin difficult then don't consider the other two; Liathach, in particular, is much more difficult. Most of the scrambling on the horns can be bypassed, but even these alternatives are exposed so if vertigo is your problem, perhaps you should think twice about this one.

Beinn Alligin means 'the mountain of jewels'. It is definitely a gem – a mountain that allows you to get a feel for the high and wild Scottish peaks without having to be a mountaineer or to trek for miles to reach the foot of the mountain. This route involves a total ascent of 1190m and follows clearly defined paths almost all the way. Take care to follow the directions on the main summit ridge and don't be seduced by side paths that may lead to dead-end lookouts but also to potential difficulties.

GETTING TO/FROM THE WALK

The walk starts from the fairly large car park beside Torridon House Bridge, about 2 miles west of Torridon village on the road to Inveralligin.

THE WALK

From the bridge (which affords a good view of the impressive waterfall and gorge on Abhainn Coire Mhic Nòbuil), follow a path signposted to Coire Dubh, up through Scots pine woodland and out into open moorland. Straight ahead is the blunt western wall of Beinn Dearg, while to the right is the western end of Liathach and, to the left, Beinn Alligin itself. About 200m further along, go through a gate in a deer fence and continue for almost 950m to a footbridge. From here the path leads roughly north, towards the eastern end of the horseshoe ridge.

Climb along the crest of the broad and very steep ridge, using your hands to help negotiate some rocky steps, aiming for the three **Horns of Alligin**. You reach the base of the first horn 1½ to two hours from the start. You can scramble over this and the next two rocky peaks (taking care on the steep descent of the first pinnacle), or follow the path on the left that skirts their south side. After the third horn, drop to a small col then climb again, swinging to the northwest to keep right of the steep drop down into the corrie. To your right (northeast) the view really begins to open out, revealing a beautifully jumbled mosaic of lochans, moors and smaller peaks, with Loch Maree beyond and the town of Gairloch visible on the coast.

It is a short distance to the summit of **Sgurr Mhór** (986m), three to four hours from the start. With the extra height the view is almost completely wraparound, with range upon range of wonderful peaks in every direction. Most notable are the Cuillin peaks on the Isle of Skye to the southwest, and the summits of Beinn Eighe to the east, the quartz scree mantle making them appear snowcapped.

From the summit head southwest down a grassy slope, keeping the corrie edge to your left. If visibility is poor, take real care on this section as the top of **Eag Dhubh**, the giant gash that dominates the view from below, is lurking in wait, to trap unwary walkers in mist. If the day is clear, the cliffs on either side of the gully frame the view of the glen far below, a classic among Scottish mountain vistas. *Don't* try to descend this way.

Beyond Eag Dhubh go steeply up again, over large boulders, to reach the summit and trig point of **Tom na Gruagaich** (922m) and more good views (one to 1½ hours from the summit of Sgurr Mhór). Descend steeply south into Coir nan Laogh on a worn path beside several small, gurgling streams. The

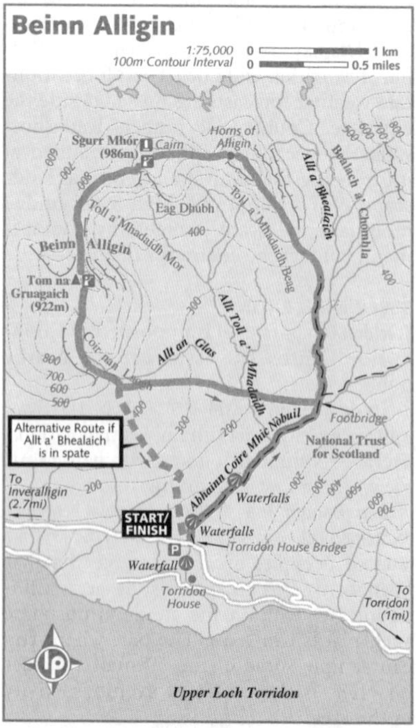

steep walls of the corrie funnel you down to a rocky plateau. Here, if Abhainn Coire Mhic Nòbuil isn't in spate, steer a course slightly south of east to reach Allt a' Bhealaich just above the footbridge. Cross it to reach the path followed on the way up and retrace your steps to the car park. Otherwise, head southeast to avoid crags on the broad spur and to find a stile over the long deer fence on the eastern fall of the spur. Follow rough paths back to the road opposite the car park. The descent from Tom na Gruagaich should take around two hours.

LIATHACH

Duration	7–8 hours
Distance	6 miles (9.5km)
Difficulty	demanding
Start/Finish	Allt an Doire Ghairbh parking area
Nearest Town	Torridon (p227)
Transport	private

Summary A sensational walk with lots of exposed scrambling on one of Scotland's most challenging mountains. The views make this a truly memorable day.

Immediately to the north of Loch Torridon, a massive, 3-mile-long wall of rock pinnacles and buttresses sweeps up to an average height of more than 900m. The south face of this massif is littered with crags and boulder fields, and has no obvious line of weakness. The northern side is even more intimidating, with several brooding corries ringed by cliffs. This is Liathach (pronounced 'lee agagh') and the traverse of its ridge is one of the Scotland's classic mountain challenges. Its name translates simply as 'greyish one'.

The ascent is steep and unrelenting and the main ridge is exposed. The crux of the route is negotiating Am Fasarinen's Pinnacles, which are reached after the ascent of Spidean a' Choire Léith (1055m/3460ft), the main summit on the massif. The descent described is direct and convenient, but rather cruel to the knees and legs after a tough day. The kinder alternative is simply to follow the mostly grassy broad ridge west from Mullach an Rathain, down to the Inveralligin/Diabaig road. However, this is rather a long way from the start, so best suited to a party with two cars.

The traverse should be reserved for a dry summer day with good visibility and light winds. Wet ground can make the muddy paths and the rock treacherous.

GETTING TO/FROM THE WALK

The walk starts and finishes at a small informal parking area on the southern side of the A896 immediately west of Allt an Doire Ghairbh. This is about 2.5 miles east of Torridon village (on foot or by car) and 700m east of Glen Cottage. To walk to Torridon at the end of the day, turn right along the road instead of left; Torridon is just 1 mile along the road.

THE WALK

Map p230

Leave the road along a clear cairned path beside Allt an Doire Ghairbh. The path zigzags the steep slopes on the eastern side of the burn. The climb begins almost immediately and, though the path is well constructed, there are a couple of short scrambles over rock outcrops. An hour of steep ascent will bring you onto gentler slopes in Coire Liath Mhór, where the encircling buttresses, terraces, gullies and scree slopes seem to offer no easy access to the ridge above.

From this point the path is no longer constructed but continues distinctly as an eroded trail. The gradient soon increases again as you climb steadily north under the impressive eastern face of Spidean a' Choire Léith. Swing abruptly to the east under a prominent gully and climb steeply along grass slopes for a short distance. Turn north and climb directly through rock outcrops (care is required in places) to reach the ridge at a bealach (pass) just west of Stùc a' Choire Dhuibh Bhig, two to 2½ hours from the start. If the ascent to here proves difficult and worrying then do not continue beyond Spidean a' Choire Léith, and follow the line of ascent to return to the start.

It is worth climbing east along the ridge as far as the cairned summit of **Stùc a' Choire Dhuibh Bhig** (915m) for the superb view of Beinn Eighe's sweeping ridges and scree. The view west to Spidean a' Choire Lèithe is a classic photo point on Liathach. Allow an hour for this detour.

From the bealach where you arrived at the crest, follow the ridge easily west to where it narrows just before the first of the two tops between here and Spidean a'

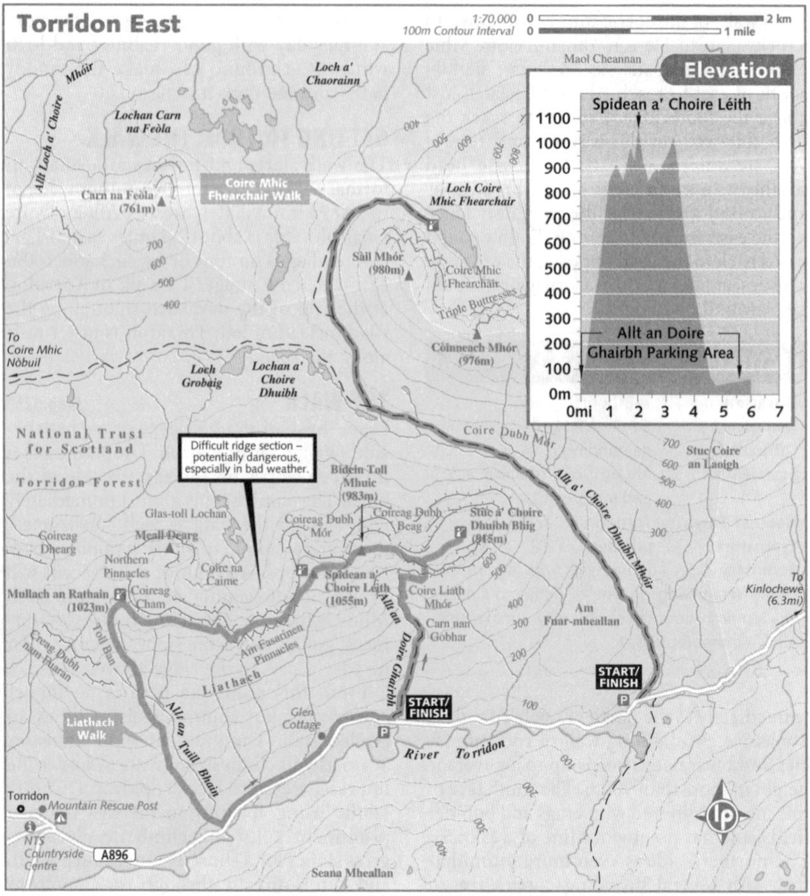

Choire Lèith. Either scramble easily along the crest of this short, knife-edged section or traverse a path just beneath to the south. Climb easily across the two tops and descend steeply to a notch in the ridge where steep gullies meet at a sharp point. The easiest route down into the notch is along the crest of the ridge, but paths do run out to the right before contouring back left into the notch along a worrying and tremendously exposed ledge.

The climb from the notch to the summit of **Spidean a' Choire Léith** is quite straightforward, the last section crossing large slabs and blocks. The views are superb, encompassing all the summits of Torridon to the Great Wilderness beyond and culminating in the jagged spine of An Teallach. To the south the rugged quartzite summits of the Coulin Forest (an ancient, hunting-related name) seem like foothills and, beyond them, the summits of Glen Affric and Mulladorch stretch across the horizon. On a very clear day you can even detect the whaleback of Ben Nevis on the horizon.

Back on Liathach, descend southwest from Spidean a' Choire Lèithe, crossing awkward scree slopes to reach a grassy shoulder just before Am Fasarinen's Pinnacles. At this point a path begins to contour across the southern slopes just below the top of the ridge, while another stays on top to meet the first difficulties head on. The first path can be followed all the way around the pinnacles and is certainly the easiest option, despite the exposure. Take great care as a simple slip could be fatal.

Meanwhile, the direct line of the ridge is entertaining without being unduly difficult as far as a notch at the halfway mark. The contouring path also passes this notch and if you wish to save a bit of time but still tackle the most difficult scrambling, take that path as far as here. There are two options for getting out of the notch and onto the easier ridge above, neither of them easy. There is either a passable, sloping stone gully around to the left or a route up the rock wall to the right. The scramble out of this notch is more akin to an 'easy' graded rock climb; don't tackle it unless you know what you're doing and are relaxed on steep and exposed rock.

Once past the pinnacles, a steady climb brings you to the summit of **Mullach an Rathain** (1023m), with more good perspectives over the other Torridon summits. Don't be tempted to scramble out onto the northern pinnacles as they are difficult and the rock is quite loose. The descent into the Toll Ban runs southwest down a stony ridge then turns southeast and follows an eroded path very steeply down scree slopes. The rest of the descent to the A896 follows this path and is remarkably easy considering the ruggedness of the surroundings. The road is reached 1½ to two hours from the summit of Mullach an Rathain. Turn left at the road and follow it for 1 mile to return to the start.

COIRE MHIC FHEARCHAIR

Duration	4½–4¾ hours
Distance	8 miles (13km)
Difficulty	moderate
Start/Finish	Coire Dubh parking area
Nearest Town	Torridon (p227)
Transport	private

Summary A beautiful, low-level walk to one of the most outstanding corries in Scotland, through impressive mountain glens and wild moorland with the chance of seeing red deer.

Hollowed out of the west end of the Beinn Eighe massif by the glaciers of the last Ice Age, Coire Mhic Fhearchair is one of Scotland's most impressive corries. This walk takes you through the wild heart of Torridon, with the brooding buttresses and pinnacles of Liathach's north face as company for most of the journey.

The walk follows paths constructed and maintained by the NTS, which owns and manages most of the country you'll pass through, except Coire Mhic Fhearchair itself. The total ascent for the route is 510m.

GETTING TO/FROM THE WALK

The walk starts and finishes at Coire Dubh parking area on the A896, 3.5 miles east of Torridon village. The parking area, popular on weekends, is on the northern side of the road, just before a bridge, and is marked by a signpost, 'Public Footpath to Coire Mhic Nòbuil'.

THE WALK

Map p230

Follow the well-constructed path away from the parking area and begin to climb steadily towards Coire Dubh Mór, the prominent cleft between Liathach and Beinn Eighe. The path stays well above Allt a' Choire Dhuibh Mhóir, thundering down through a small gorge to the right. About 40 minutes of steady climbing brings you to a flatter section right under the massive eastern prow of Liathach. In another few minutes cross Allt a' Choire Dhuibh Mhóir on good stepping stones. This may be difficult and potentially dangerous if the river is in full spate, in which case you'll need to follow the south bank of the river to ford it close to the junction with the path going up to Coire Mhic Fhearchair.

A gradual ascent, passing several small lochs, then brings you up through Coire Dubh Mór to a path junction marked with a small cairn. Already you have fine views of the northern corries and buttresses of Liathach, which stretch in an unbroken line of impregnability for almost 3 miles.

Turn right at the junction (the other path continues down into Coire Mhic Nòbuil) and begin climbing steadily around the western flank of Sàil Mhór. The path, though constructed, is quite strenuous in places but the views opening out across Coire Mhic Nòbuil and Beinn Dearg more than compensate for the effort. About 40 minutes from the stream crossing, the path swings around to the east and climbs steeply beneath impressive cliffs. A series of waterfalls drops down on the left and a final steep climb brings you suddenly onto the boulder-strewn rock slabs on the shores of **Loch Coire Mhic Fhearchair** (two to 2½ hours from the start).

From this point you can take in the view or explore further along the rough ground on either side of the lake. The alpine atmosphere of this place is quite special, with the imposing 300m-high Triple Buttresses at the very back of the corrie taking pride of place. Not long after WWII a Lancaster bomber crashed into the west buttress, killing the crew. Parts of the wreckage can still be seen in the far west gully. To the north and west there are excellent views across the wilderness of lochans and bog between Beinn Dearg, Baosbheinn and Beinn an Eoin. Retrace your steps to the parking area.

MORE WALKS

THE FANNICHS

The Fannichs is a compact mountain range several miles south of Ullapool with nine Munros (the highest being 1110m Sgurr Mór), fine corries and high buttresses and an atmosphere of airiness and space. Of many possible routes, a 10.5-mile (17km) circuit takes in three summits and a fine mountain loch; allow seven to eight hours. An alternative is to stay low and walk in to Loch a' Mhadaidh and return on the stalkers' path, an easy–moderate scenic walk of three to four hours.

The walk is in the **Lochluichart Estate** (☎ 01997 414242), where stalking takes place from mid-August to 21 October.

Use OS Explorer 1:25,000 map No 435.

The walk starts at a small, unmarked parking area on the A835, 12.5 miles southeast of Ullapool and 2.5 miles east of Braemore Junction. Approaching from that direction you will pass a conspicuous parking area on the right, east of the junction. About 1.2km further on, a track leaves the road on the left and there is room to park several cars.

THE GREAT WILDERNESS

À Mhaighdean & Ruadh Stac Mòr

These two Great Wilderness peaks are probably the most remote in Britain; you'll need to walk at least 10 miles (16km) from the nearest road to reach the foot of the mountains. À Mhaighdean (967m/3172ft) and Ruadh Stack Mòr (918m/3011ft) are two of the toughest on the Munro baggers' list. You can do them in a single day, but only with a predawn start, covering 27 miles in 14 hours. Ordinary mortals camp at Carnmore and carry a day-pack for the climb itself; start at Corrie Hall and follow the Great Wilderness Traverse (p218) to a jumping-off point. Either way, the northwest ridge of À Mhaighdean is superb. From the intervening col, there's an awful lot of scree on the way up to Ruadh Stac Mòr. Use OS Landranger map No 19; consult Cameron McNeish's *The Munro Almanac* for more detail.

TORRIDON

Beinn Eighe

The Torridon giant Beinn Eighe is a sprawling mass of deep corries and scree-covered ridges, with no fewer than seven summits achieving Munro status. It is possible to reach all these in a single day, but a less demanding, though still strenuous and entirely worthwhile, alternative is to go for the highest and most impressive peaks, concentrated in the western half of the massif. Starting from the A896, halfway between Torridon and Kinlochewe (near Loch Bharranch), follow a path to Coire na Laoigh and climb to the summit of Spidean Coire nan Clach (977m). Then follow a fine ridge west to reach the peaks encircling Coire Mhic Fhearchair (p231). Descend into the corrie then follow the path out through Coire Dubh Mór, reaching the road 1 mile or so west of the start. Total distance is around 12 miles (19.5km) and total ascent is 1300m; allow at least eight hours. Carry OS Explorer 1:25,000 map No 433.

THE NORTHEAST

Beinn Dearg

In the northeast corner of Wester Ross, the grey, scree-covered dome of Beinn Dearg (1081m/3556ft) towers above a sea of remote ridges and peaks. It's a popular summit, but in poor weather navigation on its featureless summit plateau can be tricky. You can start at a parking area on the A835 Inverness–Ullapool road at the southeastern end of Loch Droma. Allow seven to eight hours for the 11-mile (17.5km) route.

Use OS Landranger 1:50,000 map No 20; once again, consult Cameron McNeish's *The Munro Almanac*.

THE SOUTH

Maol Chean-dearg

The peaks of the Coulin Forest are largely overshadowed by the giants of Torridon, just to the north across Glen Torridon. However, the Coulin peaks offer a wilder walking experience, with fewer people. The highest Coulin summit, Maol Chean-dearg (933m/3060ft), is easiest approached from the south. Begin at the A890 where it crosses the Fionn-abhainn River, just east of Lochcarron. This village has accommodation and a shop; Strathcarron station on the Inverness–Kyle of Lochalsh line is about 1 mile away. The route is 10 miles (16km), has a total ascent of over 900m and should take eight hours. Although the walk mostly follows good paths, navigation on the higher ground can be a real challenge. Use OS Landranger 1:50,000 map No 25.

Western Isles

The very name Western Isles (Eileanan Siar) expresses remoteness, difference and mystery, qualities that soon become real, almost tangible. There's always something special about travelling to islands and you soon realise these isles are strikingly different from each other; from the peatlands of north Lewis and the rocky mountains of Harris, to the mosaic of water and land in the Uists, and the compactness of Barra. However, they all share two qualities: an extraordinary sense of space in the vast sky and the limitless ocean, and a feeling of stretched time. Western Isles communities are lively and dynamic, but there is a relaxed feeling of unhurriedness. Waymarked walks with strong historical and natural-history themes are scattered throughout the isles, and there are enough hills, glens, rocky coasts and vast sandy beaches for months of exploration on foot.

The Isle of Lewis can seem rather barren at first, but head for the coast to dispel this illusion – in the far northeast, and facing the wild Atlantic out west, you will find rugged cliffs, secluded coves and excellent walking. Harris, Lewis' southern neighbour, is the most mountainous of the isles, containing dozens of impressively rocky, steep-sided peaks, including Clisham (799m), the highest in the Western Isles. Continuing south, North Uist is mostly billiard-table flat but a few small, attractive hills poke their heads up skywards, notably Eaval, almost surrounded by water. A long chain of mountains dominates slender South Uist, among which Hecla is a formidable objective. Furthest south, Barra is a delight, with superb sandy beaches and a central knot of rolling hills affording great panoramic views.

HIGHLIGHTS

- Discovering a fascinating variety of historical features on the **Tolsta to Ness** (p237) walk on Lewis' northeast coast
- Revelling in the wild, rugged mountainscapes of Harris from the summit of the Western Isles' highest peak, **Clisham** (p245)
- Gazing down at the extraordinary water-and-rock patchwork landscape from **Hecla** (p249) in South Uist
- Wandering along vast white-sand beaches on the isle of **Barra** (p251)

- www.visithebrides.com
- www.thewesternisles.co.uk

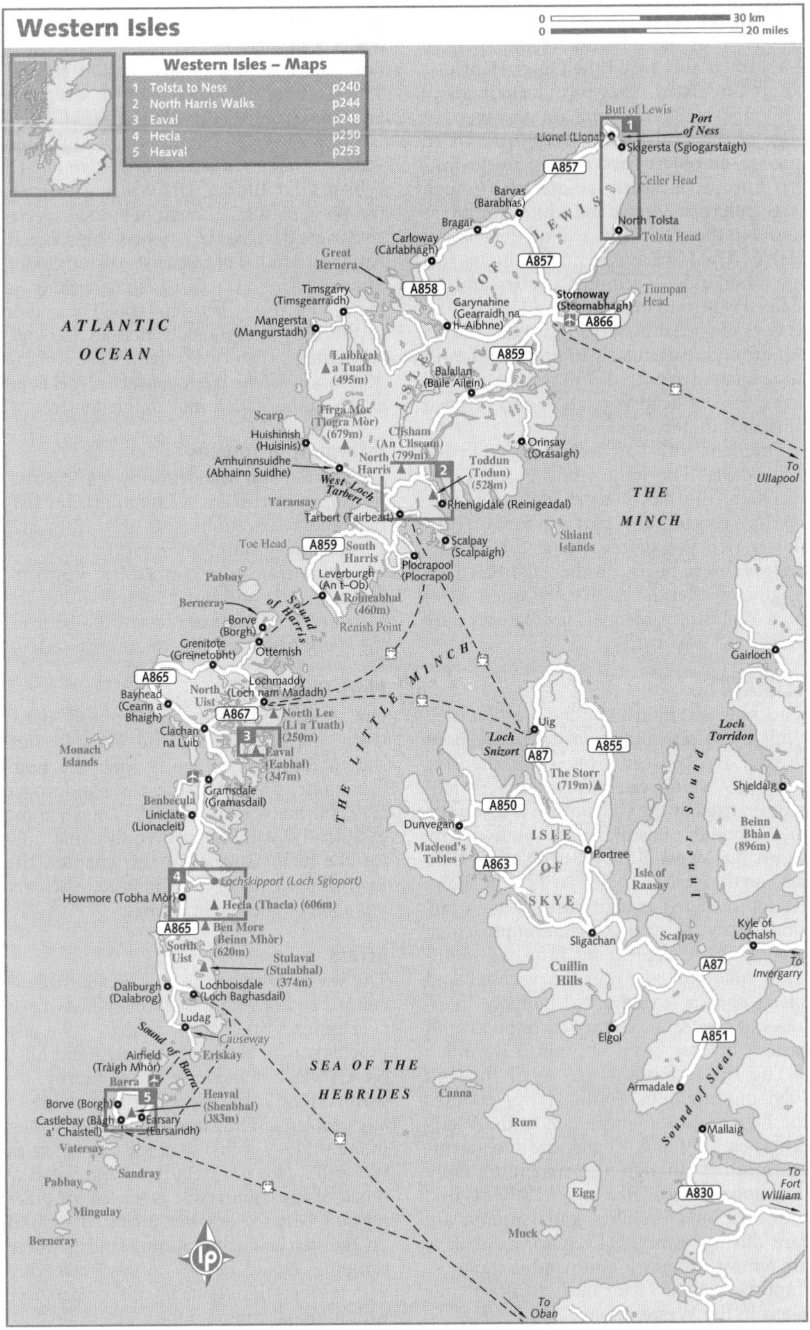
Western Isles
0 30 km
0 20 miles
Western Isles – Maps
1 Tolsta to Ness p240
2 North Harris Walks p244
3 Eaval p248
4 Hecla p250
5 Heaval p253
ATLANTIC OCEAN
THE MINCH
THE LITTLE MINCH
SEA OF THE HEBRIDES
ISLE OF LEWIS
ISLE OF SKYE
Butt of Lewis
Port of Ness
Lionel (Lional)
Skigersta (Sgiogarstaigh)
Celler Head
North Tolsta
Tolsta Head
Barvas (Barabhas)
Bragar
Carloway (Càrlabhagh)
Great Bernera
Timsgarry (Timsgearraidh)
Mangersta (Mangurstadh)
Garynahine (Gearraidh na h-Aibhne)
Stornoway (Steornabhagh)
Tiumpan Head
Laibheal a Tuath (495m)
Balallan (Baile Ailein)
Scarp
Huishinish (Huisinis)
Tirga Mòr (Tiogra Mòr) (679m)
Clisham (An Cliseam) (799m)
North Harris
Amhuinnsuidhe (Abhainn Suidhe)
West Loch Tarbert
Toddun (Todun) (528m)
Orinsay (Orasaigh)
Rhenigidale (Reinigeadal)
Taransay
Tarbert (Tairbeart)
Scalpay (Scalpaigh)
Shiant Islands
Toe Head
South Harris
Plocrapool (Plocrapol)
Pabbay
Leverburgh (An t-Ob)
Roineabhal (460m)
Renish Point
Berneray
Sound of Harris
Borve (Borgh)
Otternish
Grenitote (Greinetobht)
Bayhead (Ceann a Bhaigh)
North Uist
Lochmaddy (Loch nam Madadh)
North Lee (Li a Tuath) (250m)
Clachan na Luib
Eaval (Eabhal) (347m)
Monach Islands
Gramsdale (Gramasdail)
Benbecula
Liniclate (Lionacleit)
Lochskipport (Loch Sgioport)
Howmore (Tobha Mòr)
Hecla (Thacla) (606m)
Ben More (Beinn Mhòr) (620m)
South Uist
Stulaval (Stulabhal) (374m)
Daliburgh (Dalabrog)
Lochboisdale (Loch Baghasdail)
Ludag
Causeway
Sound of Barra
Eriskay
Airfield (Tràigh Mhòr)
Barra
Heaval (Sheabhal) (383m)
Borve (Borgh)
Castlebay (Bàgh a' Chaisteil)
Earsary (Earsairidh)
Vatersay
Sandray
Pabbay
Mingulay
Berneray
Canna
Rum
Eigg
Muck
Uig
Loch Snizort
The Storr (719m)
Dunvegan
Macleod's Tables
Portree
Isle of Raasay
Inner Sound
Loch Torridon
Gairloch
Shieldaig
Beinn Bhàn (896m)
Sligachan
Cuillin Hills
Scalpay
Kyle of Lochalsh
Elgol
Armadale
Sound of Sleat
Mallaig
To Ullapool
To Invergarry
To Fort William
To Oban
A857
A858
A866
A859
A865
A867
A87
A855
A850
A863
A851
A830

ENVIRONMENT

Of the 50 or more islands of the Western Isles, often also called the Outer Hebrides, 12 are populated. They form a chain about 130 miles (209km) long on the western edge of the British Isles. Greyish Lewisian gneiss, the oldest rock type in northwestern Europe, is nearly ubiquitous, though large outcrops of pink and white granite are found in the mountains and on the coast of Harris. The last Ice Age honed the narrow mountain ridges, sculpted corries and U-shaped valleys in hilly areas, and left behind masses of glacial material in valleys and on flat ground. Particularly in northern Lewis, large areas are covered with peat – dark soil composed of dead vegetation and of great botanical importance.

Dramatic cliffs and deep inlets typify the east coasts. The long sandy beaches and machair (the flat, coastal plain, where a mixture of sand and peat produces fertile, flower-rich grasslands, home for numerous species of birds) on the Atlantic coasts originated after the last Ice Age when skeletons of innumerable marine creatures were pulverised into sand.

CLIMATE

One thing is certain about the Western Isles' climate – its variability from day to day, hour to hour and between areas within the isles. Relatively warm water from southern latitudes carried by the Gulf Stream is accompanied by mild, moisture-laden southwesterly winds that expend the greater part of their load on the western coast, leaving only showers for sheltered eastern parts. 'Mare's tail' clouds across the vast sky herald approaching processions of depressions from the southwest, followed by lower, hazy cloud and sheets of rain streaking the horizon. Interludes of dry, calm weather correspond with easterly breezes, bringing summer warmth.

The driest months are April through July; mountainous South Harris endures the highest rainfall anywhere in the Western Isles. July and August are the warmest months, though the maximum only occasionally struggles above 20°C. Gales, prevalent in December and January, are rare during summer. Even so, calm days are almost unknown and wind is the most important single factor likely to affect your plans in the Western Isles.

INFORMATION

Maps & Books

For planning and familiarisation the OS Travel – Road 1:250,000 map No 3 *Western Scotland & the Western Isles* is good.

The Scottish Mountaineering Club's Hill-walkers' Guide *The Islands of Scotland* by DJ Fabian, GE Little and DN Williams includes the Western Isles. Though published several years ago, the basic facts remain unchanged. Among a handful of specialist walking guides, Mike Williams' *Western Isles*, describing 34 mostly shortish walks, stands out. For a guide to the isles' exceptionally rich archaeological heritage, Historic Scotland's *The Ancient Monuments of the Western Isles* by Noel Fojut et al is authoritative and comprehensive.

Information Sources

The official **Visit Hebrides** (www.visithebrides.com) website is useful for accommodation listings and reservations, transport links and general background information.

Public transport timetables, covering flights, ferries and buses to and within the isles, are available from local TICs or from the **Western Isles Council** (www.cne-siar.gov.uk).

Place Names

On street and roadside direction signs, Gaelic names either stand alone or are shown more prominently than the English name. Similarly, the OS Landranger 1:50,000 maps show Gaelic names almost exclusively, with English equivalents only for the major towns. In this chapter, the English place names are followed, wherever possible, by the Gaelic names.

Access

The walks described in this chapter follow defined and/or recognised routes. Elsewhere, as a general rule, you shouldn't strike any problems with access to the coast and hills. Nevertheless, if there's a house nearby, it's worth calling in and checking that there aren't any problems. The same applies to camping in the wild – ask first then leave your site as you find it (see p21). On Barra and Vatersay much of the countryside is fenced for grazing; it's best to seek out unfenced ground on the machair (coastal grasslands), where camping should be OK. Always take care with fences – find a gate or stile, or step over with minimal strain on the wires.

SUNDAY IN THE WESTERN ISLES

The Western Isles is the stronghold in Scotland of the Free Church, its origins lying in a mid-19th-century schism in the Church of Scotland. Later differences led to the establishment of several smaller churches, including the Free Presbyterian Church and the United Free Presbyterians.

Their congregations have built many remarkable churches on Lewis and Harris in particular, standing stolidly against the elements. The Bible is central to their beliefs, which require observance of the Lord's Day, Sunday, as a day of rest and devotion. Consequently, there are no bus services on Sunday, almost all shops and petrol stations are closed and only a handful of hotels provide meals for nonresidents. Some B&B proprietors prefer not to welcome or farewell guests on Sunday. You'll see signs prohibiting sport and even the use of children's playgrounds. However, Stornoway airport handles Sunday flights and the ferry company, CalMac, having desisted from Sunday sailings for decades, was both reviled and praised when it inaugurated services between Harris and Berneray and the Isle of Skye in 2006.

Things are different on South Uist and Barra, where most people adhere to the Roman Catholic faith.

In today's materialistic, sceptical world, these beliefs may seem anachronistic but their adherents in the Western Isles nonetheless deserve respect for their practices.

LEWIS

Lewis (Leodhas) is the most populous of the Western Isles, with Stornoway, the capital, on the east coast and several villages sprawled along the west side. North Lewis' empty hinterland is speckled with myriad lochs surrounded by almost featureless peaty moorland; the south is rockier and hillier. Everywhere the coast is exceptionally scenic, with cliffs punctuated by narrow inlets, bays and sandy beaches.

PLANNING

Guided Walks

The **Royal Society for the Protection of Birds** (RSPB; ☎ 07798 667751) puts on free guided walks on Lewis, usually lasting a couple of hours; details should be available from the Stornoway TIC (p238).

GETTING AROUND

If you're staying for only a few days, hiring a car may be more economical than bringing one on the ferry. Of the several hire companies in and around Stornoway, **Arnol Car Rental** (☎ 01851 710548; www.arnolmotors.com) delivers to the airport and ferry terminal. Small cars cost around £26 per day.

Buses link Stornoway to outlying areas, although you'll need to study the timetable carefully to ensure you aren't stranded late in the day; remember, buses *don't* run on Sunday.

TOLSTA TO NESS

Duration	4–4½ hours
Distance	10 miles (16km)
Difficulty	moderate
Start	Garry Beach
Finish	Skigersta
Nearest Towns	Stornoway (p238), Ness (p239)
Transport	private

Summary Spectacular coastal scenery, remnants of summer shielings, superb views of Sutherland mountains and abundant sea birds.

This walk is inspired by the waymarked route from Garry Beach (Tràigh Ghearadha), north of the village of New Tolsta (Bail' Ur Tholastaidh), north to the district of Ness (Nis) and the village of Skigersta (Sgiogarstaigh). The greater part of the waymarked route stays well inland from the cliff tops, crossing the peaty moorland. Thus it misses the very fine coastal scenery of cliffs, stacks, rock islets and deep inlets (geos) and the companionship of the sea birds – stiff-winged fulmars, skuas, gulls and cormorants. Seals can often be seen basking on the rocks at the foot of the cliffs.

The walk described here leaves the waymarked route early on and stays close to the cliffs, but take care as the cliffs drop vertically into the sea 50m or more below. Although there isn't a continuous path, on the whole the going underfoot is across grassland with only a few boggy patches. At either end of the walk, the way is along minor vehicle tracks, used for access to peat diggings or for gathering sheep. The walk can be done in either direction – there's not much to differentiate.

Alternative An out-and-back walk from Garry Beach to Dibidale (Dhiobadail) would take in the best of the coastal scenery and the easiest going underfoot. The distance is 10 miles (16km), for which you should allow at least four hours.

HISTORY

During this walk you'll see evidence of strikingly different aspects of Lewis' history. Precariously situated on cliff tops are the remains of at least two Iron Age promontory forts, Dùn Othail and Dùn Filiscleitir (c 500 BC). Similarly located, atop a rock stack at the southern end of Garry Beach, is Caisteal a' Mhorair (Mormaer's Castle), probably dating from the 13th century.

Shieling settlements have been an integral part of island life; there are three along the route of this walk. Shielings (small stone cottages), some quite elaborate, some pretty basic, provided shelter while islanders were fishing or tending and gathering sheep.

Lord Leverhulme, a wealthy English magnate, bought Lewis and Harris in 1918 and launched ambitious plans to provide jobs for all, mainly by developing the fishing industry. One of his many projects was building a road from Tolsta to Port of Ness, but it only got as far as Abhainn na Cloich, barely 3 miles out. Two fine bridges survive as memorials to the scale of his vision. He ran into opposition from landless soldiers returning from WWI, for whom possession of land was more important than modern fishing ports. Then, finding himself in deep financial difficulties, Leverhulme offered Lewis to its people; apart from Stornoway, there were very few takers. He died in 1925.

PLANNING

Maps

The OS Landranger 1:50,000 map No 8 *Stornoway & North Lewis* covers the walk and shows the waymarked route. Alternatively, use OS Explorer 1:25,000 No 460 *North Lewis*.

NEAREST TOWNS

Stornoway (Steornabhagh)

☎ 01851 / pop 6000

Far and away the largest town in the Western Isles, Stornoway is anything but a metropolis and feels very much like a country town. When making your plans, remember that some B&B hosts prefer not to welcome or farewell guests on Sunday and that shops are closed on Sunday (see the boxed text on p237); some may also be closed on part or all of Wednesday. The sole exception is the **Sandwick Rd filling station** (🕑 10am-4pm Sun).

Stornoway TIC (☎ 703088; info@visithebrides.com; 26 Cromwell St) stocks maps, books and public transport timetables and can make accommodation reservations.

Baltic Bookshop (☎ 702802; 8 Cromwell St) is particularly good for local references, and sells maps as well.

One of the very few places in the Western Isles where you can buy gas canisters for camping stoves is **Sportsworld** (☎ 705464; 1-3 Francis St).

SLEEPING & EATING

Laxdale Holiday Park (☎ 703234; www.laxdaleholidaypark.com; 6 Laxdale Lane; unpowered/powered sites for 2 £8/10, dm £12), about 1.5 miles north of Stornoway, has plenty of camping space. The compact bunkhouse has four-person rooms and a kitchen, and there's a barbecue area.

Stornoway Backpackers (☎ 703628; www.stornoway-hostel.co.uk; 47 Keith St; dm £10) is only five minutes' walk from the ferry, in a traditional cottage. The rooms certainly aren't cramped and a light breakfast is thrown in.

Dunroamin B&B (☎ 704578; www.dunroaminbandb.co.uk; 18 Plantation Rd; s/d £25/56, dinner £15) is centrally located, and serves a particularly good breakfast.

An Leabharlann Coffee Shop (☎ 708631; 19 Cromwell St; mains to £3; 🕑 10am-5pm Mon-Sat; 💻), an extension of the public library, serves a wide variety of snacks and offers excellent value for money.

Thai Cafe (☎ 701811; 27 Church St; mains £6-8; 🕑 lunch & dinner Mon-Sat) is a real find on the far side of the Minch, with genuine, quality Thai cuisine; bring your own drinks.

Stornoway Balti House (☎ 706116; 24 South Beach; mains £7-12; 🕑 lunch & dinner) is a Stornoway institution. Its extensive menu has something for everyone with a taste for curries and the like.

SHORT WALK

The gently undulating coastal fringe of west Lewis spills over into an intricately indented coastline, cluttered with stacks, precipitous clefts, small coves and beaches. The waymarked **West Side Coastal Walk** from Bragar to Garenin explores the most impressive stretch, the best of which lies between the villages of Dalbeg (Dialbeag) and Garenin (Gearrannan), a 4-mile (6.3km) walk; allow two hours. Use either OS Landranger 1:50,000 map No 8 or OS Explorer 1:25,000 map No 460. There are car parks at the end of the Dalbeg road (off the A858) and about 1.5 miles northwest of Carloway (on the A858) near the entrance to **Na Gearrannan Blackhouse Village** (☎ 01851 643416; www.gearrannan.com; ⌚ May-Sep). Lived in until the early 1970s, this village has been faithfully restored and is well worth a visit, as is the **Blackhouse Café and Restaurant** (☎ 07921 854470; breakfast £3, lunch £5, dinner mains £11-13; ⌚ café 10am-5pm Mon-Sat, restaurant dinner Thu-Sat). Here too is the **Garenin Hebridean Hostel** (www.syha.org.uk; dm £8), in one of the restored cottages.

From the Dalbeg car park walk up the road to a sharp left bend; cross a footbridge below to the right and begin to follow green waymarker posts, generally along a fence on the seaward side, well inland. The route crosses undulating countryside and descends to Dalmore (where there are toilets). Go up steps beside the more recent of the two cemeteries. Soon, excellent views north open up. Cross a wide, shallow glen, pass a rocky cove and climb, mostly close to the coast, on firm dry ground. Then come more undulations and the route passes the deep inlet of Fibhig, its cliffs busy with sea birds. With fine views in abundance, continue generally west and southwest, then south. Descend across a shallow glen, go up to a crest then down to Garenin village.

For self-caterers there's a Somerfield supermarket opposite the exit from the ferry terminal, and two Co-op supermarkets, one opposite the TIC and the other at the northern end of town.

GETTING THERE & AWAY

Fares on the following routes vary widely between seasons and days of the week.

British Airways/Loganair (☎ 0870 850 9850; www.britishairways.com) operates flights from Glasgow (one hour, four flights Monday to Saturday) and Inverness (40 minutes, four flights Monday to Saturday).

British Midland (☎ 08706 070555; www.flybmi.com) flies daily from Edinburgh (1¼ hours).

Eastern Airways (☎ 08703 669100; www.easternairways.com) links Aberdeen and Stornoway (one hour, daily Monday to Friday). **Highland Airways** (☎ 0845 450 2245; www.highlandairways.co.uk) operates between Inverness and Stornoway (40 minutes, three flights Monday to Saturday).

Caledonian MacBrayne (CalMac; ☎ 08705 650000; www.calmac.co.uk) operates a ferry service between Ullapool and Stornoway (passenger/vehicle £12/56, 2¾ hours, at least two daily Monday to Saturday). Island Hopscotch fares will save you considerable sums of money if you're making more than one crossing.

Scottish Citylink (☎ 0870 550 5050; www.citylink.co.uk) bus services from Edinburgh, Glasgow and Inverness connect with the ferries at Ullapool.

Ness (Nis)

☎ 01851

Ness is a district rather than a particular village. Its several villages, with few facilities, are scattered along the northernmost miles of the A857.

SLEEPING & EATING

Galson Farm Guest House (☎ 850492; www.galsonfarm.freeserve.co.uk; South Galson; dm/s/d £9/45/80, evening meal £20) is a beautifully restored property a short distance from the A857, 6 miles (10km) southwest of Lionel. Rooms in the guesthouse are large and luxurious; the small bunkhouse has a kitchen.

The **Cross Inn** (☎ 810152; Port of Ness; bar meal mains to £10) is the nearest pub for refreshments after the walk.

The nearest shop to the end of the walk is a licensed grocer at Swainbost (Suainebost), about 1.5 miles southwest along the A857 from its junction at Lionel (Lional) with the B8015 Skigersta road.

GETTING THERE & AWAY

Galson Motors (☎ 840269) runs bus service W1 between Stornoway and Port of Ness (£3,

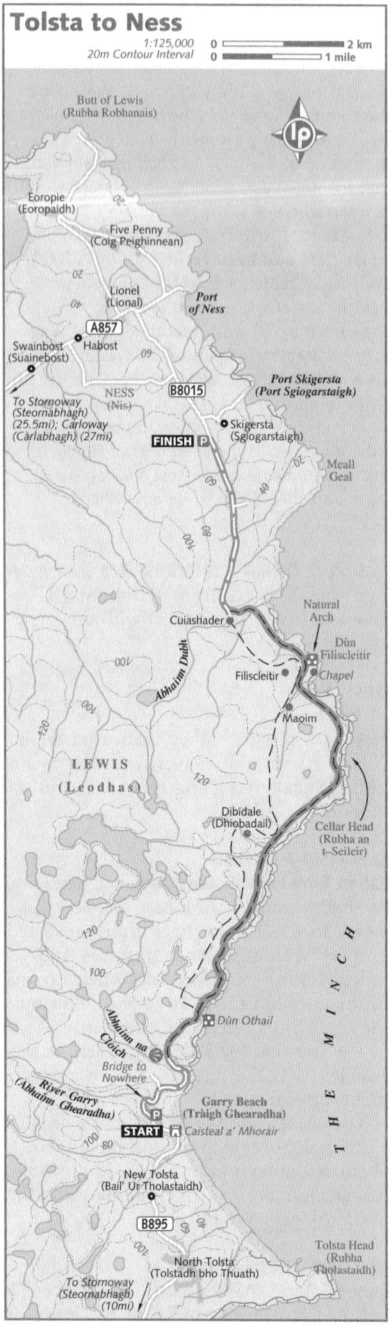

one hour, at least four services Monday to Saturday).

GETTING TO/FROM THE WALK

Western Isles Council (Comhairle nan Eilean Siar; ☎ 709747) operates bus service W5 from Stornoway to the village of New Tolsta (£2, 50 minutes, Monday to Saturday). To reach the start of the walk from New Tolsta, simply walk north out of the village along the main (and only) road; it descends quite steeply to sea level and parallels the coast to the car park above Garry Beach, 800m from the village.

By car, follow the A857 north from Stornoway for just over 1 mile to Newmarket. Turn right along the B895 and follow it to the car park above Garry Beach, about 800m beyond New Tolsta.

From the car park at the end of the walk near Skigersta it is 2 miles along the B8015 to the junction with the A857 at Lionel. **Galson Motors** (☎ 840269) buses on service W1 stop at Lionel en route to Stornoway (£3, one hour, every two hours weekday afternoons, one service Saturday afternoon).

THE WALK

From the car park at Garry Beach set out along the rough, sealed road as it dips down to cross the incongruous Bridge to Nowhere across River Garry (Abhainn Ghearadha). Past the river, the road becomes more of a vehicle track heading to the coast. From here, on a clear day, some of the Sutherland peaks can be seen across the Minch. Beyond the concrete bridge across Abhainn na Cloich (where the waterfall is best seen slightly downstream), the route is marked by green posts with a yellow band. After about 50m the driest ground should be upslope from the marked route, leading northeast across moorland. Aim for a post on a heathery knoll and pick up the path on the seaward side of the knoll. A little further on, past **Dùn Othail**, a prehistoric fort on a rocky promontory, the waymarked route swings away from the coast to cross the moor. Instead, stick to the much more scenic coast where more-or-less-continuous paths, made by sheep and walkers, follow the cliff tops. The panorama of mountains across the eastern skyline changes constantly as you move north.

After nearly 2 miles of fine walking above the crinkled coastal cliffs, you come to the ruins of a stone cottage on a grassy knoll (about 1¾ hours from the start). The knoll overlooks the steep-sided glen of **Dibidale**, the site of a shieling village. Drop down to cross the burn at a confluence, following waymarker posts, and climb steeply up the other side to a cluster of ruined shielings. The marked route continues its inland course. If you're pursuing the independent coastal way, you'll find that the path of sorts is much less obvious from here, across grassland and above the many spectacular geos in the cliff line.

Turn inland to cross the next sizable stream below the place shown as Maoim on the OS map. Here you might find, and wonder about, the remains of a cluster of curious stone structures built into the steep slope near the burn. Up the other side you come to the remains of a tiny chapel, built in the 1920s for the residents of the surrounding village of **Filiscleitir** (about two hours from Dibidale). Dùn Filiscleitir occupies an improbable site at the cliff edge, overlooking a spectacular **natural arch**. Here you can rejoin the marked route, following a vehicle track that leads inland, or stay with the coast to Abhainn Dubh then heading west to reach the vehicle track at the former shieling village of **Cuiashader**. From here it's about an hour's walk to the parking area at the end of the sealed road near the village of Skigersta.

HARRIS

Harris (Na Hearadh) adjoins Lewis, occupying the southern third of their island. Its name probably comes from an old Norse word that means 'the higher parts'. The Lewis/Harris boundary runs through Loch Seaforth, across Loch Langavat's southern end and west along the northern shores of Loch Resort.

Rock is the overwhelming feature of the landscape – there's plenty of water too, in freshwater and sea lochs, but it's the surreal, glaciated moonscapes that distinguish Harris from the rest of the isles. The north of Harris is wilder and more mountainous, with Clisham (799m) being the highest peak in the Western Isles, and several other 700m-plus mountains towering over long, deep glens and remote lochs. South Harris has plenty of respectable, though lower, mountains and is renowned for the magnificence of its west-coast beaches and machair.

This section describes two walks in north Harris, one following a historic path to an isolated settlement, with high- and low-level options, and the other to Clisham. There are more suggestions in the boxed texts on p246 and on p254.

PLANNING

Guided Walks

The **RSPB** (☎ 07798 667751) runs free guided walks on Harris, usually lasting a couple of hours; details should be available from the Tarbert TIC (p242).

RHENIGIDALE PATH

Duration	4–4¼ hours
Distance	7 miles (11km)
Difficulty	moderate
Start/Finish	Lacasdale Lochs bridge
Nearest Towns	Tarbert (p242), Rhenigidale (p243)
Transport	bus

Summary Follow a historic path through magnificent mountain and coast scenery to the isolated hamlet of Rhenigidale, with the chance to explore a deserted village or climb the rugged peak of Toddun.

Until 1990 Rhenigidale village (Reinigeadal) could only be reached on foot along rough paths, which were hazardous in winter, or by boat. The new road over the mountains made life much easier for the residents, but perhaps took away some of the magic of the place for visitors. Most of the old path survives and provides an outstandingly scenic walk up and over a rugged ridge and steeply down to the shores of Loch Trolamaraig. The path is easy enough to follow, although boggy and rocky in places; around 400m of ascent is involved.

Rhenigidale sits on the northern shore of Loch Trolamaraig and close to the entrance to Loch Seaforth, which bites deep into the interior of Harris. In the sheltered northwestern corner of Loch Trolamaraig is a luxuriant botanical oasis (by Harris standards) with willow, aspen and fragile primroses, protected from the wind and nourished by a rushing stream.

HERBERT GATLIFF – VISIONARY

Herbert Gatliff, an Englishman born near the end of the 19th century, dedicated most of his life to young people and the youth-hostel movement. He discovered the Western Isles in the late 1940s and was completely captivated; annual visits followed for the next 20 years. Convinced that the isles were the ideal place to establish simple hostels, he tried unsuccessfully to persuade the SYHA to extend its empire.

Undaunted, Gatliff seized an opportunity to open a hostel at Rhenigidale. An empty thatched cottage was soon made ready and opened in Easter 1962, when access was only on foot or by boat. Howmore Hostel, also a thatched cottage, followed in 1964. The next year, a hostel was opened on the island of Scarp (off Harris' west coast) but it closed in 1969 when the islanders moved across to Harris.

Herbert Gatliff died in 1977 but his work is carried on by the Gatliff Trust, in partnership with the local crofters who own the hostel buildings. In 1987 the SYHA adopted the hostels, the main benefit being publicity. Running of the hostels stayed with the crofters and the **Gatliff Hebridean Hostels Trust** (www.gatliff.org.uk; 30 Francis St, Stornoway).

The four Hebridean hostels – Garenin, Rhenigidale, Berneray and Howmore – provide no-frills accommodation with basic facilities, including heating (although not central heating), and an indefinable atmosphere of camaraderie and freedom.

Alternatives Using Rhenigidale as a base, there's scope for at least two walks in the vicinity. This first is to Toddun (Todun; 528m), wedge-shaped and precipitous, but a surprisingly approachable peak. Standing apart from the main north Harris mountains, Toddun affords spectacular all-round views (see p244).

You can make it a full day by descending west from Toddun, about 150m north of the summit. From the glen below, continue over An Reithe, from where a broad gully, cutting diagonally across its western face, leads down to the southern end of Loch an Reithe. Then it's over Stralaval (Strathabhal; 389m) and down to the path in lonely Glen Lacasdale, which provides an easy stroll down to the Tarbert–Scalpay road, about 800m west of the start of the path to Rhenigidale. This option takes six hours to cover the 11 miles (18km) and involves 1010m of ascent.

Another possibility is to visit the deserted settlement of Molinginish (Molingeanais), perched above Loch Trolamaraig opposite Rhenigidale (see p244). This walk could be incorporated in the return to Lacasdale Lochs, in which case the overall distance is 8.5 miles (13.5km).

HISTORY

Rhenigidale originated in the 1820s as a new home for crofters evicted from the Forest of Harris (estate), the area along the Huishinish (Huisinis) road (B887) west of Tarbert. Early in the 20th century around 90 people lived in Rhenigidale, occupying 17 houses, most of which are still standing. They were expert boat handlers as all their supplies, including peat (for fuel) and seaweed (for fertiliser), had to be shipped in from Tarbert.

Molinginish was settled around the same time as Rhenigidale; at least 12 families lived there, enough to support a school. The village was abandoned in 1965.

PLANNING

Maps

Consult either OS Explorer 1:25,000 No 456 *North Harris* or OS Landranger 1:50,000 map No 14 *Tarbert & Loch Seaforth*.

NEAREST TOWNS

Tarbert (Tairbeart)

☎ 01859 / pop 480

The main town on Harris, Tarbert straddles a narrow neck of land between north and south Harris, with the Atlantic Ocean to the west and the Minch to the east. Leverburgh, a small village on the south coast, has an interesting history connected with Lord Leverhulme (p238), and is another accommodation possibility.

Tarbert's **TIC** (☎ 502011; tarbert@visithebrides.com; Pier Rd), near the ferry terminal, opens for late-arriving ferries. It stocks maps and a small range of books and can help with accommodation reservations. A useful resource for Leverburgh is the local website, www.leverburgh.co.uk.

Harris Tweed Shop (☎ 502493; Main St) carries books on Harris and the other Western Isles. *Harris in History & Legend* by Bill Lawson, the well-known local expert, provides an excellent introduction to the area.

SLEEPING & EATING

There are no formal camping grounds on Harris; the nearest is in Stornoway on the Isle of Lewis.

Am Bothan Bunkhouse (☎ 520251; www.ambothan.com; Ferry Rd, Leverburgh; dm £14), 20 miles southwest of the town, is easily the best hostel on Harris, especially if you're heading for the Berneray ferry. Facilities are excellent.

Avalon Guest House (☎ 502334; www.avalonguesthouse.org; 12 West Side; s/d £28/50, evening meal £15) has a fine outlook over inner Loch Tarbert. Though small, rooms are well equipped.

Ceol na Mara (☎ 502464; www.ceolnamara.com; 7 Direcleit; s/d £35/60, dinner £20) is a few miles south of Tarbert, in a superb location, and comes highly recommended as setting the standard for all B&Bs.

Firstfruits (☎ 502439; Pier Rd; lunch mains £4-7, dinner mains £7; lunch Mon-Sat, dinner Tue-Fri), opposite the TIC, is an excellent cottage tearoom and restaurant. You need to book for dinner – the menu changes daily and always includes a vegetarian dish. Bring your own drinks; corkage is not charged.

Clisham Keel Restaurant (☎ 502364; Pier Rd; mains £8-17; lunch & dinner), in the Macleod Motel opposite the ferry terminal, has standard fare, with seafood and steak specialities. Vegetarian dishes rise above the ordinary and bottled Hebridean ales are available.

Munro's off-licence grocery has a butcher section.

GETTING THERE & AWAY

CalMac (☎ 08706 650000; www.calmac.co.uk) runs daily ferries between Uig on the Isle of Skye and Tarbert (passenger/car £9/39, 1¾ hours). Coming from North Uist, you'll sail on the CalMac ferry via a fascinating route across the islet-studded Sound of Harris from Berneray to Leverburgh (passenger/car £6/25, one hour, up to four daily).

Hebridean Transport (☎ 01851 705050) bus service W10 links Stornoway with Tarbert (£3, one hour, four services Monday to Saturday) and Leverburgh.

Tarbert is 37 miles (59km) from Stornoway along the A859, almost all of which is a good two-lane road.

Rhenigidale (Reinigeadal)

The only place to stay in Rhenigidale is the **Rhenigidale Hostel** (www.syha.org.uk; dm £8), simple accommodation with a special tranquillity. You need to come self-contained with a sleeping bag and supplies; there isn't a shop in the village. As a Gatliff Hebridean hostel (see the boxed text, opposite), bookings are not accepted – first come, first served. The nearest telephone is at the Maaruig (Màraig) junction, less than 1 mile down the Rhenigidale road from the A859 and 2.5 miles from Rhenigidale.

GETTING THERE & AWAY

Rhenigidale is at the end (about 3 miles) of a minor road, which branches from the A859 between Ardvourlie (Aird a' Mhulaidh) and the B887 junction.

Harris Car Services (☎ 01859 502221) operates a minibus service between Rhenigidale and Tarbert Pier (£2, 30 minutes, two services Monday to Saturday). Seats are limited and must be booked the night before for the morning run, or by 3pm latest for the late-afternoon service.

GETTING TO/FROM THE WALK

The walk starts and finishes at a car park (signposted 'To Youth Hostel') on the Tarbert–Scalpay (Scalpaigh) road, just across the bridge over the stream flowing out of Lacasdale Lochs, 2 miles from Tarbert.

Scalpay Community Minibus (☎ 01859 540356) does the run between Tarbert and Scalpay, passing the start of the walk (£1, five minutes, four services Monday to Saturday).

THE WALK

Map p244

From the car park the track starts to climb almost straightaway, near the tumbling Abhainn an t-Sratha. After about 40 minutes you reach a fairly broad saddle (where there's a large cairn) on the long ridge between Beinn a' Chaolais to the south and Trolamul to the north. Within five minutes, you pass a neat cairn on the right, marking the start of the path to Molinginish (see the Side Trip on p244). The Rhenigidale path soon copes with the extremely steep drop to the shore of **Loch Trolamaraig** in a series of extraordinary zigzags, through broken cliffs lower down, to a bridge across Abhainn Cheann a' Locha, the stream in rugged Glen Trolamaraig, with a shingle beach nearby (25 minutes from the saddle).

The path rises sharply from the bridge but soon heads down across the spur to a gated stream crossing. Continue up, soon past the silent remains of the village of **Garry-aloteger** (Gearraidh Lotaigear), with substantial stone cottages and stone-walled enclosures. The low, parallel ridges in the nearby fields were 'lazy beds' – humps laboriously created by hauling loads of seaweed to enrich the poor soil for the cultivation of potatoes and animal fodder. From here it's a short distance along the narrow, grassed path cut into the slope, up to the road. **Rhenigidale** is barely 800m down the road (about 50 minutes from the shingle beach). Return to Lacasdale Lochs bridge by the same route.

SIDE TRIP: TODDUN

3 hours, 4 miles (6.5km), 550m ascent

From the road west of Rhenigidale, follow the path signposted to Urgha and Tarbert (the path followed on the main walk), through the remains of Garry-aloteger, across a bridge and leave the path 10m further on. Walk north up the broad spur to a fence; bear left and follow it generally west until you meet a fence running north-south. Cross this fence then climb to the well-defined ridge and follow it generally northwest, shortly crossing another fence. Keep to the highest ground – it's surprisingly easy to find a way up through the scattered crags to the summit ridge. Go on to the survey cairn sheltered by a circular stone wall on the summit of **Toddun** (an hour from the main path). Among many other places, you can gaze upon the mountainous massif to the north, dominated by Clisham; the Shiant Islands to the east; and the South Uist 'hills' to the south. Retrace your steps to Rhenigidale.

SIDE TRIP: MOLINGINISH

3 hours, 5 miles (8km), 150m ascent

Follow the approach path from the road west of Rhenigidale, to go down past Garry-aloteger and on to the bridge over Abhainn

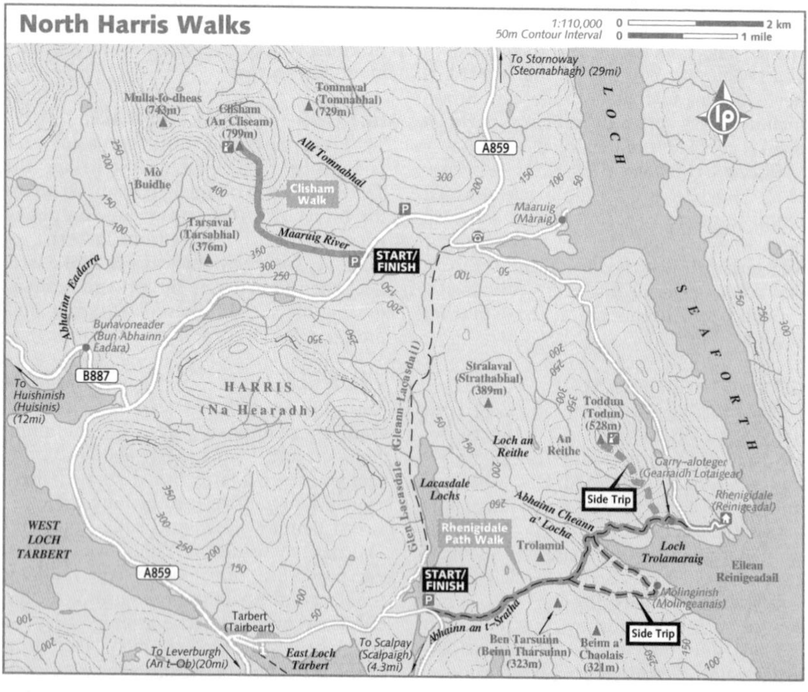

Cheann a' Locha. The Molinginish path takes off a short distance up from the shingle beach and soon becomes clear as it cuts across the precipitous slope; it's narrow, rocky and boggy in places. The second stream crossing needs *great care*, making use of slender rocky ledges. After about 35 minutes the path starts to descend and suddenly the ruined and roofed cottages of Molinginish materialise, crammed into a small, partly sheltered glen right down to the edge of the shingle beach, with the lazy beds above.

For the walk through to Lacasdale Lochs (or to make a round walk back to Rhenigidale), cross the burn and pick up the track through a large gap in the fence across the slope. The track is wide and still in good condition, with few bogs to negotiate as it rises west across the moorland. Allow about 30 minutes up to the saddle and the cairned junction with the main Rhenigidale path.

CLISHAM

Duration	3½–4 hours
Distance	4 miles (6.5km)
Difficulty	moderate
Start/Finish	Maaruig River bridge
Nearest Town	Tarbert (p242)
Transport	bus

Summary The Western Isles' highest peak – a steep, rocky, straightforward ascent for superb all-round views of peaks, lochs and deep glens.

Clisham (An Cliseam; 799m/2622ft) is well worth climbing for the exceptional views on the clear, not-too-windy days that do happen from time to time on Harris. The meaning and derivation of its name is uncertain, but an educated opinion has it being of Norse origin and possibly meaning 'rocky cliff'.

The peak dominates a complex array of narrow, granitic ridges and peaks rising steeply from the western shore of Loch Seaforth and overlooking West Loch Tarbert to the southwest. To the west, Clisham's massif is separated from another magnificently rugged group of peaks by a long, deep, north–south glen.

The conventional approach up the southeastern ridge from the A859 is straightforward, although almost unrelentingly steep; the total ascent is 640m. There is a clear enough path over some of the lower, boggy ground and high on the main ridge. If the ground is seriously wet, a recommended variation is the spur of the southern side of Maaruig River, a steep climb to a point west of the rocky bluff of Sròn Carsaclett. Then head northwest and west to gain the steep slopes of Clisham itself.

Alternative Experienced and agile walkers can take a different approach, from Bunavoneader (Bun Abhainn Eadara) on the Huishinish road, via Mó Buidhe, Mullafo-dheas (743m) and the scrambly ridge east to Clisham, returning via Tarsaval.

PLANNING

Maps

Use either OS Explorer 1:25,000 map No 456 *North Harris* or OS Landranger 1:50,000 map No 14 *Tarbert & Loch Seaforth.*

GETTING TO/FROM THE WALK

The walk starts at a parking area on the northern side of the A859 at the Maaruig River bridge, about 1 mile west of the turn-off to Rhenigidale. The **Hebridean Transport** (☎ 01851 705050) bus on the Stornoway–Tarbert–Leverburgh service (see p243) stops at the Rhenigidale turn-off.

THE WALK

Map p244

From the car park a slightly muddy path leads generally northwest, tending west, above the Maaruig River. The path isn't always easy to follow but it's not difficult to make your way up to the broad saddle at the foot of Clisham's steep southern slopes. From here, make good use of grassy leads northwards among the boulders and scree to gain the skyline ridge, gradually changing direction to climb northwest.

Once the ridge narrows and becomes distinct, a clear path materialises and leads along the slender rocky spine to the compact summit of **Clisham**; the survey (trig) cairn is surrounded by a sheltering stone wall (about 1½ hours from the start). On a good day there isn't much of the Western Isles you can't see from here, and the view extends east to the more prominent peaks in Wester Ross and Sutherland. Return to the start by the same route – more or less!

SHORT WALK

The peninsula at the southwestern extremity of north Harris, sheltering **Hushinish** (Huisinis), offers scenic, low-level walking along the rugged coast, with fine views of the uninhabited island of Scarp. A 5-mile (8km) walk following an old track to secluded beaches can painlessly last all day in good weather. Access is via the B887 from the A859 (2.5 miles north of Tarbert); it ends at a car park (with toilets) 14 miles (22.5km) west. A **Western Isles Council** (☎ 01859 502213) bus runs between Hushinish and Tarbert (£2, 45 minutes, three services Monday to Friday during school terms, two services Tuesday and Friday during school holidays). Use OS Landranger 1:50,000 map No 13.

Begin by following a sandy vehicle track north to the coast; go through a gate to the east at the seaward end of a fence and the old track soon becomes clear. It crosses the steep, rugged hillside, close to a sheer drop to the sea in places, then traverses a potentially marshy saddle. From here it virtually disappears. Descend to the shore of Loch na Cleavag and go on past a white cottage, across drier ground to Loch Cravadale; the sandy beach at the head of the loch is a few minutes south. To continue, cross Loch na Cleavag's outlet then follow its northern shore west. From the northwest corner, near a tiny beach, head northwest across the short grassy sward to the beautiful creamy white sands of Tràigh Mheilein. Walk southwest then turn inland near a knot of sheep pens. Make your way across country, over the crusty hill (Gresclett) from where it's a short descent to the saddle where you rejoin the outward route to return to Hushinish.

NORTH UIST

At first North Uist (Uibhist a Tuath) seems to comprise just water separated by scraps of rock and soil. But there is actually lots of dry ground (mainly in the northwestern quarter), some small but attractive mountains, miles of magnificent beaches on the north coast and a rugged eastern coastline. Beyond the principal town of Lochmaddy (Loch nam Madadh), which takes its name from the extraordinary, island-studded sea loch, there are a few villages on the western side and many houses and crofts scattered in between. North Uist's identity as an island is perhaps slightly compromised by the modern, but extremely convenient, causeways linking it to Berneray (Bearnaraigh) in the north and Grimsay (Griomasaigh) and Benbecula (Beinn na Faoghla) in the south.

PLANNING

Guided Walks

Check at the Lochmaddy TIC (opposite) for details of the **RSPB's** (☎ 0779 504 7294) summer program of guided walks on North Uist.

Information Sources

The community website www.uistonline.com is a useful source of information about the island and includes accommodation listings.

GETTING THERE & AWAY

British Regional Airlines (☎ 0870 850 9850; www.britishairways.com) inter-island flights from Stornoway land at Benbecula airport, between North and South Uist (two flights Monday to Friday). **British Airways/Loganair** flies between Glasgow and Barra via Benbecula (two flights Monday to Friday). **Highland Airways** (☎ 0845 450 2245; www.highlandairways.co.uk) flies daily between Benbecula and Inverness. Buses meet most flights to take you to Lochboisdale or Lochmaddy for onward connections north or south.

EAVAL

Duration	3½–4 hours
Distance	8 miles (13km)
Difficulty	moderate
Start/Finish	Drim Sidinish
Nearest Towns	Lochmaddy (opposite), Clachan na Luib (opposite)
Transport	private

Summary The highest peak in North Uist gives a superb panoramic view of the maze of lochans and land that comprise the Uists, and as far south as the Isle of Rum.

At 347m (1138ft), Eaval is famous for sometimes featuring on the route of the Hebridean Challenge, an annual team marathon from Barra to Lewis, involving running, cycling and kayaking. Consequently, there's a clear, if often muddy, path all the way from the end of the Locheport road at Drim Sidinish (Druim Saighdinis). It might not be particularly high but the summit affords outstanding views near and far. The unavoidable causeway not far from the start should be dry except after heavy rain and at very high tide. The walk described involves 350m of ascent and is a simple out-and-back route.

The name Eaval, from two Norse words *ey fjall*, meaning 'island fell' or 'hill', accurately describes its situation. With the waters of Loch Obisary (Obasaraigh) and several smaller lochs on three sides, and Loch Eport (Euphort) and the open sea also nearby, Eaval is almost an island. Rising steeply on all sides, it dominates the south-eastern corner of North Uist.

Alternative With suitable transport arrangements, a through walk is possible, descending southwest from the summit to the shore of the narrow strait between North Uist and Grimsay. You can then work your way around the long, deep inlet of Oban nam Muca-mara and finally head cross-country to the end of a minor road at Cladach Chairinis, which is about 1 mile from the A865.

PLANNING

Maps & BOOKS

Eaval is on the OS Landranger 1:50,000 map No 22 *Benbecula & South Uist*; the adjoining map to the north, No 18 *Sound of Harris & St Kilda*, is useful for orientation and identification of local landmarks. Alternatively, use OS Explorer 1:25,000 map No 454 *North Uist & Benbecula*.

North Uist in History & Legend by widely published Bill Lawson is both informative and entertaining.

NEAREST TOWNS

Lochmaddy (Loch nam Madadh)

☎ 01876

A quiet village on the east coast enjoying a superbly scenic setting beside the islet-studded loch, Lochmaddy is the port for North Uist.

The **TIC** (☎ 500321; lochmaddy@visithebrides.com) opens for late ferry arrivals and has a pretty good range of books and maps.

SLEEPING & EATING

Lochmaddy Hotel (☎ 500331; www.lochmaddyhotel.co.uk; s/d £51/96, mains £8-12; lunch & dinner), a traditional building on the outside, up-to-date within, specialises in seafood.

Taigh Chearsabhagh (☎ 500293; mains £2-4; 10am-5pm Mon-Sat;) is a museum, arts centre, café and community meeting place rolled into one. The café offers brilliant home baking and great coffee.

There's a small grocer's shop near the post office.

GETTING THERE & AWAY

CalMac (☎ 08705 650000; www.calmac.co.uk) operates the ferry to and from Uig on the Isle of Skye (passenger/car £10/46, 1¾ hours, at least three daily). Coming from South Harris, catch the small CalMac vehicle ferry from Leverburgh to Berneray (passenger/car £6/25, one hour, up to four daily).

Various bus companies operate between Berneray and Lochmaddy, with connections southwards; for details consult the **Western Isles Council** (www.cne-siar.gov.uk) guide to *Bus and Ferry Services, Uist and Barra*.

By road, Lochmaddy is on the A865, 6 miles (9.5km) from Otternish and 50 miles (80km) from Lochboisdale.

Clachan na Luib

☎ 01876

Clachan na Luib is a scattering of houses around a major road junction (A867 and A865), 7.5 miles (12km) south of Lochmaddy, at a point where North Uist is almost split in two. There's plenty of accommodation to the northwest, along the A865, and south towards Grimsay and Benbecula. The following is just a tiny selection.

SLEEPING & EATING

Shell Bay Caravan & Camping Site (☎ 01870 602447; shellbaylin@aol.com; Liniclate, Benbecula; unpowered/powered sites for 2 £12/14) on the southwest coast of the island of Benbecula, is the nearest camp site and has good facilities.

Taigh Mo Sheanair (☎ 580246; carnach@amserve.net; Carnach; dm £14;) means 'my grandfather's house' in Gaelic, as the owner proudly proclaims. It's a comfortable hostel, right beside a lovely sandy beach west of Clachan na Luib.

Temple View Hotel (☎ 580676; www.templeviewhotel.co.uk; Carinish; s/d £50/90, mains £8-15; lunch &

dinner), more than a century old, beside the main road, has beautifully furnished rooms. Local seafood is a speciality in the comfortable lounge diner.

The small licensed Clachan Stores at Clachan na Luib sells maps and sandwiches. There is a larger Co-op supermarket at Sollas on the north coast.

GETTING TO/FROM THE WALK

The walk starts at the end of the B894, which branches off the A867 800m northeast of the A867/A865 junction at Clachan na Luib, or 6.7 miles (11km) southwest along the A867 from its junction with the A865 near Lochmaddy. The road end is 5 miles (8km) from the A867.

THE WALK

From the car park go through a gate beside the nearby cottage. Cross a field, through another gate and then follow an old track, which leads down to a small cove with an old stone pier on Loch Eport. Head east on a grass track to a larger cove, with a ruined cottage on the far shore, and on to a boulder causeway. From here continue southeast towards the prominent bulk of Buraval (Burabhal). A path, easy to follow most of the way, leads above the very convoluted shores of **Loch Obisary** and across the lowermost slopes of Buraval.

Cross the boggy ground between the northern end of Loch Surtavat and the corner of Loch Obisary to the foot of the spur falling precipitously to the north. Broad ribs of rock make for a surprisingly easy, although consistently steep, climb. About two hours from the start you should reach the trig point on the summit of **Eaval**. The panoramic vista takes in an extraordinary range of features – the north Harris 'hills', the Black Cuillins on Skye and an incredible mosaic of rock, grass, water and scattered houses.

On the return it's much easier to pick the best route than it was on the way up; continue around Loch Obisary and back to the start (about 1½ hours from the summit).

SOUTH UIST

With a remarkably smooth western coast and crumpled eastern shore, South Uist (Uibhist a' Deas) is quite unlike the other isles because of its long, slender shape. There is much to interest walkers here: numerous rugged peaks, the wild and remote east coast, and the long, long beaches of the Atlantic coast. Causeways link the isle to Benbecula in the north and Eriskay (Eiriosgaigh) in the south. South Uist's population is scattered along the main road, which runs the length of the island. This road demarcates the settled western fringe from the rugged, almost empty country of rock, water and peat to the east. Lochboisdale (Loch Baghasdail), the main town, is near the southern end of the island.

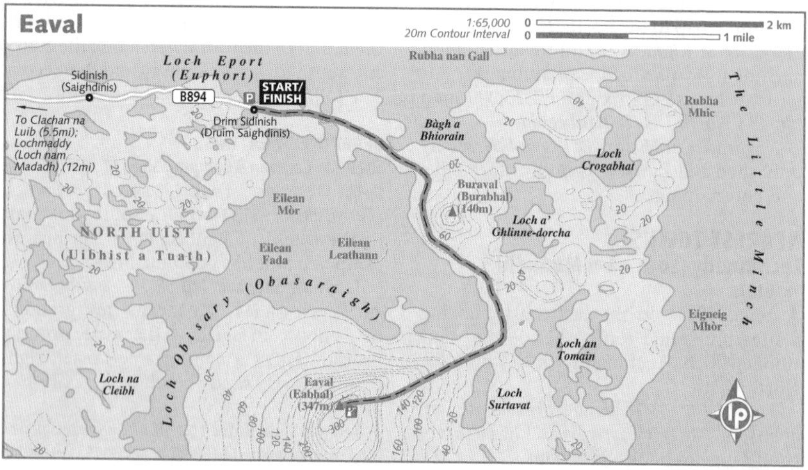

For information about the island, check the community-based site www.uistonline.com.

HECLA

Duration	7–7½ hours
Distance	10.4 miles (16.5km)
Difficulty	demanding
Start/Finish	Lochskipport
Nearest Towns	Howmore (right), Lochboisdale (right)
Transport	private

Summary A challenging and highly rewarding walk to the second-highest peak on South Uist, with fantastic, wide-ranging views.

The name Hecla (Thacla; 606m/1988ft) is of Norse origin and means 'serrated' or 'comb-like'. It's only a few metres lower than its southern neighbour Beinn Mhòr (620m). Made of Lewisian gneiss, Hecla stands at the northern end of a very rugged cluster of peaks and ridges in central South Uist, between Loch Skipport in the north and Loch Aineort in the south. It rises very steeply from the sea and tapers west to a flat coastal plain. Two fine corries, reflecting the work of glaciers during the last Ice Age, bite deep into its northern face.

If you're drawn more to climbing Beinn Mhòr, the highest peak on the island, it must be said that Hecla offers a more interesting and equally scenic outing. The walk described here is a fairly straightforward out-and-back route from Lochskipport (Loch Sgioport) to its north. Involving 600m of ascent, it's graded as demanding due to the rough ground traversed and the intricate route-finding through broken cliffs. There's a track along the shore of Loch Skipport and indeterminate paths on higher ground, but no beaten highways.

Alternatives There is scope for varying this route. A round walk is possible via the long spur extending northwest from Hecla's summit to Maoil Daimh then (having negotiated the not-too-formidable crags) northeast across the lochan-strewn moor to the shore of Loch Skipport. The full round of South Uist's highest peaks, taking in Beinn Corradail en route to Beinn Mhòr, is a challenging walk, covering a lot of rough ground and narrow ridges on Beinn Corradail.

PLANNING

Maps

Carry either the OS Explorer 1:25,000 map No 453 *Benbecula & South Uist* or the OS Landranger 1:50,000 map No 22 *Benbecula & South Uist*.

NEAREST TOWNS

Howmore (Tobha Mòr)

☎ 01878

Howmore is a typically diffuse village along and west of the A865, roughly midway between the north and south coasts and almost directly west of Hecla.

SLEEPING & EATING

Howmore Hostel (www.syha.org.uk; unpowered sites for 2 £8, dm £8), one of the Hebridean Hostels (see the boxed text on p242), less than 1 mile west of the A865, offers simple accommodation in traditional stone cottages (one of them thatched). Facilities include a shower but you'll need to bring your own sleeping bag. Bookings are not accepted – it's first come, first served. The warden, a local crofter, calls each evening to collect fees. There's plenty of space around the cottages to pitch a tent.

Caloraidh B&B (☎ 710224; 3 Milton; s/d £28/50) is 7 miles (11.2km) south of Howmore, with two very comfortable rooms; expect a warm welcome and an excellent breakfast.

Ben Mhor Stores, just south of the turn-off to the hostel, is a well-stocked licensed grocery.

GETTING THERE & AWAY

Howmore is about 6.7 miles (10.5km) south of the Benbecula causeway and about 12 miles (19.5km) north of Lochboisdale.

Lochboisdale (Loch Baghasdail)

☎ 01878

The principal town on South Uist, Lochboisdale is focused on the ordinary business of island life. The **TIC** (☎ 700286; lochboisdale@visithebrides.com; Pier Rd) offers the usual range of services.

SLEEPING & EATING

Lochside Cottage (☎ 700472; loch-side_cottage@tiscali.co.uk; s/d £23/46), beside its own fishing loch, is 1.5 miles west of the ferry terminal.

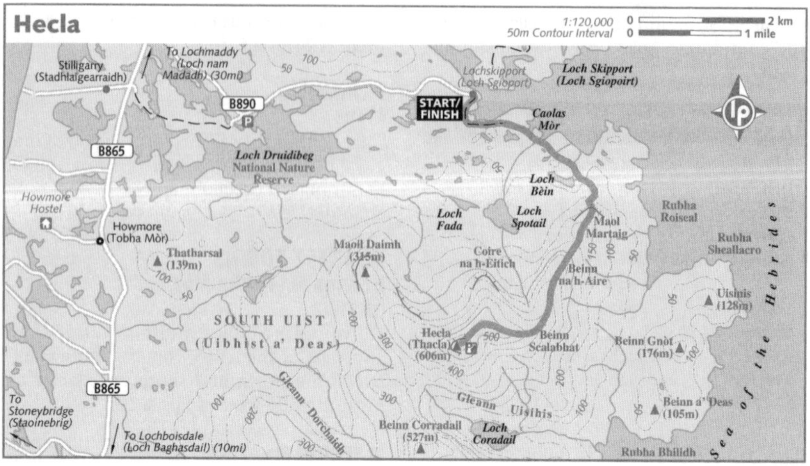

Polochar Inn (☎ 700215; www.polocharinn.co.uk; Pollachar; s/d £40/70, lunch mains £6-8, dinner mains £9-12), 7.5 miles southwest of town, has grown from the original 1695 inn to a popular, friendly, very relaxed place overlooking the Sound of Barra. The food is great; chips are banished, local produce is foremost, and the chefs are not afraid to experiment – imagine monkfish marinaded in basil and ginger.

There's a Co-op supermarket at Daliburgh, near the junction of the A865 and the B888 to Eriskay.

GETTING THERE & AWAY

CalMac (☎ 08705 650000; www.calmac.co.uk) operates a ferry service between Oban and Lochboisdale (passenger/car £21/77, 5½ hours, four weekly). There's also a link with Castlebay on the Isle of Barra (passenger/car £6/35, two hours, three weekly).

GETTING TO/FROM THE WALK

The walk starts and finishes at Lochskipport, at the end of the B890, which branches from the A865 about 2 miles (3.5km) north of Howmore. Lochskipport is 4 miles (6.5km) from the A865. Park beside the road.

THE WALK

Follow the road to a point about 120m beyond the end of the sealed section and turn off right (south) along a wide path. It's clear enough as it skirts the shore of Loch Skipport to the ruined stone buildings on the western side of Caolas Mòr. From here, keep close to the shore and cross the stream issuing from Loch Spotail. Go up the slope on its far side then head southeast across moorland, over a small stream draining a tiny, diamond-shaped lochan, and on to cross the burn from Loch Bèin just below the outlet (about an hour from the start).

Keep seaward of the cliffs above Loch Bèin and a surprisingly easy line of ascent opens up, through the crags of **Maol Martaig**. Cairns, not always in line of sight, mark the way over the highest ground, although there's no continuous path, up to Beinn na h-Aire. Once you reach this rocky eyrie the rest of the walk is relatively easy, over not-such-rough ground to the minor summit of Beinn Scalabhat (1½ hours from Loch Bèin). Traverse the southern slope of the ridge to reach the next cairn-crowned top (564m) then dip across the bealach and go up to the rock-and-grass summit of **Hecla** (35 minutes from Beinn Scalabhat). There's a veritable feast of islands and mountains in the view, notably Skye's Red and Black Cuillins and flat-topped MacLeod's Tables to the east, and the Harris 'hills' in the north.

The descent is much easier, threading together a line of grass, rock and heather, down to Maol Martaig. From here, drop down to the west initially then swing north to avoid the almost unbroken cliffs on the north face of this bump, and go on to the north shore of Loch Bèin (nearly two hours from the top). The direction is then northwest, past two small lochans and across

Loch Spotail's outlet stream; a path of sorts leads to the next small inlet. Continue generally close to the shore, past another tiny bay on the western shore of Caolas Mòr, then head west through a shallow valley. Pass the substantial ruin of a stone cottage and cross another shallow valley, where the track that you followed earlier in the day becomes clear. Follow it back to the start (1¼ hours from Loch Bèin).

BARRA

Barra (Barraigh) and neighbouring Vatersay are the southernmost of the inhabited Western Isles and the most westerly populated part of Scotland. They have a unique edge-of-the-world feeling; here you can be most keenly aware of the power and vastness of the Atlantic Ocean. There's plenty of good walking on both islands, with the central undulating ridge, outlying 'hills' and beaches in the north, and mountain and beach walks on Vatersay (Bhatarsaigh) linked to Barra by a causeway.

Barra is about 8 miles (13km) long and 7 miles (11km) wide. A rugged, rocky ridge of Lewisian gneiss stretches north to south for nearly its full length, with the highest point, Heaval (Sheabhal; 383m) at the southern end. The northern tip, centred around Eoligarry (Eòlaigearraidh), which is all low hills and machair, is joined to the rest of the island by two vast beaches (one serving as the island's airfield) and a slender strip of dry land. In the southwest corner, Ben Tangaval (Beinn Tangabhal; 333m) forms a spectacular bulwark against the Atlantic Ocean. Typically, the east coast is rocky, indented and relatively sheltered, while the west coast is graced by superb beaches and fine stretches of machair, carpeted with wildflowers during summer.

PLANNING

There's no formal camping ground on Barra; discreet wild camping on unfenced ground (usually close to the beaches) is OK; take care to leave no trace of your presence.

Maps

You'll need either OS Landranger 1:50,000 map No 31 *Barra* or OS Explorer 1:25,000 map No 452 *Barra & Vatersay*.

Information Sources

The island's own website, www.isleofbarra.com, provides an informative introduction to Barra and includes a detailed accommodation list.

GETTING AROUND

The island's bus services, run by **H Macneil** (☎ 01871 810262) and **R Macmillan** (☎ 01871 890366) operate Monday to Saturday and are frequent enough; buses connect with arriving and departing ferries and flights. There's also a **taxi service** (☎ 01871 810590) or you could **hire a bike** (☎ 01871 810284) to get around, so your own four wheels aren't essential, especially if you're not tied to a tight timetable. Public transport timetables are available from the TIC in Castlebay (p252).

HEAVAL

Duration	3½–4 hours
Distance	5.5 miles (9km)
Difficulty	moderate
Start	Craigston
Finish	Castlebay (p252)
Transport	bus

Summary Heaps of variety in the climb to Barra's highest peak: unsurpassed all-round views, prehistoric and more recent features and the moorland ridge dissected by deep passes.

It's easy enough to dash up and down Heaval (Sheabhal; 383m) from the road crossing the southern foot of the mountain, but the approach described here, along the island's central spine, is more scenic and varied and involves less seriously steep climbing. Although it is quite a popular walk, there isn't a continuous defined path, nor any cairns other than on the summits; most of the going is over grass and broken rock. The total ascent is 555m.

Near the start of the walk you'll pass a restored, thatched cottage (*dubharaidh* in Gaelic), which houses a museum about island life; it's open most days in summer. Further on, the route takes you past Dùn Bharpa, a Neolithic (Stone Age) chambered burial cairn, built around 5000 years ago. High on the steep southern slopes of Heaval stands Our Lady of the Sea, a marble statue of the Madonna and child, symbolising the islanders' main religious faith; it's not easy to find, being off the best line of descent.

Alternative It's perfectly possible to make this walk into a superb full-length traverse by starting on the A888 at its highest point, between Beinn Chliaid to the north and Beinn Bheireasaigh to the south. In the absence of a defined path, head generally south, with many subtle variations, to join the main walk at Grianan. Allow about three hours for this 6.5-mile (10.5km) route.

NEAREST TOWN

Castlebay (Bàgh a' Chaisteil)

☎ 01871

Castlebay, a large village rather than a town, and huddled around the sheltered harbour in the south, is the 'capital' of Barra. The helpful **TIC** (☎ 810336; castlebay@visithebrides.com; Main St; daily), just north of the ferry pier, opens for late ferry arrivals, stocks maps and books and can handle accommodation bookings.

SLEEPING & EATING

Dunard Hostel (☎ 810443; www.dunardhostel.co.uk; Castlebay; tw & d £30) is a small, friendly place close to the ferry terminal.

Faire Mhaoldonaich (☎ 810441; www.fairemhaoldonaich.com; Nasg; s/d £28/50) overlooks the bay from the road to Vatersay. The rooms are pleasantly furnished (ask for No 2) and breakfast is first-rate.

Ocean View B&B (☎ 810590; www.beatonbarra.co.uk; Borve (Borgh); s/d £22/40, dinner £7) is a great place for watching sunsets and enjoying good breakfasts.

Castlebay Hotel (☎ 810223; mains £9-15; lunch & dinner) specialises in local seafood, which it does very well indeed, using a range of sauces to complement cockles and crab. Vegetarians will have to hope they're happy with the lone offering.

For self-catering supplies, there's a Co-op supermarket, a licensed grocer and Barra's community shop, Co-Chomunn Bharraidh.

GETTING THERE & AWAY

The timetable's warning 'Barra Flights are subject to Tide' isn't a joke. Barra's airport is Tràigh Mhòr ('big beach'). **British Airways/Loganair** (☎ 0870 850 9850; www.britishairways.com) operates flights from Glasgow (£75, one hour, two flights Monday to Saturday). This service also links Barra and Benbecula (£30, 20 minutes). There's a small tearoom at the airport.

CalMac (☎ 08705 650000; www.calmac.co.uk) ferries from Oban (passenger/car £21/77, 5¼ hours, at least three weekly) and Lochboisdale (passenger/car £6/35, 1¾ hours, at least three weekly) call at Castlebay.

SHORT WALK

The small island of **Vatersay**, tied to Barra by a causeway southwest of Castlebay, is graced by three outstandingly beautiful beaches, all in its gently undulating southern half. Walking here is delightfully easy, mostly across short, cropped grass. A 4-mile (6.4km) waymarked walk circuits this part of the island and affords fine wide views, especially south to the uninhabited islands of Pabbay and Mingulay; allow two to 2¼ hours. Carry OS Landranger 1:50,000 map No 31. Buses operated by **R Macmillan** (☎ 890366) and **H Macneil** (☎ 810262) operate between Castlebay post office and Vatersay village, about 400m south of the start of the walk (20 minutes, at least three services Monday to Saturday). There are no shops on the island; a small café may be open at the northern end of Vatersay Bay.

The walk is waymarked from a small car park on the east side of the road, 400m north of the village. Soon you pass the Annie Jane memorial then drop down to Bagh Siar (West Bay). At its southern end cross a stile at a fence corner, traverse the slope and go up to the slight remains of Dun Bhatarsaigh. Descend south across a tiny burn then go southeast to an old grassed stone wall; turn right up to a standing stone. Climb a little then continue north and east across country to overlook Bagh a'Deas; descend to the shore. From the eastern end of the bay, go up across grassland. Soon you're above a wide glen, where the skeletal remains of Eorisdale village stand gauntly near the shore. Turn north across a slight saddle then swing gradually west to follow the shore of Vatersay Bay. Eventually, walk along the beach to a wide gap in the fringing dunes to reach the car park from where you started.

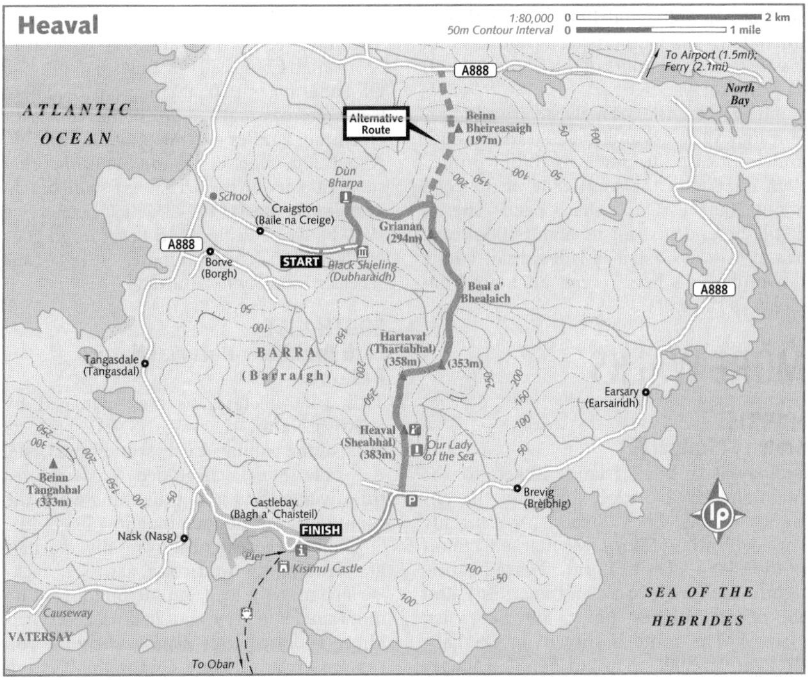

From the north, a CalMac ferry plies between Eriskay (linked to South Uist by causeway and bridge) and Ardmhor on Barra (passenger/car £6/18, 40 minutes, four daily).

GETTING TO/FROM THE WALK

The walk starts at the end of the minor road through the village of Craigston (Baile na Creige), where there's an informal car park. Alternatively, catch a Castlebay–Eoligarry bus (£1, seven minutes, at least three Monday to Saturday), get off at the junction on the main road and walk nearly 1 mile to the start.

THE WALK

From the end of the sealed road continue along the vehicular track to a point opposite the black shieling on the right. Go through a gate and head up the hillside with a fence on your left; follow it northeast then north for a short distance. Look out for a prominent waymarker post up to the right; continue to it then go on to **Dùn Bharpa**, crossing a stile over a fence en route (about 45 minutes from the main road). Sitting in a shallow gap in an east–west ridge, the dùn is a large, sprawling mound of small stones, with a huge capstone (or lid) on top.

Go back over the stile then head east across flattish moorland to the foot of the very steep western side of the central ridge. Climb up a broad, grassed gully to the obvious gap on the ridge then south and up to the summit of **Grianan** (294m), about an hour from the dùn. Descend steeply to Beul a' Bhealaich, taking care not to overshoot and finish up east of and below the gap. From the gap, angle up the steep, grassy and rocky hillside, southeast then south to a minor summit at 353m (marked with a miniature cairn). Then go sharply down, across a narrow slit as the ridge bends markedly to the west, and up to the main top of **Hartaval** (Thartabhal; 358m), an hour from Grianan. From here the ridge regains its north–south orientation as you dip across a gap then quickly dispose of the final climb to the survey cairn on **Heaval** (Sheabhal; 383m). The view is unsurpassed – from the mountains of Harris to the southernmost isles of Mingulay and Berneray (both uninhabited), and with Castlebay and Kisimul Castle (ancestral home of the Clan Macneil) at your feet.

The descent is extremely steep and unrelenting, over grass and rock. Heading south and southeast, aim for a small but prominent quarry on the south side of the road about 200m east of a sharp bend. There's a stile here, or use a gate about 100m east. The centre of Castlebay is less than 1 mile downhill from here (about an hour from Heaval's summit).

MORE WALKS

HARRIS

Scalpay (Scalpaigh)

Scalpay is a small island, linked to the mainland by a bridge, guarding the entrance to East Loch Tarbert. A scenically varied, 8-mile (13km) waymarked circuit of the island takes in Eilean Glas, a historic lighthouse (one of Scotland's earliest), and the island's highest point, Ben Scoravick (104m). The route is shown on OS Landranger 1:50,000 map No 14. The **Scalpay Minibus** (☎ 01859 540356) plies between Tarbert and the main village (£1, 25 minutes, at least three services Monday to Friday); **North Harris Motor Services** (☎ 01859 502250) does the run on Saturday. To reach the start, follow roads from the village ('Baile') to Outend, where there's a small car park. The route starts about 30m back along the road; generally, it's easy to follow.

The only potentially confusing section comes after you've left the lighthouse. Return to the gate in the stone wall and turn right immediately. Follow the wall almost to its end then pick up the waymarker posts on the slope ahead. They end near the outlet of Loch an Duin. Follow a vehicle track to a minor road; it leads to the main road above North Harbour. Turn left to return to the village or the car park. There aren't any cafés or pubs on the island; **Scalpay Mini Market** (🕑 Mon-Sat) sells takeaway rolls and hot drinks.

Toe Head (Goban Tobha)

Toe Head, the northwest extremity of Harris, offers a variety of walks: an easy ramble to a tiny chapel on the southern shore (3.2 miles/5km); a longer and rougher return walk around the east and north coast to Toe Head (8.6 miles/14km); and a climb to 365m-high Chaipaval (4.2 miles/6.6km). Use OS Landranger 1:50,000 map No 18. These walks are approached from the village of Northton, 2 miles northwest of Leverburgh. About 30m short of the road end, there's a small car park on the left above a small beach. **Hebridean Transport** (☎ 01851 705050) bus service W10 between Tarbert and Leverburgh goes via Northton (£3, 33 minutes, at least four services Monday to Saturday).

SOUTH UIST

Loch Druidibeg National Nature Reserve

This 1660-hectare reserve, managed by Scottish Natural Heritage (SNH), protects most of the habitats easily seen in the Uists. A 5-mile (8km) self-guided walk explores this diversity and is just the thing when the mountains are clouded in; allow 2½ hours.

The reserve extends from the machair grassland on the west coast, across a brackish lagoon to the loch and surrounding peaty moorland. Extensive and shallow, Loch Druidibeg is dotted with islands. On some you can see a relatively rare sight in the Western Isles, trees (juniper, willow and rowan), and one is home to a colony of heron. One of Scotland's few native populations of greylag geese lives around the loch. Beside the Lochskipport road a small plantation includes the only mature Scots pine in the Uists; if you're here in early spring you might just hear a cuckoo. On the moorland, red grouse and deer are possible sightings, and it's easier to hear the lonely piping of the golden plover than to see the bird itself.

The most convenient place to start the walk is from a car park on the Lochskipport road, which branches from the A865 road 4.7 miles south of the Benbecula causeway. Walk back along the road; cross the main road and continue west to the start of the waymarked section, near Loch Druidibeg on the left. For more information visit **SNH's office** (☎ 01870 620238) at Stilligarry (Stadhlaigearraidh), beside the A865.

BARRA

Eoligarry (Eòlaigearraidh)

The northern tip of Barra has two of the island's most important historic sites. Here, a 6-mile (9.5km) partly waymarked walk

WESTERN ISLES

starts and finishes at the former South Uist ferry pier. It visits a cemetery in which are the remnants of St Barr's Chapel (Cille-Bharra), dating from early Christian times, and a small building protecting some fascinating ancient carved stones. Next comes Dun Scurrival (Dùn Sgùrabhal), an Iron Age fort, then it's over Ben Eoligarry (102m) and down to the long Tràigh Eais and back past the airport. Use OS Landranger 1:50,000 map No 31. Buses operated by **R Macmillan** (☎ 01871 890366) and **H Macneil** (☎ 01871 810262) link Castlebay and Eoligarry (£2, 30 minutes, at least three services Monday to Saturday). If you go by car, try to time the walk to coincide with the arrival of a flight at Barra airport (Tràigh Mhór), a truly amazing sight.

Northwest

The north of Scotland, beyond a line joining Ullapool in the west and Dornoch Firth in the east, is the most sparsely populated part of the country. Sutherland is graced with a generous share of the wildest and most remote coast, mountains and glens. At first sight, the bare 'hills', more rock than earth, and the maze of lochs and waterways may seem alien – part of another planet – and unattractive. But the very wildness of the rockscapes, the isolation of the long, deep glens, and the magnificence of the indented coastline can exercise a seductive fascination. The outstanding significance of the area's geology has been recognised by the designation of the North West Highlands Geopark (see the boxed text on p264), the first such reserve in Britain. Intrusive developments are few, and many long-established paths lead into the mountains and through the glens.

This chapter focuses on a variety of walks in Sutherland's northwest corner. Incomparably beautiful Sandwood Bay is the highlight of a superb coast walk to Cape Wrath, Scotland's most northwesterly point. Ben Loyal, overlooking the small village of Tongue on the north coast, is an intriguing peak, topped by a cluster of granite tors. The ascent of Quinag, a striking mountain in the heart of the Assynt district, is nowhere near as difficult as it looks. By way of contrast, secretive Eas a' Chùal Aluinn, Scotland's highest waterfall, is reached only after a trek across wild moorland. Suggestions for other walks sustain the infinite variety that characterises Sutherland, and include the delightful Falls of Kirkaig, south of Lochinver, and the distinctive, seemingly inaccessible peak Stac Pollaidh.

HIGHLIGHTS

- Walking along the pristine beach at **Sandwood Bay** (p261), en route to the towering cliffs at northwestern Cape Wrath
- Pottering about among the breezy pinnacles and crags of **Ben Loyal** (p262)
- Venturing deep into a rocky mountain wilderness to stand atop **Eas a' Chùal Aluinn** (p265), Scotland's highest waterfall
- Capturing the amazing patchwork panorama of lochans, hills and crumpled coastline from **Quinag** (p267)

- www.visithighlands.com
- www.assynt.info

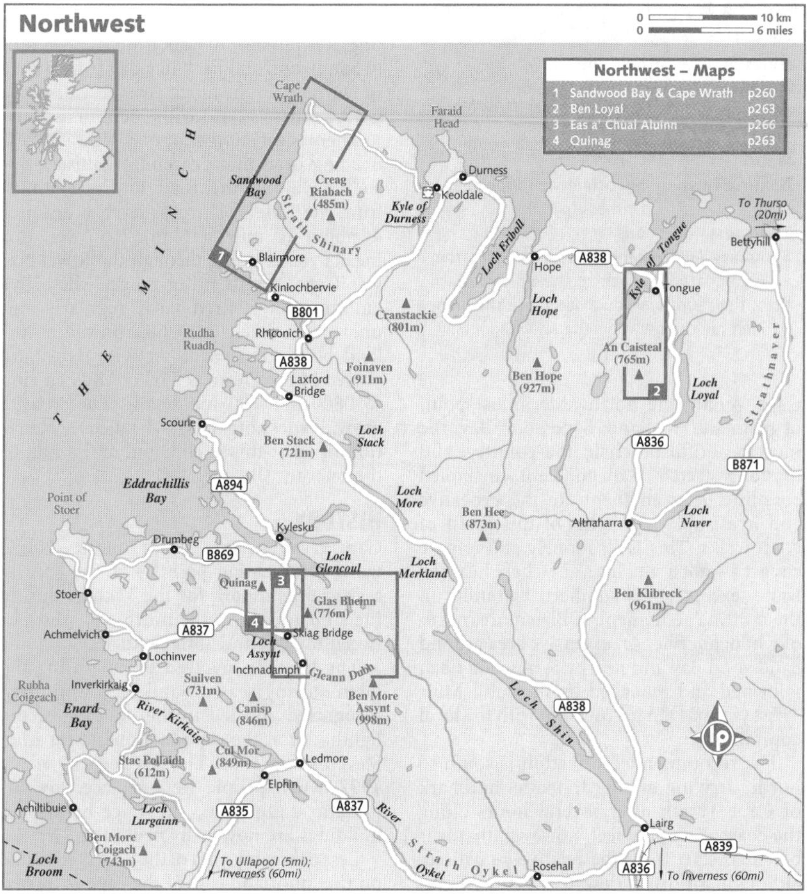

INFORMATION

Maps & Books

For use during route planning, and for general orientation while you're on the walk, the OS Travel – Road 1:250,000 map No 2 *Northern Scotland* is ideal.

The Scottish Mountaineering Club's published guide, *The Northwest Highlands*, which is jointly authored by DJ Bennet and T Strang, is a very authoritative read. It also manages to capture the scenic magic of the area extremely well.

The Pathfinder guide, *Skye and the North West Highlands*, by John Brooks and Neil Wilson, includes details on 13 walks within the northwest area. *Walks West Sutherland*, by Peter and Rosemary Koch-Osborne, is another option, which provides succinct descriptions of 23 walks in the region.

Information Sources

To access general information on things such as accommodation listings and booking facilities throughout the northwest area, try going to **VisitHighlands** (☎ 0845 2255 121; www.visithighlands.com), a really useful offshoot of VisitScotland.

Traveline Scotland (☎ 0870 608 2608; www.travelinescotland.com) provides public transport timetable information. **Highland Council's** (☎ 01463 702660; public.transport@highland.gov.uk) free *Public Transport Timetable: Sutherland* is invaluable, and is available from TICs.

SANDWOOD BAY & CAPE WRATH

Duration	6½–7 hours
Distance	14 miles (22.5km)
Difficulty	moderate
Start	Blairmore
Finish	Cape Wrath
Nearest Towns	Kinlochbervie (opposite), Durness (p260)
Transport	bus

Summary An outstanding coastal walk, from an incomparable beach to the northwestern tip of the country, through a remote and uninhabited area of great beauty and wildness.

Cape Wrath, the northwesternmost point of mainland Scotland; Sandwood Bay, the most beautiful beach in the country; and the long stretch of magnificent, unspoiled coastline between them are the evocative and irresistible highlights of this finest of coast walks. This is also lonely and remote country – not a soul lives anywhere near the route, except at its southern extremity in the crofting settlement of Blairmore, north of Kinlochbervie. An extensive area around Sandwood Bay and nearby Sandwood Loch is owned and managed by the John Muir Trust (see p31) in partnership with the local community.

The recommended direction is south to north, arriving at the dramatic landmark of Cape Wrath after several hours along the coast. You may feel, however, that it is better to start from the relatively civilised, although forlornly deserted, Cape Wrath lighthouse and to walk into the wilderness. Another factor to consider is the moorland trek between Sandwood Bay and Blairmore, which some may find desolate.

Alternatives If you're fit you could do the walk from Blairmore to Cape Wrath and back in a day, but camping at Sandwood offers the chance of an almost unique experience in Scotland – beach camping, and being lulled to sleep by the soothing music of the waves. Thus, you could spread the walk over a much more leisurely three days: one into Sandwood, another to the cape and back, and a third back to Blairmore. Choose your pitch with care, steering well clear of the fragile dunes. If there's enough driftwood to make a good fire, light it on bare sand.

In midsummer, and transport permitting, it is possible to walk from Cape Wrath to Sandwood and back in a day from a base in Durness on the north coast; the distance is 19.5 miles (32km) with 300m of ascent.

There is yet another option, although one needing even more careful organisation – walking along the road to Cape Wrath from the Kyle of Durness ferry, a distance of about 10 miles (16km). However, this means you're going through the Royal Navy's Cape Wrath firing range, where live ammunition is fired fairly regularly and unexploded shells may lurk on the moorland beside the road. 'Activity dates' are posted at the Durness TIC or you can ring ☎ 0800 833 300 for details. The website www.durness.org has a detailed explanation of what this is all about and a link to the relevant site.

HISTORY

Cape Wrath's name comes from the Norse word for 'turning point' – it was clearly a crucial landmark for the Vikings during their incursions in the north and west between the 9th and 13th centuries.

The hazards involved in navigating the often stormy seas around here were long recognised and led to the building of the lighthouse at the cape by Robert and Alan Stevenson in 1828. The last keepers left by 1997, when people were replaced by automatic equipment; the once-handsome buildings are now sadly neglected.

Less peaceably, part of the Balnakeil Estate on the moorland east of the cape is owned by the Ministry of Defence and has served for decades as a bombing range where live ammunition is used. The ministry claims, nevertheless, that wildlife flourishes and the landscape has been preserved.

People evicted from their lands on the north coast settled around Sandwood (and Sheigra to the south) in the 1820s, but their descendants were ejected in 1847 and the area repopulated with sheep. Sandwood Lodge, built during the 19th century (now roofless but stable), was used by shepherds until the 1950s. The land was returned to local people 50 years later. The John Muir Trust purchased the 4650-hectare Sandwood Estate in 1993. It extends from Sandwood Loch and Strath Shinary south to Loch Clash at Kinlochbervie and inland for up to 6 miles (10km). Essential to the management of the estate is the participation of local crofting communities through a special committee.

ENVIRONMENT

Along the coast, the cliffs, deep inlets (geos) and the offshore stacks and islets are predominantly sandstone, mixed into ancient gneiss, the most widespread rock type. At Cape Wrath the red gneiss cliffs soar to a height of about 120m. A few miles east, at Kervaig, are reputedly the highest coastal cliffs in mainland Scotland, at 284m. Glaciers and ice sheets left their mark in sculpting the river valleys; large gneiss boulders perched on sandstone platforms were left behind by retreating glaciers.

The peatlands, sand dunes and machair (coastal grasslands) from Sandwood to Sheigra, and the dunes and machair between Sheigra and Oldshoremore (all within the John Muir Trust's Sandwood Estate) are protected in two Sites of Special Scientific Interest. The machair, found only in relatively few places along the west coast and in the Western Isles, comes alive between late June and August with carpets of globeflower, bell flower, vetch, knapweed and orchid.

PLANNING

What to Bring

If you're planning to camp at Sandwood Bay, a fuel stove is an absolute must, as are a trowel (there are no toilets) and a bag to carry out all your rubbish. Water containers will be handy; some camp sites are close to the limited supplies of freshwater but they're midge havens in summer. For more information, contact the manager of **Sandwood Estate** (☎ 01971 521459); he will also be able to fill you in on guided walks around the estate during June and July.

Maps

The walk is covered by the OS Explorer 1:25,000 map No 446 *Durness & Cape Wrath*, and the OS Landranger 1:50,000 map No 9 *Cape Wrath*.

NEAREST TOWNS

Kinlochbervie

☎ 01971

Principally a fishing village, Kinlochbervie is dominated by large port facilities around the sheltered harbour. The nearest ATM, TIC, camping ground and hostel are in Durness (p260).

Braeside B&B (☎ 521325; s/d £23/46) is a friendly, long-established place in the village centre.

Old School Restaurant & Rooms (☎ 521383; www.oldschoolhotel.co.uk; Inshegra; s/d £40/70, mains £9-18; dinner) occupies a former primary school that served the local community for nearly a century. Accommodation is in an adjacent modern building, where some rooms look out across Loch Inchard.

Kinlochbervie Hotel (☎ 521275; www.kinlochberviehotel.com; s/d £55/90, mains £9-17; lunch & dinner)

WHERE NOT TO CAMP *Sandra Bardwell*

The shore of Sandwood Loch seemed an idyllic camp site – right beside a freshwater supply, where we could also take a dip after a warm day's walk. But we were still pretty naive about camping in Scotland during summer – we'd heard about midges but hadn't much idea about where they lived.

So we pitched the tent beside the tranquil, reed-fringed loch then spent the day walking up to Cape Wrath and back. We returned to the tent in the early evening and the breeze that had kept us cool on that warm July day had died. We lit the stove for a brew but, within a minute, were reduced to futile, flailing anguish as the black clouds of voracious insects swarmed upon us – even into our mouths.

Clearly, cooking a meal would be impossible, so instant relocation was the only answer. All the unpacked gear was frantically stuffed into our packs and we ran across the dunes to the beach and its midge-free expanses of bare sand. All that remained was the dome tent, its inner already lying in a heap on the sand. So, we pulled out the pegs, crawled inside and picked it up, and once again ran for the beach, seeing the way through the tent's cream panels. Our only regret was that someone didn't arrive with a camera, or preferably a video recorder, to immortalise the sight of a dome tent with four brown legs, moving at high speed through the Sandwood dunes.

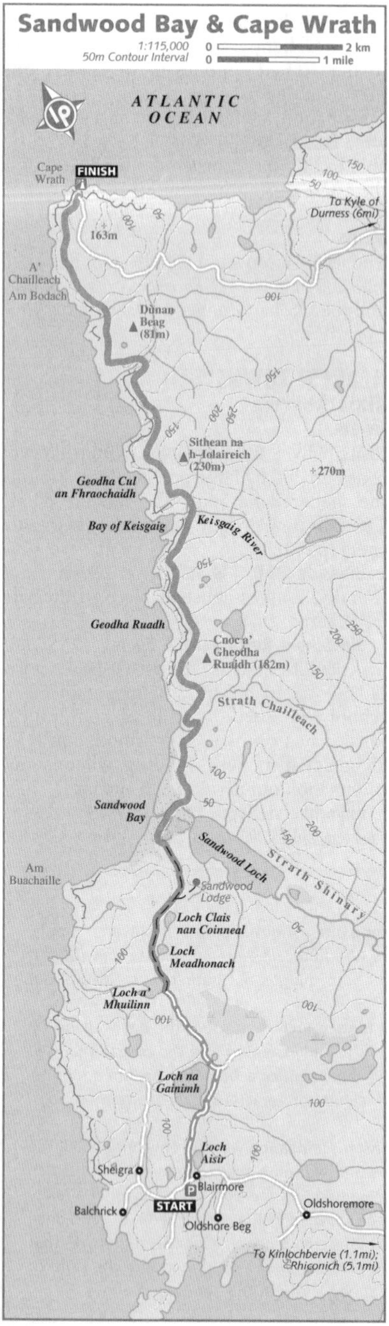

Sandwood Bay & Cape Wrath

occupies a scenic position on the Sheigra road, just north of the village. Fresh local seafood is a highlight of the thoughtfully put together restaurant menu.

Bervie Stores (daily, 12.30-2.30pm Sun), a small Spar supermarket, sells maps, among other things.

For transport information see Getting There & Away for Durness (below).

Durness

☎ 01971 / pop 363

A surprisingly large, spread-out village on the coast, Durness lays unbeatable claim to being the most northwesterly village in Britain.

The **TIC** (☎ 511259; www.visithighlands.com; daily Jun-Sep, Mon-Sat Apr, May & Oct) is at the eastern end of the village and houses a small display about local places of interest and sells maps and books. The local website www.durness.org is a rich source of background information. There's an ATM at the village store.

SLEEPING & EATING

Sango Sands Camping Site (☎ 511761; Sangomore; unpowered/powered sites for 2 £10/13), near the TIC and beside the main road, has plenty of grassy pitches and uninterrupted ocean views.

Durness SYHA Hostel (☎ 0870 004 1113; www.syha.org.uk; Smoo; dm £12), overlooking the sea, is about 1 mile east of the village on the main road beside the collection of fluttering flags.

Corrie Lochan B&B (☎ 511341; www.corrielochan.co.uk; s/d £27/50), a few hundred metres south of the village, has pleasantly appointed rooms and a large lounge facing the sea.

Balnakeil Bistro and Craft Shop (☎ 511232; Balnakeil craft village; mains £5-9; lunch & dinner;), barely 1 mile west of town, is a refreshingly homely place serving freshly prepared, mainly traditional dishes.

Sango Sands Oasis (☎ 511222; mains £7-9; lunch & dinner to 7.30pm), next to the camping ground, is usually busy; the bar meals are bog-standard but plentiful.

The **Spar** (Mon-Sat) village store sells camping gas and liquid fuel for stoves. There's also Mather's licensed grocers opposite the TIC.

GETTING THERE & AWAY

Tim Dearman Coaches (☎ 01349 883585; www.timdearmancoaches.co.uk) runs a seasonal service between Inverness and Durness (£18, five hours) via Lochinver, Inchnadamph and Kinlochbervie. The Monday-to-Saturday service operates late April to late September, and the Sunday service in July and August.

GETTING TO/FROM THE WALK

To the Start

The walk starts at Blairmore, a hamlet on the Kinlochbervie–Sheigra road, 3.4 miles (5.4km) from Kinlochbervie. There are public toilets, a car park and a public telephone.

A subsidised **taxi service** (☎ 521477) operating in the Kinlochbervie area (daily except Tuesday and Saturday) can take you to (and from) Blairmore (£1). Call the evening before to arrange a pick-up. Full details are given in the Highland Council's *Public Transport Timetable: Sutherland*, available from TICs.

From the Finish

If you are walking north from Sandwood Bay, be sure to contact the ferry and bus operators in advance to ensure they are waiting for you.

The **Cape Wrath minibus service** (☎ 511343) bounces its way along the rough road to the lighthouse from the ferry jetty on the western shore of the Kyle of Durness (£5, 40 minutes, around eight daily Easter to September).

Kyle of Durness ferry (☎ 511376) meets the minibus and crosses the Kyle to the jetty at Keoldale (£3, 10 minutes, around eight sailings daily, Easter to September), at the end of a minor road, which branches off the A838 about 2 miles south of Durness.

THE WALK

From the Blairmore car park, set out along the unsealed road signposted to Sandwood. This road, used by crofters tending their sheep, leads across the rather featureless moorland, which is enlivened by several nearby lochs. It becomes a path at Loch a' Mhuilinn. Little more than 1 mile further on, the path (much of it repaired and built by John Muir Trust volunteers) curves round a steep-sided hill on the left and starts to descend, affording the first glimpse of the beach at Sandwood Bay.

A flat, grassed area with old, stone-walled enclosures is a possible camp site. Water should be available from the small burn near the roofless cottage about 200m to the south; otherwise you'll have to go right down to peat-dark Sandwood Loch, although it may be slightly brackish. The shore of Sandwood Loch may seem like an idyllic camp site but beware the midges (see the boxed text on p259).

The path leads down through marram-grassed dunes to the beach at **Sandwood Bay**, a superb sweep of pinkish-cream sand (about 1¾ hours from the start). The towering rock stack of Am Buachaille stands guard close to the cliffs that extend southwest from the sands.

Walk north along the beach, cross the outlet from Sandwood Loch on stepping stones and go up the steep, sandy slope ahead, through a gap in the low cliffs. Cross a patch of grass and make your way through the jumble of rock slabs and boulders down to a shallow valley, then along the cliff edge to Strath Chailleach.

Cross the stream at the top of the cascades and follow the spur leading northeast for about 500m then turn generally north to skirt the steep-sided Cnoc a' Gheodha Ruaidh on its seaward side. Keep close to the cliff edge, across a dip above Geodha Ruadh and up past the next hill.

At the top of the long slope down to the **Keisgaig River**, there's a good view of a remarkable rock stack on the northern side of the bay, its profile resembling a rather sullen face. Just above the river is a low, turf-roofed stone shelter, somewhat the worse for wear (2¼ hours from Sandwood Bay). There's space for a tent or two nearby if you want to camp.

Cross the river just above the cascade coursing down onto the shingle beach and climb up the very steep slope. Steer a course west of Sithean na h-Iolaireich to overlook the superb vertical, dark-pink cliffs in **Geodha Cul an Fhraochaidh**.

Continue along the cliff tops, mainly across bare, stony ground for 1 mile or so, to the top of the next descent to the unnamed burn immediately south of Dùnan Beag. Detour inland (northeast) around the cliffs lining the seaward reaches of the burn to a small stream junction; cross over and head back towards the cliffs.

There's a potential camp site at the next stream crossing (north of Dùnan Beag), a short distance inland. A bit further on, the two remarkable rock stacks A' Chailleach and Am Bodach (the 'old woman' and 'old man') dictate a photo stop. If you look back (south) from here on a clear day, Sandwood Bay is visible.

Continue across a small burn towards the lighthouse, keeping close to the cliffs. Skirt the walled enclosure around the buildings, which are now forlornly deserted, to reach the courtyard in front of the **lighthouse** and the end of the walk (about 2½ hours from the Keisgaig River).

BEN LOYAL

Duration	6–6½ hours
Distance	8 miles (13km)
Difficulty	moderate
Start/Finish	Ribigill access road
Nearest Town	Tongue (right)
Transport	private

Summary A steep climb to one of the most attractive and intriguing peaks in the north, with fine views in all directions.

Ben Loyal is often called the 'Queen of Scottish Peaks'. It's thought that the name Ben Loyal comes not from some dutiful subject but from the Norse *laga fjall* meaning 'law mountain' – where laws were once promulgated. Whether or not you think any mountain should be female rather than male, let alone royal, it is indeed a fine peak. Standing proudly alone above rather desolate moorland to the south, its spectacular, cliff-lined western flank majestically overlooks the Kyle of Tongue and the coast to the north. At 765m (2509ft), Ben Loyal's summit, An Caisteal, has the status of Corbett. However, the mountain is well worth climbing for its own sake, irrespective of its title and designation.

With a longish, gracefully undulating summit ridge, crowned by clusters of granite tors, five separate summits make up Ben Loyal: Sgòr Chaonasaid (712m), Sgòr a' Bhatain (708m), An Caisteal ('the castle'; 765m), Beinn Bheag (744m) and Carn an Tionail (716m). There are also two outliers above the western crags – Sgòr a' Chleirich and Sgòr Fhionnaich.

Consisting of granite (specifically syenite), Ben Loyal stands alone in an area composed principally of schist and sandstone. The belt of birch trees fringing the western slopes is also unusual in the north, so much of which is treeless.

The most popular approach is from the village of Tongue to the north. Farm tracks and rough, discontinuous moorland paths lead up onto the mountain, where the going is much easier. Having gained the summit, you could spend time exploring the individual summits and peering down into the rugged corries on the western face of the mountain. The walk involves 750m of ascent.

PLANNING

Stalking

During the stalking season, from mid-August to mid-October, walkers are asked to avoid areas where stalking activities are taking place on a particular day. The number to phone to find out what's happening is ☎ 01847 611291.

Map

The OS Explorer 1:25,000 map No 447 *Ben Loyal* and OS Landranger 1:50,000 map No 10 *Strathnaver* cover the walk.

NEAREST TOWN

Tongue

☎ 01847

A scattered village, Tongue overlooks the Kyle of Tongue. Seemingly in the middle of nowhere, the village is itself dramatically overlooked by Ben Loyal. The one bank here does not have an ATM.

SLEEPING & EATING

Tongue SYHA Hostel (☎ 0870 004 1153; www.syha.org.uk; dm £12), near the causeway across the Kyle of Tongue, has up-to-date facilities and fine panoramic views.

Rhian Guest House (☎ 611257; www.rhiancottage.co.uk; s/d £37/54) is just south of the village in a traditional Highland cottage.

Ben Loyal Hotel (☎ 611216; www.benloyal.co.uk; s/d £50/70, mains £6-16; lunch & dinner) commands fine, wide views, and the menu is more imaginative than many, especially in the treatment of traditional dishes and presentation of vegetables.

For supplies, there's **Tongue Stores & Post Office** (Mon-Sat) and **Burr's Stores** (daily, noon-2pm Sun) at the northern end of the village.

GETTING THERE & AWAY

You need to be really dedicated to reach Tongue by public transport. Catch the mid-morning **First ScotRail** (☎ 0845 755 0033; www.firstscotrail.com) train from Inverness to Thurso (£15, four hours) then **Royal Mail Postbus** (☎ 0845 774 0740; www.postbus.royalmail.com) 136 from there to Tongue (£4, 1¼ hours) about 1½ hours later. The return connection necessitates double the waiting time in Thurso.

By road, Tongue is at the junction of the A838 from Durness and the A836 from Thurso and Lairg.

GETTING TO/FROM THE WALK

You can walk or drive the 3 miles (5km) south from Tongue along a minor road to the entrance to Ribigill Farm (there's a sign 'Ribigill' on the farm gate), where there is limited roadside parking.

THE WALK

From the turn-off to Ribigill Farm head south along the private road. Bear left at the first fork (after about 650m) then, on a bend with a large derelict stone cottage on the left, continue straight on along a farm track towards Ben Loyal. As the track starts to cross the low spur, ignore another track to the right and continue south. The track is clear enough across the moorland, where there are some boggy patches. Stepping stones take you across Allt Lòn Malmsgaig. Just before you reach stone-built Cunside cottage, at the foot of Ben Loyal's northern slopes, a path leads south along a narrow bank. It fades as you start to gain height steeply up the grassy moorland slope with a small stream on the left. Cross this stream after a while and continue up to the broad gap in the ridge, Bealach Clais nan Ceap. A fairly clear path leads up the slope on your right (west), above the morass in the bealach (pass), towards a cluster of low, broken cliffs. Again the path fades; evidently walkers take various ways up the steep slope. Try to avoid the wettest ground by the cliffs, making your way up to the wide, shallow valley cradling Loch na Creige Riabhaich. Continue generally northwest up to the main ridge, where a path goes north to **Sgòr Chaonasaid** (2½ hours from the start). Here there's good entertainment, scrambling around the small tors on

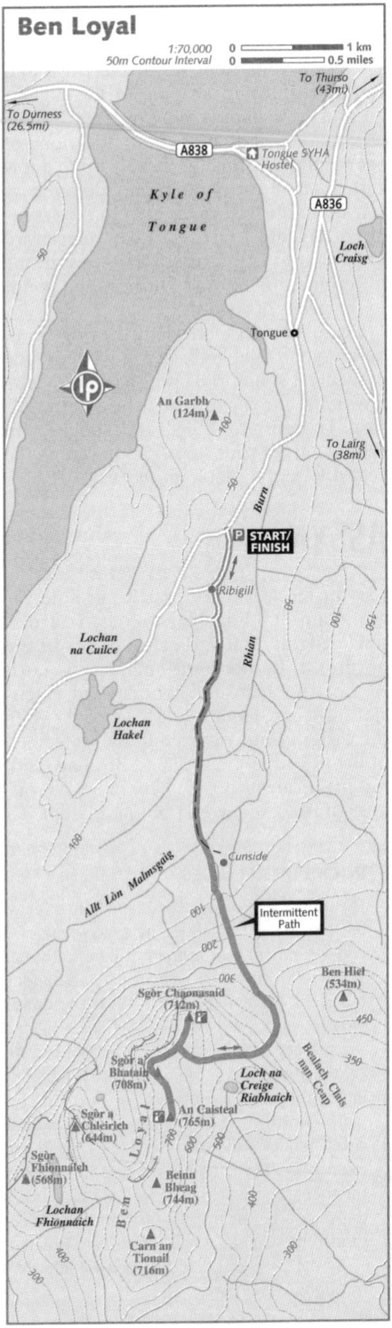

the summit to find the best outlook across Tongue and the Kyle of Tongue.

Retrace your steps down the ridge and continue along it, keeping to the highest ground – the path is more or less continuous. Gain height past the twin knobs of Sgòr a' Bhatain then go steeply up to a low cliff, where a rocky ramp provides an easy way up to the well-made cairn on the summit of **An Caisteal**. On a clear day you can see as far east as Duncansby Head, west to the towering cliffs beyond Durness and south to the peaks of Assynt.

There is a path south along the ridge from here – you could walk to the western side of the next summit, Beinn Bheag, for views down into the rugged corrie below An Caisteal. To return to Ribigill and Tongue, you simply retrace your steps – appreciating the very different outlook on the way.

ASSYNT

Assynt, the legendary practice ground for mountain-building Norse gods, is a distinct geographical and cultural area in the northwest. Its northern boundary is Loch A' Chairn Bhain and its eastward extensions Lochs Glendhu and Glencoul, while the eastern limit runs along the watershed of Beinn Uidhe, Conival and Breabag (and, for practical purposes, Ben More Assynt, though it's actually east of that divide). To the south, Loch Veyatie, Fionn Loch and the River Kirkaig separate Assynt from the district of Coigach. The coast forms its western boundary. The two possible meanings of Assynt – 'rocky' from a Norse word or 'in and out' from the ancient Gaelic – neatly summarise the area's unique landscape of rock and water, a fascinating and wildly beautiful walkers' heartland.

PLANNING

Maps & Books

Both walks in this section are covered by the OS Explorer 1:25,000 map No 442 *Assynt & Lochinver* and OS Landranger 1:50,000 map No 15 *Loch Assynt*.

Exploring the Landscape of Assynt: A Walker's Guide & Map Showing Rocks & Landscape of Assynt & Inverpolly, published by the OS and British Geological Survey, comprises a small guidebook describing 10 walks and a 1:50,000 map on which the routes are outlined. If you're particularly interested in geology, this is a must-have.

Little Assynt Estate: Connecting People to the Land by Robin Noble and Malcolm Bangor-Jones is beautifully illustrated and written. Though it relates specifically to the estate (see p271), it's worth having just for the photographs.

Guided Walks

The Assynt Field Centre, based at **Inchnadamph Lodge** (☎ 01571 822218; www.inch-lodge.co.uk;

ROCKS OF ALL AGES

The northwest corner of Scotland is an open-air geological display *par excellence*. Rocks define the basic shape of the landscape everywhere of course, but mostly they're blanketed by vegetation and settlement. But in the northwest, both are fairly thin on the ground.

Therefore the area was an obvious candidate for Scotland's (and Britain's) first Geopark. Established in 2004, the **North West Highlands Geopark** (☎ 01571 844000; www.northwest-highlands-geopark.org.uk; Culag Bldg, Lochinver) joined 25 partners of the **European Geoparks Network** (www.europeangeoparks.org), endorsed by Unesco. All are coalitions of local communities (rather than central governments) committed to celebrating their distinctive geological heritage and to achieving sustainable development.

The North West Highlands Geopark extends from the Summer Isles in the south to the north coast, and from the west coast to a ragged northeast–southwest line from just east of Loch Eriboll to Knockan. The latter boundary follows the line of the Moine Thrust, a geological feature marking the titanic westward movement of rocks soon after the coalescence of the British landmass. Within the park are vast massifs of the most ancient of rocks, Lewisian gneiss, clumps of Torridonian sandstone (Quinag, Cape Wrath) and isolated exposures of limestone (Durness).

By the time you read this, several information panels should have been installed at key sites throughout the park.

Inchnadamph), runs guided walks and courses on local geology and wildlife.

Assynt Visitor Centre (below) is where you'll find the local **Highland Council rangers** (☎ 01571 844654), who lead a varied program of guided walks in summer. The Assynt representative of the **Royal Society for the Protection of Birds** (☎ 01571 844374) also runs walks in nearby woodlands.

ACCESS TOWNS

Lochinver

☎ 01571

Lochinver is a sizable village on the sheltered upper reaches of Loch Inver; originally a fishing village it is now the centre of the lively tourist industry in Assynt.

The **Assynt Visitor Centre** (☎ 844330; www.assynt.info; Main St; Mon-Sat Apr-May, daily Jun-Oct) has an excellent range of books about the area, first-class displays about local history and wildlife, and a natural-history reading room, ideal for a wet day. The daily weather forecast is prominently available. There's an ATM at the bank near the port. **Inverbank** (Mon-Sat;) newsagency sells maps and books.

SLEEPING & EATING

Shore Camping and Caravan Site (☎ 844393; unpowered/powered sites for 2 £6/8) has plenty of space for tents right on the shore. There's a small shop; fish and chips and the like are available in summer.

The nearest hostel is **Achmelvich Beach SYHA Hostel** (☎ 0870 004 1102; www.syha.org.uk; dm £12), in the beach-side hamlet of Achmelvich a few miles northwest of town. It's close to the beautiful white sandy beach, and can be as peaceful as they come.

Veyatie B&B (☎ 844424; www.veyatie-scotland.co.uk; 66 Baddidarrach; s/d £38/56), at the very end of the road on the north side of Loch Inver, enjoys a spellbinding view of the Suilven and Canisp peaks. Breakfast is better than most, and is served on a splendid selection of crockery from nearby Highland Stoneware.

Riverside Restaurant (☎ 844356; Main St; mains £10-20; dinner) is the celebrated place to eat in Lochinver. It's famous for its savoury and fruit pies (which you can take away or even have posted home) and specialises in locally caught fish. The **Conservatory** (mains £6-10; lunch & dinner) also serves the pies, of which venison and cranberry is highly regarded, and light meals.

Caberfeidh Restaurant (☎ 844321; Main St; mains £9-15; lunch & dinner) serves standard bar meals, including a seafood platter, and is the best alternative if you find the Riverside is overflowing.

Along the main street is a **Spar** (Mon-Sat) supermarket and a butcher-greengrocer. The smaller **Inver Stores** (daily) is about 800m along the Baddidarrach road.

GETTING THERE & AWAY

Lochinver is on the A837, 10 miles (16km) west of the Skiag Bridge junction with the A894. The **Tim Dearman Coaches** (☎ 01349 883585; www.timdearmancoaches.co.uk) Inverness–Durness service stops at Lochinver (£14, three hours, daily July to September, no Sunday service April and May).

Inchnadamph

Inchnadamph is simply a hotel, bunkhouse and a handful of houses, situated all by themselves beside the A837 north of the Ledmore junction.

Inchnadamph Lodge (☎ 01571 822218; www.inch-lodge.co.uk; dm/s/d £14/25/40) offers B&B in small dorms or doubles, or you can do your own cooking. There's a small shop nearby that sells groceries, frozen food, beer and wine.

The **Tim Dearman Coaches** (☎ 01349 883585; www.timdearmancoaches.co.uk) Inverness–Durness service (£13, 2½ hours, daily July to September, no Sunday service April and May) will pick up and drop off at Inchnadamph on request.

EAS A' CHÙAL ALUINN

Duration	5¾–6¼ hours
Distance	10.4 miles (16.7km)
Difficulty	moderate
Start/Finish	Loch na Gainmhich car park
Nearest Town	Lochinver (left)
Transport	bus

Summary A ruggedly scenic walk to the top of the highest waterfall in Scotland, in one of the wildest corners of Sutherland.

Eas a' Chùal Aluinn (which means 'beautiful slender waterfall') is the highest waterfall in Scotland, with a drop of 204m, most of it in three long streams with a broad cascade at the base. It may lack the sheer dramatic force of the Falls of Glomach (p179) but the setting is wild and beautiful in a strangely compelling and desolate way.

Essentially, the walk is a crossing of the rocky ridge, pockmarked with lochans and encrusted with cliffs and scree, rising precipitously from the shores of Loch Glencoul and Loch Beag and its tributary Abhainn an Loch Bhig in the north and east. On the western side, the ridge rises from north-flowing Unapool Burn and from the many streams that empty south into Loch Assynt.

Eas a' Chùal Aluinn spills over a weakness in the long line of cliffs rising from Abhainn an Loch Bhig. Miraculously, in an otherwise almost treeless area, spindly birch clings to the cliffs, permanently dampened by the fall's spray.

The path to the falls from the A894 is well-trodden, across rough, rocky ground that is boggy in places. On a fine day you could spend an hour or more exploring the cliff tops and seeking out better vantage points for the falls. The main walk is described as an out-and-back trip from the road. A through route, deeper into the wilderness, to Inchnadamph and mostly on clear paths is outlined as an alternative. While you're there it's well worth the effort to duck up to Glas Bheinn (opposite), a peak affording fine views.

PLANNING

Stalking

During the stalking season (mid-August to mid-October) walkers are asked to avoid areas where stalking is taking place on the day, although access remains open on the main paths. Information about activities and recommended walking routes in the area is available from **Assynt Estates** (☎ 01571 822208).

GETTING TO/FROM THE WALK

The walk starts at a signposted car park on a sharp bend in the A894, above the northwestern corner of Loch na Gainmhich. The Tim Dearman Coaches Inverness–Durness service (see p260) will stop as close as safely possible to the car park; the timetable should give you plenty of time to do the walk. The same service stops at Inchnadamph if you decide to tackle the alternative through walk.

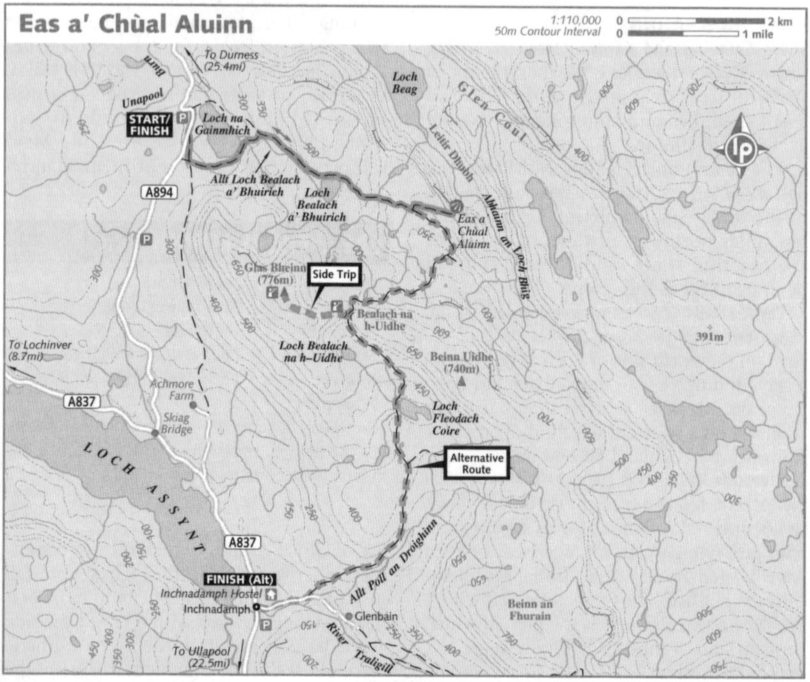

THE WALK

From the car park walk south along the road for about 200m and diverge down an old track to the left. It crosses a small stream then rises to meet an east–west path; turn left. The path descends to and parallels the shore of Loch na Gainmhich for about 150m then starts to rise northeast, crossing a small stream and leading on to Allt Loch Bealach a' Bhuirich. Cross and continue north briefly to meet a narrow path on the left. Walk up the northern side of a rugged, rocky valley, with fine views of the corries on the north face of Glas Bheinn, and on to dark, peaceful **Loch Bealach a' Bhuirich** (1¼ hours from the start). The bealach itself is above the loch to the east.

The path, now cairned, wastes no time in losing height down to a nameless tributary of Abhainn an Loch Bhig. Cross the burn on stepping stones and continue beside it downstream (not on the northern side as shown on the OS map). Go across very peaty ground, through a line of low cliffs and down to near the edge of the main cliff, high above Abhainn an Loch Bhig. Continue to the right (southeast) for about 250m to a good vantage point for **Eas a' Chùal Aluinn** (1¼ hours from Loch Bealach a' Bhuirich) – it's next to impossible to safely get a good close-up view. A series of graceful, steep cascades fall to the green, flat-floored glen of Abhainn an Loch Bhig, meandering into tranquil Loch Beag and overlooked by cliffs on its far side.

Retrace your steps to the car park and main road.

ALTERNATIVE ROUTE: TO INCHNADAMPH

3½–4 hours, 5.5 miles (8.7km)

Return almost to the stepping stones and, in a peaty spot between two crags (the left one topped with a cairn), turn left. A path materialises in a very short distance and rises southeast then south up a rocky spur. It crosses a shallow valley and continues rather deviously to overlook a pair of lochans. Turn right at a cairned path junction and go between these lochans then up the wild, rocky glen feeding them towards the cliffs ahead (south). The path, clear enough on the ground, is sparsely cairned. Take care to find a right-hand turn in the path, then cross a stream on mossy stepping stones and continue up to a rock shelf at the base of the steep, scree-strewn slopes. The path zigzags up to **Bealach na h-Uidhe** (1¾ to two hours from the waterfall), a fine lookout over the country to the south.

The path drops straight down from the gap. On the edge of the scree on the steep slope to the left, the path bends left (southeast) across a rocky shoulder then south down to Loch Fleodach Coire, becoming increasingly clear and intermittently cairned. Continue across two burns entering the loch then cross the burn flowing from the loch. Make your way through a maze of peat hags up to a broad spur, past a small lochan and on to a path junction where there's a stone shelter, used by stalkers. From here the path makes a well-graded descent into the glen of Allt Poll an Droighinn and on to meet the Gleann Dubh vehicle track near a bridge. Turn right and walk down to the Inchnadamph car park (1¾ to two hours from the bealach).

SIDE TRIP: GLAS BHEINN

1–1¼ hours, 2 miles (3km), 150m ascent

From a large cairn at Bealach na h-Uidhe, head west up over grass then scree and some boulders on the narrow ridge to the broad summit plateau. There isn't much of a path but it's easy walking, mainly on grass, to a subsidiary top on a low cliff line bisecting the plateau. Descend slightly from here, past a tiny lochan on the left, then up over shattered rock to the 2m-high cairn on **Glas Bheinn** (776m). The views of Quinag and Suilven are truly awe-inspiring. All the mountains to the north can be seen and the view east, on a good day, extends to Ben Wyvis, not far from Inverness.

QUINAG

Duration	4¼–4½ hours
Distance	6.5 miles (10.4km)
Difficulty	moderate–demanding
Start/Finish	Cnoc a'Choilich car park
Nearest Town	Lochinver (p265)
Transport	private

Summary Enjoy the ease with which you can explore one of the more formidable of Assynt's magnificent peaks, and the superb wraparound views.

Quinag (pronounced 'koon-yak', from the Gaelic for 'milking pail') is a uniquely Y-shaped mountain barricaded by terraced sandstone cliffs and overlooking Loch Glencoul to the north and Loch Assynt to the south. It has three distinct tops: Spidean Coinich (764m) on the southern leg of the Y, separated by deep Bealach a'Chornaidh from Sàil Gharbh (808m) on the northeastern arm and Sàil Ghorm (776m) to the north. So steep and cliff-bound are almost all the mountain's slopes that it's a minor miracle walkers can reach any of the summits. Fortunately, the southeastern spur yields easily and the rest of the upper reaches don't present any serious difficulties. There are a few airy places nevertheless, so consider your route carefully if you suffer from vertigo. The views from the high ground are ample reward: long swathes of coastline, tiny settlements, Loch Glencoul, Ben More Assynt and all the distinctive peaks west of the main road. With luck you may also meet a ptarmigan or two, remarkably fearless birds though difficult to spot with their camouflage suits of grey-black and white.

The route described here crosses two of the three summits – Sail Ghorm would entail an extra 1.9 miles (3km), more than an hour of walking, and about 140m of extra ascent on top of the 860m you would already have climbed.

Quinag and its surrounds, from the shores of Loch Glencoul south to the middle of Loch Assynt, were added to the John Muir Trust's (p31) portfolio of estates in

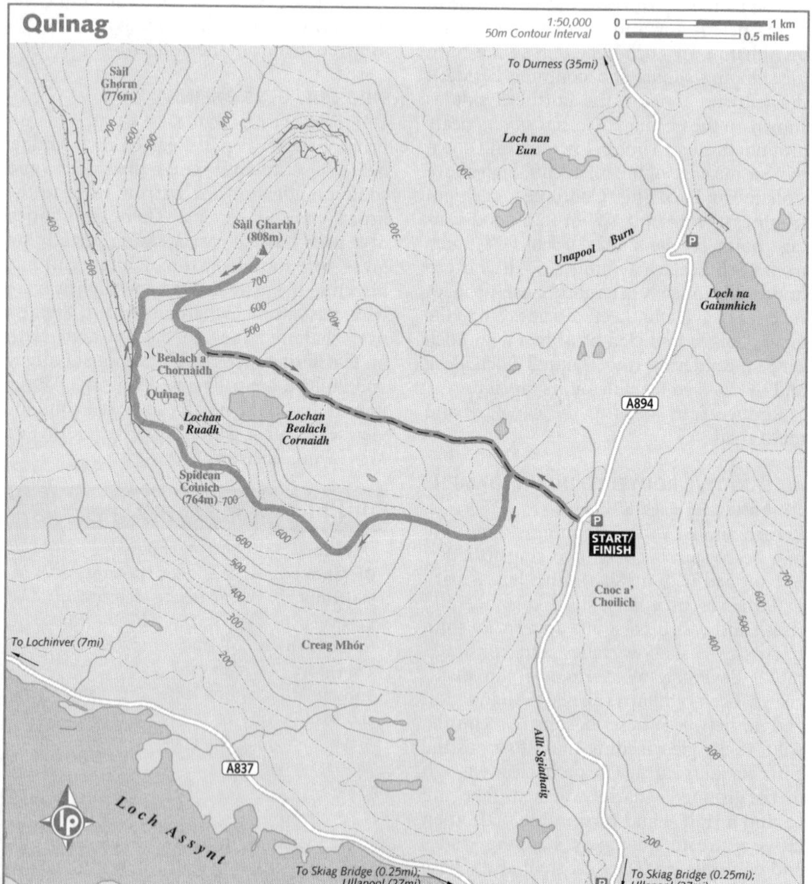

SHORT WALKS

Faraid Head

The wide sandy beaches and marram-grassed dunes northwest of Durness (p260) offer delightful walking at any time of year, and especially when the tide is right out. Views of the coastal cliffs across Balnakeil Bay are superb, and the water looks tempting, though it's not exactly warm. Allow an hour or more for a delightful 3-mile (5km) partly circular walk from the car park overlooking the beach, about 800m beyond Balnakeil craft village and opposite a stone-walled burial ground. The relevant OS Landranger 1:50,000 map is No 9. A defence establishment monopolises the top of Faraid Head so access to the head itself is out of bounds (for more information about access, go to www.durness.org).

From the car park (where there's an information board) walk along the beach. If the tide is in, pick up a road at the northern end of the beach and follow it north. Diverge where it turns east for close-up views of Faraid Head. If the tide is out, stick to the beach as far as boulders spread across the sand; gain the low cliff top and walk along sheep-cropped grass, generally close to the edge, northwest to a low point. Turn east and climb to a vantage point for fine views of the cliffs at Faraid Head, much frequented by fulmars, gulls and other sea birds. For the return, either loop back to the beach or head across to the road that leads to the defence site and follow it through dunes and across grassy fields, back to the beach and car park.

Falls of Kirkaig

These beautiful cascades and waterfalls on the tumbling River Kirkaig, in the shadow of the extraordinary peak Suilven, are the focus of a 5.5-mile (9km) walk along mostly good paths from near **Achins Bookshop & Cafe** (☎ 01571 844262; www.scotbooks.freeuk.com; snacks & light meals £3-5; 🕑 10am-5pm Mon-Sat) – yes, a bookshop with a fine selection of Scottish titles in the middle of nowhere, and a homespun, popular café next door.

The walk starts and finishes at a car park beside a bridge over the River Kirkaig on the eastern edge of the hamlet of Inverkirkaig, 2.5 miles south of Lochinver (p265) on the narrow, winding road to Achiltibuie. Allow two hours for the walk, which involves 200m of ascent, and consult OS Landranger 1:50,000 map No 15.

From the car park a sign points you through a small gate to a vehicle track, past a plaque in memory of the poet and lover of all things in Assynt, Norman MacCaig. Within 200m, bear right along a path through mature birch wood, carpeted with primroses, violets and wood anemones in spring. About 12 minutes out, the path starts to gain height and, 15 minutes further on, swings northeast to cross moorland. After a while the dome and pinnacles of Suilven appear. Soon the path forks; bear right with the sign to Falls of Kirkaig. Descend to informal vantage points across the impressive cascades feeding the falls, which plunge into a wide pool. Retrace your steps to the bookshop.

2005. The estate was purchased at the express wish of its previous owners – and with the crucial help of a huge private donation – in a bid to ensure its future guardianship. In turn, the Trust has pledged to involve local people in the management of the estate.

GETTING TO/FROM THE WALK

The car park at the start and finish is on the eastern side of the A894 Ullapool–Durness road, 2.3 miles north of the junction with the A837 Lochinver road; it is not marked by a standard blue parking sign.

THE WALK

From the car park, walk south along the road for around 30m, then turn off along a path which crosses Allt Sgiathaig on a footbridge. Follow the pathway – generally northwest and west – across moorland. Just 10 minutes out, leave the path where rock slabs appear on the left (south); a cairn marks the spot. Continue generally southwest past a nameless, reedy lochan, across a small burn and turn west as soon as possible to walk up the almost unbroken tiers of sandstone slabs along the northern rim of the ridge. Thirty minutes from the main path a shallow gully intervenes; turn southwest briefly to gain the broad, partly grassed ridge. Retrieve the westerly course over rocky ground; the path comes and goes but what looks like a large cairn on the western skyline serves as a beacon. It turns out to be a small circular shelter. Continue up to a crest, through a break in the rampart of grey crags. Drop down to a small saddle then head northwest, soon steeply up a clear path, to the flat summit of **Spidean Coinich** (764m), 50 minutes from the shallow gully. The marvellous view embraces the classic Assynt patchwork of land and water below the peaks of Suilven and Canisp, and Cul Mor to the south.

Descend from the southern edge of the summit – which involves some very steep work over slightly exposed crags – then follow the narrow ridge, which is a bit of a scramble in places. Go down steeply, now on the distinctive pinkish Torridonian sandstone, to Lochan Ruadh in a broad saddle. Then comes another up, mostly on grass, to a small, nameless pinnacle. Drop down to **Bealach a'Chornaidh** (40 minutes from Spidean Coinich). From a distance the next climb looked hair-raisingly steep and barred by low cliffs; the reality is nowhere near as bad. The path leads steeply up to the cliffs, where one slightly awkward move can easily be bypassed to the right. Higher up, go over the top of a rocky knoll on the main ridge, or bypass it on the eastern side, to a broad saddle with a curious pavement of sandstone slabs. Continue up the rocky ridge onto the fine-grained grey sandstone capping the flattish summit of **Sàil Gharbh** (808m), where a survey pillar lurks inside a stone shelter (40 minutes from the saddle).

Retrace your steps to the broad saddle then head generally southwest on a well-used path down and across the steep slope to meet a path in the corrie, about 150m east of Bealach a Choinich (30 minutes from the top). The path, vague in places over wet ground, leads southeast and east, across the wide hanging valley cradling Lochan Bealach Cornaidh, down to and across a knobbly plain to a lochan-studded plateau. Here the path becomes firm for the last mile or so beyond low-lying ground, and on to the road (50 minutes from the path junction).

MORE WALKS

ASSYNT

Ben More Assynt

From the west, Ben More Assynt (998m/3273ft) hides behind its satellite Conival (987m), so that they seem to merge into one huge mass of shattered quartzite. Doing both peaks (they're Munros) in a day makes for a fairly long and strenuous, but outstandingly scenic, walk of 10.4 miles (16.5km) involving 1100m of ascent; allow seven to 7½ hours. Most folk do it as a there-and-back trip; the views on the way back are completely different from those on the way up – after the incredible summit panorama, right across Scotland. Provided you keep to the standard route via Gleann Dubh, access during the stalking season is not an issue. Use OS Landranger 1:50,000 map No 15.

The walk starts and finishes at the car park at the entrance to the Inchnadamph Hotel, beside the A837 between Ledmore and the Lochinver turnoff.

Glen Canisp

A public footpath provides an outstandingly scenic walk of 14 miles (22.5km) across wild, rugged moorland, beside remote and beautiful lochs and past two of the north's prominent landmarks, Canisp and Suilven. It involves only 220m of ascent; allow 6½ to seven hours for the moderate–demanding outing. Alternatively, the walk could be split into two, to simplify transport arrangements, perhaps making Lochan Fada or Loch na Gainimh the turnaround points, depending on where you are based. From either direction, you can have a go at Canisp (846m) or Suilven (731m); for details of the latter see opposite. Lochinver (p265) is a convenient base for the walk. Use OS Landranger 1:50,000 map No 15.

Since fording the outlet stream from Lochan Fada can be hazardous after rain, when the stepping stones can be about 50cm under water, keep this walk for a fine, dry spell. Elphin, near the starting point, is on the A835, about 15 miles (24km) north of Ullapool and 2.4 miles (4km) west of Ledmore and the A837. The walk starts 100m east of the bridge over the Ledmore River, about 1.2 miles east of Elphin on the A835. There is no formal car park nearby but there is space for three cars beside a gate 300m east of the bridge. The walk finishes at a junction with the A837, marked by a public footpath sign to Ledmore, at the southern end of Lochinver. There is a car park about 200m to the right.

Suilven

Suilven (731m) is perhaps the icon for the northwest – its extraordinary terraced sandstone dome looming over Lochinver is a calendar staple. It's quite a complex mountain, however, with a longish, bristly ridge tapering away from the dome, Caisteal Liath – its highest point.

The main approach is from Lochinver, along the road to Glencanisp Lodge, then the vehicle track southeast as far as the southern end of Loch na Gainimh. An all-too-well-used path goes up to Bealach Mór, from where the summit is easily reached. A full traverse of the ridge, southeast from the bealach, calls for some scrambling and a head for heights. The walk is covered by OS Landranger 1:50,000 map No 15. The Scottish Mountaineering Club's guide *The Northwest Highlands* has a useful description.

Suilven is within a large estate purchased by the local **Assynt Foundation** (☎ 01571 844392; www.assyntfoundation.co.uk) in 2005.

Point of Stoer

If mist or low cloud rule out hill walking, then the Old Man of Stoer, a towering sea stack, and the spectacular coastline around Point of Stoer, northwest of Lochinver, are ideal. Whatever the weather, the views of the Assynt peaks are magnificent. An easy–moderate 5-mile (8km) round walk from Stoerhead lighthouse takes you along the cliff tops to the point then back over two grassy, heathery 'hills' – Sidhean Mòr and its nameless satellite, topped by a communications tower.

At the lighthouse car park a sign points to the Old Man of Stoer; follow well-used paths as close as safely possible to the cliff edge to the point nearest the Old Man, beyond which the path is less clear.

Turn off the A837 just north of Lochinver along the B869 coastal road. Follow it for 6 miles through the villages of Clachtoll and Stoer to the signposted turnoff to the lighthouse. Follow this road north to an intersection at Achnacarnin; turn left (as indicated) and continue to the lighthouse car park. The nearest places for refreshments are at Lochinver or Drumbeg, about 8 miles east along the B869. Use OS Landranger 1:50,000 map No 15.

Little Assynt Estate

This estate, a few miles east of Lochinver, is owned by the local Culag Community Woodland Trust; its aims are to restore the natural heart of the estate with extensive tree plantings and to make it more accessible. Two waymarked routes have been developed through the low, grassy hills, past the remains of shielings (small farming settlements), secluded lochans and small birch woods. The 1-mile (1.6km) Leitir Easaidh is an all-abilities path; the other, to Loch an t-Sabhail and back, is a circular walk of around 3 miles (4km). They're described in a beautifully illustrated brochure, available from the Assynt Visitor Centre (p265).

Stac Pollaidh

Stac Pollaidh (612m), or Stac Polly, is perhaps the most distinctive peak among the remarkable group of mountains north of Ullapool, and the most accessible. An isolated, comb-like peak west of Elphin, it rises precipitously above Loch Lurgainn to the south and from a maze of lochs and rock to the north, and affords panoramic views as fine as those from many peaks hundreds of metres higher. An excellent path climbs round the steep eastern flank and up to the top from the north; a western extension makes a round walk possible.

The path starts at a formal car park beside the single-track road to Achiltibuie, which branches from the A835 between Ullapool and Elphin. Achiltibuie, a small village overlooking the Summer Isles in outer Loch Broom, is the nearest village and a good base for walks in the area. Allow about three hours for the 2.5-mile (4km) walk; consult OS Landranger 1:50,000 map No 15.

Northern Isles

Though they're lumped together for convenience as the Northern Isles, the island groups of Orkney and Shetland proudly maintain their distinctive identities. Orkney is very green, with lush fields cropped by sheep and cattle. Across 60 miles of turbulent Atlantic Ocean, Shetland's colours are browns and blues rather than green, it's more rugged, has a real edge-of-the-world feel and relates at least as much to the Nordic world as it does to Scotland. The islands do share superb coastal scenery, with seemingly endless miles of cliffs, inlets, stacks, offshore islets and the finest coastal walking in the entire country (and in Britain). Both island groups are crowded with archaeological sites, many of exceptional significance, and home to huge sea-bird populations. Add the occasional display of the aurora borealis (the northern lights), endless summer daylight hours and exceptionally friendly and welcoming locals, and you have two inspirational walking destinations.

In Orkney, it's almost obligatory to visit Hoy, the largest Orkney isle, and to walk out to the spectacular northwest coast to see the iconic sea stack, the Old Man of Hoy. Orkney Mainland's west coast offers outstandingly scenic walking, with some of the finest sea stacks, deep inlets and secluded coves found here. The island of Westray not only has spectacular coast walking but is also home to vast sea-bird colonies. On Shetland's northernmost island, Unst, Hermaness National Nature Reserve is a bird-watchers' delight and a coast-walking destination *par excellence*. On the Muckle Roe and Eshaness peninsulas you will find what we believe is the finest coast walking anywhere in Scotland – completely unspoiled and incomparably beautiful.

HIGHLIGHTS

- Saying hello to the famous **Old Man of Hoy** (p275)
- Exploring **Yesnaby's** (p278) awesome geos, stacks and cliffs, which are among Scotland's finest
- Peering at puffins and gazing at gannets in their thousands at **Hermaness** (p286)
- Marvelling at remnants of ancient volcanoes along the magnificently rugged **Eshaness** (p289) coast

- www.visitorkney.com
- www.visitshetland.com

INFORMATION

Maps

For a topographic overview of the islands, OS Travel – Road 1:250,000 map No 2 *Northern Scotland* is ideal. Red Books' 1:160,000 *Orkney & Shetland Islands Leisure & Tourist Map* is better for overall trip planning.

ORKNEY

There is something almost mystical about the wild and beautiful Atlantic archipelago of Orkney. Beginning just 6 miles north of mainland Scotland, 68 islands, of which 19 are inhabited, stretch northeast for around 50 miles towards Shetland. Many of the islands are flat, or have low, gently sloping hills, patchworked with heather and grass moorland and green cultivated fields dotted with sheep and cattle (the ratio of humans to cattle is 1:5). Hoy is the exception; its steep-sided hills include Ward Hill (479m, p277), the highest in all Orkney. Here you'll also find some of the highest vertical sea cliffs in Scotland (and Britain) and the famous sea stack, the Old Man of Hoy (p275). The islands are endowed with the richest concentration of prehistoric archaeological sites in Europe and it's rare not to pass a few such sites on any walk you undertake. Sea cliffs in their infinite variety and scenic beauty are ever-present on every walk, and

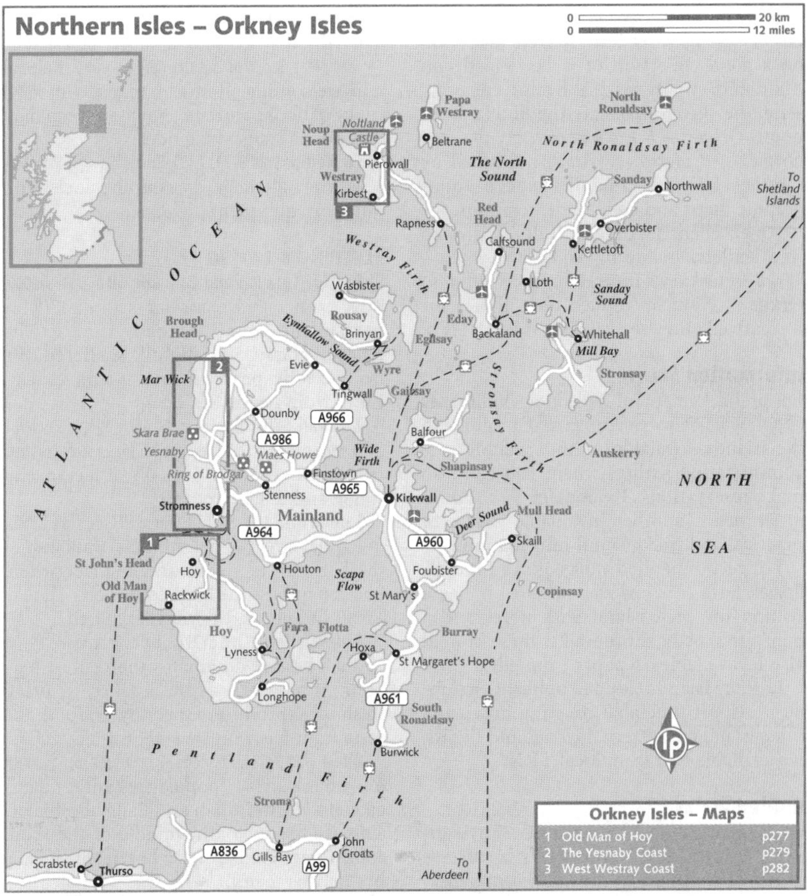

vast numbers of sea birds are constant companions, especially on Westray walks.

Considering its northerly latitude, Orkney experiences a surprisingly temperate climate, with mild winters and cool, damp summers. Wind is its most predictable feature, with fronts regularly sweeping in from the west or southwest, bringing wet and windy weather. This is typically followed by cold northwesterlies driving the odd squally shower of rain or hail. Showery days can make for exhilarating walking, with stormy seas sparkling under crystalline blue skies.

PLANNING

Books

Handy pocket-sized *Walks – Orkney* by Felicity Martin succinctly describes 40 outings, from short strolls to full-day walks. *Orkney on Foot* by Kate Barrett takes you on a good collection of walks, mostly on Mainland; written in a lively, engaging style, the sketch maps are the book's weak point. *Orkney – 8 Environment Walks* and *Orkney – 8 Heritage Walks,* published by Orkney Islands Council, feature topographic maps and concise descriptions.

An excellent set of beautifully illustrated free leaflets, including *Hidden Orkney – Wildlife*, *Orkney's Birds*, *Orkney's Cliffs* and *Orkney's Flora*, introduce their topics informatively; they're available at local TICs.

Information Sources

For preliminary planning contact **VisitOrkney** (☎ 01856 875056, www.visitorkney.com). Its guide to the islands, available online, includes accommodation listings where you can also make reservations. Its booklet *The Islands of Orkney* is another invaluable source of practical and background information.

For recommended walks, go to the **Walk Orkney** (www.walkorkney.com) website. It has a section for each island with notes and a map for mostly short walks; these should also be available on paper from TICs.

Orkney Islands Council publishes a public transport timetable covering buses and inter-island and external ferries and flights; it's available free from local TICs.

Guided Walks

OCEAN (Orkney Community Environment Awareness Network) is a diverse group of community and official organisations that stages a program of guided walks and tours to natural and cultural heritage sites throughout Orkney. Groups include the Royal Society for the Protection of Birds (RSPB) and Historic Scotland. For more information contact **Scottish Natural Heritage** (SNH; ☎ 01856 875302; 54 Junction Rd, Kirkwall) or pick up a copy of the program at local TICs.

ACCESS TOWN

Kirkwall

☎ 01856 / pop 6210

The capital of Orkney, Kirkwall is a rather prosaic commercial centre (apart from the area around magnificent St Magnus Cathedral), though it does have a wide range of services and good transport connections.

INFORMATION

The **TIC** (☎ 872856; www.visitorkney.com; 6 Broad St; 🕒 daily May-Sep, Mon-Sat Oct-Apr) is very helpful and welcoming. It stocks maps, a modest range of books and can provide a town map and public transport guide.

EG Kemp (☎ 872137; 31 Bridge St; 🕒 Mon-Sat) sells the full range of camping fuels, and outdoor equipment.

SLEEPING & EATING

Pickaquoy Caravan and Camping Site (☎ 879900; Pickaquoy Rd; unpowered/powered sites for 2 £7/10) is next to the large Pickaquoy Centre. The fenced, grassy and slightly sheltered site isn't exactly peaceful, but is convenient. Enter from Peerie Sea Loan.

Kirkwall SYHA Hostel (☎ 0870 004 1133; www.syha.org.uk; Old Scapa Rd; dm/d £13/26) is a fair step from the harbour. Unusually, it has several single and double rooms.

Lerona B&B (☎ 874538; Cromwell Cres; s/d £30/50), in a quiet street seven minutes' walk east of the harbour, is a comfortable place where you can browse the large collection of books about Orkney; breakfast is excellent.

Kirkwall Hotel (☎ 872232; Harbour St; mains £9-14; 🕒 lunch & dinner) dominates the central harbour front. Great pride is taken in using fresh local produce, especially seafood; the restaurant has won several awards.

Dil Se (☎ 875242; 7 Bridge St; mains £9-16; 🕒 lunch & dinner) is a stylish, popular restaurant dedicated to North Indian and Bangladeshi cuisine. Go for one of the middle-of-the-road, subtly flavoured dishes; hot really means hot on this menu!

For groceries, **Somerfield** (Pickaquoy Rd) and **Co-op** (Pickaquoy Rd) supermarkets are close together.

GETTING THERE & AWAY

British Airways/Loganair (☎ 0870 850 9850; www.britishairways.com) flies daily to Kirkwall from Aberdeen (50 minutes), Edinburgh (1½ hours), Glasgow (1½ hours), Inverness (45 minutes) and Sumburgh on Shetland (35 minutes). Fares fluctuate widely according to date and time of departure. Kirkwall airport is 2.5 miles from the town centre; Orkney Coaches operates a connecting bus service to the town centre (£1, 15 minutes, Monday to Saturday).

NorthLink Ferries (☎ 0845 600 0449; www.northlinkferries.co.uk) operates the service between Aberdeen and Kirkwall (passenger/car/two-berth cabin £24/85/106, six hours, Tuesday, Thursday, Saturday and Sunday), and on to Lerwick in Shetland. For its Scrabster–Stromness service see p279.

Pentland Ferries (☎ 831226; www.pentlandferries.co.uk) runs a small car ferry from Gills Bay, east of Thurso, to St Margaret's Hope on South Ronaldsay (passenger/car £12/28, one hour, four daily), across what the company claims is the calmest stretch of the notorious Pentland Firth. Booking is essential

John O'Groats Ferry (☎ 01955 611353; www.jogferry.co.uk) provides a passenger-only service between John O'Groats and Burwick on South Ronaldsay (£16, 40 minutes, up to four daily May to September). A connecting bus service takes you to Kirkwall.

OLD MAN OF HOY

Duration	5½–6 hours
Distance	13.6 miles (22.1km)
Difficulty	moderate
Start/Finish	Moaness pier, Hoy (p276)
Transport	ferry

Summary A close encounter with Orkney's famous landmark, impressively high sea cliffs and the chance to climb Hoy's highest hill.

Hoy, the second-largest Orkney isle, is by far the most rugged. Long, steep-sided, broad-backed ridges dominate the island, rising from deep, wide valleys. Ward Hill (479m), the highest point in all of Orkney, rises sharply from the northeastern coastal fringe, and gives superb views across the isles and south to the mainland. The Old Man, all 137m of him, is the tallest sea stack in Europe. Consisting of thin slabs of sandstone, it stands close to colourful, near-vertical cliffs, 200m or more high.

A fair proportion of the island is protected in the Hoy Nature Reserve, owned and managed by the RSPB. The upland moors provide ideal nesting sites for several hundred pairs of great skua (bonxie), while fulmars, puffins, guillemots, razorbills and kittiwakes jostle for space on the cliffs. Another inhabitant of the moorlands that you'll undoubtedly meet if you climb Ward Hill is the mountain hare. In spring it's grey-white, in transition from its winter coat to the brown summer garb.

BEWARE OF THE BONXIE

The great skua, known as a bonxie in the Orkneys, is one of the most formidable and aggressive sea birds in the world. Surpassed in size and power only by the great black-backed gull, the great skua commonly attacks other birds in flight to force them to drop their catch. They even attack and kill gannets, hanging on to a tail or wingtip until the gannet has to ditch. Until the early 20th century the great skua's only breeding colonies in the British Isles were on Unst and Foula in Shetland. They have since spread across Orkney and into northern mainland Scotland.

If you find yourself too close to a skua nest (on the ground in moorland) you may be dive-bombed. The huge birds approach out of a dive at speeds of up to 50mph but rarely make direct contact. Still, it can be an unnerving experience and the best defence is to wave a walking pole above your head to ward off sharp beaks. If you happen to stray into a colony you could find yourself under attack on all fronts!

In Hermaness Nature Reserve (p286) in Shetland, skua have become accustomed to humans so will rarely attack. Of the other sea birds you're likely to encounter in the Northern Isles, only terns are as aggressive in defending their nests, often pecking with their small, very sharp beaks. The best strategy is to steer well clear of all ground-nesting bird colonies. You have been warned!

The walk is described as an out-and-back jaunt from Moaness pier, used by the ferry from Stromness; an ascent of Ward Hill is suggested as a side trip. Should you prefer a shorter walk, you can start and finish at Rackwick, a settlement on Hoy's south coast, directly accessible by car, or by minibus from Moaness. Allow 2½ to three hours for this 5-mile (8km) walk. If you're prepared to arrive at Rackwick with enough food and gear to stay overnight, you can patronise the SYHA hostel there; it's possible to camp nearby and use hostel facilities.

PLANNING

Maps

Use either OS Explorer 1:25,000 map No 462 *Hoy* or OS Landranger 1:50,000 map No 7 *Orkney – Southern Isles.*

NEAREST TOWN

Hoy

☎ 01856

Hoy is the general name for the thin scattering of cottages and farms on the hillsides above Moaness pier. There are no shops on Hoy so bring all the supplies you'll need.

Hoy Outdoor Centre (☎ 873535; www.syha.org.uk; dm £12) is 15 minutes' walk uphill from the pier, near the prominent church. Run by the Orkney Islands Council Education Dept, it has small en suite rooms and excellent facilities.

WATCH YOUR STEP!

During all the walks in this chapter you'll inevitably be going along, or close to, the edge of high sea cliffs, which are generally unfenced and, in places, loose and crumbling. This sort of walking is potentially hazardous, especially where nesting sea birds invite a closer look from the cliff edge. Be careful and err on the side of caution, especially when the wind is strong. Accidents have occurred when people wearing waterproof outer gear have slipped on steep slopes above the cliffs – the combination of shiny fabric and wet grass can be lethal.

Another, less obvious, hazard is rabbit burrows, found anywhere in sandy ground; they're far from obvious and could easily cause a sprained ankle.

Quoydale B&B (☎ 791315; quoydale@supanet.com; s/d £25/46, dinner £10) is a working farm all by itself overlooking Burra Sound; the bedrooms are a bit of a tight fit and you share a bathroom.

Rackwick SYHA (☎ 873535; www.syha.org.uk; dm £8) is a small hostel in a great location, at the start of the path to the Old Man.

Orkney Ferries (☎ 872044; www.orkneyferries.co.uk) operates a passenger ferry between Stromness and Moaness pier (£7 return, 25 minutes, four services Monday to Friday, two Saturday and Sunday). **Albert Clark** (☎ 791315) meets most ferries in his minibus and plies the road to and from Rackwick (£5).

Alternatively, if you fancy exploring the island yourself, Orkney Ferries vehicle ferry goes from Houton, east of Stromness, to Lyness in southeastern Hoy (passenger/vehicle return £7/20, 45 minutes, six services Monday to Friday, four Saturday, five Sunday).

THE WALK

From Moaness pier walk up the single track road leading generally west. Follow it for 1.5 miles, ignoring left and right turns, climbing gently at first then more steeply past a church. At the top of the hill (40 minutes from the start) the road turns right and a good track continues straight on towards the gap between Cuilags on the right and Ward Hill on the left. Follow the track to **Sandy Loch**, where it deteriorates to a rough, wide path. This gains height steadily through the impressive glen, eventually reaching the watershed, from where it drops purposefully past the small glen known as Berrie Dale to the west, which shelters hardy dwarf birches, the most northerly native woodland in Scotland. The path improves as you descend and there are bridges across the burn. An hour from Sandy Loch turn right at a minor road then shortly right again to reach the youth hostel.

The signposted path starts on its south side; go through a gateway and up past a small cottage on the right. Turn left beside a fence then right briefly. Turn left again to cross a burn, then pass behind a cottage and within 50m bear right uphill. The path angles up the slope, below another cottage, to a gate, going on to moorland. The path, nice and clear now, curves round

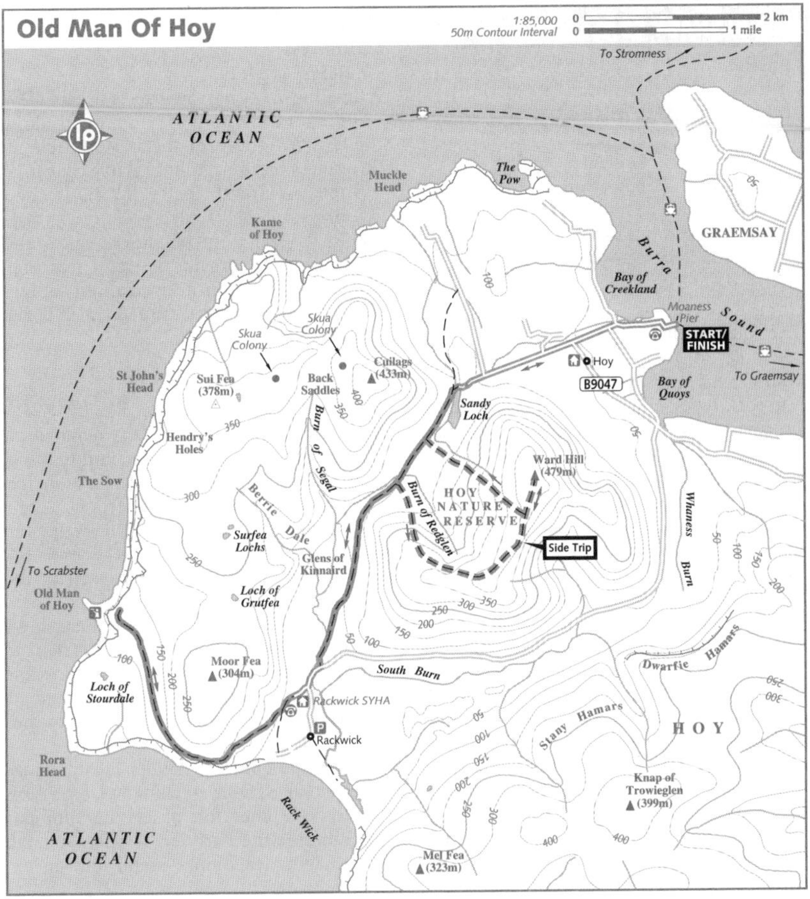

the hillside. Turning north, the topmost layers of the Old Man appear above the cliffs – if you didn't know it was there, you'd wonder what on earth this isolated block of rock was. A wide path, rocky in places, leads north across moorland and on to the cliff-top viewpoint for the Old Man and adjacent cliffs.

Retrace your steps to Rackwick and on to Moaness pier.

SIDE TRIP: WARD HILL

2 hours, 3.1 miles (5km), 330m ascent

The map suggests a traverse from the junction of the Moaness path and the Rackwick road, but the ridge here is covered with fairly deep heather, and only the uplands offer relatively easy walking across rocky ground, strewn with flat grey sandstone slabs. The most direct approach is from a large cairn beside the path, just south of the Burn of Redglen. It is simply a matter of climbing steeply to the ridge, then heading east and northeast along the undulating ridge to the summit of **Ward Hill**, which is topped by a cairn and a survey pillar inside a low, circular stone shelter. On a clear day you can see virtually all of Orkney, as well as the mainland in the general vicinity of Duncansby and Dunnet Heads. From the first bump with a cairn south from the summit descent northwest, regaining the path a short distance south of Sandy Loch.

THE YESNABY COAST

Duration	5–5½ hours
Distance	12.5 miles (20km)
Difficulty	moderate
Start	Bay of Skaill
Finish	Stromness (right)
Transport	bus (seasonal)

Summary One of Scotland's premier coastal walks, along spectacular cliffs and past sea stacks, with long sea views.

The southern half of Mainland's west coast resembles an awesome geological exhibition, with extensive displays of different features and rock types, and evidence of a variety of processes. The cliffs aren't particularly high, compared with Hoy's west coast, but they're impressively rugged, tilt alarmingly towards the sea, sheer in many places and constantly lashed by waves and spray. Sea birds do nest here but in comparatively small numbers. Landward of the cliff edge the mainly grassy slopes rise quite steeply and make for really easy walking. In the later stages it's necessary to take to the shore, where field fences around Breck Ness run along the edge of the low cliff, and to walk across flat rock slabs. The state of the tide shouldn't matter, though with a heavy sea and high tide, you'd be lucky to escape the occasional wetting.

The walk starts near Orkney's best known archaeological site, Skara Brae, a part of the Neolithic Heartland World Heritage site. As northern Europe's best preserved Neolithic village, it deserves to be on your must-do list in Orkney.

PLANNING

Maps

Use either OS Explorer 1:25,000 map No 463 *Orkney – West Mainland* or OS Landranger 1:50,000 map No 6 *Orkney – Mainland*.

NEAREST TOWN

Stromness

☎ 01856 / pop 1610

A small town of narrow streets, steep alleyways and rather dour grey buildings along the western shore of the Bay of Ireland, Stromness has a beguiling, gritty charm.

Stromness Travel Centre (☎ 850716; www.visitorkney.com; NorthLink ferry terminal; daily May–mid-Sep, Mon-Sat mid-Sep–Apr) stocks maps and books and can provide a useful free map of the town. Two more specialised sources of books are **John Rae** (Victoria St) and **JL Broom** (Victoria St).

SLEEPING & EATING

Ness Point Camping & Caravan Site (☎ 873535; unpowered/powered sites for 2 £7/10) is perched on a breezy point at the southern end of town, though stone walls provide some shelter and the views of Hoy are superb.

Stromness Hostel (☎ 850589; www.stromnesshostel.co.uk; Hellihole Rd; dm £11, d with bathroom £24) is five minutes from the docks along the main street.

Ferry Bank B&B (☎ 851250; 2 North End Rd; s/d £30/50) overlooks the harbour and is flanked by its own large garden. It's impossible to fault this superb establishment and its breakfast is unsurpassed for variety and presentation.

Julia's Cafe & Bistro (☎ 850904; 20 Ferry Rd; mains café £5-10, bistro £10-18; café to 5pm, bistro dinner Thu-Sun) is a cheerful, deservedly popular place beside the harbour. It offers a small but imaginative dinner menu and an extensive wine list.

Stromness Hotel (☎ 850298; Victoria St; mains £7-17; lunch & dinner) dates from the beginning of the 20th century and has a measure of old-fashioned atmosphere and charm. The menu includes Orkney and Orient dishes served up generously; local beers are available on tap.

SKARA BRAE – WORLD HERITAGE SITE

For thousands of years Skara Brae was covered by sand until it was exposed by a severe storm in 1850. It is the best-preserved Neolithic village in northern Europe and offers a remarkably detailed insight into the thriving communities that lived in Orkney 5000 years ago. It is part of the Neolithic Heartland World Heritage site.

A visit to **Skara Brae** (☎ 841815; admission £7), managed by Historic Scotland, is a wonderful, thought-provoking start to the Yesnaby walk. The visitor centre there has informative displays and a sizable shop; the official guide to Skara Brae is among the many publications available.

Stock up with basic supplies at the **Co-op** (North End Rd) supermarket but for Orkney delicacies head for the **Stromness Deli** (Victoria St) or **Argo's Bakery** (Victoria St).

GETTING THERE & AWAY

NorthLink Ferries (☎ 0845 600 0449; www.northlinkferries.co.uk) operates a car ferry service between Scrabster, near Thurso on the mainland, and Stromness (passenger/car £15/45, 1½ hours, six services Monday to Saturday, four Sunday).

An **Orkney Coaches** (☎ 870555; www.rapsons.co.uk) bus service links Stromness and Kirkwall (£3, 30 minutes, hourly Monday to Saturday, six services Sunday).

GETTING TO/FROM THE WALK

Orkney Coaches (☎ 870555; www.rapsons.co.uk) operates a seasonal service (one service Monday to Friday, three Sunday, May to September) linking Skara Brae with Kirkwall (£3, 1¼ hours) and Stromness (£2, 20 minutes).

By car, turn off the A967 Kirkwall–Birsay road towards Bay of Skaill along the B9057 and follow signs to the bay at subsequent junctions; there's a parking area (with toilets) overlooking the beach.

THE WALK

Walk along Bay of Skaill beach, past **Skara Brae**; at the western end of the beach cross the shingle, pass a roofless stone building and follow a path beside a fence. Cross some rocks and scramble up to the open cliff top. Soon you pass Yettna Geo, crowded with birds. Climb to the cairn at **Row Head** (59m), from where the Old Man of Hoy comes into view. Continue southeast; about an hour out, Ness of Ramnageo bites deep inland. In places wind has stripped away the grass cover, creating a patchwork of flat rocks and grass, dotted in spring with pink thrift. It's easy enough to follow a narrow path close to the cliff edge for the best views. At an east–west barbed-wire fence, a signpost 'Footpath to Broch of Borwick' is on the far side; fortunately the stile is nearby to the right. The crumbling remains of the Iron Age **broch** sit on a small knoll; the entrance is intact so you can inspect its double-wall construction. Cross Bor Wick; stay above the fence to avoid barbed wire above a yawning drop near the end of the small headland. Continue the short distance to **Yesnaby** car park, beside the derelict WWII buildings, crossing the fence near its seaward end (35 minutes from Ness of Ramnageo). Information boards here describe local geology, history and wildlife.

Cross a small bay and diverge to the headland topped by a cairn for awesome views of

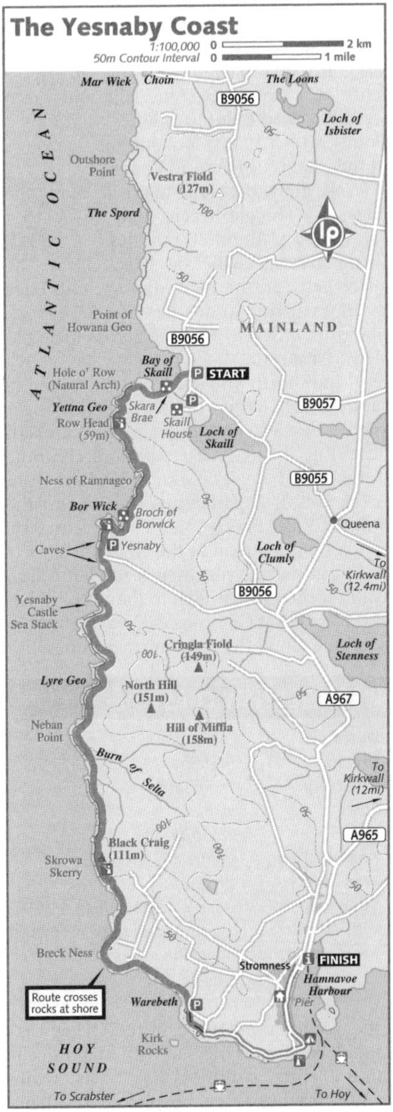

nearby cliffs. Gain height and you soon come to Garthna Geo, sheltering the elegant, grey **Yesnaby Castle** sea stack. Continue up, though a gate and on past deep Lyre Geo. Stick to the lower path to see the next (nameless) castle or sea stack in a shallow inlet close to Neban Point, much larger and more colourful than Yesnaby Castle, its horizontal strata exactly matching those of the point (one hour from Yesnaby). Soon, descend slightly to cross the wide shallow glen of Burn of Selta; beyond the third small stream crossing, go over a fence at a makeshift stone stile and climb steadily to **Black Craig** (40 minutes from Neban Point), with a WWII lookout, for fine views of the islands of Hoy and Graemsay.

Walk down the slope to a path along the edge of a shingle beach, then go up to a low cliff top. About 30 minutes from Black Craig, past a corner at Breck Ness, the space between the fence and the cliff edge disappears, so take to the shore-level rock platform with easy walking across huge flat slabs. Around a shallow point, stay at sea level and shortly you reach an intermittently sandy beach. When the fence is no longer visible above (about 250m from Warebeth beach) go up to a clear path and continue to the Warebeth car park (30 minutes from Breck Ness). A path leads on, around the point at Pulse Skerry, past a large cemetery. Join a bitumen road at the golf course for a few hundred metres, then a hard-surfaced path for the short stretch to the car park beside Ness Point Camping & Caravan Site (or continue along the road into Stromness).

WEST WESTRAY COAST

Duration	3–3½ hours
Distance	5.5 miles (8.8km)
Difficulty	moderate
Start	Kirbest
Finish	Noup Head
Nearest Town	Pierowall (opposite)
Transport	private

Summary A first-class coastal cliff-top walk with countless thousands of sea birds for company and wonderfully wide views.

Often called the 'Queen of the Orkney Islands', Westray is blessed with magnificent coastal cliffs, countless sea birds, white sandy beaches, very hospitable residents and an infectious atmosphere of peace and contentment.

Noup Cliffs Nature Reserve, cared for by the RSPB, is renowned for its wealth of bird life. The horizontal beds of old red sandstone on west Westray's sea cliffs have been weathered by the elements, creating perfect nesting sites. The numbers are amazing; at the height of the breeding season these cliffs are home to around 60,000 guillemots (known as aaks in Orkney), 30,000 pairs of kittiwake, 3000 pairs of fulmar, several thousand puffins (known as the tammy norrie) and 1700 razorbills. Just inland from the cliffs, on the exposed coastal heath, about 20,000 arctic terns and 1000 pairs of great skua make their nests. In midsummer the combined impact of bird calls and their wheeling and diving, not to mention the smell, makes for a memorable experience.

Five defined walks have been developed on the island, exploring many places of interest, including the walk described here and the Castle O'Burrian (or Puffin) walk (p282). They're all outlined in free leaflets available from **VisitOrkney** (☎ 01856 875056; www.visitorkney.com) or locally.

Most of the way on this route you're on short, cropped grass; elsewhere it's bare or rocky ground underfoot. The route is not waymarked but there's a more-or-less-continuous path, and several stiles help to define the best route. If you use the alternative car park, Bis Geos, towards the northern end of the walk (see Getting to/from the Walk on p279), you'll have an extra 2 miles (3km) to walk from Noup Head; alternatively, you could follow the short waymarked path north from the coast near Bis Geos up to the car park, saving 1.9 miles (3km). In the absence of a lift from the end of the main route, it's 4 miles (6km) from the lighthouse back to Pierowall.

PLANNING

Maps

Use either OS Explorer 1:25,000 map No 464 *Orkney – Westray* or OS Landranger 1:50,000 map No 5 *Orkney – Northern Isles.*

Guided Walks

Westraak (☎ 01857 677777; www.westraak.co.uk; Quarry Rd, Pierowall) offers guided walks on the island; the owners are exceptionally knowledgeable and their tours are highly recommended.

Information Sources

Westray & Papa Westray Tourist Association (☎ 01857 677777; www.westrayandpapawestray.com; Quarry Rd, Pierowall) is a good place to start.

For information about the nature reserve, contact the **RSPB** (☎ 01856 850176; orkney@rspb.org.uk; 12-14 North End Rd, Stromness).

Westray Heritage Centre (☎ 01857 677414; admission £2; daily Jul-Aug, Sun & Mon, Tue-Sat afternoon Sep-Jun), next to the Pierowall Hotel, houses award-winning displays about the island's cultural and natural heritage.

NEAREST TOWN

Pierowall

☎ 01857

Pierowall, the only village on Westray, is a friendly place, spread around the sandy Bay of Pierowall. The bank opens only on Wednesday and Friday; a cash-back service from British banker's cards is available from Rendall's Store.

SLEEPING & EATING

The **Barn** (☎ 677214; www.thebarnwestray.com; Chalmersquoy; unpowered sites for 2 £10, dm/d £12/24) occupies a converted stone barn, complete with stone slab roof. Excellent facilities include double rooms and a campers' kitchen; the camp site itself is sheltered. The owners are very knowledgeable.

No 1 Broughton (☎ 677726; www.no1broughton.co.uk; No 1 Broughton; s/d £25/50) is a restored mid-19th-century Orkney house with large bedrooms, the walls of which are adorned with some of the host's artworks. Breakfast in the sunny conservatory features homemade bread and preserves.

Pierowall Hotel (☎ 677472; www.orknet.co.uk/pierowall; s/d £32/56, mains £5-11; lunch & dinner) has comfortable rooms and is justly famous for its fish and chips. The fresh, melt-in-the-mouth fish (several varieties are available) and thick chips are served up generously and are exceptionally good value. It also does takeaway fish and chips, wine and spirits.

Haff Yok Café (Quarry Rd; mains £2-4; lunch), run by the Westraak people (opposite), sells maps and crafts. Snacks and light meals are truly homemade, using local products, including bread. The name comes from the days when farms were worked with yoked horses; farmers would take a break for a snack between meals.

Rendall's (Mon-Sat, Sun afternoon May-Sep) and **Tulloch's** (Mon-Sat, Sun afternoon May-Sep) stores both have a fair range of groceries. The bakery is by the pier.

GETTING THERE & AWAY

Loganair (☎ 01856 872494; orkneyres@loganair.co.uk) operates flights from Kirkwall to Westray (£31, 20 minutes, daily except Wednesday).

Orkney Ferries (☎ 01856 872044; www.orkneyferries.co.uk) runs services from Kirkwall to Rapness on the southern tip of Westray (passenger/car £7/15, 1¾ hours, three services Sunday to Friday, two Saturday).

Westray Bus (☎ 677450) links Rapness and Pierowall and meets most ferries (£2, 20 minutes, three services Monday, Wednesday and Thursday, two Tuesday, Friday, Saturday and Sunday, May to September).

Failing all else, **Westraak** (☎ 677777) or **No 1 Broughton** (☎ 677726) can provide a taxi service.

GETTING TO/FROM THE WALK

As this is a linear walk, you need to plan carefully if two cars are available. To reach the start, follow the B9067 south from near Pierowall to a T-junction; turn right. At the next junction, turn right towards Kirbest. There's a small parking area on the south side of the road, beside the entrance to the last farm. The road to Noup Head is signposted in Pierowall; the last 2 miles are very rough. Out of respect for your car you can park at Bis Geos (Backarass on the OS map).

THE WALK

From Kirbest set out along the farm access track; bear left at the farm buildings then bend right past a cottage. Drop down to the left and go through a kissing gate. Follow a path between fenced fields, cross a stile and continue in the same direction to another one. A clear path crosses the slope to Inga Ness, all flat, wave-washed rock shelves, then turns north and the objective, Noup Head lighthouse, comes into view. Gain a little height and pass the head of Whey Geo, its thin slices of sandstone encrusted with sea birds. Beyond a slight dip, cross a stile and go up to a pair of stiles, side by side (40 minutes from Kirbest). You can diverge east here, steeply up to the summit of **Fitty Hill** (169m), the highest point on Westray, for great views of almost the entire island,

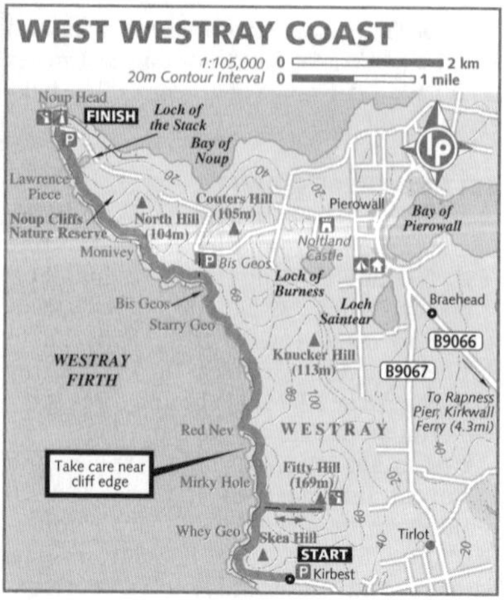

flat little Papa Westray and much else; allow 30 minutes for this return jaunt.

Cross another dip then go up past Red Nev, densely populated with birds. Soon the route starts to subtly veer northwest. Descend across a burn; look back here to spot a good example of a **natural arch**. Then swing around a fairly wide geo harbouring a small stack; cross a stile and continue on the seaward side of the fence. Soon you reach the first of Bis Geos. An hour from the Fitty Hill stile, you come to a small green sign on a stile post indicating a Westray walk to the right (the Noup Head loop); this leads to the alternative car park at Bis Geos.

Continue uphill, past Monivey's sea-bird colonies and through a line of cliffs to a plateau cradling Loch of the Stack. One more short climb takes you to a survey pillar (76m), from where it's a hop and a step to the **Noup Head lighthouse** car park.

SHETLAND

The Shetland isles are the most northerly outpost of the British Isles, are closer to Norway than to mainland Scotland and lie on the same latitude as southern Greenland. Of the 100 or more islands in the group, 15 are inhabited, the largest being Mainland, where the capital Lerwick lies on the east coast. With the exception of Fair Isle and Foula, the isles are clustered companionably close together. The 930-mile-long (1500km) coastline is crumpled, deeply indented, awesomely rugged and littered with stacks, geos, gloups, skerries and cliffs teeming with sea birds; indeed, the isles are internationally renowned among bird-watchers. The sea is everywhere and it's impossible to hide more than 3 miles from the water's edge.

Shetland has been settled since prehistoric times and evidence of early inhabitants is plentiful in cairns, standing stones and brochs. The Vikings took over Shetland around AD 700 and it remained under Norse rule until 1469 when the islands were presented to Scotland as part of a royal

SHORT WALK – CASTLE O'BURRIAN, WESTRAY

Of all the sea birds on view around the Scottish coast, the puffin is probably the most endearing, with its penguin-like bearing, bright red feet and colourful summertime beak. Encounters can be virtually guaranteed (especially between May and July, ideally in the afternoon) on this 3.4-mile (5.5km) circular walk. You should allow around 1½ hours to complete the walk. It starts at Rapness Mill, a short distance northeast of the B9066, about 6 miles southeast of Pierowall. Use OS Landranger 1:50,000 map No 5.

Walk past what was Rapness Mill (the skeletal wheel is still in place) and go through a gate and along a path. In a few minutes you reach the shallow inlet in which stands the castle, a thick-set rock stack and puffin residence, pockmarked with the birds' burrows. Continue generally east and you may spot a few outcast puffins on the cliffs ahead. The path turns southeast at Stanger Head and the island of Sanday comes into view. About 40 minutes from the start, at a stile above Geo of Rustling Stones (on the North Sea), turn right along a grassed track. It becomes a road and leads to the main road; cross and continue to the beach of Bay of Tafts – on the Atlantic Ocean. Walk along the sand, exiting through a gap in the fringing dunes, and passing Rapness cemetery en route to the main road. Turn left and follow it for about 300m back to the road leading to Rapness Mill.

dowry. Shetlanders are proud of their distinctive history and culture and generally regard themselves as Shetlanders who happen to be part of Scotland.

The isles have their fair share of damp, foggy weather but clear, sunny days are by no means exceptional. Wind is a constant presence, from every direction, so you need to have good protective clothing. Midsummer is the ideal time to visit, when the sun is above the horizon for up to 19 hours and the other five hours are far from dark – the 'simmer dim' in local parlance. This is also the peak time for bird-watching. It's not exactly hot – maximum daily temperatures rarely exceed 18°C.

Walking here is first, last and foremost coastal; in fact, the isles collectively are the best venue for coast walking in Scotland, being second-to-none in beauty, infinite diversity and ease of access.

PLANNING

Books

Orkney & Shetland, in SNH's *Landscape Fashioned by Geology* series, explains the processes that created the indented coast, and describes the different types of rock. The islands are rich in archaeological sites, so consider either *The Ancient Monuments of Shetland* by Noel Fojut and Denys Pringle, or Anna Ritchie's *Shetland* in the *Exploring Scotland's Heritage* series, both by respected professionals in the field.

The isles are a bird-watcher's paradise, so *Where to Watch Birds in Shetland* by Hugh Harrop is invaluable. It includes lists of species, useful maps and illustrations. *Shetland's Wild Flowers* by D Malcolm has good, clear photos and brief descriptions.

An alternative to most of these is an excellent series of leaflets, produced by Shetland Amenity Trust and others and available from TICs, covering many topics including wildflowers, the seashore and the several districts within the isles.

For walks, Peter Guy's seven-volume series *Walking the Coastline of Shetland* is ideal. The maps are fairly basic but the information certainly isn't. They're illustrated with contemporary and historic photos. *Walk Shetland*, a pack of 13 plastic cards, each with brief notes and a rough map, is good for ideas that you can follow up elsewhere, but the notes aren't very helpful.

WICKS, GLOUPS & NOOSTS

The Northern Isles' (especially Shetland's) Norse heritage strikes you as soon as you open a map. Maritime and land features bear unfamiliar and often unpronounceable names. The reasons for this lie in the distant past. Norse settlers arrived in the Northern Isles around AD 800 and stayed for several hundred years; their language, Old Norse, soon displaced Pictish and Gaelic. Its continuing and extensive use in place names should guarantee permanence but its future as a spoken language (Norn) is less certain. It is in everyday use among Shetlanders but is taught only to a limited extent in local schools. Here's a guide to the more common terms.

- **ayre** sand or shingle beach
- **-bister, -sta** farm
- **brough, burgi, burra** broch, or watch tower
- **dale** valley
- **-garth** fence, enclosure
- **geo** narrow inlet
- **gloup** cleft with land bridge at seaward end
- **hamna** harbour
- **holm** small island
- **houbie** lagoon
- **ness** headland
- **noost** skerry
- **papa** celtic priest, monk
- **quoy** cattle enclosure
- **voe** creek, bay
- **wick** bay, inlet

Guided Walks

The Shetland ranger service runs programs of guided walks in north and south Shetland; contact **Shetland Amenity Trust** (☎ 01595 694688) for details.

Information Sources

VisitShetland (☎ 08701 999440; www.visitshetland.com) produces a guide to accommodation and services, available both online and in hard copy, and can handle accommodation reservations.

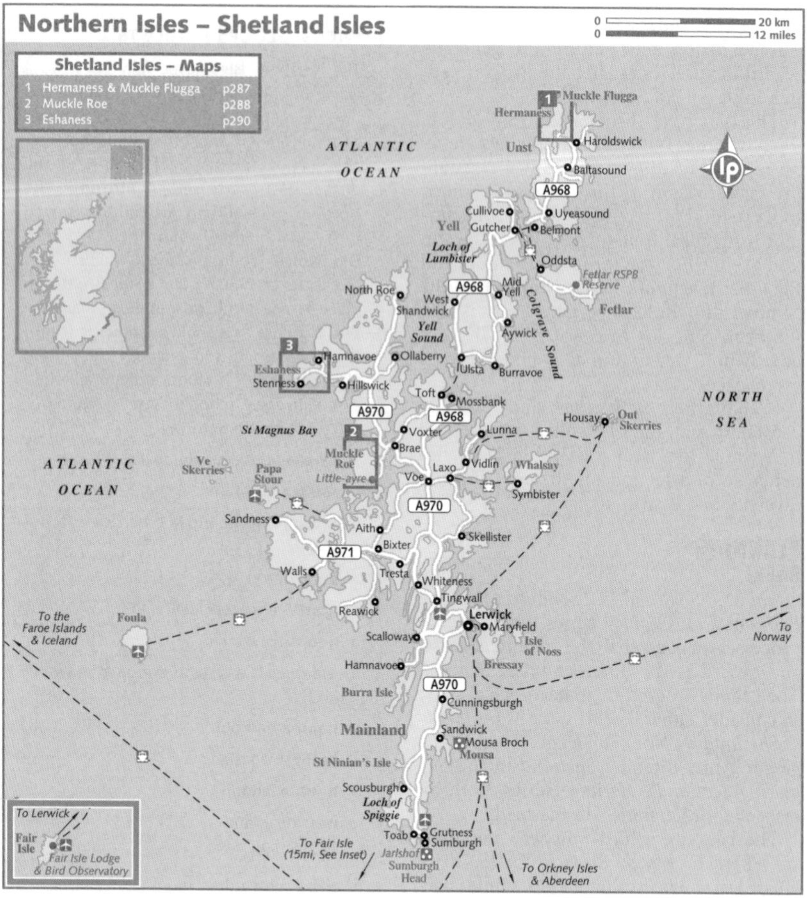

If you're particularly interested in wildlife, check **Nature in Shetland** (www.nature-shetland.co.uk), an independent site that's particularly good for the latest sightings and links to local groups.

So you know what you're in for, have a look at www.northisles-weather.co.uk – it's more useful than the usual publicly available forecasts.

Shetland's annual walking festival, held in September, has become an institution and attracts many people from far afield. Knowledgeable locals act as guides on a wide variety of walks, and social events keep you up late most evenings; check the 'Walk Shetland' link on VisitShetland's website.

GETTING AROUND

Although there's an extensive network of public buses throughout the islands, the timetables to more remote areas don't really make for a relaxed walking holiday, so you're better off bringing your own car or hiring one locally. Try **Star Car** (☎ 01595 692075; www.starcar.co.uk; 22 Commercial Rd, Lerwick) or **Bolts Car Hire** (☎ 01595 693636; www.boltscarhire.co.uk; 26 North Rd, Lerwick). Car fuel is around 10p a litre more expensive than on the Scottish mainland.

ACCESS TOWN

Lerwick

☎ 01595 / pop 6830

The capital of Shetland, Lerwick is by far the largest settlement of the islands. The old

SHETLAND'S SECRETIVE WILDFLOWERS

Sea birds are Shetland's outstanding natural attraction, closely followed by the magnificent coastline. Wildflowers may not register high on such a list, but Shetland does have them, even if only 400 species have been recorded, a number that's comparatively low on account of the islands' northerly location and severe climate.

Yet, between May and September you will find vividly colourful displays in many places. On and near coastal cliffs, mats and clumps of sea pink (thrift) are particularly striking. In sheltered sites, look for purple-flowering thyme and magenta-coloured red campion. Moorlands are brightened by the white 'balls' of bog cotton, yellow bog asphodel, heathers and spotted orchids.

Beautifully illustrated brochures about wildflowers are available free from TICs.

town, with its intriguing alleys and closes, is clustered around the busy harbour. Suburbs and commercial areas are spread further along the bay and up the surrounding hillsides.

INFORMATION

Lerwick TIC (☎ 08701 999440; www.visitshetland.com; Market Cross; ⌚ daily Apr-Oct, Mon-Fri Nov-Mar) is very helpful and well organised. It can book accommodation for you; pick up the public transport timetable for inter-island ferry information.

Shetland Times Bookshop (☎ 695531; www.shetland-bookshop.co.uk; 71-79 Commercial St) stocks a huge range of books about Shetland and the wider world.

SLEEPING & EATING

Clickimin Caravan & Campsite (☎ 741000; www.srt.org.uk; Lochside; unpowered/powered sites for 2 £7/11) is a small site with grassy pitches overlooking the eponymous loch. Washing and showering facilities are in the nearby Clickimin Complex, where you can also have a swim and patronise **Horizons Cafe** (mains to £6; ⌚ to 8pm) for snacks and full-scale meals.

Lerwick SYHA Hostel (☎ 692114; www.islesburgh.org.uk; King Harald St; dm £16) occupies Islesburgh House, built in 1907 for a herring fisheries magnate. It's been refurbished to provide quality accommodation in largish dorms. The downside is its popularity with groups. Within is the House Cafe for inexpensive snacks and light meals (to £3).

Seafield Farm B&B (☎ 693853; Seafield Rd; s/d £23/46) enjoys a great location overlooking Brei Wick; relax in the conservatory in this home away from home. Rooms are larger than average and neatly furnished.

Osla's & La Piazza (☎ 696005; 88 Commercial St; breakfast £5-6, lunch mains £4-10, dinner mains £8-17) is a popular place in the centre of town from which you won't emerge feeling underfed. Go for a pizza baked in the authentic Italian pizza oven. Vegetarians will have to make some inventive choices.

Monty's Bistro (☎ 696555; 5 Mounthooly St; lunch mains £7-8, dinner mains £10-17; ⌚ lunch Tue-Sat, dinner Mon-Sat) is unquestionably the place to eat in Lerwick. In the brightly decorated, not-too-crowded bistro, choose from a small menu featuring the best local produce enhanced by Mediterranean flavours. Don't miss the rosemary bread, baked on the premises daily.

The **Co-op** (Holmesgarth Rd) supermarket is at the northern end of town, while Somerfield is close to the A970 roundabout at the southern end.

GETTING THERE & AWAY

NorthLink Ferries (☎ 0845 600 0449; www.northlinkferries.co.uk) operates a daily service departing from Aberdeen via Kirkwall (passenger/vehicle/two-berth cabin £32/112/106, 12½ hours).

British Airways/Loganair (☎ 0870 850 9850; www.britishairways.com) operates daily flights from Glasgow (three hours), Edinburgh (2¼ hours), Aberdeen (1¼ hours) and Inverness (1¾ hours) to Sumburgh, Shetland's main airport, 25 miles from Lerwick, on the southern tip of Mainland. Fares vary considerably according to season and special conditions.

Atlantic Airways (☎ 01737 214255; www.flyshetland.com) does a direct flight from London Stansted to Shetland (1¾ hours, Monday and Friday late June to October).

John Leask (☎ 693162) operates the bus service between the airport and Lerwick (£3, 45 minutes, six services Monday to Friday, four Saturday and Sunday).

HERMANESS & MUCKLE FLUGGA

Duration	3–3¼ hours
Distance	5.5 miles (9km)
Difficulty	easy
Start/Finish	Hermaness National Nature Reserve car park
Nearest Town	Haroldswick (right)
Transport	private

Summary An exhilarating walk through Hermaness, home to vast numbers of sea birds, overlooking Muckle Flugga and Out Stack, the northernmost points of the British Isles.

Every year, between May and August, more than 100,000 sea birds – puffins, great skuas, fulmars, gannets, guillemots and razorbills – come to the rugged granite and gneiss cliffs in Hermaness National Nature Reserve on the island of Unst to breed. The air is loud with their calls and the distinctive aroma of guano wafts across the cliffs. Unst is the most northerly inhabited island in Scotland; Muckle Flugga ('big, steep-sided island') lighthouse, improbably perched on a rock stack a mile or so off the coast, is the first and last signal on British land.

Protection of sea birds here dates right back to the early 19th century, when the local landowner realised that the great skua population had been reduced to just three pairs – thanks mainly to taxidermists and egg collectors. His personal crusade ensured the species' survival; today about 700 pairs nest on the moorland. The lighthouse was completed in 1858 by David Stevenson. In 1869 his famous nephew Robert Louis paid a visit Unst, which is said to have inspired him to draw his map of *Treasure Island*.

Most of this walk is waymarked and sections of boardwalk make for dry crossings of the boggy bits. The western stretch passes above sheer cliffs up to 170m high, where considerable care is needed; this is not the place to be in strong winds.

PLANNING

Maps

Use either OS Explorer 1:25,000 map No 470 *Unst, Yell & Fetlar* or OS Landranger 1:50,000 map No 1 *Shetland – Yell, Unst & Fetlar*.

Information Sources

SNH's **Hermaness Visitor Centre** (☎ 01595 693345; www.nnr-scotland.org.uk; ⏲ Apr-Oct), in a former lightshore station, is a couple of minutes' walk from the start of this walk, and is well worth a visit to find out more about the flora and fauna of the area.

For a more general run-down on the whole island, go to www.unst.org.

NEAREST TOWN

Haroldswick

☎ 01957

Haroldswick is a small collection of houses gathered around a shingle beach, and the closest settlement to Hermaness. Here you'll find **Unst Heritage Centre** (admission £2; ⏲ 11am-5pm May-Sep), which houses displays featuring local history, and where you can purchase local crafts. There's a cash machine inside the **P&T Coaches depot** (⏲ Mon-Sat), near the Hagdale turn-off, about 1 mile south of Haroldswick.

Beyond Haroldswick is Baltasound, 2.5 miles south, which is Unst's largest village, with the island's sole post office.

SLEEPING & EATING

Gardiesfauld Hostel (☎ 755259; www.gardiesfauld.shetland.co.uk; Uyeasound; dm £11, unpowered sites for 2 £8) is the nearest hostel to Haroldswick, around 10 miles south. It enjoys an uninterrupted sea view and has a well-set-up kitchen; the hostel's rules prohibit alcohol.

Joan Ritch (☎ 711323; Gerratoun, Haroldswick; s/d £20/40, dinner £6) is Scotland's most northerly B&B, in a traditional crofter's cottage, in the most peaceful of locations. You'll be made most welcome, and will be well looked after at dinner.

Clingera Guest House (☎ 711579; clingera@btopenworld.com; Baltasound; s/d £25/50) has large, comfortable rooms in a modern family home.

Baltasound Hotel (☎ 711334; s/d £53/86, lunch £3-5, dinner mains £6-8), the nearest hotel (and the most northerly in Britain), is popular with tour buses and offers good, plain fare, using local produce wherever possible.

Wind Dog Cafe (☎ 744321; Gutcher; lunch £2-4, dinner mains £10-12), right beside the Yell-Unst ferry terminal, offers homely, good-value fodder.

Northern Lights Cafe (mains £6-8; ⏲ lunch & dinner) occupies space in the Uyeasound public hall, though the enthusiastic proprietor expected to open in Baltasound as Northern Lights Bistro in 2007. The food is truly homemade, using as much local produce as possible. The bistro will include a gallery featuring local artists.

Skibhoul Store (Baltasound; Mon-Sat), in a two-storey, 19th-century stone building, has its own bakery and sells maps and books. There's a small self-service café under the same roof for hot drinks to wash down something from the bakery.

GETTING THERE & AWAY

You first need to cross from Mainland (Toft) to Ulsta on the island of Yell by the **Orkney Ferries** (☎ 722395; www.orkneyferries.co.uk) service (driver/vehicle return £3/7, 20 minutes, half-hourly). The next crossing is from Gutcher (Yell) to Belmont on Unst (free, 10 minutes, half-hourly).

You can fly to Unst with **British Airways/ Loganair** (☎ 0870 850 9850; www.britishairways.com) but you would then be relying on taxis to take you from and to the airport, and probably to and from the walk.

GETTING TO/FROM THE WALK

The walk starts and ends at the Hermaness National Nature Reserve car park 3 miles northwest of Haroldswick, along the single-track road signposted to Burrafirth.

THE WALK

From the car park, go through a gate and follow a well-made gravel path up the hillside above Burra Firth, and then down to Burn of Winnaswarta. A short distance on, bear left at a junction. The pattern of the next stage soon takes shape: sections of boardwalk separated by a grass-and-heather-moorland path. Dark-brown great skuas nest here; they'll probably skim low enough to let you know they're around, but are unlikely to practise their notorious dive-bombing antics (see the boxed text on p275).

Reaching the crest (45 minutes from the start) is a startling experience: suddenly you're on the edge of nowhere, being welcomed by a dapper puffin or two, and surrounded by sea, sky, black cliffs and birds. Turn left here to reach **Neap** (170m), the highest of the cliffs, which is especially good for gannets. Continue along or near

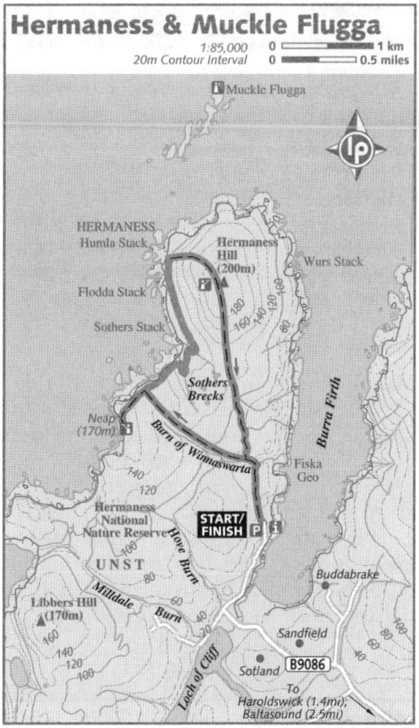

the cliff edge. There's no formed path but the trodden way is clear enough, down over two burns then up across the steep hillside, past more puffin burrows and cliff-ledge nesting sites, with fine views of the stack-littered coast to the south. The best place for puffins is near a fenced-off chunk of unstable cliff; these most endearing of birds seem to be putting on a show just for passers-by. **Muckle Flugga** lighthouse, and Out Stack just to its north, soon come into view and you reach a familiar waymarker post (30 minutes after reaching the cliff edge). It takes a while to accommodate to the acute sense that you've come to the edge of everything.

Follow the posts right up the steep flank of **Hermaness Hill** to its summit (200m), which is around 15 minutes' walk from the waymarker post, from where most of Unst is in view, notably Burra Firth and the lochans of Sothers Brecks below. Descend along the line of boardwalks and paths to a junction, and here turn left and return to the start (35 minutes from Hermaness Hill).

MUCKLE ROE

Duration 3¼–3½ hours
Distance 7.5 miles (12km)
Difficulty moderate
Start/Finish Little-ayre
Nearest Town Brae (right)
Transport private
Summary An exceptionally scenic walk along a rugged and intricately indented coast with wide-ranging views along the central west coast of Mainland.

Muckle Roe is an island, though a bridge has long since replaced the original stepping stones that connected it to the west coast of Mainland. It's a wonderfully rugged area of craggy red and green hills, lochans and, naturally, magnificent coast.

The route of this walk invites further exploration and variation, by venturing out onto each and every headland, climbing the several small hills and lingering at the secluded coves and beaches, so you could easily spend the whole day here.

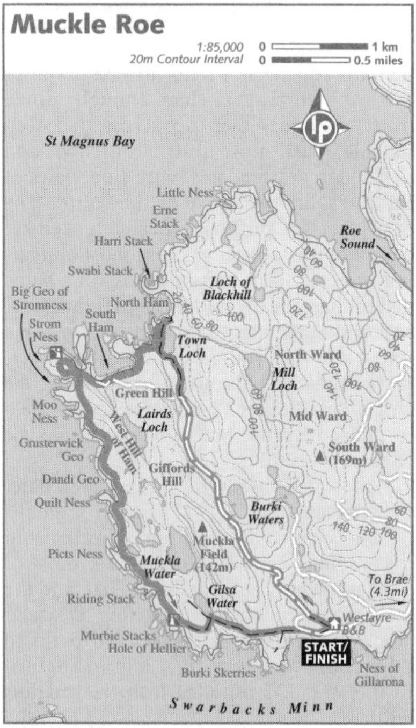

PLANNING

Maps

Use either OS Explorer 1:25,000 map No 469 *Shetland – North West* or OS Landranger 1:50,000 map No 3 *Shetland – North Mainland.*

NEAREST TOWN

Brae

☎ 01806 / pop 660

Brae is a scattered village mainly housing workers at the nearby Sullom Voe oil terminal. It's strung out along the A970 from Lerwick. More attractive Hillswick (opposite) isn't too far away (10 miles) to serve as a base for this walk.

SLEEPING & EATING

Westayre B&B (☎ 522368; www.westayre.shetland.co.uk; Muckle Roe, Brae; s/d £24/50) is right beside the start of the walk, 4.5 miles from Brae, with superb coastal views, a lovely garden and perfect peace and quiet.

Mid Brae Inn (☎ 522634; mains £7-13; lunch & dinner) has a traditional-style lounge bar-dining room. It specialises in seafood and local lamb and there's an unusually wide choice for vegetarians.

Brae Stores (daily) stocks a small range of goods; it's licensed and operates a cash-back service with a British banker's card.

GETTING THERE & AWAY

To reach Brae by car, follow the A970 west and north from Lerwick, a distance of 25 miles.

GETTING TO/FROM THE WALK

The walk starts and finishes at a small roadside parking area at Little-ayre, 4.5 miles from Brae, at the end of a quiet single-track road signposted to Muckle Roe.

THE WALK

Go through a gate near the parking area where signposts point to 'Lighthouse' and 'Hams'; shortly, follow a track to the right towards Hams. It leads northwest up the wide glen, across a broad saddle, then gradually down past Burki Waters and on to a wider, more fertile glen. At a junction near a stream crossing, continue straight on, over a stile beside a large green shed, through a gateway and on, beside a small burn. Soon you'll reach a stile next to a gate at the northern end of Town Loch (one hour from the start). Below, the sheltered inlet of **North Ham** dictates a break on green grass beside bleached shingle and deep-blue water reflecting brick-red and black cliffs and stacks.

Continue south up the slope from the stile and along the cliff top, past deep, colourful geos then down, from near a ruined stone building, to **South Ham**. From the further shingle beach, follow a track up to a gate then swing left (more or less west) uphill to a roofless stone cottage. Climb to the crest to overlook the Big Geo of Stromness, where there's a stack in the making on the southern cliff line. Cross a stile over a fence in a slight dip then go up to the elongated ridge that is West Hill of Ham.

From a large cairn (45 minutes from North Ham) drop down to the head of Dandi Geo. The route continues in undulating fashion, past a lochan and on until the beacon above Murbie Stacks comes into view. Follow the ridge crest to a wide glen and walk across to the **beacon**, a lovely spot for a spell (40 minutes from the cairn). Head north and northeast up the glen; keep east of a cairn on the crest and follow a path across the slope above Gilsa Water to its outlet. From here a clear path leads east, keeping below the high ground to the north, past a nameless beach, across moorland then steeply down to another strand. Follow a path on the seaward side of a low hill, through a gate; the car park is nearby (50 minutes from the beacon).

ESHANESS

Duration	2¼–2½ hours
Distance	5 miles (8km)
Difficulty	easy
Start/Finish	Eshaness lighthouse
Nearest Town	Hillswick (right)
Transport	private

Summary A circuit taking in some of the finest coastal cliffs in Shetland, a geologists' paradise with sea views far and wide.

Eshaness means 'headland of volcanic rock' and here, on the west Mainland coast, you can see graphic, colourful evidence of Shetland's fiery ancient past. Volcanoes spewed lava and ash over the surrounding land about 370 million years ago; the various types of rock that subsequently formed – black basalt, lighter-coloured tuff and dark, pinkish rhyolite – can be seen. Indeed, it's the best geological showcase of its kind in Britain. An information board at the start of the walk describes all this in vivid detail.

The walk described here isn't waymarked but there are stiles across the fences along the way and the going underfoot is unbelievably easy, as if you're wandering a golf course.

PLANNING

Maps

Use either OS Explorer 1:25,000 map No 469 *Shetland – North West* or OS Landranger 1:50,000 map No 3 *Shetland – North Mainland*.

NEAREST TOWN

Hillswick

☎ 01806

Hillswick is small, dispersed settlement in a very picturesque setting on the shores of Ura Firth on northwest Mainland. It can serve as a base for the Muckle Roe walk (opposite) and for the Ness of Hillswick walk (p291). Brae Stores (10 miles southeast) provides a cash-back service on British bankers' cards.

SLEEPING & EATING

Braewick Cafe & Caravan Park (☎ 503345; Braewick; unpowered/powered sites for 2 £5/10, lunch £3-7) has a fantastic view of sea stacks and rugged coastline. Genuinely homemade snacks and light meals are available and you can make a reservation for an evening meal. Campers' facilities are immaculate.

Johnny Notion's Camping Böd (☎ 01595 694688; shetlandamenity.trust@znet.co.uk; Hamnavoe; dm £8) is named in honour of the local man who invented his own inoculation against smallpox. Modernised since it was home for fishermen and their gear during the fishing season, it has a single bedroom and no electricity. BYO bedding, eating and cooking utensils and food. It's 1.5 miles down the Hamnavoe road, off the road to Eshaness.

Almara B&B (☎ 503261; www.almara.shetland.co.uk; Upper Urafirth; s/d £25/50) looks out across the firth. Be assured of a warm welcome and the opportunity to gain insights into life from a Shetlander's point of view; breakfast is first-rate.

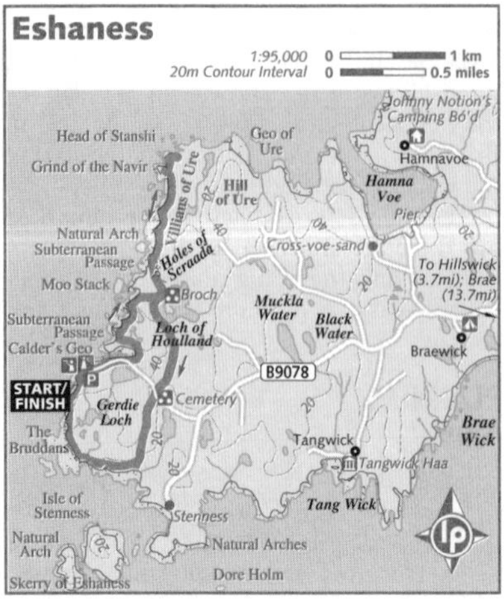

Da Böd Cafe (☎ 503348; mains £4-7; lunch & diner Sat & Sun May, Wed-Sun Jun-Sep) is an excellent, discreet vegetarian café on the seafront, and is linked to the Hillswick Wildlife Sanctuary. It's not licensed but you can BYO.

The small shop is below the prominent (former) St Magnus Hotel.

GETTING THERE & AWAY

To reach Hillswick by car, simply follow the A970 west and generally north from Lerwick, a distance of 37 miles.

GETTING TO/FROM THE WALK

The walk starts and finishes at Eshaness lighthouse, where there's plenty of parking space. From Hillswick, follow the B9078 for about 5 miles to a junction; continue on a minor road to the lighthouse.

THE WALK

Set out north, close to the cliff edge, soon skirting deep Calder's Geo then passing two tranquil lochans. Fulmars and kittiwakes squat on the precipitous cliffs and narrowest of ledges on massive **Moo Stack**, pitted with caves and natural arches. Then come the wonderfully named Villians of Ure: several hundred metres of volcanic crags, cliffs and small stacks. About 45 minutes from the lighthouse, you come to the northernmost point of the walk, dramatic **Head of Stanshi**, waves pounding the black offshore crags.

Retrace your steps as far as the stile from which Loch of Houlland is visible to the south. Cross it and steer a course to the relatively high ground above the loch's western shore. Soon you almost trip over the most amazing **gloup**, though you should have been warned by the deep, subterranean booming of waves bursting through a passage between the sea and this inland chasm. Continue to the western shore of **Loch of Houlland**, where the vestigial remains of an Iron Age broch sprawl on a small

SHORT WALK – BURRA ISLE

Burra Isle, south of Scalloway (the ancient capital of Shetland), is comprised of four peninsulas, which are all linked by the slenderest of causeways or dykes. The most southwestern of them has a wonderfully remote atmosphere and boasts a superb coastal walk. This 4-mile (6.4km) circuit of a low-lying grassy islet takes in remarkably varied coastal scenery and delivers up a fine range of wide views.

To reach the island from Lerwick, follow the A970 to the head of East Voe of Scalloway, then turn south to Burra Isle. Continue via Bridge End through the hamlet of Papil to a small parking area at the road end. In Scalloway there are two shops, Scalloway Hotel and **De Haaf Restaurant** (☎ 01595 880747; NAFC Marine Centre), renowned for its fish and seafood. Use OS Landranger 1:50,000 map No 4.

Go through a small gate to a vehicle track. Cross the sandy isthmus, go through another gate and head south past a roofless stone building. The next gate is slightly uphill. Continue past a row of roofless cottages, through a gate; the last gate is about 250m further on. Walk south across open ground and follow the shoreline, past the colourful Bight of Sandy Geos. Continue southwest, along much rockier coast. Climb to a knoll above the sheer cliffs of Groot Ness then descend to and pass a lochan. Go up to a cairn on the Heugg, a narrow promontory. Turn southeast to gain a nearby knoll then head northeast to the highest point locally, which is particularly good for views north. From here, descend to a stile near the seaward corner of a fence and make a beeline for the isthmus to return to the start.

promontory. Further on, cross a stile over a dyke, then head south across open grassland. With luck you'll reach the lighthouse road just east of Loch of Framgord (40 minutes from Head of Stanshi), where there's a fine view of the famous Dore Holm stack, which resembles a horse drinking.

Drop down to a walled burial ground; in here the prominent vertical headstone remembers unlucky Donald Robertson, whose doctor prescribed Epsom salts but gave him lethal nitre. Continue across country on the uphill side of the burial ground, cross the crest and descend towards the Isle of Stenness. Gradually veer west to parallel the scenic rocky shore, west then north. One last climb takes you up to South Head of Caldersgeo, from where it's not far to the lighthouse (45 minutes from the burial ground).

MORE WALKS

ORKNEY

Mainland

Mull Head Local Nature Reserve, at the northern tip of the east coast of Mainland, protects a variety of habitats and geological formations, and a probable Norse chapel. A 3.5-mile (5.6km) circular walk takes in these features and gives fine views of islands to the north. The route is signposted at crucial junctions and there's the odd length of boardwalk over some potentially boggy places. Allow about 1½ hours; use OS Explorer 1:50,000 map No 6. From Kirkwall follow the A960 to St Peters Pool; continue along the B9050 and signposted minor roads to a car park.

Stronsay

This peaceful farming island has broad sandy beaches, a bird reserve, impressive rock formations and some good coastal walking. The Odin Bay footpath is in the south of the island. It encompasses heritage sites, a Norse harbour and the Vat of Kirbuster, Orkney's most spectacular natural arch. The footpath is 4 miles, but the complete circuit from Whitehall (the island's capital) is 10 miles. **Orkney Ferries** (☎ 01856 872044; www.orkneyferries.co.uk) runs ferries to Whitehall from Kirkwall. Use OS Landranger 1:50,000 map No 5.

Sanday

Sanday is an island of pristine white-sand beaches that might be more at home in the Caribbean. The island is almost entirely flat and hosts several impressive archaeological sites, including a 5000-year-old chambered cairn. A signposted walk makes a 3.5-mile (5.5km) circuit around Backaskaill Bay in the east of the island. For further information, pick up *The Sanday Trail* brochure from TICs in Stromness or Kirkwall. **Orkney Ferries** (☎ 01856 872044; www.orkneyferries.co.uk) runs regular ferries to the island from Kirkwall. Use OS Landranger 1:50,000 map No 5.

SHETLAND

Ness of Hillswick

This spectacular headland is just south of Hillswick village (p289). A short but very scenic route passes good cliff scenery and Neolithic and Bronze Age remains; you may also see otters in the more sheltered waters. The walk starts and finishes in Hillswick; allow around two hours to complete the 5-mile (8km) circuit. Use OS Landranger 1:50,000 map No 3.

St Ninian's Isle

Here you'll come across the ruins of a 12th-century church and may also see puffins and skuas near the cliff tops. The main feature of this short but extremely scenic walk is the beautiful sand-and-shell isthmus that gives access to the island. The walk starts and finishes at Bigton on south Mainland; allow about 1½ hours for the 3.8-mile (6km) circuit. Use OS Landranger 1:50,000 map No 4.

Gloup Ness, Yell

The north coast of the island of Yell is rugged, indented and there's even a beautiful sandy beach. A 5.3-mile (8.6km) circuit leads west from near Breckon Sands along the coast to Gloup Ness, south to a memorial to 58 fishermen who drowned nearby in 1858, then back over Scordaback (113m) for the views. The route is waymarked as far as the memorial. Use OS 1:50,000 map No 1. Access is from the A968 along B9082 (near the ferry terminal). After 4.3 miles turn right to Breckon Sands; park at the farm house. For refreshments, there's the Wind Dog Cafe at Gutcher (p286).

Walkers Directory

CONTENTS

PRACTICALITIES

- Pick up a copy of *tgo* magazine – 'by hillwalkers for hillwalkers' – for news, walk ideas, gear and book reviews; its Scottish coverage is usually better than the otherwise recommendable *Trail* and *Country Walking* magazines.
- Buy or watch videos on the PAL system.
- Plug into a square three-pin adaptor (different from the Australian three-pin) before connecting to the electricity supply (240V, 50Hz AC)
- Scotland uses the metric system for weights and measures, except for road distances (in miles) and beer (in pints).

ACCOMMODATION

Visitors are spoilt for choice of accommodation in Scotland. You can camp in the wild or stay at bothies for free. Budget travellers (spending £5 to £20 per person per night) have the choice of camping grounds, hostels and, increasingly rarely, inexpensive B&Bs. Midrange travellers (£20 to £45 per person per night) will find a plethora of comfortable B&Bs, guesthouses and small hotels. At the top end are luxury B&Bs, guesthouses and, of course, hotels. B&Bs, guesthouses and hotels (and the odd hostel) usually serve breakfast; the more you pay, the greater the choice.

Prices are higher during the busy season (June to September), peaking in July and August when some establishments will not take single-night bookings. At other times, special deals are often available at guesthouses and hotels. Many smaller establishments close between November and March, particularly in remote areas.

VisitScotland's (www.visitscotland.com) tourist information centres (TICs) and website provide an accommodation booking service (£3 per reservation, local and national). Alternatively, you can use the site to obtain contact details and make the bookings yourself, possibly saving quite a few pounds.

Bothies

These are privately owned, simple shelters in remote areas. They're not locked, they're free and you can't book a space. You'll need your own cooking equipment, sleeping bag and mat, map, lighting and food. They are not meant for extended stays – two nights at the most. Many are maintained by the **Mountain Bothies Association** (www.mountainbothies.org.uk). For details about staying in bothies, see p21.

Camping & Caravan Parks

There are plenty of camping and caravan parks in most parts of the country, though they're rather scarce in the Northern and Western Isles. For many, caravans and campervans are the main business, and tents are allocated only limited space. However, around major walking areas you will find sites with (usually) well-grassed spaces for tents. Tariffs vary from £10 to £16 for two people occupying an unpowered site; you'll pay an extra few pounds for an electrical hook-up. Hot showers are free in some places, others charge a modest fee. Camper kitchens, where you can cook and wash up under cover, are fairly rare; most parks do have laundries, where a wash and spin-dry costs around £3. On-site shops and cafés are quite common, especially at sites well away from a town or village. Many sites participate in VisitScotland's grading scheme and are listed in its *Caravan and Camping Parks Map*, published annually.

WILD CAMPING

The scope for wild camping – in the hills, glens and along the coast – is almost infinite. However, keeping in mind the changeable climate and the favourite haunts of midges (see the boxed text, p313), you will need to choose your site carefully. See also p21 for some camping tips.

Guesthouses & B&Bs

B&Bs are a Scottish institution and their hosts' hospitality is almost legendary. At the very least you'll have a bedroom in a private house, a shared bathroom and breakfast, either cooked or continental. Pay a little more and you'll enjoy an en suite room with TV and tea- and coffee-making facilities and a wider choice for breakfast. The best have a separate sitting (lounge) room for guests, where you can relax and enjoy a cup of tea in comfort. In popular walking areas some establishments have a drying room, and the hosts will provide a pick-up and drop-off service and a packed lunch; look for the 'Walkers Welcome' symbol in accommodation guides. Expect to pay as little as £22 and as much as £40 per person per night for a B&B. Many of those in more remote locations offer a two-, three- or even four-course evening meal, usually excellent value, ranging from around £12 to £25.

Guesthouses are larger than B&Bs, and perhaps a little more formal, but not necessarily any more luxurious. Pubs may also offer relatively inexpensive B&B accommodation, which can be convenient, with room and meals under one roof, but they may not be as peaceful as a private home. Rates start at about £26 per person per night.

Single rooms are scarce and some hosts are reluctant to let a twin room to one person, even in the off-season, without charging a supplement of as much as £10.

Hostels

Scotland's many hostels offer inexpensive accommodation and are great places for meeting fellow travellers and walkers. The standard of facilities is generally very good; it's fast becoming the norm for hostels to have small dorms with en suite. Kitchens are provided for self-catering and many hostels provide internet access.

From May to September, and on public holidays, hostels can be booked solid, sometimes by large groups, so book well ahead.

The **Scottish Youth Hostel Association** (SYHA; ☎ 0870 155 3255; www.syha.org.uk; 7 Glebe Cres, Stirling FK8 2JA) operates a wide variety of reasonably priced hostels from one end of the country to the other. They range from the brand new Edinburgh Central palace (opened in 2006), to a magnificent mansion beside Loch Lomond, to small, homely hostels at Inverey in the Cairngorms and Broadford on the Southern Upland Way. The average tariff during summer is around £14; an online booking service is available. A booklet listing the hostels is widely available from the hostels themselves and from TICs.

Many of the numerous independent hostels belong to **Scottish Independent Hostels** (SIH; www.hostel-scotland.co.uk; PO Box 7024, Fort William, PH33 6RE), an association that represents only hostels that have been approved by SIH's independent assessor. Most are privately owned and the majority are family run. The greatest concentration is across the Highlands; they're very scarce south of Glasgow and Edinburgh, and in the far north. SIH's

WALKING CLUBS

If you're a sociable type, joining a walking club can make all the difference to your enjoyment of exploring Scotland on foot. There are scores of clubs across the country (though they are mainly in the more populous central regions) which run regular programs of walks and, usually, social events throughout the year. Some may also offer instruction in navigation (maps, compass, GPS). Walks are always organised and led by competent and experienced members, and are graded in much the same way as the walks in this book.

The **Ramblers Association** (☎ 01577 861222; www.ramblers.org.uk) has more than 50 groups around Scotland, while the **Scottish Mountaineering Council** (www.smc.org.uk) website has links to many other clubs.

Blue Hostel Guide, a free brochure with full details of more than 120 hostels, is available from TICs or direct from the association.

In Shetland, you'll find *böds* (camping barns). All are in historic buildings and, usually, remote locations. They offer rather spartan accommodation – a roof over your head, running water and lighting. You'll need a sleeping bag, mat, cooking equipment and food. Contact **Shetland Amenity Trust** (☎ 01595 694688; www.camping-bods.co.uk) for more information

Hotels

Generally at the more expensive end of the accommodation scale, hotels range from rather impersonal international-style hotels in the cities and near airports, to magnificent mansions in spectacular locations, to homely, small inns, usually also in great, and quite often remote, settings.

BUSINESS HOURS

Approximate standard opening hours are as follows:

Cafés 9am to 5pm; in large towns and cities some open for breakfast from about 7am. If licensed they may also stay open for dinner.

Pubs & Bars 11am to 11pm (some to midnight or 1am) Monday to Saturday, 12.30pm to 11pm Sunday; lunch is served noon to 2.30pm, dinner 6pm to 9pm daily.

Restaurants Noon to 3pm for lunch, 6pm to 9pm or 10pm for dinner.

Shops At least 9am to 5pm Monday to Saturday; many also open Sunday, typically 11am to 5pm. Supermarkets stay open to 8pm and a few city and large-town supermarkets open 24 hours.

CHILDREN

It's true that walking with your kids is very different from walking as you knew (and loved) it before they came along. If you can adjust happily to living with children, you'll probably enjoy walking with them.

'Kids, they slow you down,' you'll often hear, and that is never more true than when you're walking. There is an age, however, when children can match your pace exactly: when you're carrying them all the way. A good quality specialist child carrier is worth its weight in chocolate (or beer, depending on your tastes). All carriers on the market have to meet strict safety criteria, and are designed to carry a maximum load of 20kg. Inevitably, children's increasing weight, and a growing determination to get down and do everything for themselves, spells the end of that transitional phase. Once your first child is too big or too independent for the carrier, usually around the age of four years, you simply have to scale down your expectations of distance and rate of progress.

This is when the fun really starts. No longer another item to be carried, or at least not all the time, a walking child must be factored into your planning at the most basic level. Rather then get partway into a walk and ask yourself in desperation, 'Why on earth are we doing this?', make that the first question you ask, at home. While any walking that is driven by adult statistics – miles covered, peaks bagged – isn't likely to work with kids, other important goals take over: fun and a sense of something accomplished together, and joy in the wonders of the natural world.

Easy and small is a good way to start; plan (or hope) that more adventurous, longer walks will come later. Even if you were out every weekend before you had kids, once or twice per month will probably be enough, at least to start with. Too hard and too often, and what should be fun can become an ordeal for all, especially the youngster, who could well be put off completely for life.

Don't overlook time for play. A game of hide and seek during lunch might well be the highlight of your child's day on the walk. A few simple toys or a favourite book stowed in your pack can make a huge difference. Play can also transform the walking itself: a simple stroll in the outdoors becomes a deer/otter/badger hunt in an enchanted wonderland, or a crab chase along the coast. Company can be all-important, however well you get on together; consider inviting a couple of friends or cousins to share the fun. Plan to finish the day with a treat; there are plenty of good tearooms where everyone can enjoy a drink and a sticky cake.

For the sake of sanity and general contentment, and to avoid any resentment of missed opportunities, you may need to plan to do some walks *without* children. This is harder to arrange away from home and the regular, trusted network of family, friends and babysitters. You may be able to take advantage of local child-minding services;

consult your accommodation hosts and/or the local TIC, preferably in advance.

There is another alternative. If you're desperate to stretch your legs and climb a Munro/Corbett/any hill at all that's simply beyond you as a family, split up for a few hours. Find a short but suitably challenging walk – maybe a peak close to a road or on a side trip – and take turns. Consider whether you could take your walking holiday with another young family, to enlarge the pool of both walkers and carers, and to give the kids company of their own age.

These days some outdoor gear shops have a special section decked out with brightly coloured, functional kit for kids, mainly small packs, clothing and footwear. It might seem expensive, but it will help to ensure that they keep warm and dry, all-important in ensuring their enjoyment. It's worth remembering that shoes (trainers) are much more comfortable than boots, especially for younger children.

Following is a selection of walks in this book that we recommend for children:

Edinburgh & Glasgow Lothian Bents & Links (p48), Falls of Clyde (p56), Along the Greenock Cut (p53), North Berwick Law (p50), Arthur's Seat (p50), the Whangie (p59).

The South Grey Mare's Tail & White Coomb (p73), Eildon Hills (p79), Burnmouth to St Abb's Head (p81), Tweed Valley near Peebles (p84).

Central Highlands & Islands Cock of Arran (p101), Heights of North Sannox (p103).

Lochaber & Glen Coe Glencoe Lochan (p133), Steall Meadows to Glen Nevis on the Ring of Steall (p128).

The Cairngorms Linn of Dee Circuit (p154), Loch Muick (p164), Loch an Eilean (p151).

Highland Glens Individual days of Great Glen Way (p168), Aberarder to Lochan a'Choire on the Creag Meagaidh walk (p184), the Other End of the Caledonian Canal (p188).

Isle of Skye The Quiraing (p209), Coral Beaches (p210)

Wester Ross Beinn Eighe Mountain Trail (p225), Coire Mhic Fhearchair (p231).

Western Isles Scalpay (p254), Hushinish (p246), Eoligarry (p254), Loch Druidibeg National Nature Reserve (p254), Toe Head (p254), Vatersay (p252), West Side Coast (p239).

Northwest Sandwood Bay & Cape Wrath (p258), Point of Stoer (p271), Stac Pollaidh (p271), Faraid Head (p269), Falls of Kirkaig (p269).

Northern Isles Old May of Hoy from Rackwick (p275), West Westray Coast (p280), Castle O'Burrian (p282), Mull Head Local Nature Reserve (p291), Muckle Roe (p288), Eshaness (p289), Hermaness & Muckle Flugga (p286), Burra Isle (p290), St Ninian's Isle (p291).

As far as travelling is concerned, child concessions for accommodation and transport are often available. Discounts may be up to half the adult rate, although the definition of 'child' varies from under 12 to under 16 years of age.

The Lonely Planet guide, *Travel with Children*, contains plenty more useful advice and information.

CLIMATE

'Varied' accurately describes the many moods of Scotland's cool, temperate climate. The weather can change more than once during a day, and usually changes from one day to the next. There are also wide variations over small distances; one glen may languish under cloud and drizzle, the next may be basking in sunshine. As some locals say, 'If you don't like the weather, come back this afternoon'.

Country-wide, May and June enjoy the lowest rainfall. Scotland's west coast is wettest (between 150cm and 200cm annually) exposed as it is to moisture-laden winds and weather fronts from the Atlantic. The east is much drier, with an average rainfall around 65cm. Storms are rare between May and August, but become increasingly commonplace towards winter (December to February), especially in the Western and Northern Isles.

Considering Scotland's northern position (Edinburgh is on the same latitude as Moscow), you'd expect a cold climate. However, thanks to prevailing southwesterly winds warmed by the Gulf Stream, the climate is relatively mild. Summer (June to August) temperatures average between 16°C and 19°C in the west and in the Highlands. During prolonged spells of warm southern airflow, the thermometer can rise well into the 20°Cs and temperatures around 30°C are not unknown.

For more detail see the climate charts on p296.

Weather information

The **Met Office** (☎ 0870 900 0100; www.metoffice.com) is the government's meteorological agency, and issues Mountain Area forecasts for two regions: West Highlands (Northwest Highlands, Skye, Lochaber, the Trossachs) and East Highlands (east of Rannoch Moor and including the Cairngorms). These daily forecasts include the extent of low cloud,

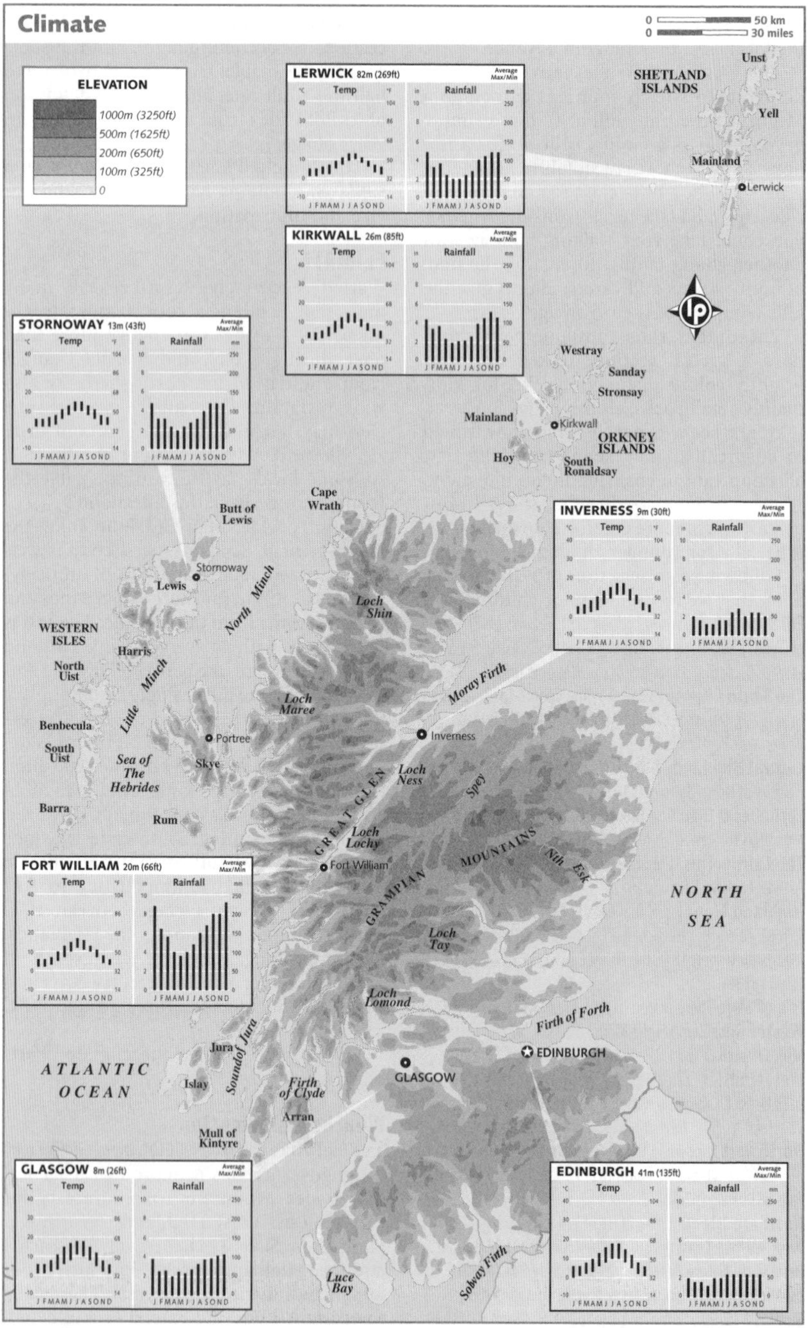
Climate
0 50 km
0 30 miles
ELEVATION
1000m (3250ft)
500m (1625ft)
200m (650ft)
100m (325ft)
0
LERWICK 82m (269ft)
KIRKWALL 26m (85ft)
STORNOWAY 13m (43ft)
INVERNESS 9m (30ft)
FORT WILLIAM 20m (66ft)
GLASGOW 8m (26ft)
EDINBURGH 41m (135ft)
Average Max/Min
Temp
Rainfall
J F M A M J J A S O N D
SHETLAND ISLANDS
Unst
Yell
Mainland
Lerwick
Westray
Sanday
Stronsay
Mainland
Kirkwall
Hoy
ORKNEY ISLANDS
South Ronaldsay
Cape Wrath
Butt of Lewis
Stornoway
Lewis
North Minch
Loch Shin
WESTERN ISLES
Harris
North Uist
Little Minch
Loch Maree
Moray Firth
Benbecula
Portree
Inverness
South Uist
Sea of The Hebrides
Skye
Loch Ness
Spey
Barra
Rum
GREAT GLEN
Loch Lochy
Fort William
MOUNTAINS
Nth Esk
GRAMPIAN
NORTH SEA
Loch Tay
Loch Lomond
Firth of Forth
EDINBURGH
Jura
ATLANTIC OCEAN
Islay
Sound of Jura
Firth of Clyde
GLASGOW
Arran
Mull of Kintyre
Luce Bay
Solway Firth

visibility, wind, temperature and a general outlook. Four webcams on the website are fragmented and of little use.

The more specialised **Mountain Weather Information Service** (www.mwis.org.uk) offers a better service for walkers and climbers. It covers five regions, including the south, with data for wind, wetness, cloud, sunshine, air clarity and temperature. Some of the webcams, including those on Ben Nevis and Beinn Alligin in Wester Ross, are useful.

Print-outs of local forecasts are usually available from TICs or visitor centres in mountain areas, and from some hostels; generally, such sources are mentioned in the walks chapters in this book.

CUSTOMS

Travellers arriving in the UK from other EU countries don't have to pay tax or duty on goods for personal use. Travellers from outside the EU can bring in specified quantities of duty-free alcohol and cigarettes, and £145 worth of all other goods, including gifts and souvenirs.

For details of restrictions and quarantine regulations, see the website of **HM Revenue and Customs** (www.hmrc.gov.uk).

EMBASSIES & CONSULATES

UK Embassies Abroad

Following is a selection of British embassies and high commissions abroad.

Australia (☎ 02-6270 6666; www.britaus.net; Commonwealth Ave, Yarralumla, Canberra, ACT 2600)
Canada (☎ 613-237 1530; www.britainincanada.org; 80 Elgin St, Ottawa, Ontario K1P 5K7)
France (☎ 01 44 51 31 00; www.amb-grandebretagne.fr; 35 rue du Faubourg St Honoré, 75383 Paris)
Germany (☎ 030-20457-0; www.britischebotschaft.de; Wilhelmstrasse 70, 10117 Berlin)
Ireland (☎ 01-205 3700; www.britishembassy.ie; 29 Merrion Rd, Ballsbridge, Dublin 4)
Netherlands (☎ 0070-427 0427; www.britain.nl; Lange Voorhout 10, 2514 ED, The Hague)
New Zealand (☎ 04-924 2888; www.britain.org.nz; 44 Hill St, Thorndon, Wellington).
USA (☎ 202-588 7800; www.britainusa.com; 3100 Massachusetts Ave NW, Washington, DC 20008)

Consulates in Scotland

Most overseas diplomatic missions are in London, but several countries also have consulates in or near Edinburgh.

Australia (☎ 0131 624 3333; 93 George St, EH2 3ES) Passport applications and document-witnessing only; for emergencies contact the **Australian High Commission** (☎ 020-7887 5335) in London.
Canada (☎ 0131 473 6320; Festival Sq, 50 Lothian Rd, EH3 9WJ)
France (☎ 0131 225 7954; 21 Randolph Cres, EH3 7TT)
Germany (☎ 0131 337 2323; 16 Eglinton Cres, EH12 5DG)
Ireland (☎ 0131 226 7711; 16 Randolph Cres, EH3 7TT)
Netherlands (☎ 0131 220 3226; Thistle Ct, 1-2 Thistle St, EH2 1DD)
USA (☎ 0131 556 8315; 3 Regent Tce, EH7 5BW)

FOOD & DRINK

Scotland has become a gourmet's destination, as the country's excellent range of top-quality fresh meat, seafood, cheeses and vegetables (increasingly including organic produce), and the skills and enthusiasm of chefs in restaurants and pubs, has become widely known.

Locally grown beef and lamb are much sought after, as is venison, a leaner meat from red deer. Haggis, that much-maligned Scottish icon, can be very enjoyable if it's properly prepared and cooked. Scottish wild salmon is famous but scarce and expensive, while shellfish is widely available, as is brown trout and smoked fish. Many of the best cheeses come from the islands, notably Arran, Bute, Mull and Orkney.

Scotland supports a thriving brewing industry, with the mass market dominated by McEwens, Scottish & Newcastle, Tennent's and Youngers. There's a bar-full of small breweries, literally from one end of the country to the other, producing an amazing array of real ales – for our pick of the best ales, see p298. They're free of hangover-inducing preservatives and some are served in pubs by hand-pump from the cask; many more are available in bottles.

Whisky and Scotland are synonymous, and you can't leave without trying a dram or two of single malt; it's the more expensive variety, but infinitely superior to blended whisky. The more fiery malts come from the islands – Islay, Skye and Orkney. Strathspey produces lighter, less peaty drams.

Eating out

If you're staying in towns and villages during your walks, there will usually be a choice between dinner in a pub or restaurant/bistro. Bar suppers (as they're called) in pubs are usually good value, and the best of them can be surprisingly good, with imaginative combinations of ingredients and sauces, far removed from the once-traditional chips-with-everything approach. There are plenty of small restaurants around the country which are dedicated to using fresh local produce whenever possible, and which offer very affordable menus, the equal of any fancy place in the cities. Almost all larger villages and towns have either an Indian or Chinese restaurant (or both), and at least one takeaway place, usually a 'chippie' (fish and chip shop); the well-known fast-food chains are very thin on the ground away from the major centres. The recommended establishments in the regional chapters are listed in order of cost, with the least expensive first. See p294 for standard opening times.

Vegetarians, and to a lesser extent vegans, are well looked after these days; it's rare to find a menu that doesn't include at least one vegetarian dish, though it does help if you cultivate a devotion to pasta and curries.

Self-catering

You will find at least one supermarket in larger towns where you can stock up before

TOP FIVE REAL ALES *Sandra Bardwell*

Scores of real-ale breweries in Scotland produce an extraordinary range of wonderful beers, including lagers, Pilsners, Scottish ales, wheat beers, dark ales, and some using traditional ingredients such as heather and even seaweed. Many are so distinctive that they deserve to be imbibed at a particular time – before, during or after dinner. Here is a highly personal guide to five of the best, in alphabetical order (as order of merit is impossible!), and some recommendations for others well worth trying.

- **Belhaven Pilsener** (www.belhaven.co.uk) Made at Dunbar in East Lothian, this beer is orange-gold with up-front hops so it's very dry, even tart. A great thirst quencher after a walk.
- **Cairngorm Trade Winds** (www.cairngormbrewery.com) Made at Aviemore, this multi-award winner has a high proportion of wheat and corn. The surprise ingredient is elderflower, which really hits you at first, but soon merges with plenty of hop flavours. Very refreshing and thirst-quenching.
- **Isle of Arran Dark** (www.arranbrewery.com) A lovely, deep golden-brown, this is a bit thin at first for a dark beer but becomes very fruity as you sip. Ideal after dinner, served at room temperature.
- **Innis & Gunn Oak-aged Beer** (www.innisandgunn.com) An amazing ale; at 6.6% it's stronger than most and very, very smooth, having been matured in oak barrels, residing in Edinburgh, for 30 days. This rich, raisin-sweet beer is definitely one for slow after-dinner sipping.
- **Orkney Red MacGregor** (www.orkneybrewery.co.uk) Orkney does several fine beers, including this one, which is deep cedar in colour, rich, creamy and full of fruit. One to have with puddings.

Of the many others, **Broughton** (www.broughtonales.co.uk) in the Borders pays tribute to writer John Buchan – also celebrated on the John Buchan Way (p76 – with Greenmantle. **Caledonian** (www.caledonian-brewery.co.uk) Golden Harvest organic ale is full of lemons and limes. **Heather Ale** (www.heatherale.co.uk) is perhaps the most innovative of all, with its delectable Fraoch, using heather, and Grozet, made with gooseberries. **Harviestoun**, at Dollar below the Ochil hills, offers Old Engine Oil and Bitter & Twisted (among others) – much more than mere marketing gimmicks. The **Black Isle Brewery** (www.blackislebrewery.com) near Inverness specialises in organic ales, notably a wheat beer and Red Kite, both superb thirst quenchers. At Uig on the west coast, **Isle of Skye** (www.skyebrewery.co.uk) has a great range, including Black Cuillin and Red Cuillin – what else would you drink after a stroll in those rugged mountains? Last, but certainly not least, Britain's northernmost brewery, **Valhalla** (www.valhallabrewery.co.uk) on Unst in Shetland, produces a small range, of which Old Scatness, made with bere meal (an ancestor of barley), stands out as an after-walk beer.

Slàinte!

heading out into the wilds, though even very small villages almost always have a small shop that carries a basic range of supplies, as do some large camping grounds. These sources are listed in the respective town/village entries in the regional chapters. If you're planning to camp, specialised freeze-dried meals are only available in outdoor gear shops but it doesn't take much imagination (and much less cash) to do interesting things with, for example, pasta, packaged sauces and a few vegetables. See p317 for information about availability of fuel for camping stoves.

WATER

Most walks cross at least one burn, from which you could be tempted to drink long and deep. Remember, however, sheep are almost ubiquitous and deer are widespread here. Consequently, the chances of watercourses being contaminated by animals, alive or dead, are quite high. While many walkers do drink from burns in remote areas, it's better to play safe and either carry your own drinks on a day walk or boil water if you're camping. For information about purification methods see p312).

HOLIDAYS

Public Holidays

Although bank holidays are general public holidays in the rest of the UK, in Scotland they apply only to banks and some other commercial offices. Bank holidays happen at the start of January, the first weekend in March, the first and last weekend in May, the first weekend in August and on Boxing Day. Christmas Day, New Year's Day and 2 January, and Good Friday and Easter Monday are also general public holidays.

School Holidays

School is out for two weeks at Easter, from early July to late August, one week in October, and two or three weeks around Christmas. These are always busy times, particularly in summer, when locals holidaying in Scotland are joined by visitors from Continental Europe and the world at large. Accommodation is harder to come by and it's well worth booking ahead.

INSURANCE

Travel-insurance policies are many and various, and should routinely cover medical expenses, theft or loss, and cancellation of, or delays in, your travel arrangements. The international student-travel policies handled by STA Travel and other reputable student-travel organisations are usually good value.

Make sure the policy includes health care and medication in the countries you may visit on your way to/from Scotland (see also p310).

As some policies specifically exclude 'dangerous activities', which may include walking, make sure you'll be covered for everything you plan to do, especially as some don't cover ambulances, helicopter rescue or emergency flights home.

INTERNET ACCESS

The best places to check email and surf the internet are public libraries. Almost every town and many villages have at least a couple of terminals, use of which is available either free or for a modest fee. Larger TICs across the country also have internet access, as do most large youth hostels.

There are also internet cafés in the cities and some large towns that are generally good value, charging up to £5 per hour.

MAPS

Buying Maps

Ordnance Survey (www.ordnancesurvey.co.uk) maps are available online and from outdoor gear shops, newsagents, bookshops and TICs.

Harvey (www.harveymaps.co.uk) maps can also be purchased online and from TICs in the areas they cover.

Large-Scale Maps

For the great majority of walks in this book, two OS series are recommended – the Landranger 1:50,000 and the Explorer 1:25,000. With a contour interval of 10m, the superb Landranger maps contain an enormous amount of tourism-related information, including the location of TICs and car parks. Around 85 maps cover the country. The Explorer series comes in single- and double-sided formats and is the ideal walking map, though you may need more than one for a given walk where a single Landranger would suffice. If you feel particularly indulgent, succumb to the temptation of an

MAPS IN THIS BOOK

The maps in this book are intended to show the general route of the walks described and are drawn to a metric scale. They are not sufficiently detailed for route-finding or navigation. For this you will need properly surveyed maps at an adequate scale, showing all (or most) relief features. They are recommended in the Planning section for each walk.

A map legend appears on the inside front cover.

Explorer – Active map, printed on waterproof paper with a coating that allows you to write all over it. Active maps cost almost twice as much as standard Explorer maps.

All 85 Landranger maps can also be purchased on four CDs from **Anquet Maps** (☎ 0845 330 9570; www.anquet.co.uk); individual 1:25,000 (with 3D virtual landscape) and national park maps can also be downloaded (at a steep price).

Independent map publisher, Harvey, produces a wide range of walking maps in its Superwalker (1:25,000), Outdoor (1:40,000) and Summit (1:12,500) series. These excellent maps, with 10m contours, are printed on waterproof paper and contain loads of useful information. Areas covered include Torridon, the Cuillin (Skye), Ben Nevis, Cairn Gorm, Lochnagar, Arran, Pentland Hills and Galloway Hills. Harvey has also mapped the Great Glen, West Highland, Speyside and St Cuthbert's Ways in its 1:40,000 Route series.

Small-Scale Maps

Britain's official map maker, the Ordnance Survey (OS), publishes 1:250,000 maps in its Travel – Road series, three of which cover Scotland. They are contoured and ideal for finding your way around the country.

Other regional maps, usually available at TICs, may be a better bet, though you could finish up with a backpack full of maps.

MONEY

Britain's currency is the pound sterling (£), which comprises 100 pence (p).

Three Scottish banks issue their own bank notes. You shouldn't have trouble changing them immediately south of the Scotland–England border, but elsewhere it may be difficult. All UK banks will accept the notes but overseas banks will not.

Exchange rates are listed on the inside front cover of this book. For a guide to costs see p18.

ATMs

You'll usually find at least one automatic teller machine (ATM, also known as cash machines) in small towns and some villages, sometimes inside a shop or service station. Cash withdrawals may be subject to a small charge, but most are free.

Credit Cards

Visa and MasterCard are widely accepted, although some places charge a fee for using them. Charge cards such as Amex and Diners Club may not be accepted in small establishments or off the beaten track. It's best to combine plastic and travellers cheques so you have something to fall back on if an ATM swallows your card or local banks don't accept it.

Moneychangers

The best places to change currencies are the bureaus de change at international airports. They charge less than most high-street banks and cash sterling travellers cheques for free. Elsewhere, you will probably have to pay outrageous commissions and fees.

On the Walk

If you're doing day walks from a base in a town or village, cash shouldn't be a problem. On long-distance walks make sure you have enough to cover the expected costs of accommodation and meals. B&Bs and small youth hostels don't usually take credit cards; cheques drawn on local accounts are OK if backed by a guarantee card.

Travellers Cheques

In Scotland, banks charge to cash travellers cheques, so it's best to cash them at a bureau de change at an international airport.

TELEPHONE

To call Scotland from abroad, dial your country's international access code then ☎ 44 (the UK country code), then the area code (dropping the first 0) followed by the telephone number.

In the UK, local calls are charged by time; national calls by time and distance. The cheapest times to ring are from 6pm to 8am Monday to Friday and from midnight Friday to midnight Sunday.

Public phones take either cash or credit cards; some take both. The minimum charge on BT phones is 30p, which buys you 15 minutes for local and national (Britain-wide) calls.

The following are codes to be aware of:

☎ 0800	toll-free call
☎ 0845	local call rate
☎ 0870	national call rate
☎ 090/091	premium rate

To call abroad from Scotland, dial ☎ 00, followed by the country code, area code (drop the first 0 if there is one) and number. Direct dialling is cheaper than going via the international operator (☎ 155).

MOBILE PHONES

Mobile phone numbers usually begin with ☎ 07. Scotland uses the GSM 900/1800 network, which covers the rest of Europe, Australia and New Zealand but isn't compatible with the North American GSM 1900. If you have a GSM phone, check with your provider about using it in the UK, and beware of calls being routed internationally, which is very expensive for a local call. You can buy a 'pay-as-you-go' phone for as little as £40. See p315 for advice about using your mobile during a walk.

TIME

Summer Time (daylight-saving time) has been used in Britain since WWI. Clocks are put forward one hour during the last weekend in March and put back one hour during the last weekend in October. This means that, during Summer Time, Britain is one hour ahead of GMT. As a standard, New York is five hours behind GMT and Sydney is 10 hours ahead.

Most public-transport timetables use the 24-hour clock but it's rarely used in everyday conversation; people refer to 9am or 9pm.

TAKING PHOTOS OUTDOORS *Gareth McCormack*

For walkers, photography can be a vexed issue – all that magnificent scenery but such weight and space restrictions on what photographic equipment you can carry. With a little care and planning, however, it is possible to maximise your chance of taking great photos on the trail.

Light & Filters In fine weather, the best light is early and late in the day. In strong sunlight and in mountain and coastal areas, where the light is intense, a polarising filter will improve colour saturation and reduce haze. On overcast days the soft light can be great for shooting wildflowers and running water, and an 81A warming filter can be useful. If you use slide film, a graduated filter will help balance unevenly lit landscapes.

Equipment If you need to travel light carry a zoom in the 28–70mm range, and if your sole purpose is landscapes consider carrying just a single wide-angle lens (24mm). A tripod is essential for really good images and there are some excellent lightweight models available. Otherwise a trekking pole, pack or even a pile of rocks can be used to improvise.

Camera Care Keep your gear dry – a few zip-lock freezer bags can be used to double wrap camera gear and silica-gel sachets (a drying agent) can be used to suck moisture out of equipment. Sturdy cameras will normally work fine in freezing conditions. Take care when bringing a camera from one temperature extreme to another; if moisture condenses on the camera parts make sure it dries thoroughly before going back into the cold, or mechanisms can freeze up. Standard camera batteries fail very quickly in the cold. Remove them from the camera when it's not in use and keep them under your clothing.

For a thorough grounding in photography on the road, read Lonely Planet's *Travel Photography* by Richard I'Anson, a full-colour guide for happy-snappers and professional photographers alike. Also highly recommended is the outdoor photography classic *Mountain Light* by Galen Rowell.

TOURIST INFORMATION

VisitScotland (☎ 0845 225 5121; www.visitscotland.com; Ocean Point One, 94 Ocean Dr, Leith, Edinburgh EH6 6JH) is the country's official tourist agency. It does handle post and telephone enquiries, but you'll probably do better by contacting local sources (listed in the Information Sources sections, and in individual towns in the regional chapters).

TICs in cities and large towns are open daily from around March to October, and Monday to Saturday from October to March. In smaller places most are usually open only from Easter to September or October.

Many of the local TICs are, for better or (probably) worse, hooked up to centralised call centres, which deal with phone enquiries. Face-to-face, you can expect friendly, helpful service.

VISAS

Visa regulations are subject to change so it's essential to check with your local British embassy before leaving home. Currently, if you're a citizen of Australia, Canada, New Zealand or the USA, you can stay for up to six months without a visa, but are not allowed to work. EU citizens do not need a visa to enter the country. For more information, see **UKvisas** (www.ukvisas.gov.uk).

WALKING FESTIVALS

A distinctively Irish event, walking festivals have caught on in Scotland with a vengeance. Not quite a contradiction in terms, although walking can be a very serious business for some, festivals typically comprise day and evening programs, spread over a weekend or even a week. During the day there'll be one or more guided walks, ranging from easy to demanding, and in the evening a variety of entertainment is usually put on, including illustrated talks, exhibitions, BBQs, dinners and that Scottish speciality, a *ceilidh*, which is part-party, part-concert. Does it cost anything (apart from accommodation and meals)? Yes and no – some organisers charge participants for each of the walks, others don't.

Mountain film festivals are another growth industry, having expanded from the Dundee original. Their focus is pretty wide (covering the spectrum of outdoor adventure activities) but always includes mountaineering and climbing. Programs include lectures (often by famous 'names'), exhibitions and, of course, social events, without which any festival would be incomplete.

The festivals listed below are all well established, so the contact details should hold good. If not, then the **VisitScotland** (www.visitscotland.com/walking) website may be useful; alternatively, check with a local TIC.

EDINBURGH & GLASGOW

Edinburgh Mountain Film Festival (www.edinburghmountainff.com) In a city with some experience in festivals, this one takes place in October with the focus on adventure in a program of films, lectures and exhibitions.

THE SOUTH

Moffat Walking Festival Usually takes place in October, and features walks along rivers and in the hills, including the several Corbetts in the area, and sections of the Southern Upland Way (p63). Contact the **Moffat TIC** (☎ 01683 220620; www.visitmoffat.co.uk) for details.

Newton Stewart Walking Festival (☎ 01671 402770; www.newtonstewartwalkfest.co.uk) Around May, this makes the most of the nearby Galloway Hills and forest park, and includes challenging mountain walks (such as the Merrick, p72) and a variety of low-level walks along the coast and to archaeological and historic sites.

Scottish Borders Walking Festival The pioneer in Scotland in the mid-1990s, this week-long festival happens during early September. St Cuthbert's Way (p85) and the Borders Abbeys Way (p86) are hardy annuals, plus there's the Cheviot hills, and easy valley and river-side walks. For information see **Scottish Borders Tourist Board** (☎ 0870 608 0404; www.visitscottishborders.com).

CENTRAL HIGHLANDS & ISLANDS

Crieff & Strathearn Drovers' Tryst (www.droverstryst.co.uk) Many of the walks at this festival commemorate the cattle drovers of yesteryear, for whom Crieff was the crossroads of their long journeys across Scotland. The festival takes place during October.

Dundee Mountain Film Festival (www.dundeemountainfilm.org.uk) This festival has been going for years, usually in late November, with films on skiing, Himalayan expeditions and polar exploration, as well as trade stands.

LOCHABER & GLEN COE

Fort William Mountain Festival (www.mountainfilmfestival.co.uk) Staged in the self-styled outdoor capital of Scotland, the festival happens in the second half of February and offers films, talks, book readings and exhibitions.

THE CAIRNGORMS

Aviemore Mountain Film Festival (www.amff.co.uk) Over a March long weekend, this festival presents top-class productions featuring many adventure sports, including mountaineering and climbing.

Aviemore Walking Festival (PO Box 5349, Aviemore PH22 1YG; www.aviemorewalking.com) May is the month for this feast of Munros (including Ben Macdui, p150), the Speyside Way (p163) and shorter strolls through forests and beside rivers, mostly in Cairngorms National Park.

Ballater Royal Deeside Walking Week This well-organised event has walks ranging from Munro ascents to long glen walks following old rights of way, mostly in Cairngorms National Park. Mountain guides, full-time rangers and local residents with specialised knowledge lead the walks. Information can be obtained at ☎ 013397 55467 or www.royal-deeside.org.uk.

Blairgowrie Walking Festival (www.walkingfestival.org) Taking place in early October at the foot of the Angus Glens on the southern fall of the Cairngorms, this festival offers climbs of Munros and Corbetts or, less strenuously, a walk along the Cateran Trail. Information can also be obtained from the **Blairgowrie TIC** (☎ 01250 872960).

Spirit of Speyside Walking & Wildlife Festival (☎ 01343 557147; www.walkingfestival.net) Encouraging the use of public transport is another theme at this Speyside festival, in late August. The walks are either along the Speyside Way (p163) or, more remotely and adventurously, in the Glenlivet estate.

HIGHLAND GLENS

Caithness & Sutherland Walking Festival (☎ 01847 851991) During early May, walks are led by Royal Society for the Protection of Birds and Forestry Commission rangers and members of the Caithness Field Club.

Glen Affric Walking Festival (☎ 01456 476363; lebrunshenval@hotmail.com) All the low- and high-level walks are in Glen Affric National Nature Reserve, highlighting the long-term conservation work in the area.

NORTHERN ISLES

Shetland Walking Week By far the most distant festival, this one has developed a surprisingly strong following. During early September, the program of walks includes the highest hill in Shetland and Hermaness National Nature Reserve. Contact the **Lerwick TIC** (☎ 08701 999440; www.visitshetland.com) for details.

Transport

CONTENTS

GETTING THERE & AWAY

AIR

Airports & Airlines

Scotland has four main international airports. London is the major UK gateway for long-haul flights.

Aberdeen (code ABZ; ☎ 0870 040 0006; www.aberdeenairport.com)
Edinburgh (code EDI; ☎ 0870 040 0007; www.edinburghairport.com)
Glasgow (code GLA; ☎ 0870 040 0008; www.glasgowairport.com)
Glasgow Prestwick (code PIK; ☎ 0871 223 0700; www.gpia.co.uk)
London Gatwick (code LGW; ☎ 0870 000 2468; www.gatwickairport.com)
London Heathrow (code LHR; ☎ 0870 000 0123; www.heathrowairport.com)

THINGS CHANGE...

The information in this chapter is particularly vulnerable to change. Check directly with the airline or a travel agent to make sure you understand how a fare (and ticket you may buy) works and be aware of the security requirements for international travel. Shop carefully. The details given in this chapter should be regarded as pointers and are not a substitute for your own careful, up-to-date research

Many airlines service Scottish airports. The main ones are the following.

Aer Arann (airline code RE; ☎ 0818 210210; www.aerarann.com)
Aer Lingus (airline code EI; ☎ 0845 973 7747; www.aerlingus.com)
Air France (airline code AF; ☎ 0845 084 5111; www.airfrance.com)
Air Transat (airline code TS; ☎ 0870 556 1522; www.airtransat.com)
American Airlines (airline code AA; ☎ 0845 778 9789; www.aa.com)
bmibaby (airline code WW; ☎ 0870 264 2229; www.bmibaby.com)
British Airways (airline code BA; ☎ 0845 773 3377; www.britishairways.com)
British European (airline code BE; ☎ 0870 567 6676; www.flybe.com)
British Midland (airline code BD; ☎ 0870 607 0555; www.flybmi.com)
Continental Airlines (airline code CO; ☎ 0845 607 6760; www.continental.com)
Eastern Airways (airline code T3; ☎ 0870 366 9100; www.easternairways.com)
easyJet (airline code U2; ☎ 0870 600 0000; www.easyjet.com)
KLM UK (airline code UK; ☎ 0870 507 4074; www.klmuk.com)
Lufthansa (airline code LH; ☎ 0845 773 7747; www.lufthansa.com)
Ryanair (airline code FR; ☎ 0870 156 9569; www.ryanair.com)
Zoom Airlines (airline code OOM; ☎ 0870 240 0055; www.flyzoom.com)

Australia & New Zealand

Many airlines compete on flights between Australia and New Zealand and the UK, and there is a wide range of fares. Round-the-world (RTW) tickets are often real bargains and can sometimes work out cheaper than a straightforward return ticket.

AUSTRALIA

Flight Centre (☎ 131 133; www.flightcentre.com.au)
STA Travel (☎ 1300 733 035; www.statravel.com.au)

NEW ZEALAND

Flight Centre (☎ 0800 243 544; www.flightcentre.co.nz)
House of Travel (☎ 04-496 3010; www.houseoftravel.co.nz)

BAGGAGE RESTRICTIONS

Airlines impose tight restrictions on carry-on baggage. No sharp implements of any kind are allowed onto the plane, so pack items such as pocket knives, camping cutlery and first-aid kits into your checked luggage.

If you're travelling with a camping stove you should remember that airlines also ban liquid fuels and gas cartridges from all baggage, both check-through and carry-on. Empty all fuel bottles and buy what you need at your destination.

Canada
Zoom Airlines flies direct to Glasgow from Vancouver, Toronto, Calgary and Halifax. Charter operator Air Transat links Toronto to Edinburgh and Glasgow, and Calgary and Vancouver to Glasgow.

Travel CUTS (☎ 1-866 246 9762; www.travelcuts.com) is Canada's national student travel agency and it has offices in all the major cities.

Continental Europe
Major airlines run several direct flights daily to Edinburgh from Amsterdam, Frankfurt, Geneva, Hamburg, Paris and Rome. Budget airlines fly direct to Glasgow and/or Edinburgh from Cologne-Bonn, Geneva, Milan, Nice, Rome and Zurich.

England & Wales
BA has flights to Glasgow and Edinburgh from London, Bristol, Birmingham, Cardiff, Manchester, Plymouth and Southampton, and to Aberdeen and Inverness from London.

EasyJet flies from London to Edinburgh, Glasgow, Inverness and Aberdeen; bmibaby has flights from East Midlands and Cardiff to Edinburgh and Glasgow. Eastern Airways flies from Norwich to Edinburgh, and from various English airports to Aberdeen and Inverness. Ryanair flies from Liverpool to Inverness.

Good UK travel agencies include **STA Travel** (☎ 0131 226 7747; www.statravel.co.uk) and **Trailfinders** (☎ 0141 353 2224; www.trailfinders.com).

Ireland
BA flies from Belfast and Derry to Glasgow, and from Belfast to Aberdeen and Edinburgh. EasyJet has direct flights from Belfast to Glasgow, Edinburgh and Inverness. There are daily flights from Dublin to Edinburgh and Glasgow with Aer Lingus and BA. Ryanair flies from Dublin to Glasgow Prestwick, Edinburgh and Aberdeen. British European flies from Cork and Shannon to Glasgow and Edinburgh via Birmingham. Aer Arann flies from Dublin to Inverness.

The youth and student travel agency **USIT** (☎ 01-602 1904; www.usitnow.ie) has offices in most major Irish cities.

USA
Continental flies daily from New York (Newark) to Glasgow and Edinburgh. **STA Travel** (☎ 800 781 4040; www.statravel.com) has offices in major cities.

LAND
Bus
Buses are normally the cheapest way to reach Scotland from other parts of the UK. The main operators, **National Express** (☎ 0870 580 8080; www.nationalexpress.com) and its subsidiary **Scottish Citylink** (☎ 0870 550 5050; www.citylink.co.uk), run regular services from London and regional cities in England, Wales and Northern Ireland. Citylink operates a daily service linking Dublin and Edinburgh.

Silver Choice Travel (☎ 01355 249499; www.silverchoicetravel.co.uk) operates a daily overnight service between London and Glasgow/Edinburgh. **Megabus** (☎ 0900 160 0900; www.megabus.com) offers inexpensive fares from London to Glasgow, Edinburgh and Inverness.

Car & Motorcycle
Drivers of EU-registered vehicles must carry registration papers and have insurance; the vehicle must have a nationality plate. The International Insurance Certificate (Green Card) isn't compulsory but is excellent proof that you're covered.

Train
Travelling to Scotland by train is usually faster and more comfortable, but more expensive, than by bus. The train is also a competitive alternative to air travel on the London–Edinburgh route. Timetable and fare information for all UK trains is available from **National Rail Enquiries** (☎ 0845 748 4950; www.nationalrail.co.uk).

CONTINENTAL EUROPE

You can travel from Paris or Brussels to London Waterloo (in 2½ hours) on the **Eurostar** (UK ☎ 0870 518 6186, France ☎ 0892 35 35 39; www.eurostar.com), but to reach Scotland you'll have to transfer to Kings Cross or Euston stations to connect with Edinburgh or Glasgow trains. Total journey time from Paris is about eight hours.

UK

GNER (☎ 0845 722 5225; www.gner.co.uk) operates frequent services between London Kings Cross and Edinburgh. The **Virgin Trains** (☎ 0845 722 2333; www.virgintrains.co.uk) service between London Euston and Glasgow is slower.

First ScotRail (☎ 0845 755 0033; www.firstscotrail.com) runs the *Caledonian Sleeper* service connecting London Euston with Edinburgh, Glasgow, Fort William and Inverness. Services to Edinburgh from elsewhere in England and Wales usually involve at least one change. First ScotRail also does Rail and Sail deals between Edinburgh and Glasgow and Belfast on the Stena Line ferries.

SEA

Superfast Ferries (☎ 0870 410 6040; www.superfast.com) runs a car ferry between Zeebrugge in Belgium and Rosyth, 12 miles northwest of Edinburgh.

Car ferry services from Northern Ireland to Scotland are run by **Stena Line** (☎ 0870 570 7070; www.stenaline.com) between Belfast and Stranraer, and **P&O Irish Sea** (☎ 0870 242 4777; www.poirishsea.com) between Larne and Troon, and Larne and Cairnryan. Standard and high-speed ferries ply the Stranraer and Cairnryan routes. There are also Rail and Sail deals with Stena and First ScotRail between Edinburgh and Glasgow and Belfast.

GETTING AROUND

Public transport is generally good in Scotland but costly compared with other European countries. Buses are usually the cheapest way to travel, but also the slowest. With a discount pass, trains can be competitive; they're also quicker, though you may still need to catch a bus to reach walking areas.

Traveline (☎ 0870 608 2608; www.travelinescotland.com) provides timetable information for all public-transport services in Scotland, but can't give fare information or book tickets.

AIR

Flying is a pricey way to cover relatively short distances, and only worth considering if you want to visit the Western or Northern Isles.

Loganair (☎ 0870 850 9850; www.loganair.co.uk) is the main domestic airline, providing flights from Glasgow, Edinburgh and Inverness to the islands.

British Midland (☎ 0870 607 0555; www.flybmi.com) flies from Edinburgh to Stornoway. **Highland Airways** (☎ 0845 450 2245; www.highlandairways.co.uk) operates flights from Inverness to the Northern and Western Isles.

BOAT

The main ferry operators are **Caledonian MacBrayne** (CalMac; ☎ 0870 565 0000; www.calmac.co.uk) for the west coast and islands, and **NorthLink Ferries** (☎ 0845 600 0449; www.northlinkferries.co.uk) for Orkney and Shetland. Calmac's Island Rover ticket gives unlimited travel on its ferry services. It also offers more than two-dozen Island Hopscotch tickets, with lower fares for various combinations of crossings; these are listed on the website and in its timetables booklet, available from TICs throughout Scotland. NorthLink ferries sail from Aberdeen and Scrabster on the north coast to Orkney, from Orkney to Shetland, and from Aberdeen to Shetland. See the various destinations for full details of services and fares.

BUS

The national network is operated by **Scottish Citylink** (☎ 0870 550 5050; www.citylink.co.uk), with reliable buses serving all main towns. Elsewhere, you'll have to switch to local services. During summer, seats are at a premium, so it's a good idea to make reservations at least a few days ahead.

Some remote villages can only be reached by **Royal Mail postbuses** (☎ 0845 774 0740; www.postbus.royalmail.com). These are usually minibuses used for delivering and collecting mail and following circuitous routes. While timetables usually suit reaching the start of a walk, you might be left in the lurch at the end of the day, so check carefully before boarding.

SHEEP MAY SAFELY ROAM

Driving to many of the walks in this book will take you through areas where sheep, and occasionally cattle, graze unconfined, particularly in the Western and Northern Isles.

Sheep are irresistibly attracted to roads on wet or cool days, when the bitumen surface is the driest and/or warmest place for miles around. During April and May, beware of very young lambs – they have no road sense at all.

In fenced farming country, stock are often moved along public roads while going from one field to another. If you do come upon a flock on the move, the only thing to do is to wait for it to pass around you, or until the farmer waves you on.

During the long hours of summer daylight, stock are easy to see if you're driving in the evening. But from late September, wandering stock can be a hazard, especially dark-coated animals. One Western Isles farmer hit upon the idea of painting the horns of a prized black sheep luminous orange to warn drivers of its presence! You have to wonder whether this was a status symbol or an embarrassment for the sheep.

Haggis Scotland (☎ 0131 557 9393; www.haggisadventures.com) and **MacBACKPACKERS** (☎ 0131 558 9900; www.macbackpackers.com) offer jump-on, jump-off minibuses, running from Edinburgh to Inverness, Ullapool, Skye, Fort William, Glencoe and Glasgow. Tickets are valid for up to three months. Bear in mind that you'll still need onward connections from most of these places.

Bus Passes

The Scottish Citylink Explorer Pass can be bought in the UK by both UK and overseas citizens. It offers unlimited travel on all Scottish Citylink services within Scotland for three of five consecutive days, five of 10 consecutive days, and eight of 16 consecutive days. It also entitles you to discounts on various regional bus services, on CalMac ferries and at SYHA hostels. It's not valid on National Express coaches.

Scottish Citylink offers 20% discounts to holders of the Euro<26 card, and the **Young Scot card** (☎ 0870 513 4936; www.youngscot.org).

CAR & MOTORCYCLE

Travelling by car or motorcycle allows you to travel quickly, independently and flexibly. Indeed, your own wheels are essential to reach the start of a fair proportion of the walks in this book.

Scotland's roads are generally good and far less busy than those in England, so driving is more enjoyable. Motorways (designated 'M') are toll-free dual carriageways, limited mainly to central and southern Scotland. Main roads ('A') are dual or single carriageways and are often busy. Secondary roads, most of which are designated 'B', wander between villages, and are quieter – some, mainly in the Highlands and islands, are only a single lane with passing places. Remember that passing places are not only for allowing oncoming traffic to pass, but also for overtaking. Check your rear-view mirror frequently and pull over to let faster vehicles pass if necessary. It's illegal to park in passing places. In the Highlands and islands there's the added hazard of sheep wandering onto the road; be particularly wary of lambs in spring (see the boxed text, above).

At around £1 per litre (equivalent to about US$4 for a US gallon) petrol is expensive by American or Australian standards; diesel is slightly more expensive. Distances, however, aren't great. Prices rise even more as you travel further from the main population centres and are up to 10% higher in the Western Isles. In remote areas, petrol stations are few and far between and are sometimes closed on Sunday.

Driving Licence

A foreign licence is valid in Britain for up to 12 months from time of entry into the country. If bringing a car from elsewhere in Europe, make sure you're adequately insured.

Hire

Car rental is relatively costly and often you'll be better off making arrangements in your home country for a fly/drive deal. The international rental companies charge from around £160 a week, plus insurance, for a small car (Ford Fiesta, Peugeot 106); local companies such as **Arnold Clark** (☎ 0845 607 4500; www.arnoldclarkrental.co.uk) start from £160 a week including insurance.

Following are the main international hire companies:

Avis (☎ 0870 606 0100; www.avis.co.uk)
Budget (☎ 0870 153 9170; www.budget.co.uk)
Europcar (☎ 0870 607 5000; www.europcar.co.uk)
Hertz (☎ 0870 844 8844; www.hertz.co.uk)
Thrifty (☎ 01494 751600; www.thrifty.co.uk)

TICs have lists of local car-hire companies. To rent a car, drivers must usually be aged 23 to 65; outside these ages, special conditions or insurance requirements may apply.

If you plan to visit the Western or Northern Isles, it will probably be cheaper to hire a car on the islands, rather than pay to take a rental car across on the ferry.

Parking

In virtually all towns you'll find off-street parking areas, which operate a pay-and-display system. In major centres there are also long-stay car parks.

In the countryside, at the starting and finishing points of popular walks, there's usually a formal car park, increasingly with a voluntary payment facility.

Road Rules

Anyone doing a lot of driving should buy the *Highway Code*, available from major bookshops. Vehicles drive on the left-hand side. Front seat belts are compulsory, and if belts are fitted in the back seat they must be worn. The speed limit is generally 30mph in built-up areas, 60mph on single carriageways and 70mph on dual carriageways. You give way to your right at roundabouts (traffic already on the roundabout has right of way). Motorcyclists must wear helmets.

It is a criminal offence to use a hand-held mobile phone or similar device while driving; this includes while you are stopped at traffic lights or stuck in traffic.

When driving you're allowed a maximum blood-alcohol level of 35mg/100mL.

HITCHING

Hitching is never entirely safe in any country and we don't recommend it. Travellers who hitch take a small but potentially serious risk. However, many people choose to hitch, and the advice that follows should help to make their journeys as fast and safe as possible.

Hitching is fairly easy in Scotland, except around big cities and built-up areas, where you'll need to use public transport. Although the northwest is more difficult because there's less traffic, waits of more than two hours are unusual (except on Sunday in 'Sabbath' areas).

It's against the law to hitch on motorways or their slip roads; make a sign and use approach roads or service stations.

TRAIN

Scotland's rail network extends to all major cities and towns, but the railway map has a lot of large blank areas in the Highlands and Southern Uplands, where you'll need to switch to bus or car.

For information on train timetables contact one of the following.

First ScotRail (☎ 0845 755 0033; www.firstscotrail.com)
National Rail Enquiries (☎ 0845 748 4950; www.nationalrail.co.uk)
Traveline Scotland (☎ 0870 608 2608; www.travelinescotland.com)

There are two classes of train travel: first and standard. First class is 30% to 50% more than standard but, except on very crowded trains, isn't really worth the extra money.

Reservations

First ScotRail operates most train services in Scotland. Reservations are recommended for intercity trips, especially on Fridays and public holidays; for shorter journeys, just buy a ticket at the station before you depart, or on the train if the station is not staffed.

Among the bewildering array of ticket types, Saver tickets can be used on any day and with few time restrictions.

Train Passes

First ScotRail offers a range of good-value passes. You can buy them at BritRail outlets in the USA, Canada and Europe, at the **British Travel Centre** (Regent St, London), at train stations throughout Britain and from **First ScotRail telesales** (☎ 0845 755 0033).

The Freedom of Scotland Travelpass gives unlimited travel on all ScotRail and Strathclyde Passenger Transport trains, plus NorthLink ferry services and on First Edinburgh buses serving the Borders. It's available for four days' travel out of eight, or eight days out of 15 consecutive days. The Highland Rover pass covers travel from Glasgow to Fort William, and from Inverness to Kyle of Lochalsh, Thurso, Aviemore and Aberdeen, and free travel on the Fort William to Inverness, Isle of Skye and Thurso to Scrabster buses, plus a discount on NorthLink ferry services. It allows four days' travel out of eight.

While the prices represent a great saving, you'd have to do a lot of travelling to get full value, and probably not as much walking as you might like.

Health & Safety

CONTENTS

In Scotland you're more likely to sprain an ankle out in the 'hills' than succumb to a dreaded illness. If you take care to treat the water you drink along the way, cover up on sunny days and exercise sensible precautions when walking, this chapter will be the least read in the whole book.

BEFORE YOU GO

While excellent medical services are readily available in Scotland, prevention is the key to staying healthy during your visit. A little planning before departure, particularly for any existing medical conditions, will save trouble later. Bring medications in their original, clearly labelled containers. A signed, dated letter from your physician describing your medical conditions and medications, including generic names, may also be useful. If you use syringes or needles, be sure to carry a physician's letter documenting their medical necessity. Pack a spare pair of contact lenses and/or glasses, and take your optical prescription with you.

INSURANCE

If you're an EU citizen, a European Health Insurance Card (EHIC), available from health centres or, in the UK, post offices, covers you for most medical care. EHIC will not cover you for non-emergencies, or emergency repatriation. If you're a citizen of a non-EU country, find out whether there is a reciprocal arrangement for free medical care between your country and the UK. If you do need health insurance, make sure you take out a policy that covers you for the worst possible case, such as an accident requiring an emergency flight home. Find out in advance if your insurance policy will make payments directly to providers or reimburse you later for overseas health expenses.

MEDICAL CHECK LIST

This is a list of items to consider including in your medical kit – consult your pharmacist for brands available in your country.

- ☐ Acetaminophen (paracetamol) or aspirin
- ☐ Adhesive or paper tape
- ☐ Antibacterial ointment for cuts and abrasions
- ☐ Antidiarrhoeal drugs (eg loperamide)
- ☐ Anti-inflammatory drugs (eg ibuprofen)
- ☐ Antihistamines (for hay fever and allergic reactions)
- ☐ Bandages, gauze swabs, gauze rolls
- ☐ Elasticised support bandage
- ☐ Iodine tablets or water filter (for water purification)
- ☐ Nonadhesive dressings
- ☐ Oral rehydration salts
- ☐ Paper stitches
- ☐ Permethrin-containing insect spray for clothing, tents and bed nets
- ☐ Scissors, safety pins, tweezers
- ☐ Sterile alcohol wipes
- ☐ Steroid cream or cortisone (for allergic rashes)
- ☐ Sticking plasters (Band-Aids, blister plasters)
- ☐ Sutures
- ☐ Thermometer

See also the equipment check list, p317.

RECOMMENDED VACCINATIONS

No vaccinations are required to travel to Scotland. However, the **World Health Organi-**

zation (WHO; www.who.int) recommends that all travellers should be covered for diphtheria, tetanus, measles, mumps, rubella, polio and hepatitis B, regardless of their destination.

INTERNET RESOURCES
A wealth of travel advice is to be found on the internet. The **WHO** (www.who.int/ith) publishes *International Travel and Health*, a handy volume that is revised annually and is available free online.

FURTHER READING
Hillwalking by Steve Long et al is the official handbook of the Mountain Leader and Walking Group Leader Schemes; it's an excellent reference, written by experts.

IN SCOTLAND

AVAILABILITY AND COST OF HEALTH CARE
Excellent health care is readily available and pharmacists can give valuable advice about minor illnesses and sell over-the-counter medication. They can also advise you when more specialised help is required and point you in the right direction.

Preparing for a Walk
It's always a good idea to know what to do in the event of a major accident or illness. Consider doing a recognised basic first-aid course before you go, and/or including a first-aid manual with your medical kit (and reading it).

INFECTIOUS DISEASES
Giardiasis
Giardiasis is a potential risk only in areas where water supplies may be contaminated by human or animal faeces or dead animals, so drinking untreated water is not recommended. Use water filters and boil or treat water with iodine to help prevent the disease. Symptoms consist of intermittent foul-smelling diarrhoea, abdominal bloating and wind. Effective treatment is available (tinidazole or metronidazole).

Lyme Disease
This is a tick-transmitted infection that may be acquired through contact with vegetation or merely walking in areas inhabited by red deer or sheep. The illness usually begins with a spreading rash at the site of the tick bite, and is accompanied by fever,

COMMON AILMENTS

Blisters

To avoid blisters make sure your boots are well worn in before you set out. Your boots should fit comfortably with enough room to move your toes; boots that are too big or too small will cause blisters. Make sure socks fit properly and are specifically made for walkers; even then, make sure there are no seams across the widest part of your foot. Wet and muddy socks can also cause blisters, so even on a day walk, pack a spare pair of socks. Keep your toenails clipped but not too short. If you do feel a blister coming on, treat it promptly. Apply a simple sticking plaster or, preferably, a special blister plaster that acts as a second skin.

Fatigue

More injuries happen towards the end of the day rather than earlier, when you are fresher. Although tiredness can simply be a nuisance on an easy walk, it can be life-threatening on narrow, exposed ridges or in bad weather. You should never set out on a walk that is beyond your capabilities on the day. If you feel below par, have a day off. To reduce the risk, don't push yourself too hard – take a rest every hour or two and take a good-length lunch break. Towards the end of the day, reduce the pace and increase your concentration. You should also eat and drink sensibly throughout the day; nuts, dried fruit and chocolate are all good energy-giving snack foods.

Knee Strain

Many walkers feel the judder on long, steep descents. Although you can't eliminate strain on the knee joints when dropping steeply, you can reduce it by taking shorter steps that leave your legs slightly bent and ensuring that your heel hits the ground before the rest of your foot. Some walkers find that tubular bandages help, while others use high-tech, strap-on supports. Walking poles are very effective in taking some of the weight off the knees.

headache, extreme fatigue, aching joints and muscles and mild neck stiffness. If untreated the symptoms usually resolve over several weeks, but disorders of the nervous system, heart and joints may develop later. Medical help should be sought immediately as treatment works best at an early stage. For more information and advice go to www.bada-uk.org.

ENVIRONMENTAL HAZARDS

Bites & Stings

BEES & WASPS

Stings from bees and wasps are usually painful rather than dangerous. However, people who are allergic may suffer severe breathing difficulties and need urgent medical care. Calamine lotion or a commercial sting-relief spray will ease discomfort, and ice packs will reduce the pain and swelling.

SNAKES

The adder is the only poisonous snake you're likely to encounter in Scotland, and its venom is rarely fatal; an antivenin is usually available.

Immediately wrap the bitten limb tightly, as you would for a sprained ankle, and then attach a splint to immobilise it. Keep the victim still and seek medical help. Tourniquets and sucking out the poison are comprehensively discredited.

TICKS

You should always check all over your body and clothing if you have been walking through a potentially tick-infested area (especially overhanging vegetation), as ticks can cause skin infections and other more serious diseases, such as Lyme disease (p311). Ticks are most active from March to September, especially where there are plenty of sheep or deer. It's wise to wear trousers, gaiters and a long-sleeved shirt, and to apply insect repellent in areas where ticks are likely to be prevalent.

If you find a tick attached to your skin, press down around its head with tweezers, grab the head and gently pull upwards. Avoid pulling the rear of the body as this may squeeze the tick's gut contents through the attached mouth into the skin, increasing the risk of infection and disease. Smearing chemicals on the tick will not make it let go and is not recommended. Spread antiseptic cream over the bite area.

> **WATER**
>
> Tap water in Scotland is safe to drink, but all other water should be treated. This can be done by boiling it for around five minutes, filtering it or chemically disinfecting it (with iodine tablets, available from outdoor gear stores and pharmacies) to prevent diarrhoea and Giardiasis. Prolonged use of iodine, for several weeks, can be harmful; use a filter instead.

Dehydration & Heat Exhaustion

Potentially dangerous and generally preventable, dehydration is precipitated by excessive fluid loss. Sweating and inadequate fluid intake are the most common causes among walkers. Other important causes are diarrhoea, vomiting and high fever. The first symptoms are weakness, thirst and passing small amounts of very concentrated urine. This may progress to drowsiness, dizziness or fainting upon standing up and, finally, coma.

It's easy to forget how much fluid is lost through perspiration while you're walking, particularly if a strong breeze is drying your skin quickly. You should always maintain a good fluid intake – a minimum of 3L a day is recommended.

Dehydration and salt deficiency can cause heat exhaustion. Salt deficiency is characterised by fatigue, lethargy, headaches, giddiness and muscle cramps; adding extra salt to your food should be sufficient – taking salt tablets isn't necessary.

Hypothermia

Hypothermia is a significant risk whenever the weather turns cold, wet and windy, which can happen at any time of the year. Strong winds produce a high chill factor that can cause hypothermia even in moderately cool temperatures. Early signs include the inability to perform fine movements (such as doing up buttons), shivering and a bad case of the 'umbles' (fumbles, mumbles, grumbles, stumbles). The key elements of treatment involve moving out of the cold, changing out of wet clothing into dry warm clothing (especially windproof and waterproof layers), wrapping-up in a sleeping

MEGABITES FROM MIDGES

Tourist literature promoting Scotland, and the western Highlands and islands in particular, is still coy about mentioning an unavoidable and less-than-delightful fact of the country's summer life: midges.

The midge is a pin-head-sized, black insect, which gathers in dense, dark clouds and swarms on humans (and animals), making life a misery. The insect can detect its prey from up to 100m away by scent and shape, and can also let other midges know about the 'find'.

Midges usually appear in early June and blight the countryside until the first chilly weather of autumn. They congregate wherever there's damp or wet ground, in rushes and sphagnum moss. They're most active in the early morning and evening, and on overcast days. Fortunately, they don't like wind, dry ground, bright sunshine or a scent emitted by some lucky people, who remain untouched while their companions are being attacked.

The bite causes an itchy reaction in most people, which can last from several minutes to several hours. Scratching the bite only prolongs the itch. It is best to brush rather than slap them away, so as not to spread the saliva.

Stories abound about the desperate measures taken to escape the biting hordes – immersion in the sea, or donning gloves and balaclava to eat a meal outdoors. Some people swear by swallowing heaps of vitamin C, others add liberal amounts of garlic to their meals.

The best protection is to cover your arms and legs, and wear a hat with a fine netting veil, available at outdoor gear shops. Insect repellents containing DEET (diethyl toluamide), DMP (dimethyl phthalate) or natural oils (such as bog myrtle and neem) should keep your skin midge-free for a few hours. Burning coils impregnated with repellent are an effective weapon, especially at camping grounds. It's best to avoid sheltered, windless sites when you stop for lunch or to pitch a tent. Midges rarely venture indoors – your last refuge.

The creatures have an ecological niche as food for some species of birds, bats and worms, and insectivorous plants such as sundews love them. Midge larvae in turn feed on other organisms in the soil (where they live for about 10 months after the eggs hatch).

Attempts to eradicate midges from their natural habitat have adversely affected other wildlife, and research into harmless and 100% effective methods of protection continues. For a good laugh, and more information, track down Alasdair Roberts' book *Midges*.

bag if available and ingesting fuel (water and high-energy, easily digestible food). With severe hypothermia, shivering stops. This is a medical emergency requiring immediate medical attention in addition to the above measures.

Ultraviolet (UV) Light Exposure

Surprisingly perhaps, Scotland has a high rate of skin cancer. You should certainly monitor your exposure to direct sunlight; slap on sunscreen and a barrier cream for your nose and lips, wear a broad-brimmed hat and protect your eyes with high-quality sunglasses with UV lenses, particularly when walking near water, sand or snow. Ultraviolet exposure is greatest between 10am and 4pm, so be particularly vigilant about skin exposure during these times. Always use 30+ sunscreen, apply it 30 minutes before going into the sun and repeat regularly to minimise damage.

TRAUMATIC INJURIES

Major Accidents

Falling or having something fall on you, resulting in head injuries or fractures, is always possible, especially if you're crossing steep slopes or unstable terrain. Following is some basic advice about what to do if a major accident happens; detailed first-aid instruction is outside the scope of this book. If someone suffers a bad fall:

- Make sure you and other people with you are not in danger.
- Assess the injured person's condition.
- Stabilise any injuries, such as bleeding wounds or broken bones.
- Seek medical attention (see p315).

If the person is unconscious, immediately check their breathing (clear the airway if it's blocked) and check whether there's a pulse by feeling the side of the neck rather than the wrist. If there is a pulse but no breathing, start mouth-to-mouth resuscitation immediately. In these circumstances the patient should be moved as little as possible, just in case their neck or back is broken.

Check for wounds and broken bones; if the victim is conscious, ask where pain is felt. Otherwise, gently inspect the person all over (including the back and back of the head), moving them as little as possible. Control any bleeding by applying firm pressure to the wound. Bleeding from the nose or ear may indicate a fractured skull. Don't give the person anything by mouth, especially if they're unconscious.

You will have to manage the person for shock. Raise their legs above the level of the heart (unless their legs are fractured); dress any wounds and immobilise any fractures; loosen tight clothing; keep the person warm by covering them with a sleeping bag or dry clothing; and insulate them from the ground if possible, though do not heat them.

Some general points to bear in mind:

- Simple fractures take several weeks to heal, so they do not need fixing straight away, but they should be immobilised to protect them from further injury. Compound fractures (those associated with open wounds) need urgent treatment.
- If you do have to splint a broken bone, remember to check regularly that the splint is not cutting off the circulation to the hand or foot.
- Most cases of brief unconsciousness are not associated with any serious internal injury, but any person who has been knocked unconscious should be watched for deterioration. If they do deteriorate, seek medical attention straight away.

Sprains

Ankle and knee sprains are common injuries among walkers crossing rough ground. To help prevent ankle sprains, wear boots that have adequate ankle support. If you do suffer a sprain, immobilise the joint with a firm bandage and, if feasible, immerse the foot in cold water. Once you reach shelter, relieve pain and swelling by keeping the joint elevated for the first 24 hours and, where possible, by applying ice to the swollen joint. For severe sprains, seek medical attention.

SAFETY ON THE WALK

By taking a few simple precautions, such as those listed in the boxed text on opposite, you can significantly reduce the odds of getting into difficulties. A list of the clothes and equipment you should carry is on p317.

CROSSING STREAMS

Sudden downpours can speedily turn a small burn into a raging torrent. If you're in any doubt about the safety of a crossing, look for a safer passage or wait. If the rain is short-lived it may subside quickly.

If you decide it is essential to cross (late in the day, for example), look for a wide, shallow stretch of the stream rather than a bend. Take off your trousers and socks, but keep your boots on to prevent injury. Put dry, warm clothes and a towel in a plastic bag near the top of your pack. Before stepping out from the bank, unclip your chest strap and hip belt. This will make it easier to slip out of your pack and swim to safety if you lose your balance and are swept downstream. Use a walking pole as a third leg on the upstream side, grasped in both hands, or go arm in arm with a companion, clasping each other at the wrist, crossing side-on to the flow, taking short steps.

LIGHTNING

If a storm brews, avoid exposed areas. Lightning has a penchant for crests, lone trees, small depressions, gullies, caves and building entrances, as well as wet ground. If you are caught out in the open, try to curl up as tightly as possible with your feet together and keep a layer of insulation between you and the ground. Place metal objects such as metal-framed backpacks and walking poles away from you.

RESCUE & EVACUATION

If someone in your group is injured or falls ill and can't move, leave somebody with them while another person goes for help. They should take a clear written description of the condition and location of the victim (as a six- or eight-figure grid reference), and of the terrain should a helicopter be needed. If there are only two of you, leave the injured person with as much warm clothing, food and water as is sensible to spare, plus a whistle and torch. Mark their position with something conspicuous – an orange bivvy bag or perhaps a large stone cross on the ground.

Emergency Communications & Equipment

MOBILE PHONES

Although mobile-phone coverage in walking areas in Scotland is generally good, there are still gaps and it's very unlikely to reach glens and corries. Reception may be good on high points but the strength of transmission can't be guaranteed. When you ring the **emergency services** (☎ 999, 112), ask for the service required (mountain rescue, ambulance) and be ready to give information on where the accident happened, how many people are injured and the injuries sustained. If a helicopter needs to come in, explain the terrain and the weather conditions at the accident site.

GPS RECEIVERS

Global Positioning System (GPS) receivers (see p318) may help you avoid some emergency situations, though there is no substitute for common sense and map and compass skills.

DISTRESS SIGNALS

If you need to call for help, use these internationally recognised emergency signals. Give six short signals, such as a whistle, a yell or the flash of a light, at 10-second intervals, followed by a minute's rest. Repeat the sequence until you get a response. If the responder knows the signals, this will be three signals at 20-second intervals, followed by a minute's pause and a repetition of the sequence.

Search & Rescue Organisations

In Scotland, search-and-rescue operations for walkers are coordinated by the police, and involve the local volunteer mountain-rescue team, and possibly a search-and-rescue dog team and an RAF helicopter. You can be connected to a police station by ringing ☎ 999 or ☎ 112 from either a landline or a mobile phone and asking for mountain rescue.

WALK SAFETY – BASIC RULES

- Allow plenty of time to complete a walk before dark, particularly when daylight hours are short.
- Study the route carefully, noting the possible escape routes and the point of no return (where it's quicker to continue than to turn back). Monitor your progress against the time estimated for the walk, and keep an eye on the weather.
- It's wise not to walk alone. Always leave details of your intended route, number of people in your group and expected return time with someone responsible before you set off; let that person know when you return.
- Before setting off, make sure you have the relevant map, compass, whistle, spare clothing, adequate food and water and that you know the local weather forecast for the next 24 hours.

HELICOPTER RESCUE & EVACUATION

If a helicopter arrives on the scene, there are a couple of conventions you should know. Standing face on to the chopper:

- Arms up in the shape of a letter 'V' means 'I/We need help'.
- Arms in a straight diagonal line (like one line of a letter X) means 'All OK'.

For the helicopter to land, there must be a cleared space of 25m x 25m, with a flat landing-pad area of 6m x 6m. The helicopter will fly into the wind when landing. In cases of extreme emergency, where no landing area is available, a person or harness might be lowered. Take extreme care to avoid the rotors when approaching a landed helicopter.

Clothing & Equipment

CONTENTS

Mishaps that befall walkers in Scotland can often be traced to unsuitable equipment or to underestimating the difficulty of a walk or the fickleness of the weather. Walking anywhere in the country should never be treated lightly and it makes sense to start with the most suitable kit for the type of outing. If it's not up to the mark, you can risk a cold and miserable day; in extreme conditions, it can mean the difference between life and death.

Good footwear, a rain jacket, overtrousers and a sweater or fleece jacket are the key items. Even if you already have some or all of these, check they don't need replacing. You don't have to spend a fortune; indeed, the most expensive may not be the best. The following section is not exhaustive. Browse product reviews in local walking magazines or consult staff in reputable outdoor gear shops for advice before you buy.

CLOTHING

Layering

A secret of comfortable walking is to wear several layers of light clothing, which you can easily take off or put on as you warm up or cool down. Most walkers use three main layers: a base layer next to the skin; an insulating layer; and an outer, shell layer for protection from wind, rain and snow.

For the upper body, the base layer is typically a shirt of synthetic material that wicks moisture away from the body and reduces chilling. The insulating layer retains heat next to your body, and is usually a windproof fleece jacket or sweater. The outer shell consists of either or both a windproof top or a waterproof jacket that also protects against cold wind.

For the lower body, the layers generally consist of either shorts or a pair of loose-fitting trousers, 'long-john' underwear and waterproof overtrousers.

Footwear

Runners (training shoes) are OK for walks in this book graded easy or moderate. However, you'll probably appreciate, if not need, the support and protection provided by proper boots for the demanding walks. Nonslip soles (such as Vibram) provide the best grip.

Buy boots in warm conditions or go for a walk before trying them on, so that your feet can expand slightly, as they would on a walk. Most walkers carry a pair of sandals to wear at night or during rest stops. Sandals are also useful when fording waterways.

Gaiters

Gaiters help to keep your feet dry in wet weather and on boggy ground; they can also deflect pebbles or small stones and maintain leg warmth. The best are made of strong fabric, with a robust zip protected by a flap, and have an easy-to-use means of securing them around the foot.

Overtrousers

Choose trousers with slits for pocket access and long leg zips so that you can pull them on and off over your boots.

Socks

Walking socks should be free of ridged seams in the toes and heels.

Waterproof jacket

Ideal specifications are a breathable, waterproof fabric, a hood that's roomy enough to cover headwear but still allows peripheral vision, a capacious map pocket and a heavy-gauge zip protected by a storm flap.

EQUIPMENT

Backpack

For day walks, a day-pack (30L to 40L) will usually suffice, but for multiday walks you will need a backpack of between 45L and 90L capacity. Even if the manufacturer claims your pack is waterproof, use heavy-duty liners.

EQUIPMENT CHECK LIST

This list is a general guide to the things you might take on a walk. Your list will vary depending on the kind of walking you want to do, whether you're camping or planning to stay in hostels or B&Bs, and on the terrain, weather conditions and time of year.

Clothing

- ☐ boots and spare laces
- ☐ gaiters
- ☐ hat (warm), scarf and gloves
- ☐ overtrousers (waterproof)
- ☐ rain jacket
- ☐ runners (training shoes) or sandals
- ☐ shorts and trousers
- ☐ socks and underwear
- ☐ sunhat
- ☐ sweater or fleece jacket
- ☐ thermal underwear
- ☐ T-shirt and long-sleeved shirt with collar

Equipment

- ☐ backpack with waterproof liner
- ☐ first-aid kit*
- ☐ food and snacks (high energy) and one day's emergency supplies
- ☐ insect repellent
- ☐ map, compass and guidebook
- ☐ map case or clip-seal plastic bags
- ☐ plastic bags (for carrying rubbish)
- ☐ pocket knife
- ☐ sunglasses
- ☐ sunscreen and lip balm
- ☐ survival bag or blanket
- ☐ toilet paper and trowel
- ☐ torch (flashlight) or headlamp, spare batteries and globe (bulb)
- ☐ water container
- ☐ whistle

Overnight Walks

- ☐ cooking, eating and drinking utensils
- ☐ dishwashing items
- ☐ matches and lighter
- ☐ sewing/repair kit
- ☐ sleeping bag and bag liner/inner sheet
- ☐ sleeping mat
- ☐ spare cord
- ☐ stove and fuel
- ☐ tent, pegs, poles and guy ropes
- ☐ toiletries
- ☐ towel
- ☐ water purification tablets, iodine or filter

Optional Items

- ☐ backpack cover (waterproof, slip-on)
- ☐ binoculars
- ☐ camera, film and batteries
- ☐ candle
- ☐ emergency distress beacon
- ☐ GPS receiver
- ☐ groundsheet
- ☐ mobile phone**
- ☐ mosquito net
- ☐ notebook and pen
- ☐ swimming costume
- ☐ walking poles
- ☐ watch

* see the Medical Check List (p310)
** see Mobile Phones (p301)

Fuel

The easiest type of fuel to use is butane gas in disposable containers; true, it doesn't win many environmental points but it's much easier to come by than liquid fuels. The most widely-used brands are Coleman and Camping Gaz, available from outdoor gear shops and, in some remote areas, from small supermarkets.

Liquid fuel includes Coleman fuel, methylated spirits and paraffin. Again, outdoor gear shops, possibly hardware stores or even small supermarkets are the best places to look for it. You may be able to obtain

NAVIGATION EQUIPMENT

Maps & Compass

You should always carry a good map of the area in which you are walking (see p299), and know how to read it. Before setting off on your walk, ensure that you are aware of the contour interval, the map symbols, the magnetic declination (difference between true and grid north), plus the main ridge and river systems in the area and the general direction in which you are heading. On the trail, try to identify major landforms such as mountain ranges and valleys, and locate them on your map to familiarise yourself with the region's geography.

Buy a compass and learn how to use it. The attraction of magnetic north varies in different parts of the world, so compasses need to be balanced accordingly. Compass manufacturers have divided the world into five zones. Make sure your compass is balanced for your destination zone. There are also 'universal' compasses on the market that can be used anywhere in the world.

1 Base plate
2 Direction of travel arrow
3 Dash
4 Bezel
5 Meridian lines
6 Needle
7 Red end
8 N (north point)

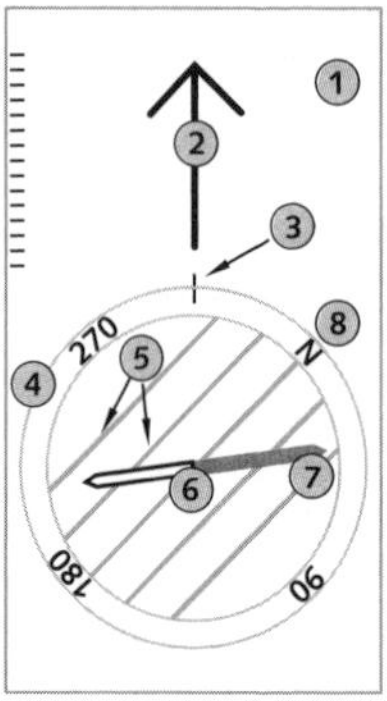

How to Use a Compass

This is a very basic introduction to using a compass and will only be of assistance if you are proficient in map reading. For simplicity, it doesn't take magnetic variation into account. Before using a compass we recommend you obtain further instruction.

Reading a Compass

Hold the compass flat in the palm of your hand. Rotate the bezel (4) so the red end (7) of the needle (6) points to the N (north point; 8) on the bezel. The bearing is read from the dash (3) under the bezel.

Orienting the Map

To orient the map so that it aligns with the ground, place the compass flat on the map. Rotate the map until the needle is parallel with the map's north/south grid lines and the red end is pointing to north on the map. You can now identify features around you by aligning them with labelled features on the map.

small quantities of unleaded petrol from service stations.

Airlines prohibit the carriage of any flammable materials and may well reject empty liquid-fuel bottles or even the stoves themselves.

Sleeping Bag & Mat

Down fillings are warmer than synthetic for the same weight and bulk but, unlike synthetic fillings, do not retain warmth when wet. Mummy-shaped bags are best for weight and warmth. The given figure (-5ºC, for instance) is the coldest temperature at which a person should feel comfortable in the bag (although the ratings are notoriously unreliable).

An inner sheet will help keep your sleeping bag clean, as well as adding another layer of insulation. Silk 'inners' are the lightest, but you can also get them in cotton or synthetic fabric.

Self-inflating sleeping mats work like a thin air cushion between you and the ground; they also insulate from the cold. Foam mats are a low-cost, but less comfortable, alternative.

Stoves

Fuel stoves operate on butane gas, Coleman fuel (white gas), unleaded petrol, methylated spirits (ethyl alcohol) or paraffin. In general the liquid fuels are efficient and inexpensive, while gas is more expensive, but cleaner and still a reasonable performer. However, the gas canisters can be awkward to carry on walks, and present a potential litter problem.

Taking a Bearing from the Map
Draw a line on the map between your starting point and your destination. Place the edge of the compass on this line with the direction of travel arrow (2) pointing towards your destination. Rotate the bezel until the meridian lines (5) are parallel with the north/south grid lines on the map and the N points to north on the map. Read the bearing from the dash.

Following a Bearing
Rotate the bezel so that the intended bearing is in line with the dash. Place the compass flat in the palm of your hand and rotate the base plate (1) until the red end points to N on the bezel. The direction of travel arrow will now point in the direction you need to walk.

Determining Your Bearing
Rotate the bezel so the red end points to the N. Place the compass flat in the palm of your hand and rotate the base plate until the direction of travel arrow points in the direction in which you have been walking. Read your bearing from the dash.

GPS

Originally developed by the US Department of Defense, the Global Positioning System (GPS) is a network of more than 20 earth-orbiting satellites that continually beam encoded signals back to earth. Small, computer-driven devices (GPS receivers) can decode these signals to give users an extremely accurate reading of their location – to within 30m, anywhere on the planet, at any time of day, in almost any weather. The cheapest hand-held GPS receivers now cost less than US$100 (although these may not have a built-in averaging system that minimises signal errors). Other important factors to consider when buying a GPS receiver are its weight and battery life.

Remember that a GPS receiver is of little use unless used with an accurate topographical map. The receiver simply gives your position, which you must then locate on the local map. GPS receivers will only work properly in the open. The signals from a crucial satellite may be blocked (or bounce off rock or water) directly below high cliffs, near large bodies of water or in dense tree cover and give inaccurate readings. GPS receivers are more vulnerable to breakdowns (including dead batteries) than the humble magnetic compass – a low-tech device that has served navigators faithfully for centuries – so don't rely on them entirely.

Tent
A three-season tent will fulfil most walkers' requirements. The floor and the outer shell, or fly, should have taped or sealed seams and covered zips to stop leaks. The weight can be as low as 1kg for a stripped-down, low-profile tent, and up to 3kg for a roomy, luxury, four-season model. Dome- and tunnel-shaped tents handle windy conditions better than flat-sided tents.

BUYING LOCALLY
The British brands of clothing and equipment prominently displayed in outdoor gear shops in Scotland are generally designed and manufactured to high standards. A decision to purchase gear here will probably depend very much on the exchange rate available when you are looking into buying stuff, and whether you consider you will be getting value for money. Outdoor gear shops are listed in the town descriptions in the regional chapters wherever they're readily accessible. You can, of course, do some online browsing beforehand. The main outlets in Scotland are listed below.

Blacks (www.blacks.co.uk) Stores in Aviemore, Edinburgh, Glasgow, Fort William and Inverness.
Ellis Brigham (www.ellis-brigham.com) Stores in Aviemore and Fort William.
Nevisport (www.nevisport.com) Stores in Aviemore, Edinburgh, Fort William, Glasgow and Inverness.
Tiso's (www.tiso.com) Stores in Edinburgh, Glasgow, Inverness and Stirling.

It's worth noting that gear hiring services are very few and far between.

Language

CONTENTS

Scottish Gaelic (*Gàidhlig* – pronounced *gallic* locally) is spoken by about 80,000 people in Scotland, mainly in the Highlands and islands, and by many native speakers and learners overseas. It is a member of the Celtic branch of the Indo-European family of languages, which has given us Gaelic, Irish, Manx, Welsh, Cornish and Breton.

Although Scottish Gaelic is the Celtic language most closely associated with Scotland, it was quite a latecomer to those shores. Other Celtic languages in the form of Pictish and Brittonic had existed prior to the arrival and settlement by Gaelic-speaking Celts (Gaels) from Ireland from the 4th to the 6th centuries AD. These Irish settlers, known to the Romans as Scotti, were eventually to give their name to the entire country. Initially they settled in the area on the west coast of Scotland in which their name is perpetuated, Earra Ghaidheal (Argyll). As their territorial influence extended so did their language, and from the 9th to the 11th centuries Gaelic was spoken throughout the country. For many centuries the language was the same as the language of Ireland; there is little evidence of much divergence before the 13th century. Even up to the 18th century the bards adhered to the strict literary standards of Old Irish.

The Viking invasions from AD 800 brought linguistic influences which are evident in many of the coastal place names of the Highlands.

Gaelic culture flourished in the Highlands until the 18th century and the Jacobite rebellions. After the Battle of Culloden in 1746 many Gaelic speakers were forced from their ancestral lands; this 'ethnic cleansing' by landlords and governments culminated in the Highland Clearances of the 19th century. Although it is still studied at academic level, the spoken language declined, being regarded as a mere 'peasant' language of no modern significance.

It was only in the 1970s that Gaelic began to make a comeback with a new generation of young enthusiasts who were determined that it should not be allowed to die. People from all over Scotland, and indeed worldwide, are beginning to appreciate their Gaelic heritage.

After two centuries of decline, the language is now being encouraged through financial help from government agencies and the EU. Gaelic education is flourishing from playgroups to tertiary levels. This renaissance flows out into the field of music, literature, cultural events and broadcasting.

The Gaelic language has a vital role to play in the life of modern Scotland.

MAKING CONVERSATION

Good morning.
Madainn mhath. — madding va

Good afternoon/Good evening.
Feasgar math. — fesskurr ma

Good night.
Oidhche mhath. — uh eech uh va

How are you?
Ciamar a tha thu? — kimmer uh ha oo?

Very well, thank you.
Glè mhath, tapadh leat. — gley va, tappuh let

I'm well, thank you.
Tha mi gu math, tapadh leat. — ha mee goo ma, tappuh let

That's good.
'S math sin. — sma shin

Please.
Mas e do thoil e. — mahs eh doh hawl eh

Thank you.
Tapadh leat. — tappuh let

Many thanks.
Mòran taing. — moe ran ta eeng

You're welcome.
'Se do bheatha. — sheh doh veh huh

I beg your pardon.
B'àill leibh. — baaluv

Excuse me.
Gabh mo leisgeul. — gav mo lishk yal

I'm sorry.
Tha mi duilich. — ha mee dooleech

Do you speak (have) Gaelic?
A bheil Gàidhlig agad? — uh vil ga lick ackut?

Yes, a little.
Tha, beagan. ha, beg an
Not much.
Chan eil mòran. chan yil moe ran
What's your name?
De an t ainm a tha ort? jae an tannam uh ha orsht?
I'm...
Is mise... is meeshuh...
Good health/Cheers!
Slàinte mhath! slahntchuh va!
Goodbye. (lit: Blessings go with you)
Beannachd leat. b yan achd let
Goodbye. (The same with you)
Mar sin leat. mar shin let

FOOD & DRINK

I'm hungry.
Tha an t-acras orm. ha an tac russ orrom
I'm thirsty.
Tha am pathadh orm. ha am pah ugh orrom
I'd like...
Bu toigh leam... boo tawl lehum
I don't like...
Cha toigh leam... chah tawl lehum
That was good.
Bha siud math. va shood ma
Very good.
Glè mhath. gley va

a biscuit	*brioscaid*	briskatch
bread	*aran*	aran
broth/soup	*brot*	broht
butter	*ìm*	eem
cheese	*càise*	kashuh
cream	*bàrr*	baahrr
dessert	*mìlsean*	meehlshuhn
fish	*iasg*	eeusk
meat	*feòil*	fehyawl
oatcakes	*aran coirce*	aran korkuh
peas	*peasair*	pessir
porridge	lee *lite*	chuh
potatoes	*buntàta*	boontahtuh
salmon	*bradan*	brahdan
vegetables	*glasraich*	glasreech

a cup of coffee	*cupa cofaidh*	coopa cawfee
a cup of tea	*cupa tì*	coopa tee
black coffee	*cofaidh dubh*	cawfee dooh
black tea	*tì dhubh*	tee dhooh
with milk	*le bainne*	leh bahnyuh
with sugar	leh *le siùcar*	shooh car
a glass of water	*glainne uisge*	glahnyuh ooshkuy
a glass of wine	*glainne fìon*	glahnyuh feeuhn
beer	*leann*	lyawn
red wine	*fìon dearg*	feeuhn jerrack
white wine	*fìon geal*	feeuhn gyahl
whisky	*uisge beatha*	ooshkuy beh huh

LANGUAGE

Glossary

Some English words and phrases commonly used in Scotland will be unknown to visitors from abroad, even if English is their first language. There are also many walking and geographical terms, often derived from ancient and endemic languages, which you're likely to come across during your travels. We have translated some of these terms here. Lonely Planet's *British Phrasebook* provides an in-depth introduction to the British English language.

AA – Automobile Association
abhainn – river; stream
allt – river; stream
aonach – ridge
arête – narrow or sharp ridge separating two glacial valleys

bag – to reach the top of a mountain or large hill
bàn – white
bank holiday – public holiday (when banks are closed)
beag – small
bealach – pass between hills
beinn – mountain
ben – mountain
bidean – peak
bitumen – road-surfacing material; asphalt; Tarmac
bonxie – great skua (a bird – Orkney Islands)
bothy – simple hut in the hills used by walkers (and shepherds and others)
broch – ancient circular dry-stone tower, large enough to serve as a fortified home
burn – stream

cairn – pile of stones to mark a path or junction; peak
clan – group of people claiming descent from a common ancestor
cnoc – rounded hillock
coire – high mountain valley; cirque; *corrie*
col – the lowest point of a ridge connecting two peaks
contour interval – vertical distance between contour lines on a topographical map
Corbett – hill or mountain between 2500ft and 2999ft high
corrie – semicircular basin at the head of a steep-sided valley, usually formed by glacial erosion; cirque; *coire*
crag – rocky outcrop
croft, crofting – plot of land and adjacent house, worked by occupiers
cull, culling – systematic reduction of deer population as part of a wildlife management program

dearg – red; reddish
Donald – Scottish hill between 2000ft and 2499ft high
dram – whisky measure
druim – ridge
dubh – dark; black
dùn – fortress; fort
dyke – stone wall

eas – waterfall
eilean – island
estate – large (usually) area of landed property
EU – European Union
exclosure – fenced enclosure to protect internal trees from external grazing stock

fionn – white
firth – river estuary
fraoch – heather

geal – white
gendarme – large block (of rock) barring progress on a narrow ridge
geo – very narrow coastal inlet or chasm
GGW – Great Glen Way
ghillies – estate employees who guide hunters and anglers
glas – grey; grey-green
glen – valley
gloup – blowhole (Northern Isles)
GNER – Great North Eastern Railway
gorm – blue
gully – small, steep-sided valley

hag – mound of *peat*, usually in bogs
hamlet – small settlement

hillwalker – person who enjoys walking in the 'hills' of Scotland
horseshoe – curved or circular route up one ridge and down another, round a valley
HS – Historic Scotland

inch – island
inn – pub, usually with accommodation
inver – river mouth

JMT – John Muir Trust

ken – head (noun); know (verb)
kin – head (noun)
kirk – church
kissing gate – swinging gate in fence, built to allow people through, but not animals or bicycles
kyle – narrows; strait

lairig – pass (mountain)
law – round hill
LDP – long-distance path
linn – waterfall
loch – lake
lochan – small lake
lock – section of canal that can be closed off and the water level changed to raise or lower boats

machair – area of sandy, calcium-rich soil, confined to the west coast, extending inland from the beach and very rich in summer wildflowers
màm – rounded hill; pass in the hills
MBA – Mountain Bothies Association
MCoS – Mountaineering Council of Scotland
meall – lumpy, rounded hill
mheadhoin – middle; central
mhor – big; great
midge – minute, biting insect, irresistibly attracted to humans in damp, moist areas on dull, still days
MoD – Ministry of Defence
moor – open, treeless area
mor – big; great
moraine – ridge or mound of debris deposited by retreating glacier
moss – bog; morass; mire
Munro – mountain over 3000ft high
Munro bagger – someone who deliberately sets out to reach the top of a *Munro*

ness – headland
NNR – National Nature Reserve
NP – National Park
NTS – National Trust for Scotland

off-licence – shop selling alcoholic drinks to take away
OS – Ordnance Survey

passing place – area beside a *single-track road* where vehicles can wait for others to pass, allowing the smooth flow of traffic in remote areas
peat – compact, brownish deposit of partially decomposed vegetable matter saturated with water, and used as a fuel when dried; see also *hag*
Pict – early Celtic inhabitant
postbus – mail delivery van, which also carries passengers

RA – Ramblers Association
RAC – Royal Automobile Club
real ale – any beer that is allowed to ferment in the cask, contains no chemicals or additives and, when served, is pumped up without using carbon dioxide
RSPB – Royal Society for the Protection of Birds
rubha – headland

sàil – long mountain slope; heel
scrambling – using hands for balance and/or to enable movement upwards on rock
sealed road – road surfaced with *bitumen*
sea stack – pillar of rock rising from the sea
sgurr – pointed hill or mountain
shieling – traditional stone cottage used in summer for fishing or tending herds in remote areas
single-track road – sealed road, one-lane wide with regularly spaced passing places
SMC – Scottish Mountaineering Council
SNH – Scottish Natural Heritage
sròn – ridge running off mountain top; nose
SROWAS – Scottish Rights of Way & Access Society
stalking – hunting of deer for sport and/or to control population
stell – small corral for sheep etc
stile – set of steps enabling crossing of a fence or stone wall
stob – peak
strath – broad, flat river valley
SUW – Southern Upland Way
SWT – Scottish Wildlife Trust
SYHA – Scottish Youth Hostels Association

TIC – tourist information centre
torr – small hill
tràigh – beach
trig point – survey pillar or *cairn*
true left/right bank – side of the river as you look downstream
tryst – cattle market

VAT – value-added tax
voe – large bay or sea inlet (Northern Isles)

WHW – West Highland Way
wick – bay (Northern Isles)
woodland – forest

Behind the Scenes

THIS BOOK

This guidebook was commissioned in Lonely Planet's Melbourne office and produced by the following:

Commissioning Editor Ben Handicott
Coordinating Editors Andrew Bain, Pat Kinsella
Coordinating Cartographer Andrew Smith
Coordinating Layout Designer David Kemp
Senior Editor Helen Christinis
Managing Cartographer Mark Griffiths
Assisting Editor Peter Cruttenden
Assisting Cartographers Jody Whiteoak, Erin McManus
Cover Designer Wendy Wright
Project Managers Eoin Dunlevy, Craig Kilburn

Thanks to Carol Chandler, Sally Darmody, Brendan Dempsey, Quentin Frayne, Jennifer Garrett, Laura Jane, Glenn van der Knijff, Wayne Murphy, Trent Paton, Paul Piaia, Wibowo Rusli, Fiona Siseman, Celia Wood.

THANKS

SANDRA BARDWELL

Staff at some TICs were especially helpful, particularly Robbie at Brodick, Hazel in Lerwick and Susan at Drumnadrochit. Richard Means (Dumfries & Galloway Ranger Service), Mike Baker and Keith Robeson (Borders Ranger Service) unstintingly gave advice and up-to-date information, as did Pete Crane (Cairngorms National Park), Lyndy Rennick (Galloway Forest District), and Polly Farmer (Atholl Estates Ranger Service). Sarah and Dave put me right in the Ochils, where Jetta's and Bramble's companionship in the snow was greatly appreciated; Jetta also provided invaluable route advice. Anne unearthed useful archaeological information; Jan and Alan updated Islay; Fiona liberated the photocopier. Fraser's willingness to impart his knowledge of Highland cairns, and Roddy's contribution on the Gaelic language are highly valued. B&B ladies' hospitality is legendary: Morag went much further when I was stranded by heavy snow; Debbie and James welcomed us warmly, and on Shetland Marcia and Joan enriched our visit with insights into island life. The whole project would have faltered without the enthusiastic help of Ann Miles, Duncan Macdonald, Gavin Miles, Noel Fojut and Peter Wilkes in checking several walks. Thanks to Ben for another fantastic LP assignment, and to Andrew (Bain) for excellent editorial work and to Andrew (Smith) for first-rate cartography. I would undoubtedly have fallen by the wayside without Hal's companionship, support and help in many ways, including the housework.

OUR READERS

Many thanks to the travellers who used the last edition and wrote to us with helpful hints, useful advice and interesting anecdotes:

Stuart Bell, Michael Holden, Leslie MacKay, Rona McIntyre, Katharina Menzel, Thomas Murray, Johanna Puesche, Rebecca Ross, Elizabeth Silva, Mary Stacey

THE LONELY PLANET STORY

The story begins with a classic travel adventure: Tony and Maureen Wheeler's 1972 journey across Europe and Asia to Australia. There was no useful information about the overland trail then, so Tony and Maureen published the first Lonely Planet guidebook to meet a growing need.

From a kitchen table, Lonely Planet has grown to become the largest independent travel publisher in the world, with offices in Melbourne (Australia), Oakland (USA) and London (UK). Today Lonely Planet guidebooks cover the globe. There is an ever-growing list of books and information in a variety of media. Some things haven't changed. The main aim is still to make it possible for adventurous travellers to get out there – to explore and better understand the world.

At Lonely Planet we believe travellers can make a positive contribution to the countries they visit – if they respect their host communities and spend their money wisely. Every year 5% of company profit is donated to charities around the world.

ACKNOWLEDGMENTS

Many thanks to the following for the use of their content:

Globe on back cover ©Mountain High Maps 1993 Digital Wisdom, Inc.

This book includes mapping data reproduced by permission of Ordnance Survey on behalf of HMSO. © Crown copyright 2006. All rights reserved. Ordnance Survey Licence number 100031848.

SEND US YOUR FEEDBACK

We love to hear from travellers – your comments keep us on our toes and help make our books better. Our well-travelled team reads every word on what you loved or loathed about this book. Although we cannot reply individually to postal submissions, we always guarantee that your feedback goes straight to the appropriate authors, in time for the next edition. Each person who sends us information is thanked in the next edition – and the most useful submissions are rewarded with a free book.

To send us your updates – and find out about Lonely Planet events, newsletters and travel news – visit our award-winning website: **www.lonelyplanet.com/feedback**.

Note: we may edit, reproduce and incorporate your comments in Lonely Planet products such as guidebooks, websites and digital products, so let us know if you don't want your comments reproduced or your name acknowledged. For a copy of our privacy policy visit www.lonelyplanet.com/privacy.

Index

000 Map pages
000 Photograph pages

D

INDEX

INDEX

000 Map pages
000 Photograph pages

INDEX

INDEX

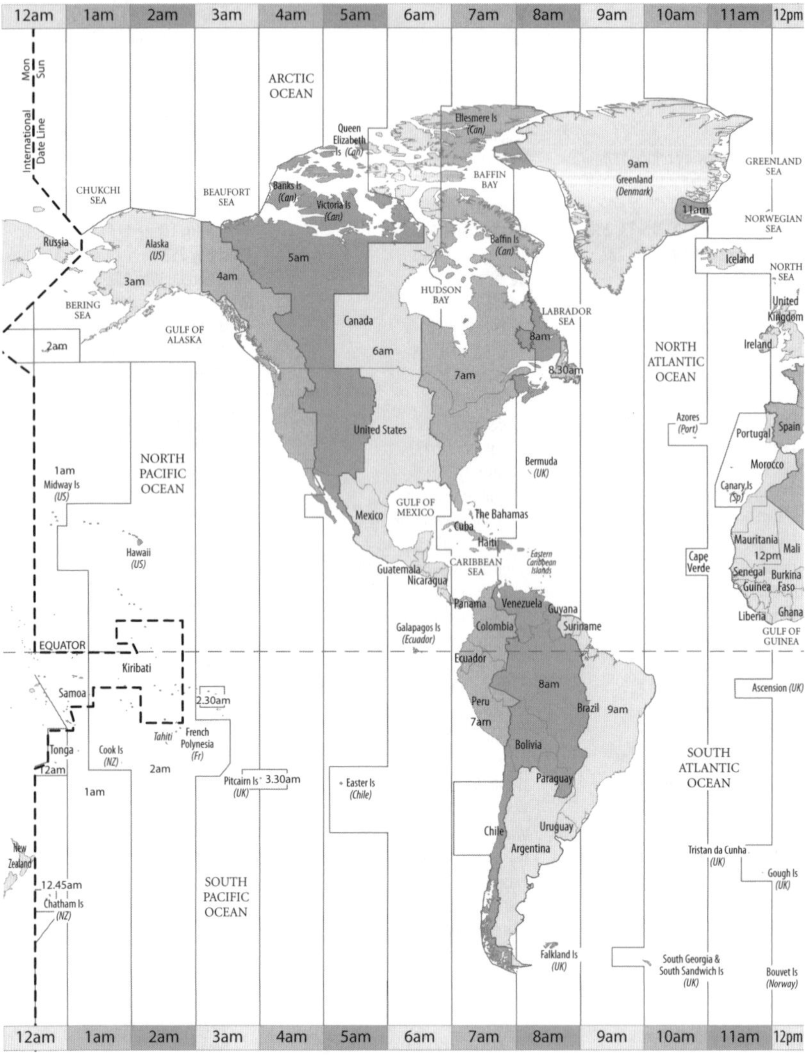
12am
1am
2am
3am
4am
5am
6am
7am
8am
9am
10am
11am
12pm
Mon
Sun
International Date Line
ARCTIC OCEAN
Queen Elizabeth Is (Can)
Ellesmere Is (Can)
9am
Greenland (Denmark)
GREENLAND SEA
CHUKCHI SEA
BEAUFORT SEA
Banks Is (Can)
Victoria Is (Can)
BAFFIN BAY
11am
NORWEGIAN SEA
Russia
Alaska (US)
3am
4am
5am
Baffin Is (Can)
Iceland
NORTH SEA
BERING SEA
HUDSON BAY
United Kingdom
Canada
LABRADOR SEA
GULF OF ALASKA
2am
6am
8am
Ireland
NORTH ATLANTIC OCEAN
7am
8.30am
Azores (Port)
United States
Portugal
Spain
NORTH PACIFIC OCEAN
1am
Midway Is (US)
Bermuda (UK)
Morocco
Canary Is (Sp)
GULF OF MEXICO
Mexico
The Bahamas
Cuba
Haiti
Hawaii (US)
Eastern Caribbean Islands
Mauritania
12pm
Mali
Cape Verde
Guatemala
CARIBBEAN SEA
Nicaragua
Senegal
Burkina Faso
Guinea
Panama
Venezuela
Guyana
Galapagos Is (Ecuador)
Colombia
Suriname
Liberia
Ghana
GULF OF GUINEA
EQUATOR
Ecuador
Kiribati
8am
Samoa
2.30am
Ascension (UK)
Peru
Brazil
9am
7am
Tahiti
French Polynesia (Fr)
Tonga
Cook Is (NZ)
2am
Bolivia
SOUTH ATLANTIC OCEAN
12am
1am
Pitcairn Is (UK)
3.30am
Easter Is (Chile)
Paraguay
Chile
Uruguay
Argentina
Tristan da Cunha (UK)
New Zealand
12.45am
Chatham Is (NZ)
SOUTH PACIFIC OCEAN
Gough Is (UK)
Falkland Is (UK)
South Georgia & South Sandwich Is (UK)
Bouvet Is (Norway)

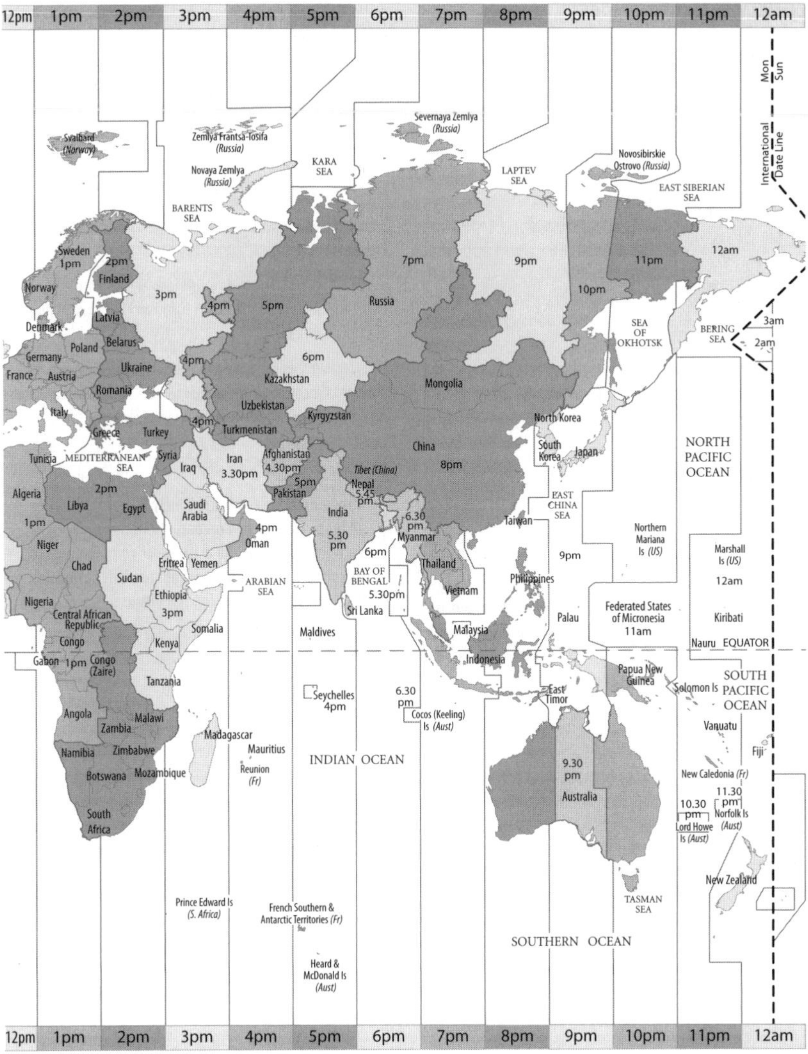
12pm
1pm
2pm
3pm
4pm
5pm
6pm
7pm
8pm
9pm
10pm
11pm
12am
Mon
Sun
International Date Line
Svalbard (Norway)
Zemlya Frantsa-Iosifa (Russia)
Novaya Zemlya (Russia)
Severnaya Zemlya (Russia)
KARA SEA
BARENTS SEA
LAPTEV SEA
Novosibirskie Ostrovo (Russia)
EAST SIBERIAN SEA
Sweden 1pm
Norway
Finland
2pm
Denmark
Latvia
Belarus
Germany
Poland
France
Austria
Ukraine
Romania
Italy
Greece
Turkey
Tunisia
MEDITERRANEAN SEA
Syria
Iraq
Algeria
Libya
Egypt
1pm
Niger
Chad
Sudan
Eritrea
Yemen
Ethiopia
3pm
Somalia
Nigeria
Central African Republic
Congo
Kenya
Gabon
Congo (Zaire)
Tanzania
Angola
Zambia
Malawi
Namibia
Zimbabwe
Botswana
Mozambique
South Africa
Madagascar
Mauritius
Reunion (Fr)
Prince Edward Is (S. Africa)
3pm
4pm
Russia
Kazakhstan
Uzbekistan
Turkmenistan
Kyrgyzstan
Iran 3.30pm
Afghanistan 4.30pm
Pakistan
Saudi Arabia
Oman
ARABIAN SEA
India 5.30 pm
Nepal 5.45 pm
Tibet (China)
China
Mongolia
Myanmar 6.30 pm
BAY OF BENGAL
Sri Lanka 5.30pm
Maldives
Seychelles 4pm
Thailand
Vietnam
Malaysia
Indonesia
6.30 pm
Cocos (Keeling) Is (Aust)
INDIAN OCEAN
French Southern & Antarctic Territories (Fr)
Heard & McDonald Is (Aust)
North Korea
South Korea
Japan
Taiwan
EAST CHINA SEA
Philippines
Palau
East Timor
Papua New Guinea
9.30 pm
Australia
SEA OF OKHOTSK
BERING SEA
3am
2am
NORTH PACIFIC OCEAN
Northern Mariana Is (US)
Marshall Is (US)
Federated States of Micronesia 11am
Kiribati
Nauru
EQUATOR
Solomon Is
SOUTH PACIFIC OCEAN
Vanuatu
Fiji
New Caledonia (Fr)
10.30 pm
Lord Howe Is (Aust)
11.30 pm
Norfolk Is (Aust)
New Zealand
TASMAN SEA
SOUTHERN OCEAN

LONELY PLANET OFFICES

Australia
Head Office
Locked Bag 1, Footscray, Victoria 3011
☎ 03 8379 8000, fax 03 8379 8111
talk2us@lonelyplanet.com.au

USA
150 Linden St, Oakland, CA 94607
☎ 510 893 8555, toll free 800 275 8555
fax 510 893 8572
info@lonelyplanet.com

UK
72-82 Rosebery Ave,
Clerkenwell, London EC1R 4RW
☎ 020 7841 9000, fax 020 7841 9001
go@lonelyplanet.co.uk

Published by Lonely Planet Publications Pty Ltd
ABN 36 005 607 983

Cover photographs: Standing Stones, Isle of Arran, Kevin Schafer/Agefotostock (front); lone hiker on a raised beach, Isle of Jura, Graeme Cornwallis/Lonely Planet Images (back). Many of the images in this guide are available for licensing from Lonely Planet Images: www.lonelyplanetimages.com.

Printed through The Bookmaker International Ltd
Printed in China